TAKING STOCK

A Larry McMurtry Casebook

SOUTHWEST LIFE AND LETTERS

A series designed to publish outstanding new fiction and nonfiction
about Texas and the American Southwest and to present
classic works of the region in handsome new editions.

General Editors
Suzanne Comer, Southern Methodist University Press
Tom Pilkington, Tarleton State University

Photo by Lee Harmon

TAKING
STOCK

A Larry McMurtry Casebook

EDITED BY CLAY REYNOLDS

Contributing Editors

JAMES WARD LEE ▪ TOM PILKINGTON

ERNESTINE P. SEWELL ▪ MARK BUSBY

ROBERT FLYNN ▪ DON GRAHAM

Accompanying Essay: HAMLIN HILL

Bibliography: CHARLES WILLIAMS

SOUTHERN METHODIST UNIVERSITY PRESS ▪ DALLAS

First edition, 1989

Requests for permission to reproduce material from this work should be sent to:
Permissions
Southern Methodist University Press
Box 415
Dallas, Texas 75275

Library of Congress Cataloging-in-Publication Data

Taking stock : a Larry McMurtry casebook / edited by Clay Reynolds ;
contributing editors, James Ward Lee . . . [et al.] ; accompanying
essay, Hamlin Hill. — 1st ed.
    p.   cm. — (Southwest life and letters)
   Bibliography: p.
   ISBN 0-87074-291-4. — ISBN 0-87074-261-2 (pbk.)
   1. McMurtry, Larry—Criticism and interpretation. 2. Southwestern
States in literature. I. Reynolds, Clay, 1949–   . II. Series.
PS3563.A319Z85   1989
813'.54—dc20   88-43316
                                                          CIP

Copyright acknowledgments for reprinted essays appear on pages 448–450.

*For my wife and family
and all those who have to learn to live with
Texas's writers . . . and scholars*

CONTENTS

PREFACE AND ACKNOWLEDGMENTS

My introduction to McMurtry came during my senior year at Quanah High School. Linda Traylor, who also happened to be my first cousin by marriage, handed me a dog-eared, coverless paperback with the remark that I might find it interesting since it was set "around here." The "around here" she referred to was what we in the valley of the Prairie Dog Fork of the Red River called "West Texas" with an obviously derisive sneer at the Trans-Pecos region, Panhandle, and Caprock. (El Paso, for our money, was somewhere out near Mexico and unworthy of further geographic distinction.) West Texas, as it always has, began on the outskirts of Fort Worth and centered on the 100th Meridian. The paperback in question was, of course, *Horseman, Pass By,* Larry McMurtry's premiere novel; and even though I was never a fan of the traditional Western, modern or otherwise, I was entranced. Along with John Knowles, McMurtry was my most astounding literary discovery in high school.

Some years later when I traveled to Archer City with a college buddy from there, I was introduced to McMurtry quickly and anonymously. ("This is Larry McMurtry," my friend said and then ignored me as he tried unsuccessfully to ingratiate himself with the novelist.) I was more than a little overwhelmed. It wasn't so much that he was a "real" writer—I had rather self-consciously attended lectures and readings by Ginsberg, Snyder, Albee, and other "real" writers who wore turtlenecks and long hair and Hush Puppies and sandals and *looked* like "real" writers—it was more that he was a writer from Texas, my Texas, West Texas. Writers weren't supposed to come from there.

It perhaps is understandable, then, that when *The Last Picture Show* was being assigned in my college English courses, I felt somewhat smug about my foreknowledge of McMurtry's brilliance; after all, I was the only one who knew that Thalia was the name of a ghost town in Foard County. I also felt a kinship with the author I had barely met, for he knew how a blue norther could freeze a man between the house and the barn and what a careless weed was and what manure smelled like in the summer sun and how religion and gossip and football were the treble fuels of small-town life; and he wasn't afraid to write about people who also knew those things, people I had grown up with and around, people from my Texas.

My interest in McMurtry continued through the viewing of his first films (I had been forbidden to see *Hud,* as were most of the teens in Quanah when it came to the Chief Drive-In, but I made the San Antonio premiere of *The Last Picture Show*), through *In A Narrow Grave,* which I devoured like a chicken-fried steak with cream gravy, and through *Lovin' Molly,* which I saw with Judy, my wife-to-be, because I was a Tony Perkins fan and she liked Blythe Danner; I became so excited to discover that it was based on a McMurtry novel, I neglected to notice the serious flaws in the picture. My first Ph.D.-level seminar paper was on McMurtry, much to the amusement of my professor, "Jersey" Joe Millichap, who nevertheless encouraged me; and my first professional publication, a review of *Terms of Endearment* in *Southwest Review,* confirmed and validated my interest in this Texas writer whose works I had been aware of at least as long as I had known Shakespeare or James Joyce (Joyce was also on the forbidden list in Quanah).

At the 1987 meeting of the Texas Institute of Letters in San Antonio, Suzanne Comer surprised me by announcing that SMU Press was interested in a project I had proposed by letter some weeks before: a collection of reprinted articles on the works of Larry McMurtry. I was flattered; I was also cocky: After all, how much material could there be? The biggest problem was going to be gathering the cooperation of the supporting and contributing editors. I was wrong.

After a cursory look through major indexes and bibliographies, I put together a checklist of secondary materials on Larry McMurtry. There were about thirty items, and I estimated that a more careful check might reveal as many more. I hired a graduate student of mine, Charles Williams, to do that "more careful check," with the promise of small remuneration for his bibliographic efforts. I estimated that it might take him a week—two, if he got his Hemingway paper in on time.

What evolved from Mr. Williams's check, however, is the more than fifty manuscript pages of secondary bibliography published at the end of this volume. I never dreamed that McMurtry had excited such a widespread variety of commentary from so many periodicals and journals. Mr. Williams's yeoman effort to identify and track down every source who has published, however briefly, on McMurtry's work has kept him busy checking, verifying, and correcting for nearly two years. The bibliography's scope and breadth is testimony enough that McMurtry has outgrown Texas and is truly established as a national literary figure.

I am also grateful for the enthusiastic response of the six contributing editors I invited to participate in selecting the forty-one essays that are assembled in this volume. Professor James Ward Lee leads off with his discussion of McMurtry's essays and the general critical reaction to his overall work. Lee's early editorial work with McMurtry criticism gives him a precise understanding of the novelist's career and his evolution from "minor regional novelist" to national literary figure; he offers an insight into McMurtry's particular role as novelist *extraordinaire* and as unofficial and sometimes controversial spokesman for Texas letters. Tom Pilkington, a well-recognized critic and scholar of Southwestern and Texas writing, follows Jim Lee with an assessment of McMurtry's early novels, the "Thalia Trilogy." Pilkington's insightful look at the unusual reception these first three works had, not only in Texas but across the country, suggests the antecedents that emerge so forcefully in McMurtry's later fiction. Following Pilkington is Ernestine P. Sewell, a well-known student of Southwestern folklore and American studies as well as literature and author of one of the few essays McMurtry has publicly extolled for its excellent treatment of his fiction. Her analysis of the "Houston Trilogy" points out that these three novels constitute a departure for McMurtry, not only from the agrarian themes and "Cowboy-God" myth that permeate his earlier work, but also from Texas itself as the novelist traveled first to Hollywood and then to Washington, D.C. Sewell's perceptive treatment of the trilogy, however, suggests that the departure may be more philosophical than physical and that McMurtry was working his way rapidly to the urban themes which would soon emerge in his fiction.

Mark Busby, whose work on Preston Jones and other Western American writers is well established, takes on a section devoted to what is often referred to as the "Trash Trilogy," novels which McMurtry now asserts represent a transition for him and which eventually brought him back to his inspiration and his voice if not to Texas. Although often maligned as the weakest efforts in McMurtry's canon, these novels, as Busby argues, are important parts of a novelist's development. They have a value to McMurtry's developing career and as examples of fiction of the late seventies and early eighties; but they also are works of fiction with a unique integrity and quality of their own. Don Graham, the widely published critic of the Hollywood Western and Texas films in general, devotes his section to the four feature films which have been based on McMurtry's works. Graham's introductory essay examines the contrasts between the two early movies, made in black and white and heavily overlaid with the country-and-western motifs of the fifties, and the two later films, both shot in color with the added glitz of big-name stars and slick formats. And Robert Flynn, another novelist from that particular region of Texas which he, McMurtry, and I understand as being "West," Chillicothe, Texas, offers his unique understanding of what it means to be a novelist from Texas. His section's examination of McMurtry's newest novels brings the critical appraisal of the novelist full circle.

Each of these contributing editors has devoted considerable time and attention to McMurtry's work through published articles and reviews as well as in open and closed forum discussions, formally and informally, of his novels and his impact on American and Texas letters. Finally, but no less significantly, Professor Hamlin Hill, the internationally acclaimed critic of the works of Mark Twain and Western American literature, adds his assessment of McMurtry's status as an American author in an essay written especially for this volume. Hill's point of view is not so much that of a Texas critic evaluating a Texas author; instead his essay presents the opinion of one who has been concerned with American literature on a larger if not grander scale and who now assesses McMurtry's status in the full spectrum of the American tradition.

Taking Stock is the result of these scholars and writers' work; it is a text which sets out not to be the "final word" on McMurtry but rather to offer an evaluation of "first words," a cultural examination of a writer in emergence whose value to greater American letters is reflected in what critics had to say about him as his career developed. The text offers a resource, a starting place for future critics who are interested in what case has been made for McMurtry's fiction in the past three decades. This volume is, then, a casebook, a tracing of the developing career of an author who for several years was regarded and, indeed, regarded himself as a "minor regional novelist," but who in recent years has emerged as a major voice on the American literary scene.

My deep thanks go out to all of the eight scholars, writers, and editors whose work on this volume increases its integrity and adds immeasurably to its overall worth through their selections of materials for inclusion in the text and through their original contributions and comments on McMurtry's work. It is my hope and the hope of all the contributors to this volume that it will make accessible the material criticism and comment on the works of Larry McMurtry so that the opinions of those who have studied his fiction and essays for almost three decades can be utilized properly as further work on his books is continued.

A word needs to be said about the selection of the essays for reprinting and the overall organization of the volume. A number of options concerning organization presented themselves at the outset. As Professors Sewell and Busby pointed out early on, overlapping was going to be unavoidable if the book proceeded chronologically, ordering the sections of the volume according to the publication sequence of McMurtry's books. For example, Janis P. Stout's fine article could appear in Professor Sewell's section almost as readily as it appears in Professor Lee's. However, I still felt that the chronological method was the most utilitarian and would best serve the purpose of the text. Hence, with the exceptions of the section dealing with essays and "general criticism" and the one dealing with the films, edited by James Ward Lee and Don Graham, respectively, the book follows, generally, the publication order of McMurtry's canon to date.

After the secondary bibliography was established, I selected a body of work to submit to each of the six section editors for their consideration. I made no eliminations on the basis of point of view or quality of content; rather, I included in each editor's pool any review, essay, or article which treated any of McMurtry's work with any substance beyond a simple plot summary or "blurb-type" recommendation. Although I made suggestions by way of adding to an editor's consideration list material which turned up after the selections were made, no articles or reviews have been eliminated from their final selections for their sections purely because of editorial discretion on my part.

Another word might be added about the sources for the material chosen for consideration for reprinting. The purpose of the text was to focus on material published in journals, reviews, and little magazines, including those of a regional nature and of limited circulation wherein a great deal of criticism of McMurtry's work lies. No excerpts from either of the two published books by Charles D. Peavy and Lera Patrick Tyler Lich devoted exclusively to McMurtry have been included; this is by editorial design. Likewise, collections of essays devoted largely or in part to McMurtry were excluded from consideration on the grounds that many of the essays were themselves reprints and that most of the books are still in print and generally available. To reproduce them here would, I believe, be redundant.

Excerpts from the out-of-print monographs by Raymond L. Neinstein and Thomas Landess are exceptions to this policy, made on the grounds that these works are virtually impossible to obtain outside of special collections in most academic libraries. Other exceptions include, on the special request of Don Graham, a piece by Pauline Kael, originally published in *Film Quarterly* and revised and reprinted in *I Lost It at the Movies* (Boston: Little, Brown, 1965), and, on the special request of Mark Busby, an article by Brooks Landon originally published in the *Dictionary of Literary Biography Yearbook: 1980*. With these exceptions, the exclusion of printed books and chapters of books remains consistent through the volume as the concentration of the contributing editors was directed toward periodical and journal criticism.

Some of the reprinted material contained herein has been authored by the contributing editors themselves. To a great extent, this is unavoidable, as a large body of the criticism concerning McMurtry's work has been written by the very people who are involved in the creation of this volume, particularly Professors Graham, Sewell, Pilkington, Busby, and myself. At no point, however, was an editor faced with the difficulty of having to decide whether or not to include his or her own work for reprint. Although it is understood that to reprint materials by the very people whose names appear on the editorial staff of a volume risks charges of self-indulgence, I am convinced that the decisions made in each case were born out of the critical integrity and academic detachment that make these editors the proper choice for work on this volume in the first place.

No work of this nature is completed without the input and help of a number of people. In particular I would like to thank the Board of Regents and Faculty Senate of Lamar University in Beaumont, Texas, for providing me with a Faculty Developmental Leave during the fall semester, 1987, during which I completed a great deal of the work of assembling and reading material for this text. A special thanks also goes to Linda Dietert, Librarian for Interlibrary Loan Services at the

Gray Library on the Lamar campus, her technical assistant, Billie Avery, and Inez Duranleau, a student assistant. Also I want to thank the University of North Texas, especially Dr. Kenneth E. Lavender, University Bibliographer for the University of North Texas, and his assistant, P. Martin Sarvis, who were helpful in securing and verifying unpublished and out-of-print materials that would not have been available otherwise, and who aided Mr. Williams in confirming bibliographic entries. Additional help in assembling and confirming bibliographic items was provided by several people who are specifically acknowledged by Mr. Williams in his essay introduction to his bibliography. Further help in gathering and locating bibliographic materials was provided by Judyth Rigler, Book Editor for the *San Antonio Express News* and author of a regular book review column, "Lone Star Library," Robert Compton, Book Editor for the *Dallas Morning News,* Jane Tanner, Editor of *Texas Books in Review,* Sally Dooley, Editor of *Review of Texas Books,* and Jim Harris, Editor of *Southwest American Literature.* Many other editors, authors, and scholars too numerous to mention but representing universities, libraries, and publications from coast to coast graciously provided information and leads for tracking down published material on McMurtry's work, and their assistance is likewise appreciated.

Finally, a heartfelt acknowledgment and appreciation must be offered to the editorial staff at Southern Methodist University Press, particularly Suzanne Comer, Keith Gregory, and Freddie Jane Goff, whose willingness to undertake this project and careful editorial work and assistance provided a stimulation and inspiration to bring together materials for scholarly use in a practical and, we hope, informative manner. Simply putting up with the volumes of correspondence and working with the sheer weight of material involved in this text is worthy of high praise.

It is the hope of the editors of this volume that work on Larry McMurtry will continue both in print and during the meetings of professional associations and learned societies. His importance not only to Texas but also to American letters seems to be self-evident, with enthusiasm for his books continuing to grow as we enter the last decade of the century.

CLAY REYNOLDS

T A K I N G

S T O C K

An Introduction

CLAY REYNOLDS

Much of what needs to be said about Larry McMurtry has already been said. Indeed, the editors who have contributed original essays to this volume of previously published criticism and comment on McMurtry's canon have devoted a considerable amount of time and energy to saying and writing what they thought—good and bad— about this comparatively young and possibly only genuine superstar in Texas's literary firmament. That no fewer than two dozen articles, reviews, and essays by these writers appear in the bibliography of criticism of McMurtry's work indicates their strong and lasting interest in his writing, and numerous other important Southwestern critics for a number of years have also followed McMurtry's progress from an unknown, minor regional novelist to a major contemporary American writer.

When gathered together in groups of two or three, the scholars represented in this volume would likely agree more often than not on virtually any general point—pro or con—raised about McMurtry, even if they might not arrive at a consensus about which of his novels is the "best" or "worst" of his work, about where he is going, literarily, or, for that matter, where he currently stands in the American, or even Texas, literary scene. Indeed, one of the major issues facing any critic of McMurtry's work is just how seriously to take his novels or his critical pronouncements.

An honest question at the outset of the volume, then, is what value a survey of the criticism of McMurtry's work might have, particularly when it focuses on a career that is apparently still developing, on a novelist who is still emerging. The Pulitzer Prize certainly has been an impetus for more and sometimes better work by other writers; it almost never has been the hallmark of retirement when the author is still writing, still active in letters, still able to notch a best-seller list, and still keeping both his detractors and his admirers guessing as to what his next step might be. The answer to the question is that Larry McMurtry is a special case. He is special not only because he is a Texan and has become the most prominent Texas author in a half century if not ever, but also because his work has had a national impact. For some he is a new addition to their home libraries; but to a good many readers and not a few critics, he is an old hand with whom they have been familiar since the early sixties when *Horseman, Pass By* made its quiet appearance on the Southwestern literary scene.

McMurtry's novels have been made into four feature-length motion pictures; a TV miniseries has been drawn from another. Additionally—and perhaps as a more important if less sensational point—his novels and essays have formed the bases for numerous seminar papers and professional meeting discussions, to say nothing of published critical essays and reviews; they also have proven useful as the subjects of more than a dozen graduate theses and doctoral dissertations. These points, in and of themselves, do not make McMurtry unique. Certainly any number of contemporary authors could make the same claim about their work, and most of them will never be the subject of a text of critical essays. McMurtry's books, however, have been consistently taught on college campuses for twenty years; and for at least the past fifteen, any literary conference with a section on contemporary or especially Western or Southwestern literature has had a disproportionately large number of papers on the works of Larry McMurtry.

From another point of view, one has only to acknowledge that, like it or not, Larry McMurtry is Texas's most prominent, most successful, and, to a certain degree, most controversial native literary son. Not since J. Frank Dobie has any popular author been so closely identified with Texas (and Dobie, candidly, was never that popular outside academic circles, especially outside Texas); and with exceptions such as William Faulkner, few American writers have managed to use their regional identities so completely, unless, of course, their regions are centered in New York City. Notably, few writers, Texan or otherwise, have so successfully exploited the Southwest as a realistic place instead of something that looks more like Monument Valley or the Southern California desert or, more commonly, something fabricated by a Yankee set designer on a Hollywood sound stage. McMurtry's novels—even those set in the alien climes of Hollywood and Washington, D.C.—concern themselves with Texas in an almost umbilical attachment to the real place that is the author's motherland. Significantly, the center of McMurtry's geographical and fictional place is not in the more romantic vistas of the Western alkali deserts or the post-oak shaded limestone caverns of the Hill Country; it's not in the various "cradles of Texas Liberty," either—San Antonio, Austin, Southeast Texas, and the central prairies—nor is it high on the Panhandle's flatness or down in the Rio Grande Valley's lushness. Originally McMurtry's place finds its center west and a touch north of Fort Worth, east and a touch south of Amarillo, smack-dab between the cedar ridges of the Palo Pinto Country and the loamy sloughs of the Red River Valley. It is a land geographically isolated from the rest of the state, culturally anonymous, yet blessed with a unique heritage of frontier development, of cotton, cattle, and oil, of a unique kind of boom and bust that has made life there uncertain in the best of times, impossible in the worst. From that base, McMurtry did eventually expand his center to take in Houston, Austin, the Valley, the western *Llano* and its vastness; and ultimately he touched on California, Washington, and the Midwest. But somehow there is always a trail leading back to Texas in his work.

Themes, symbols, imagery, and direct connections between non-Texans and Texans-in-exile as they appear in his novels direct all eyes if not all sentiments, positive and negative, toward the Lone Star State. He exposes misconceptions about some stereotypes and affirms the worst characteristics of others. For all of McMurtry's characters, however, Texas is more than a geographic reality; it is a state of mind, and its influence on the entire nation is no less today than it was when it was shoe-horned into the Union and spawned "Mr. Polk's War" some one hundred forty years ago. Its uniqueness and variety—cultural and geographic—is as profound in the late twentieth century as it was when Crockett, Bowie, and Houston came here. It's no paradise on earth; in many ways, it's not as nice a place as most of the rest of the country; but in the novels of Larry McMurtry, it takes on a palpable shape which is readily if sometimes uncomfortably identifiable.

This tends to give native Texans, particularly those who are literary critics and commentators, a proprietary feeling where McMurtry's fiction is concerned. It also creates a divisiveness among those who have any opinion concerning McMurtry or his work. Although, as James Ward Lee and others have pointed out, McMurtry devoted almost a decade to building a reputation as the "Peck's Bad Boy" of contemporary fiction—"I don't sign paperbacks, posters, or other effluvia," he is quoted as having said at a college reading in the seventies, a period of time when he had "left Texas" and set himself up as a merchant and artist-in-exile in far-off Washington—during the past decade the author has come home, both metaphorically and physically, to deal with the land that spawned him, not only in his fiction, but face to face, man to country, author to subject. The result is that now in the wake of a major novel that is completely Texan in subject matter, tone, and theme, McMurtry has created a conundrum for critics. Even those who agree on general points about his literary worth often dispute what his books are saying and, not incidentally, which of the baker's dozen says it best.

In short, no one who has read and thought critically about the work of Larry McMurtry is without an opinion about it, usually a strong one; and these opinions, particularly the newer ones, are often rendered without the benefit and the focus of the body of criticism which has gone before. Aside from the obvious point that such knowledge prevents a rehash of what has already been said—and published—placing this body of comment into an accessible form will help those who continue or are just now beginning to read McMurtry's work to come to a larger assessment of its value and to try to understand what message he has for his audience and how to interpret that message in light of his canon.

When he emerged almost thirty years ago with *Horseman, Pass By,* Larry McMurtry was often considered to be a talented flash in the pan, a writer whose literary light would be as brief as it was brilliant, a clever small-town storyteller whose novels contained more sizzle than steak. His first books stood up well to the test of scholarly inquiry, although more than a few agreed with Kerry Ahearn who complained, "McMurtry must decide whether he wishes to be a serious writer or an exploiter of methods others have used better" (127), and many enthusiastic readers eagerly awaited his next volume in anticipation of a new voice from Texas that could elevate the cowboy bumpkin and crass millionaire stereotypes to higher levels of literary status. After his fourth novel, *Moving On,* appeared, though, many felt that he was on the way out of the fiction business for good. After all, as some reviewers pointed out, there's only so much one can say about a small town and a way of life no one cares about, including the folks who live there; overly complicated, absurdist stories about zany sexual maniacs and egocentric graduate students were better left to the French and English writers, respectively.

Now, however, almost thirty years after *Horseman, Pass By* and in the light of the nation's most prestigious literary prize, McMurtry has emerged as a writer who uses his own particular techniques well enough. He has exploited his particular approaches to fiction in spite of complaints about shallow, one-dimensional characters by demonstrating that it is they, not the plot or the themes, that form the center of his fiction. The notion asserted by Thomas Dubose that the "overriding image" of his earlier books was less a view of a realistic small town and ranching community and more "of the stupidity and myopia of Thalia" (45) has been sublimated to a more serious consideration of this Texas writer who has fleshed out the caricatures to original individuality by showing him or her to be too pathetic and too yearning, too self-consciously romantic to have but one dimension. As Louise Erdrich points out in her *New York Times* review of *Texasville*, "He doesn't ask us to feel sorry for his characters, but to laugh at their crude one-liners and to be appalled at, and yet admiring of, their raw material decadence." When McMurtry goes after characters he is as tenacious as the Texas Ranger of a century ago: He knows his man, or woman, and he grabs hold of the trail and won't be shaken by idle caveats from readers who would rather see him fit into a mold better suited to a Dobie or L'Amour or even the shallower and erroneous visions of Edna Ferber and James Michener. A reader who has followed McMurtry down his fictional trail might discover that the rigidity of the author's characterizations is less fabricated than genuine. His characters may refuse to follow the tenets of logic and order that people seem for some reason to expect to find in an illogical and disordered universe, but their behavior somehow seems more homey than humdrum, more significant than stilted, more real than romantic, for it is they and not their creator who insist on the rigid molds into which they are often stuffed like a fat oilman into his designer jeans.

In the past five years, the debate over McMurtry's literary status has gained momentum as his novels have gained discovery and popularity. The nature of academic criticism is such that the artistic worth of a writer is often determined less by the power of his prose and more by the quality or even quantity of the scholarly comment made about him, in print, in something university administrators enjoy referring to as "peer reviewed" and "refereed" journals and periodicals. But much of the criticism of McMurtry's work has appeared in smaller academic journals which have been willing to devote space to the study of a "minor regional novelist" who as yet has not been worthy of discussion in the pages of the *PMLA*. Some of the best criticism, in fact, rests between the pages of *Western American Literature, Southwest Review, The McNeese*

*Review, Southwestern American Literature, RE: Arts and Letters, The
Texas Review, The Texas Observer,* and *Cross Timbers Review;* and
while McMurtry's works appear as the subjects of articles and reviews in the more prestigious if not more substantial *Commonweal,
Texas Monthly, Nation, Saturday Review,* and even the *New York
Times,* among other national magazines and journals, it seems that
the most incisive criticism by those scholars who have sought to
explicate McMurtry's work and find a truer worth in it than is nor-
mally suspected in books by novelists who are merely popular is hard
to find in the average library. Certainly, those who will determine
McMurtry's role in literary posterity, Texan or otherwise, are just
now emerging, and some of them have never even heard of many of
the publications which have carried reviews and full articles on Mc-
Murtry's work. With deference to those who admire him as well as to
those who feel he will never rise to a sufficient level of literary importance, this collection is offered to help them see what has been said
about Larry McMurtry's published work. After looking at this selection of "first words" and examining it in light of what he has done
over the past three decades, it may be easier to determine whether
Larry McMurtry's novels are merely heat lightning or whether they
constitute a bona fide and lasting Texas thunderstorm.

The facts of Larry McMurtry's life are fairly well known, but it
might be useful to rehearse them. Born in 1936 in Wichita Falls,
Texas, Larry McMurtry grew up in Archer City, Texas, where he was
graduated an honors student from high school. His father and uncles
were cattlemen who dated their heritage to Charles Goodnight's era.
McMurtry has described himself as a "herder of words"; unable to
master the finer points of ranch work, he discovered books and, hence,
a career in letters. He earned a B.A. from North Texas State College
(now the University of North Texas) and an M.A. from Rice University, where he also taught briefly as a graduate assistant. As the recipient of the Wallace Stegner Fellowship in 1960, he attended Stanford
University. He has been an instructor or lecturer at Texas Christian
University and Rice University, and a visiting professor at George
Mason College and American University. Although he spends a good
deal of time on college campuses lecturing and reading and seems
comfortable among academics and students, a few minutes' conversation with him reveals that he is first and always a writer. He is often
better read than the professors who interview him, but he does not
flaunt his erudition; rather, his attitude is that of the visiting author, a
man whose profession is writing fiction, and he exudes no pretensions

to the academy, though he likely could make the claim more easily than many novelists who hold professorial rank.

Although McMurtry once wore a T-shirt that read "Minor Regional Novelist," he has perhaps been the best-known living Texas author for more than two decades. That comes as a surprise to a good number of people who have only just discovered that he exists and may be a significant contemporary American writer. However, few people outside Texas can name anyone else who has such a close tie to the state, and McMurtry's reputation, minor, regional, or otherwise, has been fairly well established in national literary circles for more than twenty years.

His first novel, *Horseman, Pass By,* won the Jesse H. Jones Award of the Texas Institute of Letters in 1962; filmed as *Hud,* it won two Academy Awards. He became a Guggenheim Fellow in 1964, and his second novel, *Leaving Cheyenne,* was filmed as *Lovin' Molly* in 1974. His third novel, *The Last Picture Show,* completed what is called the "Thalia Trilogy"; it was filmed in 1971 and won three Oscars. *The Last Picture Show* was widely taught on college campuses during the late sixties and early seventies and established for McMurtry a loyal following among those who believed that his talent would soar as he matured and continued to write.

In a collection of essays, *In a Narrow Grave: Essays on Texas,* and later in a celebrated 1981 *Texas Observer* article, McMurtry calls for Texas writers to turn from the antique myths of the rural past and to seek plots and characters and literary inspiration in modern Texas's urban, industrial present. He also deprecates his earlier works as being juvenile and lacking in scope, calling them "modern westerns."[1] In his next series of novels, the "Houston Trilogy," McMurtry began to take his own advice. *Moving On, All My Friends Are Going to Be Strangers,* and *Terms of Endearment,* published between 1970 and 1975, move his artistic focus out of Texas to California and ultimately to the American Midwest. Only one of these, however, *Terms of Endearment,* created any serious literary interest, and it also was the only one to be filmed. The movie won four Golden Globe Awards, the New York Film Critics Circle Award, and five Academy Awards, including "Best Picture of the Year" for 1983. By 1983, however, few remembered that there had been a novel by that name, and even fewer recalled that it was written by the Archer City novelist who had also penned *Hud* and *The Last Picture Show.* Actually, all four films were more closely associated with their stars and directors (Paul Newman, Melvyn Douglas, Patricia Neal, and Brandon De Wilde in *Hud,* directed by Martin Ritt; Ben Johnson, Beau Bridges,

and Cybill Shepherd in *The Last Picture Show,* directed by Peter
Bogdanovich; Beau Bridges, Tony Perkins, and Blythe Danner in
Lovin' Molly, directed by Sidney Lumet; and Shirley MacLaine, Debra Winger, and Jack Nicholson in *Terms of Endearment,* directed by
James L. Brooks) than with the Texas writer who created the films'
characters and stories. But as McMurtry has often noted in his
essays and lectures on his own movies, such is the nature of Hollywood. With the exception of *Lovin' Molly,* which he has disowned as
an unmitigated disaster in the application of an author's fiction to
the screen, he expresses no regrets.[2] By the close of the 1980s, however, any number of people were speaking of the "passing by" of this
bright young novelist who had failed to sustain the successes of his
first books in his subsequent fiction and seemed to be thinking of
film rights before he considered fictional quality.

For about fifteen years during this period and up until the recent
past, McMurtry lived in Washington, D.C., where he owns a rare book
shop, Booked Up, which now has branches in Dallas, Houston, and
Los Angeles. His leaving Texas elicited a cry of protest from Texas
literary types who saw his traveling away from the state as a kind of
metaphoric abandonment of his roots, an exile that was potentially
permanent after his celebrated 1981 *Texas Observer* attack on Texas
letters. It seemed to confirm the opinion that he was abandoning
Texas as he had accused the "Cowboy-God" as well as Teddy Blue and
Charles Goodnight of doing in *In a Narrow Grave* (xv). Others, however, saw McMurtry's deliberate "moving on" as a part of a process of
literary maturation. Janis P. Stout, for example, explains the importance of the journey as metaphor in his fiction, and her comment could
almost be as accurately applied to McMurtry himself:

> In the first two novels, the impulse to journey is chiefly a desire for
> experience, and the more fully a character identifies himself with
> the ranching way of life the less he travels. The journeys of *The Last
> Picture Show* are sporadic and frustrated expressions of an urge to
> find an alternative to an empty and deadening life. But, the last
> two novels share a use of journeying as a metaphor for modern life
> itself, which is seen as being impoverished by the demise of the old
> traditions and the lack of new structures of meaning and
> allegiance. (38)

The "last two" novels Stout refers to were the first two volumes of the
"Houston Trilogy," completed by *Terms of Endearment,* but finishing
that cycle of books did not satisfy McMurtry's wanderlust. During
this time he also wrote screenplays and adaptations for film. His

next three novels, *Somebody's Darling, Cadillac Jack,* and *The Desert Rose*—published 1978–1983—attracted only minor critical interest and were dubbed the "Trash Trilogy" even by his most ardent admirers who believed that perhaps he had indeed shot his bolt with *The Last Picture Show* and was writing now out of frustration and a sense of fading laurels. His claim that *The Desert Rose* was the most significant book he had written and his personal favorite as well fell on deaf ears who perceived the narrow account of a Las Vegas showgirl as the worst kind of literary pandering and possibly the last gasp of a regional novelist whose inspiration along with his style had "gone south," while his focus and interest seemed to move west. Pleas came from numerous critics and fans for him to "return to Texas" in form, content, and subject matter; there was a growing feeling that Larry McMurtry had traveled too far and stayed away too long. Some saw *Cadillac Jack* as a self-parody of the author's own dilemma, a story of the "Cowboy-God" brought low— trapped in the Yankeefied North, unable to find happiness in a yuppie-infested world where he is forced into humiliating self-caricature, yet unwilling to swallow his pride and return to his roots where he can, at last, be understood if not happy. But if McMurtry paid any attention to such criticism, he failed to show it. Instead, he insisted that he was suffering from Valley Fever, a curious, debilitating disease he contracted in the deserts between California and Texas, an illness that left him exhausted and disoriented, unable to make public appearances, almost unable to write. Even so, he steadfastly and quietly worked his way back to health and home in his own good time, and when he finally crossed the Red River with a national literary trophy under his rope, his return was hardly that of a prodigal.

Lonesome Dove, the story of two old Texas Rangers, Augustus McCrae and Woodrow Call, who embark on an improbable cattle drive in the mid-1870s, created a large popular sensation; in spite of a derisive accusation of its Saturday-afternoon-matinee derivative nature by such critics as Don Graham, it won for McMurtry the Pulitzer Prize for fiction in 1986 and was filmed for a television miniseries in the spring of 1989. Not incidentally, it spawned dozens if not hundreds of scholarly papers, particularly from graduate students and junior as well as senior professors who seemingly had just discovered that McMurtry had "literary quality," and the number of theses and dissertations begun on his work increased proportionately. To put it colloquially, his stock had risen along with his star, and the time seemed right for him to capitalize on it.

McMurtry now resides at least part of the time on a ranch he owns near his home town of Archer City. He followed *Lonesome Dove* with

Texasville, a novel that returns to Thalia and picks up the characters from *The Last Picture Show* some thirty years and considerable financial boom and bust later, and *Film Flam: Essays on Hollywood,* a collection of previously published essays concerning McMurtry's career as a screenwriter, his experiences in Hollywood, and his assessment of film, both his own and others'. Neither of these books pleased either his admirers or detractors, for neither approached what many saw as a fundamental use of the frontier myth or any other motif which has been consistently identified as a basis for his fiction. On one level at least, *Texasville* has been called an ugly little romp through a dirty little oil town whose inhabitants have discovered that in the eighties it's acceptable to enjoy illegal drugs and illicit sex, to tell dirty jokes in mixed company, and to swear loud and often in public; for most critics' money, it was an unworthy complement to the "Thalia Trilogy." Others, however, found the book delightfully funny and in keeping with McMurtry's sense of black humor and satiric fun-poking at contemporary small-town life in the Southwest. Likely, there is validity in both opinions, but *Texasville* fell short of the critical success of most of its dozen predecessors on McMurtry's publications list.

In the fall of 1988, he published *Anything for Billy,* a first-person narrative account of a dime novelist's experiences with a character loosely based on Billy the Kid. Early notices run the gamut from praise to blame. Jack Butler, for example, in the *New York Times Book Review* suggests: "Like Faulkner, McMurtry is weaving a complete history . . . he has been alternating the Old Wild West with the West of the present or near-present, connecting time past to time not realized," and Butler concludes, "The book seems to be Mr. McMurtry's examination of his own relationship to his material." Yet Ron Hansen, writing for *Book World,* complains, "The novel seems hastily written, incidentally researched, and too easily trumped up at times, as if Larry McMurtry's only intent was a romp and a recreation" (13). Critics Tom Pilkington and Lee Milazzo took the book to task for a variety of faults in reviews in the Dallas newspapers, while reviewers for *Time* and *Newsweek* seemed willing to forgive it, even to like it a bit. *Texas Monthly* writer Suzanne Winckler may well speak for the majority when she dubs the novel "a peculiar little book."

Regardless of immediate critical response, however, *Anything for Billy* may well prove to reach further than any previous McMurtry novel in many ways and to be more important for the effort. It ties thematic threads together, unifies character traits that have run throughout his work from *Horseman, Pass By* through *Lonesome Dove*

and even into *Texasville,* and solidifies his long-standing argument
that the frontier myth is a vapid, hollow illusion that is in the final
analysis more destructive than useful. Viewed in that sense, the novel
becomes one of the most important works he has written yet; whatever
reputation it enjoys among a popular audience, and whatever
McMurtry's intention may be for future fiction, *Anything for Billy*
emerges in many ways as one of the most satisfying and mature books
in his canon.

If criticism can be compared to an industry, then one of the easiest
products to manufacture is the essay devoted to defining McMurtry's
use of themes and myth, particularly the frontier myth. Consistently,
he has dealt with the absurdity inherent in the conflict between past
and present as values and human relationships evolve. Almost as often, he has confronted the problem of the frontier as it exists both
historically and in the recollected idealization of those who are direct
heirs to it as well as those whose "frontier experience" is confined to
country-and-western music and Saturday afternoon matinees. As
Christopher Baker has pointed out, "McMurtry's novels record the
dilemmas of those who must live in the moral and emotional vacuum
left after the death of this age of exuberance" (47); but Baker also
notes that the sensational gunfights in Main Street, the Indian attacks, the cattle stampedes, while actually a part of Western history,
were hardly the norm. Boredom, ignorance, poverty, hardship, isolation, loneliness, drudgery, and harsh weather were the commonplace
experiences of life on the frontier. It is the illusion rather than the
reality that has formed the idea of the now lost "age of exuberance"
which, in fact, never existed. Even so, Baker goes on, there are inherent values in the myth which those who believe in it cling to in spite of
the fact that they feel the same privations that their ancestors faced,
only in a different way:

> The values of the frontier still seem desirable, but no longer
> attainable. His characters are crossing a new frontier which has
> less freedom, fewer clearly defined principles, and greater personal
> anonymity than the old. There is isolation, but it is internal, not
> geographical; there is restlessness, but it is spiritual more than
> economic; there is resistance to control and defiance of authority,
> but without a corresponding social bonding in either family or
> friendship to balance that rebellion. (53)

In *Horseman, Pass By, The Last Picture Show,* and to a lesser degree
in *Leaving Cheyenne,* McMurtry points out that the privations of the

frontier continue to exist in the West today and that the more
"exuberant" facets of that romantic age are no more in evidence now
than they were then; but he addresses this "internal isolation" indirectly, often treating it in a satiric, absurdist tone that reveals the
shallowness of the myth when it is applied even in good faith. But it is
at the end of *Horseman, Pass By* that McMurtry's spokesman and
narrator, Lonnie, sets the pattern that his creator, the novelist himself, would follow in search of the story of the modern frontier, a place
where big cars and school busses have replaced cow ponies and herds
of buffalo. As Mark Busby points out,

> When Lonnie climbs into that cattle truck for a ride to Wichita
> Falls as the novel ends, he will not light out for the circuit that
> Jesse followed. Instead, he will head for the cities which have now
> filled the wide-open spaces of the old frontier. There he can pursue
> the books now open to him. There he will become the writer of his
> own story. There he will escape the stifling, strangling world of the
> diminished frontier. (10)

At least part of McMurtry's apparent purpose in his early novels is to
reveal the "diminished frontier" in all its faded exuberance and false
glory. But it might be dangerous to read too much of McMurtry's
philosophy into Lonnie, the frontier's orphan. And there's Hud to
consider, as well as Homer Bannon. They don't "light out" either, and
unlike Huck Finn, they have no fear of being "sivilized." Homer
doesn't fear it because he prefers dying to living to see it come about;
Hud welcomes its coming, because he is confident that he represents
the "new frontier" and a whole new set of phony values that will likely
fade more rapidly than those surrounding the myth of the "Cowboy-
God" that Homer represents. Hud, however, is prepared to take it as it
comes, to gamble it away if he has to; for unlike Homer and unlike
Lonnie, Hud understands that a symbol is only a symbol, that pragmatism and hard reality have more substance than myths of any
stripe. There is nothing quixotic about Hud: He is the antithesis of
Homer, an Outlaw-God who rises Phoenix-like from the ashes of the
"diminished frontier," the grave of the Cowboy-God, the rancher-
stockman of the legendary past. He understands his image, whence it
came and what it requires of him; he accepts its negative aspect, and
he is prepared to live up to it or, failing that, to try something else.

When the picture is deepened and complicated by the rest of the
"Thalia Trilogy," a pattern tends to emerge concerning the conflict
between the practical realities of the present and the romanticized
ideals of the frontier past. Certainly Sam the Lion's death in *The Last*

Picture Show is as much the end of an era as Homer's death is in *Horseman, Pass By*. But Sonny, Sam's melancholy and somewhat unwilling heir to the myth, and Duane, a Hud-like realist who will have what he wants regardless of who is hurt by it, ultimately remain in Thalia, appropriately near Idiot's Ridge, even though they are far less ready to face what might come than their spiritual benefactors, something that is revealed clearly in the seriocomic picture of decadence in *Texasville*. There, Duane whiles away his wasted opportunities by pot-shooting at a doghouse and enduring insults from his wife and children, and Sonny sits in the ruins of the old picture show and reruns ancient westerns in his head. Like Hud, Duane keeps looking for a way to turn adversity to advantage; like Homer and Sam the Lion, Sonny is passing by, seeking escape from the present's unalterable tragedies by reaching back into a past that was as imaginary as were the grainy reels of *Red River* and *They Died With Their Boots On*.

By looking at McMurtry's treatment of this conflict across the entire spectrum of his fiction, one can see that the decadence is more than personal; it is pervasive and a part of a fictional universe McMurtry has not so much created as reported in his novels. What he sees when he looks at the modern frontier is, perhaps, less forgiving than what Lonnie would see once he had read a bit and looked back in anger; but somehow it seems true even in its most exaggerated absurdities.

Unconventional and often unerotic sex, phony academics, parochial art, pretentious wealth, and a particular kind of Southwestern culture which McMurtry has called "*echt*-Texas" emerge often in his fiction of the seventies as he moves away from the rural settings along Idiot Ridge and into the urban environments of Houston, Los Angeles, and Las Vegas. In a metaphoric way, though, these elements are the same as those found in his earlier work. "We too are symbolic frontiersmen, most of us," McMurtry has written about the modern Texas urbanite, "attempting to keep the frontiersman's sense of daring and independence by seeking these qualities, not in the life of action, but in the life of the mind." The difference is that he handles the thematic shift from a rural to an urban setting with sublime and often satiric treatment as his characters attempt to find something concrete in the confusing array of changes that so often beset them. In fact, they often seem to be nothing more than displaced rural folk who find themselves confronted with confusing urban wonders; but at bottom, they discover that big-city human behavior is different only in its concrete manifestations. The city, in short, is just a larger version of the small town, and the foibles and follies of McMurtry's urbanites are magnified to the same degree that the number and size of buildings and streets is multiplied in a metropolitan environment. "It is still daring enough, in Texas, to commit oneself to a life of the mind," McMurtry writes, "and it is our only corollary to that other kind of daring—a kind that has a small place in his land of cities" (*ING* 137). The rural frontier of the past may be gone along with dirt soddies and the open range and the Cowboy-God, but the values of the frontier are still pervasive in the tree-lined avenues of River Oaks and Highland Park where the Outlaw-God seems to have the upper hand, for the moment at least.

It may be that oil derricks have replaced cattle herds, and Cadillacs have replaced horses; but in the private clubs and fancy restaurants, in the urban barrios, and along the honky-tonk strips of Fort Worth and Wichita Falls, the sense of isolation and desperation, of boredom and frustration, of hardship and emotional deprivation keeps his characters at the mercy of phony, fabricated images of themselves. Such images are based almost entirely on a rural archetype and a set of small-town values that never really existed but that somehow belong to a nostalgia which associates itself with bucolic visions and a simpler time. The frontier myth and its chief gods seem to demand a tribute of codified behavior that somehow doesn't fit a modern, urban Texas, although it is offered there without a question as to its suitability or appropriateness. The result is that most of McMurtry's characters seem, more often than not, to be tragically off balance and comically bewildered.

In fact, bewilderment, as a consistent state of mind, is a far more important and accessible image in McMurtry's fiction than any of the grander notions of the frontier myth his critics have identified. His characters are caught up in a world that is changing faster than they can comprehend, and even though they tell themselves that they are hanging on to that which is of value from the past while dealing with the ever changing present, they seem overwhelmed by the failure of such notions to save them from themselves and from their own self-destructive inclinations. Tim Summerlin notes, "A journey through McMurtry's novels is a journey through a gallery of the dispossessed" (23). What Summerlin fails to note, however, is that the symbolism is largely perceived by the characters themselves, perhaps not with Hud's callous clarity, but at least with a sense of self-indulgent irony which fails to relieve their confusion but does give an illogical sense of order to their universe. "Nobody," McMurtry asserts, "watches TV westerns as avidly as cowboys" (*ING* 27); is it any wonder, therefore, that even "Urban Cowboys" pattern their lives after images which they have been taught are positive and heroic? "The myth of the clean-living cowboy devoted to agrarian pursuits and the rural way of life is extremely limiting," he recently told a *New York Times* reporter. "You're dealing with a romanticization. The flaws in the structure are rarely described, are rarely pointed out. I don't think these myths do justice to the richness of human possibility" (Rothstein). Instead, therefore, of being one-dimensional and flat, as some critics have asserted, McMurtry's characters actually may be rounder and more real than they first appear since they are attempting to deal with changes that take place so rapidly that all they can do is hang onto what traditional ideas they have collected and hope that everything, like a blue norther, will blow over and leave behind warmth and light and, not incidentally, "human possibility."

"Demons haunt these characters," Summerlin goes on; "they often fail as if to spite themselves. McMurtry's heroes and heroines may be wilful, but they are seldom profoundly sure of themselves" (26). The results of this "wilful" bewilderment and profound lack of self-assurance are often comic, but they are sometimes tragic, and they are always frustrating. When he's at his best—as in *The Last Picture Show* or *Lonesome Dove*, for example—McMurtry's comedy relieves his tragedy—as comedy is meant to do—and reveals the strength of the human spirit as the most pathetic victims of life's confusion learn to laugh or at least to snarl and accept their bewildering dilemmas. The acceptance won't make the problem go away any more than it will cure Homer's cattle or bring back the oil boom and save Duane's life-style; nor will it make the problem easier to accept any more than it will alter Emma Horton's cancer and assuage Aurora Greenway's guilt. It won't make a good life for Gus and Call up on the plains, and it won't give Cadillac Jack a reason to sober up and come home and face the reality of his roots. But it does suggest a consistent theme in McMurtry's works and reveals a deeper, more significant, and more consistent use of the frontier myth than might be first apparent.

Such revelations, however, are not sufficient to explain McMurtry's fiction for most of his critics. Themes of the "Journey as Metaphor," the "Cowboy-God," the "Urbanization of Texas," and "Death and Initiation" have all been identified in McMurtry's novels by astute critics. Their arguments are convincing, but sometimes they seem to miss the obvious. Perhaps, as James Ward Lee and others have suggested, McMurtry is still a searching and callow writer, one who is unsure exactly where the myth is going and how it will ultimately develop in American culture. Tom Pilkington and others have also suggested in discussion that McMurtry doesn't intend for his derision of the frontier myth and attendant themes to be taken seriously, or at least at face value. Perhaps he *is* putting us on; perhaps what he is dealing with is something besides the myths and themes themselves, those ideas that rise to the surface of his fiction and catch the eye and stimulate handy criticism. Dave Hickey notes, "There is a tremendous amount of emotional energy surrounding the 'bold horseman and gallant lady' myth, and the sentiment, if not the myth, is authentic" (15). Maybe it is that authenticity that McMurtry is exploiting in his fiction. Maybe he is trying to show Texans, and by extension, Americans, that myths are what people make them and make of them; and too often, they are made too important. Or, perhaps, one should take McMurtry at his word when he says that when he completes a book, he is done with it and he doesn't care to think about it any more.

There is no doubt, as Raymond C. Phillips among others has pointed out, that McMurtry has an ambivalent attitude toward the frontier and its attendant myths and the hold it has over contemporary Americans. Phillips states that Thalia, the setting for four of McMurtry's novels, is based on a Greek word meaning "the blooming one" (36), an allusion with ironically tragic overtones; but the name is also that of the Muse of Comedy, and no one who has read McMurtry's novels can deny the importance of his sense of humor to his stories. More than one critic has gone to lengths to try to find in McMurtry a consistent statement of what he thinks is positive in Texas and the Southwest and its attendant myths and to reconcile it with his acrimonious attack on Texas letters and his attempt to divorce himself from the image of a fictional chronicler of the modern frontier, an author of "modern westerns," steeped in its traditions and burdened by its history.[3] "I had begun to suspect," McMurtry wrote twenty years ago, "that home was less a place than an empty page" (*ING* 86). As critics hovered like buzzards over a native son who had lost his way home, what they perceived as McMurtry's final literary gasp, the "empty page" he couldn't fill, the analysis of his use of the frontier myth and its passing as a principal theme in his work became the mainstay of their eulogies for this once and future Texas author. Such inquiry is, perhaps, a worthy scholarly enterprise, but it is also premature. Many of the assertions that underlay the best critical elegies, including Charles D. Peavy's important Twayne book study, were scattered to the four winds when McMurtry breathed new life into the Western and "returned to Cheyenne," literally, by writing *Lonesome Dove*.

Lonesome Dove is more than a return to the frontier myth and Texas as subject matter. The story of two "over the hill" Rangers who come out of retirement to drive a massive herd of cattle north to a promised land where they hear from a disreputable old comrade there is sweet water and good grass and harmony is dripping with the stuff of which myth is made. But *Lonesome Dove* is also pure fiction with little or no basis in fact, and its relationship to the romantic frontier ideals is far more tenuous than it appears at first. As Don Graham has pointed out, in the context of really first-rate cattle drive novels such as *North to Yesterday* by Robert Flynn and *Train to Ogallala* by Benjamin Capps, *Lonesome Dove* "begins to seem like a novel too crowded with incidents, with everything that could possibly happen on one drive but never did. Still, it's not a bad read, and that apparently was McMurtry's main goal from the beginning" (12). Even Ernestine P. Sewell's apology that "History . . . is not McMurtry's territory: storytelling is" (220) does not completely address the problems that the novel raises with regard to its treatment of the frontier and its archetypal images and myths.[4]

In the larger context of McMurtry's entire canon, however, *Lonesome Dove* might be seen as a significant part of his thematic development. In fact, from one point of view, it might be seen as a kind of megapreamble to the book that would form a much more concise and incisive treatment not only of the frontier myth but also of those who would perpetuate it in fiction, legend, and ultimately in attempts to adapt it as an answer to the problems that present themselves to modern characters facing modern dilemmas. In that sense and on that level, *Lonesome Dove* has to exist as pure fiction, fantastic and overdone as it sometimes is, just as *Texasville* and certain odd scenes from *Moving On* and *All My Friends Are Going to Be Strangers* and *Terms of Endearment* tend to exaggerate modern bewilderment in order to demonstrate the significance of that same conflict between romanticized ideals of the past and pragmatic realities of the contemporary present. At bottom, in each case, what is left is isolation, loneliness, frustration, and, if the characters are lucky, humor or at least irony as they continue to attempt to define themselves in the light of fabricated gossip and idly concocted reputations. And in that sense, and to a certain extent on that note, *Lonesome Dove* and *Texasville* join the rest of McMurtry's fiction to set the stage for a dusty and lonely finale to the frontier myth which is recounted in *Anything for Billy*.

"My first concern has commonly been with textures, not structures," McMurtry wrote (*ING* 142). He has elsewhere lamented his carelessness in forgetting in *Lonesome Dove* that the huge cattle herd would have to cross railroad tracks somewhere in Kansas, and more than one critic has noted other "technical errors" in history, dates, and other assorted details in that and other novels.[5] Taking on the story of

Billy the Kid—one of the best-known if not most often biographed outlaws of the Old West—invites careful research if the plausible re-creation of history is the novelist's aim; but in a way, McMurtry's choice of this particular hero leaves him free to invent that which he doesn't already know. What emerges from McMurtry is less historical than imaginary, but in the first place it's supposed to be, and in the second place, the accepted and popular "facts" of many if not most Western legends are more imaginary than real as well. In the case of William Henry Bonney (aka Henry McCarty, Billy McCarty, Henry Antrum, William Antrum, Billy Antrum, etc.), few "facts" can be absolutely established, and what is known has, as McMurtry's narrator says of the boy he befriends and follows until his death, washed away and left him "a pure, clean legend" (300).[6]

In many cases, fictional imaginings are less interesting than historical truth. As much can be correctly said about the film *The Life and Times of Judge Roy Bean,* for example, where John Huston's direction and the historically embellished script by C. L. Sonnichsen (who knew better) proved to be far less spectacular or entertaining than the actual career of the colorful "Law West of the Pecos." The same might be said of *The Alamo,* a film sufficiently far off the historical mark to offend almost any Texan, but of sufficient impact on the public (and the Daughters of the Texas Revolution) to merit placement of a painting based on the movie (complete with the recognizable faces of Laurence Harvey, John Wayne, and Frankie Avalon) in the chapel of that most hallowed Texas shrine. But in other works such as Clifford Irving's *Tom Mix and Pancho Villa,* Thomas Berger's *Little Big Man,* or William Harrison's *Burton and Speke,* or the films *Butch Cassidy and the Sundance Kid,* or *Bonnie and Clyde,* the purpose of the art form is directed more toward entertainment than information. If loose adaptations of historical facts are acceptable in the name of excitement, action, and adventure, to say nothing of sensationalism and titillation, they should be taken in the same light-hearted way as such fluffy Hollywood fun as *Viva Max!, The Sugarland Express,* or *The Texas Chainsaw Massacre* have been: bad art sometimes, but good entertainment always. Conversely, films such as *Heartland, The Grey Fox,* and *The Ballad of Gregorio Cortez* are virtual documentaries, reenactments that leave as much to guesswork as actual accounts do.

"If you actually read the biography of any of the famous gunfighters," McMurtry says, "they led very drab, mostly very repetitive, not very exciting lives. But people cherish a certain vision, because it fulfills psychological needs. People need to believe that cowboys are simple, strong and free, and not twisted, fascistic and dumb, as many

cowboys I've known have been" (Rothstein). McMurtry's purpose in
Anything for Billy is neither to pander to such "psychological needs"
nor to document the history of a particular outlaw *cum* legend, but
rather to use whatever elements of history may be ascertained as
the basis for a good story, a story which is more interesting than and
has less to do with Billy the Kid the legend than Billy the Kid
the legend had to do with William Bonney, or whatever his favorite
name was—and less to do with either the legendary or the historical
figure *per se* than it does with an analysis of the folly of frontier myth
and the futility of its continued application.

Within a year after his death, at least ten accounts of Billy the
Kid's life were published, the first appearing just three weeks after he
was shot. One, *An Authentic Life of Billy the Kid,* was ghosted in 1882
for Sheriff Pat Garrett, the man who shot Billy, by the sheriff's friend
Ash Upson. Charles Angelo Siringo, the famed Pinkerton detective
who tracked Butch Cassidy and other desperadoes, devoted one of his
seven books on the West to Billy, of whom he wrote that the Kid was
"a prince of a human being who got off on the wrong foot." No fewer
than a dozen motion pictures have been made concerning the Kid's
exploits at least in part, including *The Left-Handed Gun* (a misconception apparently based on a bad illustration in the *Police Gazette;*
the most accepted accounts note that he was right-handed) and *Pat
Garrett and Billy the Kid,* starring Kris Kristofferson, James Coburn,
and, improbably, Bob Dylan. The grave site at Fort Sumner, near
where Sheriff Pat Garrett killed Billy, and also the old Court House in
Lincoln have become museums and tourist attractions, the latter complete with bullet holes and markers to indicate where deputies J. W.
Bell and Robert Olinger died during the Kid's last escape.[7]

Although McMurtry borrows liberally from the popular and historical accounts of Billy the Kid, he makes no pretense of trying to patch
them into the fabric of his book. Instead, his narrator, Benjamin J.
Sippy, dime novelist, world traveler, and Philadelphia socialite, uses
what he wants to tell his story of the West's most famous gunman since
Wild Bill Hickok. Sippy disputes that which contradicts and ignores
the rest without explanation or apology. Hence, Stinking Springs, the
site of a famous shoot-out between William Bonney and a feuding faction, becomes Skunkwater Flats, where Billy Bone and a collection of
loosely aligned gunfighters are beset by cowboys hired to ride them
down and kill them. Charles Bowdrie, the first man killed in that foray,
becomes Barbecue Campbell; Pat Garrett becomes Tully Roebuck;
John Chisum, rancher and Territorial power mogul, becomes Will Isinglass, an intelligent and farsighted man but a creature impervious to

evil and capable of almost superhuman frontier feats—and, significantly, the villain of the piece. Billy himself never uses any of his several aliases but is known by one and all in the novel simply as Billy Bone, a young man consciously in search of his destiny.

Other connections with accepted history appear obliquely in McMurtry's account: The famous escape from the Lincoln County Jail where Billy kills Bell—renamed Snookie Brown—is present, but McMurtry neatly avoids the sensational shooting down of Olinger and the derisive breaking up of the weapon before an hour's cavort through the building. Instead, Billy Bone falls under his horse and makes his getaway ignominiously across the saddle of his sometime lover and Isinglass's outlaw illegitimate daughter, Katie Garza. Additionally, McMurtry avoids the complications of the Lincoln County War, which becomes the Whiskey Glass War, a simpler conflict centering on Isinglass's attempt to run buffalo hunters and gunfighters off his three million acres. Other well-known legends surrounding the life of William Bonney are also omitted, and McMurtry allows his own Billy to establish his reputation as a cold-blooded murderer through fictional atrocities that are no less bloody than those of the historical record. "Everyone in the West had heard of him," Sippy explains, "and plenty of people in other parts of the world as well. Since Wild Bill Hickok had let himself get killed in South Dakota two years before, I doubt there was a gunfighter alive with a reputation to match Billy's" (13). But Sippy also wants it established that this is a "true" account, not authorized perhaps, but certainly accurate: "Newspapermen and historians," Sippy argues, "jealous of the fact that novelists get to make things up and they don't, encroach into fiction whenever they think they can get away with it" (357). In this book the novelist encroaches into history and makes things up, and likely he does more justice to the story of Billy the Kid than any of Billy's biographers ever did. Billy Bone's story may not be actual, but it certainly is true in the novelistic sense; and in its particulars, it is likely no less factual and no more fantastic than any of the "authorized" or "authentic" accounts that have gone before.

That the story begins with Sippy meeting Billy who comes "walking out of a cloud" (11) is significant; for Sippy is truly the protagonist of this novel. He is a man enchanted with half-dimers, dimers, and double-dimers—pulp Westerns—to the extent that when he cannot find a new one for sale he turns to writing them to satisfy his longing for Western adventure, for a nineteenth-century version of the frontier myth that is no closer to actuality than is the twentieth century's version. To Sippy,

Billy the Kid is not simply a young man "off on the wrong foot": He is a legend come to life. Like Sancho Panza behind Don Quixote, Sippy guides his mule Rosie—not Rosinante—behind Billy and the Kid's sidekick, Joe Lovelady, a hapless Texas cowboy whose association with Billy is almost as inexplicable as Sippy's. Indeed, the only explanation Sippy gives is that he "just followed along with Billy as he rode the bloody trail—a wandering boy one step ahead of his doom" (87).

Deliberate allusions to Cervantes are not new for McMurtry. Confessing to a fascination with *Don Quixote de la Mancha* since the age of twelve (*ING* 139), McMurtry has used the theme before. Ernestine Sewell notes that the absurdity as well as the romantic hopelessness of Cervantes' work can be discerned in several of McMurtry's novels, most particularly in *Lonesome Dove* (221), and certainly there are elements of it in *Moving On* and *All My Friends Are Going to Be Strangers* as well. In this newest book, the allusion is brought to light in a clear and well-defined series of references as Sippy wonders several times if his fascination with this ill-fated youngster's dance of death is not purely "quixotic" and governed by some misguided sense of romantic delusion of his own. Such thoughtful insights are hardly accidental, and they point out the fact that whereas Billy may be the character of focus of *Anything for Billy,* Sippy's role rapidly gains importance. Ultimately, Billy's story becomes subordinate to and dependent upon Sippy's. As in *Horseman, Pass By, All My Friends Are Going to Be Strangers,* and *Cadillac Jack,* the narrator's own bewilderment and dilemmas are those of the greatest interest as the story unfolds. As in the case of Melville's "prudent and safe" lawyer observing Bartleby's road toward a melancholy death, the impact of the story's events is told most significantly on the teller; and in this case the important detail is that the teller, Sippy, is himself a novelist and a fabricator of an imaginary frontier myth which he now is witnessing in the flesh.

McMurtry's sense of humor emerges quickly in the supporting cast of frontier characters, but there is no outrageous satire here such as may be found in *Moving On* or *Texasville.* Neither is there a Charlene Duggs or Frank Fartly or Khaki Descartes or Uncle Ike Spettle; there is no attempted sex with postholes and gas tanks, no overburdening of the plot with a collection of improbable events, no outlandish collection of snippy insults to offset the grimy story at hand. Sippy records the vast emptiness of the *Llano Estacado,* speaks of the loneliness and privations of following his nineteenth-century knight errant in search of some vague, romantic notion of destiny, and catalogues those he encounters by listing names that sound gritty in their authenticity:

Hill Coe, Pleasant Burnell, Wild Horse Jerry, Simp Dixon, Happy Jack Marco, Moss Kuykendall, Ike Pumpelly, Vivian Maldonado, Des Montaignes, and the cameo portraits of an Apache chief named Bloody Feathers and hired gun named Long Dog Hawkins. Comical tidbits mentioned in other works do appear, such as the camel ridden by Mesty-Woolah, Isinglass's pet Islamic African murderer, recalling Uncle Laredo's humped legacy from the ill-fated experiment by the U.S. Cavalry in the post–Civil War Southwest. And even the notion of trying to capture some relic of Billy the Kid's life recalls Jack McGriff's idea of an authentic cowboy boot display in a Washington, D.C. gallery.

But unlike other McMurtry heroes who journey in search of escape, Sippy has come to the West somewhat by accident. The death of his butler whose chore it was to fetch the latest pulp novels as soon as they hit the newsstand near the Sippys' Philadelphia home combines with his wife's callous disregard for his interests by throwing out his entire library of Westerns, and he takes a boat for Galveston and then a stagecoach for El Paso, which is where he meets up with Billy. At this point he is a successful author of what he calls "booklets," some sixty-five of them, with characters whose names—Orson Oxx, for example—sound a good deal like McMurtry's previous casts of crazy characters and their zany, onomatopoeic monikers. There is some confusion about Sippy's attempt to rob a train, which also plays a part in his coming west, but it is less Sippy's past than his present and, indeed, his coming to understand the true nature of the frontier which concern the tale at hand.

Sippy is a man of wealth and intelligence. He seeks a validation of his mental picture of the real frontier and the myths it has spawned, and he has left behind false comfort and a cold and unfaithful wife. He has nothing to lose by throwing in with Billy but his life, and he counts that a small price to pay to watch an archetype in the making. He rides along and becomes a witness to Billy's final days. He can see the destruction coming and, again like Sancho Panza, he attempts to advise his companion of the foolishness of his ways, advice to which Billy responds with the comment, "Nobody knows what I'm like. . . . Nobody knows—but they will before I'm through" (162). But like Don Quixote, Billy is blind to his true nature himself. He is just discovering the image of the Outlaw-God, and as with the Spanish knight's desperate battles with windmills and herds of sheep, this frontier gunman is desperate to fulfill his destiny. Ostensibly, then, the story focuses on an outlaw who is attempting to live up to a reputation, a legend, of which he is acutely aware; but beneath that surface, the story is that of a writer, a man whose attempt to tell what really happened, to expose the truth behind the myth is frustrated because actuality sometimes is not as interesting as fiction, especially when the fiction becomes a part of a greater myth that defies any facts that might confuse it.

Sippy becomes so caught up in the myth as it forms in front of him that he finds himself unable to deny or decry it. He pauses several times to complain, "They've all [the historians] made a study of it, you see, whereas I was there. The very fact that I *was* there is the only fact they can't dispute—just makes them edgy; in fact, it makes them jealous and produces much resentment" (209). But what Sippy does not understand—and what McMurtry understands very well—is that Sippy's "facts" have less to do with Billy the Kid and his bloody ride to infamy than with a much larger story, something that is so pervasive that mere facts cannot dispute or correct it without destroying it.

On the surface of the book, McMurtry offers a cracking good yarn that is reminiscent in its ironic narrative detachment of Mark Twain's account of the bewildered Easterner encountering the "civilization" of Europe and the Holy Land in *Innocents Abroad* or the frontier wilderness of the American West in *Roughing It*. As he plods along on his mule behind Billy, Sippy's comments and complaints about the lack or quality of the available food balance in ironic understatement neatly against the real and present dangers of a wild and untamed land: "The beauty of the country was surpassing, with antelope frolicking near and the grass so endless. Yet, within a day, I had seen three men meet their deaths. I was beginning to have to reckon with the fact that I was riding around in a place where it was rather hard to last" (132). Here and throughout the book, the reported dialogue is as rustically realistic as Sippy's own texture is an accurate reflection of nineteenth-century formal prose style such as might be found in Twain, Howells, or even the early Henry James. McMurtry might play fast and loose with history, but when it comes to exposition and technique, he has clearly done his literary homework.

Further, irony and satire, hyperbole and comic understatement invade Sippy's descriptions of the filthy and illiterate nature of most of the men and women he encounters, the superstition and fragile egos of the simple gunfighters and cowboys, including Billy, and the fascination they all seem to have with their own reputations as well as with their roles in the myth that has already grown up about the Southwest and those who inhabit it. Sippy's comments are grounded in commonplace observations typical of a well-educated man of his era. He refers to New Mexico Territorial Governor Lew Wallace's epic *Ben Hur* as nothing but a "fat double-dimer set in Roman times" (134), and he describes an afternoon just across the Rio Grande in Mexico as being so "hot and still you could hear a watch tick from thirty yards away" (151). For once, openly, citizens of the Lone Star State are viewed in terms that strip away the romance and leave a vicious and somber picture: "Texans," Billy comments at one point, "are speedy and mean. If they don't kill you standing they'll kill you running" (140); and Katie Garza explains to Sippy that she fears the law "because I'm brown, and that's Texas across the river" (158). The West Sippy encounters and chronicles, then, is rife with an already well-developed image, and it is the sustaining of that image, the living up to that reputation that motivates the characters.

Indeed, it is the imagery associated with the idea of reputation that underscores the major thesis of the book and gives it meaning beyond its surface story. Billy, according to Sippy, is nothing more than a roughly handled and bewildered boy so concerned with living up to the legend that has developed around his name that he consciously tries to become the outlaw he is supposed to be, ultimately with horrible success. After one of Billy's particularly heinous murders, Sippy comments: "He had become what he had long been supposed to be: a cold killer. Four days ago his reputation had only been built on gossip and exaggeration: but Jody Fay lay dead outside the cabin, and that was not gossip" (203). Billy's yearning for a reality to match his reputation is in conflict with his sense of commonplace practicality. Although he is a bloody killer, he also is a naïf, a child whose bewilderment at life is tempered only by his complete disregard for anyone else's right to the same confusion:

> In general Billy tended to do all his thinking when he was miserable, and then all his thinking centered on his misery. He may have given some thought to Katie and Cecily occasionally; he may have spared a little for Joe Lovelady at some point; but Billy Bone didn't spend many hours thinking about his fellow human beings. The notion that they had some sort of a right to life probably never entered his head, and might have struck him as comical if it had. (290)

That McMurtry, through Sippy, can create a character of such low degree, a man with so casual a disregard for life and such offhand willingness to kill, is remarkable enough; but to do so and at the same time capture the affability and likability that William Bonney was supposed to have indicates the depth of characterization that emerges from this novel. It also indicates the strength of the frontier myth in contemporary times. Sippy follows Billy down his bloody trail, watches him gun down innocents and play the outlaw his reputation says he is; but he also notes the sadness inherent in the role Billy feels forced to portray: "I'm getting too big a reputation. . . . Sometimes I wish they'd just let me fall" (275). Sippy makes no apology for Billy. In spite of the ruthlessness and psychopathic, homicidal tendencies he discerns in this young anti-hero, he confesses the depth of his compassion for the doomed youth early on in his account: "When I think of Billy Bone giggling at one of his own little sallies, I soon grow blind with tears—sentimental, I guess. But there was a time when I would have done anything for Billy" (12).

This might appear to be an anomaly, a deliberate attempt to satirize the subject of the novel as well as the narrator. Yet most of the "heroes" of the Old West, the men and women whose names are synonymous with the myth and its archetypal Outlaw-Gods—the Earps, Doc Holliday, John Wesley Hardin, Wild Bill Hickok, Jesse James, Belle Starr, or more recently, Bonnie and Clyde, John Dillinger, Pretty Boy Floyd—were often bloody, sociopathic outlaws whose disregard for human life in no way diminishes their reputations as giants and heroes in an American—and Southwestern—Olympiad that has little room for "good guys" and lives built on proper behavior and law-abiding good citizenship. Even Gus and Call, as former Texas Rangers, "lawmen," blithely engage in rustling, lynching, and homicide all in the name of some sort of frontier code they are only dimly aware of. In portraying this enigmatic villain, McMurtry touches the very heart of the matter of the frontier myth. William Bonney was a young man who captured the American imagination by virtue of his evil deeds and derring-do; but Billy Bone, McMurtry's real and tangible villain, is little more than a sad, frightened boy who is driven by the image of himself others—such as Sippy—have created. By cracking the image, McMurtry reveals that the values inherent in the myth of the frontier never really existed, and the genuine values of that historical period were never worth very much beyond their immediate application to a time and place and people of a century ago. He exposes the notion that the Outlaw-God, like the Cowboy-God, was manufactured, fabricated, and false. Whether he came out of a cloud or not, the Outlaw-God was no less bewildered by the frontier myth and its uselessness in a practical world than a later generation of "symbolic frontiersmen" would be.

Sippy is not dealing with a myth either in the person of Billy or in the setting of the Old West which he, as a novelist, is partly responsible for creating. Instead, he is a witness to the concrete reality of life and death on the frontier, a participant in a violent struggle that is as difficult to accept as it is to report clearly. "It's a melancholy thing," he comments after a bloody shoot-out that sees most of Billy's friends killed, "because hard though they were, I liked those gunmen who died in that windy gully. They only warred on one another, as near as I can see, and they brought some spirit to the ragged business of living, a spirit I confess I miss" (211). Even after Isinglass captures him and announces an intention to hang him unless the Easterner can entertain him with "yarns" in the manner of Scheherazade to prevent the old rancher's post-supper indigestion, Sippy has trouble divorcing himself from the practical realities of the present. Instead of wild adventure, cold and impersonal death seems to be all around him; harshness and cold acceptance of violence and murder inform this supposedly romantic world. The real frontier he came west to discover is a dark and bloody place, dirty and ignorant and gritty, yet somehow determined to sustain its hold on the American imagination and to cement itself permanently into the greater context of fundamental American values.

Thus, McMurtry underscores his old point about the reality of the frontier belying the myth. In order to assert their independence against the bewildering changes they perceive in their world, the gunmen have rebelled; Sippy notes that they have a "determination to defy any order, no matter who it came from, or what the consequences" (199). Such a rebellion becomes meaningless in an ordered universe and a logical world. It isn't anarchy; it is a blind assertion of independence against the kind of confusion that pulls men down. In a way, it is the same sort of reaction McMurtry demonstrates in Homer Bannon's initial refusal to destroy his cattle, particularly the one remaining Longhorn, in Sam the Lion's ultimate philosophical acceptance of time's erosion of the country's beauty, in Uncle Roger Wagonner's antique methods of running his ranch, and even in Will Isinglass's refusal to abide any question of his authority as he attempts to hold onto an impossible amount of land in the face of a closing frontier.

On this level, *Anything for Billy* resembles a kind of culmination of McMurtry's best work as first revealed in *The Last Picture Show* and possibly in *Lonesome Dove* as well. The book does nothing to reinforce the frontier myth; nor does it adequately explain exactly why it arose or where it came from. On the contrary, it demonstrates that the myth was as much a fabrication then as it is now. *Anything for Billy* is a satiric slap not only at those who seek it, in general and specifically in his and others' works, but also at those who perpetuate it through their constant reliance on it to save their characters and present some phony set of values in their writings. The novel exposes one of the

West's most infamous and inexplicable legends as little more than a boyish humbug, a juvenile delinquent with a ten-gauge shotgun. Billy Bone is a likable youth, no less uncertain and bewildered than Hud or Duane, and like those two anti-heroes of McMurtry's earlier works, Billy strikes out blindly when he is confronted with a conflict between what he is supposed to be and what he really is. Virtually a legend in his own time, he and the rest of the outlaws work to become what they think they are supposed to be, even if it means killing and hurting other people.

The lesson of McMurtry's philosophy remains clear: Legends are too easily made too much of. He reminds us in this story of the frontier of Mark Twain's essay on the medieval world in *A Connecticut Yankee in King Arthur's Court* or, more recently, of Thomas Berger's satiric *Arthur Rex*. These more modern versions of Camelot suggest that it was nothing but a collection of drafty stone huts inhabited by illiterate and bloodthirsty barbarians for whom a harsh and hopeless life was tempered only by a superstitiously oriented and vague grasp of their destinies as knights in a primitive Christian kingdom. They are hardly Malory or Tennyson's shining-armor heroes. The Old West and its heroes and villains are not the Round Table and its knights, but the frontier myth is no less pervasive in or important to American culture than the Arthurian legend is to Western culture generally, and its ideals and values survive to intensify modern bewilderment as they are misunderstood and misapplied to modern dilemmas.

In a sense, then, *Anything for Billy* tends to bring McMurtry's novels and the themes he has expressed through them for the past thirty years full circle. In several of the characters there also is a sense of fulfillment of previous characterizations which perhaps were left incomplete or only partly resolved before. In Katie Garza, for example, one can find traits of Molly, Jacy, Emma, Jean Arber, and Lorena, those "wilful women" whose determination to discover happiness is doomed almost before it starts and who become bamboozled by love and victimized by the very men they seek to control. But Katie is less wilful and more self-assured than previous heroines. Her killing of Billy—an act she performs because she cannot stand to see him shot by someone who does not love him—is testimony as much to her strength as to her vulnerability. In Cecily Snow, the shades of Lois Farrow, Patsy Carpenter, Aurora Greenway, Cindy Sanders, Karla Moore, and Clara, Gus's long-lost love in *Lonesome Dove*, emerge, although Snow is possibly less likable, less imposing, less sympathetic in this hard, almost cruel manifestation. She is a woman whose only reaction to watching a beheading by Isinglass's African henchman, Mesty-Woolah, is that the African "besplotched her father's chicken house with Joe Lovelady's blood" (250), and for whom love, sex, is merely "coupling," a means of controlling men, none of whom she wants, all of whom she uses.

In these two women is the combined image of McMurtry's frontier female archetype, women who he says "got along okay with their husbands until they learned they were supposed to have orgasms too, after which there was generally confusion and distress," women whose mothers were pioneers and who couldn't "make the leap" into the image that was created for them and found themselves lost and as bewildered as their husbands (*ING* 69). In *Anything for Billy* the women—even La Tulipe, the seer who recalls such philosophically oriented characters from Halmea to Ruth Popper to Aurora's maid— are catalytic; but they are not central, for McMurtry understands and points out in a way he hasn't since *Horseman, Pass By* that the frontier myth is, if anything, a male myth, the archetype a male archetype. The West might not be hard on horses, because they were valuable, he has written, but with women, it was a different story (*ING* 68). Women may be consorts, even conduits, for men and the actions they take; their stories may form the centerpiece of a novel, and their actions may ultimately determine a plot's outcome; but the story of the West—mythical, frontier, modern, urban—remains a man's story. Annie Oakley was a side-show attraction; Buffalo Bill was a hero.

Will Isinglass's character also fulfills a McMurtry type of long-standing duration: the rancher, stockman, Cowboy-God. Already an anachronism in a rapidly civilizing frontier, Will struggles fruitlessly to hang onto the past and the values associated with despotic power and absolute control through strength. He acknowledges that the future is upon him, slipping around the empty *Llano Estacado* and closing his future along with the frontier. He tells Sippy that he might consider becoming a schoolteacher in the Territory, although there was no need for one "just now," as there were no schools "just yet." In Will's character is the taciturn, stoic, almost masochistic old cowman whose reputation for taking a hard line strikes fear and respect into all who have heard of him. But fear and respect are not sufficient deterrent to rebellion, and it is rebellion that will ultimately shut down the man and leave only the legend to stand as that part of the myth.

"Old Whiskey," as Isinglass is called, is as indifferent to violence and ruthlessness as are the men he tracks and kills, including his foil and alter ego, Joe Lovelady, the proper but put-upon cowboy who is no less determined to live up to his fabricated image than anyone else and no less bewildered by the failure of his efforts. Isinglass is set in his ways—rejecting Cecily's tortoise soup for his regular steak and chili— and determined to keep things the way they are for as long as he can. He fears only murder in his sleep and is as impervious to eating ground glass as he is to the hatred that is universally felt for him. He brooks no betrayal, but he expects it and deals with it harshly when it comes. He tolerates no opposition, but he anticipates it and strikes it down as ruthlessly as he can when he finds it. Clearly modeled on the darker and perhaps truer sides of men like John Chisum and Charles Goodnight, Will Isinglass also possesses traits of Homer Bannon and Uncle Laredo from McMurtry's previous books, but he bespeaks something of Boog Miller and Vernon Dalhart as well in the more comic manifestations of the millionaire rancher/oilman who is the ruler of all he surveys. Again, as an archetype, the Cowboy-God Isinglass is harder and more evil than those who would inherit the myth and the image. He hands it down to men who are as tough but not as wise as their benefactor, and they, in turn, will pass it along to the Homers, Sam the Lions, Uncle Roger Wagonners, and even the Sonnys, men who keep the wisdom if they lose the grit or even the sanity that made the frontier their domain and kept them tall in the saddle as the new era dawned around them. Isinglass's ignominious end—pumping bullets into an automobile that runs away with him and mortally injures him—is as significant a comment on the end of the frontier and the Cowboy-God as Billy's emergence from a shadowy cloud is a comment on the elusiveness of the Outlaw-God's true nature.

In the character of Billy, as noted, Hud, Duane, and even a bit of Sonny Shanks and Cadillac Jack show through as he attempts to live up to some idea of himself, an idea of the Outlaw-God he hasn't even created but in which he believes fatally and with all his heart. But there is more here than that. In Billy we find the irresponsibility of Flap Horton and even a touch of Jake Spoon, men whose yearning for something they cannot define in no way offsets their attempts to grasp that which presents itself and to hang on tight until a better opportunity comes along. Billy blunders through and lives for the moment; he seeks destruction mechanically; he knows that at some point he will die violently, and he does everything he can to invite such an end in order to fulfill his destiny, to make the gossip true. It is an admirable determination, although a foolish one, yet it is an *idée fixe*, a hobgoblin not of a little mind but of a little myth that promises a place in posterity for anyone who can endure the pain.

Billy wants greatness, but he is willing to settle for the reputation of having it. He desires happiness, but he acknowledges that true contentment is no more real than the false image he attempts to live up to. He differs from Hud only in that he is willing to meet his fate head on and will not try to wriggle out of it and cut a new deal when he is called to pay up. His death completes his story and is concrete enough to be real, but even the factual circumstances of who kills him must be altered to fit a legend that has yet to be written. That, too, is the price of being an archetype.

But it is in the character of Sippy, the narrator and certainly the main character of this novel, that the ultimate importance of *Anything for Billy* is revealed, at least insofar as McMurtry's canon to date is concerned. Benjamin J. Sippy, novelist and manufacturer of a myth he has to go west to find in order to confirm his account, emerges from this novel as a mature Lonnie, a more confident Danny Deck, and, perhaps, a sadder but wiser authorial voice for contemporary Texas novelist Larry McMurtry. Sippy is involved in the action of the novel, but clearly, he is not a part of the story of Billy Bone. Instead, he is the main character of the story within the story, the account of how one writer comes to terms with his own lack of worth as a creator of a phony myth and finally understands how dangerous the worship of false gods can be. Like Lonnie, he has run away to write his own stories and to discover the "open books," but what he finds is reality, a flesh-and-blood boy who is caught up in an image men like Sippy have created. Like Danny, he becomes disillusioned, desirous of being swept away, if not by the Rio Grande, at least by the very real violence and brutal harshness of the frontier he discovers, but what he finds is a deeper and more meaningful romance, one that is not dependent on illusions but rather on courage and compassion even in the face of certain death. It is an initiation, a rite of passage for the author of potboiling pulp Westerns. Such initiations for McMurtry's characters, Kenneth W. Davis remarks, "are marked by overwhelming feelings of loss and of alienation. In keeping with his characterization of his region, the deaths he records as occurring there are violent and the initiations which result from them are traumatic" (29–43). Like Gus, Sippy learns that he must come to terms with the traumatic and tragic reality around him, not as a detached observer and reporter, but rather as an involved and active player in the bewildering drama of life as it unfolds.

More than any other McMurtry character or narrator, Ben Sippy seems to speak directly to the problems inherent in the conflict between the rural frontier past and its attendant myths and values and the modern urban present with its consistent rejection of reality in favor of misapplied and bewildering ideals and images that never existed in the first place. "I'm interested in how legends arise," McMurtry says. "Here was a man, a boy, really, who had a short life. How could he have produced a legend, and a bibliography with thousands of items in it? There's an element of sheer publicity in it" (Rothstein). Thus, Benjamin Sippy speaks directly for McMurtry's argument against the exploitation of the hollow myths of the frontier. Sippy claims that he invented "Billy the Kid," or at least the sobriquet, and that men like Tully Roebuck stole it from him; but, in the final analysis, they were welcome to it. He says, "No one wanted my new knowledge, my human depth—they only wanted my old silly heroes— or, failing that, Pinkertons" (363). It would, he understands at least, ultimately please Billy Bone to have lived and died up to the image that he sought so fatally; it would be a disservice to discredit that image by showing him to be the slight, bewildered boy he actually was.

Hence, *Anything for Billy* may be read as a coming together of several themes and ideas McMurtry has consistently expressed in his fiction and essays for almost thirty years. By putting his narrative voice into the past where his protagonist can observe the archetype in the making, he exposes the fruitlessness of the myth and the shallowness of its roots. A stronger and more clear statement of this argument, possibly McMurtry's real message, cannot be found in any of his previous novels, even in *Lonesome Dove* and *The Last Picture Show;* yet without those two demonstrations of McMurtry's thesis concerning the frontier myth and the vagaries of the rural past, *Anything for Billy* likely could not have been written. At the very most, it would exist only as a curious and entertaining yarn, possibly shot through with too much sentimentality and an excessive penchant for casual violence.

Looking at the rest of McMurtry's canon as a prologue to this novel, however, sheds a brighter light on this Texas novelist's treatment of the modern West, the new frontier. Aside from shadowy peeks at Philadelphia and Galveston in the 1880s, there are no cities in *Anything for Billy,* and there are none in *Lonesome Dove* or *Texasville.* Jack McGrath winds up in a small-town motel in Colorado, and McMurtry himself has relocated at least semipermanently to Archer County where he continues to run his urban bookstores while he writes in the shadow of the Cowboy- and Outlaw-Gods who once ruled the frontier. Whether he will essay forth with a new look at these old themes once more is anyone's guess, but in this most recent novel, he has stated his message concisely and with a firm conviction that archetypes and myths, symbols and images, reputations and legacies are strong stuff, not to be taken lightly and never to be accepted wholesale.

Although Larry McMurtry's writing has remained regional in tone and setting, there is no doubt that he is more than merely a Texas novelist who has achieved major recognition. McMurtry's contributions to the evolution of American fiction are profound, and the major question about his status as a contemporary writer is how long-lived his impact will be. Poised as he currently is with two post-Pulitzer novels and a book of essays to his credit, he still represents an enigmatic author whose work excites study and causes debate. Almost without exception, those who have followed his career await his next publication with anticipation and not a little dread. Where he goes from here may, indeed, validate or render useless the criticism that has gone before.

Where McMurtry will go from here, however, is not within the scope of this volume. The concern here is with where he has been, with what of value has been said about him while he was there, and with several important questions that are central to any assessment of his work thus far. This volume is, then, a kind of critical taking stock of his current status as a contemporary American and, not incidentally, Texas author. What is vital at this point, from a reader's perspective, is not to speculate on what he might do with his next book, but rather to examine what he has done that is worthwhile and to present a case for further critical evaluation and study of the works of Larry McMurtry.

NOTES

1. Larry McMurtry, "Ever a Bridegroom: Reflections on the Failure of Texas Literature," *Texas Observer* 23 Oct. 1981: 7–19; sufficient ink has been spilled discussing McMurtry's observations in this essay to obviate a lengthy discussion here. For a more thorough debate of McMurtry's points and other Texas critics and authors' reactions to them as well as other literary matters, see Tom Pilkington and Craig Clifford, eds., *Range Wars: Heated Debates, Sober Reflections, and Other Assessments of Texas Writing* (Dallas: Southern Methodist UP, 1988).

2. For a discussion of McMurtry's attitude toward *Lovin' Molly*, see "Approaching Cheyenne . . . Leaving Lumet. Oh, Pshaw!" in *Film Flam: Essays on Hollywood* (New York: Simon and Schuster, 1987).

3. See note 1, above.

4. Sewell's essay, incidentally, was named by McMurtry as being one of the best interpretations of his work that he had read during a meeting of the Western American Literature Association's meeting in Lincoln, Nebraska, in November 1987.

5. Less would be made of McMurtry's lapses from historical accuracy in film and fiction, perhaps, if he had not himself made such a stir about the complete ignorance of Texas geography, style, language, culture, and life-style reflected in *Lovin' Molly*. In *Film Flam*'s essay on the subject, noted above, he takes director Sidney Lumet harshly to task for his use of Bastrop, Texas, as a setting for Archer County, his dressing of the ranch-oriented characters in shoes rather than boots, and for a host of other inaccuracies and errors. "Here's HUD in Your Eye" and "Cowboys, Movies, Myths, & Cadillacs: An Excursus on Ritual Forms in the Western Movie," essays in *In a Narrow Grave: Essays on Texas* (3–30), address the same problems in association with the filming of *Hud* and in general. For another and, perhaps, less subjective discussion of the anachronisms and errors included in *Lovin' Molly,* see Larry L. King's article, "Leavin' McMurtry" (*Texas Monthly* [March 1974]: 70–78) and Don Graham's essay, "Filming McMurtry: The Regionalist Imperative," included in this volume.

6. Parenthetical citations from *Anything for Billy* in this essay are taken from advance uncorrected reader's proofs of the novel provided by Simon and Schuster and page numbers may not conform to those in the final, printed first edition.

7. Although historians and biographers vary in their treatment of the incident, all seem to agree that Billy's celebrated escape from the Lincoln County Court House came about after he somehow obtained a pistol and used it to shoot Deputy Sheriff J. W. Bell while being escorted to the privy. Billy then returned to the upstairs quarters where he was being held and shot Deputy Sheriff Robert Olinger as he returned from eating a meal across the street. According to one popular version of the story which is indicated by plaques and historical markers in Lincoln, New Mexico, he shot Olinger from the courthouse balcony with the deputy's own shotgun, which was loaded with dimes. Billy then supposedly broke the weapon into pieces and threw them at the body, admonishing the corpse that he would never use that weapon again. He then ransacked the courthouse and terrified the townspeople for about an hour, stole a horse, and made his way to a friend's ranch near Fort Sumner, New Mexico, where Sheriff Pat Garrett tracked him down on the night of July 11, 1881. Garrett supposedly shot Billy to death without announcing who he was or what he wanted. According to his own boast, Billy the Kid had killed twenty-one men, "one for every year I've been alive," although historians and biographers differ on the actual figure. He is buried at Fort Sumner, and his tombstone has been stolen and recovered at least twice. At least some locals around Fort Sumner claim that the body is missing from the grave, although there is no official record of the grave itself having been disturbed apart from the theft of the stone.

Biographical information on William Bonney is not hard to come by, but sources are at wide variance on any number of particulars. Among the best sources for factual data such as it can be established are the following: *They "Knew" Billy the Kid: Interviews with Old-Time New Mexicans,* ed. Robert F. Kadler (Santa Fe: Ancient City, 1987); *The Reader's Encyclopedia of the American West,* ed. Howard R. Lamar (New York: Crowell, 1977); C. L. Sonnichsen and William V. Morrison, *Alias Billy the Kid* (Albuquerque: U of New Mexico, 1955); Stephen Tatum, *Inventing Billy the Kid: Visions of the Outlaw in America, 1881–1981* (Albuquerque: U of New Mexico, 1982); and Jon Tuska, *Billy the Kid: A Bio-Bibliography* (Westport,

CT: Greenwood, 1983). Among these, Tuska's volume probably offers the most comprehensive bibliography and references to sources, fictional and historical, concerning the life of William Bonney.

WORKS CITED

Ahearn, Kerry. "More D'Urban: The Texas Novels of Larry McMurtry." *Texas Quarterly* 19.3 (1976): 109–29.

Baker, Christopher. "The Death of the Frontier in the Novels of Larry McMurtry." *McNeese Review* 28 (1981–1982): 44–54.

Busby, Mark. "Damn the Saddle on the Wall: Anti-Myth in Larry McMurtry's *Horseman, Pass By.*" *New Mexico Humanities Review* 3.1 (1980): 5–10.

Butler, Jack. "The Irresistible Gunfighter." Rev. of *Anything for Billy. New York Times Book Review* 16 Oct. 1988: 3.

Davis, Kenneth W. "The Themes of Initiation in the Works of Larry McMurtry and Tom Mayer." *Arlington Quarterly* 2.3 (1970): 29–43; rev. and rpt. as "Initiation Themes in the Cowboy Trilogy" in this volume.

Dubose, Thomas. "*The Last Picture Show:* Theme." *Re: Artes Liberales* 3 (1977): 43–45.

Erdrich, Louise. "Why Is That Man Tired?" *New York Times Book Review* 19 Apr. 1987: 7.

Graham, Don. "*Lonesome Dove:* Butch and Sundance Go on a Cattledrive." *Southwestern American Literature* 12.1 (1986): 7–12.

Hansen, Ron. "The New Adventures of Billy the Kid." Rev. of *Anything for Billy. Washington Post Book World* 9 Oct. 1988: 1+.

Hickey, Dave. "McMurtry's Elegant Essays." *Texas Observer* 7 Feb. 1969: 14–16.

McMurtry, Larry. *Anything for Billy.* New York: Simon and Schuster, 1988.

———. *In A Narrow Grave: Essays on Texas.* New York: Simon and Schuster, 1968.

Phillips, Raymond C. "The Ranch as Place and Symbol in the Novels of Larry McMurtry." *South Dakota Review* 13.2 (1975): 27–47.

Rothstein, Mervyn. "A Texan Who Likes to Deflate the Legends of the Golden West." *New York Times* 1 Nov. 1988: C17+.

Sewell, Ernestine P. "McMurtry's Cowboy-God in *Lonesome Dove.*" *Western American Literature* 21 (1986): 219–25.

Stout, Janis P. "Journeying as a Metaphor for Cultural Loss in the Novels of Larry McMurtry." *Western American Literature* 11 (1976): 37–50.

Summerlin, Tim. "Larry McMurtry and the Persistent Frontier." *Southwestern American Literature* 4 (1974): 22–28.

Winckler, Suzanne. "The Old West, The New South." Rev. of *Anything for Billy. Texas Monthly* Oct. 1988: 146+.

S P E A K I N G
P L A I N

The Essays and the General Criticism

JAMES WARD LEE

Larry McMurtry's essays, like his novels, present the author's many faces: the brilliant adolescent (the mature, reflective thinker); the show-off self-promoter (the self-effacing judge of his own work); the propagandist for himself and his friends (the balanced, judicious critic); the blistering satirist (the sentimentalist of the Dobie school). McMurtry is compassionate on occasion (but intolerant much of the time). An intellectual from the nation's capital (but only a few steps removed from the rodeo arenas and paper-napkin cafes of Archer County), Larry McMurtry is an acute observer of the Hollywood scene (as witnessed by country-boy novelist and redneck Texan).

The many faces of McMurtry appear in the novels and films, and in the essays that he has published for more than twenty-five years. It is hard to know how many sides to McMurtry there are. His novels can be divided into as many categories as a critic chooses—the Westerns, the city novels, the potboilers, the feminist works, the satires, and the work of West Coast glitz. His essays treat such subjects as screenwriting, sex in Archer County, Texas, the ignorance of Texas writers, Texas states of mind, and the "ego-zoo" of Hollywood ("in which egos are allowed to stroll around in their natural habitats" [*FF* 35]). His themes—in novels and essays alike—range from the changing West to the emergence of urbanism in Texas to the futility of life in little towns. His characters include tough cowboys like old "Wild Horse" Homer Bannon, Gideon Fry, and Woodrow Call; villains like Hud; loving women like Patsy Carpenter, Molly White, and Emma Horton. His novels abound in victims—Halmea, Ruth Popper, and the sensitive McMurtry-like figure Lonnie Bannon. It is hard to say whether the novels or the essays show the real McMurtry—or McMurtrys. In fact, the many shifts in McMurtry's themes, settings, subjects, and styles account for the thinness of the general criticism on his novels.

The fact that Larry Jeff McMurtry is now on the bad side of fifty does nothing to diminish his reputation as "the marvelous boy" of Texas letters. Like Audie Murphy, who always played "the kid" in Westerns, McMurtry is saddled with an image of eternal adolescence. Part of the reason is that his early novels, written when he was barely out of his teens, are still his most memorable (Pulitzer Prize notwithstanding), and one can't discount the effect a 1962 give-'em-hell speech to the Texas Institute of Letters had on his statewide reputation as a bad boy (he was then about twenty-six). And then there was the 1967 attack on Dobie, Bedichek, and Webb that branded McMurtry as a "young gunslinger" among the Old Guard. But most important in keeping McMurtry's artist-as-a-young-man reputation alive is his own view of himself as an always emerging writer. For most of his career, he has spoken of himself in essays as someone on the verge of new adventures in writing; and there is nothing in his career as a novelist, essayist, or screenwriter that would belie his constant search for newness and growth. He is always on the verge of discovery, always looking forward.

Despite the world-weary aloofness that he projects when he speaks to an audience, his writings always reveal that he is dreaming of a better next book, some perfect McMurtry novel still to be written. But who can guess what it will be? He offers prescriptions for the kind of novel that Texas should write—not novels of farm and ranch life (those he puts into the category of "Country-and-Western literature") but novels about "the less simplistic experience of city life." He dismisses his early works as "juvenile," saying of *Horseman, Pass By* and *Leaving Cheyenne* that "both incorporate, at best, a 22-year-old's vision" (*FF* 129–30). And of *The Last Picture Show* he says, "It was the flattest and most hastily written of my books—dashed off, in fact, in a fit of pique at my hometown—and by the time it was published, I had ceased to think well of it" (*FF* 18). The essays promise urban novels like *All My Friends Are Going to Be Strangers* and *Terms of Endearment,* but the books that appear after his call for an abandonment of the pastoral and bucolic are *Lonesome Dove, Texasville* (an even more dashed-off sequel to *The Last Picture Show*), and his newest novel, *Anything for Billy*. What happened to the McMurtry prescription to cure what ails Texas letters by going urban? Where are the complex city novels? Has the *enfant terrible* of Texas letters struck again to confuse and confound friend and foe alike? You bet!—to use a C-and-W expression. One thing is sure, McMurtry's next novel after *Anything for Billy* could be set in Washington or Buenos Aires or Crystal City, Texas. Its main character could be a resuscitated Charlie Goodnight (who has appeared more than once in McMurtry's works) or a Mexican bracero or Mary Queen of Scots. Larry Jeff the Kid is not to be taken for granted.

Most of McMurtry's essays may be found in two volumes, one old and one new. The older book is *In a Narrow Grave,* made up of magazine essays that came out between 1965 and 1968, the date of the book's publication. The newer volume is *Film Flam,* comprised of essays that were mostly written in the late sixties and early seventies. *Film Flam* is devoted solely to the movies, while *In a Narrow Grave* discusses literature, filmmaking, travel, McMurtry family history, and some of the byways of Texas life.

For most of the last twenty years, I have considered *In a Narrow Grave* to be callow comments on subjects that McMurtry knew less about than he thought. Now, I am not so sure that I was right. Tom Pilkington, who wrote a defense of McMurtry as essayist a good many years ago, "The Cowboy and the Dirt Farmer," tried for years to tell me that I was wrong. But *callow* was my word, and I was sticking to it. Naturally, I was too red-blooded an American to reread the volume before affirming my pronouncements. Now that I have reread *In a Narrow Grave* (the same weekend I read *Film Flam*), I am coming closer to Pilkington's position, but not all the way. Some of the essays in both volumes *are* callow or mean-spirited or careless. For the most part they are good pieces of writing that make more sense than I was willing to admit in my own callow days. But there are still some of the essays that betray a lack of thought or a general cussedness or a refusal to see things from any viewpoint but McMurtry's own. Since I have admitted all those faults in my own estimation of McMurtry, I ought to be more forgiving of him. And God knows I would hate to have all my random writings hauled out and scrutinized by someone as mean-spirited as I have been about Larry Jeff. But I will say in my own defense that I have made no effort to get my juvenile maunderings into hard covers and offer them to the reading public at one whack, let alone two. That is just inviting trouble. (Besides, I don't know a publisher who would gamble good money on my maunderings, juvenile or otherwise.)

McMurtry's most famous essay—at least in Texas literary circles
—is one that does not appear in either of the two volumes mentioned
above. "Ever a Bridegroom: Reflections on the Failure of Texas Literature" appeared in the *Texas Observer* in October 1981. It is the essay
that finally "tore it" with some of his most fervent admirers but probably established him as a hero with the *Texas Observer* crowd who have
always been embarrassed about what they perceive as the cornpone
image projected by many Texans.

"Ever a Bridegroom" was read to an audience at the Fort Worth Art
Museum, not a stone's throw from Texas Christian University, where,
if memory serves, McMurtry was once held in low esteem by some of
the stricter and more proper faculty members. McMurtry was teaching there when *Horseman, Pass By* came out. The word I have is that
Mabel Major, who loved and taught and fostered Texas literature in
the Dobie manner, was so appalled by the novel that she simply
checked it out of the library and refused to return it. When beseeched
to let the library have the book back, Major invoked her faculty privilege for long-term loans, and that was that. Mabel Major was not alive
when "Ever a Bridegroom" was read in Fort Worth, but one has to
wonder if McMurtry was still remembering his days at the Fort Worth
school. And still getting even. Getting even is one of the things that
seems to mark a great many of McMurtry's writings. In addition to
the "pique" that provides a subliminal score for *The Last Picture
Show,* there seems to be a good deal of mean-spiritedness in many of
the essays and in some of the novels, especially *All My Friends Are
Going to Be Strangers* and *Terms of Endearment.*

It is hard to tell whether the ruckus over "Ever a Bridegroom" was a
reaction to certain snide passages (some mightily true) or to his reac-
tivating the attack on the famed trio, Dobie, Bedichek, and Webb, or to
the general contempt he seems to feel for the idea of such a thing as
"Texas letters." To demonstrate what I mean by his snideness, let me
cite his final comment on Katherine Anne Porter. After quoting
Gertrude Stein's famous comment on Oakland, California—"There is
no there there"—he goes on to say, "I feel very much the same way
about the fiction of Katherine Anne Porter. The plumage is beautiful,
but plumage, after all, is only feathers" (9). I am not at all sure that he
is wrong, but the sentence falls into the category of the gratuitously
catty, as does his remark that Madison Cooper's novel *Sironia, Texas*
is "the book that makes the best doorstop" (18). In the area of Dobie's
reputation, McMurtry has not wavered a bit since his 1967 article
"Southwestern Literature?" He calls Dobie's works "a congealed
mass of virtually undifferentiated anecdotage: endlessly repetitious,

thematically empty, structureless, and carelessly written" (8). Such a sentence is almost certain to get worshippers of the "Holy Trinity" working alive like maggots. Even after all these years, followers of the "Three Men in Texas" brook no criticism of this trio of Golden Oldies. When a whippersnapper like Larry Jeff comes around calling them the Larry, Curly, and Moe of Texas letters, look out for eye-gouging and head-knocking. And on the matter of Texas literature, McMurtry is still of the opinion that it doesn't amount to anything. McMurtry says that there are no major writers: nothing written in Texas will last for more than ten years. And another thing: Texas writers too often write about the wrong stuff (the sweet but retrograde pastoral) instead of facing the "less simplistic" life of the cities; Texas writers have not read enough; Texas's "best writers' approach to art is tentative and intermittent: half-assed to put it bluntly. . . . The majority of our most talented writers have not yet produced even one book with a real chance of lasting" (18).

Naturally, such comments as those—and there are more, some even harsher—are certain to produce a reaction, a series of reactions. "Ever a Bridegroom" was hardly out before Bryan Woolley, a novelist and newspaperman, wrote a column for the *Dallas Times Herald,* entitled "Nuts to You Too, Mr. McMurtry." Woolley says that every few years "McMurtry feels the need to defecate on Texas." Woolley accuses Larry Jeff of the "very provincialism he decries," and closes his attack on McMurtry with this comment: "A Texas writer should do what any decent writer does: Write what he feels compelled to write. . . . and let McMurtry go on whining, if that's what he wants to do." Woolley's response is to McMurtry's presuming to prescribe subjects for Texas writers, a prescription that calls for an abandonment of books about the life of bucolic pleasures. McMurtry put it this way: "Why are there still cows to be milked and chickens to be fed in every other Texas book that comes along? When is enough going to be allowed to be enough?" ("Bridegroom" 10).

Of course, Woolley is right in reacting against McMurtry's trying to dictate the subject matter of Texas writing. McMurtry is on shaky ground in attacking books about the land, the farm, the ranch, the Piney Woods. Who is to say that a great novel must be about a particular subject or set in an urban area? I can't believe that McMurtry really thinks that. Nor do I think that McMurtry believes that city life is more complicated than rural life. It is not. It is easier to hide in the city than in the small town or the country. McMurtry's novels about life in and around Archer City prove that and show how complicated rural life can be. His assertion that "urban life offered me richer possibilities as a novelist" ("Bridegroom" 10) is not borne out by his writing. And, much as he hates it to be said, his best work has not been about city life.

In addition to Bryan Woolley's acerbic column, there were other voices to be heard from. The *Dallas Morning News*'s Kent Biffle devoted a couple of articles in the *Focus* section to the tempest. Under the headline "Bulldozing Texas' Literary Landscape," Biffle quoted comments from other Texas writers about McMurtry's essay. Dan Jenkins said, "Obviously, the man likes boring books. He writes boring books, and that's why he likes boring books." Francis Abernethy, inheritor of J. Frank Dobie's post as secretary-editor of the Texas Folklore Society, defended Dobie, and called McMurtry

> a rather superficial and condescending sort of reviewer . . . I think that something in Texas bit him in the gizzard and he's still trying to get even. It's like a kid who's 40 years old and is still talking about how bad his mother treated him. . . . Even before I read [McMurtry's article], I considered McMurtry a very uneven and mediocre writer at best. He was saved by having some damn good movies spin off his books. These were movies that gave his characters a lot more depth and his settings a lot more reality than his novels did.

A. C. Greene, who was castigated by McMurtry in "Ever a Bridegroom" for some of the choices he made in *The Fifty Best Books on Texas,* responded to the McMurtry article in a mild way: "Larry McMurtry always has been a demanding critic of his native state, especially of its literature: sometimes outrageous, occasionally outlandish, but penetrating and uniquely personal. . . . His weakness as a critic comes at those points where he seems to deny anyone the right to have a differing opinion."

The funniest response to the whole McMurtry *contretemps* came from Panhandle journalist and novelist Al Dewlen, who wrote a letter to the editor of the *Dallas Morning News* telling how McMurtry's

> cold dismissal of me as a writer, and of my novels as insignificant, shocked me and gave me gas. I've never met McMurtry, never abused him, never read him. So I can't believe he owes me insult. But he does owe me. The amount is $1,000, plus interest compounded since February 1962.

Dewlen goes on to tell how his novel *Twilight of Honor* was slated to win the Texas Institute of Letters Award for 1962. His agent had been alerted that Dewlen should be present at the banquet to receive it.

Dewlen had a "tailor make me a shimmering new suit warranted to bedazzle" the TIL. When he got to Dallas, he found people avoiding him. Then, he says:

> Evelyn Oppenheimer, intrigued by how the mere sight of me put [TIL President] Frank Vandiver to flight and sent [Secretary] Lon Tinkle ducking into restrooms, started poking around . . . and found that I had indeed won the best book prize. But the selection group, which had a distinct TCU taint, had reconvened and reconsidered. The reasoning was that since *Twilight of Honor* was a national best seller, I didn't need the money. But a young TCU-connected writer with a struggling book called *Horseman, Pass By* did need it, desperately. So, my prize would be re-awarded to Larry McMurtry.
>
> I declined to hold a press conference on the whole affair. Nevertheless, my name was scrubbed from the TIL's book of life. But I did feel mighty good about how my $1,000 was helping out old Larry. The fact is, I never intended to ask for my money back, not until I read last Sunday's *News.*

Margaret Hartley, a member of the judging committee, denied Dewlen's assertions and disputed the TCU taint. George Williams of Rice and Martin Shockley of North Texas State University did not respond to Dewlen's charge. The truth is probably as Margaret Hartley tells it. The misinformation probably came from Dewlen's agent and editor (who cancelled out on coming to Dallas at the last minute, saying he had contracted mumps). Dewlen learned later that the editor had not had mumps at all, which furthered his suspicions. It is likely that someone in New York jumped to a conclusion and misinformed Dewlen. Maybe.

One interesting note from Hartley's letter is that she says the McMurtry acceptance speech "took pot shots at the TIL and, in one sentence, at me personally." The stories, true or false, add to the McMurtry legend.

The essays that appeared in *In a Narrow Grave* back in 1968 struck just the right note among the *Observer* crowd of the sixties, the Texas liberals who had been fighting against "Old Texas" since the fifties. Here was a major Texas writer who had shown himself ready to abandon the usual Texas shibboleths, bite the hand of the Texas Institute of Letters, and take a swipe at "the Texas way." Larry the Kid would not hesitate to satirize LBJ and Sam Rayburn and the snuff-dippin' way of life lived by the rubes who ran the Texas Legislature. He was Young Lochinvar rough-molded by Archer County and North Texas

State College, planed and smoothed by Rice Institute, and polished to a veneer by Leland Stanford Junior University. The voice of Texas Past had been Dobie's; the voice of Texas Future would be Larry Jeff's. At least that is what the Scholz Beer Garden crowd and the college intellectuals thought.

But it never really worked out that way. Larry would not play the role that fate and Ronnie Dugger had assigned him. He taught at TCU briefly and then appeared to find a home at Rice. For a while. Then he decamped suddenly and established a bookstore in "fashionable" Georgetown (no other adjective is ever applied to that District of Columbia suburb). A faculty member at Rice told me that McMurtry's departure was stealthy, that he had been gone for some time before the administration tumbled to the fact that he was now running a bookstore in the Federal District and not teaching classes in English behind "the Wall." There must be more to this story than I was told. Again, here is an addition to the McMurtry legend. In any event, McMurtry was no longer available to Texans on their home ground, no longer one of the Billy Lee Brammers or Larry Kings ready to take up the cudgels of culture against the Texas Philistines.

But no matter about place of residence, Texas is in McMurtry's soul and always has been. He says, in the Introduction to *In a Narrow Grave,* that Texas may be a boring place "to move to, [but] it is not a boring place to be rooted. . . . Living here consciously uses a great deal of one's blood; it involves one at once in a birth, a death, and a bitter love affair" (xv). McMurtry tells of the god Hercules leaving Antony at the end of Shakespeare's play and sees in the Shakespearean scene a metaphor that fits his Texas: "[W]hat is the name of the god who now abandons Texas? Sometimes I see him as Old Man Goodnight, or as Teddy Blue, or as my Uncle Johnny . . . but the one thing that is sure is that he was a horseman, and a god of the country" (xvii). So, as the god abandons Texas, so does its most famous literary son. *In a Narrow Grave* is McMurtry's farewell to Texas—at least for a long while. As he tells in the book's Introduction, his Texas—real or imagined—is in a state of sudden change. The Texas of the future, he says, "is probably going to be a sort of kid brother to California, with a kid brother's tendency to imitation" (xv). And so McMurtry left the Texas that was becoming a kid brother to the Golden State. Maybe McMurtry saw Texas the way Joyce saw Dublin. It was a subject for literature, but it had to be written about from afar.

The essays in the volume range from the dispassionate and often cutting to the sentimental. "Here's HUD in Your Eye" is a humorous and biting picture of movie making in the Panhandle. The Amarillo matrons spend night after night circling the motel where Paul Newman stays, figuring ways to break into his room. The Hollywood types who come to the Panhandle to make the movie are shown warts and all. Only McMurtry is a sensitive observer. In fact, one of the things I dislike about the book is the lofty air that the essay often takes toward its material. In "The Old Soldier's Joy," his picture of the Old Fiddler's Reunion in Athens, Texas, is definitely from the point of view of the superior and sensitive observer of rubes and boobs. Written for the intellectually toney *Texas Quarterly,* the essay takes a satiric view of a minor East Texas celebration. McMurtry finds little to amuse him in Athens. His condescension is evident. He says, near the end of a day of observation, that "the one really lovely woman I saw that day" came on stage to sing:

> All day I had watched graceless bodies and resigned faces, but her face was not resigned, merely sorrowful. . . . what one noticed most in her was a combination of melancholy and weariness—the tired, composed weariness of someone who has lived a long while in the love of people whose capacities were smaller than her own. (106)

This is the kind of observation that "the sensitive" love. I find the whole comment disagreeable. Who can say that the singer has "lived a long while in the love of people whose capacities were smaller than her own"? What does this Kahlil Gibran gibberish mean anyway? I find "The Old Soldier's Joy," "Here's HUD in Your Eye," and "Eros in Archer County" unpleasant. "Eros" is an anatomy of sex among the ranch boys and must have caused sniggers among the English majors and Texas liberals when it appeared. "Love, Death, and the As-trodome" is a commentary on Texas Vulgar, Houston style. It doesn't take much imagination to figure what McMurtry's attitude is toward a room big enough to play baseball in. The article—written for the *Texas Observer*—was just the thing for the times, but now that every-one has an indoor ball-field, the amazement that everyone felt for the Harris County Domed Stadium has worn off.

The best of the essays in *In a Narrow Grave* are "Southwestern Literature?," "A Handful of Roses," and "Take My Saddle from the Wall: A Valediction." "Southwestern Literature?" is an early version of "Ever a Bridegroom." In it, McMurtry discusses the Texas litera-ture that he has read. That he went to the trouble to read all of Dobie, Bedichek, and Webb says a great deal about his diligence. The trouble is that he pontificates on Texas writers without having read some of the best ones. (The same failure can be noted in "Ever a Bride-groom.") What he has to say about the "Old Three," as their admirers still love to call them, is accurate and acute, I think. Dobie is unreadable today except by the most dedicated of Texana-philes; Webb is a good historian but not much of a literary figure; and Bedichek was a man of small and precious output. In "Southwestern Literature?"— once he has disposed of Dobie and his followers—McMurtry takes the pompous English major's approach to the writing about the state. He feels called upon to argue that Texas has produced no Dickens, no Balzac, no Yeats. To say that there is not "real greatness" in Texas writing is one of those parlor games that elitists play when deciding how many "true artists" existed between Chaucer and Shakespeare. If we start asking questions about greatness in literary periods, we might ask some of the following: How many major figures are there in American literature? How many of them came before 1850? Excessive worry about major figures is a pastime for rainy afternoons in the faculty lounge.

"A Handful of Roses" is McMurtry's assessment of the "character" of Texas cities. Dallas is "uneasy," its culture and sophistication are "mostly hybrid, not indigenous." Houston is "one of the last places left where men so simply go for their guns when an argument gets hot" (127). San Antonio "transcends" Texas. Austin is a city of "Wives, legislative, academic, or miscellaneous, some of them long in the tooth and lean in the shank, others graceful and nervous as does, but all of them, it sometimes seems, dedicated to the principle that the horn is always greener on the other guy" (133). These are the cliches that the *Texas Observer* and Scholz Beer Garden crowd have always mouthed about the cities of the state. (And probably about its women. I really can't say about that.) Nothing is new here, but at least McMurtry writes it all well.

And, finally, there is the most admired of all the McMurtry essays, "Take My Saddle from the Wall: A Valediction." This is McMurtry's farewell to a favorite uncle, a man who was the original of many characters in the novels. Uncle Johnny was a cowboy, a survivor, a Texan who lived before Texas was degraded and changed, a man of character and fortitude. He had "the look of a man who saw life to the last as a youth sees it, and who sees in any youth all that he himself had been" (172). Uncle Johnny is what Larry Jeff wants to be and wants to celebrate. The essay is good, and it gives a good insight into what McMurtry values in the Texas past.

"Cowboys, Movies, Myths, and Cadillacs: An Excursus on Ritual Forms in the Western Movie" is, as the title states, an essay on film. It is an interesting and serious discussion of what the rituals in the Western movies imply. It was published in *In a Narrow Grave* but would have fitted nicely in *Film Flam,* a book of essays devoted either to films that McMurtry saw or to his involvement in film as novelist or screenwriter. As is always the case with McMurtry's writings, the less he is personally involved, the more balanced the writing is. Several of the essays are narratives about McMurtry's adventures as a novelist whose work was being adapted or as a screenwriter himself. But a number of the essays are pure film criticism—the sort of thing that Pauline Kael writes for the *New Yorker.* Almost all the entries were first published in *American Film,* though a couple appeared in other magazines, and the final article was printed privately by the author.

Many of the essays are of the same vintage as those in McMurtry's first book. He admits in the Foreword that he had forgotten many of the essays and thought of them as coming from a typewriter other than his own. But a reader of McMurtry's works can spot the similarities of style and content between these and the ones reprinted in *In a Narrow Grave.* The several essays on McMurtry's involvement with Hollywood are exactly like the piece on the filming of *Hud.* His *Film Flam* essay on Sidney Lumet's version of *Leaving Cheyenne* is as acerbic as anything McMurtry has ever written. The Lumet movie, entitled *Lovin' Molly,* deserves the McMurtry treatment, for it is widely acknowledged to be one of Hollywood's worst movies. Most of McMurtry's novels lent themselves to filming, and most of those made into movies were in the same class as the novels themselves. McMurtry and others have praised some of the movies highly. But not *Lovin' Molly.*

The best essays in *Film Flam* are those where McMurtry can bring to bear his considerable learning in literature, both written and filmed. And there is no question that McMurtry is a well-educated critic of literature and film. He can usually talk on equal terms with professors of English or professors of film history and theory. He has read widely, and he has thought about what he has read and seen. Here is a paragraph from "The Situation in Criticism: Reviewers, Critics, Professors" that demonstrates something of McMurtry's intellectual interest in literary and film criticism:

> T. S. Eliot and the New Critics chipped away at the author's privileged position as a critic of his own work, but it remained for Northrop Frye to utterly destroy this privilege. *The Anatomy of Criticism* was as devastating an attack on authorial authority as, say, *The Origin of the Species* was on biblical authority. Frye cooly pointed out that it is ridiculous to grant authors or auteurs special privileges in regard to the criticism of their own work. An author who criticizes his own work is merely one of his own critics, not

necessarily the best. Authorial comment is seldom descriptive
enough to suit Frye; too often it falls off into value judgment, and
the *Anatomy* banishes the old criticism of value judgments, mere
footnotes in the history of taste, and replaces it with the study of
genres, modes, and structures. (77)

I don't cite this paragraph to show that McMurtry has some revealed brilliance or that he has mastered the arcana of modern theory.
It does show that McMurtry is interested enough in critical theory to
read the major texts and think about them. Whether he can apply
what he knows to his own writing and to Texas literature is sometimes
in question, however. He derides *Horseman, Pass By* and *Leaving
Cheyenne* and seems to think better of *Terms of Endearment* than
many others do. And he is never loath to speak with definiteness on
his writings, though I suppose he does not forget that as author he is
only one critic of many. I find his criticism of film to be professional
and well thought out. I don't think *Film Flam* is an outstanding work
of film criticism, but some of the individual pieces are thoughtful,
informed, and well written.

Only a handful of articles or reviews have commented formally on
McMurtry's essays. Tom Pilkington offers one of the only extended
commentaries on *In a Narrow Grave,* and the *Texas Observer* piece is
predictably laudatory. I doubt that the essays of McMurtry—unless
he produces another "Ever a Bridegroom"—will draw much commentary from critics, academic or journalistic. For one thing, he doesn't
write many nowadays and, with his success as a novelist, he may write
even fewer in the future.

There are probably several reasons that critics have produced so
little good general criticism on his novels. For one thing, McMurtry is
hard to pin down, for he keeps changing the venue: country to small
town to city to small town to country. If a writer won't settle down to
a steady viewpoint or a certain area or a general thematic stance,
writers of criticism are left scratching out particular small issues. I
think another reason the criticism is so thin is that McMurtry has not
been a writer of repute long enough to stimulate much criticism by the
average English professor. Instead of someone's devoting a great deal
of study to McMurtry and producing article after article the way one
might do on, say, Faulkner, what we get is the "occasional" article
written to be read at a regional meeting. Time constraints make the
writer think in terms of the twenty-minute paper (ten pages). The
writer finds a motif in two or three of the novels and packages a neat
idea for a short essay. Since McMurtry has not long been a writer of

national reputation, even the small-compass articles are few. In any case, there is very little general commentary on the McMurtry canon—if I may use such an inflated term. One final reason for the lack of criticism is that Texas literature, about which McMurtry has said so much, is only now achieving respectability. Critics like Don Graham, Tom Pilkington, Mark Busby, and some others included in this volume are still in the process of leading the way toward a disciplined study of Texas writing—and of McMurtry in particular.

WORKS CITED

Biffle, Kent. "Bulldozing Texas' Literary Landscape." *Dallas Morning News* 8 Nov. 1981: G1+. Includes quotations by Francis Abernethy, A. C. Greene, and Dan Jenkins.

Dewlen, Al. "The McMurtry Case, Chapter 2." *Dallas Morning News* 22 Nov. 1981: G1+.

Hartley, Margaret. "On McMurtry: Some Final Words." *Dallas Morning News* 29 Nov. 1981: G1+.

McMurtry, Larry. "Ever A Bridegroom: Reflections on the Failure of Texas Literature." *Texas Observer* 23 Oct. 1981: 1, 8–19. Rpt. in *Range Wars: Heated Debates, Sober Reflections, and Other Assessments of Texas Writing.* Ed. Craig [Edward] Clifford and [William] Tom Pilkington. Dallas: Southern Methodist UP, 1989.

_____. *In a Narrow Grave: Essays on Texas.* Austin: Encino, 1968.

_____. *Film Flam: Essays on Hollywood.* New York: Simon and Schuster, 1987.

Woolley, Bryan. "Nuts to You Too, Mr. McMurtry." *Dallas Times Herald* 22 Nov. 1981: R4.

There are relatively few general studies of McMurtry's works compared to the amount of criticism of his individual titles. A number of journal entries treat a particular theme as it appears in more than one novel, and the editors have reprinted several in this volume. Tim Summerlin's "Larry McMurtry and the Persistent Frontier" is typical of the kind of general study that exists. Summerlin traces the theme of the disappearing frontier through the five novels and one volume of essays that had appeared by 1974. Janice Stout's 1976 essay, "Journeying as a Metaphor for Cultural Loss . . ." is a discussion of journeying as a "resonating device" that echoes America's own tendency to "wester" when faced with cultural impoverishment. Like the two mentioned above, Raymond C. Phillips, Jr.'s "The Ranch as Place and Symbol . . ." is limited in its scope, concerning itself with the ranch as the "vortex . . . about which everything moves" in McMurtry's first five novels. And, finally, Billie Phillips's "McMurtry's Women . . ." is an exploration of three kinds of love exemplified in McMurtry's females. Phillips sees the women in the author's first five novels as being either "searchers, settlers, or travelers," all of whom fail in some measure to "experience authentic love." Each of the four essays furthers our understanding of McMurtry's works, but none aims at more than one idea, at more than a small explication of the writer's canon.

The criticism devoted to the two volumes of essays is even more limited. Tom Pilkington's article on the essays of Larry King and McMurtry—only the McMurtry half is printed here—is the only piece that goes beyond the transitory review. Pilkington argues that McMurtry's *In a Narrow Grave* is among the finest essays to come out of the state. Equally laudatory is the brief *Texas Observer* notice of McMurtry as essayist by Dave Hickey. The context of the times should not be forgotten in judging the *Observer* reviews of *In a Narrow Grave*. This was the era when Dobie, Bedichek, and Webb were the preeminent spokesmen for Texas cultural affairs. McMurtry's iconoclasm fitted well with that of the *Observer*. Donald Barthelme's "Terms of Estrangement" is a response to McMurtry's celebrated "Ever a Bridegroom," which continued his attack on Dobie et al. and went on to more damning of Texas writing. Barthelme takes issue with McMurtry's assessment of Texas writing as hopelessly third-rate.

The only piece worth noting on McMurtry as a film critic is Bruce Bawer's review of *Film Flam* that appeared in *The New Criterion.*

Bawer's thorough commentary on the book of essays concludes that McMurtry's own atypical experiences in Hollywood have led him to generalize without having been more than an amateur in the film business, but, Bawer says, the book "succeeds quite nicely as a charming and funny personal account."

. .

Larry McMurtry and the Persistent Frontier
TIM SUMMERLIN

Wandering between two worlds, one dead,
The other powerless to be born.
   —Matthew Arnold, "Stanzas from the Grande Chartreuse"

For some writers "home" is only the place they come from, while for others it is a part of their blood and infused in their senses. The upper Midwest is the setting for a handful of Hemingway's stories, but he adapted easily to Paris, Spain, Italy, or the Florida Keys. William Faulkner, on the other hand, needed go no further than his native Mississippi for the source and setting of his essential work. Larry McMurtry, author of five novels and one book of essays over the last dozen years, falls clearly into the latter category. Reared in Archer County, Texas, a plains region in which dwindling post oak gives way to the grasses and mesquites of West Texas and which has become familiar to millions of Americans through the film, *The Last Picture Show,* McMurtry has created a fictional world inspired and shaped by the Southwest.

This is not to say that Larry McMurtry is a writer of Westerns. There are no gunfights on Main Street, ambushes in box canyons, or even big cattle drives in his writings. The old West is dead and he is very concerned with the living. His relation to the heroic vision of freedom, courage and the self-sufficiency of man and horse that we call the myth of the cowboy is vividly described in McMurtry's introduction to his volume of essays, *In a Narrow Grave.* He likens the disappearing myth to the departure of the god, Hercules, from the doting Antony: "That god is riding fast away," he says, "and will soon be out of sight and out of hearing." But if the days of Oliver Loving and Old Man Goodnight are gone, many customs, traditions, and attitudes of their era linger on in their descendents, even when they have packed up and moved to the big city. This anachronistic but continuing mind-set McMurtry calls "symbolic frontiersmanship," and there is nothing closer to the heart of his fictional world than the pathos and tensions it creates. He may address himself directly to the problem of the old cowboy caught in a changing world or, more indirectly, he may treat the mores of a small town, the relation of the sexes, or the consciousness of a writer within the context of the disappearing frontier. That Texas frontier, though, always looms large.

The archetypal image of the god's departure for McMurtry comes from an old story which recurs in his writings of a ragged group of Indians who left their reservation to beg a buffalo from Charles Goodnight. When the old man finally relented, they dragged the buffalo out and amid shouts and yells killed him, a pitiful attempt to relive past glory. McMurtry traces the Indians' symbolic bloodlines in the rodeo rider reduced to driving a train in Hermann Park and frequenting the bars of South Houston, where a great deal of "symbolic frontiersmanship" is practiced to the danger of the habitués. He traces them in ranchers whose lordship of the land is successfully challenged by government control and the oil wells which have usurped the range. He even finds them in a young novelist whose imagination is haunted by his ninety-year-old uncle, a rancher to whom he returns in search of some clue to his own character.

A journey through McMurtry's novels is a journey through a gallery of the dispossessed, a wide assortment of "symbolic frontiersmen." *Hud*, originally entitled *Horseman, Pass By*, treats most directly the fate of the cowboy in the twentieth century. It pits old Homer Bannon, loyal to the earth and his own moral code, against his stepson, Hud, who embodies the westerner's instinct for survival and contempt for authority, and both these men against a government which demands that their diseased cattle be destroyed. Time is a villain in the elegiac *Leaving Cheyenne* through the inexorable drying up of the cowboy's "blood's country and his heart's pastureland." Gideon Fry, Johnny McCloud, and Molly Taylor, lifelong friends and lovers, form a sort of composite mind of the West: Gid, ambitious, sober, and conscience-haunted; Johnny, boyish and unreflective; and Molly, warm and giving, suggestive of whatever is best in the land. *The Last Picture Show* portrays life in one of the hundreds of vacant-faced towns one encounters across the state, casting a cold eye on the stifling sexual customs and narrowmindedness which reaffirm the homelessness of young Sonny Crawford.

Rural residents are not alone finding their vision of freedom and self-discovery in the vast plains of the Southwest comprised by time and man. McMurtry's most recent novels pass to the dispossessed in the urban setting of Houston with forays as far away as California. *Moving On* depicts the restlessness of a young couple, Jim and Patsy Carpenter, and explores their vague disquiet perhaps too thoroughly, to the point of tedium. Born too early to fit into the drug culture or the world of the flower children, they cannot find strong roots in an older tradition either. Danny Deck, protagonist of *All My Friends Are Going to Be Strangers,* moves in a similar environment, with an ancestral past which belongs to the soil and a present which includes all the giddy trappings of a successful first novelist and screenwriter. He can be comfortable in neither world. All of these characters live to some degree in a state of flux, a state suggested by each of the book titles; perpetual restlessness is their fate.

McMurtry does create people whose world is stable or who, at least, have come to terms with life. The old people who most perfectly embody the myth of the cowboy have a steadiness and tenacity which is enviable. The loyalties of Homer Bannon, the Carpenters' Uncle Roger Wagonner, and Gideon Fry to their land and their close-grained sense of integrity are unshakeable. A very different but equally solid bedrock of personality is found in the characters of Hud and Danny Deck's ancient Uncle Laredo. Hud was born out of his era and Uncle Laredo has long outlived his, but both have the energy and ruthlessness to have carved empires out of the West. Theirs is the kind of mastering passion which knows "no variables," in Danny's words, the kind necessary to those who would make life theirs.

It is an enormous leap from these primitive figures to the insouciant chaos of the modern multiverse, but those at home in one sphere share something with those who are comfortable in the other. The secular person is as confident of the superiority of his way of life as the committed cowboy is of his. His may be based on the admittedly shaky principles of agnosticism and may even be precariously close to the edge of nihilism, but it is, he believes, the only enlightened response to the age of relativity. The supreme image of this ethos for McMurtry is California. It is urban, plural, volatile, sensual and blithely free of the "mystery and guilt," the "fear, remorse, and shame," to use the language of *Moving On,* that characterize the more backward segments of society. Californians have left the childhood of the race behind and advanced to a fantastically healthy, if sometimes bland, state. See Clara Clark, for instance, the California-bred graduate student of *Moving On:*

Movies seldom moved her—very little *did* move her, though she was not unfeeling. It was as if her needs were purely metabolic, she was too nearly complete, too fully possessed, to need very much emotionally. Food, sleep, a job, sex, pleasant company: those were her needs. She was not dramatic, not neurotic; ultimately, she was athletic.

It is this direction that the future lies. McMurtry suggests, in passing, some of the human wreckage that washes up in the wake of the accelerated pace of society—those who cast their lot with California but lack the constitution to see it through. Patsy Carpenter's younger sister, Miri, is a failed hippie and drug enthusiast. Danny Deck's movie mentor has the Hollywood style down pat, even to the eccentricity of keeping a 22-pound pet rat, but his chronic discontent indicates that he has not been able to maintain the Californian's uncluttered psyche.

This breezy world, however, is at the fringe of McMurtry's true country. His protagonists are typically a step or three further back in social development and many degrees less confident of themselves than is the quintessential Californian, but they do not fit into the older world either. Often they are literally homeless. Such homes as McMurtry does portray are typically fractured. The Bannons exist in an uneasy truce, broken by the book's end. One recalls the picture of Homer and his wife sitting in the same room, he listening to "Fibber McGee" and she to "Break the Bank," with the two radios blaring away in competition. Both Gideon Fry's and Molly Taylor's mothers died young, and his father is stern while hers is an out-and-out tyrant. Sonny Crawford's mother is dead, and his drug-addicted father remains in the shadows—as a highschooler, Sonny lives in a rooming house. The Carpenters ignore or endure their parents, and Danny Deck considers himself the family "black sheep." Little security or sense of community is provided by the family in McMurtry's novels, echoing their general preoccupation with outcasts. As the novelist comments, in a significant metaphor, "Not long after I entered the pastures of the empty page I realized that the place where all my stories start is the heart faced suddenly with the loss of its country, its customary and legendary range."

Lonnie Bannon, the narrator of *Hud,* is such a victim. Though he loves his grandfather, he realizes that they live in "separate times," and he cannot feel the old man's identity with the soil. He is awed by Hud's brutal vitality but unwilling to try to match it. He hears the trains at night, thinking of all the romantic cities they travel to, embroiders on his memory of a visit to Fort Worth, and, finally, when he seems the "only one left," heads off to try to relieve that unscratchable itch. Sonny Crawford also knows what it is to feel like "the only human creature in the town." Like other Thalians, he is victimized by repressive sexual myths that seal people into their separate emotional compartments. Conscious enough to realize the viciousness of the life and to see himself implicated, Sonny knows no way out of his discomfort.

Even those protagonists a generation or two removed from rural life are hobbled by expectations and prejudices that unfit them to be true golden people. Patsy Carpenter and Danny Deck customarily speak in the theological categories which a restive Ralph Waldo Emerson called "rotten language," and which reveal them to be less than liberated. No one ever engages in sex, it seems, who is not "seduced," and unmarried people living together are only half-jokingly said to be "living in sin." Sex is not finally a simple athletic engagement for them, though both Patsy and Danny can at times engage in the therapy of pure sensation. There remains a shroud of "mystery and guilt" about it, an inheritance from the ethos of Sonny Crawford, Gideon Fry and Lonnie Bannon.

Demons haunt these characters; they often fail as if to spite themselves. McMurtry's heroes and heroines may be wilful, but they are seldom profoundly sure of themselves. Sonny, Lonny, Molly, Patsy, Danny—all are disposed to be confused, to blame themselves. Patsy cannot be gracefully affectionate in public regardless of her wishes. Danny lives on Fig Newtons in a rundown hotel when he can easily afford comfortable surroundings. Some vague uneasiness, some atavistic fear that when things fall too easily into one's lap disaster is near, haunts them. Perhaps it is an inheritance from those pioneer ancestors living in an uncertain land who knew that ideal weather conditions one year bespoke drought the next. It may be ancient, unshakeable fear of hubris and the consequences of pride. Perhaps their bones hint what Gideon Fry's father drummed into his head: "Why, any damn fool can enjoy himself," he said. And what then is life for? "Fight it. Fight the hell out of it."

Fight it or enjoy it or, what is more likely, work out an uneasy accommodation of the two philosophies—whatever they do, these protagonists are alike in suspecting that life will never be a dependable ally. McMurtry is drawn to characters who are unrequited dreamers with visions of a life, a style, or a lover of ideal proportions which will never be found. They are awed by, sometimes admire, the Huds and Sonny Shankses, champion cowboys with the insolence necessary to get their own way, but they cannot be these people. They have too much in common with the Jessie Logans and Pete Tatums, marginal people, losers in life, to be swaggering heroes. They cannot create or purchase, finally, perfection, untainted success, or a sense of completion.

For Lonnie Bannon the plight is summed up in the plaintive wail of "Fräulein" with its image of the remote, unattainable beauty, "far across the distant waters." Molly Taylor, prevented by her own whims and Gid's unyielding conscience from living with her "favorite," decides, "I don't know that there are situations where you can completely win. Not where you can completely win something important." *Moving On* is full of things not completely won—flaws prevent nearly every relationship from ripening into maturity. Ruth Popper, Sonny Crawford's middle-aged lover, answers his confusion with a non-answer: "Never you mind." She might just as well speak to Danny Deck, the *schlemiel* who is repeatedly told, "You'll never learn," and who, indeed, in his twenty-three years never does learn what it takes to survive. None of his images of human happiness or successful living will stand for even five minutes. Flight to California is futile when the "genie" of a brooding, ungenerous Texas looms over him, awaiting vengeance on anyone so foolish as to believe escape from its dominance is possible.

If any of McMurtry's characters are saved, they must surely be those few who retain a grace after passing through the fire of human loss. *The Last Picture Show* gives us Sam the Lion, an old man who has endured the almost unbelievable experience of the loss of three teenage sons and the madness of his wife, outrageous even by McMurtry's standards of family instability. Throughout this he has somehow been able to retain the distinction between "trashy behavior" and human decency, and, even more striking, he still has a sense of romance. There is an unquenchable flame of life in an old man who can claim of a girl he had loved years before, "Being crazy about a woman like her's always the right thing to do. Being a decrepit old bag of bones is what's ridiculous." Joe Percy, the Hollywood script writer who befriends Patsy Carpenter, lives in a world aeons away from that of Sam the Lion, but he plays much the same role in his. Not surprisingly, he has lost the one true love of his life to cancer. He lives his life and practices his trade, treating himself with humor and others with impeccable respect, a bastion of sanity amid the emotional lunacy of his surroundings. There are a few other ministering angels in McMurtry's novels, people redeemed by a tender imagination or compassion for others. But such knowledge does not given them protection against life. They remain, like all of the people the novelist cares about, supremely vulnerable.

McMurtry's own saving graces are a sure sense of his subject matter and the means to approach it. He has suggested a personal literary theory in *In a Narrow Grave*, expressing his faith in "the creation of characters" and narrative as essential to fiction even if both are depreciated by modernist theory. In another essay he remarks that prose "must accord with the land" and contrasts the spare style appropriate to the Southwest with the sinuosity and density of Faulkner in the forests of Mississippi. Both points are apropos to McMurtry's work. His clean-swept narrative is ideally suited to the expression of the simple things he loves—the smell of a big breakfast cooking, the taste of a freezerful of ice cream, the feel of a horse in the morning, and the austere geometry of the rancher doing his work. When I saw *The Last Picture Show* I recall hearing the audience laugh when Ben Johnson commented about the scenery around a stock tank, "Ain't it beautiful?" I knew the writer must have expected a laugh—mesquites are not the universal ideal of beauty—but I also suspected he sympathized more with his character's response than with that of the audience. McMurtry shies away from portentous symbols, preferring images which resonate with quiet human significance. There are, for instance, the recurring images of Fort Worth, the great glittering outside world; Old Man Goodnight and his buffalo, a tale of loss; or the broken keg of molasses, a monstrous accident that meant a long winter with no sweets.

Appropriately, Larry McMurtry's most persuasive scenes are those unadorned and quiet moments when two souls meet on a familiar turf. The previously mentioned scene of Sam the Lion and Sonny Crawford at the stock tank is such a one; Patsy Carpenter and her friend Emma Horton contemplating their "undisciplined squads of emotions" in a Houston park is another. As the two women talk, their ineptness and the unassaultable elusiveness of life are mirrored in the Hortons' young son, frustrated in his efforts to play basketball with the older boys. McMurtry accomplishes more in one scene such as this than in a hundred pages of description of the vague unrest and minor irritabilities in which the novel indulges. These are the moments which contain what McMurtry calls the "silence where fiction starts," a sort of respectful reticence before the unfolding of human drama. It is a silence present in all of his best work whether it be found on Idiot Ridge or Bissonnet Street. There is more than a little of the austerity and quiet of the Southwest in it.

If the god has departed entirely, should his scribe remain behind? Writing in 1968, McMurtry suggested that the loss of one's range created "defeats that are tragic in quality." Both Patsy Carpenter and Danny Deck, since that time, have had strong suspicions that their problems, tormenting as they seem, are more trivial than tragic, and enormous only because they themselves are unable to direct their feelings appropriately. Perhaps it is coincidence that McMurtry has left

the state and now lives, as I understand, in the Washington, D.C.
area. Possibly he is seeking some other theme more appropriate to
the age. But then, there is nothing necessarily parochial about the
conflict of a world which refuses to conform itself to the individual's
emotional makeup. One can find excellent company for him in American literature alone. Hawthorne, Twain, James, Fitzgerald, and
Hemingway come to mind quickly. Possibly, just as he followed his
Homer Bannons, his Huds, and his Lonnies from Archer County to
Houston and California, he will now extend his pilgrimage and seek
them in their nation's capital. As anyone who has followed the Water-
gate hearings can testify, they should be found in ample abundance.
One only hopes he is not too far away to hear the call of his "genie" if
it has something valuable to say.

Journeying as a Metaphor for Cultural Loss in the Novels of Larry McMurtry

JANIS P. STOUT

Northrop Frye writes in *Anatomy of Criticism,* "Of all fictions, the
marvellous journey is the one formula that is never exhausted."[1] I
would add that the aimless journey, wandering, is also a timeless
formula and one with a relatively constant meaning. This archetypal
structure, the journey, variously pervades and controls the novels of
Larry McMurtry and extends their import beyond the limits of a
regional commentary.

McMurtry's five novels have not generally been considered in relation to archetypes but rather in relation to the more limited patterns
afforded by their Texas setting and its distinctive heritage.[2] Regarded
in regional terms, the novels show considerable variation, as the impulse to mythicize the forebears and to assess present life by its departure from their model, evident in *Horseman, Pass By* and *Leaving
Cheyenne,* yields, in *The Last Picture Show,* to a virtually unrelieved
distaste for the moribund small-town life which succeeded that austere
heritage and, in the last two novels, to a radical dissociation from any
cultural heritage.[3] This growing disaffection is fittingly manifested in
the successively greater predominance of journey structures which, increasingly, describe the circuitous patterns of aimless wandering.

In a comment appended to *Horseman, Pass By* McMurtry said,
"In my own generation of adolescents the shakeup [of an urbanizing

society] manifested itself as a consuming restlessness—an urge to be on the move." As a member of that generation of adolescents in Texas, I can testify to the accuracy of his remark and to the consuming importance of the automobile. The degree of its dominance is a crucial factor in McMurtry's novels. The one novel which largely antedates that dominance, *Leaving Cheyenne,* shows the strongest attachment to place and to a stable and traditional pattern of life, ranching. To the adolescents of *The Last Picture Show* and to Hud, of *Horseman, Pass By,* the automobile offers escape. But to the characters of the two novels of contemporary urban life, *Moving On* and *All My Friends Are Going to Be Strangers,* neither the goal nor the repellent impulse for escape is clear. In simple uncertainty, they practically live in their cars. Since the preparation of this study, the third in what appears to be McMurtry's trilogy of Houston, *Terms of Endearment,* has been published. In this novel, one character does literally live in his car. This growth in the dominance of the automobile, as well as the varying modes of the journey motif in the novels and the cultural dissolution they signify, can be seen to occur in three distinct phases, and it is in this sequence that I would like to consider McMurtry's work. In the first two novels, the impulse to journey is chiefly a desire for experience, and the more fully a character identifies himself with the ranching way of life the less he travels. The journeys of *The Last Picture Show* are sporadic and frustrated expressions of an urge to find an alternative to an empty and deadening life. But the last two novels share a use of journeying as a metaphor for modern life itself, which is seen as being impoverished by the demise of the old traditions and the lack of new structures of meaning and allegiance.

The youthful protagonists of the two early novels,[4] which chronicle the decline of the ranching tradition, keenly feel the urge to be off, to broaden their horizons. To them, journeying means adventure. But both are caught between this urge and the equally strong allegiance to values represented by their ranch homes. Thus, Lonnie, of *Horseman,* is caught between loving admiration for his grandfather, Homer Bannon, and a reluctant attraction to his stepuncle, Hud. Sitting at night on the front porch with Granddad, he "could watch the cars zoom across the plains—north to Amarillo or Raton, south to Dallas or Houston or Fort Worth" (p. 4). These are the magic names of his world, representing all that adventurous adult life from which he is still shut out, and Lonnie endows passing trains with the mystery these relatively far-off cities hold for him: "I could see the hundred lighted windows of the passenger cars, and I wondered where in the world the people behind them were going night after night. To me it

was exciting to think about a train" (p. 4). Lonnie's restlessness manifests itself in his driving fretfully between ranch and town, but there
is nothing new he can learn in Thalia and almost nothing to do. It is
not that Lonnie is a rebel against his origins; he "really liked" Thalia
but "just didn't want it for all the time" (pp. 57–58). What he does
want is acquaintance with the wider world that essentially represents
adulthood.

The catalyst for this wish is Jesse, a forlorn drifter, whose talk
makes Lonnie "itch to be off somewhere . . . to go somewhere past
Thalia and Wichita and the oil towns and Sno-Cone stands, into
country I'd never seen" (p. 22). Jesse had been to "practically ever
town in Texas, big or little," a fact that makes him a virtual Sinbad in
Lonnie's eyes, and "just hearing the names was enough to make me
restless" (p. 93). But Jesse explicitly warns him against a rootless life:

> "You boys think stayin' in one place is tiresome, just wait till you
> see that goddamn road comin' at you ever mornin'. And still comin'
> late that evenin' and sometimes way into the night. I run that road
> for ten years and never caught up with nothin'." (p. 94)

When the destruction of Homer Bannon's herd forces Jesse to set out
for yet another place to pick up work, he reiterates:

> "It don't hurt to take a little look around. . . . Just don't turn into
> an old loose horse like me. You're better off to stop somewhere,
> even if it ain't no paradise. . . . I went all over this cow country,
> looking for the exact right place an' the exact right people. . . .
> But that's going at it wrong. I shoulda just set down an' made it
> right wherever the hell it was." (p. 148)

There is no real danger that Lonnie will look indefinitely for a perfect
place, since he has already seen his "exact right place," the ranch,
destroyed. That destruction cannot be blamed on any one person or
cause, but is an inevitability arising ultimately from the mysteries of
disease and proximately from modern technology, in the form of government veterinarians who can order a man's herd destroyed.[5] But
Hud is associated with the process of change; when he gains control of
the ranch he will surely allow drilling for oil, a disruption of the
ranching way that Homer Bannon has steadily resisted. Hud bears a
more direct guilt as well, however, since his rape of Halmea, the winsome black cook who embodies the fecundity of the earth itself, forces
her to leave the ranch. With her powerful attractive and sustaining
force removed, and with the herd destroyed and his grandfather dead,
Lonnie sets out, apparently, to follow Jesse's nomadic example.

The implications of this concluding departure, however, are not entirely unambiguous. Certainly he has lost his cultural roots, but it is implied that personal allegiances may nevertheless provide him a secure sense of identity. Jesse had earlier told Lonnie he had "better stay till your Granddad gets back on his feet a little" (p. 148). That is, loyalty to an individual might provide anchorage. The idea is not developed, and we have little basis for speculating on the nature and duration of Lonnie's venture into the wider world. But I take it that this is one implication of his concluding comment on the trucker with whom he rides out of town: "he reminded me of someone that I cared for, he reminded me of everyone I knew" (p. 179). So long as the faces of strangers remind Lonnie of those he has cared for, he will have a tie to a special place where he belongs.

A similar theme appears in *Leaving Cheyenne* as McMurtry moves back to give, from the carefully distinguished points of view of his three central characters, an account of the regional development from the relative stability of the early twentieth century to the town-centered transience of approximately the same period as that of *Horseman, Pass By*. Against a background of the move away from the land, he projects a drama which affirms allegiance to one's own place. That allegiance is developed and examined in the novel both directly and by means of the paradigmatic relationships of three male characters—the rancher Gid and the cowboy Johnny, each of whom narrates a section, and the footloose oilfield hand Eddie—to Molly, an idealized development of the mother-earth associations surrounding Halmea in the earlier novel.

In the long opening section—which pointedly antedates the local impact of the automobile though not the impulse of youth to venture from home—Gid and Johnny are eager to see new places. Like Lonnie in *Horseman*, they have an initiation into the "sophisticated" adult world when they take cattle to market in Fort Worth. Lonnie had chanted the magical place names of Texas; for Gid and Johnny the idea of adventure is summed up in one name: the Panhandle. The high bald plains connote the essence of old-time drifting cowboying, the symbolic Cheyenne of the title.[6] But for both—Johnny, who "didn't feel like he belonged to any certain place," and Gid, who "was just tied up with" Archer County (p. 93)—the venture to the plains is presented so as to debunk the romance of journeying. After Gid's feat of breaking nineteen wild horses in one day come a dull round of work and simple homesickness, and Gid returns home because, he says, "home was where I belonged" and "it was my country and my people" (p. 93).

After this trip to the plains, both Gid and Johnny stay close to the ranch which Gid has inherited from his father. For Gid, this is largely because he has been bitten by "the land bug" (p. 129). But Johnny's true "blood's country" or "heart's pastureland" (p. v) is cowboying itself, rather than any particular place. He is held to Archer County by love of Gid and Molly. It is largely because of this difference in motivation that Johnny (who appropriately has the last word in the novel) is most nearly the ethical center of the book. Gid is too self-centered to receive the reader's full approval, but Johnny unstintingly spends himself in love of the others.

The relationship of the two men to Molly is presented as an analogue to their relationship to the land. Molly, who dislikes travelling and never in her life goes past Oklahoma, is as freely giving and sustaining as the earth. The identification is repeatedly stressed, both through the speaker's comments and through visual effects, and a moral hierarchy is established among Gid, Johnny, and Molly's husband Eddie, on the basis of both relationships. Eddie is an exploiter who uses Molly as a tool for pleasure: she says that he "done what he pleased, and when he got done he stopped" (p. 174). As a "damn greasy oilfield hand" (Gid's words, p. 53), he takes what is immediately profitable from the land and cares no more about it. Of the three, only Eddie (who is thus the clearest precursor in the early novels of McMurtry's later wanderers) would "go crazy if he couldn't get off and run around" (p. 115). For Eddie, journeying does not serve the educative function that it does for Johnny and Gid, but is a way of life in itself because he has never established any stable tie which constitutes his identity. Gid is a possessor, who wants to own land and marry Molly, and can never reconcile his conscience to simple enjoyment. Johnny is an enjoyer of Molly, not a possessor; a cowboy, not a rancher.

But it is Eddie, Gid's grasping wife, and her crafty brother that represent the wave of the future; the ideal of simple cowboying and all it has come to represent in the novel are an anachronism. The tone of the work, despite the gritty realism of its depiction of ranch work, is strongly elegiac.[7] At the end, when Gid suffers a fatal accident while working on his father's home ranch, his wife is away on another in a series of vacation trips. Johnny and Molly, who continue their devotion to the old ways and the old love, are aged vestiges of a dead past.

The Last Picture Show is dominated tonally not by nostalgia, but by McMurtry's antipathy to the small-town life he describes. Thalia has become a place to be escaped, and restlessness dominates. Sonny, another late-adolescent, who is the nearest in the book to being a central character, first appears in the opening chapter struggling to get his old pickup to run. It is a prophetic detail, for Sonny will never be able to escape. But during the novel he and various other adolescents of Thalia travel to California, to Mexico, to Fort Worth, and continually back and forth between Thalia and Wichita Falls, in their search for amusement. Even for athletic events their team has to drive to towns like Paducah, "well over a hundred miles from Thalia" (p. 57). Sonny, appropriately, earns money driving a truck (in a typical satirical thrust, for Frank Fartley, who sells bottled gas).

Their circuitous travels, always ending in Thalia again, are parallel in futility with their ventures into sex. As Peavy says in his article "Coming of Age in Texas," adolescents and adults alike turn to sex as their "only outlet for frustrations, loneliness, boredom, even hatred"— just as they turn to aimless jaunts. The association of the two is emphatic. The teenagers typically engage in petting and what serves for love-making in car seats, and it is in Sonny's truck bed that they set the hapless defective Billy onto the town's cheap whore Jimmie Sue. Jacy becomes aroused only on the school bus when all the class are watching, but when she and Duane finally have their tryst in a California motel room during the senior trip she is peevish and Duane can't perform. When Duane and Sonny drive to Matamoros for a weekend of dissipation, Sonny finds that although he "had driven five hundred miles to get away from Thalia" the squeaking springs in a prostitute's crib "took him right back" (p. 139). He goes to sleep without sex. Later he runs away with Jacy to Altus, Oklahoma, to get married but is picked up by police before the consummation because Jacy had left a note to insure that they would have no wedding night.

It is the return from the trip to Matamoros that brings the deepest grief and frustration for Sonny. When he and Duane drive back into town, they are told that Sam the Lion, the vigorous old man who has been Sonny's surrogate father, has died. Only Sam—the true hero of the novel, if it can be said to have one at all—appears to possess self-knowledge, and to him alone (besides the detached and often sardonic narrative voice) is given the right to make knowing, ironic comments on life. Sam is never seen to wander, but reliably inhabits his pool hall and its environs, dispensing a rough sort of care to the town youths, especially to poor Billy. By the end of the novel, a few have escaped, but Sonny, physically crippled by his past and emotionally dependent on an older woman, is left in dusty Thalia, owner of Sam the Lion's pool hall and custodian of Billy. But he is not allowed even that solace of continuing Sam's care of the defective boy, for Billy is killed—appropriately enough, by a cattle truck, the embodiment of that tradition that in its passing has so crushed those left behind. Sonny's last act is to start out of town in his truck, but finding nothing but emptiness all around answering the emptiness within, he returns in fear to the older woman who has loved him and who can now only wish she had a message of wisdom.

The reader is left to wonder if Sonny's return to Thalia will mean his digging in and making a life, as Sam had, but he has not seemed to possess the needed vitality to combat such desolate circumstances. Doubly orphaned because his real father long ago abdicated his responsibilities and his effectual father, Sam the Lion, is dead, Sonny lacks a past which can provide him an identity and a role in his shabby present. The most visible sign of his regional past in the entire novel is the cattle truck that kills Billy. The basis of Sonny's problems, that is, is a radical cultural discontinuity. It is this lack of a meaningful past, present, or future that creates the restlessness increasingly evident in McMurtry's adolescents. Lacking significant temporal orientations, they are thrown back onto a spatial search that is equally unsatisfactory because they are not equipped with the capacity to set goals or make distinctions. Thus they find all places much alike and much like Thalia: they wander.

In *Moving On* and *All My Friends Are Going to Be Strangers,* McMurtry has moved even further from the traditional cultural roots of his region. None of the characters in these two novels has any sense of a usable past, and none is purposefully directed toward the future. They inhabit the burgeoning cities of Texas with no apparent means of orienting themselves and nothing to engage them but endless, unsatisfying motion—as the title *Moving On* well indicates. The problem, of course, is that they are not moving on toward anything. The journey pattern so insistent in McMurtry's first three novels has in these become dominant, as the characters drive endlessly and pointlessly around the country chiefly between Texas and California.[8] Not surprisingly, novels so constituted lack cohesive form; or rather, their forms may be described as being imitative to a radical and destructive degree.[9]

The primary action of both novels is completely divorced from ranching, the traditional, land-based way of life that provides a relatively stable background for the first two novels. In *Moving On,* ranching is transformed into rodeoing, itself a transient way of life. Real ranching appears only in the small spread of a stepuncle of the heroine Patsy's husband and in a vast domain, like an industrial complex, whose owner shares, in a scarcely lesser degree, the wanderlust of the main characters. Only Roger Wagonner, the elderly stepuncle, never travels. Wagonner is an embodiment of lost but still respected virtues; a parallel figure in *All My Friends,* the narrator's Uncle L, is a ludicrous eccentric running an insane parody of a ranch. But either way, both are vestiges of the past, unable to hand on its values. Danny, the narrator, says of his Uncle L, "Once he was dead, I would never get a chance to visit anyone remotely like him—that was certain. There was no one remotely like him" (p. 150). Significantly, both old ranchers are without legitimate heirs; Roger Wagonner must leave his ranch to Patsy, who is of no blood kinship to him and can hardly guess what she will do with the land.

Aside from these ranching relics, the two novels are populated by nomads. In both, university life is a way-station for academic migrants and those who have not yet decided where they want to go. Both casts of characters are quite large, since people drift into and out of the main characters' lives, seemingly for no particular reason, as they wander. Prominent in *Moving On* are an aunt of Patsy's who speeds in her Cadillac from store to store and a rodeo star named Sonny Shanks who drives recklessly around the western half of the country in a customized hearse in which, fittingly, he is killed in a Hollywood freeway accident involving "only nine cars" (p. 664). That he had used the hearse for random seductions is also strikingly fitting, underscoring as it does the instability of patterns of sexual behavior in both of these novels. They are as fully cut off from the moral past as they are from the ranching past. Action develops as encounter, involvement (often sexual), and estrangement. Danny Deck, narrator and hero of *All My Friends,* is hopelessly subject to random emotional entanglements, all of which prove destructive as well as transient, because he has no basis for judging others or the quality of his own response to them. Like the journey structure of which it is a function, this pattern of emotion-laden encounter that litters the novel with undeveloped characters can be seen as a functional form clearly and poignantly indicative of the protagonist's cultural malaise. He feels, he says, "dislodged" (p. 47), and stability in his personal relationships is as impossible as fixity in place.

Patsy and Jim, of *Moving On,* fully equal both the restlessness and the sexual disorder apparent in Danny Deck. Following the rodeos for Jim's transient interest in photography means virtually living in their car. The book opens with Patsy sitting in it outside an arena in Merkel, Texas, and the rodeo calendar takes them not only through Texas but on a circuitous route through the other Western states, to Wyoming, and south again to Houston. Jim is "a fantastic marathon driver" (p. 52) whose one sentimental attachment is to his old car. It is a measure of his radical dissociation from his personal past that, before leaving for California on a trip from which he never returns, he buys a new car. Similarly, since Danny Deck, of *All My Friends,* has personified his old car as El Chevy and every phase of his story has been tied up with the car, his abandonment of it near the end of that novel seems a momentous act.

None of the characters in either novel travels with fixed purpose—their wanderings are not quests—nor is even the motive of escape clearly defined. Rather, like Patsy's husband Jim, they travel out of vague dissatisfaction with life as they find it and uncertainty as to what they want to do. When Jim drives, not for the first time, to California, he suspects "almost the whole distance" that he is "going the wrong way" but cannot decide to turn back because "there was always a chance that the place he was looking for would appear somewhere ahead" (p. 640). Similarly, when Patsy's lover drives rather indifferently away from Houston and their relationship, "lights of the towns, at a distance in the darkness, distinct as stars, were always more beautiful than the empty towns themselves" (p. 609). It is a statement that could apply to them all. Typically, Hank is driving toward the Plains without plan or any purpose except change.

Patsy herself, the heroine of *Moving On,* is to some extent an exception to this dispiriting pattern. When she goes to California, she has a purpose, to retrieve her strayed sister, and she accomplishes it. However, she too is very unstable; she is never able to sort out her feelings for either her husband or her lover, or for any of several other men to whom she feels drawn, and at one time she moves into a large house she and Jim had foolishly bought only because she can't think of anything better to do. The book ends in hopeful affirmation of her impulsive warmth, however, with Patsy in possession of Jim's uncle's ranch, surrounded by a small circle of friends, and committed to them and to the future, in the form of her own child and the baby with which her sister is pregnant. The last chapter shows her strolling around the neighborhood in which, however haphazardly, she has settled, in the company of the few people about whom she cares.

Danny Deck, of *All My Friends,* never reaches even Patsy's degree of stability in interpersonal relationships. He does, however, gain a fuller vision of his cultural loss than any other character in either of these last novels. Danny's name is first encountered near the end of *Moving On* when Patsy's friend Emma expresses her grief for him. He had "disappeared" leaving no trace but his car (p. 783). That disappearance, in *All My Friends,* follows an account of Danny's wanderings between Texas and California after he sells his first novel and quits school. But he never discovers for himself any goal or allegiance, personal or professional. Even his devotion to being a writer is only moderate and extremely uncertain; the creation of art cannot by itself provide stability to one who so lacks cultural resources, and his second novel is a burden Danny is compelled to "drown" at the end of the book. Similarly, McMurtry's construction of novels by no apparent principle but random accretion appears to be a self-defeating enterprise. The pattern of transient involvement in both these late novels is brilliantly indicative of the cultural shortcoming McMurtry indicts, as well as of the particular dilemmas of Danny Deck and the others; unfortunately, this expressive form, by its very nature, is destructive of the overall novelistic structure and renders the work a chronicle of tedium. One thinks, by contrast, of the tight structures of *Horseman, Pass By* and *Leaving Cheyenne.* McMurtry seems to be saying that their kind of neatness is available only to an art of nostalgia, that an art honestly treating the present flux, at least as he experienced it in Texas, is foreordained to fragmentation. If so, he is offering a bleak aesthetic vision.

The ending of *All My Friends* is problematic but clearly related to McMurtry's use of journeying as a metaphor for cultural loss. The puzzle is that Danny apparently drowns himself in the Rio Grande, but his death would violate all conventions of first person, past tense, narration. It is clear that a wish for self-annihilation has seized Danny as he enters the river in order, he tells himself, to wade across to Mexico. Recognizing in midstream that his own inadequacies will continue to plague him wherever he is, he rejects that idea, destroys his novel, turns briefly upriver toward the direction of his own memories but, finding them too troubling, turns again downriver toward the Gulf and the great names of history. Now he wants only "to flow" (p. 246). Though some of his meditations here seem to indicate return and renewal after the immersion in the river, the predominant quality is renunciation of his life, which is symbolized in the names of his friends and the "dim bank of Texas" (p. 247). He seeks dissolution in rivers and in the great sea of the unreachable past.

The sense of finality, hence of death, is accented by the preceding abandonment of his car, which itself seems near death. Leaving "El Chevy," he states solemnly, "I didn't feel like driving any farther anyway. . . . I was tired of driving. It had stopped being fun" (p. 235). He says that the car now "could be free" and adds, "I wouldn't need him again" (p. 235). One recalls that the folk-song metaphor for death in *Leaving Cheyenne* is turning one's horses free. The implication is that by giving up his means of journeying, Danny is giving up living.

The quality of Danny Deck's journeying, as of Patsy's and the journeying of numerous minor characters in the earlier novels, has been circuitous wandering. In *Leaving Cheyenne,* Gid and Johnny travel only to learn the lessons proper to youth; they have a source that draws them back and a feeling of belonging when they get there. In *The Last Picture Show* only Sam the Lion knows his place and keeps it. In the last two novels figures out of the Texas past who bear marginal resemblance to Sam, the old ranchers, are anachronisms. The young central characters of all five novels have either loose ancestral ties or none at all, as fathers or father surrogates die partway through the action of all except the last novel. Lacking any sense of continuity with the past or of belonging to the life of any particular place, McMurtry's protagonists are, to a progressively greater degree after *Leaving Cheyenne,* left to wander inconclusively.

One might assign biographical significance to this feeling of rootlessness. McMurtry himself left Texas, and thus his familial and professional roots, a few years ago to work near Washington, D.C. He has made it clear that he can no longer find his home state a viable place to live; he is a "happily exiled native son."[10] Yet his tone when writing of the ranching past of Charlie Goodnight, the Palo Duro, and his own ancestors, in both his recent *Atlantic* article and the earlier essay "Take My Saddle from the Wall: A Valediction," is elegiac, uncolored by irony. It seems clear from these expository writings that his imagination responds warmly to a past that is dead and that, unable to appropriate any usable cultural heritage in the absence of that past, he finds himself lacking a sense of home. His "hardest task" as a writer, he says, has been to "convince myself that the Texas I have lived in and in some sense known was as legitimate and as worthy of attention as the Texas that existed before my time."[11] One senses this divided relation also in his uneasy bearing of the label "regional writer," which he mentions derisively in his essay "Southwestern Literature?"[12]

We have every reason to believe that these personal tensions have very directly become embodied in McMurtry's novels. All of them, for instance, are peopled by characters clearly drawn from the author himself and his sizable clan. People who live near Archer City, the basis of fictional Thalia, say that townspeople are clearly recognizable in *The Last Picture Show.* This biographical nexus, as well as the uncomfortable accuracy with which McMurtry has depicted and ridiculed his Texas scene, points indeed to the view of his work as a well-crafted, regional social analysis. It is as a realist working in a localized mode that he must initially be read. But his choice of allusive and thematic patterns extends the significance of his work beyond the scope of documentary or localized satiric interest. The initiation patterns of his novels, for instance, are universalizing, as are the literary allusions which link the personal emotions revealed in *Leaving Cheyenne* to those of people far removed in time and place. In that same novel, the structural indications of a cyclical vision of human life also extend the reverberation of the drama beyond its indisputably pungent localization.

McMurtry's recourse to the archetype of journeying is another, and a more significant, resonating device. As we have seen, the journeying impulse is closely related to the specific cultural impoverishment McMurtry exposes. But through the journey pattern these novels join a longtime tradition of literary journeys, a tradition which has appeared in epics of all literatures but has been a particularly characteristic American form because of the peculiarities of the nation's history. Indeed, the insistence with which McMurtry's characters strike out for the High Plains or for California links these novels to the heritage of westering and to the great California dream. Like other Americans throughout our history, these Texans define their values spatially. The loss of traditional values involves his fictional people in fruitless geographical search and a permanent restlessness.

NOTES

1. Frye, *Anatomy of Criticism* (Princeton: Princeton University Press, 1957), 57.

2. See, for example, Thomas Landess, *Larry McMurtry* (Austin: Steck-Vaughn, 1969). However, the initiation theme in his first three novels is examined by Kenneth W. Davis in "The Themes of Initiation in the Works of Larry McMurtry and Tom Mayer," *Arlington Quarterly*, 2 (1970), 29–43, and more fully by Charles D. Peavy in "Coming of Age in Texas: The Novels of Larry McMurtry," *Western American Literature*, 4 (1969), 171–88.

3. McMurtry's novels, cited parenthetically, are *Horseman, Pass By* (New York: Harper and Brothers, 1961); *Leaving Cheyenne* (New York: Popular Library, 1963); *The Last Picture Show* (1966; New York: Dell, 1974); *Moving On* (1970; New York: Avon, 1971); and *All My Friends Are Going to Be Strangers* (1972; New York: Pocket Books, 1973).

4. *Leaving Cheyenne*, of course, is not a book about youthful characters only, but takes its people through to old age. Indeed, its humorous portrayal of the crotchets of Gid and Johnny as old men—and, in particular, their endless talks— seems to me its finest achievement.

5. Beyond the veterinarians, the responsibility rests upon Homer Bannon himself, since it was he who insisted on buying the cattle that later proved infectious. In this respect, the destruction of the herd implies the inability of any human being to sustain what Jesse calls "the exact right place," or "paradise."

6. One should add that, on another level, Cheyenne is simply youth.

7. Cf. James K. Folsom, *The American Western Novel* (New Haven: College and University Press, 1966) on the characteristic elegiac tone of the Western.

8. In his essay "Southwestern Literature?" McMurtry asks, other than in Texas, "where else except California can one find a richer mixture of absurdities?" *In a Narrow Grave* (New York: Simon and Schuster, 1968), 54.

9. Reviews have been almost uniformly unfavorable. See, for example, Thomas Landess's review of *Moving On* in *Southwestern American Literature*, 1 (1971), 38–39, and William T. Pilkington's of *All My Friends* in the same journal, 2 (1972), 54–55. McMurtry himself has stated that he is more interested in textures than in structures.

10. McMurtry, "The Texas Moon, and Elsewhere," *Atlantic*, 235 (March 1975), 29–36.

11. *Atlantic*, 235, p. 29. He adds that one thing he knows about the past Texas is "that its roads were not all filled with Oldsmobiles, as they are today."

12. This essay, as well as "Take My Saddle from the Wall," appears in McMurtry's *In a Narrow Grave*.

The Ranch as Place and Symbol in the Novels of Larry McMurtry

RAYMOND C. PHILLIPS, JR.

In his essay on the contemporary literary heritage of the Southwest, Larry Goodwyn singles out Larry McMurtry as the young novelist "most embattled in terms of the frontier heritage."[1] By "frontier heritage" Goodwyn means treating the history of the Southwest as "the *unexamined* legend—the propagandistic Anglo-Saxon folk myth," which is pastoral, masculine, and racialistic.[2] Those writers who stay within this legend produce a literature of nostalgia that is largely affirmative, that perpetuates frontier romanticism. The newest generation of southwestern writers, however, has approached the legend and its myths in a skeptical mood: they "are asking radically different questions both about the nature of human experience and the functions of a received heritage in informing that experience."[3]

McMurtry, born in 1936 in Archer County, Texas, the author of five novels and a collection of essays, is very much representative of this new generation. That he is "embattled" can be seen by closely examining the significance that the ranch, both as place and as symbol, plays in his fiction. One finds that the ranch represents a stationary vortex, a cluster of values, about which everything moves. It is home, the place to revere, the place to protect, to flee from, to return to. It is the place to die. Usually peaceful and harmonious, offering psychological shelter, the ranch also can be the site of ultimate ineffectuality. It can be at the center of McMurtry's fictional world, or it can hover on the fringes. Finally, the ranch points up the ambivalence that McMurtry feels about the frontier legend.

Although written after the publication of his first three novels, McMurtry's essay "Take My Saddle from the Wall: A Valediction"[4] most clearly expresses his ambivalence about the Texas past and present. In the essay he remembers how "As a boy, riding across the lower field, I would sometimes look back at the speck of the ranchhouse and imagine that I heard the old man's dinner call carrying across the flats" (p. 552). He recalls that the glory of the cowboy was his horsemanship; he writes of the cowboy's disgust with farming, his romanticizing of women, his stoical acceptance of life, his strength of character, his intolerance, his refusal to become domesticated, his violence, his pantheism, and, finally, his essential "dream of innocence and fullness never to be redeemed" (p. 569). The center of this world is not the Clarendon Country Club where in July, 1965, the heroic Uncle Johnny and the McMurtry clan held their last reunion, but the ranch that they built and lived on. McMurtry, who never could braid a rope, loves this world and the people in it, yet he wants his saddle taken from the wall. The problem, according to Goodwyn, is "the beguiling simplicity with which McMurtry takes down his saddle in his mind while his heart immediately replaces it." Goodwyn contends that "a writer simply cannot afford such innocence in respect to his own point of view."[5] "Innocence," however, may not be the accurate term for McMurtry's "embattled" position; instead, his career suggests an awareness of his ambivalence and some confusion as to how to come to grips with it.

Horseman, Pass By,[6] his first novel, shows McMurtry staking out the area in and around the imaginary north-central town of Thalia (really Archer City, his home town) as his fictional territory.[7] Lonnie Bannon, the young narrator of the novel, writes very early in the novel that from his grandfather's ranch, "we could watch the cars zoom across the plains," that he could hear the trains fly by, that he "could see the airplane beacons flashing from the airport in Wichita Falls" (pp. 6–7). Lonnie dreams of the day "when I would have my own car, and could tear across the country to dances and rodeos" (p. 77). Very quickly, then, McMurtry introduces what becomes one of his crucial themes: the tension between the values centered in the ranch, the symbol of the Old West, values developed principally in Homer Bannon, and the values, the demands, and the expectancies of the more frenetic and transient world that lies beyond.[8]

While later novels leave the immediate world of the ranch, *Horseman, Pass By* is set almost entirely on the Bannon Place, ruled over by old Homer Bannon, a life-long cattleman. Homer loves the land and, as Lonnie remembers, "was always studying it" (p. 138). Homer

rejects the suggestion that he lease part of his ranch to the oil companies: "I guess I'm a queer, contrary old bastard, but there'll be no holes
punched in this land while I'm here" (pp. 87–88). His love of the ranch
is not sentimental: "There's so much shit in the world a man's gonna
get in it sooner or later, whether he's careful or not" (p. 104). Very
much aware that ranching has changed, Homer keeps an old Hereford
bull and two longhorn steers around "to remind me how times was"
(p. 45). Still, he does not dwell on the past: "If the times come when I
get to spend my time lookin' back, why, I'd just as soon go under"
(p. 103). Homer, the durable representative of the past, faces one of his
greatest challenges when the hoof-and-mouth disease infects his herd.
While waiting for the results of the tests that will determine the fate
of his herd—the week or so that it takes for the verdict to come in
emphasizes the inexorable winding down of all that he has built—he
angrily refuses to follow Hud's suggestion that he unload the cattle on
unsuspecting buyers. A decent man but one who has made mistakes, a
man who has suffered through family tragedies, Homer retains his
dignity until his death. At his funeral, the minister's lies and the
undertaker's cosmetic skills cannot destroy that dignity, which grew
out of his respect for life lived on the land.

Homer's feelings for the ranch are not shared by Hud, his stepson.
Thirty-five years old, Hud resents Homer's ways. He would rather
drive his Cadillac at high speeds through the night in search of sexual
conquests. On being advised to stay home because of a storm warning,
Hud snaps: "If I sat around an' waited for every little piss cloud to
turn into a tornado, I never would go nowhere" (p. 12), a far cry from
Homer's patient acceptance of life and nature. When he does stay
home, Hud unnerves everyone who is about. At one point, he tries to
rape Halmea, the Negro cook, an extreme example of the violence he
exudes. Here, and elsewhere in McMurtry's fiction, a character embodies this sort of violence.[9] The violence of the nineteenth century
West, patterned and ritualized in the literary and cinematic treatments of the frontier legend, gives way to a more subtle and ominous
violence in McMurtry's work. More often than not, this contemporary
violence is sexual, stemming in part from a loss of reverence for the
land and the ensuing rootlessness.

Both Homer and Hud, the older and the middle generations, serve
as models for young Lonnie to follow. Lonnie is attracted to both:
when he rides his horse across the big valley pasture in the early
morning he shares his grandfather's love of the land; on the other
hand, he has an "itch to be off somewhere, with a crowd of laughers
and courters and beer drinkers, to go somewhere past Thalia and

Wichita and the oil towns and Sno-Cone stands, into country I'd never seen" (pp. 75, 21). Lonnie, restless and confused, senses the psychic disarray and gloom that has settled over the Bannon ranch, much in the same way that Huck Finn feels the cultural malaise along the Mississippi River. Lonnie, for instance, is disturbed by the moods of Jesse, the hired hand, who admits to having botched up his life because he "went all over this cow country, looking for the exact right place an' the exact right people" (p. 121) without ever finding it or them. Halmea's homelessness bothers Lonnie, too. She is both substitute mother and sexual woman for him, but when he tries to find her again after she leaves the ranch, she has gone north. At one point, Lonnie feels so pent up that he goes off in the night and shoots some animals, only to lament his senseless slaughter: "Things used to be better around here . . . I feel like I want something back" (p. 74).

What he wants back, of course, becomes impossible to have when his grandfather dies and when he realizes that nobody will be able to stop Hud from taking over the ranch. All that Lonnie has at the end is the warm and good memory of his grandfather, the horseman, passing by his window early in the morning, the horseman who "had always held the land, and would go on holding what he needed of it forever" (p. 140). As presented in the novel, then, the ranch is the good place as long as it was ruled over by Homer Bannon. It was no utopian retreat but a place where hard work, good luck, and patience yielded a life worth a man's living. What Hud will do with the ranch is problematical, of course, but it is doubtful whether he will cherish it the way Homer did. Lonnie, his travelling over, might be man enough and smart enough to right any damage that Hud might do. Perhaps his experiences outside of the ranch will temper his late adolescent enthusiasm for a good time. In any event, McMurtry's examination of the frontier legend succeeds; his characters embody the tensions inherent in the legend: primarily, the clash between those who love and respect the land and those who treat it unfeelingly.

Leaving Cheyenne, [10] McMurtry's second novel, treats ranch life from the early 1900s until about 1960. The setting is the same north-central cattle country as in *Horseman, Pass By,* the cast of characters is still fairly limited, and the ranch still functions as the central symbol of the story. That McMurtry is striving for a broad symbolic effect is apparent from the epigraphs that introduce each of the three sections of the novel. The epigraph for the whole novel, a four line verse about leaving Cheyenne, refers to "that part of the cowboy's day's circle which is earliest and best: his blood's country and his heart's pastureland" (Foreword). These words suggest that near-magical attraction to the land, to

Texas, that one finds in, say, Sara Orne Jewett's treatment of the Maine coast in *The Country of the Pointed Firs*. Such an attempt generally carries with it the risk of sentimentality, a risk avoided by McMurtry. *Leaving Cheyenne* has an understated, flat quality to it— the flatness often found in the old photographs of the family album. The pace of the novel is slow (again one is reminded of Jewett's novella); one expects more from the novel than it delivers, yet the "cowboy's blood country" is undeniably there. The second epigraph, immediately preceding Part One, which is titled "The Blood's Country," refers to the "high lean country" that is "full of old stories" (Foreword). The land and the closely connected lives of three people, then, is what the novel is all about.

The epigraph for Part Two, from Shakespeare's Sonnet 64, emphasizes a major theme in McMurtry's fiction: the passing of time and the changes that ensue: "Ruin hath taught me thus to ruminate, / That Time will come and take my love away" (p. 135). Crucial to McMurtry's treatment of the Southwest is the presence of an eroded myth, but a myth that refuses to vanish no matter what the ruin of Time does to it. Two epigraphs introduce Part Three, one the Wife of Bath's bittersweet statement that although her youth is gone, she has had her world and will do the best she can: "The flour is goon, ther is namoore to tell; / The bren, as I best kan, now moste I selle"; the other Teddy Blue's request that when his life is over "go turn / my horses free" (p. 191). By quoting both from Chaucer and from a western folk source, McMurtry enriches the texture of his novel.

Leaving Cheyenne is the story of Gid, Molly, and Johnny, three Texans born around the turn of the century. In their late teens or early twenties when the novel begins, the three friends, evincing an uncommon love for and loyalty to each other, live out lives of mixed blessings and tragedy. Both men share the love of Molly, each fathering a son by her. Molly, with more than a bit of the Wife of Bath about her, possesses a resilience befitting her demotic background. "In some ways an updated version of the legendary dance-hall girl so familiar to lovers of the classic Western romance," the judgment of Thomas Landess,[11] Molly, nevertheless, emerges as a complex figure with an inner strength very closely dependent on her loyalty to her father and to the land on which she lives.

It is in Gid's section, Part One, that McMurtry develops the mystique of the ranch and the land. Old Mr. Fry, Gid's father, wants above all else to have his son perpetuate the ranch that he has spent his life building. He resents Gid's restlessness, his desire to go up to the Panhandle and do some cowboying: "Why, any damn fool can enjoy himself. What makes you think life's supposed to be enjoyed anyhow?" (p. 27). Mr. Fry, like Homer Bannon, knows the high price exacted in running a successful ranch. When he becomes too ill to continue, Mr. Fry kills himself. In his suicide note, he says, "I think I'll go out on the hill and turn my horses free" (p. 107). By invoking the words of Teddy Blue, Mr. Fry places himself within the traditions of the past and he impresses them on his son. He ends his note with an order for Gid to fix the windmill, another way of ensuring that Gid remembers where his obligations lie—with continuing the existence of the ranch. That Gid fulfills his obligations is emphasized at the end of the novel when he insists that he and Johnny repair the same windmill; Gid, too old and ill for such hard work in the hot sun, falls and injures himself, dying a short time later. In the delirium before his death, Gid confuses the fall with being thrown from a horse years before, thereby linking his earlier skills in horsemanship with the demands his father placed upon him to keep the ranch going.

As a young man and before he becomes the rancher his father wants him to be, Gid suffers a great deal, not only because of his difficulty in winning Molly but also because of his longing to be a free roaming cowboy like Johnny. When the two young men go up to the Panhandle, Gid gets a taste of cowboying; on the Grinsom place, he breaks a string of eighteen horses in one day. He likes cowboying, but he soon becomes homesick: "I just minded feeling like I wasn't where I belonged. . . . That country might not be very nice and the people might be onry; but it was my country and my people, and no other country was" (pp. 93–94).

One attraction for Gid, of course, is Molly, who serves both men as lover and as confidant. Molly, quite ordinary in some ways, takes on an archetypal significance in several places in the novel, most clearly, perhaps, when she and either Gid or Johnny go fishing at the tank on the Fry ranch. The tank, along with the windmill a literal reminder of the cattleman's efforts to reckon with the aridity of the Southwest, is the idyllic retreat in most of McMurtry's fiction. It is here that Molly, now the Temptress, invites Gid to skinny-dip with her, in effect, to submerge and to lose his innocence beneath the life-giving water of the tank. He refuses because "I just know what's right and what ain't" (p. 32). Somewhat later, after finding out that Molly has married Eddie, an oil-field worker, Gid retreats to the tank to brood about his missed opportunity to win Molly for himself. Johnny also takes Molly to the tank to fish after she tells him about Jimmy's (Gid's son by Molly) decision to become a homosexual. In this scene, Molly, grieving for her lost sons (both had been killed in the war),

seems more the Earthmother now; "The tank was still as a mirror"
(p. 180) and she and Johnny pass the long afternoon together. Molly
sews a rip in Johnny's shirt while he sleeps, they swim, shoot at some
cowchips, and finally, they eat. The entire scene has a slowed down,
elegiac quality to it, but, at the same time, it is a powerful celebration
of life and of the need to endure. Much of Molly's strength seems to
emanate from the life-giving water of the tank. The tank, however, is
but a part of the ranch, just as being able to go there very often is but a
part of life.

Although the three characters live close to the land, it alone cannot
sustain them. Both Gid and Molly suffer from loneliness. Gid misses
Johnny when they are apart as young men, and after he marries
Mabel, an ungenerous and overly proud woman, he continues to need
Molly. Molly loses her father, to whom she was very close, a husband,
and both of her sons. After visiting her, whether to sleep with her, to
repair her windmill, or merely to talk to her, Gid says something like:
"She always stood right where you left her, as long as she could see
you. . . . Molly was just as permanent as my land" (p. 133). This
picture of Molly, alone but enduring, one finds again and again in the
novel. She has a remarkable ability to articulate her feelings. When
her Bible-pounding son Jimmy tries to make her feel guilty of adultery, she answers him in much the same way that the Rev. Casey
explains his new ways in *The Grapes of Wrath:* "But words is one thing
and loving a man is another" (p. 169). With such a simple power as
this, Molly can fight her loneliness. Johnny, one of the men she sleeps
with, is a cowboy-drifter who takes life easy. If he suffers from loneliness, we are not very aware of it. He has no desire to own land or to
gain power. Sleeping with Molly presents him with no moral problems: "it's enjoyable . . . I ain't gonna bother to look no farther than
that" (p. 189).

"The earth endures and the stars abide, but where are the old men,"
to paraphrase the earth-song in Emerson's "Hamatreya." So it is in
Leaving Cheyenne. Gid, Molly, and Johnny grow old and, as Johnny
complains to Molly, "Now we both just got yawny" (p. 234). While the
passing of time is noticeable in Parts One and Two, it is most apparent
in Part Three, the section narrated by Johnny. His narration seems
almost too slack and rambling. Landess, for instance, in finding
Johnny's drawn-out account of the automobile accident unjustified
thematically, accuses McMurtry of wandering "into the tangled
thicket of redundancy."[12] A defensible criticism, to be sure, but it is
possible that McMurtry is trying to suggest the slowed down lives
of the characters. Gid, his health growing poorer, reminisces and

complains more. Molly also reflects about the passing of time; she recalls the time her father brought home a barrel of molasses only to have it accidentally spilled all over the ground.[13] Johnny humors Gid when he laments the passing of the West as they had known it, but Johnny also recalls the past with sadness. Both men realize they aren't as strong as they once were; in going out to round up a milk cow, they have trouble saddling their horses and then they muff the job. Gid, though greatly weakened after a stay in the hospital, insists on doing the chores about the ranch, but, as Johnny notes, he "wasn't the hand he used to be" (p. 241). Like his father, Gid stubbornly keeps on. When he becomes mortally hurt in falling from the windmill, he, in a sense, takes his own life. His half-delirious remark to Johnny on the way to the hospital—"Ain't this been a hell of a time?" (p. 246)—is a fitting remark for an old cattleman to make about his and Molly's and Johnny's lives on the land.

It is Molly, however, who dominates the last section of the novel and who most appropriately characterizes the spirit of the novel. After Gid's death, Johnny spends the night with Molly. He wakes up next to her in bed and is a bit non-plused to see that he has an erection. Molly, still the archetypal Earthmother, smiles at him and says: "That's nature. . . . And you better not waste it, either" (p. 249). With Molly, here and elsewhere in the novel, McMurtry reworks the "unexamined myth" of the West. He advances a woman to the forefront of what had usually been a man's world. Molly, her unabashed sexuality emulating the zest for living embodied in the Wife of Bath (remember the epigraph), challenges the ruin of time, the wearing down and the losses of her sixty-two years. Indomitable, she remains on her land and in her house, and when Johnny, at the end, remembers her sitting in her blue and white dress on the schoolhouse steps nearly a half century before, the novel comes full circle with the cowboy's "blood's country and his heart's pastureland" intact.

In his next novel, *The Last Picture Show,*[14] McMurtry turns from the ranch to the town of Thalia, to whom the novel is "lovingly dedicated." Thalia, as has been pointed out more than once, is the Greek Muse of comedy and pastoral poetry; the name comes from the Greek *Thaleia,* meaning "the blooming one." Thalia, Texas, however, does not bloom at all. In fact, as Sam the Lion says, "The oil fields are about to dry up and the cattle business looks like it's going to peter out" (p. 53). The inhabitants of Thalia, both young and old, find the place lonely and dreary. Sonny, the central character, excuses a night of whoring and drinking at Ft. Worth with these words: "at least we got to go *somewhere*" (p. 56). Life is so bad sometimes that the boys of Thalia visit the stockpens to copulate with a heifer, an action hardly befitting the pastoral myth the town's name suggests. For Lois Farrow, the hard-drinking mother of Joey, the town's dream girl, Thalia and the land around it are "flat and empty, and there's nothing to do but spend money" (p. 42). McMurtry relentlessly hammers home the negative points of the town; Landess is correct in calling the novel a satire with one-dimensional and stylized characters which gives the book the flavor of Sinclair Lewis's novels.[15] Consider, for instance, Sonny's first girl friend, Charlene Duggs. Charlene, a bovine, gum-chewing girl, spends most of her time sitting in a beauty shop reading movie magazines. Full-breasted, Charlene is a flat character, sometimes amusing to the reader but hardly interesting.

Part of McMurtry's strategy in satirizing Thalia is the inclusion of a great many sexual, even scatological, passages. In his first two novels, to be sure, one finds sex, but beginning with *The Last Picture Show,* McMurtry stresses more and more the sexual manifestations of life in the West. I suggested earlier that violence is linked with sexuality; people commit violence against the integrity of someone else, and they do it sexually. Such is the case here. The boys of Thalia lead the unsuspecting half-witted Billy to Jimmie Sue Jones, the obese town whore. The wealthier teenagers from Wichita have nude swimming parties and "screw" each other; Coach Popper, a latent homosexual, cracks obscene jokes with his players; Lois Farrow sleeps with another man; and on and on it goes. In describing all of this, McMurtry uses very frank language (in his last two novels, the language is even more frank, causing discomfort to some readers).[16] Since most of the novel deals with high school students, a group that finds sex especially interesting, the language mostly rings true. The upshot of this heavy emphasis on sex is that it calls into doubt the sanctity of the West advanced in *Horseman, Pass By* and in *Leaving Cheyenne.*

Towering over everyone else in *The Last Picture Show* is Sam the Lion, the owner of the town's pool hall and movie house. Sam embodies whatever good is left in Thalia: he "took care of things" (p. 7), he always bets on the high school teams no matter how inept they are, he never goes to bed at night until Billy is safe, and, in general, he sympathizes with the young people who have to grow up in that town. The essential goodness of Sam's values is best seen in his reaction to the trick the boys play on Billy with the whore: "Scaring an unfortunate creature like Billy when there ain't no reason to scare him is just plain trashy behavior. I've seen a lifetime of it and I'm tired of putting up with it" (p. 92).[17] Sam belongs to the older generation that has roots in the land. He belongs with those other representatives of the frontier myth whose lives testify to the positive force of the West: Homer Bannon, Mr. Fry, and even Gid and Molly.

Every year or so, Sam would take Sonny and Billy out to a tank on land he once had owned to do some fishing. The last time he does this, he reminisces about the past; he tells Sonny of a day twenty years before when he had brought "a young lady swimming here. It was after my boys were already dead, my wife had lost her mind" (p. 123). The woman, we learn later, was Lois Farrow for whom Sam was the only good thing in her life. Once again a tank takes on symbolic importance. Although the ranch is gone, the values residing in it live on at the tank. Sonny's "pissing off the dam" (p. 122), just the way Sam once did, and his renewing the life of Ruth Popper, the coach's wife, just as Sam made Lois feel "worthwhile," offer the possibility that life in Thalia is not entirely hopeless after all, no matter how depressing and provincial it may seem. Sonny might take up the values of Sam, just as in *Horseman, Pass By* Lonnie holds out hope that Homer Bannon's life was not in vain. With his characterization of Sam the Lion and with his unmistakable elevation of the redemptive qualities of the ranch-tank, McMurtry keeps his saddle on the wall.

McMurtry's first three novels are geographically limited and rather sparsely peopled. Not so his fourth, *Moving On,*[18] a rambling story that moves over much of the West and that has some twenty important characters in its nearly 800 pages. One gets to know the people of the rodeo world, from Sonny Shanks, the World Champion horseman, to Peewee Raskin, a fledgling and usually inept bareback rider. Then, there is the Rice University graduate school circle presided over by Bill Duffin, an English professor. Joe Percy represents the Hollywood scene; Eleanor Guthrie, the wealthy Texan; Patsy's parents, the moderately wealthy; Roger Wagonner, the rural and the struggling; Stone, the spaced-out, beat San Francisco world; and fleetingly, other characters represent still more facets of the contemporary West. So immense and so panoramic is *Moving On* that it is impossible here to examine it thoroughly, yet so crucial is it to an understanding of McMurtry's attempts to deal with the frontier myth that I must present more details than was necessary before, commenting as I go along.

Moving On is primarily the story of Patsy Carpenter's search for a meaningful life in the modern West. Married but a year to Jim, a wealthy young man who is conducting his own search for a vocation, Patsy accompanies him on the rodeo circuit. Jim is trying to become a photographer; riding in an old Ford, the Carpenters encounter a world they have never known: fast sex, violence, different value systems altogether. Most perturbing to Patsy is Sonny Shanks, the champion cowboy, who, forsaking a horse except in the ring, drives from rodeo to rodeo in a white Cadillac hearse. Sonny uses the hearse for publicity but also as a place for his sexual conquests. With the hearse, McMurtry suggests the death of the cowboy as the frontier myth had pictured him, especially at the end of the novel when Sonny, high on amphetamines, dies in a freeway collision with a car full of hippies. In a way, Sonny's hearse is a ranch house on wheels, which moves over the land but which has no secure ties to it. Patsy comes to hate the rodeo world; when, for example, she hears of two cowboys almost killing an old man by mistake, she says: "It's not just two especially dangerous cowboys, it's some sort of insane violence this life seems to breed" (p. 170). Another form of violence encountered in the rodeo world is sexual; Sonny tries to seduce Patsy very soon after meeting her. Bored and lonely when she isn't afraid, Patsy finds one man on the circuit who impresses her favorably: Pete Tatum, a rodeo clown, but even he would like to take her to bed.

After two months of following the rodeos, Patsy and Jim return to Houston, where Jim, disenchanted with photography, enters graduate school at Rice University (where McMurtry himself studied and taught). Although they have no financial worries and even though Jim quickly becomes a favorite of Prof. Duffin, Patsy finds no self-fulfillment in Houston. In fact, she cries more in Book II than in any other part of the novel, on some twenty-one different occasions.[19] She does attract men easily: Flap Horton, her best friend's husband, Bill Duffin, Hank Malory, all want to seduce her. Jim, his interests elsewhere, mostly ignores her, driving her finally to Hank, a graduate student friend of his. Book II has a wide variety of sexual activity and frank language in it. Flap and Emma Horton have sexual intercourse on the floor of their apartment; Clara Clark is known as a three orgasm girl; Bill Duffin fondles his wife in a very intimate way; Joe Percy, the screenwriter, tries but fails to copulate successfully with Patsy's Aunt Dixie; Hank works very hard in trying to convince Patsy to sleep with him; and so on. McMurtry spares the reader none of the vivid details of this sexual three-ring circus. Toward the end of Book II, Patsy and Jim have a baby boy, but not before Jim goes off to Mexico for a one night stand with a whore. It would take a team of social-psychologists to explain all of the reasons for this sex, but it seems that McMurtry is connecting the abundant sexuality here and elsewhere in the novel with the loss of meaningful values and the consequent malaise he finds existing in the contemporary West. That this may well be the case becomes probable by analyzing what happens to the ranch and its value system, but, first, a few more words about Patsy's search.

Book III opens with Patsy feeling a nameless restlessness. Jim is off in Amarillo helping Sonny Shanks make a movie, and, before too long, Patsy begins to sleep with Hank, who at least can make her feel like a woman sexually. While she and Jim grow more apart, McMurtry allows the reader brief glimpses into the other characters' lives. Jim, for instance, visits Eleanor Guthrie at her ranch (which is huge and efficiently managed), where each tries to seduce the other without success. Interestingly enough, her attempt to seduce him occurs at a tank on the ranch, which, in the context of *Moving On*, tends to subvert the positive image of the tank in the earlier novels. Eleanor's needs, though, are understandable: she realizes that she is aging and that Sonny, her lover, always thinks of himself first, of her second. By the end of Book III, then, the Carpenter's marriage is in near hopeless disarray with no positive values available to remedy it.

Things get worse in Book IV. Jim, discovering Patsy's affair with Hank, begins one of his own with Clara Clark, and they leave for Los Angeles, where Jim gets a job with IBM. Patsy and her son move into the Duffin house, which the Carpenters had bought in happier times, but all through the second winter in Houston, Patsy feels depressed. She next goes to California at the urging of her parents in order to rescue her sister, Miri, who has become pregnant, probably by a black man. Patsy's frenetic few days in California allow McMurtry a chance to present what can only be described as a corrupt and debased world. Patsy finds Miri high on drugs, starving, and filthy. While tracking her down, Patsy sees a group of Hell's Angels and their women in a park openly fondling each other's sexual parts. A far cry from Hud's pinching Halmea's breast, this scene is part of a pattern that pictures the modern West as spiritually different from the romanticized and sentimentalized West of the "unexamined frontier legend." The novel closes with Patsy daydreaming about an imminent trip to Uncle Roger's ranch, which is northwest of Thalia and which earlier in the novel had been willed to her and to Jim. In other words, Patsy is still searching, still moving on, when the novel ends.

The above summary of *Moving On* has excluded any mention of Uncle Roger's ranch, not because it lacks importance but because it is so crucial to an understanding of McMurtry's reading of the modern West that it requires separate treatment. A highly mobile, sexually obsessed, often corrupt society as drawn by him, the West would seem to have no time and no room for the positive values of the frontier myth. Such is not the case. There all the time, in north-central Texas not too far from Thalia, sits Roger Wagonner's ranch. Roger, widowed eleven years before, lives alone. He admits to being "pore": "I been at it fifty years and get worse at it every year. Least that's the way it looks in the bankbook" (p. 51). His house is plain, he drives an ancient Chevrolet pickup, and, in Patsy's opinion, he fries his eggs hard as stones. A man of common sense, he speaks softly and simply. He lives close to the land, raises his cattle, endures stoically whatever life offers, and, above all else, remains loyal. Although the moral center of the novel, he does not strike heroic poses, nor does he exhibit any unusual facility with his words. Patsy visits the ranch four times: twice with Jim, at the beginning of the novel and at the end of the rodeo section, then with her son Davey the following summer when Jim is in Amarillo making the movie, and, finally, to attend Roger's funeral. And, we remember, she is looking forward to visiting the place again when the novel ends.

These visits provide Patsy, the new woman of the West, with an opportunity to learn about the Texas that has closer and stronger ties with the old West. In the course of the novel Patsy travels thousands of miles; at the ranch the rhythms of life are slower. Roger gets up with the sun to feed the chickens and to milk his cow; Patsy, on her first visit, watches him from her bedroom window, much in the same way that Lonnie watches his grandfather ride beneath his window in *Horseman, Pass By.* The Wagonner house is filled with memories. Roger and his wife had argued for thirty-five years about salvation and sin, and though she has been dead for eleven years, Roger continues the argument: "In a way it's even better than having her here. I always win the argument" (p. 187). As one expects, Roger enjoys recalling the past; "After a while it seemed to Patsy that he was delivering an elegy" (p. 187), which saddens her. Because she finds him "a lovely man" (p. 190), Patsy, after the second visit, invites Roger to come to see her and Jim in Houston. At the end of Book II, he drives down to see Davey because he "always liked to keep tabs on my kin" (p. 384). That he would drive so far at his age in his old truck confirms the high opinion that Patsy has of him. He wants her to bring Davey to the ranch so he can "start 'em riding" (p. 387). Roger has a strong attachment to the ranching West, and he seems bent on maintaining this vital connection by teaching horsemanship, the highest skill in the old West, to little Davey.

By the time of her third visit to the ranch, Patsy's marriage is severely threatened and she has become involved with Hank Malory: "She was alone with Davey and didn't really know where *she* was going . . . or what she was going to do" (p. 490). Soon after her arrival, Roger suggests that they go horseback riding; he brings out his wife's saddle for Patsy, and they go off across the fields, with Davey riding in front of Roger. The ride is a pastoral interlude; it is an idyllic affirmation of the Old West. Although an old man, Roger skillfully rounds up a stubborn cow that had wandered off. Patsy, impressed by his skill and struck by the beauty of the land and sky, feels a sense of great well-being. After supper, Roger tells her he would like to leave his ranch to her and Jim, "to keep it in the family somewhere" (p. 497). When he learns of the state of Patsy's marriage and of her relationship with Hank, Roger refuses to pass judgment or to advise her. All he wants to know is whether Hank is a scoundrel. Before Patsy leaves for home, Roger tells her to "Bring old Davey back to see me before he gets too old to ride double" (p. 500). Roger will never see Patsy and Davey again because he dies the following March. Although his presence quantitatively in the novel is small, Roger plays a very important role. His quiet resoluteness, his love for the land and for his family, and his sincerity stand in sharp contrast to the corruption and the machinations of the larger world beyond the ranch.

When Patsy returns to the ranch to attend the funeral and to take care of the affairs of the inheritance, she both affirms and denies the spirit of Roger's generosity. She realizes that his gift "had shown a faith in them [Patsy and Jim] that they had not lived up to" (p. 699). Nevertheless, she arranges for the disposition and care of the animals with the help of a neighbor. She eats the last of the peanut butter that she and Jim had bought on their first trip there; McMurtry mentions the peanut butter each time Patsy visits the ranch, thereby reminding us of the passing of time and, in an unobtrusive way, of the gulf between the Carpenter's lives and Roger's (he cannot understand anyone eating such food). Hank arrives the following morning (Patsy had invited him), and he and Patsy renew their sexual activities, first in the bedroom, then in the front seat of the Ford (the very car in which she and Jim had first kissed), and finally on Aunt Mary's couch. Their intercourse in the Ford takes place at a tank located on the ranch, which, like Eleanor Guthrie's attempted seduction of Jim earlier in the novel, amounts to a debasement of the positive values associated with the tanks in the other novels. Similarly, their use of Aunt Mary's couch violates the love and respect that had been Roger's and Mary's for over thirty years. After Hank leaves, Patsy cleans out the Ford, washes the dishes, and tidies up the house, suggesting, symbolically at least, her partial awareness that what she and Hank had done defiled Roger's memory. Patsy's inability to commit herself fully to the ranch and its values persists to the end of the novel; in contemplating another visit she wonders whether it would be better to go with Davey and share his delight at the cows or to go alone and meet Hank for another sexual spree. She cannot decide, and, it appears, neither can McMurtry. One thing is clear, what Goodwyn says: that "the frontier ethos, removed from the center of his work, continues to hover around the edges."[20]

Towards the end of *Moving On* Emma Horton tells Patsy of her brief affair with Danny Deck, a young writer who had lived in Houston for a time but who had disappeared and is presumed to be dead. McMurtry's most recent novel, *All My Friends Are Going to Be Strangers*,[21] involves Danny's search for love as he wanders from Texas to California and back. The novel is set a year or two before *Moving On*. Danny, referred to as "the best young writer in the state" (p. 10), marries Sally, whom he has known but a couple weeks, has his first novel accepted, and then leaves Houston for California. Shortly afterwards, Danny and Sally split up, and Danny begins living alone in a grubby hotel. For diversion, he plays ping-pong with Wu, a Chinese friend who is studying English literature. Next, Danny falls in love with Jill Peel, a girl who does drawings for animated cartoons. Their relationship is a good one, but it does not last. Following a night during which he gets high on some Mexican mushrooms, Danny drives back to Texas, where the rest of the action takes place. Up to this point, the novel is slack and not very interesting; the scene involving the flooded highway in Chapter 6 has a comic robustness about it, to be sure, but little else stands out. McMurtry's language throughout the novel and the incidents he treats are quite salacious, frequently to the degree that one suspects him of pandering to the tastes of those who frequent the bus station paperback racks.[22] Whatever his designs in this regard, McMurtry does not give a very favorable view of the contemporary West. His characters are dislocated, loveless, lonely, hostile, unfaithful, or like Danny himself, living lives that "veer crazily one way and then another" (p. 51). In this way, *All My Friends* repeats the situations and moods of *Moving On*.

On his way back to Austin Danny decides to stop off at his Uncle Laredo's ranch near Van Horn. Since McMurtry has been describing a West where the frontier myth in any positive sense has been rendered irrelevant, we expect, especially if we have read his other works, that the ranch will be a place where the old values still hold. Danny's description of the Texas sky before he arrives at Uncle L's supports this expectation: "It had such depth and such spaciousness and such incredible compass, it took so much in and circled one with such a tremendous space that it was impossible not to feel more intensely with it above you" (p. 176). This promising sky, however, belies the state of things at the ranch. Danny finds his aged uncle (he is ninety-two) presiding over a madhouse. The ranch house itself is a blackened

Victorian mansion, the living room of which still houses a grand piano and the musical instruments for a nine-piece orchestra, not to mention a stuffed lobo wolf, the last wolf killed in Pecos County. These images, and others like them, point up the demise of the Old West, its ineffectuality for today. When Danny drives up, he finds Uncle L digging a center-post hole; he has dug some 300 already. In case he ever decides to put up a fence, the holes will be ready. Danny theorizes that Uncle L really digs the holes in order to hurt the hateful earth (we recall that Homer Bannon would not allow the oil company to come in and deface his land).

Another bizarre incident occurs next. One of the Mexicans who works on the ranch throws himself on the mound of dirt next to the post hole and begins to copulate with it. Shortly thereafter, he does the same thing with the gas hole in an old, black pickup truck. Here is sexuality gone wild, comic but disgusting, as if McMurtry has become sickened of the West he has been describing earlier in the novel. Still another facet of Uncle L's incredible world is his camel herd, a vestige of the post–Civil War importation of camels into what at that time was called "the Great American Desert." There is more; piled behind the windmill are 300 manhole covers, and nearby stands Uncle L's junkyard: "twenty or thirty cars, two broken-down bulldozers, several tractors, a hay baler, a combine, and an old cattle truck" (p. 186). McMurtry's choice of images seems right out of the world of Nathanael West. The blackened house, the oversexed Mexican, the unused post holes, the manhole covers, the camels, and the junk all suggest that the frontier myth is no longer viable.

Danny provides a clue that this impression is correct. Seeing Uncle L's buffalo herd (another vestige from the past) reminds him of a story in which some reservation Indians come to Old Man Goodnight (the legendary cattleman who also kept a herd of buffalo) and asked for a buffalo. They got one and ran it down and killed it on the plains in front of Goodnight's house. Danny reflects: "To me it was the true end of the West. A few sad old Indians, on sad skinny ponies, wearing rags and scraps of white man's clothes and carrying old lances with a few pathetic feathers dangling from them, begging the Old Man of the West for a buffalo, one buffalo of the millions it had once been theirs to hunt. . . . From then on all they would have was their longing" (p. 191). It was all over for the Indians, and it seems to be finished for Uncle L and his friend Lorenzo, who both keep a nightly vigil for the reappearance of Zapata, the Mexican revolutionist, with whom they had fought. Uncle L, his mind addled by age, keeps a sack of gold in his jeep in case Zapata needs money when he comes back.

In a sense, Uncle L and Lorenzo "had made life theirs" (p. 199), as Danny claims, but, in fact, they are but variants of McMurtry's Uncle Johnny, anachronistic guardians of the unexamined myth of the Old West. Suddenly Danny realizes that he never wants to visit the ranch again.

His disillusionment becomes clearer after he leaves the ranch. In Austin, for instance, he does violence to Geoffrey, "a little thing, in greasy Levi's" (pp. 207–208) because Geoffrey was bribing Godwin, a professor Danny had met earlier in the novel. Right before he hurts Geoffrey, Danny "felt strange and a little dangerous. Zapata was about to come out of the mountains" (p. 209). In other words, Danny's (and possibly McMurtry's) disgust at the debasement of the Old West explodes into violent outrage. The curious thing is that Danny invokes Zapata to express his feelings, testifying to the vitality of the frontier myth. A few chapters later, his autograph party in a Houston book store a flop, Danny drives south with Petey, a Mexican friend who has some dope with him. Two Texas Rangers (Uncle L had been a Ranger at one time) stop the pair, find the dope, and begin to needle the two men. They chide Danny because of his long hair, ask him if he is a homosexual, hit him, and, finally, throw him over a fence onto a prickly pear cactus. The Rangers' violence further isolates Danny from the positive parts of the frontier myth. A few pages later, he "gives" his car, which he has dubbed El Chevy, to an old couple who are hitchhiking. Divested of his "horse," the images of the past lost to him after his talk with Neville, an ex-movie actor, Danny renounces writing. He "drowns" the manuscript of his second novel in the Rio Grande, and he begins to walk farther and farther into the river, thinking to himself that "I didn't see the great scenes anymore, the Old Man riding, the Old Woman [Danny's grandmother who had endured the hardships of settling the Old West] standing on the ridge, the wild scenes from the past that I usually saw when I was walking some border of my own at night" (p. 285). The novel ends with Danny wanting, above all else, to flow with the fabled Rio Grande.

Whether Danny commits suicide or not, the point is clear: the frontier myth has failed him. The old cattlemen, Homer Bannon, Gid Fry, Sam the Lion, Roger Wagonner, the positive ties to a valid life and a viable legend, have given way either to the Huds, the Coach Poppers, the Sonny Shanks, the greasy runts on motorcycles, and the Texas Rangers or to the empty and absurd hungering for the past of Uncle L and Lorenzo. While Danny Deck himself falls short as an ideal heir of the Old West, he was attuned to its harmony and to its possibilities for art. His "death," and, if it is safe to speculate, McMurtry's move to Washington, D.C., suggest at least a temporary abandonment of the legend. Nevertheless, the ranch and the land may well endure in memory, if not in fact, to challenge not only the embattled McMurtry but also other writers both now and in the future.

NOTES

1. "The Frontier Myth and Southwestern Literature," *American Libraries,* 2 (1971), 363. Part I of this essay appears in February, 1971; Part II in April, 1971.

2. Goodwyn, pp. 161–162.

3. Goodwyn, p. 363.

4. From *In a Narrow Grave: Essays on Texas* (Austin: The Encino Press, 1968), which is to be reprinted in the spring of 1974. A more available source and one cited in this article is *The Literature of the American West,* ed. J. Golden Taylor (Boston: Houghton Mifflin, 1971), pp. 550–569.

5. Goodwyn, pp. 364–365.

6. (New York: Harper and Row, 1961). I shall refer to the paperback edition: *Hud* (New York: Popular Library, 1961).

7. Except for Uncle L's ranch in *All My Friends Are Going to Be Strangers,* which is located south of Van Horn in southwestern Texas, all of the ranches in McMurtry's novels are located around Thalia, the territory he knows best.

8. The titles of McMurtry's novels suggest his fascination with change and transience. Each novel, save one, has a verb in its title: *pass, leaving, moving, going to be.* The *last* in *The Last Picture Show* implies the passing of time, the giving way to the present.

9. Few people, for instance, would want to tangle with Sonny Shanks, The Champion Cowboy, in *Moving On.*

10. (New York: Harper and Row, 1963). I shall refer to the paperback edition: *Leaving Cheyenne* (New York: The Popular Library, 1963).

11. *Larry McMurtry* (Austin: Steck-Vaughn, 1969), p. 22.

12. Landess, p. 19.

13. The molasses incident, along with many others in his novels, comes from McMurtry's family background. See "Take My Saddle from the Wall: A Valediction," pp. 561–562.

14. (New York: Dial, 1966). I shall refer to the paperback edition: *The Last Picture Show* (New York: Dell, 1966).

15. Landess, pp. 23–26.

16. In their literary history and bibliography, Mabel Major and T. M. Pearce find in *Moving On* that "The language used at all levels of society strains credibility with its coarseness." See *Southwest Heritage,* 3rd ed. (Albuquerque: University of New Mexico Press, 1972), p. 231.

17. Sam's words remind one of Nigger Jim's denunciation of Huck's actions in the fog in Chapter 15 of *Adventures of Huckleberry Finn.*

18. (New York: Simon and Schuster, 1970). I shall refer to the paperback edition: *Moving On* (New York: Avon, 1971).

19. Over the entire novel, Patsy cries about seventy times, often in moods of self-pity, often for silly reasons (see p. 15).

20. Goodwyn, p. 365.

21. (New York: Simon and Schuster, 1972).

22. See Reed Whittemore's review of the novel in *The New Republic* (April 1, 1972), pp. 28–29, a somewhat facetious and inaccurate attack on McMurtry's fiction.

McMurtry's Women: "Eros [Libido, Caritas, and Philia] in [and out of] Archer County"

BILLIE PHILLIPS

Texan Larry McMurtry has published dozens of essays and book reviews in the past twelve years: he has also published several short works of fiction, a few poems, and five novels—three of which have been adapted to the screen by people professing to like his work but producing films belying their appreciation of McMurtry. Kenneth Davis has pointed out McMurtry's themes of initiation, and Charles Peavy, in trying to prove that McMurtry is a black humorist, has quoted a few passages from *The Last Picture Show* dealing with the sexual initiation of a calf. Thus the author's work has received some critical attention. It should be noted, however, that women in the Southwest are directly involved in the rituals of initiation, and they are sometimes even more interesting than cattle. For these two reason, alone, the women in the novels deserve more attention than critics have paid them.

When I finally finished Patsy Carpenter's novel, *Moving On,* I realized that this was one of the few novels that did not belong to McMurtry's male searchers: *Horseman, Pass By* belongs to Hud and Lonnie; *Leaving Cheyenne* to Gid and Johnny; *The Last Picture Show* to Duane and Sonny; and *All My Friends Are Going to Be Strangers* to Danny.

It is for these males in the novels that McMurtry's searching, seeking women function as important directional spirits. Since the direction seldom is toward happiness, it is fairly safe to suspect that the female characters illustrate several somewhat unconventional attitudes. They also illustrate an existential tenet that the importance of life's journey lies in making that journey. Embodying, as they do, the potential for creation as well as for destruction, these women are explored but not exploited by the author. They confront traditional beliefs and typically American dreams with disquieting practicality.

Finally, McMurtry's open end plot structure bespeaks his refusal to manipulate the actions of his women in an incredible or romantic manner; for, like our own, their experiences can not always be ended by tidy conclusions.

Most of McMurtry's women are developed, complex characters who exemplify, in varying degrees, the four kinds of love that Rollo May recognizes in Western tradition: "One is sex, or what we call lust, *libido*. The second is *eros*, the drive of love to procreate . . . A third is *philia*, or friendship, brotherly love. The fourth is *agape* or *caritas* . . . the love which is devoted to the welfare of the other . . . Every human experience of authentic love is a blending, in varying proportions of these four."[1]

In addition to exemplifying these kinds of love, the women can be divided into three groups: searchers, settlers, and travellers. The searchers constantly move on and experiment with their own emotions in an attempt to achieve self-fulfillment and satisfaction. The settlers experience life and settle for a measure of self-knowledge and fulfillment—often a very small measure. The travellers make up the largest group of women. About these it may be said that "All they ever get is older and around." If that tag-line sounds familiar, you may recognize that I am following the McMurtry-approved practice of borrowing song snatches. The tag-line and other quoted lyrics in this paper belong to Kris Kristofferson.

There are two generations of travellers. To the first generation, nearing forty, wealthy, beautiful, and sexually attractive, belong such women as Dixie McCormack, Lee Duffin, Eleanor Guthrie, and Jenny Salomea. Eleanor, from *Moving On,* maintained a touch and go relationship with Sonny Shanks, World Champion Cowboy and do-it-yourself-second-hand-hearse-decorator, for fifteen years. Once Eleanor invited Jim Carpenter to her ranch. The flirtation promised to be some special kind of an opportunity for them, but after their initial, fumbling meeting, Eleanor felt that she had "lost completely all the good emotions she felt for him in Amarillo. She didn't feel that she could be good for him, gentle with him, loving or tender or wise, the mistress-mother-confidante that she had once vaguely envisioned herself. She no longer wanted to restore his confidence in himself and send him back to his young wife experienced and secure. She felt something much coarser and didn't like it at all. It was a shock, but it was there." *Eros, philia,* and *caritas* are absent from Eleanor. She only feels lust, and the realization shocks her.

The youthful second generation travellers are Jacy Farrow of *The Last Picture Show* and Clara Clark of *Moving On.* Clara is a lovely, red

haired graduate student at Rice who has come from California with
her eyes and arms wide open. Literally, Jim Carpenter drives Clara
westward from Texas back to California; figuratively, it is she—or
more accurately what she represents—driving Jim. Since Jim is ready
to try anything that will help him to "find out what he is good at," he is
anxious to follow the girl whose body promises satisfaction to him. In
a more traditional triangle, Clara would be the evil woman who steals
the husband and father from his wife, his baby, and the land which
need him.

The McMurtry triangle confronts the myth that a man will find
self-knowledge and satisfaction with his woman, his children, and his
land. In his essay, "Southwestern Literature?", McMurtry talked
about the belief that earlier Texas writers shared concerning man's
relationship to nature: "Knowledge of it made a full man, and accord
with it was the first essential of the Good Life." That McMurtry
doubts the power of the land to give man satisfaction is expressed in
that same essay: "I spent more than twenty years in the country and I
came away from it far from convinced that the country is a good place
to form character, acquire fullness, or lead the Good Life. . . .
Sentimentalists are still fond of saying that nature is the best
teacher—I have known many Texans who felt that way, and most of
them live and die in woeful ignorance. When I lived in the country I
noticed no abundance of full men."

Traditionally, family and land have held much promise in Western
literature. But McMurtry has created a series of traditionally accepted, almost stereotyped, situations in *Moving On* and has, one by
one, destroyed his own cardboard sets. Jim could have achieved very
little satisfaction and self-knowledge in Houston with his wife and
child. The situations and people in Houston are no less artificial than
the situations and people Jim meets in California. So Jim drives himself in search of an elusive dream in the company of Clara Clark, an
illusion of authentic love.

The theme of illusion was central in the earlier novel, *The Last
Picture Show,* in which the second young traveller, Jacy Farrow was
always fascinated by fantasy. Jacy, the beautiful, unloving temptress
in Sonny Crawford's paradise, Thalia, Texas, attempts awkwardly and
seldom successfully to experience her concept of love, which is *libido;*
she wants to be sexually desired. In the name of *caritas,* which she
apparently believes is a more worthy kind of love than *libido,* Jacy tells
herself that she will be good for mutilated Sonny, poor Duane, and
unattractive Lester. Jacy's idea of love has been created by what she

has seen on film and in magazines and by her mother's flamboyant sexual posturing.

At the end of the novel, when Duane asks Sonny if he has heard anything from her, Sonny replies that he guesses Jacy "just stays in Dallas all the time." There is no reason to believe that Jacy is changed or that she will ever change. She will just get older and around, a second generation Eleanor Guthrie.

Lois, Jacy's mother, might, except for one reason, belong to the group of older, first generation travellers. While Lois is promiscuous and unhappy, she has experienced what the other women have not. With Sam the Lion, Lois has experienced an authentic love, but Sam could not or would not ask her to leave Gene Farrow and to live with him. That was one of the few wrong decisions Sam the Lion ever made, but that decision was probably the one that caused Lois, who was once possessed of *libido, eros, philia,* and *caritas,* to lose all of those emotions except *libido* and to become "thing" oriented in the crudest of senses.

The second group of women, the settlers, assume as their chief, self appointed responsibilities making their men comfortable and joyful. These are women who can experience authentic love—the blending of *libido, eros, philia,* and *caritas* —such as Emma Horton. This perennial graduate school wife, who appears in both *Moving On* and *All My Friends,* is, at once and on the rim of poverty, maternal, erotic, sympathetic, and occasionally more than semi-literate.

To the males in the novels, the settlers represent admirable, ideal womanhood. They are always wherever they should be in order to minister to their men. Boots, Pete Tatum's barrel racing, beer drinking, teenaged lover-child wife in *Moving On,* wants to please Pete even more than she wants to win a barrel race.

Each of these settlers possesses a nearly perfect blend of *eros, libido, philia,* and *caritas,* but these women are surrounded by an aura of illusion, just as were the women of the first group. Molly Taylor of *Leaving Cheyenne* is an idealized woman rather than an ideal woman. She is mother, wife, lover, daughter to the men in her life. She cares for her jealous father after her mother dies; she maintains a forty-year love affair with the two fathers of her two sons. Ironically, she is never more sexually desirable to her husband, Eddie, the father of neither of her children, than when she is pregnant. Molly is an amazing woman, even for North Texas. Her literary namesake, created in Henry Fielding's *Tom Jones,* was a country girl, whose skirts were more likely up than down. McMurtry, like his own countryman, Frank Norris, has attempted to create an *alma,* a soul of the country. Molly Taylor can comfort and excite the men for whom she must always "be doing." She views her men in friendship and as a sister views her brother, as a lover views her beloved, and as a mother views her children.

Charles Peavy has called Molly a mother surrogate.[2] She was McMurtry's second mother surrogate, Halmea of *Horseman, Pass By* being the first. Ruth Popper is still another such character. Ruth is a more credible creation than Molly, largely because she is not a beautiful woman until she assumes the beatific aura of a lover to Sonny Crawford.

In his essay, "Coming of Age in Texas," Peavy argues that Sonny's maturation owes much to this relationship with Ruth Popper. It is true that her authentic love was a pleasant experience for Sonny, but it is likewise true and should be noted that Sonny does not learn the wonderful secret which he needs to know, the secret that has taken Ruth forty years to learn. Even though the secret was "on the tip of her tongue," Ruth "lost the words." This settler was unable to pass knowledge on to Sonny.

While these women who experience authentic love—Lois, Genevieve Morgan, Emma, Boots, Ruth Popper, and Molly—find some measure of satisfaction, theirs are not permanently life-giving, joyful relationships. In other words, except for the somewhat idealized Molly Taylor, Larry McMurtry has treated human relationships realistically. His women do not "live happily ever after" just because they can experience love and they deserve happiness.

It is also highly doubtful that the man who has been subjected to one of these Southwestern settler's authentic loves lives happily. When Pete Tatum is last heard from, he is on his way to becoming a used car salesman for Boots' father in Fort Worth; he has resigned his clowning and is resigning himself to accepting the position he has often rejected.

Molly Taylor would not marry Gid; so he married a cold, unfeeling woman with whom he never realized joy. Sonny rejects both Ruth and Genevieve because he probably senses they can not provide him with post-maturation love. Flap Horton is regularly escaping from Emma's cozy kitchen to fish with his father in *All My Friends,* and when he is a middle-aged graduate student in *Moving On,* Flap shoots himself. The irony is that his garage, in which he shoots himself, is steps away from the kitchen of his fertile goddess, Emma. It is a kitchen that has been a very special room for Danny Deck during his troubled attempts at being father, lover, and husband to four different females. Yet the arms of Emma and her capacity for authentic love do not satisfy Flap.

And, after one sexual experience with Emma, Danny Deck knows that he will never repeat the intimacy with her.

Of all McMurtry's women, the searchers are the characters who are the least traditional and who most challenge understanding. They are the most interesting characters; for it is in the potential of these women that the male characters look for authentic, productive love and satisfaction. The searchers, like most of the other characters, are realistically drawn. Involved with the problems that concern today's women, they have their freedom and are not sure what to do with it. While their potential for authentic love is suggested, they do not experience that love in the novels. They do have the capacity for destruction, and that capacity is always illustrated. The three women who form this group are Patsy Carpenter of *Moving On* and Jill Peel and Sally Bynum Deck of *All My Friends Are Going to Be Strangers.*

Sally and Jill possess the four kinds of love, although it would take their combined possessions to make an authentic love. Jill, the Oscar-winning cartoonist whom Danny Deck lives with for awhile in California, can not experience joy in her sexual relations with Deck. Concerned for his welfare, desiring to care for him, she is filled with both *caritas* and *philia,* but she is without *libido* and *eros.*

The time Jill and Deck spend together is a period of creativity when both artists create, but they do not achieve happiness. Ironically, Deck's human creation, his daughter, is carried and nourished not by Jill but, instead, by Sally, who feels neither the *caritas* nor the *philia* that Jill feels toward Danny.

The third member of the group, Patsy Carpenter, possesses the necessary emotions that one should feel in order to experience an authentic love, but Patsy can not get the emotions together. She is the embodiment of lust when she is with Hank Malory, Jim's fellow graduate student. She occasionally embodies *eros* in her relationship with Jim and their son, Davey. With her friend, Emma, and Emma's children, Patsy expresses *philia; caritas* is evident in her relationship with her sister, Miri, Miri's lover (Eric), and Davey. Patsy, an intelligent and beautiful young woman, has her choice of sexual partners and friends; she has money, family, a son, and a maid who adores her, but Patsy does not feel fulfilled as wife, mother, friend, and lover.

Although Patsy spends much time travelling in what seems to her to be a circular journey ("All we've done is circle around"), she is the character who learns more about herself and her situation than any of the other women in the novels. Toward the end of her search, which has taken almost eight hundred pages to chronicle, Patsy's knowledge is evident. She knows that her parents' realized dream of wealth has not given them satisfaction. She finds out that sex, money, scholarship or professional competence do not necessarily provide the searcher with satisfaction. Patsy's associates in Houston are morally weakened because they hold on to these traditional, panacean goals without believing personally in their efficacy.

Patsy may have recognized something that can redeem the hopes and dreams of her generation. She may have the secret that will show the searchers the way to their goals; for Patsy recognizes in her sister's lover, Eric, a strong man who may provide new blood for a weakened line. With new blood and the old land that Roger Wagonner has left them, Patsy's vision may materialize. On the other hand, Patsy's dream may be one more of several illusions in the novels; for McMurtry did not tell the story of the dream come true.

One of the suggestions that stays with the reader of Larry McMurtry is this: the combination of an authentic love, self-knowledge, and satisfaction is an elusive dream. Many of the women who possess authentic love lose it or have it ruined. The strong, intelligent women find little or no satisfaction in what is traditionally recognized as the accepted fruition of an authentic love—marriage and a family. The husbands of the searchers, Jim Carpenter and Danny Deck, and the lovers of these women become neither the satisfied men nor the creative artists they would like to become. Deck, because he is a fragmented, frustrated man, destroys the offspring of his liaison with Jill Peel in one of the most recently recorded literary infanticides: he drowns his second novel in the Rio Grande. Then McMurtry leaves Danny Deck, literally, in midstream.

It is not a lack of structural artistry that causes the author to end his novels where more traditional writers begin theirs. In 1967, McMurtry expressed his interest in exploring, for the richness of their "textural possibilities," "situations in which a person loves or is loved by more than one person. One man loves two women, one woman loves two men, etc."[3] When one person is in love with two or more people, at the same time, his personality and his emotions are more than likely fragmented.

McMurtry's exploration of heterodox love relationships in his last two novels, *Moving On* and *All My Friends,* leaves the reader with the chaotic experiences of fragmented characters and a series of disquieting assumptions: Patsy's dreams may never be fulfilled; [Deck's] suicide may lie at the end of the unsatisfied artist's life. More comfortable endings might have had the characters illustrating modern lyrics such as,

> Soon as I was better,
> I was movin' on,
> Gettin' it together,
> Getting' good and gone . . . .

But, for an optimistic reader, it is both difficult and necessary to remember that McMurtry has no novel titled either *Going Someplace* or *Getting There*.

Instead, he chooses the open end plot to reflect today's society. His choice illustrates his refusal to sacrifice the realistic treatment of plot and characters for complacent romance.

Because he has been realistic in his exploration of love relationships, McMurtry has recorded the incomplete searches of some characters who never experience authentic love, who never achieve complete satisfaction, but who see visions and learn much. He has also created a group of settlers, who experience authentic love but who do not experience the realization of dreams, and, finally, he has presented the travellers, those women whose experience with love is succinctly expressed by Dixie McCormack, moving on through a red light: "'Oh, hell,' she said, 'I'll stop twice as long at the next one.'"

NOTES

1. *Love and Will* (New York: W. W. Norton & Company, Inc.), 1969, pp. 37–38.
2. "Coming of Age in Texas: The Novels of Larry McMurtry," *Western American Literature.* 4 (Fall 1969), 188.
3. *Collage* (May 1967), p. 8 as quoted in "Coming of Age in Texas: The Novels of Larry McMurtry," pp. 175–76.

From

The Dirt-Farmer and the Cowboy: Notes on Two Texas Essayists

TOM PILKINGTON

The essay is not a form that most Texas writers find congenial. Like the people from whom they spring, they are apparently too impatient and too inclined toward action and violence to feel at home in such a leisurely, introspective genre; their tastes in both fiction and nonfiction run more to fast-paced narrative. It is an event of some importance, therefore, when two Texans publish, within a period of a few months, collections of essays which seem more substantial than anything produced recently by local novelists. I refer to *And Other Dirty Stories* (New York, World Publishing Company), by Larry L. King, and *In a Narrow Grave: Essays on Texas* (Austin, The Encino Press), by Larry McMurtry, both of which appeared in 1968. . . .

Unlike King's essays, which vary widely in subject matter and quality, the essays which comprise Larry McMurtry's *In a Narrow Grave* all develop in some way a single topic, and all are of consistently high quality. In fact, *In a Narrow Grave* is in every way (save one perhaps) superior to *And Other Dirty Stories*. First of all it holds together better; for a collection of essays, the way it holds together is almost miraculous. It is better organized, tighter, more economical. McMurtry's style is more polished than King's, and despite King's deservedly widespread reputation as a humorist, McMurtry is wittier; *In a Narrow Grave* contains none of those gratuitous attempts at humor that mar parts of *And Other Dirty Stories*. McMurtry's perceptions, and his relating of them, are more incisive and thought-provoking.

Only in the area of subject matter, it seems, does King have the advantage, and even there personal preference might dictate the opposite judgment. King, faced with the necessity of putting his prose on the national publishing market, has for the most part chosen to treat subjects of general interest; McMurtry, I suppose because the material interests him, is content to ruminate about what it means to be a Texan, how the state got the way it is, the changes it is undergoing. McMurtry's subject, as he well understands, has built-in limitations that are difficult to overcome. "I have begun to wonder," he says at one point, "if it is possible to write a discursive book about Texas which will not turn out to be simply a book for Texans, or, more narrowly still, a book for Texas intellectuals" (p. 44). Publishers probably wonder the same thing; King was able to find a national publisher for his book, while McMurtry apparently could enlist only a regional one for his. (The term "regional publisher" is not intended to denigrate the Encino Press, which has earned a wide reputation for the high quality of its books; it does suggest, though, certain distribution and sales restrictions. From the standpoint of physical appearance, *In a Narrow Grave*—when compared with *And Other Dirty Stories* or, come to think of it, when compared with almost any other book I have seen recently—takes the prize hands down. Its excellent format, type, paper and binding make it a very handsome volume indeed.)

Larry McMurtry, in any event, is not one to fret over the limited distribution facilities of a regional publishing house. Being a writer, he says, he likes to talk to himself anyway. McMurtry is a young Texas writer and intellectual who has taken the second of the alternatives mentioned earlier: he has chosen not only to write about the state, but to live in it. "Let those who are free of Texas," he says, "enjoy their freedom" (p. 31). Obviously, McMurtry is not free. He is thoroughly aware of his state's publicized weaknesses, but most writers must have a place—a homeland in which they and their characters can sink their roots—and McMurtry's is Texas. The impulse to write *In a Narrow Grave* was in part, he reveals, the desire to understand more fully "the place where my characters live" (p. ix).

From having read his book, I think McMurtry must have the ideal temperament for accommodating himself to the stay-at-home alternative. As is the case with King's collection, his prose reflects the tone of his work as a whole: it is smooth and relaxed. It has a kind of intensity, but there is nothing in it of the threatened explosiveness that characterizes King's style. His attitude toward the current Texas scene is one of tolerant amusement, with perhaps a touch of acid. Probably he has known his share of embarrassment and outrage, but these are wearing emotions; sanity and good health require a more temperate outlook. On the surface at least, he appears not to be irritated very much about anything, least of all the doings of his fellow Texans. He does not even worry that his mother may be frowning on something he has written. He seems very sure of himself, and his comments have an air of crisp authority. Occasionally he is almost cocky—as, for instance, in his peremptory dismissal of Dobie, Webb and Bedichek, the holy trinity of Texas letters. One reason, I think, that he can write about his native state with absolute certainty (though the reader does not always receive his judgments with the same degree of certainty) is because he has been tested severely; he has been able to look upon Texas in the harsh light of day, to see all her warts and wrinkles and to love her still. "Living here," he writes, "uses a good deal of one's blood; it involves one at once in a birth, a death and a bitter love affair" (p. xv).

But if the author admits to having an ambiguous love affair with his homeland, it is the birth and the death that he is most concerned with. The birth is what the state is becoming, the death what it once was. That sounds like a simple statement, but as McMurtry rightly perceives, it encompasses scores of connections, complications and tensions; if correctly extended and elaborated upon, it explains many of those things about modern-day Texas that mystify and confuse people from other states. It is the central, recurring theme which holds together the disparate parts of *In a Narrow Grave,* and it is implicit in the author's relation that at first he had thought of calling his book *The Cowboy in the Suburb;* he finally settled on the present title (which comes from an old cowboy song: "In a narrow grave just six by three / We buried him there on the lone prairie . . .") because he wanted "a tone that was elegiac rather than sociological" (p. xv).

Certainly *In a Narrow Grave* is elegy; in a sense it is a wave of goodbye to a code and a way of life that are rapidly vanishing from the face of the earth. It is not, however, sentimental. McMurtry is no romantic yearning to retreat into the womb of time. His attitude toward the past and present is what any sensible man's would be—it is ambivalent. "I am critical of the past," he writes, "yet apparently attracted to it; and though I am even more critical of the present I am also quite clearly attracted to *it*" (p. 141). But if the reader must detect the author leaning in one direction or the other, it is easy enough to see that he inclines to the past. "The death," he writes elsewhere, "moves me—the way of life that is dying had its value. Its appeal was simple, but genuine, and it called to it and is taking with it people whom one could not but love" (p. xv). He says that he expects very little from the birth, except a kind of "kid brother" imitation of California. "One sometimes wonders," he muses, "if Bowie and Travis and the rest would have fought so hard for this land if they had known how many ugly motels and shopping centers would eventually stand on it" (p. 75). But the motels, shopping centers and sprawling housing developments are portents: they foretell the state's future, and most certainly they will wax larger and gaudier, even as they multiply.

McMurtry is the descendant of a clan of cattlemen, men who operated ranches in Archer County and later in the Panhandle. His family's position in society was somewhat more secure and respected than that of the King family, and their contrasting family backgrounds may account for the manifest differences between him and his colleague. McMurtry refers at one point to an uncle who was part owner of a bank, and all of his relatives were well-established, if not wealthy ranchers. His leisurely style, his confident and authoritative tone, his calm acceptance of an imperfect social environment—all of these are appropriate to a man who thoroughly knows himself and his "blood's country" (to use Judith Wright's phrase), even though that country is now in a sense occupied territory. Anyway, it is natural, considering his origins, that McMurtry's conception of past and present should be embodied in the mythical figure of the cowboy, and that he should identify with that figure (just as it is natural that, to some extent, King should be driven by memories of his dirt-farming childhood). As *In a Narrow Grave* shows, he was nurtured from his earliest years on the philosophy of the cowboy, and he seems to have incorporated into his writings something of the self-sufficiency extolled by that philosophy.

The stereotyped cowboy—the free horseman of the open range—is, of course, familiar to all; he has become part of our national mythology. McMurtry concedes that the image is romantic, therefore distorted, but contends that it is nonetheless useful. It is, after all, based on reality, and it is that reality which he wants to follow to its source. Through movies and literature, personal experiences, the testimony of family and friends and the reminiscences of old-timers, he traces out the lines of the cowboy myth. He lists and discusses some of its essential elements, one of the most important of which is the fact that the cowboy was first and foremost a horseman. The cowboy could fail in almost any field, but he dared not be found deficient in horsemanship. The horse in large measure created the myth, because it gave the cowboy a physical and psychological elevation—a perch from which to look down upon the pedestrian world and to which, just as importantly, the world had to look up. This circumstance explains, among other things, the cowboy's legendary contempt for the farmer, who had to grub his living from the soil, and the ambition of so many farm boys to become cowboys probably indicates that the farmer accepted the contempt as justified.

The cowboy was indeed a unique individual, a man who looked at life in a special way. But the time has almost arrived when we can say that he no longer exists. Most of the large ranches have been broken up, and the wide open spaces have been greatly diminished. The cowboys (and the dirt-farmers, too, for that matter) have moved to town and to the suburbs. The adjustment to city life has not been easy, nor is it yet complete. Texas towns and cities enthusiastically support rodeos, pioneer celebrations, old fiddlers' reunions and dozens of other spurious fiestas and fandangos, all of which bear noisy witness to a chronic nostalgia for the past and for open country. Texans are rural people suddenly set down in an urban environment, and they must practice, in McMurtry's words, "symbolic frontiersmanship" to maintain even a partial sense of balance. Much of the peculiarity of Texans as a "class," McMurtry believes, can be traced to the fact that they are undergoing a physical and psychological transition of staggering proportions.

That fact may explain, for example, the well-known tendency for Texans to resort to easy violence. Houston, currently the writer's hometown, provides a paradigm: "One cannot help believing that Houston's astonishing homicide rate is related to its equally astonishing rate of growth. A great many Houstonians are still in the process of transition from country ways to city ways. They are not yet urban, but they are no longer quite country, either. Many of them are poor, and the unaccustomed urban pressures frustrate them severely. To let off steam they go to honky-tonks—dance halls for country people who are no longer in the country. . . . In such a place, with a little beer under his belt, a man is apt to find that his frustrations are uncontainable: he has more steam to let off than he had realized, and he may let it off by shooting some poor bastard whose plight is little different from his own" (p. 127). That transplanted cowboy or farmer, blazing away in one of the state's notoriously dangerous taverns, evokes a common and unforgettable image. He is a kind of microcosm of Texas as a whole.

In a Narrow Grave develops several aspects of this theme of transition, showing how it affects movies, the state's literature, the quality of life in its cities, the McMurtry family. One of its more illuminating explorations is into a virtually uncharted wilderness: the sexual attitudes and practices (and recent changes therein) of the state's villages and rural areas. As anyone who grew up in a place like Archer City will attest, it takes a hardy spirit and strong stomach to hack one's way through the thickets of small-town eroticism. In his novels McMurtry has demonstrated that he possesses the requisite tenacity. In "Eros in Archer County," one of the essays in *In a Narrow Grave,* he shows that he can think as well as observe. I confess that, in reading his novels, I was not always certain as to just what he was driving at. But much in the novels that at first seemed irrelevant or superfluous is in the essay amply justified. Stated simply, the author's contention is that during most of the twentieth century Texans have been singularly confused and distressed by changing relations between the sexes and that tension between present reality and the persistence of ingrained assumptions from the past has created a backlog of inhibitions and psychological suffering that will require many years and a great deal of patience to relieve.

Most of the ideas that McMurtry examines in *In a Narrow Grave* are not new; in one form or another they have been tossed around by the state's intellectuals for quite some time now. McMurtry's, however, is the first reasonably full treatment of them that I have seen in print. For that reason I may have overestimated the worth of his book. I also may have been unduly swayed by the originality of much of his evidence, the freshness of his insights and the grace and precision with which he expresses himself. If so, I must plead guilty to that most dreaded of critical felonies—over-enthusiasm. My only defense is that it seemed to me, as I read the book, that to get there the firstest with the mostest should be a guiding principle of literary creation, as well as of warfare.

I will readily concede, however, that it is probably far too early to make anything more than a shaky judgment concerning the ultimate value of either of the two books I have discussed. Again, I can only indicate my personal response to them, which was one of pleasure and delight. I think that I learned a few things in reading them and experienced an occasional shock of recognition. What more can one ask of a book? If I have seemed more critical of King's book than of McMurtry's, it is only because I read them back to back, and unfortunately King's suffered by comparison; in any other company, it would have, I am certain, shone more brightly. I have not in these comments tried to psychoanalyze anyone or to read his mind, tasks I have neither the desire nor the competence to perform. I have wished only to provide possible guidelines for thinking about the careers and most recent books of two Texas writers. I suppose what I have been trying to say is this: that, in the case of these writers, and not unreasonably in the case of many other Texans as well, their choice between the two alternatives outlined above has been determined, in large measure, by their confidence (false or otherwise) in their place in the scheme of things. Reduced to its essentials, that is scarcely a startling proposition, but tangled in the complexity of human behavior, it is not, I think, self-evident. I do not mean to imply by the foregoing discussion that dirt-farmer and cowboy are comprehensive categories that explain everything about Texas, its past and present alike; they are merely useful literary and social archetypes, and they should be used in the same general way that one employs terms such as "nervous middle class" and "complacent aristocracy" in talking about English literature and society. As classifications they are not very precise, and they await, I realize, further definition and elaboration.

Before concluding, I want to point out a revealing quirk that, oddly enough, characterizes both writers. The essay is apparently so unfamiliar and demanding a form that both are quick to apologize for anticipated failures; they apologize even when the reader feels that no apologies are necessary. Very early McMurtry expresses the belief that perhaps he "should have left them [the essays] to rot in the fields . . ." (p. viii). Later he says that one of his "covert purposes in writing this book was to find out for myself if nonfiction could be as interesting and rich a mode as fiction." He professes to believe his experiment a failure: "I was not long in discovering that it wasn't going to work for me" (p. 138). King's variation on the theme is his repeated, and only half-facetious, assurances that he is just a country boy trying to make a living and the reader should not expect his book to win a Nobel Prize.

Neither work, I predict, is going to win a Nobel Prize. Perhaps neither will win even a local award, though McMurtry's collection probably deserves at least a regional commendation of some kind. The writers' modesty, therefore, is in a way a hedge against the possibility of their books' future obscurity. But considered within the context of their careers to date, the note of deprecation that recurs throughout their essays seems, to this observer at least, all but inexplicable. Certainly King's discursive prose is far better than his first, and so far only, novel (*The One-Eyed Man*), which is, to put it gently, mediocre. McMurtry has done somewhat better with his fiction, but I cannot help feeling that people will be reading "Eros in Archer County" and some of his other essays when *Horseman, Pass By* and *Leaving Cheyenne* and *The Last Picture Show* have been long forgotten. One could hardly claim, on the basis of these two collections, that an essayical tradition in Texas literature has been firmly established. One can only believe, as I do, that a promising and rousing start has been made.

McMurtry's Elegant Essays

DAVE HICKEY

"There was blood on the saddle,
and blood on the ground.
And a great,
big puddle of blood all around.
Oh pity the cowboy
all bloody and red,
Cause a bronco fell on him,
and squashed in his head.
—"Blood on the Saddle"

Excluding professors who, being slaves to tastes more bland than theirs, must coat their tongues and follow their noses up the ladder toward administration, we all judge the books we read. If we don't there's hardly need for more than one. And this judgment, as arbiters of taste will tell you, is fairly arbitrary. What I would suggest, to make literary judgment at least as fair as arbitrary, is a scoring method similar to that used in competition diving, wherein the diver's score is multiplied by a difficulty-factor according to the demands of the dive he has chosen.

If this method were adopted, the difficulty-factor for Larry McMurtry's *In a Narrow Grave* would be large indeed. Here is an honorable and self-effacing novelist who has chosen to publish an honest set of personal essays about Texas, and to publish it *in* Texas, thus depriving himself of that audience which so happily plunked down ten bucks to chart with William Manchester the stations of the cross on a Humble map of downtown Dallas. Moreover, he writes this book without once treading wittily on this state's most prominent and well-trod feet of clay. In short, McMurtry is no Uncle Clem (the local equivalent of an Uncle Tom) telling deppity sherf stories in the cloisters of the Time-Life Building. Such gallantry approaches foolishness.

Granted, some of the book is unfair and none of it is scandalous, but none of it is dull either, and even the gratuitous portions serve a certain cathartic function. Everyone, for instance, knows that Frank Dobie and Walter P. Webb were pedestrian writers, however equestrian their subject, and that neither of them—in that great string band in the sky—will ever even qualify to carry Gibson's harp, but it's nice to see it documented. Especially here in Austin, hub of the Pancho industry, where beef jerky is transubstantiated into sacred cow and served in boxed editions.

But what is most delightful about this book is McMurtry's voice, educated, indirect and full of surprising turns and modulations that are simply not in his novels. Looking back from *In a Narrow Grave* to the novels and reading a few passages here and there, the innocent bumpkins who narrate the McMurtry novels seem terribly stagy and posed. It makes you wonder about the novelistic convention which requires a writer to divest himself of half of his vocabulary and a proportionate amount of brains when he approaches a character less learned than himself. Certainly it is a feat of skill to approximate primitive speech, whether it is worth doing or not is another question. (I'm reminded of Raquel Welch's recent impersonation of Katharine Hepburn, which, assuming the common man has better taste than do literary critics, will hopefully not become part of her repertoire.) In McMurtry's book, by speaking in his own voice, he gains access to levels of irony which enable him to engage subjects charged with sentiment without collapsing, or rising (according to your taste) into sentimentality.

It has often been noted, and McMurtry notes it himself, that Texas is hell on women and horses. What hasn't been noted, probably since it isn't very important, is that there is some retribution, since women and horses are hell on Texas writers. Confronted with subjects equine or feminine or both, your average Texas writer's mind is turned to cream-of-wheat, his heart to tapioca; his wit abandons him as he enters and his prose falls back on that earliest of models: the radio evangelist, and women and horses, those two despotic servants of the frontier, are bathed more often than not in the rhetorical blood of the lamb. This is a general characteristic. It is avoidable only by keeping Old Ralph in the pasture and Dolly Sue out of the stock tank. Even Terry Southern can get smarmy about a horse, though he keeps safe distance.

McMurtry doesn't completely avoid the problem, nor should he.

There is a tremendous amount of emotional energy surrounding the "bold horseman and gallant lady" myth, and the sentiment, if not the myth, is authentic. It is interesting to note, though, that only on the subject of women and horses does the prose in this book begin to sound like "fiction" and not like McMurtry; but in this book McMurtry triumphs and laconically assures us that the gallant ladies turn brackish and bitter on occasion, and that bold horsemen have been known to get their heads squashed.

And finally, if there is anything in this book which reveals the quirks and cadences of this culture, it *is* McMurtry's voice. You could learn as much about Texas if the book were about Indianapolis, because McMurtry would find the same faces there, lined with contemplation of their defeat, the same droll embarrassing innocence; he would record, I believe, the same laconic conversations since his voice is half of them. As lovely as the evocation of the flat-country is in this book, the real truth of it, or so it seems to me, is in the selectivity of McMurtry's eye and, most basically, in the nature of his humor. Like all good cowboy humor it is based of self-deprecation and baroque similitude, and it is a terribly decorous form of amusement. The self-deprecation inevitably reflects a sublime and non-assertive confidence in the self, and the far-fetched similitudes display (as much as anything can) a serious desire to please rather than instruct.

But the very tact and decorum of this voice leaves McMurtry open for that most terrible of literary disasters. Having spoken well in the Texas language and about the local soil, and having spoken truly about his own responses to it, there will be those who will praise or accuse him of have spoken the "Truth"—of, in the current idiom of sincerity, "telling it like it is," this being one of the cheapest ways a blind eye can rob a writer of his individuality and appropriate his vision.

Writers who speak in their own voice are awfully vulnerable to this kind of banditry, and the best of the self-dramatists—Byron, Wilde,

Dylan Thomas—have been forced to ridiculous extremes in their attempts to make the public—truth-seekers to the man—accept their words as good but not necessarily as true. In fact, the primary attraction of the personal essay, which is hardly anything but an expanded aphorism, is that it is *not* generally true. If it were, it would hardly be worth saying.

McMurtry's voice, for instance, with its patience, its non-assertiveness and decorum is absolutely incapable of capturing or sympathizing with the bravado and energy and pure visual spectacle of a modern city. Although he is perfectly aware of this attraction, even talks about it, his ideal city is a bunch of ranch houses with streets between them and an area devoted to dark, quiet *cantinas*. Every morning everyone takes the commuter train out to the number ten pasture and saddles up Old Ralph.

Now this is as good an idea for a city as any, and it enables McMurtry to generate a lovely sense of what it is like in those Texas cities which most closely approximate that idea. Those cities which *are* cities get short shrift in this book. They are guilty of "boosterism." For myself, I couldn't conceive a city more guilty of vulgar boosterism than Elizabeth's London, unless it was Lorenzo de Medici's Florence; nor could I conceive of a more arrogant booster than Augustus, who boosted Virgil, unless it was Pope Julius, who boosted Michelangelo all the way to the ceiling. At any rate, both of them make Roy Hofheinz look like the soul of restraint, Astroturf and all, and the point is not that McMurtry is wrong, which he isn't, but that he is McMurtry, and the contradictions in the book define the strategy by which he, personally, confronts the world.

It is really wonderful, for instance, that he can deplore the puritanism of Archer County in one essay, then turn up in another deploring the promiscuity of faculty wives in Austin. (This observation, by the way, dates McMurtry's stay in Austin. Since then, either the quality of faculty wives has gone down, or the standards of philandry gone up—or, and this is more likely than both, the number of willing distaff undergraduates has so multiplied that the wives have been left with their strawberry facials.)

In any case, this is a damned amusing book, and the effect of it on me was surprisingly similar to the effect of Norman Mailer's *Armies of the Night*. How amazing to discover that the novelist's life is more interesting than his dreams, that his friends are more interesting than his characters. This is rarely the case—but, then again, it is rarely today. There is a Chinese curse which goes: "May you live in

interesting times." It is a curse on fiction writers, but not on writers
in general, and never on writers as elegant as McMurtry. It would be
ironic, but not unusual if McMurtry survived with the Astrodome
rather than the high lonesome. You can't look forward to the fact, but
you can look forward to the telling of it.

Terms of Estrangement
DONALD BARTHELME

The time was October 1981; the vehicle, the by-then venerable *Texas
Observer*. The message was that Texas writers, at best, might aspire to
the second-rate. In fact, Larry McMurtry implied, Texas had no literature that you didn't have to tie a pork chop to its head to get the dawg
to read it. According to McMurtry, the Houston poet Vassar Miller
was the only world-class writer in the state.

The response from the Texas literary community was striking.
Four writers in Abilene stopped drinking, cold turkey. John Graves
grasped his posthole digger and swore a mighty swear. Max Apple
asked himself, "Am I an apple, or merely a dumb withered raisin?"
Larry King considered taking the veil; he put on the veil, took off the
veil, put on the veil again, and decided, finally, that the veil was not
for him. Laura Furman called up Rainer Maria Rilke in heaven and
asked him what to do next. Charlie Smith began running eight miles
every day before dawn with a Purdey shotgun clenched between his
teeth. Beverly Lowry ordered up a railroad car of vitamin B from the
Upjohn concern. Shelby Hearon spit in the eye of the editor of the
New York Times Book Review, on the theory that a certain *virtù*
attaches to offending the gods. From El Paso to Hemphill, from Dalhart to Rio Grande City, it was crisis time for Texas quality lit.

I disagree with McMurtry; I think that taking the thing state by
state, there are more good writers in Texas than anywhere in the
country save New York and California. New York is a special case, our
Paris; you go to have your corners knocked off. When I first lived
there, two decades ago, I was one night congratulated by a prominent
poet on my "rural irony"; being from Texas, you're a natural target.
California has movie money, and since most writers make less than a
tenth-level lawyer, that is of interest.

Those peculiarities aside, one must ask: What has Nevada done for
literature lately? Who's the Alaskan Tennyson? McMurtry acknowl-

edged the geographical fallacy in his argument (indeed, his argument, considered in this way, disappears) but wanted to make it anyhow. The gravamen of his complaint, made not for the first time, was that he had had high hopes for us and that we had disappointed him. Perhaps his hopes were grandiose, or perhaps his definition of Texas literature was too narrowly drawn. We've done at least as well as Rhode Island, we're pushing Wyoming to the wall. . . .

The question of who is, and who is not, a Texas writer intrudes here. In 1915, in Galveston, my grandfather began building a raft. There was a terrible hurricane in the Gulf, and a raft must have looked, at the time, like a pretty good idea. My grandfather owned a lumberyard, as it happened, and had thoughtfully repaired thither to build the raft. The men laid out the two-bys and nailed them together and debated which way the planking should run, drank whiskey, and generally had a high old time, with the waters rising and the wind howling around them. The women, my grandmother among them, played cards (probably liars' poker). Fifty years ago, in 1935, my father, an architect, took his wicked pencil in hand and designed the Hall of State for the Texas Centennial Exposition. I was pulling catfish out of the Guadalupe when A. C. Greene, a much younger man, was still trying to understand those funny curly fingerlike things at the end of his feet. Am I, then, a Texas writer? Because I don't deal much in the specifics of place, McMurtry suggests (in an otherwise generous critique) that the answer is no, not really. I would hope that a more liberal definition of what is Texian would prevail—it would be healthier.

Another atmospheric disturbance, parallel in a way, blew up about a year ago when Don Graham complained, in the *Texas Humanist*, about all the new writers in the state who came here from someplace else. "Fern-bar writers," he called them, whatever that may mean. (Did he mean faggot homosexual queer pansy fairies? And if so, why didn't he say so?)

Mr. Graham seems to believe that new arrivals, new citizens parking their tired, dusty, rump-sprung Honda Civics in the back streets of Austin and Dallas and Houston, are not good for the state's literary culture, that they in some way dilute it or render it less authentic. This betrays a weak notion of historical process. Not true of America, not true of Texas. A "pure" Texas literature would probably be written in Coushatta. What we want are people who can speak a little Coushatta, a little Big Spring, a little Brit lit crit, a little Hebrew, a dash of salsa.

There's a great painting by the Armenian immigrant Arshile Gorky, who died in 1948, titled "How My Mother's Embroidered Apron

Unfolds in My Life," in which the wonder of possibility and the to-be-dreaded movement of time are stunningly present. Gorky saw many things about America that no one else had ever seen, and he had to come from far away to do it. A rich and vital culture accepts all gifts.

Tinsel Talk

BRUCE BAWER

Larry McMurtry, who is known primarily as the author of a number of elegiac, Texas-sized novels about his native Lone Star state, has also had something of a second career as a writer of movies, and (briefly) a third career as a writer of articles and columns based on his experiences as a writer of movies. His unpleasantly titled new collection, *Film Flam*—what a tongue twister!—consists of twenty-one opinionated pieces, most of them originally published in the magazine *American Film,* that render a writer's-eye view of what folks in Los Angeles like to refer to as "the industry" (a locution which, for me, always brings to mind images of Jane Fonda and Robert Redford sweating it out on an assembly line).

Among the subjects that McMurtry treats in these essays are the problems of adapting one's own novel for the movies, the advantages of writing screenplays away from Los Angeles, the fun of screenwriting, the L.A. ambience, and the unreadability of most film scripts. McMurtry describes an afternoon he spent with Diane Keaton and her nonagenarian grandmother in Pasadena, compares and contrasts *Seven Beauties* and *All the President's Men* (he feels that the former has "radiance of spirit" and "greatness of heart," and the latter doesn't), and reviews two books on the relation between novels and their film adaptations. He writes endlessly about his novel *The Last Picture Show* and the movie that Peter Bogdanovich made from it. (He seems to think that we are all extremely familiar with this movie, and that our appetites for details about its genesis are insatiable. By the end of the book one is sick to death of reading its very title.) Some of his essays are forthrightly reactionary: he complains about the unfilmability (as well as the unreadability) of such postwar novels as *Gravity's Rainbow* and *The Sot-Weed Factor,* and (in two separate essays) laments the "disappearance of love" and the "disappearance of grace" from the cinema. He also discusses the lack of beauty and feeling in pornographic movies and laments the departure of movie

theaters, particularly drive-ins, from the rural middle-American landscape. And he offers critiques of two movies that were made from his
own novels: Peter Bogdanovich's adaptation of *The Last Picture Show*
gets very high marks, while Sidney Lumet's *Lovin' Molly,* derived from
McMurtry's *Leaving Cheyenne,* gets very low marks.

Film Flam is itself something of a flimflam. At times one finds
oneself thinking that McMurtry's most impressive talent is his ability
to ramble on at such length about so many inconsequential and overly
familiar topics. Every so often, moreover, one has the feeling that one
is reading a sentence, a passage, that one has already read in a previous essay—if not one of McMurtry's, then perhaps one of Gore
Vidal's. Nonetheless, the book is consistently readable and diverting,
and often, even when he is saying something one has heard before, one
finds oneself admiring the way he says it. In a piece called "The Dead-
line Syndrome," for instance, he writes that *The Last Picture Show*

> was exactly the kind of novel from which good movies are made—
> that is, a flatly written book with strong characterizations and
> a sense of period and place. Films like *The Blue Angel, Jules and
> Jim,* and *Treasure of Sierra Madre* were made from just such
> books—books that offer a director no stylistic resistance whatever.
> Towering classics always have a style, and adapting them is like
> attempting to translate poetry, only more difficult. Poetry is at
> least being taken from language to language, whereas a film
> adaptation attempts to take something from language to image.
> The director, like the translator, may take a free approach, or he
> may try to be literal, but if he hopes to find a cinematic counterpart
> to a literary style he can only count on being frustrated. True
> equivalents simply don't exist, and the book that best lends itself to
> filming, in my view, is the book from which one can abstract a
> place, a period, and a story for which the director can feel free to
> develop a style of his own.

Such passages notwithstanding, McMurtry, as the book's title suggests, finds the film business mostly absurd and its productions most
meretricious, a verdict with which one can hardly disagree. He has
particularly harsh things to say about the place of the writer in the
business. For instance, in "No Clue: Or Learning to Write for the
Movies," the book's lead piece, he argues that "[o]f the many crafts
necessary to the making of motion pictures, that of the screenwriter is
easily the most haphazard, the most impressionistic, and the most vulnerable. Screenwriting, so far, has no rationale, no theory, and, at best,
an indifferent, pedestrian craft-literature." He complains that "[t]he

vast bulk of the industry's writing chores is still divided between smart-
assed amateurs (the novelists) and dull-witted hacks: in other words,
between people who are given little chance to treat screenwriting as
other than a joke, and the peons of the system, who can only treat it as a
job." For his own part, McMurtry does not hesitate to treat the business as a joke: he concludes the essay by remarking that, "Fitzgerald,
West, et al., not to the contrary—light comedy is the proper mode in
which to consider the writer's role in Hollywood."

McMurtry, in short, doesn't take Hollywood very seriously (or, at
least, doesn't want to *seem* to). Disconcertingly, however, he doesn't
take his pieces—or the essay form in general—very seriously either.
In his foreword, he describes his novels as "the marriages and great
loves" of his imagination, and the columns and articles contained in
Film Flam as "quick tricks and one-night stands, the offspring of
opportunity rather than passion." He confesses that

> [r]eading the pieces in galley was a surprise, not because they were
> better than I had hoped or worse than I feared, but simply because I
> had forgotten most of them completely. The emotion one invests in
> a novel weights any rereading with memory—the memory, at least,
> of what one felt for, and hoped for, its characters. But these essays
> evoke no characters and involved no long or loving invention. They
> moved quickly from head to typewriter and from typewriter to
> mailbox, to return in their present form as from a blank in my past.

Reading this passage, one is simultaneously impressed by McMurtry's
honesty and struck by his nerve: after all, if these pieces are too
ephemeral to have left a lingering impression even in *his* memory, then
where on earth does he find the audacity to hawk them to us in
hardcover? In one of them he dismisses bound collections of screenplays as "non-books"; even the published script of *Citizen Kane,* he
says, is a non-book. What, one wonders, if its contents are indeed so
utterly forgettable, does that make *Film Flam?*

Yet the book, in truth, has more to recommend it than McMurtry's
foreword would lead one to believe. And the reader who is aghast at
McMurtry's flippant attitude toward his essays soon realizes that
self-deprecation is one of McMurtry's favorite devices: he seemingly
never fails to take advantage of an opportunity to put his own work
down. For example, in his essay on *Lovin' Molly,* he says that his first
two novels, *Horseman, Pass By* (which became the Paul Newman
movie *Hud*) and *Leaving Cheyenne,* "incorporate, at best, a 22-year-
old's vision," and that he is not "overjoyed to see the literary results of
[that vision] applauded." In another essay he remarks that "[w]hen

Hud was released, I used to shock people a good deal by saying that I thought the movie was better than the book" (although Martin Ritt, the film's director, "still managed to cripple the film dramatically by chaining himself hand and foot to the ass-backwards structure of my novel"). And he confesses that, when writing the screenplay of *The Last Picture Show,* he realized how weak the book was. To be sure, he wasn't very happy with the novel to begin with: "It was the flattest and most hastily written of my books—dashed off, in fact, in a fit of pique at my hometown—and by the time it was published I had ceased to think well of it." But it wasn't till he went back to the novel to adapt it for Peter Bogdanovich that McMurtry saw just how lousy it was. All at once he realized that it was "a novel about a middle-aged courtship in a small town," and that he'd made a mistake in focusing on "those uninteresting kids" who were his major characters.

Why does McMurtry keep running himself down? Part of it is doubtless sheer native honesty. Part is probably egocentrism: to read a few of the pieces in *Film Flam* is to realize that self-deprecation provides authors with a simple means of writing endlessly about themselves without seeming narcissistic. Part of it is that McMurtry likes the idea of shocking people, likes being viewed as a plainspoken maverick who lives and works and thinks at a considerable remove from the mendacious conformists of Hollywood. And part of it is, I think, that McMurtry, a scion of a big ranching clan, and nephew to a goodly number of macho cattle barons, is secretly embarrassed to be a *writer,* of all things. He doesn't want us to think he's interested in *art,* for God's sake, or to confuse him with those effete types that populate New York and L.A. (McMurtry now lives in Washington, D.C.) In a piece called "Movie-Tripping: My Own Rotten Film Festival"—the longest piece in the book, by the way—he proudly chronicles a weekend that he spent watching seventeen crummy movies in Times Square, movies with names like *Fuzz* and *Eroticon,* like *The Night Evelyn Came Out of the Grave* and *Tarzan's Jungle Rebellion.* Why did he waste a weekend in such a manner? Well, for one thing, he seems to *like* crummy movies. And crummy theaters, too: "I have always hated art theaters, art audiences, screening rooms, suburban theaters, and, indeed, decorous moviegoers of any ilk; apparently some severe Methodist suspicion of all fanciness still lurks in my psyche." He extols "fringe theaters" in "border areas," theaters that appeal to "anyone with either a taste for street life or participatory theater." "[T]hese," he writes, "are the places to see movies. The audience will more than compensate for whatever turgidities there may be in the film."

In this essay, at any rate (he seems less fatuous elsewhere), McMurtry views film at its best not as art, or as an attempt at art, or even (for that matter) as entertainment, but rather as an occasion for lowbrow socializing. To him, *art* is a dirty word: he likes watching movies with children because they "are even less polite to art than I am," and likes watching them with "the proletariat" because "[a]rt is a meaningless word to them." McMurtry complains that "there is just too much art—far more, at least, than *I* can use, either as a writer or as a person." And he doesn't buy the notion of art as a form of truth: "[F]or a novelist to suppose that he is wedded to Truth is a flat absurdity. A novelist works with lies. The more constant he is to his craft, the deeper into lies it will lead him. To pretend otherwise is to misunderstand the game of fiction entirely. . . . Pigs is pigs, and a lie is a lie—as Protestantism has always insisted." But it's not a temptation to lie that compels good authors to write fiction; it's the desire to capture a universal truth that lies beyond the mundane facts of their everyday lives. And it is because sensitive and intelligent readers recognize these truths as truths—because, in other words, good serious fiction strikes chords of recognition in the depths of their souls—that they are capable of an intense emotional response to such fiction. (Indeed, McMurtry himself admits as much when he observes that the film of *The Last Picture Show* was successful largely because it reminded its jaded, anomic audiences of "what it had been like to feel.")

Some of McMurtry's generalizations about the film world are, to say the least, dubious. "Writers," he pronounces, "have not made a habit of rushing unbeckoned to Hollywood. . . . As ambassadors of the word, they respectfully wait to be summoned." Perhaps this is true of the handful of successful novelists like McMurtry who moonlight as screenwriters; but the vast majority of screenwriters have indeed rushed unbeckoned to Tinseltown for the express purpose of churning out screenplays and submitting them, unbidden, to producers. The chief problem here, and elsewhere in *Film Flam*, is that McMurtry consistently generalizes about Los Angeles and the film business on the basis of his own somewhat atypical experiences. Not once does he show any sign of ever having swapped anecdotes with other screenwriters—or, for that matter, of having any real interest in another writer's experiences.

Equally dubious is McMurtry's belief that most filmmakers "inhabit an ivory tower of literacy." "The comments filmmakers hear," he grumbles, "are those of their friends, their eminent critics, their intelligent and educated patrons; they remain largely unaware of the *illiterate* response to what they are doing, and perhaps never really confront the more primitive resources of film." Now there are a number of things wrong with the contemporary American film, but in these days of Goonies and Gremlins and Rocky Balboa and Conan the Barbarian, excessive literacy certainly isn't one of them. Nor are most filmmakers out of touch with the unlettered masses. On the contrary, I suspect that most good screenwriters would say that for an illiterate response, one usually need not go further than the powers that be at one's own studio. These are the people whose comments the typical "film artist" hears most regularly, and to whom he is obliged to pay the most attention. They are people who are desperate to reach the lowest common denominator, who are most comfortable with dialogue rich in four-letter words and street slang, and who—when writers try to slip intelligent, witty dialogue into a script—will remark that it's "too *uptown.*" Given this state of affairs, McMurtry's remarks about untapped "primitive resources" are little short of incredible.

But to respond to McMurtry's provocative comments with such arguments is probably to take *Film Flam* more seriously than it is intended to be taken. Though at times, to be sure, McMurtry presents himself as a bona fide critic of films and of books about film, and as an inside observer of life in the film community, more often he wants us to see him as a less-than-serious outsider—a good old boy from Texas, as it were—who has spent some time in the exotic land of Hollywood, and is eager to retail his impressions and chronicle his adventures. McMurtry is, in short, a storyteller at heart, and *Film Flam,* though it fails to be the enlightening volume of commentary upon the business of filmmaking that one might have hoped it to be, succeeds quite nicely as a charming and funny personal account.

D O I N G

W I T H O U T

The Thalia Trilogy

TOM PILKINGTON

It is now evident that Larry McMurtry's writing career is not all of a piece. Like most of us whose lives have spanned as many as four or five decades, McMurtry, in his life and in his art, has passed through various phases and stages. Though McMurtry at present is perhaps in many essential ways the same person as the McMurtry of thirty years ago, he plainly has said and done things in the past that are in conflict with what he is saying and doing today. Though in his public pronouncements he attempts to gloss over the contradictions that crop up with ever-increasing frequency—for example, the nasty things he said in 1981 about the Texas literary scene versus his current role as benevolent godfather of Texas letters—the contradictions will out for all that.

Such observations are not meant in any way to be critical of McMurtry. Why should we expect the author to be a model of consistency when none of the rest of us can claim purity of action and motive? McMurtry has the same right, as did Emerson, to renounce that "foolish consistency" that inhibits intellectual and personal growth. Better still, in rejecting the demands of those who wish to impose a continuity between the McMurtry of five, ten, twenty years ago and the McMurtry of today, he might do well to adopt the pointed brevity of Whitman: "Do I contradict myself? Very well, then, I contradict myself."

To this juncture McMurtry's career as a writer may be divided into three fairly distinct periods. The first, from the late 1950s to the late 1960s, encompassed the composition and publication of his first three novels, plus the 1968 collection, *In a Narrow Grave: Essays on Texas*. McMurtry himself has said that 1968 is a clear line of demarcation in his life and literature: "*In a Narrow Grave,*" he commented in 1981, "was my formal farewell to writing about the country" ("Bridegroom" 10). Though *Lonesome Dove* (1985) and *Texasville* (1987) would seem to invalidate this statement, it was no doubt, in 1981, sincerely offered.

The second stage of McMurtry's career began about 1970, when the writer moved to Washington, D.C. He had already written fiction set in cities—Houston, in particular; later Hollywood, Washington, and Las Vegas would also supply settings for novels. For whatever reasons—many claimed it was because he had abandoned his "true" subject[1]—McMurtry's talents as a writer seemed, in the 1970s, to dwindle book by book. In the early 1980s the author himself was glum about the quality of his achievement. "It took me," he said at the time, "until around 1972 to write a book that an intelligent reader might want to read twice, and by 1976 I had once again lost the knack" ("Bridegroom" 17). Something that was overlooked in the controversy surrounding McMurtry's 1981 "Ever a Bridegroom" is that in the essay he appeared, if one reads between the lines, even more convinced of his own "failure" than that of his fellow Texas writers.

Oddly the breakthrough book—the one that sent his career hurtling into the triumphs of the mid- to late 1980s, the third and, to this point, final phase—was *The Desert Rose* (1983), the story of an aging Las Vegas showgirl. *The Desert Rose* is, to put it charitably, a mediocre novel; for McMurtry, however, it was obviously an important work. He has claimed that the novel "was written in three weeks" ("Preface" 5). Writing the book in such a burst seems to have unclogged the pipeline, so to speak—to have allowed him to regain the "knack" he thought he had lost. In the last five years, a Pulitzer Prize, TV miniseries and movie contracts, and contracts with the Book-of-the-Month Club and the Literary Guild have accrued with dizzying speed. Since the early 1980s McMurtry has enjoyed a somewhat unexpected reconciliation with the Texas culture he once fled and a newfound fellowship with the Texas writers he once scorned. Maturity and recognition, both financial and critical, seemingly have mellowed the acerbic McMurtry of earlier years.

It is important, however—important for both McMurtry and the reading public—to remember that he *was* at one time a literary outlaw, a youthful buccaneer churning the once-placid waters of Texas literature. But the writer's attitude toward the first phase of his career remains peculiar; for twenty years now he has continued to make statements about the early novels—*Horseman, Pass By* (1961), *Leaving Cheyenne* (1963), and *The Last Picture Show* (1966), the so-called Thalia Trilogy—that suggest he would gladly burn, if possible, all existing copies of them. He consistently denigrates the books. For instance, he has dismissed *Horseman, Pass By* as "a piece of juvenilia" ("Bridegroom" 11). Of Molly Taylor, the much-admired heroine of *Leaving Cheyenne*, he has said that she is "a male journalist's fantasy" ("Approaching Cheyenne" 66). Other expressions of the author's contempt for the books could easily be assembled.

There are probably some understandable reasons why McMurtry feels this way about his early novels. First, many readers preferred—at least up to the publication of *Lonesome Dove* in 1985—*Horseman, Pass By* and *Leaving Cheyenne* over any of the writer's subsequent novels. McMurtry has frequently and publicly complained of this (in his view) unreasonable preference. Despite his complaints many of us staunchly maintained over the years an admiration for his first two books. We failed to appreciate the psychological imperative that was the subtext of McMurtry's disdainful comments: few writers can continue to struggle with their craft if they become convinced their powers are diminishing rather than growing. In praising *Horseman, Pass By* and *Leaving Cheyenne*, we were telling McMurtry his best work was behind him, a judgment he rightly disputed.

Second, considerable evidence suggests that getting the early novels published caused the young writer a good deal of pain. In the case of *Horseman, Pass By*, the first novel, there was, by his own admission, "editorial conflict over the book" (Bennett 25). According to Charles D. Peavy, who has examined relevant correspondence and papers housed in the University of Houston library, the manuscript was rewritten at least five times. Style was revamped; dramatic scenes—such as a devastating "cyclone"—were deleted; and point of view was changed from third person to first (134). The author eventually agreed to most editorial demands because he wanted the novel to be published, but he never came to believe in the rightness of the changes. Thus McMurtry's professed dislike for *Horseman, Pass By*.

It seems to me beyond question that *Horseman, Pass By* is McMurtry's tightest, most structurally sturdy narrative. I think all those revisions and rewritings—and probably most of the editor's suggestions as well—made it a better book. At any rate, by 1980 McMurtry would tell an interviewer he no longer had "editorial difficulty with anyone. . . . So little that one hardly knows if the editors are reading"

(Bennett 26).[2] Such neglect is a shame because *any* writer can benefit from good editorial advice, from sympathetic—and, maybe even better, unsympathetic—readings of his or her manuscripts. McMurtry especially has never been a good judge of what is good and what not so good in his own work—but then neither was Mark Twain. He has trouble knowing when enough is enough. Even *Lonesome Dove* could have been a better novel had some courageous editor firmly insisted the author discard about three hundred well-chosen manuscript pages, thus eliminating at least one superfluous subplot. In any event, the documented conflicts with editors over the first three novels no doubt make the books something less than golden in the writer's memory.

I believe the third—and perhaps most important—reason McMurtry refuses to acknowledge the worth of his early novels is that they are plainly a young man's books. All three were written when he was still in his twenties. They are obviously the products of a precocious talent, but all show a young writer groping for a subject and an appropriate vision through which to interpret that subject. Given the age of the author at the time of their composition, they also exhibit predictable attitudes: nostalgia, sentimentality, preoccupation with the past, both family and regional.

The sophisticated McMurtry who in recent years has hobnobbed with the likes of Diane Keaton and Cybill Shepherd and Virginia hunt-country aristocrats is probably more than a tad embarrassed by them. They no longer—nor should they—reflect his world view. The point is, though, the early novels exist; the author, however much he might like to do so, cannot take them back. They are works of art (flawed, to be sure) that have a life of their own. Many readers, young and old alike, still respond to their power. Instead of sneering at them, the author would do well simply to accept them for what they are and own up to them without embarrassment.

Certainly a strong case can be made in favor of both the historical and esthetic importance of the early novels. Historically, they played a crucial role in the evolution of Texas fiction over the last few decades. Up until 1961, when McMurtry's *Horseman, Pass By* appeared, Texas writing had been rather reticent and genteel in its treatment of what most Texans considered unsuitable subjects. Billy Lee Brammer's *The Gay Place* was also published in 1961. Together McMurtry and Brammer—the two, incidentally, were briefly roommates when both were living in Austin in the early 1960s (McMurtry *ING* 134)—dragged Texas literature, kicking and screaming, into the twentieth century. In language, subject matter, and thematic concerns, their novels are, for better or worse, thoroughly modern.

McMurtry, the boy wonder of Texas letters, and Brammer, the politician-turned-novelist, seemed to delight in shocking by telling the raw, unvarnished truth. They told us, for instance, what life in 1950s Texas had *really* been like. Between them they covered the demographic spectrum—from Brammer's jaded politicos and urban cosmopolites to McMurtry's West Texas swains and rustic bumpkins. (When, as in *The Last Picture Show,* Thalia teenagers see Wichita Falls teenagers as the ultimate in worldliness and sophistication, we are clearly in the presence of serious social deprivation.)

Both McMurtry and Brammer brought news previous reports on life in Texas had usually left out: specifically that s-e-x was everywhere—city, small town, ranch. Many were horrified. No doubt they were mostly horrified at seeing the message boldly proclaimed on the printed page. There is the oft-told story, for example, of Lyndon B. Johnson's admonishing his one-time friend and aide, "Billy Lee, I tried to read your book but didn't get past the first ten pages because of all the dirty words."[3] Another story, one I can verify since I was a student at Texas Christian University in 1961 when McMurtry's *Horseman, Pass By* was published, has to do with Mabel Major, a teacher at TCU and a pioneer scholar of Southwestern literature. (Ironically McMurtry at the time was an instructor of English at that university.) Major checked out the library's copy of *Horseman, Pass By* on faculty loan and refused to return it. TCU students, she huffed, ought not be exposed to such trash.[4]

J. Frank Dobie's reactions to McMurtry's and Brammer's novels are perhaps the best barometer as to how much of a threat the upstarts represented to the Texas literary establishment.[5] In 1961 Dobie was nearing the close of a long reign as Texas's unofficial literary arbiter. (He died in 1964.) He owned copies of both books and peppered their pages with decidedly hostile annotations (Graham 6–9). Dobie was apparently offended by the language of the books and by their frank descriptions of the characters' sexual escapades. In the case of McMurtry he no doubt believed the young writer was impinging on his, Dobie's turf—ranching and its attendant way of life. In a sense Dobie was probably justified in his anxiety: after 1961 Texas writing has not been the same.

Esthetically McMurtry's early novels attained a level of artistry that few previous works of Texas literature could match. While far from flawless, they are alive; they emanate passions the author undoubtedly experienced as he composed them: nostalgia, longing for an irrecoverable past, and, in *The Last Picture Show* anyway, bitterness, hatred, and contempt. Since they were written by a young man, they feature, for the most part, young men as major characters. In fact, it is a commonplace among critics of the early novels that their primary theme is the initiation of those young men into adulthood. Peavy asserts, as an example of this view, that "the most important theme of the first three novels is the male protagonists' achievement of manhood . . ." (57).

Peavy also notes, however, that when McMurtry's "male characters have left the precarious time of adolescence and have become, at least physiologically, adult men, they often remain psychologically fixed in an extended adolescence" (77). Precisely. The main theme of the novels, then, is not the successful initiation of the male characters, but their *failure* to achieve maturity. At the end of *Horseman, Pass By* Lonnie Bannon is a confused seventeen-year-old, still befuddled by the enigma of Hud; we can only guess at his future, but it is clear he has a lot of growing up to do. Sonny Crawford, in *The Last Picture Show,* arrives at an alienation so acute it might almost be described as a psychosis. Gideon Fry, in *Leaving Cheyenne,* becomes a responsible adult, at least in the eyes of the community. But it can scarcely be said he attains emotional maturity; his "adult" years are marred by misery and unhappiness, by feelings of love and guilt he is not capable of dealing with.

The question is, Why do these characters, as well as others in McMurtry's fiction, never become adults in any meaningful sense of the term? Is it simply that in the modern world most people—most Americans anyway—never "grow up"? That may be part of the answer, but the full explanation may be more complicated. The problem with the young men in McMurtry's early novels is that they lack a secure sense of identity, any semblance of self-definition; they have no feeling of belonging, of having a "place," emotional as well as social and geographical. Most of them are essentially parentless, and they live in a fluid and uncertain environment. According to Raymond L. Neinstein, "Displacement is the central concern" of the early novels (i). If we define the word "displacement" metaphorically as well as literally, it supplies a clue to the characters' stunted growth.

Christopher Baker is on target, it seems to me, in invoking the sociologist Robert E. Park's concept of "the marginal man" to diagnose the protagonists' emotional deficiencies. The marginal man, in Park's formulation, emerges from the breakdown of a traditional society "as a result of contact and collision with a new invading culture." He is "a man on the margin of two cultures and two societies," and he is troubled by "spiritual instability, intensified self-consciousness, restlessness, and *malaise*" (qtd. in Baker 52). The condition of marginality, then, by adding more stress to the usual burdens of adolescence and of life generally, obviously retards emotional growth rather than assists it.

It is not surprising that McMurtry's young men, trapped between two cultures—between the mythic rural past and the rootless urban future—fail to grow and mature. (Even Gid, in *Leaving Cheyenne*, is torn asunder by the conflict between his own highly traditional views on sex and marriage and the kind of unconventional, "modern" love Molly offers him.) Inevitably the author's young men, displaced and on the margins of a brave new—and scary—world, fall victim to alienation and feelings of loneliness and aloneness. Lonnie, in *Horseman, Pass By*, more than once says he is "lonesome" (57) or has "the blues" (84). The very first sentence of *The Last Picture Show* strikes the same chord: "Sometimes Sonny felt like he was the only human creature in the town" (5). Nothing in Sonny's subsequent experiences, not even his affair with Ruth Popper, alleviates his loneliness; in fact, in the end he comes to the full realization of "how hard it was to get from day to day if one felt hopeless"(206).

The most pervasive and crippling emotion the characters from the early novels must come to terms with is, as several critics have remarked, a sense of loss. At one point in *Horseman, Pass By*, Lonnie tells Halmea, "Things used to be better around here . . . I feel like I want something back." Halmea retorts, "You mighty young to be wantin' things back" (88). Later, Lonnie, on discovering his grandfather is dead, says, "I needed him," and he asks Hud, "[W]hat will I do?" Hud replies, "You'll do without like the rest of us . . ." (159). Hud's flip response conceals a perception of the world of the early novels that is of great importance: it is one of the modern individual's major tasks, the novels imply, to learn to "do without" that which has been lost. Lonnie observes, concerning all the people he knows, that they "wanted more and seemed to end up with less; they wanted excitement and ended up stomped by a bull or smashed against a highway . . . whatever it was they wanted, that was what they ended up doing without" (145).

But what, aside from unfulfilled personal desires, has been lost? What has been left behind? For many of the characters in McMurtry's early fiction, a stunning loss has been the frontier—or at least the living myth of the frontier and the freedom, openness, and opportunity the land had supposedly promised the pioneers who settled West Texas. "All through my youth," McMurtry once recalled, "I listened to stories about an earlier, purer, a more golden and more legendary

Texas that I had been born too late to see" ("Texas Moon" 29). As a young writer McMurtry, conditioned by the tales of elder kinsmen, often waxed nostalgic in his portrayal of cowboys and frontiersmen— particularly old ones: Homer Bannon in *Horsemen, Pass By*, Adam Fry in *Leaving Cheyenne*, Sam the Lion in *The Last Picture Show*, sympathetic characters embodying all the positive aspects of frontier values.

In the early novels the land is still there, as are a few of the men of stature and integrity it shaped. What is different is that frontier freedom has given way to a rudimentary yet suffocating society that attempts to impose a totally different set of values and mores. The author's people in the early fiction often suffer from a feeling of living in a lesser time, an age in which the frontier and its values have been betrayed, even perverted. Of the novels of the the 1960s *The Last Picture Show* supplies the most wickedly damning criticism of that betrayal.

Set in a town, Thalia, rather than on a ranch, *The Last Picture Show* indicts Thalia in about every way possible for deadening and constricting the lives of its citizens, for making those lives as drab and gray as the West Texas sky during a spring duststorm. In Thalia in the 1950s, the frontier imperative to establish a moral order in the wilderness has resulted in a social and ethical code so oppressive that it stifles spontaneity and engenders, in many, ennui: "[L]ife is very monotonous," says Lois Farrow. "Things happen the same way over and over again. I think it's more monotonous in this part of the country than it is in other places. . ." (43). The cowboy's famous (or notorious) attitude toward women—a kind of respectful uneasiness—has evolved into sexual misunderstanding that exacts a terrible emotional toll from both sexes. For the townspeople, the soured residue of frontier values in the middle of the twentieth century is a bitter draught to swallow—though they drink it, for the most part, without realizing there are alternatives.

Perhaps McMurtry's richest study of what has happened to the frontier tradition in modern times is his first book, *Horseman, Pass by*. The three major characters—Homer Bannon, who is eighty years and more in age; thirty-five-year-old Hud, his stepson; and seventeen-year-old Lonnie, Homer's grandson—are, as more than one commentator has pointed out, three versions of the cowboy at different ages. What they have in common is that all now live in the twentieth century at a time when the cowboy way of life is, practically speaking, dead.

Homer, however, had been born in the 1860s and had grown up in the old times—had once been known as "Wild Horse" Homer Bannon.

He had built a ranch and assembled a considerable herd of cattle on his hardscrabble West Texas land. He is a man of honor and principle who loves the land and the animals he works with. He will not allow oil wells to be drilled in his soil, since he believes such exploitation would be contrary to nature's intention as to how the land should be used. Obviously he is a man living out of tune with the times. Fittingly—and inevitably—Homer, like his cattle, is destroyed at the end of the novel, another remnant of the frontier that has passed from the scene.

Hud, Homer's stepson, is a frustrated frontiersman who, living in the mid-1950s, has no geographic frontiers to conquer. So, for Hud, sex becomes a frontier. He invests most of his time and energy in sexual conquest. Hud is inconsiderate, selfish, and cynical. He bull-dozes and uses other people to get his way. He is more than a touch mean. In Hud, then, the aggressive self-sufficiency of the frontiers-man has been transformed into singleminded viciousness. At novel's end Hud has apparently acquired control of Homer's ranch. We as-sume, now Homer is out of the way, that oil wells will be punched in the land. Probably Hud is destined to become an eccentric oil tycoon; he will not, however, be a rancher in the sense that Homer was.

For Lonnie, the youngest of the three, living on the land, as his grandfather had done, is never a viable possibility. Lonnie admires his grandfather, and he is fond of the ranch and the horses and cattle it harbors. But he appears to realize his future lies elsewhere. Oppor-tunity, for Lonnie, lies in the city, not in the distant plains and moun-tain. From time to time in his narration Lonnie recalls his infrequent visits to Fort Worth, his only taste of city life to this point. He remem-bers wandering through the streets after dark, enjoying "the shatter of those nights: things were moving around me, and it was exciting" (96). At the close of *Horseman, Pass By* Lonnie has left the ranch, his grandfather dead, Hud now in control. His future is uncertain, but it seems fairly sure it will be spent in cities.

In this fictional portrait of three generations of a West Texas fam-ily, therefore, we have a clear allegory of the fate of frontier values in the twentieth century. Homer doggedly holds onto the values because he is too old to adapt to any other way of life. Hud betrays the values, perverts them, out of spite and ignorance; in a way he is as much a man living out of his time as is old Homer. It is Lonnie, intuiting rather than articulating the perversion that Hud represents, who re-jects the sad, undernourished life the frontier experience spawned on the Texas prairie. Lonnie, because of his youth and inexperience, is only partly aware of his dissatisfaction with the repressive society of rural and small-town West Texas, but he knows at some level that, for him, the frontier must be a realm of the mind and the spirit rather than of the land.

The sensational and superficial significance in the state's literature of McMurtry's *Horseman, Pass By* and Brammer's *The Gay Place* is the open and (to some) outrageous manner both authors treated the hitherto taboo subject of sex. The books' really lasting significance, however, is much more subtle: they sounded a note that had seldom been heard in Texas writing before 1961. They implied that what has been lost is not just the frontier and its values, but all values—that the only principle by which one can now live is the assumption there are no absolute values.

It is hardly a startling revelation to say that the mode of thought predominant in modern European and American literature and intellectual life is, for lack of a better term, existentialism. Writers and thinkers often acquire their existentialist views secondhand, often in diluted or distorted form, but the idea of life and the universe as being essentially absurd and meaningless is a common thread that runs though most important twentieth-century literature. A concomitant theme is that of coping with chaos, of "doing without" in the profoundest sense of the phrase, of the individual's escaping the abyss by generating purpose and meaning from hard-won interior battles.

Is this not the message of the great modernist writers from earlier in the century? Eliot, Fitzgerald, Hemingway—and others? These writers saw the old world of faith and certainty lying shattered and broken at their feet and attempted to solve the riddle of how best to live in the new world of doubt and disorder. Eliot's answer was conservative, even reactionary; Fitzgerald and Hemingway faced the problem more honestly, bravely and with stiff upper lips, though, like the little boys they sometimes resembled, their lips trembled now and again.

Ideas often have a hard time finding their way across the Red River, so it took a while for existential angst to ooze into the state's life and literature. Once it did, however, beginning in the early 1960s, it quickly spread across Texas, if we may judge by the literature, from city to small town, even to isolated farms and ranches. Without pushing the analogy too far, it seems that Brammer and McMurtry were Texas's Fitzgerald and Hemingway at a time when we had little in the way of the modern literary spirit.

Clearly Brammer thought of himself and his work in Fitzgeraldian terms. (*The Gay Place* takes its title from a phrase in a little-known Fitzgerald poem.) Brammer's novel depicts Gatsbian decadence mired in despair as thick as molasses. For example, Neil Christiansen, the protagonist of the book's second section, contemplates the dissolution of his marriage: "[H]e was able, finally, to realize his loss, to feel the great gap in himself. Not so much long gone youth as adulthood never quite attained. For all his good intentions, there had been only a kind of chic faithlessness in between, randy and frivolous. . . . Moving into the center of the city he smoked the last of his cigarettes and thought about their deeply violated selves" (281–82).

I could easily quote a dozen or more passages from *The Gay Place* that say roughly the same thing: once there was strong support for right conduct, but now the centrifugal force of modern life has splintered into an irresistible moral shiftlessness. A "lost generation" aura, undoubtedly a calculated effect, hangs over the novel. "You are all a depressed generation" (477), says one of the characters in reference to the book's sizable cast of desultory hedonists, an obvious allusion to Gertrude Stein's description of American expatriates in 1920s Paris.

Rereading McMurtry's early novels recently, I could not help thinking of Hemingway. I do not mean to imply any specific debt on McMurtry's part to Hemingway's style, techniques, or subject matter, but there are nonetheless some striking correspondences. For instance, the rodeo in *Horseman, Pass By* functions in much the same way as does the fiesta in *The Sun Also Rises:* as an interlude of ritual, tradition, and order in an otherwise random succession of monotonous and meaningless events. "Since it all came like Christmas, only once a year," says Lonnie, "I was careful not to let any of it pass me by" (99). And is not the scene in *The Last Picture Show* in which terminally depressed Sonny sits with the waitress Genevieve in the all-night cafe reminiscent of "A Clean, Well-Lighted Place," one of the classic works of twentieth-century existentialist fiction? "The window by the booth was all fogged over, but the misted glass was cold to the touch, and the knowledge that the freezing wind was just outside made the booth seem all the cozier" (27).

Brammer apparently wrote himself out with *The Gay Place;* at any rate, he did not publish another book before his death in 1978 at age forty-eight. Since the appearance of *Horseman, Pass By* in 1961, on the other hand, McMurtry has brought out thirteen additional volumes— some good, some bad, but none surpassing his initial effort. Whatever McMurtry thinks of them today, *Horseman, Pass By* and the other two novels of the 1960s remain a cornerstone of his reputation and achievement as a writer, and as I have tried to show, they are landmarks in Texas's literary history.

Of the three early novels *Horseman, Pass By* is the best because it is the most tightly controlled and structurally sound. *Leaving*

Cheyenne almost attains a similar level of artistry, but there are at
least two weaknesses in the 1963 novel that diminish its impact. The
first is the uneven quality of the book's three segments. The second,
related problem—and on this point I agree with McMurtry—is
Molly. Molly has elicited lavish praise from many critics—Peavy
judges her a "magnificently realized character" (47)—but I don't buy
Molly for a minute. Indeed the middle section, which she narrates, is
easily the least convincing part of the novel.

There are many believable and sometimes fascinating women in
McMurtry's early fiction—Halmea, Ruth Popper, Genevieve, Lois
and Jacy Farrow—but Molly is not among them. The fatal flaw of
characterization is that she is basically a one-dimensional person, a
"giver," as Adam Fry calls her, who gives far too much to "sorry
bastards that don't deserve it" (175). Even Mabel Peters (later Mabel
Fry), who appears briefly in only a few scenes, is more plausible, as a
woman and as a human being, than is Molly. Still, as Neinstein asserts, *Leaving Cheyenne* succeeds, despite the difficulties the character of Molly creates, "at a mythic level. It satisfies . . . even while we
doubt the probability of the love story, because it is dealing, through
the romance-plot, with the myth of the end of the West" (13).

Esthetically *The Last Picture Show* is the poorest of the early novels. It is episodic and sprawling and as such anticipates the formless-
ness of several of McMurtry's later books; in this regard the movie
version of *The Last Picture Show* is superior to the novel because it is
more focused and powerful in conveying its message. Moreover, the
depiction in the book of small-town Texas life in the 1950s wobbles
unsteadily among realism, satire, and poison-pen caricature. At any
given point in the story the reader is hard pressed to say which approach the author is employing.

The one element of the work that seems exceptionally good is characterization. While some of the people are stereotypes and Sam the
Lion is something of a sentimentalized indulgence, many vivid and
interesting characters emerge from the tale. The women in the narrative are well drawn, but then so too are the men—Abilene, Duane
Moore, Gene Farrow, Lester Marlow, even Billy, the village idiot. The
fate of Sonny, more or less the focal character of the story, is unfortunately all too believable.

At novel's end Sonny finds himself in a no-exit situation. He cannot
join the army, like his buddy Duane, because of his injured eye, and he
is much too passive to go out into the world to seek his fortune. He will
remain in Thalia, but since he has graduated from high school and is

no longer on the football team, he feels that he is a nonperson in the town. Even the countryside—beloved by Homer Bannon and Adam and Gid Fry and Molly and Johnny McCloud—seems threatening and sinister. Driving in his pickup near the close of the narrative, Sonny becomes "scared. . . . As empty as he felt and as empty as the country looked it was too risky going out into it—he might be blown around for days like a broomweed in the wind" (217). Sonny's existence has shrunk and diminished almost to the vanishing point. It is a sad, bleak story, but one that continues to be enacted, many thousands of times over, even in the late 1980s.

None of McMurtry's early novels sold well, and yet they established him, almost immediately, as Texas's rising star in the American literary heavens—an ascent only recently culminated. He was extraordinarily fortunate that all three were translated into motion pictures and that two of the three films were both critical and popular successes. For two decades McMurtry was known to most literate Americans primarily as a writer who had produced fiction on which some good movies were based. A reconsideration of the early novels as literature, however, reaffirms their status as autonomous works of art. Despite their nostalgia and sentimentality, despite the fact their creator would apparently disown them if he could, they continue, as we near the end of the twentieth century and confront a world far removed even from the one sketched in the novels, to speak to readers in a strong and passionate voice.

NOTES

1. One critic, whose explanation is fairly typical, claims that "as McMurtry leaves the ranch country of his youth . . . his writing becomes more analytical and sociological," and thus less energized and powerful (Peavy 107).

2. On the subject of editing, McMurtry's and others', I am compelled to chide the author for carelessness with details. I do not wish to nitpick, but it is more than a little annoying to run across such anachronisms as the following: In *Horseman, Pass By* old Homer's precise age remains uncertain; at one point he is said to be "eighty-two years" (26), but elsewhere his birth and death dates are given as 1868–1954 (168). Most of the first section of *Leaving Cheyenne* supposedly takes place in and around the year 1924 (194), smack in the middle of prohibition; yet on different occasions Gid and Johnny frequent public bars in Henrietta and Fort Worth. Molly buys her first (and only) automobile in early fall 1941. A couple of months earlier both her sons had "volunteered" for military service (164). A limited peacetime draft had been initiated in 1940, but there were few volunteers to the armed services before America's entry into the Second World War in December 1941. In *The Last Picture Show* Duane at the end of the novel has joined the army to go fight in

Korea. The Korean War ended in July 1953; several times in the book there is mention of the fact that Coach Popper's favorite television show is *Gunsmoke,* a program that first aired in September 1955.

3. Al Reinert, a friend of Brammer's, isolates Johnson's sanctimonious rejection of *The Gay Place* as *the* turning point in Brammer's writing career—and, by implication, his life. "He never," Reinert claims, "completely believed in himself as a writer again" (xxv).

4. Major later summed up in print her impatience with McMurtry's depiction of Texas life in his books: "The language used at all levels of society strains credibility with its coarseness" (Major and Pearce 231).

5. Admittedly there had been, in Texas writing, a few antecedents to McMurtry and Brammer, but by the early 1960s they were nearly invisible and certainly did not pose a threat to the hegemony of Dobie and his friends. For example, Philip Atlee's *The Inheritors* had created a controversy in 1940 by recounting the scandalous doings of 1930s Fort Worth teenagers. Though McMurtry has dismissed *The Inheritors* as being "wooden as any plank" ("Bridegroom" 12), Atlee was obviously attempting to write fiction in a mode that McMurtry and Brammer, two decades later, would seize as their own.

WORKS CITED

Baker, Christopher. "The Death of the Frontier in the Novels of Larry McMurtry." *McNeese Review* 28 (1981–82): 44–54.

Bennett, Patrick. "Larry McMurtry: Thalia, Houston, and Hollywood." *Talking with Texas Writers: Twelve Interviews.* College Station: Texas A&M UP, 1980.

Brammer, Billy Lee. *The Gay Place.* 1961. New York: Vintage, 1983.

Graham, Don. "J. Frank Dobie: A Reappraisal." *Southwestern Historical Quarterly* 92 (1988): 1–15.

McMurtry, Larry. "Approaching Cheyenne . . . Leaving Lumet." *New York* 29 Apr. 1974: 64–66.

———. "Ever a Bridegroom: Reflections on the Failure of Texas Literature." *Texas Observer* 23 Oct. 1981: 1+.

———. *Horseman, Pass By.* 1961. College Station: Texas A&M UP, 1985.

———. *In a Narrow Grave: Essays on Texas.* Austin: Encino, 1968.

———. *The Last Picture Show.* 1966. New York: Penguin, 1979.

———. *Leaving Cheyenne.* 1963. New York: Penguin, 1979.

———. "Preface." *The Desert Rose.* 1983. New York: Touchstone, 1985. 5–8.

———. "The Texas Moon, and Elsewhere." *Atlantic Monthly* Mar. 1975: 29–36.

Major, Mabel, and T. M. Pearce. *Southwest Heritage: A Literary History with Bibliographies.* 3rd edition. Albuquerque: U of New Mexico P, 1972.

Neinstein, Raymond L. *The Ghost Country: A Study of the Novels of Larry McMurtry.* Berkeley, CA: Creative Arts, 1976.

Peavy, Charles D. *Larry McMurtry.* Boston: Twayne, 1977.

Reinert, Al. "Introduction." *The Gay Place.* By Billy Lee Brammer. 1961. Austin: Texas Monthly P, 1979. v–xxvii.

Larry McMurtry's three novels published in the 1960s, mainly no doubt because they have been around longer, have elicited a good deal more criticism than has any trio of his later works. The winnowing process with regard to that criticism, therefore, involved hard decisions. The pieces that follow are intended to represent a cross section of critical approaches to and interpretations of the early novels.

"Elegy and Exorcism: Texas Talent and General Concerns," by Dave Hickey, was first published in 1967. Though only part of it deals with McMurtry's fiction (specifically with *The Last Picture Show*), Hickey's essay, somewhat abridged as it appears here, is an excellent introduction to the status of Texas writing in the mid-1960s, shortly after McMurtry had burst onto the scene. Raymond L. Neinstein's monograph *The Ghost Country: A Study of the Novels of Larry McMurtry* focuses on the disorienting recognition of McMurtry's characters that the "old myth" is dead and that there is now nothing "really powerful enough to provide a center, a new myth . . ." (iii). In the segment excerpted in this volume, Neinstein analyzes how this theme is woven into *Horseman, Pass By* and *Leaving Cheyenne*.

Larry McMurtry, by Thomas Landess, is a sharply critical pamphlet that appeared in 1969 as part of the Southwest Writers Series. In the reprinted excerpt, Landess discusses the difficulties in growing up encountered by the male characters in *Leaving Cheyenne* and *The Last Picture Show;* the critic attributes these problems to inadequate father-son relationships. Clay Reynolds, in "Showdown in the New Old West: The Cowboy vs. the Oilman," discerns two myths—one of the past, one of the present—embodied in the stereotypes of the cowboy and the oilman. Reynolds traces the confusing impact these figures, and all they represent, have on Lonnie in *Horseman, Pass By* and Sonny in *The Last Picture Show.*

Using the theories of historian Frederick Jackson Turner and sociologist Robert E. Park, Christopher Baker, in "The Death of the Frontier in the Novels of Larry McMurtry," tallies the emotional price of living in a historical "vacuum" left by a departed way of life. Baker draws his examples primarily from *The Last Picture Show*, with reference also to *All My Friends Are Going to Be Strangers*. Kenneth W. Davis's "Initiation Themes in McMurtry's Cowboy Trilogy," a revised version of Davis's 1970 article "The Themes of Initiation in the Works of Larry McMurtry and Tom Mayer," does not offer an original thesis, but Davis nonetheless argues logically and persuasively. He asserts that experiences with sex and death are major factors in the initiation into adulthood of the young men in McMurtry's early fiction.

In "Damn the Saddle on the Wall: Anti-Myth in Larry McMurtry's *Horseman, Pass By,*" Mark Busby contends that a widely held critical assumption—that McMurtry's first novel implicitly and nostalgically longs for a return to a glorious past—is simply wrong. On the contrary, Busby says, *Horseman, Pass By* clearly rejects a bankrupt and now useless mythos. Donald E. Fritz's "Anatomy and *The Last Picture Show:* A Matter of Definition" claims *The Last Picture Show* is, according to Northrop Frye's categories of fiction, an "anatomy" rather than a novel. It is so, Fritz believes, because McMurtry's overriding concern in the book is to depict "the sexual attitudes and activities of Texas in the 1950's."

・ ・

From
Elegy and Exorcism: Texas Talent and General Concerns
DAVE HICKEY

I was beginning to realize, most unwillingly, all the things love could not do. It could not make me over, for example. It could not undo the journey which had made me such a strange man and brought me to such a strange place.

I am afraid that most of the white people I have ever known impressed me as being in the grip of a weird nostalgia, dreaming of a vanished state of security and order, against which dream, unfailingly and unconsciously, they tested and very often lost their lives.

—James Baldwin, Nobody Knows My Name

I

If you have been to a family reunion in Texas or the South, you have seen them. If you have been to a picnic in a brush-arbor, you have seen them at their best—those hard old women, vain in their maternity, strong in their piety, their hair blue with rinse or yellowing into its terminal discoloration. You have seen them spreading platters of fried chicken and milk-glass bowls of ambrosia on red-check tablecloths, and you have seen their husbands too: the pale ones, broken by drudgery, the corners of their mouths stained by tobacco juice, perhaps an ear chewed by cancer; and the gregarious ones, the charming failures in their houndstooth jackets, smelling of bay rum and bourbon as they trade jokes in the sycamore shade; and the successful ones, growing fat and bleak on the nothingness of their achievement, drawing circles in the dust with the toe of a Johnson & Murphey shoe. And how these men are fawned over by the old ladies—hugged, patted, kissed, flattered, and plied with mind-numbing quantities of food! Yet you never have the faintest doubt where the power lies. You are seeing the last days of the rural matriarchy, and these old women are the last of the matriarchal tyrants whose feminine myths have kept their men in a state of flattered, bedazzled subjugation for nearly a century.

The women didn't plan it that way, of course. The men had tried to make an empire and had made only a desert; the women had tried only to endure, and with the failure of each succeeding enterprise of the men, the women gathered power unto themselves and their institutions. Causes might be lost, holes come up dry, the cattle market might fall, the rain refuse to, crops might burn in the field or wash away, but the family, the village, and the church in their conservative tenacity endured. They were doomed to prevail because Texas and the South never offered a lasting answer to the man's imperative question, *"How can I rise in the world and shape the world through which I am rising?"*

For a century and a half, in the rest of the Western World, men had found the answer to this question in science, government, industry, and the arts. Texas and the South offered instead a sequence of mercurial, violent surrogates. First there was the cotton. A man could do that, until the war with the North. Then he could fight for his country, but too soon there was no cotton and no war. So, if he had survived the war, he could retain his dignity by going to Texas and building again. But then there was a depression, another war, another depression, and finally drought. Old men trapped in rocking chairs watched their land blow away. Young men couldn't see the horizons for the dirt in the air. But the oil fields had opened by now and man could try his hand at that. It offered more possibilities for motion, adventure, and freedom than dirt-farming or shop-keeping. But the eastern corporations were coming even from the beginning and, returning from the second war, the young men found the corporations had triumphed. So Texas emerged from that war with a host of honored dead, a host of men with dead professions (ex-soldiers, ex-ranchers, ex-farmers, ex-oilmen, ex-railroadmen), and a host of men whose professions had gone sour. It was a country run by tin-horn lawyers and controlled by women—but it was also a country coming out of its Middle Ages.

Even today Texas is still in the process of joining the Western World. Science, government, industry, and the arts are now open to its young men, and the new literature being produced, like that of the English Renaissance, is concerned with the masculine ego, with escape from the old women and their institutions. The sudden initiation of Texas writers into the modern world finds an analogy in the initiation of their entire society, and they are making a literature of elegy and exorcism.

This initiation into the twentieth century is the central concern of three books published by Texans this fall. William Owens' autobiographical novel, *This Stubborn Soil,* traces a boy's escape from the dirtfarm and the one-room school into the great world of intellect, action, and sidewalks. Larry McMurtry's *The Last Picture Show* is an account of two boys and a girl coming of age in a dying town and being drawn toward the growing city. Sherry Kafka, in her novel *Hannah Jackson,* tells the story of a small town matriarch and dissects the causes and effects of her tyranny. Each of these books strives for a tonal balance between elegy and exorcism, and each achieves its own kind of equilibrium, but what is most exciting about them is that you can *talk* about them; they are serious literature. Certainly no novelist enjoys providing music for critical pirouettes, but these novels, unlike the bulk of what is called "Texas writing," can withstand the strain. They deserve serious criticism, even demand it. So perhaps the day of the matriarchal book reviewer, male or female, is dying too.

II

Owens' *This Stubborn Soil* is the most mature of these books and in some ways the most disappointing. There is a sense of ending about it, as if Owens is saying to us, "I have spent a life-time learning how to write this book. Now I have written it and I am through. My childhood is exorcised. It is on paper and I am freed from it. This is how it was." . . . In *This Stubborn Soil* the exorcism is so final, the author so finally freed from his material, the work takes on the queer isolation of an historical novel.

But Owens' distance from his subject has its virtues. There is no "weird nostalgia," no sentimentality, in Owens' account of dirt-farming life in northeast Texas. Here are people and things, not characters and settings. . . . This is the book of a boy who has not learned to see "artistically," to frame everything. So farm life takes on that peculiar deadness and particularity which other writers have ascribed to it, only to contradict that ascription by inserting lush descriptions of "fog in the cotton" or "colts at play in the alfalfa," making it pastoral, which it is not.

Certainly much of this particularity derives from Owens' autobiographical intent, but it would be just as successful as pure fiction. Held together by the boys' drive to escape the farm, the book eschews "form" and "drama" and in doing so captures with real grace the inconclusiveness of everyday life. Promises are broken without atonement, things are broken and not repaired, lives are broken arbitrarily by death and accident; groundwork is laid for confrontations that don't take place, challenges are given but not met, potential friendships do not bloom. Owens' willingness to use this kind of material without "dramatizing" it gives his book a texture and authority at once organic and discontinuous. The rough shape of the book, like the fragment of a broken Christmas ornament, implies by its contours and ragged edges the missing whole. . . .

By refusing to romanticize, Owens captures as well as anyone the nature of the matriarchy which followed in the wake of the advancing frontier and the deadening effect of dirt-farming on the masculine will. There are sensitive portraits of Owens' mother and grandmother, but there is no Faulknerian "bleak grandeur" in the treatment. . . . Owens resists idealization, and this book has none of the suicidal longing for the lost village which seems to infect the writing of so many first generation urbanites. By resisting idealization he also resists the temptation to view the city as merely a corruption of the rural village. The north Texas of *This Stubborn Soil* is by no means a "vanished state of security and order"; it represents a way of living which buys its simplicity and clarity of motive at the price of moral and intellectual tyranny. Owens sees rural and urban life as two radically different things, with different virtues and different vices, and this, for me, is the happiest quality of his book.

The dichotomy between the village and the city faces any writer who tries to come to terms with Texas in the twentieth century. There has been no smooth progression from one to the other. The seeds of modern Texas were simply not in the Texas of the nineteenth century. The changes have been radical and for the most part externally enforced. Like the Soviet Union, Texas has moved from a feudal culture to a technological welfare-state in two-thirds of a century. It has been hard on the people's sense of identity, and as a result even harder on the artists. The only real form of verbal expression that shows a coherent development is popular music. When a tradition can move from the oral tradition of the cowboy songs of the nineties, find its Chaucer in Jimmy Rodgers, its Shakespeare in Hank Williams, and its Byron in Roger Miller, things are changing rapidly. Popular music, though, only reflects an idealized group of assumptions, while the novelist, supposedly, tells us what the truth is and what it means. If he doesn't do this, his novels, like Hank Williams' songs, are merely indicative and not demonstrative. If, in the face of complicated change, the novelist opts for sensibility in lieu of sense, his novels lose in authority what they gain in integrity, and this seems to be at least partially the case with *The Last Picture Show* and *Hannah Jackson*.

Larry McMurtry is easily the most talented of the three writers discussed here. He has more grace, facility, felicity, and in this case courage, since he sets himself a harder task. Where William Owens and Miss Kafka deal almost exclusively with the rural setting, McMurtry places the village, Thalia, and the city, Wichita Falls, side by side and attempts to deal with them simultaneously. He really has two stories in his novel: a village story and a town story. First there is the account of Sonny Crawford and his friend Duane, two poor boys, growing up in Thalia and learning about the world, Sonny by having an affair with the coach's wife, and both of them by having hopeless romances with Jacy Farrow, the richest, prettiest girl in town. Second there is the story of Jacy Farrow's attempts to break into "big city" Wichita Falls society, to become a part of the fast, rich crowd of city kids. McMurtry is obviously more comfortable with the first story, but unfortunately the second has more vitality and drive. Times might be changing, but the matriarchy has not lost all of its power, not in this novel anyway. Jacy Farrow and her mother, Lois, are by far the most powerful and interesting characters in the novel. Sonny and Duane, in fact, seem to belong in another book. Not that McMurtry doesn't tell both stories well, he does, but he doesn't tell them in the same way. For all his craft and sensibility McMurtry doesn't maintain intellectual and stylistic control over his interlocking stories. The book, at every point, seems about to disintegrate from centrifugal force.

Just as the styles of life in the village and the city are radically different, so are the styles McMurtry uses to portray them, so much so that the book could have been written by two authors: one writing about the men and the life in Thalia, the other writing about the women and Wichita Falls. Writing about the boys in Thalia, McMurtry is sympathetic, becoming almost identical with them. Writing about the women and Wichita Falls, he pulls back to an ironic distance and views the action non-committally. Writing about the boys, McMurtry's prose falls into their modes of expression; the style is casual and anecdotal. Writing about the women, his prose becomes tough and transparent and his style takes on drive and flexibility. It is like alternating between Sherwood Anderson and Thackeray: the difference really seems to be one of genre. Finally, reading *The Last Picture Show* is like reading a novel about a north Texas Becky Sharp with interspersed short stories about the boys back in Thalia.

Those restless, ineffectual country boys, for all the charm and humorous sexual adventures, are simply not in the same league with Jacy Farrow. In the three sections of this novel which were excerpted and published as short stories, Sonny and Duane fare very well; they are in their element as short-story characters. But when these stories are inserted into the novel, they become set-pieces, totally overwhelmed by the vitality and drive of the women. What is missing, perhaps, is some articulation of the differences which are obvious in the styles, something that might pull the book together and modulate the differences in tone, distance, and pace which make the book seem so fragile. For all the beautiful writing and sensitive observation the book lacks intellectual authority. Its attempt at exorcism, at farewell, does not succeed. For three novels now McMurtry has been bidding farewell to his childhood; the horsemen have passed by, the cowboys have left Cheyenne, the last picture show has played, but somehow McMurtry himself seems reluctant to leave. To take an appropriately rural simile, in *The Last Picture Show,* McMurtry, like a colt in foal, seems to have gotten himself "onto the ground." He is ready to run where he wants to now, and anyone who is interested in writing and in Texas should look forward to his next novel with anticipation and perhaps a little anxiety.

Sherry Kafka's *Hannah Jackson* is a fine little book, all the finer for being a first novel. It tells the story of Hannah Jackson's life in a small town not too different from Johnson City or Fredericksburg. Hannah is a religious girl, but she falls in love with a married rancher and he divorces his wife to marry her. As a result Hannah is ostracized from the church which is the center of spiritual and social life in her world. . . . Miss Kafka tells the story in a classically feminine fashion, in a sequence of short first-person accounts by various people concerned with Hannah and the town. The narrative, jumping from person to person, moves cautiously around the subject, gradually closing in and finally slaying Hannah with a delicious, almost feline, irony, kept well under control. Miss Kafka's eyes are cold, so we get sentiment without sentimentality, honesty without confession, and affection without affectation. Unfortunately we also get truism without truth.

Hannah Jackson, like *The Last Picture Show,* seems to lack intellectual authority. Miss Kafka doesn't seem to be sure what she thinks about her subject-matter, and she is unwilling to tell us what she feels, so she chooses a manner of telling which seems to rescue her from telling us either. The book, in this sense, is almost too "well written." Miss Kafka's hold on the possibilities of the novel is as tight and puritanical as Hannah Jackson's hold on her family. The material seems controlled but not under control. It is as if Miss Kafka knows that beneath her tough, clear-eyed facade, there is a heart-of-gold, or at least a nostalgia for those older, clearer days. I may be wrong, but her device of telling the story from many points of view seems less a *tour de force* than a retreat from authority, a way of avoiding articulation of feelings she knows to be unfashionable, or perhaps intellectually fragile.

The technique which seems to rescue her ultimately betrays her. . . . We have a strange feeling of equivocation which is different from the complexity she seems to intend. The novel takes on the tone of a demonstration in which the author is unsure of what is being demonstrated, or, again, of an exorcism which does not exorcise. This criticism may seem unfair of a first novel, but where bad writing can be easily dismissed, good writing demands criticism. Potentiality demands realization, and the potential of the writing in *Hannah Jackson* is considerable. A dying way of life is evoked before our eyes. The touch and smell of small-town life is here, its freedoms and tyrannies are boldly drawn; but we are given no overview. We are given no sense of how much the freedoms and tyrannies are co-extensive, and it is in this sense, it seems to me, that the exorcism fails. Miss Kafka seems to want to cast aside the cruelties of small-town life while retaining its rewards—a difficult task indeed.

III

In many ways *This Stubborn Soil, Hannah Jackson,* and *The Last Picture Show* (particularly in the Thalia sections) are old-fashioned novels in the pre-war mode of Hemingway and Fitzgerald. By moving around their subjects rather than with them, they endeavor to stop time rather than translate it. They tend toward silence rather than statement, toward classical stasis rather than movement, and in this they have nothing in common with the headlong drive of the best of the post-war novels. The novels of writers like Barth, Mailer, Heller, and Pynchon, which exist in time rather than space, which explode at the end with an authoritative, autodestructive bang, have the prodigality and daring of Elizabethan drama. They are novels of wit, intellection, and articulation. Compared to them, the novels discussed here seem timid, almost reactionary.

Of course the comparison is not fair, but the point to be made from it is. Texas is no longer an isolated and static place, no longer a colony or a ghetto, and those who wish to treat it as such must retreat into very special enclaves, as the New York writers have retreated into the Negro and Jewish ghettos. The ghetto, the farm, the wilderness, and the village are all places where there is safety from history, but Texas is no longer in its Middle Ages. What is most vivid and characteristic about this place will not stand still for the classical treatment. Modern Texas is above all *historical,* and the old forms, as Philip Rahv points out, betray a fear of history and change.

It is feared because modern life is above all an historical life producing changes with vertiginous speed, changes difficult to understand and even more difficult to control. And to some people it appears as though the past, all of it together with its gods and sacred books, were being ground to pieces in the powerhouse of change, senselessly used up as so much raw material in the fabrication of an unthinkable future.

But the future seems no more unthinkable than the gory past. The dead vary only in quantity, not in quality. And it might be that the novel, pronounced dead by those who really meant history was dead, is still alive. Bored with the past and disdainful of the future, it might again, at the risk of ephemerality and self-destruction, come to terms with the present: with the modern city, with power, history, and change. The novel might again become the barometer of society. If the novelist decides to stand again in the flux of society, in the area of maximum danger, he might begin to tell us what we are becoming rather than what we were. For Texas novelists this might require gaining identity at the expense of a dead tradition. In any case it will require, as James Baldwin has said, some realization of the things love cannot do, and a more complete exorcism from our weird nostalgia for a vanished state of security and order which never was.

From

The Ghost Country: A Study of the Novels of Larry McMurtry

RAYMOND L. NEINSTEIN

Horseman, Pass By, [1] McMurtry's first novel, begins with a return of life, a wet drizzly spring bringing new grass to a parched land. "Spring had come dry for seven straight years," Lonnie, the young narrator-protagonist remembers, "but that year the month of March was a long slow drizzle" (p. 7). Lonnie's grandfather, Homer Bannon, a character-type who will show up in one guise or another in each of McMurtry's novels, tells Lonnie "that nature would always work her own cures, if people would be patient enough, and give her time" (p. 7). Homer is the old rancher, the man whose life has been tied closely to the land and whose values derive from that bond, from the land's rhythms and cycles. The opening in a time of spring rain and the greening of the countryside stands in ironic counterpoise to the tale of the destruction of Homer and his world that is to follow. But it is consistent with that more important aspect of the story which is the burgeoning of Lonnie's young manhood and his growing away from the world which Homer represents, the mythic "Homeric" world. Yet when Homer dies, the only alternative figure left on the land is his step-son Hud, a ruthless, power-hungry modern-day rancher-cowboy in a fast Cadillac. McMurtry, in an essay on the Western as a genre, writes, "Hud, a twentieth century Westerner, is a gunfighter who lacks both guns and opponents. The land itself is the same—just as powerful and just as imprisoning—but the social context has changed so radically that Hud's impulse to violence is turned inward, on himself and his family."[2] In a later essay, speaking of his father's and his uncles' generation of Texans, McMurtry poses the question, "to whom have they left that country: myself, or Hud?" (*ING*, p. 140). His answer is that both have inherited the place, Hud to stay there, frustrated, the imaginative artist to leave and then attempt to work out the meaning of his dispossession.

The plot of *Horseman, Pass By* is quite simple. It is discovered that Homer Bannon's cattle herd has hoof and mouth disease and must be entirely destroyed. For the old rancher, who has spent a lifetime building up his herd, this destruction means his own end, and he, in fact, survives his herd only by a day. The story is narrated by Homer's grandson, Lonnie, whose story the book actually is. It begins with Lonnie feeling restless on his grandfather's ranch, eager to get away and see the rest of the world. He listens avidly to the stories told by Jesse, an old lame cowboy who works for Homer. But Jesse is beaten, his stories "never lasted long enough, and . . . always ended with him getting tireder and more sad" (p. 22). Lonnie wants desperately "to be off somewhere . . . into country I'd never seen" (p. 23). He realizes that his grandfather and he are in different worlds: "Granddad and I were in such separate times and separate places. I had got where I would rather go to Thalia and goof around on the square than listen to his old-timy stories" (pp. 23–24). But Thalia, McMurtry's fictional home town in all his books, has nothing to offer: "there would just have been Thalia to go to, just an empty court-house square to drive around" (p. 22).

There is an air of suffocating age and disability around Lonnie at the novel's beginning, in contrast to the exuberance of spring. Old Homer and Jesse both have game legs; Grandma, Homer's second wife and the mother of Hud, is going off to the hospital for an operation; Newt Garrett, the veterinarian who discovers the disease in Homer's herd, has lost his larynx to cancer and can talk only by pressing an electric buzzer against his throat. There is an eerie scene in which Newt, Homer, and Lonnie go out to look at the tell-tale dead heifer, the body of which is being eaten by buzzards. The buzzards buzz about and Newt buzzes instead of talking. The constant repetition of the word "buzz" in connection with death, carrion, cancer and hoof and mouth disease creates a low background murmur itself. In such an atmosphere the cause of the heifer's death is discovered, and the process begins which leads to the inevitable destruction of the Bannon herd.

Lonnie is not only surrounded by death, decay, and disease; he is also cut off from any models of healthy, mature male sexuality. The men around him are his elderly grandfather; Jesse, the tired, ageing, bachelor cowboy; and Hud. For all the emphasis put on him when the novel was filmed as "Hud" (a change in emphasis of which McMurtry approves, he tells us in *ING*, p. 17), Hud is, in the novel, just a stereotype, the cowboy-stud who reappears in *The Last Picture Show*[3] as the character Abilene, and in *Moving On*[4] as Sonny Shanks, King of the Rodeo. He relates to women by seducing or raping them, and to other men by beating them up, stealing their wives, beating them at pool or cards, and driving a faster car. He is ruggedly handsome, very strong, very mean, and very clever. He comes nearest to being a realized character as Sonny Shanks in *Moving On*, but by then McMurtry has had considerable practice and has also allowed himself the luxury of eight hundred pages in which to develop his characters. In *Horseman, Pass By*, Hud is a powerful force on Lonnie, but is never more than a type. What is important is that Lonnie has no decent model of manhood at a time when he crucially needs one. He simply does not know what to do with his longings, which are especially directed at Halmea, the black cook and housekeeper at the ranch, to whose brutal rape by Hud he is a fascinated witness. Afterwards, thinking back to how he stood by and watched, sickened but spell-bound, he still cannot resolve his feelings. "What bothered me was I had wanted to do pretty much the same thing to Halmea. I didn't want to do it mean, like Hud did everything, but I wanted to do it to her" (p. 107). The problem is irresolvable at the ranch, or in Thalia, where his high school buddies find their sexual outlets in blind heifers. When Halmea leaves, "I began to feel like I was the only person left in the country, and it was a shitty feeling" (p. 147). His restless impatience to be gone at the beginning of the book has resolved itself, after his grandfather's death, into a feeling that he is totally alone, gone already. "I felt lost from everybody, and from myself included" (p. 130).

Homer Bannon's decline and death are, as McMurtry admits, pathetic and unconvincing (see *ING*, p. 17). Homer is an old, but strong, rugged horseman when the book opens, working long, hard days on his ranch. Within a day after having to slaughter his herd, he is reduced to a senile little old man who falls off his own porch. Whether Hud shoots him "for kindness or meanness" (p. 144), when he is lying in a ditch, broken, bloody and delirious, Lonnie never finds out. But the important aspect of his death is that he leaves no legitimate heir, no one who will carry on as he did. His tradition dies with him; although the ranch will go to Hud, who has been trying to wrest control of it through shady legal maneuvers all along, in no sense will the traditions of the land continue. There is no one left to continue them. Hud lacks the ethics, the rugged honesty of his stepfather. The scene in which Homer shoots his three old longhorns, which he had raised himself, reminders of the old days, the cattle drives, is brutally paralleled by Hud's shooting Homer, another man's wife standing half-naked and drunk beside him in the road in the glare of his Cadillac's headlights. When Hud kills Homer, he has killed off an entire tradition, but has nothing with which to replace it.

Lonnie cannot understand his grandfather's sense of the land, but neither can he accept Hud's alternative. When he finds that Halmea has left town, he knows there is nothing to stay on for any longer. Going away, he turns his back on nothing, actually. "If Halmea was gone, they were all gone, and Thalia might as well be empty" (p. 146). He can do nothing but leave. In the cab of the truck in which he's hitched a ride away, Lonnie "sat thinking about Thalia. . . . At home it was time for the train to go by, and nobody was sitting on the porch . . . ." (p. 157). Lonnie is fast moving into McMurtry's favorite land, the pastures of nostalgia, of homesickness without a home that one is able to go back to.

There seems to be a small critical debate as to how to read the novel's ending. Thomas Landess, author of a small study of McMurtry's work, thinks Lonnie is going off "to see the urban world of cheap adventure and quick pleasure. It is Hud's world he is seeking, not Homer's."[5]

James K. Folsom, in an interesting study of *Horseman, Pass By* and *Shane* in relation to the films based on them, interprets the ending in the following way:

> Lonnie learns, through the action of *Horseman, Pass By,* the futility of his own generalized longings for escape. The world, he discovers, when viewed with, in Yeats' phrase, 'a cold eye,' is not the romantic place he had thought it was at the beginning of the novel. Captive at the beginning of the story of the common adolescent belief that somewhere there must be more 'life' than there is in one's own environment, Lonnie learns the truth symbolized by the name of the town—Thalia—where the story's action has taken place: that the stuff of life and history and epic poetry may be discovered in one's own surrounding if one has the intelligence to know where to look for it.[6]

Landess would have Lonnie learning nothing from his experiences; and Folsom would have him learning more than he actually has. Folsom bases his conclusion about the novel's ending, I suppose, on the fact that Lonnie has narrated the story. In effect, Folsom is saying, Lonnie has written a regional novel, or is now prepared to, shaped with intelligence from a cold-eyed look at his environment and his experiences in it. I think Folsom is confusing Lonnie with Larry. McMurtry may know that he has inherited the imaginative water rights to his uncles' land while forfeiting any other rights to it; it is difficult to say precisely whether Lonnie has learned this lesson. If the "stuff of life and history and epic poetry may be discovered in one's own surroundings," why, then, does Lonnie leave? What is he looking for? There seem to be as few grounds for believing Lonnie to be looking for "Hud's world" as for believing that he has outgrown his romantic illusions and is looking at the world with a "cold eye." He appears to be looking neither for Hud's world nor for Homer's, but for his own, and not with "cold eyes," but with eyes misted over with nostalgia, a blurred vision that allows us the final image of the novel in which Lonnie sees in the face of the trucker who has given him a ride, the faces of everyone he knew, "those faces who made my days" (p. 157).

Lonnie is a narrator, not a self-conscious author, at least not yet. He is a fictional device, and, as we shall see, McMurtry's use of first-person narration is a problematic one. The question always arises, in connection with first-person narratives, where is the narrator telling the story from, where does he stand in relation to the narrative? We know where, say, Jacob Horner or Todd Andrews are telling their stories from, in Barth's early novels. We know where

Holden Caulfield is, and Huck Finn. We are not sure with Lonnie. I would think he is standing pretty close to the events of his story, looking back on them all as he is leaving Thalia. He has decided to put some distance between himself and the place of his boyhood, but has not yet achieved the critical distance on the events he has been through that the author has. The problem will become more crucially relevant when we look at Danny Deck, the hero and narrator of McMurtry's fifth novel, *All My Friends Are Going to Be Strangers.*[7] At the end of that novel, Danny plunges into the Rio Grande. As we learn in *MO,* published previously but taking up events at a later date with some of the characters Danny Deck knew, Danny has simply disappeared. We don't know if he is alive or dead, but we have an entire novel narrated by him. Is he treading water, as he narrates it, in the middle of the Rio Grande? As I will attempt to show, the device of the "displaced narrator" is central to the formal and thematic concerns of *AMF;* in fact, that novel depends on this device for its very intelligibility. But, by that novel, McMurtry has taken an ironic stance toward his early literary achievements and is measuring his distance from them. A novel one imagines to be very much like *Horseman, Pass By* has been written and sold to Hollywood by the young novelist-hero of *AMF,* a hero whose giving up on that mode of fiction and whose plunge into the Rio Grande signal McMurtry's plunge into the choppy waters of neo-regionalism. In *HPB,* however, the problems of narrative stance which underlie the critical debate over the meaning of the book's ending are ones I think McMurtry neither foresaw nor intended. They are simply evidence of a young novelist's not having achieved full control of a fictional technique.

McMurtry went on, in his next book, *Leaving Cheyenne,*[8] to show that it was possible to further complicate these narrative problems, solve none of them, and still produce a fine novel. Here we have *three* first-person narrators, and it is hard to say where any of them stand in relation to their sections of the text. They are telling their life-stories, but the book ends with their birth and death dates on their tombstones. These are ghostly voices from the last mythic days, voices which have grown old, cracked and dry as they tell of their range life turning suburban, as "Gunsmoke" replaces their West.

Leaving Cheyenne presents, in episodic form, the lives of two men, life-long best friends, and the woman they both love and sleep with for forty years. Their friendship is never strained by this shared relationship with Molly Taylor; it is, if anything, strengthened. This is, of course, only possible since neither ever marries her; neither is successfully able to put a claim on her. She bears each man a son. Both sons are killed in World War II. Molly is briefly married to a disreputable character who is conveniently killed off in an oil-rig accident offstage. The two men, a rancher and a cowboy, embody the two aspects of the mythic Western horseman. The woman exists in the novel largely as a natural principle, a feature of the landscape, good to those who love her, but wild, unable to be possessed, changed, or even transported. "I'm doing just as much living right here and now as I could anywhere," Molly says (p. 216). "I can't imagine that hill without her," Johnny McCloud, the cowboy, tells us (p. 216). "I felt like Molly was just as permanent as my land," thinks Gideon Fry, the rancher (p. 133).

McMurtry, in a review of "Lovin' Molly," a film based on *Leaving Cheyenne*, calls his jealousy-free best-friends-share-one-good-woman-for-life plot a "male journalist's fantasy," and indicates that he has long since abandoned any idea as to its credibility. "What *Leaving Cheyenne* really offers is a vision of adult life in which sexuality cannot seriously interfere with friendship."[9] Emotionally, psychologically, McMurtry is right. The story is a wish-fulfillment dream, the kind American literature has often presented while showing it to be impossible of fulfillment, a dream of anxious adolescence afraid of entering the estate of manhood, having to choose between staying with one's buddies or growing up and living with women. McMurtry himself admits it is his most widely admired novel. Why? Are his admirers all naive "male journalists"? Perhaps, but a more important answer is that the novel is truly alive at a mythic level. It satisfies and convinces, even while we doubt the probability of the love story, because it is dealing, through the romance-plot, with the myth of the end of the West.

Regional fiction has long worked this way, a not very credible love story somehow containing, under pressure, a larger myth. Kirkland's *Zury Prouder*, "the meanest man in Spring County," practically becomes a mild-mannered suburban Pop barbecuing hot dogs for the kiddies out on the patio, under the benevolent influence of the "Bosting" schoolmarm Anne Sparrow.[10] And perhaps, in the 1880's, readers were moved by love once again bringing out the good in a man, while we see in Zury (short for Usury) the repression, the hardness and ruthlessness it took to conquer the Great Plains; and in Anne Sparrow we see the only force that could conquer Zury. We feel Zury's mellowing as false, romantic, tacked-on to appease readers who demanded sentiment. But the novel really lives in terms of the sexual dynamic of "place," as does *Leaving Cheyenne*.

Gideon Fry is a rancher, a land-owner, a buyer and seller of acreage, cattle, horses. Johnny McCloud is a foot-loose cowboy, his only possession his saddle, and even that was a gift from Gid. Together, the two characters add up to a composite figure: "Sometimes I see him as Old Man Goodnight, or as Teddy Blue, or as my uncle Johnny . . . but the one thing that is sure is that he was a horseman, and a god of the country. His home was the frontier, and his mythos celebrates those masculine ideals appropriate to a frontier" (*ING*, p. xv). If we see Gideon and Johnny, then, as embodiments of the mythic horseman, and Molly as, in fact, the land itself, that aspect of it which fascinated and captured the imagination of the horseman as no real woman could, we see how McMurtry is manipulating a story in which the land is at once property and wild sexuality, able to be freely loved but never possessed. Gideon, one day, surveys all the land he can see and tells Molly that, except for her small ranch, he owns it all. She tells him he'll never get her piece and she means it both ways. Wendell Berry develops the metaphor of marriage as one's tie to place, land, country, as well as to another, both ties being ground for renewal through surrender, mutual possession, the processes of fertility, death, and re-birth.[11] McMurtry's rancher, though, wants to own all the land, but can't; wants to marry the women he loves, but can't. McMurtry is limning the psycho-sexual dynamics, not only of an unreal love-triangle, but, more importantly, of the fate of the Western myth. Desire is either unfulfilled or fruitless; Molly's sons are killed off, one having turned homosexual in the Army, another and more obvious way in which McMurtry is showing us the end of the masculine ethos of the horseman. Perhaps not just the end, but the truth of the ethos, which, of course, excluded women, its bond being that of male "adhesiveness," to use Whitman's term. McMurtry had, somewhere in the novel, to show what he could not say about Gid and Johnny. And he was right in not saying, since they would have had no way of saying it themselves.

"Nobody gets enough chances at the wild and sweet," Johnny thinks to himself toward the end of the book, recalling the time when he, Gid, and Molly were young (p. 253). There is no mode for dealing with the vanished mythic energies any longer except through memory, nostalgia, and fading desire. The characters age and die; real history, war, impinges on mythology. Gid and Johnny, the old horsemen, drive through Thalia, cruising past drive-in hamburger stands, lamenting, ironically, the passing of really good Westerns. They are beset, in their old age, with automotive problems, cars breaking down. Their range has narrowed; Gid has moved into town, the owner of thousands of acres of rangeland paying off a mortgage on a "big ugly brick house." We are already on the set of *The Last Picture Show,* a novel in which bitterness is only a mask for nostalgia. The form of the regional novel is becoming exhausted and McMurtry is looking for a way out, as his young protagonists are looking for a way out of dreary old Thalia.

NOTES

1. Larry McMurtry, *Horseman, Pass By,* first published by Harper & Row, New York, 1961. I am using the British paperback edition, entitled *Hud,* London, Sphere Books, 1971. Page references are to that edition, and references will be indicated as *HPB* in the text.

2. Larry McMurtry, *In a Narrow Grave,* first published by The Encino Press, Austin, 1968, p. 24. I am using the Simon & Schuster Touchstone paperback edition, New York, 1971. Subsequent references will be indicated as *ING* in the text.

3. Larry McMurtry, *The Last Picture Show,* first published by The Dial Press, New York, 1966. I am using the British paperback edition, London, Sphere Books, 1972. References are to that edition, and will be indicated as *LPS* in the text.

4. Larry McMurtry, *Moving On* (New York: Simon & Schuster, 1970). I am using the Avon paperback (N.Y., 1971). Subsequent references will be indicated as *MO* in the text.

5. Thomas Landess, *Larry McMurtry* (Austin: Steck-Vaughn, 1969), p. 10. Landess' usually quite fine summaries and analyses are sometimes marred by careless reading. Landess has Homer Bannon dying from a fall from his horse, "the ultimate indignity to the cowboy" (p. 13). Actually, Homer's fall is much more prosaic—he falls off his porch. (Cf. *HPB,* 137, 145). In discussing *Leaving Cheyenne,* Landess has Molly marrying Eddie *after* discovering that she is pregnant. In the novel, Molly clearly allows herself to become pregnant a few months after she is married to Eddie. (Cf. *LC,* 119, 154). This is not just a quibble. Landess' reading would turn Molly into a much more calculating character than she in fact is. She doesn't marry Eddie for any particular reason, which is what Gid finds so incredibly hard to accept.

6. *Shane* and *Hud:* Two Stories in Search of a Medium," *Western Humanities Review,* XXIV, 4, Autumn, 1970, pp. 359–372. The material quoted is on p. 370.

7. Larry McMurtry, *All My Friends Are Going to Be Strangers* (N.Y.: Simon & Schuster, 1972). I am using the paperback edition, N.Y.: Pocket Books, 1973. Subsequent references in the text will be indicated as *AMF.*

8. Larry McMurtry, *Leaving Cheyenne,* first published by Harper & Row, New York, 1963. Subsequent page references, indicated in the text as *LC,* are to the Popular Library paperback edition (N.Y., n.d.).

9. Larry McMurtry, "Approaching Cheyenne . . . Leaving Lumet. Oh, Pshaw!," *New York,* Vol. 7, No. 17, April 29, 1974, p. 66.

10. Joseph Kirkland, *Zury: The Meanest Man in Spring County* (Urbana, Ill., 1956), originally published in 1887.

11. Cf. Wendell Berry, *The Country of Marriage* (N.Y.: Harcourt Brace Jovanovich, 1973).

From
Larry McMurtry
THOMAS LANDESS

It is perhaps condescending to say that *Horseman, Pass By* is merely a good *first* novel, even though the author himself has been guilty of the same condescension (see *In a Narrow Grave*). The book is more than that. It is a coherent work of fiction which gives a new life to the myth of the cowboy, a life which neither destroys the essence of that myth nor is unduly distorted by it. And it is just possible that this novel may one day be regarded as an important breakthrough in the development of a substantial literature of the Southwest. Indeed, the survival of McMurtry's reputation as a writer may be assured by the publication of this apparently frail but ultimately durable Western classic.

In many ways *Leaving Cheyenne* (1963), McMurtry's second novel, is a reprise of thematic material treated in *Horseman, Pass By*. Once again the setting is Thalia, a small community in the cattle country of North Central Texas. Once again the principal male characters are cowboys who in part represent typical figures in the evolution of the ranch from earlier times to the present. And once again the broader issue at stake is the contrast between youth and old age, or, to put it another way, the effect of the passing years on the hopes and dreams of the young. As McMurtry writes in an introductory epigraph, "The Cheyenne of this book is that part of the cowboy's day's circle which is earliest and best: his blood's country and his heart's pastureland."

Thus, to some extent, the novel is both a story of initiation and of generational conflict, and the enveloping action is that of the changing West. But structurally *Leaving Cheyenne* bears little resemblance to the earlier work. The point of view, for instance, though again that of the first-person narrator, is shared equally by the three main characters, each of whom relates a long segment of their common story. And the plot line, while almost as simple, is less sharply defined than that of *Horseman, Pass By*. The characters browse through the predictable events of their lives like lazy cattle, stopping for a while and then ambling on when the spirit moves them. No central conflict arises to dominate the action. There are only day-to-day conflicts that come, one after another, to wear down their energy and will to live. And the story stretches over several decades rather than over the relatively short span covered in the first novel.

Essentially the action concerns the friendship of Gideon Fry and Johnny McCloud and their love for Molly Taylor, a lifelong passion that is at first a threat to their own relationship and later a strange bond which unites them ever more strongly as they pass from youth to maturity and finally to old age. The youthful years are narrated by Gid, who begins his story at the age of twenty-one on election day, an occasion of some significance since it is, according to law, the day one first assumes the responsibilities of adult citizenship. But despite his legal qualifications, Gid is not yet a man, has not been "initiated." He still has much to learn about the life struggle (in his case the management of a cattle ranch), and he is still relatively innocent about matters sexual. His naiveté concerning the latter is partially explainable in terms of his environment (rural Texas in the second decade of the twentieth century) and his upbringing by a stern, pragmatic father. But even under such circumstances, he is a slow learner.

There is something of the same naiveté in the other two, though Molly and Johnny are much less ill at ease with their newly matured passions, perhaps because they have not been as inhibited by the stern example of a man like Adam Fry. In many ways Mr. Fry represents the same values that Homer Bannon stands for in *Horseman, Pass By,* but Fry is saltier and less idealized—more like the Homer that Hud sees than the hero of Lonnie's youthful imagination. For Gid finds his father's discipline hard and often unreasonable, and the boy complains constantly of the old man's niggardliness, particularly when other youngsters are driving their own automobiles. In the end, however, when his father chooses to commit suicide rather than gradually succumb to a wasting illness, Gid begins to see him as a mythic figure. And this relationship is particularly important to Gid while he is competing with Johnny in a good-natured rivalry for Molly's hand and learning by fits and starts the hard truth about ranching.

But even his father cannot help him unravel the mystery of Molly. While perfectly happy to sleep with him when the opportunity presents itself, she consistently refuses, much to his bewilderment, his offer of marriage. And she seems to bestow her favors with surprising impartiality on Gid, Johnny, and Eddie White, another young buck with an automobile and ideas. Yet her conduct is more generous than promiscuous, and her motive in refusing Gid's proposals is an altruistic one: she realizes, as does Mr. Fry, that should she marry Gid, she would destroy his friendship with Johnny, a relationship which is perhaps as important to Gid as his attachment for her.

And so, when she becomes pregnant, it is Eddie whom she marries, despite her knowledge that of the three men Gid would make the best father. Not only is the child in fact his, but also, of the three, Gid is the most sensible and reliable, the only one with a trace of the dynastic impulse to build and acquire for his children.

Gid, then, must bear two great sorrows in a brief span of time: the bewildering defection of Molly and the death of his father. So lonely and unsettled is his young life that he impulsively marries lowborn Mabel Peters, a girl who has, over the years and with monotonous regularity, offered to sell herself to him for the price of a wedding. As soon as the ceremony is performed, however, Mabel is transformed before Gid's startled eyes from a docile, submissive suppliant into an arrogant shrew—a warning to her husband and to the world that after a fierce struggle she has at last won her measure of dignity and status. Gid, whose mind is not equipped to handle such psychological subtleties, makes the best of a poor bargain and eventually establishes an uneasy peace with Mabel, who does not crave love but the respect and civility her family has never enjoyed.

After a time, because love has played an important part in his younger years, Gid resumes his relationship with Molly, now alone after the death of Eddie. Johnny, of course, has never ceased his nocturnal visits. Thus, despite the changes that a few years have wrought, the three seem to maintain their solidarity, happy with each other as if the rest of the world did not exist. Youth, it seems, can bear whatever life has to offer.

But the middle years bring new sorrows, and the world intrudes to upset their delicate relationship. Molly narrates this section, the story of life during World War II and of the changes that inevitably come with the years. For one thing, fiery lusts are cooling, and Molly must reap the first consequences of her decision to sacrifice a respectable marriage for the continuing friendship of her two lovers. She begins to feel lonely, particularly with her two sons (one by each lover) away in service; and when both boys are killed, she must endure her sorrow without the consolation of a husband by her side or the solicitude of the feminine community, from which, presumably, she has been ostracized because of her conduct.

Then too, she must live with a terrible secret—the perverse nature of her son Jimmy, who despises her since the day she tells him that Gid rather than Eddie is his true father. Jimmy becomes a religious fanatic in his adolescence and denounces his parents with the biblical rhetoric of a tenthouse evangelist, but after a few months of military combat he loses his tenuous immature faith and becomes involved with a rich homosexual, with whom he plans to live a soft postwar life as a kept man.

Once again the thematic emphasis falls on the relationship—or lack thereof—between father and son. It is the father, after all, who is best suited to guide a young man through the perils of initiation. When the mature masculine force is absent during those crucial years, a youth enters the adult world ill-prepared to meet its challenges or, worse, fails to enter it at all and languishes in the limbo of adolescence, arrested development, blind rebellion, or homosexuality. Jimmy is such a youth, and with characteristic malice he writes his mother about his plans, knowing the revelation will wound her simple sensibilities. For, with the exception of her love life, she is thoroughly conventional in all her attitudes. She believes strongly in filial piety and loves her father with fierce loyalty, despite his manifest weaknesses. She also feels a strong sense of patriotism, respects the flag, and hates her country's enemies. About God she is less definite, but by no means disrespectful. Soon after the letter arrives, she receives word that Jimmy has been killed.

Gid, whose homelife has worsened with the passage of time, believes that the death of his only son is a judgment against the sins of his youth and vows never to sleep with Molly again, a vow he keeps with the fierce determination of the rugged rancher he has become.

Of the three friends, Johnny is the most constant. The years do little more than slow him down. They effect no essential alteration in his character, nor do they change his attitude toward Molly and Gid. He is less passionate in his lovemaking perhaps, but only a little less so; and he continues to work for Gid as he has done for so many years, with no trace of envy for Gid's increasing wealth and no desire to be anything more than a cowboy with a few dollars in his pocket. Certainly he is never bothered by the ghosts which haunt both Molly and Gid, even though his own son, Joe, is killed in an air raid over Germany. For Johnny this death is simply a bad break, though he does feel some paternal pride in a brave and manly son. For Molly, however, it is a grievous wound, painful despite her simple patriotism and her strong will to endure.

In the last section, narrated by Johnny, the final dissolution of the friendship occurs when Gid, perhaps the most strong-willed of the three, falls into a critical physical decline. The tone of these closing scenes is elegiac; and even Johnny, who has never been given to regrets or to sentimental reminiscence, begins to look to the past with increasing nostalgia. Gid, however, is most affected by the coming on of old age. He is now given to long-winded tales of the past—rambling anecdotes which his friends must listen to with patient indulgence. He has also grown more stubborn and set in his ways. And his body, once a precise engine, is beginning to wear out with hard use. Here one sees the final turn of the life cycle as the day wanes and the shadows crowd in. If one eliminated the middle third of the novel, it would be difficult to find in this dying old rancher the twenty-one-year-old boy who began the narrative. Yet despite the ellipsis of many years between each of the sections, the continuity of character is remarkably maintained, and the stark image that Gid forms in the closing pages is all the more effective thematically because of its contrast with the callow youth he is at the outset.

Much of the last third of the novel is devoted to Johnny's drawn-out account of an automobile accident in which he and Gid are involved following a day of fence mending. While the incident is vivid and gives the three principals the opportunity to reveal the present state of their perennial relationship, the scene lacks the disciplined economy of the first novel. The author himself must bear part of the blame for Johnny's vocal rambling, however true to character it may be, for there is not enough thematic development in the scene to justify its length or proliferation of detail. And here the lack of a sharply defined plot line seems to lead McMurtry off the beaten path and into the tangled thicket of redundancy.

In contrast, the final pages are devoted to the rapid decline of Gid's health and his death while mending the windmill—a task which his father had assigned to him in a note of farewell at least four decades earlier. This scene of course signals the final breakup of the old relationship and, in a broader sense, the impermanence of all things natural, a theme emphasized by the epigraph at the beginning of Section II, lines from Shakespeare's Sonnet LXIV, whose theme is evanescence.

> Ruin hath taught me thus to ruminate,
> That Time will come and take my love away.

In the windmill incident, in the obvious parallel between Gid's physical decline and that of his father, in the constant reminiscence of the aging friends, and, most obviously, in Johnny's closing memory of the election day which begins the story, there is an unmistakable emphasis on the cyclic nature of life, the "day's circle" of McMurtry's prefatory epigraph. This emphasis lends to the entire narrative the quality of a tableau in which the universal experiences of love and death are frozen in a particular time and place for observation and meditation. Life and its inevitable end, then, provide the subject of this tableau—life which is the outgrowth of sexual union (love) and death which is the ultimate fruit of love. The rest—the day-to-day incidents which make up the vital activity of Gid, Johnny, and

Molly—is merely the raw material which gives substance or body to such abstractions as life and death, meaningless unless defined in concrete terms.

The significance of *Leaving Cheyenne* is broad, however narrowly limited its setting or the sensibilities of its characters. Of course this broadness has its dangers, the most obvious of which is the temptation to be undiscriminating in the inclusion of detail. Since everything, after all, can be said to relate to life or death, the natural thematic limitations which usually apply to a work of fiction might seem too nebulous here to worry about. McMurtry is obviously aware of the pitfalls, and his metaphor of the day's circle helps to organize and control his material, though, as noted above, not always successfully.

Another controlling device is the author's continuing preoccupation with the mythic cowboy, and for this reason the historian can find much of interest in the novel. For one thing, in old Mr. Fry one sees another portrait of the old-time rancher: tough, hard-working, independent, and by the same token closemouthed, penny-pinching, and undemonstrative in his relations with those whom he loves. Of course, in *Leaving Cheyenne* there is not so clear-cut a distinction between the older and the younger generation, since Gid is very like his father in the end. This similarity of character is in large measure explainable by the fact that because Gid grows up before modern urbanization has corrupted the range, his times are not as different from his father's as, say, Hud's were from Homer's.

The virtues which Mr. Fry (and later Gid) exemplify are the virtues of one type of cowboy: the would-be rancher with his pride of ownership and his dynastic impulse. Thus, old Fry watches his expenditures, not so much out of meanness of spirit as out of a desire to enlarge and protect his holdings, which are always subject to the vicissitudes of nature. Fry also wishes to pass along the ranch intact to his son, a desire common among agrarian patriarchs.

His toughness and avoidance of open affection are in part the result of a life without the tenderizing influence of a woman, the fate of every true cowboy; but these qualities are also designed to shape and temper his son for the hard struggle ahead, the struggle to hold the land and make it prosper. Gid obviously takes his father's example to heart. After an initial temptation to sell the ranch, he begins to expand his holdings, and in the end he has carved out a greater portion of the land for himself than his father left him.

Johnny McCloud, on the other hand, exemplifies an entirely different kind of cowboy: the romantic drifter who believes that ownership of land is more a curse than a blessing, since it curtails a man's freedom to move about and to take his pleasure as he sees it. Johnny is perfectly content to be a ranch hand all his life, and his pure joy of living is never corrupted by a desire for wealth and status. Unlike Gid, who is torn by pangs of puritan conscience, Johnny is able to accept the natural pleasures his senses afford him without a moment's remorse. Thus Molly finds him a carefree, unreserved lover, while Gid is comparatively restrained in his passions.

If Molly functions at all in this portrait of the vanishing frontier, she adds the image of woman to the picture. Tender, at times sentimental, she is nonetheless tough enough to bear a succession of tragedies that might easily destroy a more delicately fashioned sister from Boston or Charleston. Indeed, Molly is in some ways an updated version of the legendary dance-hall girl so familiar to lovers of the classic Western romance. Like the stereotype, she is both promiscuous and good-hearted, the constant companion of the cowboy in his search for pleasure—but, finally, the girl he never marries. Yet this description alone would be an oversimplification of Molly's nature, for her more complex human dimensions bear little relationship to the stereotype. Her devotion to her father, her lifelong struggle to preserve her own small plot of land, and her maternal love for her two sons are qualities which give her the unique vitality so necessary to memorable fictional portrayals.

Though it could hardly be termed a popular success, *Leaving Cheyenne,* like *Horseman, Pass By,* received some excellent critical reviews following its publication. It stands as evidence of McMurtry's continuing artistic development and, despite a slight tendency towards looseness of structure, compares favorably with the earlier work. On the surface its characters are less sentimentalized, since they are never quite so lyrical about their world or so self-indulgent as the teenager Lonnie Bannon. But beneath that surface toughness the same vision of the ideal cowboy still shines through, particularly in the relationships that exist among the three principals. At this stage of his career, then, despite the realistic tone of *Leaving Cheyenne,* McMurtry still has one eye on myth.

In his next novel, however, he turns his attention from the cowboy, mythic or real, to examine the sordid contemporary world which has grown out of the dust of the past. Here the open range gives way to the ugliness of oil derricks; and Thalia (named for the muse of pastoral poetry) becomes a Western version of Smalltown, U.S.A., that Madison Avenue invention with its shabby pretensions and its stultifying provincialism.

Of course, if one takes a narrow view of the term "novel," *The Last Picture Show* is not a novel so much as a satire which occasionally exhibits the essential properties of a novel—that is, an interest in the creation of credible characters and a concern for portraying human relationships as they actually exist. It is not condescending to suggest that this book is more a satire than a novel in the way that Walter Allen, for example, was condescending to Swift when he wrote in *The English Novel* (p. 30) that the author of *Gulliver's Travels* "could never have been a novelist," since satire "can only be a part of the novelist's make-up." Given the choice of being Allen's "archetypal novelist" (Daniel Defoe) or a mere satirist like Jonathan Swift, most writers would rather be Swift; but Allen's view of the novel as primarily concerned with character is highly relevant to a discussion of *The Last Picture Show.*

One suspects that in writing this book the author came to some abstract conclusions about the nature of small towns in Texas and American society in general, then set about to put these abstractions into a fictional framework that would dramatize their truth to the reader. For most of the characters in the book are one-dimensional and stylized, their humanity sacrificed to the ruthless demands of the author's sociological categories. There are significant exceptions to such a generalization, but relatively few in number.

In this respect the book resembles a good deal of eighteenth-century fiction and, more recently, the works of Sinclair Lewis, who, forty years earlier, did for the Midwest what McMurtry does in the 1960's for his native state. Indeed, the Thalia of this book resembles Lewis' small towns in a number of significant respects. First, of course, there is the hypocrisy of the community, its pretense to a respectability that is only a veneer hiding its basic materialism and sensuality. Second, there is a social hierarchy, rigid in its structure and based on nothing more than new wealth. And third, there is religion, which plays an important role in the community, not only serving the vicious status quo when occasion demands, but also retarding the intellect and blighting the natural joy of living. The picture is a familiar one to readers of American fiction over the past four decades, and such familiarity breeds contempt for the stereotype unless it is given new meaning by technical innovation or by a unique setting.

As for technical innovation, McMurtry adopts a point of view new to him but commonly used by fictional satirists. Forsaking the first person narrator used in the earlier novels, he chooses to tell the story from an omniscient viewpoint. This narrator does not, like Thackeray in *Vanity Fair,* announce his presence with the use of the pronoun "I"; but the force of his personality—sardonic, world-weary, and at times moralistic—is felt through the tone of the narrative as he constantly interjects his own ironic commentary after dramatically rendering a scene. One example should suffice to illustrate:

> . . . Coach Popper taught civics—if what he did could be called teaching—and he could not have cared less what went on.
>
> Not only was the coach the dumbest teacher in school, he was also the laziest. Three days out of four he would go to sleep in class while he was trying to figure out some paragraph in the textbook. He didn't even know the Pledge of Allegiance, and some of the kids at least knew that (pp. 37–38).

Thus, the "controlling intelligence" which orders and interprets the events is that of someone outside the action, someone contemptuous of Popper who still knows the inadequacies which the coach hides from all other characters and perhaps from himself as well. Though this narrator focuses on Sonny Crawford, an adolescent boy, through most of the action, at times he is too restricted by this limitation and skips from character to character, revealing what the reader needs to know and at times how he is to feel.

But the passage quoted above reveals more about McMurtry's technique than just his point of view. It also exemplifies the tendency towards caricature which is another important characteristic of Lewis' social satire. Herman Popper here, as elsewhere, is a deliberately overdrawn character, a monster whose exaggerated personality traits combine to form not a credible human being but the fictional embodiment of an abstraction, the prototypal Football Coach as viewed by a decidedly jaundiced eye.

Never once in the entire course of the narrative does Popper step out of the rigid role McMurtry has cast for him and assert a humanity of his own. From start to finish he is the blustering, ludicrous villain of numerous painful incidents, a mere puppet in the hands of his creator and often an excruciatingly funny figure. That he is not always as funny as he ought to be is perhaps the result of the author's heavy-handed irony in several crucial scenes. In this respect McMurtry once again resembles Sinclair Lewis, whose contempt for his creation George Babbitt occasionally shifted to his readers as well and manifested itself in a tendency to oversimplify lest some poor Babbitt-like fool miss the true purpose of the narrative. So, at times, does McMurtry seem worried that his sports-mad readership might tend to regard Coach Popper with less than the full measure of scorn he deserves.

Another technical characteristic of the typical fictional satire is its lack of any definite plot line. Instead of a carefully structured central action, there are episodes or vignettes which are designed to illustrate the abstract thesis the author wishes to promote. Here situations serve in lieu of linear plot development in order to allow the characters occasion to reveal what ideas, virtues, or vices they stand for. But these situations do not form a continuous line of action, nor do they provide for the gradual expansion of a central theme. The total picture, then, is created like an Impressionist painting, with a group of discrete incidents dotting in the larger image.

The Last Picture Show is assembled by just such a method (as are many realistic novels), and consequently plot analysis in the usual sense is of little value in understanding the work. What central action there is happens to the focal character, Sonny Crawford, and is composed primarily of sexual encounters, satisfactory and unsatisfactory. But here there is only a thread of thematic development in Sonny's changing attitude toward Ruth (the coach's wife and Sonny's most wholesome bed-partner) and not enough to give meaning to the other hunks of action and the discursive passages. Thus, the structure of the satire is predictably fragmented like most others of its type.

McMurtry's technique, then, is hardly innovative. The setting is the primary device which gives the narrative whatever freshness and vitality it possesses. Here the author's knowledge of his subject matter, his own region, comes to his aid. For Thalia is not by any means the Middlewest of Sinclair Lewis or the South of Erskine Caldwell; it has a flavor all its own which McMurtry is able to capture in his descriptive passages and in the speech of his native characters. In this respect, the book is no mere imitation of other, older models, but has some unique value, however limited, of its own.

In a work with plot and technique of little essential interest, characters are all the more important, since it is in characterization that the reader can most readily find a key to the ultimate meaning of the action. And in the creation of his characters McMurtry often proves a pure novelist in spite of himself, for a few of his principals have a complexity which makes them more than the mere stereotype that Coach Popper is. Sonny Crawford is the best example, and in him the reader can once again see the trial of an adolescent trying to achieve manhood, this time in a corrupt adult society which fails to provide a proper means of initiating him into its company. Thus, in some respects Sonny is like Lonnie of *Horseman, Pass By,* and in other respects like Tom Jones, Pip in *Great Expectations,* Huck Finn, and Holden Caulfield in *The Catcher in the Rye.* Indeed, Sonny and his

friends in Thalia are closer in type to the latter group than to the
young people in McMurtry's other novels, since in *The Last Picture
Show* the total immorality of the adult society is emphasized by way of
contrast with the vital innocence of the youths, whereas in the author's earlier works the complete degeneration of the society had not
yet been realized.

Sonny, for example, not only lacks good counsel in his adolescent
years but the bare essentials of life as well. His father, a widower and
drug addict, can neither provide him with a home nor pay for his room
and board elsewhere. Thus, Sonny lives with his friend Duane (set
adrift by a working mother) in a cheap rooming house. And the other
young people in Thalia are really no better off than Sonny and Duane,
the presence of parents in the household notwithstanding. Jacy, the
meretricious daughter of a successful oilman, is pushed towards
promiscuity by her amoral mother, who has no more regard for her
daughter's virtue than she has for her own. Billy, a benign idiot reminiscent of Faulkner's Benjy, has been deserted by an itinerant father
and now lives in the pool hall, where he earns his keep by dreamily
sweeping the floors. Even Joe Bob Blanton, son of the Methodist
preacher, is driven and harangued by his ignorant, self-righteous father, whose puritan spirit holds no room for understanding or love.

These young people, abandoned by their parents and by the community, must work out their own destinies with only the help of such
sympathetic adults as Sam the Lion—owner of the pool hall, cafe, and
movie house—who is a father substitute for all homeless boys, including Sonny, Duane, and Billy. The mother surrogate is Genevieve, a
cafe waitress who watches over the boys' diets when she can and
listens to their troubles with a woman's sympathy and tenderness.
These two provide the norm against which the rest of the adult community is measured and found wanting.

But despite the credibility of Sonny, Duane, and Ruth Popper, the
characterizations are largely given to stereotypes. Jacy, for example,
is the Spoiled Rich Girl. Brother Blanton, Joe Bob's father, is the
Fundamentalist Preacher. Genevieve is the Good-hearted Working
Girl. Billy is the Sublime Idiot. And an examination of these stereotypes reveals in an instant the socio-moral generalizations which they
illustrate. It is not difficult to tell the Good Guys from the Bad Guys.
The Good Guys are all people with little money and less social status.
The Bad Guys are rich and influential, the town's elite. Coach Popper
would seem to be an exception to this generalization, as would, perhaps, Brother Blanton, since neither could be counted among the
country club set; but in a different way each is a part of the establish-

ment, reverence for athletics and religion being a cornerstone of every Babbitt's creed.

In *The Last Picture Show,* then, a new element has entered McMurtry's fiction—a concern with such issues as class struggle and social injustice. But the story of Sonny's initiation is blurred by the presence of these additional factors rather than complemented and enriched by them. For example, McMurtry is so eager to move on to other matters that he finesses what could have been the most vital scene in the book—that of Sonny's reaction to the death of Sam the Lion, who has been the boy's one dependable link with the adult world. On returning from a trip to Mexico, Sonny and Duane discover that their friend has died, and there the chapter ends. The next chapter begins with a brief description of the funeral and Sonny's even briefer conversation with Genevieve. Then the seniors are off on their class trip, and the focus switches to Duane and Jacy in order to record the further depravities of the Pampered Princess. Judging the work as a full-blown novel, one would have to conclude that the failure to dramatize the trauma of such an important event is inexcusable, like Thackeray's closing the door on the reader just as Becky Sharp's lover, Sir Pitt Crawley, discovers that the lady has eloped with his son.

Another element which distinguishes this novel from *Horseman, Pass By* and *Leaving Cheyenne* is its extraordinary number of scatological passages. The pages abound with sexual adventures of all sorts, many of them grotesque or perverse; and the dialogue, particularly among the youngsters, is laden with obscenities. Most of the time this material is artistically justified simply by the age of Sonny and his friends. Seventeen-year-olds, after all, are preoccupied with sex and spend much of their time either talking about such matters or actually experimenting. And the language they use among themselves is seldom euphemistic. Indeed, some of the more humorous passages of the book are those in which sordid perversions are discussed with all of the casual innocence one might expect to find in a conversation about mumblety-peg. Occasionally, like a burlesque comic, McMurtry will go for the cheap laugh by interjecting unnecessary vulgarity; but for the most part, the humor is Rabelaisian and functional.

The creation of satire is the nearest thing in art to an act of the pure intellect, and probably for this reason few writers have completely mastered the genre. Swift was a great satirist, and more recently George Orwell wrote some superb examples of the type. But McMurtry in *The Last Picture Show* never quite decides whether he wants to become a satirical portrayer of the transitory social scene or to remain a novelist in the fullest sense of the word. The tension between these two fictional tendencies might be described as a tension between head and heart, the sophisticated college professor versus the range-bred cowboy, with neither emerging as victor.

WORKS CITED

Allen, Walter. *The English Novel.* New York: Dutton, 1955.
McMurtry, Larry. *In a Narrow Grave: Essays on Texas.* Austin: Encino, 1968.
————. *The Last Picture Show.* New York: Dial, 1966.

Showdown in the New Old West: The Cowboy vs. the Oilman
CLAY REYNOLDS

Along Idiot Ridge, not far from Wichita Falls, deep in the north-central Texas cattle country, lies the mythical hamlet of Thalia—named for the Muse of Comedy, and typical of the modern ranching community, embodying all the attitudes, dreams, and fears of the citizens who live in such towns from the Panhandle to the Texas Hill Country. Two novels by Larry McMurtry focus on the conflict between contradictory visions and the painful choices which two Thalia boys, Lonnie in *Horseman, Pass By,* and Sonny in *The Last Picture Show,* must make between them. These are novels of conflict between changing times, between the romantic visions of the past and the pragmatic demands of the present. Both Lonnie and Sonny represent a future generation, uncertain in its direction and in what values it will embrace, those of the romantic cowboy or those of the rough-hewn and realistic oilman.

The past romantic is revealed through the cowman or horseman, an epic figure who has worked hard and concentrated on his self-image without any real hope of ever achieving anything more from life other than some minor satisfaction of having "lived right." McMurtry enlarges this vision to include the chivalric "Code of the West," of the man who sits "tall in the saddle" and rules over the dominion of the American West. This quixotic hero has a set of rules for life which are hopelessly grounded in romantic ideals and are inherently self-defeating. Yet because he is a horseman, he follows them firmly, almost religiously, dimly realizing, perhaps, that the sweetness of life relies solely upon his having lived by this code. For the romantic horseman, honesty, integrity and stoic acceptance of life's misfortunes are part and parcel of his vision.

Opposed to the horseman is the oilman or modern rancher, a ruthless individual to whom rules are absurd, romantic obstacles. His vision is defined in the most base, materialistic terms: money, land, bigger cars, more of everything. The horseman, to him, is a bothersome antique, out of place in a modern world of profit and exploitation. The oilman wastes no time worrying about the integrity of his vision. Tangible success is the only consequence which concerns him.

The conflict between these two visions involves the teenage heroes of the two novels, and it is broadened to include not only Thalia, the dying cowtown, but also the very country and people who populate it. The symbols of the past blend oddly with the realities of the present. In *Horseman, Pass By,* for example, Lonnie notes the changing times in a world of anachronisms: "After school on the weekdays, riding the long road home through the ranches in the old yellow school bus, I watched the range change,"[1] he remarks. The fact that a youngster rides the "range" in a bus rather than on a horse indicates a conflict between two very different times. In addition to feeling the pressure of the transition from past to present, Lonnie is also torn between his affection for his grandfather, Homer, who offers him a romantic vision of the past, and Hud, his step-uncle, who offers him a pragmatic and brutally realistic vision of the present. Lonnie is in line to inherit all or part of Homer's ranch when the old horseman dies. The choice of whether he will accept along with the land the vision of the past that Homer represents or the vision of the present that Hud represents becomes a prize in a deadly game played out in the novel.

Homer is a romantic holdover from the past. He not only thinks about the past in romantic terms, he attempts to live his life as if nothing has changed. He is a cowman in the truest sense of the word, spending hours recollecting memories of the past, and in those memories, subordinating the reality of the actual experience to a nostalgic romance, fashioning them into a vision which does not recall how things were but how they are remembered. The cattle in his pastures represent a lifetime's struggle, and he reacts to the slaughter of his diseased herd with the fatalism of one who has come to expect such calamity as a normal state of affairs: "There's so much shit in the world a man's gonna get in it sooner or later," he muses philosophically.[2] Homer's conscious recognition of the futility of continuing is made more poignant because of his advanced age; he is too old to overcome this last defeat. An epic horseman, he realizes that he is beaten, and he takes over the killing of his two pet longhorns personally, for they, more than the slaughtered herd of modern short-horned cattle, represent the vision of the past—they are the last symbols of a romantic age.

Lonnie loves and respects Homer, but it is a love mixed with pity for an old man who is living outside his natural time. Though the boy realizes that the romantic past is over, he is impressed with Homer's death-grip on the values of a life which has never been kind to him. The old horseman refuses to accept any part of the present. Although the cattle are gone, the ranch still has potential, as Hud suggests, as a source of oil. Hud argues that such income could rebuild the herd, but Homer knows that he is too old and too often defeated to start over, and he regards Hud's suggestion as a violation of the strict codes by which he has lived: "What can I do with it? With a bunch of fuckin' oil wells?" he rants. "I can't ride out every day an' prowl amongst 'em like I can my cattle. I can't feel a smidgen a pride in 'em, cause they ain't none a my doin'."[3] Homer's love for what he has created, a cattle ranch, goes beyond the money in the bank or fiscal possibilities of merely owning land and not working it. Such an existence has no connection to the vision of life he perceives, and the realization that this is his only alternative proves too much for the wizened cowman. He reverts to a time when Lonnie's father was alive; and finally, after his accident, his memory takes over altogether and he goes completely back to the era when his vision was new, when the game was always played by the rules, when he was Homer Bannon, horseman.

The vision Homer offers Lonnie is not one the youth can easily accept. Homer fills each day with hard work and ends it with a grim satisfaction that there is as much or more to be done tomorrow. But Homer presses Lonnie to be all the things that cowmen must be, to live by this code, however self-defeating it may be; and he strives to show the boy how honesty, hard work and fatalistic acceptance of each day's defeat in its turn makes life worth living. But Homer's vision holds no promise of success, and Lonnie watches the old horseman die with his dreams in a frothy, dusty agony.

In contrast to Homer is Hud, the modern rancher who would be an oilman. The boasting manner, big car, flashy women with which Hud surrounds himself appeal to the adolescent more than the sweat and grime of Homer's ranch work. Hud presents an attractive image to his step-nephew, but his vision is drastically different from Homer's. Hud is marked by a ruthlessness and a sense of the practical which forbids reverie into the romance of the past. He demands the reality of the present. Though he lives on a ranch and imitates the cowman in his dress and manner, Hud lacks the integrity or the stature of an epic horseman. Homer is a cowboy who became a horseman; Hud is a cowboy who wishes to become an oilman. Herein lies the difference in how they perceive their visions. McMurtry points out: "We see Hud on horseback only twice; we think of him in the Cadillac, a machine which has a dual usefulness, just as the gunfighter's gun once had. It is both a symbol of status and a highly useful tool. But Hud is a rancher, not simply a cowboy."[4] In the lingo of the modern range, "rancher" means profiteer, not a man who lovingly works his cattle.

Homer clearly admires his step-son's physical ability, his callous manner, his tough talk, so long as they do not violate the old man's sense of honesty and respect for tradition. Hud offers Homer a flesh and blood image of the horseman's youth, but there the similarity ends. Hud's vision includes quick money, questionable ethics, and a total lack of respect for the past or the "Code of the West" kind of integrity which is the mainstay of Homer's vision.

Lonnie's admiration for Hud is tempered by disapproval of Hud's actions against Homer or Halmea, the cook. He does not totally disapprove of Hud, however; and he takes strong exception to Homer's constant comparisons of his step-son to his dead son, Lonnie's father. But occasionally Hud goes too far. When he rapes Halmea, for example, Lonnie stands in petrified horror. Although the boy holds a rifle on Hud, he is helpless to stop the crime even though Halmea has become a surrogate mother for him. He is overcome by Hud's playing out of fantasies the boy has cherished, and he is mesmerized by Hud's total disregard for any rules or codes of behavior. Lonnie also condemns Hud's disrespect for Homer, but he admires Hud's ability to avoid hard work, to go into town and pick up good times and beautiful women, to have an answer to any question or solution to any problem. Again Hud acts out Lonnie's fantasies with no thought of obeying any romanticized list of rules of conduct.

Lonnie's confusion and reluctance to make a decision as to which vision he will accept causes him to be torn apart by both of them. He longs to accept Homer's romance; but in a physical attempt to do so, by taking a predawn ride on Stranger, the old man's mount, he is thrown, as if to symbolize the impossibility of capturing the past. He could play *at* being a horseman, but he could not relive the romance as Homer envisions it. And when the rodeo comes to town, Lonnie sees that Homer's vision is as doomed as his cattle; it belongs to the past, and when it attempts to manifest itself in the present, it is as phony as the spangled shirts of the people who leave their beer-can debris along the streets of Thalia. The men and women who follow the rodeo do not even make good attempts at play *at* the past romantic. Divorced from the land, they are the "shit-kickers," "goat-ropers" and "drug-store cowboys" who have no conception of the past; they represent only a sham of Homer's vision.

Pressured to accept both visions, Lonnie finds that he cannot fully embrace either. Homer's hope of victory is dead, and Hud acknowledges no rules, no discernible values that the boy can see. He climbs atop the windmill to escape the perplexing struggle that goes on within him; but even here, perched on a symbol out of Homer's past, he is reminded of the present by the airport lights from Wichita Falls.

Whatever doubts Lonnie has about accepting Hud's vision are excised when his step-uncle shoots the injured old cowman. This action reveals Hud's basest nature. Now the step-son rancher has control of Homer's land, and nothing Lonnie can do will stop him—nothing, perhaps, except the acceptance of Homer's vision and the futile role of the cowman.

Sitting through Homer's funeral, Lonnie envisions the old equestrian form as he rode Stranger out before dawn each day to work the cattle. Passing by the window where Lonnie slept, Homer became greater than a cowman, he became the embodiment of the epic horseman who belonged to a time which was already a part of history. The vision is forgotten, however; the game is over. The mourners in the church had known a man named Homer Bannon, but they did not know what he had stood for, and they had not understood how he lived. Understanding that Homer's vision is dead and that it must be buried with him, Lonnie realizes that cruelty, greed, or even a genuine *credo* of the present is too strong for him to fight, armed only with a set of romantic values which belong to old men and memories.

Lonnie flees Thalia, leaving Hud and his land behind him. He chooses to follow neither vision, but he searches for time to think out some alternatives, to hunt for other sets of rules which will effectively save some part of Homer's vision. McMurtry's first novel, therefore, ends on a note of uncertainty as to which vision will ultimately triumph. The only certain thing is that the horseman has passed by for Lonnie and the Texas cattle country, and the vision which is left holds no attraction for any who care about the legacy of the cowman.

In *The Last Picture Show* Sonny also seeks to escape. In fact, playing the "game of escape" becomes a motivating factor in the novel's plot. Sonny's classmates have come to realize that whatever romance the land and its history once offered is dead, and they search for other visions to challenge their imaginations. For some the picture show itself offers a romantic escape from the shoddy reality of Thalia, for its silver screen becomes a window through which dreams can be seen in lands far away from the small town. For others, however, sexual fantasy becomes an escape; and although it frequently has disastrous consequences for its players, few are deterred from engaging in escapades of perversity and titillating excitement. But for Sonny, who indulges in both these escape-games, neither exercise provides satisfaction. With a dope-addict for a father, an idiot for a companion, and a wornout frycook for a confidante, Sonny searches for a vision with values and with some sense of direction.

To Sonny, Sam the Lion represents the romantic past. Though no longer a horseman, Sam embodies all the qualities of the epic figure and plays his game by rules of honesty and compassion. The same qualities are represented by Homer. For both men's personal visions are formed from the experience of having *lived* life, made mistakes, and learned the right of things. Such a code of ethics forces a man like Homer to refuse to sell his diseased herd to an unsuspecting buyer, and such a code makes Sam the Lion the defender and protector of the boys of Thalia. Everyone in town respects Sam: even those who antagonize him by teasing his retarded ward, Billy, look upon him as a wizened man who lives his life according to a sense of integrity.

When Sam reveals his midnight swim adventures to Sonny, the boy is shocked, but he understands Sam's struggle with time to keep from growing old: "'Goddammit! Goddammit!' he cursed. 'I don't want to be old. It don't fit me!'"[5] Like Homer, Sam realizes that the past is quickly slipping away from him, and he cannot relive the romance of his youth. Sonny realizes that Sam knows how to live life, that his vision, however romantic, has value; but he also knows that Sam is obsessed with dreams of an age which is gone forever. Reluctant to play a role such as Sam's, Sonny casts about for another vision which will require less of him, less experience in life, less adherence to a conflicting and impossible code; he doubts that he can live with a vision which leads to Sam's sense of honorable resignation.

Drillers from the oil fields such as Abilene pose an alternative vision for Sonny. Like Hud, Abilene drives a big car—only it is a Mercury rather than a Cadillac—and he uses a pool cue with the deftness of a gunslinger in a "B" western. Abilene has no conscious sense of codes or visions, but he assumes that he will be rich someday; and to this type of man, having money equates with living successfully. Abilene's swaggering, brawling self-assurance is more attractive to Sonny than Sam's gruff, stoic virtue. The range of the past is gone; the fences are up, and oilmen like Abilene have announced a new era wherein there are no codes, no discernible ethics at all except that the biggest and strongest take the most. Men like Abilene are the best fighters, handsomest lovers, and biggest drinkers of the former cow-town; and again Sonny balks rather than accept a vision which requires that he become something he is not.

Neither of these alternatives appeals to Sonny, in part because they require that he become strong in some way—either in character and acceptance of self-defeating codes, or in physical ability and careless regard for any sense of ethics. He refuses to make a decision at once and seeks again to escape, this time on a "binge" trip to Mexico. Even as he and Duane depart, however, they are reminded by Sam that such trips south of the border were part of the old man's youth as well; they go with his blessing. When they return, however, they find that Thalia and the decision are still there, but now Sam has died and willed Sonny the pool hall and his role as a visionary of the romantic past.

Still Sonny demurs. He seeks a final escape by marrying Jacy Farrow, who senses in the scandalous fight between Sonny and her former boyfriend, Duane—a fight in which Duane blinds his former friend with a broken beer bottle—a chance to play a game of her own. Jacy, like her mother Lois, works at building a romantic and sexy image of herself. She promotes her own legend through well-publicized escapades with her high school sweetheart, Duane, and eventually with a faster group from Wichita Falls. Ultimately she seeks to cap her career by sleeping with Abilene, who is Lois' lover as well, on a snooker table in Sam's pool hall; but this bid for notoriety is unsatisfactory, first of all because Abilene is completely unmoved by the experience and second because he shows no inclination to tell anyone about it: "If the story had got out that she had slept with Abilene on a snooker table," she thinks, "she would have been a legend in Thalia forever, but she couldn't think of any way to publicize it. Neither Abilene nor her mother were going to, that was for sure. So the whole thing was just wasted. It was disgusting."[6]

Jacy is undaunted, however; and she senses another opportunity in the frustrated Sonny, now ridiculously bandaged in one eye after his fight with Duane. Convincing him to elope with her, she leaves a note for her father, announcing that they will honeymoon in Oklahoma, hence allowing the elder Farrow to locate the couple before they can consummate their wedding vows. Even this opportunity for escape appears to be another dead end for Sonny, although Jacy sees it as a social triumph. Lois, however, changes Sonny's failure into another step toward his acceptance of Sam's vision by realizing his frustration and confusion after her husband has carried Jacy back to Texas and left the crestfallen boy alone in Oklahoma with no car and no money.

Offering him a ride back to Thalia, she seduces him, thereby at once fulfilling Sonny's fantasies about Jacy and at the same time offering him another parallel to Sam's youth; for she reveals to Sonny that she had been the unnamed partner with Sam in the midnight swims of the past.

By willing Sonny the pool hall and responsibility for the idiot Billy, Sam chose Sonny as the person to accept the vision of the past. Recognizing Sonny's feeling of inadequacy to play the role well, Sam condoned his foolish trip to Mexico and his other boyhood experiences, understanding that they all would combine to give Sonny the background he needed to carry on in the old Lion's footsteps. But in no way is Sam's understanding of Sonny's situation better defined than when the old man condones the youngster's affair with the coach's wife, Ruth Popper.

Like most people in Thalia, Ruth also seeks escape. Just as Sam seeks his lost youth and Abilene seeks wealth, Ruth seeks to recover some of the vitality of her younger days by a secret tryst with Sonny; and through such an affair, the boy gains the kind of experience upon which Sam built his own reputation. Recognizing that even though the affair is adulterous, both Sonny and Ruth need each other, Sam blesses the liaison in his own gruff way: "You might stay with her and get some good out of her while you're growing up," he counsels. "Somebody ought to get some good out of Ruth."[7] And it is to Ruth that Sonny returns after Jacy has thrown him over, after Lois has seduced him, and after the idiot Billy has died, blinded in both eyes by bandages he donned in imitation of his idol Sonny, Sam's heir.

Just as Homer's death shocks Lonnie into a decision, Billy's tragic accident brings Sonny into a sense of awareness. His indecision and reluctance to accept Sam's legacy causes his attention to wane, and it is this blindness, not that brought on by the bandages, which kills Billy. Sonny realizes that he never really had any choice at all. To become an oilman like Abilene would mean burying everything Sam stood for in the past and adopting a lonely vision concentrating on a materialistic set of values. He must learn to live life by the code Sam lived by; Abilene's alternative fades completely out of the picture. Loose and hard are the qualities of the men who hold the pragmatic vision of the present, but they lack a concept of moral values, a sense of ethics. They are also lonely. Though Sam never achieved anything of a tangible nature, he was never without the respect and love of those who knew him.

In these two novels Larry McMurtry illustrates a conflict of two modern Texans, the cowman or horseman, visionary of the past, and the rancher or oilman, visionary of the present. He pits them against each other in what becomes a life and death struggle for supremacy of vision. The protagonists of these novels, youngsters who will form the future of the Texas cattle country, find both visions unappealing; however, they are unable to come up with alternative visions, alternative codes which will permit them to create a set of values of their own. As they painfully try to reconcile the ideals of the past with the pragmatism of the present, they discover that neither vision is adequate to the needs of a modern world filled with ancient symbols and ruthless men. While Lonnie turns his back on Thalia, Sonny remains, precariously posed as a player in a futile game with no hope of victory. Yet both boys have learned that winning is less important than the play of the game itself, and that victory without ideals, romantic or otherwise, is hollow.

NOTES

1. Larry McMurtry, *Horseman, Pass By* (New York: Harper and Row, 1961), p. 5.
2. Ibid., p. 104.
3. Ibid., p. 88.
4. Larry McMurtry, *In a Narrow Grave: Essays on Texas* (New York: Simon and Schuster, 1968), p. 25.
5. Larry McMurtry, *The Last Picture Show* (New York: Dell Publishers, 1966), p. 123.
6. Ibid., p. 176.
7. Ibid., p. 125.

The Death of the Frontier in the Novels of Larry McMurtry

CHRISTOPHER BAKER

I would like to begin with four items of historical interest. Item: Between 1870 and 1885 in five of the most important cattle towns in Kansas there was an average of only 1.5 homicide "per cattle trading season." Contemporary newspapers record "no evidence that there was ever a shoot-out on main street at high noon" in either Abilene, Dodge City, Ellsworth, Wichita, or Caldwell.[1] Item: In 1858 an Austin newspaper stated that it was a "common thing here to see boys from 10 to 14 years of age carrying about their persons Bowie knives and pistols. By the time he was eighteen, John Wesley Hardin had killed twenty-five men and was said to "handle a pistol faster than a frog can lick flies."[2] Item: Interviews with persons who helped settle the Oklahoma Territory in the 1880's and 1890's recall that a dominant feature of their lives then was "the wretched loneliness and almost total lack of excitement in their lives."[3] Item: "Leadville, Colorado, one of the last 'Wild West' towns, in 1879, in addition to its 110 saloons, boasted four daily newspapers, five churches, three schools and a branch of the YMCA."[4] What these items all have in common is that each describes an aspect of the American frontier: peaceful yet violent, lonely but bustling. Together, they illustrate the paradoxical character of this much-debated element of American social growth. And the paradox continues: the Census Bureau declared in 1890 that the frontier had closed, yet the direct impact of that era has only recently begun to die out, amalgamated into lesser importance by admixture with other social and historical factors.

The novels of Larry McMurtry, who has been called the finest regional novelist Texas has produced,[5] have as a major theme the death of the frontier and its values and the impact of this death on the lives of contemporary Texans. His novels, in their dispassionate and acerbic picture of a modern urban Texas, in their lament of a lost age of strong values rooted in a life on the land, and in their contrast between the proud but outmoded ranchers and the prosperous but anxiety-ridden urbanites, all document the loss of certain frontier attitudes first outlined by historian Frederick Jackson Turner some forty years before McMurtry was born in 1936 in Wichita Falls, Texas. His first three novels, *Horseman, Pass By* (adapted for the movie *Hud* in 1963), *Leaving Cheyenne,* and *The Last Picture Show,* are all set in the prairie towns of West Texas. His last three novels leave the plains behind as he studies life in contemporary Houston and other Texas cities: *Moving On, All My Friends Are Going to Be Strangers,* and *Terms of Endearment.* McMurtry is probably the best contemporary chronicler of what has been called the "major social problem" of the Southwest, the "imperfect transition from a rural to an urban society."[6] His novels reveal not so much the death of frontier behavior, as the death of what might be called the frontier attitude—a set of expectations which defined that behavior. The underlying mood of optimism which contributed to the settling of the "free land" to the West of the Eastern seaboard during the nineteenth century counterbalanced, if it did not lessen, the frequent loneliness, isolation and nomadic existence of many of the early settlers, who also benefited from generally close-knit families and mining and cattle cooperatives. The closing of the frontier, however, brought with it the end of this

mood of popular expectation. This social disorientation in the wake of
the frontier's death is a strong contributing factor to the random
violence, personal alienation, and wandering life-style which marks so
many of McMurtry's characters. This theme could be profitably
traced through both trilogies, but I shall here focus only on *The Last
Picture Show* and *All My Friends Are Going to Be Strangers.*

Like McMurtry, Frederick Jackson Turner was raised in a region
having immediate ties to the frontier. As he grew up in the 1860's in
Portage, Wisconsin, a firsthand knowledge of the wilderness helped
impress upon him the importance of the land, and a migration into it,
as a significant social factor in American life. John Stuart Mill, Karl
Marx, Josiah Strong, and James Bryce also noted the effect of a
diminishing supply of land upon "man's social evolution,"[7] and they
were only a few of many influences which ultimately led to Turner's
paper on "The Significance of the Frontier in American History," first
read in 1893. His basic thesis is by now familiar. The westward migration of settlers, beginning in the mid-eighteenth century, introduced
the "disintegrating forces of civilization" into the wilderness as trappers, traders, and adventurers subdued both land and Indians. This
process placed a premium on individual effort. "The frontier is productive of individualism," wrote Turner. "Complex society is precipi-
tated by the wilderness into a kind of primitive organization based on
the family. The tendency is anti-social. It produces antipathy to control and particularly to any direct control."[8] Following the Italian
economist Achille Loria, Turner also seized upon the concept of available free land as a spawning ground for other related features of
American political and social behavior. While acknowledging that the
frontier experience had its negative points. Turner sees it as one
source for a host of features basic to the American "intellect": "That
coarseness and strength combined with acuteness and inquisitiveness;
that practical, inventive turn of mind, quick to find expedients; that
masterful grasp of material things, lacking in the artistic but powerful
to effect great ends; that restless, nervous energy; that dominant individualism, working for good and evil, and withal that bouyancy and
exuberance which comes with freedom."[9]

Billington suggests that Turner's concept of the frontier can be
usefully understood as both *place* (a geographical location having a
low man-land ratio) and as *process* (the act and opportunity for
self-advancement made possible by the low ratio). Men and women
moved westward driven by both a "deficiency motivation" (the desire
to escape negative social factors) and an "abundancy motivation"
(the seeking of positive factors).[10] Though the actual presence of a

"safety-valve" of available jobs and wages for Easterners once they reached the frontier is debatable, a "socio-psychological" safety-valve seems to have been at work: the settlers headed west prompted by what they hoped they would find or could create.

One reason for the paradoxical nature of the items noted earlier was the presence of at least three categories of westward travellers. The trappers, explorers, and backwoodsmen were the first to reach a frontier place and valued its freedom at the price of extreme physical isolation. The small-propertied farmers cultivated the land first infiltrated by the backwoodsmen and created a market for the services of the townspeople, whose social organizations were often as conformist as the backwoodsmen were iconoclastic. The mood within the towns was defined more by a desire for upward mobility and the accumulation of wealth, both of which helped engender conformity. Kit Carson would not have felt at home in a little house on the prairie, but both were part of the frontier ethos.

Indeed, the mountain men and trappers, even if not outlaws, scorned the more civilized towns and ranches in favor of a wandering life and were, as a contemporary traveller noted, "never satisfied if there [were] any white man between them and sundown."[11] Billington feels they were victims of *anomie*, "a state of mind in which the individual's sense of social cohesion is weakened or broken, and [which] arises when he leaves a familiar environment with a corresponding disruption of connection, social status and economic security." From the deep sense of hostility thus fostered sprang arrogance, aggression, and indolence.[12] The small ranchers were able to curb these traits somewhat by their greater acceptance of responsibility, their sense of belonging to a social group, and their need to take part in a money economy, among other reasons. Each, however, displays qualities of the character type which Georg Simmel has called "the stranger." Each is a potential wanderer, each is a newcomer to an environment of which he was not an original member, and each is not radically committed to the "unique ingredients and peculiar tendencies" of the dominant group (the townspeople).[13] It is not surprising to recall that one of the most clichéd lines in Western films has been "Howdy, stranger," or that McMurtry would entitle one of his books *All My Friends Are Going to Be Strangers.*

Such negative characteristics were outweighed by the more affirmative qualities of the frontier attitude, the values which made for "abundancy motivation." Travellers from Europe and the East noted that the frontiersmen (and they were primarily men, in both numbers and significance) exhibited great self-confidence, a desire for self-improvement, a dislike of artificiality or lying ("a man's word is his bond"), strong support of democracy and nationalism, "manliness in respect to women," practicality, materialism, restlessness, and "aggressive optimism."[14] These features found expression in all three categories of settlers; and even in the towns, which were built upon hard work, cooperation (and a sense of community) was often so strong that it was "almost stultifying in its parochialism."[15]

McMurtry's novels record the dilemmas of those who must live in the moral and emotional vacuum left after the death of this age of exuberance. What had been a transition into the "free land" has now become a transition into a "controlled land" society. In the first trilogy, the older men who see Texas, as does McMurtry, as a "lost frontier,"[16] are the only ones who remember the ideals of the open plains, but are powerless to live by them. As Turner wrote, "inherited ideals persist long after environment has changed,"[17] and McMurtry agrees when he says "the cowboy's temperament has not changed much since the nineteenth century; it is his world that has changed, and the change has been a steady shrinkage. There are no more trail herds, no more wide open cattle towns, no longer that vast stretch of unfenced land between Laredo and Calgary. . . . The effect of this has been to diminish the cowboy's sense of isolation, his sense of himself as a man alone. . . . he is being drawn toward the confusions of the urban or suburban neighborhood" (*ING*, 26).

In *The Last Picture Show*, Sam the Lion (no one knew how he got his nickname) is the owner of the pool hall and picture show in the town of Thalia, and is its last remnant of the frontier cowboy culture of the plains. A rancher and later rodeo rider whose three sons died before they reached eighteen, he now looks after the idiot Billy and is a father-figure to Duane and Sonny, two adolescents who frequent the pool hall. Sentimental, he reminisces with Sonny as the two of them sit near a watering tank, remarking "I used to own this land, you know. It's been right at fifty years since I watered a horse at this tank."[18] It was also the place where he courted women: isolated, uninhibited, romantic. Sam embodies the silent aloofness of the frontier rancher whose isolation conveys a sense of gravity and deeply held values, unlike the drifting solitude of the backwoodsmen. He "personifies the quiet masculine dignity, honesty and strength of the cowboy archetype—a vestigial remnant of the old West of the ranges amid the drab town of the new West whose boys define their masculinity through high school athletics, zoophilia and group sex."[19] To Sonny he "was the man who took care of things . . . and Sonny did not like to think that he might die" (*LPS*, 4). For these reasons Sam is far less

lonely—though alone—than the rest of Thalia's citizens. He contrasts
sharply with Herman Popper, a crude, abusive, latent homosexual who
is also the high school coach. Unlike Sam, who laments the loss of
what he was, Popper longs for what he never will be: namely, the kind
of man he sees on *Gunsmoke* each week.

The rest of the town exhibits other features of frontier behavior,
but without the corresponding frontier attitudes of optimism and self-
reliance. The loneliness of the women in this novel stems from their
emotional isolation, not a physical solitude. Popper's wife Ruth is
desperately driven into Sonny's arms in an attempt to cope with her
emptiness. Herman has ignored the tumor in her breast and complains
about the cost of her prescriptions with the false bravado of a masculinity he lacks. "I could have bought a new deer rifle with what she's
spent on pills just this last year, and I wish I had by God. A good gun
beats a woman any day" (*LPS,* 60). "The pioneer women had to cope
with deprivation and hardship," but the post-frontier woman of the
twenties and thirties, in McMurtry's opinion, found it even harder to
cope with more modern concepts of womanhood which stressed sexual
equality.[20] The men, intimidated by this unique assertiveness, retreated from the responsibilities it brought, producing a loneliness far
different from that dictated by a division of labor for the sake of
survival on the open plains. As Ruth Popper tells Sonny, "the reason
I'm so crazy is that nobody cares anything about me" (*LPS,* 58).

The town itself shares the dulling sameness which marked many
frontier towns, but again it is a product not of the move into new territory, but of the death of that sense of newness. "There ain't no sure-
nuff rich people in this town now," says Sam. "I doubt there'll ever be
any more. The oil fields are about to dry up and the cattle business
looks like it's going to peter out" (*LPS,* 62–63). Lois Farrow, the rich
wife of a boorish oilman, feels bored: "Everything's flat and empty and
there's nothing to do but spend money." In some of the most unselfish
words she ever speaks, she warns her spoiled daughter Jacy of what life
in Thalia means. "The only really important thing I came in to tell you
was that life is very monotonous. Things happen the same way over and
over again. I think it's more monotonous in this part of the country than
it is in other places, but I don't really know that—it may be monotonous
everywhere. I'm sick of it myself" (*LPS,* 49).

Duane and Sonny must cope with this stultifying dullness as they
emerge into manhood. Each is essentially an orphan; their only remaining parents have neglected them and they lack any adult model
except for Sam. Their desire to escape Thalia is not only an expression
of adolescent restlessness, but reveals the desire to seek new and

better frontiers of their own; only one of them manages to break away. They drive to the valley for a few days of liquor and sex south of the border, and to Ft. Worth for a taste of the big city. "'We got to go *somewhere*,' Sonny said." Ft. Worth "was part of the big world, and he always came back from a trip there with the satisfying sense that he had traveled" (*LPS*, 67). Duane decides there's no future in Thalia. "'There's not a goddamn thing to stay for,' he says. 'I'm going to Midland'" (*LPS*, 200). But he soon returns, disgusted with the Odessa desert, and finally enlists in the Army, bound for Korea. For Sonny, the pull of the familiar, even though depressing, is too strong to escape. His marriage to Jacy is annulled by her mother before they reach their honeymoon destination. Sam has died, and the innocent Billy is run down by a cattle truck; but Sonny cannot leave the town. Driving to work one afternoon, he stops his pickup outside the city limits, and seems threatened by what lies beyond. "The gray pastures and the distant brown ridges looked too empty. He himself felt too empty. . . . From the road the town looked raw, scraped by the wind, as empty as the country. It didn't look like the town it had been in high school, in the days of Sam the Lion" (*LPS*, 277). He returns to Ruth Popper and their reunion only deepens their private loneliness. The *anomie* Sonny feels at the end of the novel, his longing, his sense of dislocation, is not the result of his distance from a culture with whose values he strongly disagreed, as was the case with the backwoodsmen. He feels unable to leave a place which now has no values at all, and there is nothing beckoning him away from Thalia. "As empty as he felt and as empty as the country looked it was too risky going out into it—he might be blown around for days like a broomweed in the wind" (*LPS*, 277). The land still holds him, but neither he nor it is in any sense "free."

Though the inhabitants of Thalia live within the *place* of the frontier, its prosperity has long since gone and they have ceased to benefit from the invigorating frontier *process*. The characters in *All My Friends Are Going to Be Strangers* are even further removed from the frontier ethos, living their lives in Houston, Los Angeles, and New York, a fact which mirrors McMurtry's contention that "the Metropolis swallowed the Frontier like a small snake swallows a large frog: slowly, not without strain, but inexorably. And if something of the Frontier remains alive in the innards of the Metropolis, it is because the process of digestion has only just begun" (*ING*, 44). Danny Deck, the novel's hero and in places an alter-ego of McMurtry himself, has just had his first novel published, has married Sally after knowing her a week, and leaves Rice University for San Francisco. The novel revolves around Danny's aimless travels, his various sexual adventures and disintegrating marriage, and leads finally to an ambiguous ending as he wades into the Rio Grande River near Roma, drowning the manuscript of his new novel as he heads for the lights of Mexico.

Danny lacks practically all of the positive attitudes which Turner felt the frontier had bequeathed to the American individual. He is bewildered rather than optimistic, diffident rather than self-confident, expedient rather than principled, and artistic without being practical. His decision to leave Houston is clearly "deficiency-motivated." "Suddenly I didn't fit it any more," he says. "All the furniture of my life had been changed around. Sally was there, the apartment was too small, I couldn't see much of the Hortons, I had sold my novel, I didn't want to study anymore, Jenny wanted me, Godwin was around—it was all too much. Without wanting it to happen, I had let myself be dislodged. Dislodged was exactly how I felt."[21] There is no hint of a distant goal in his leaving, even though he is living out the frontier *wanderlust;* and as he leaves, he senses a loss of the one thing which really defines him—Texas itself and his ancestry there. As he drove into New Mexico, he could feel the authority of the land. "It was all behind me, north to south, not lying there exactly, but more like looming there over the car, not a state or a stretch of land, but some giant, some genie, some god, towering over the road. . . . Texas let me go, ominously quiet. It hadn't gone away" (*AMF,* 67).

Though an urbanite himself, Danny is viewed as a son of the pioneers by the city-dwellers. His wife is scandalized to discover he has shot a squirrel with his .22 and is cooking it for supper, but he is proud of his "perfect" shot, hitting a moving animal eighty-five feet off the ground with the sun in his eyes. At a cocktail party an English biologist tells him "if you propose to walk among us as an equal you must begin to cultivate one or two more of the more basic of the civilized graces." Godwin, the lecherous literature professor, mockingly defends him, saying "The boy's a frontier genius, don't you know? The fact that he farts in public is part of his appeal" (*AMF,* 41).

Danny is no hayseed, but his deep affinity for the lost life of the frontier is most clearly revealed in his respect for his Uncle Laredo, a ninety-two-year-old black sheep of the family who lives on a decrepit ranch called Hacienda of the Bitter Waters near Van Horn with three Mexican hands, all of whom he calls "Pierre." It was from his uncle that Danny thinks he inherited his good shooting eye. Uncle Laredo and his friend Lorenzo had fought with Zapata and Villa in Mexico, with the Texas Rangers, and with the Seventh Cavalry in Wyoming in 1890, and time had not mellowed him a bit. Laredo's wife Martha lived on her own ranch some miles away, their individualism so strong that not even marriage could keep them under one roof. Danny knows he doesn't live by their values and he doesn't even really like them as people, but his admiration for their tenacity and sense of identity is profound and tragic:

> I always thought of Uncle L as near death, because he was ninety-two, but it was obvious to me that that was a wrong way to think. I was probably nearer death. It was as if Uncle L and Martha and Lorenzo had already contested Time and won. The contest was over. They had made life theirs. So far as life was concerned they could go on living until they got bored with living, with butchering goats and digging postholes and cooking buffalo steaks.
>
> I felt really insubstantial. I didn't know if I would ever make life mine. Martha was right about Uncle L, though. He was an old son-ofabitch. The Hacienda of the Bitter Waters wasn't the Old West I liked to believe in—it was the bitter end of something. I knew I would never want to visit it again. (*AMF,* 170)

Uncle L is a magnificent, comical anachronism, but he possesses a greater sense of identity and vitality than Danny thinks he will ever achieve himself in his "dislodged" life.

Danny's sense of dislocation, of displacement, is a "central concern" of McMurtry's as R. L. Neinstein has noted.[22] McMurtry writes that "the place where all my stories start is the heart faced suddenly with the loss of its country, its customary and legendary range" (*ING,* 140) and his reference to the land links his characters' sense of loss to the historical change they are forced to confront. Unlike Sam the Lion or Uncle L, Danny and Sonny are, in Matthew Arnold's words, "caught between two worlds, one dead, the other powerless to be born." Danny is what Robert E. Park has called "the marginal man." "When the traditional organization of society breaks down, as a result of contact and collision with a new invading culture, the effect is, so to speak, to emancipate the individual man. . . . The individual is free for new adventures, but he is more or less without direction and control." Just such a clash, of course, is occurring as the frontier meets the metropolis. Danny is "a man on the margin of two cultures and two societies," and has links with the character type of the "stranger" mentioned earlier. Unlike the stranger, however, he lacks a private sense of values which distinguishes him from the crowd; unlike him, the stranger does not exist in a crisis of transition. "But in the case of the marginal man the period of crisis is relatively permanent"; he exhibits "spiritual instability, intensified self-consciousness, restlessness, and *malaise.*"[23] Park sees the marginal man's instability as a necessary step in the synthesis of a new stage in the progress of civilization, but McMurtry does not leave us with the sense that Danny is forging a new life for either himself or his society.

To conclude, we must return to paradoxes. McMurtry's people all possess a love-hate relationship with their native locale: a love for what it was and a hatred of what it has become. The values of the frontier still seem desirable, but no longer attainable. His characters are crossing a new frontier which has less freedom, fewer clearly defined principles, and greater personal anonymity than the old. There is isolation, but it is internal, not geographical; there is restlessness, but it is spiritual more than economic; there is resistance to control and defiance of authority, but without a corresponding social bonding in either family or friendship to balance that rebellion. McMurtry views the frontier cowboy as an essentially tragic figure, and it is hard not to conclude that the same urbanization which spelled his demise has lost in him the embodiment of certain values which it itself desperately needs.

NOTES

1. W. Eugene Hollon, *Frontier Violence: Another Look* (New York: Oxford University Press, 1974), p. 200.

2. Hollon, p. 54.

3. Hollon, p. 196.

4. Ray Allen Billington, *America's Frontier Heritage* (New York: Holt, Rinehart and Winston, 1966), p. 78.

5. Charles D. Peavy, *Larry McMurtry* (Boston: Twayne, 1977), p. 118.

6. Peavy, p. 140.

7. Billington, p. 6.

8. *The Turner Thesis Concerning the Role of the Frontier in American History,* ed. G. R. Taylor (Lexington, Mass.: D. C. Heath, 1956), p. 6. Turner's thesis as a theme in American literature is discussed in Harold P. Simonson, *The Closed Frontier: Studies in American Literary Tragedy* (New York: Holt, Rinehart and Winston, 1970).

9. *Turner Thesis,* p. 20.

10. Billington, pp. 25–26.

11. Billington, p. 42.

12. Billington, pp. 42–43.

13. Georg Simmel, "The Stranger" in *The Sociology of Georg Simmel,* trans. Kurt H. Wolf (Free Press: 1950, 1978), repr. in *The Pleasures of Sociology,* ed. Lewis Coser (New American Library, 1980), p. 237.

14. Billington, p. 59.

15. Billington, p. 144.

16. *In a Narrow Grave: Essays on Texas* (Austin: Encino Press, 1968), chapter 5. References to this book are cited as *ING.*

17. Billington, p. 26.

18. *The Last Picture Show* (New York: Dial Press, 1966), p. 153. References to this book are cited as *LPS*.

19. Peavy, p. 124, n. 17.

20. *ING*, pp. 68–69.

21. *All My Friends Are Going to Be Strangers* (New York: Pocket Books, 1973), p. 47. References to this book are cited as *AMF*.

22. *The Ghost Country: A Study of the Novels of Larry McMurtry* (Berkeley: Creative Arts Book Co., 1976).

23. Robert E. Park, "Migration and the Marginal Man," *American Journal of Sociology,* 33 (May, 1928), 200–206. Repr. in Coser, pp. 241–247.

Initiation Themes in McMurtry's Cowboy Trilogy

KENNETH W. DAVIS

In his perceptive essay "What Is An Initiation Story?" Mordecai Marcus provides a precise and comprehensive definition of the theme of initiation in fiction.[1] His basic premise, that the major element in an initiation story involves growth toward understanding, resembles Ihab Hassan's general definition of the theme of initiation as one which ". . . can be understood . . . as the first existential ordeal, crisis, or encounter with experience in the life of a youth. Its ideal aim is knowledge, recognition, and confirmation in the world, to which the actions of the initiate, however painful, must tend. It is, quite simply, the viable mode of confronting adult realities."[2] Marcus, however, particularizes his definition by distinguishing three types of initiations: *tentative,* "which lead only to the threshold of maturity and understanding but do not definitely cross it," *uncompleted,* "which take their protagonists across a threshold of maturity and understanding but leave them enmeshed in a struggle for certainty," and *decisive,* "which carry their protagonists firmly into maturity and understanding, or at least show them decisively embarked toward maturity" (Marcus, p. 204). Marcus wisely admits that in some instances overlapping occurs among these three types.

Although Marcus's three-fold examination is comprehensive, it can be used as the basis for examining McMurtry's uses of themes of initiation only if another element is added. This element involves the importance of locale, or, as Eudora Welty has said, "place," in the shaping of the nature and quality of various initiatory experiences McMurtry's characters undergo.[3]

The present day Southwest is the general locale McMurtry used in *Horseman, Pass By* (1961) which became the award-winning film *Hud, Leaving Cheyenne* (1963), and *The Last Picture Show* (1966). The specific setting for these three novels which McMurtry sometimes calls "the cowboy trilogy" is the short-grass ranching country of North Central Texas. He saw this region as in a time of transition from the age of the authentic horse-riding cowman to the contemporary age of the pickup-driving cowboy. The potential in such a setting for meaningful depiction of changing human values is great and McMurtry exploits it fully with several youthful characters who face initiatory dilemmas. McMurtry's presentations of initiations in his fictional world of changing values are at times starkly realistic; at other times, they are colored by melancholic elements of a romantic myth. Regardless of his approach, the changes he sees in the culture of his particular region serve as catalytic forces in effecting initiations and in making them unique.

In this often severe and violent North Texas ranching country, McMurtry's characters must cope with introductions to sex, with challenges to physical stamina, with loneliness, with moral choice, and with encounters with death. His young men experience sexual initiations marked by elements of violence, estrangement, and despair. These initiations are characterized by overlapping of the uncompleted and the decisive types.

Lonnie Bannon's sexual initiation in *Horseman, Pass By* is violent. Lonnie watches his step-uncle Hud rape Halmea, the Negro maid whom Lonnie had desired. Lonnie's growing acknowledgment that at the time of the rape his feelings were ambivalent is a step in his progress toward maturity. As Hud raped Halmea, Lonnie watched in horrified fascination, sensing the animal cruelty of Hud, and at the time painfully aware that Hud was having what he (Lonnie) desired (pp. 114–118). But with Lonnie there was a difference: Lonnie's longing for Halmea stemmed from loneliness and affection. His feelings were not the result of a sadistic desire to inflict pain.

The incident marked a turning point in Lonnie's life. Prior to it, he was torn between affection and respect for the strength of character he sensed in his grandfather, Homer Bannon, and admiration and envy of Hud, who represented the appeal of adult virility to a teenager longing to escape from the limitations imposed on him by his youthfulness. Two basic changes are present in Lonnie after the violence of his sexual initiation: he is more aware of the need to respect the dignity of other human beings in sexual and in other matters, and he begins to see the true nature of Hud's character. The result here is similar to that which can occur after the moment of anagnorisis in a Greek drama. From his shock and disillusionment, Lonnie Bannon gained new wisdom. He began to reject the way of Hud and to accept the way represented by Homer Bannon—the way of the old values, possibly romanticized by McMurtry, but the old values, nonetheless, of honor, of honesty, of endurance with integrity. The values Lonnie then saw clearly in his grandfather are an integral part of the myth McMurtry includes in *Horseman, Pass By* as an element deriving from the novel's locale.

In his other novels, *Leaving Cheyenne* and *The Last Picture Show,* McMurtry also writes of sexual initiations: Gideon Fry with Molly Taylor in *Leaving Cheyenne;* Sonny Crawford and his friend Duane with Jacy Farrow, and Sonny with Ruth Popper in *The Last Picture Show* —to mention only the major ones. The violence which character- ized Lonnie Bannon's initiation is absent from these later ones, but a common element is present: loneliness. All of the individuals involved are lonely characters who strive for some means, physical or spiritual, of communicating with their various partners. Their loneliness is aug- mented by the stark bareness of the region. It is a loneliness of place as well as of the heart.

Sonny's liaison with Mrs. Ruth Popper, the affection-starved wife of a brutish high school coach, provides illustration of the agonizing initiation which can result from such loneliness. When Sonny first makes love with Mrs. Popper, he is relatively unconcerned about her as a person. As their relationship continues, however, he becomes deeply aware of her needs. Later, when he seeks in Jacy Farrow a partner his own age, he suffers remorse for neglecting Ruth Popper. But until his attempt to marry Jacy Farrow is thwarted by her par- ents, he cannot fully understand or sympathize with Ruth. A pat- tern, then, has gone a full cycle: from loneliness leading to sexual union to initiation and back to loneliness more poignantly felt be- cause of the initiation. In this instance, the initiation is best catego- rized as having more qualities of the uncompleted one than of the decisive. Sonny's experiences with sex have caused him to be more concerned with others than with himself, which can be a sign of maturity, but at the novel's conclusion he continues in the struggle for certainty which Marcus described as characteristic of the uncom- pleted initiation.

Sexual initiations are not the only ones present in McMurtry's early novels. His characters also undergo ritualistic initiations involv- ing physical stamina. The importance of place in these initiations is as great as it is in sexual initiations, if not greater.

Although McMurtry does not shape a single incident of a test of physical prowess into a clearly defined initiation experience, his characters seem always aware of the importance of physical valor. At times physical strength and moral integrity become synonymous in these characters' minds. For example, in *Horseman, Pass By,* Lonnie Bannon is torn between respect for his grandfather and envious admiration of the vigorous Hud. Lonnie's growth toward maturity becomes definite when he realizes that Hud's physical prowess is not as important as Homer Bannon's moral integrity.

Examples which illustrate the pervasive influence of a belief in the importance of physical prowess may be found, also, in *Leaving Cheyenne* and in *The Last Picture Show.* Gideon Fry and Johnny McCloud in *Leaving Cheyenne* compete in physical contests to prove themselves worthy of acceptance by the adult world. Sonny and Duane in *The Last Picture Show* rebel against the emphasis placed on athletic prowess in their hometown but long for the feeling of achievement which football once gave them.

Physical stamina is valued by most of the inhabitants of McMurtry's world as an entity possessing its own importance. His characters sometimes reject the majority opinion, but they cannot ignore it. The emphasis placed on physical stamina is another example of the effect locale has in shaping the precise natures of initiations. In McMurtry's world, passage from one level of maturity to a higher one is sometimes gained only by the ability to endure physically.

Encounters with death form a third group of initiatory experiences in the trilogy. All of McMurtry's major characters endure initiations as the results of the deaths either of relatives or close friends. These initiations have many of the same elements found in sexual and physical-challenge initiations.

For Larry McMurtry's characters, initiations effected by encounters with death are marked by overwhelming feelings of loss and alienation. In keeping with his characterization of his region, the deaths he records as occurring there are violent and the initiations which result from them are traumatic.

The account of Lonnie Bannon's reaction to the death of his grandfather in *Horseman, Pass By* is McMurtry's most fully developed presentation of an initiation resulting from an encounter with death. In this episode Lonnie discovers the gravely injured Homer Bannon who has broken his leg in a fall. As Lonnie seeks to aid him, Hud and a woman with whom he is having an affair drive up and crash her car into Lonnie's pickup. Because Hud and the woman are intoxicated, they do not at first understand what has happened. When Lonnie does make clear to Hud that Homer Bannon is injured, Hud discovers that the injury is far more serious than Lonnie had allowed himself to think it was. Hud sends Lonnie to the highway to seek help. While Lonnie is gone, Hud kills Homer Bannon. Lonnie's reaction is one of overwhelming loss. He refuses to accept Hud's realistic opinion that Homer Bannon is better off dead. He says: "It woulda been all right, he woulda got well, I needed him" (p. 159).

The violent death of his grandfather occasions more for Lonnie, however, than merely personal loss and a feeling of helplessness. When his immediate grief dissipates, Lonnie begins to see the reality of his world with greater clarity than he had seen it before. He now perceives fully the harsh brutality of Hud to which he was earlier introduced while witnessing the violation of Halmea. Hud becomes the usurper who has supplanted the patriarchal Homer. In the process of gaining this realization, Lonnie's feelings are transmuted from those of personal loss to those of an almost cosmic loss and alienation. A world in itself, the world Lonnie built upon his admiration for his grandfather, is no more; and he cannot accept what instead remains.

His alienation is revealed further in his bitter rejection of the notions of some of the mourners that Homer Bannon "had gone to a better place." Of those who held this opinion Lonnie thought: "They could think so and go to hell; I don't believe it. Not unless dirt is a better place than air" (p. 166). The fulsome eulogy the minister offers also aids in the growth of Lonnie's alienation. Lonnie now knows that he loved and accepted his grandfather for what he really was and did, not for what others might have thought or wanted him to be. The violence of Homer Bannon's death thus effects a bitter, decisive initiation for Lonnie which is in harmony with McMurtry's view of the harsh nature of Lonnie's region. Complementing the somberness of his initiation is the irony that not until Lonnie has seen life taken can he appreciate what life can hold. In the early sections of the novel, McMurtry frequently has Lonnie voice desires to escape from the region to find excitement and adventure. In the novel's epilogue, Lonnie leaves, not on an adventurous quest, but in flight from a world grown empty.

Although McMurtry's treatment in *Leaving Cheyenne* of the initiation Gideon Fry experiences as a result of the suicide of his father is less intense than the account of Lonnie's bitter passage, in it are elements of violence and loss. The elder Fry was ill and elected to end his life rather than give up any of his activities. Given the conditions imposed by the locale in which he lived, it was in character for him to take his life. Another course could have seemed cowardly for one who so long displayed an indomitable will to shape his destiny in a demanding region.

The second element, the feeling of loss, grows to the point that he could have suffered the type of alienation to which Lonnie Bannon was fated. Gideon Fry, however, either must assume responsibility for continuing the operation of his father's holdings, or become a penniless cowboy. Gideon accepts adult responsibility. Thus an encounter with death in this instance ultimately forces a decisive initiation upon a youth who had earlier rebelled against his domineering father. Following his initiation, Gideon Fry becomes as strong willed as his father had been. In assuming this role, he is saved from the alienation which engulfed Lonnie Bannon. For Lonnie, there seemed to be no purposeful avenue open; for Gideon, whose initiation occurred some years before the old ranching way of life began the disintegration McMurtry chronicles, there was still a way to achieve purpose.

Two deaths in McMurtry's third novel, *The Last Picture Show*, effect an initiation which leads Sonny Crawford to a sobering awareness of reality. Although the death of Sonny's friend, Sam the Lion, was not a violent one, its effect on Sonny resembles the effect of Homer Bannon's death on Lonnie and of Fry's death on Gideon. First, there is the immediate shock and feeling of loss, then the growing realization of how meaningful life had been for the deceased. Not until after the death of Sam does Sonny learn that it was Sam who had been Lois Farrow's lover and the only man in her life with whom love had had any meaning. When the terms of Sam's will are disclosed, Sonny learns more of the concern which Sam in his eccentric way so long had felt for the people who helped make his lonely life bearable. Sonny and Billy, a feeble-minded boy, are among the beneficiaries. To them, Sam willed the pool-hall which had been Billy's only home for several years. Sonny is to be Sam's replacement as Billy's protector (p. 180).

In the process of achieving the realization of Sam's compassion, Sonny forgets at least momentarily his own dilemmas and begins to have compassion for other individuals. At this point Sonny learns what Lonnie Bannon and Gideon Fry learned: the full meaning of another individual's life often is not realized until his death forces the realization.

Billy's death in *The Last Picture Show* complements the initiation Sonny experienced when Sam died. In the weeks following Sam's death, Sonny was conscientious in his attempts to care for Billy, but could not be with him constantly. One morning before Sonny awakened, Billy began his daily ritual of sweeping the sidewalks. In his enthusiasm, he moved into the street and was killed by a cattle truck.

Sonny's immediate reaction to the sight of Billy's body is one of overpowering shock. He becomes nauseated and vomits. Then, because he cannot stand to leave Billy on the street until an ambulance can be summoned, he frantically drags him to the front of the picture show which was Billy's favorite haunt. The witnesses to this grim tableau are dumbfounded. Hurley, the trucker who accidentally killed Billy, observes: "You all got some crazy kids in this town" (p. 276). Because Hurley and the others have not shared Sonny's feelings, they cannot realize that his gesture was one compounded of agony and compassion. Sonny Crawford, at last, has experienced through a violent encounter with death, a decisive initiation which reveals to him a devastating vision of the impersonal cruelty of a fate which can strike down an innocent victim such as Billy. The novel concludes somberly with Sonny reaching out once more for understanding from an equally tormented Ruth Popper. She and Sonny feel defeated by the brutality inherent in the place where they were destined to play out their roles.

Larry McMurtry's uses of initiation themes as major components in his fiction link him with an established tradition in American letters. His youthful characters join the company of Hawthorne's Robin Molineux, Twain's Huck Finn, Crane's Henry Fleming, and Faulkner's Ike McCaslin—to mention but a few—as initiates who have gained wisdom about themselves or the world they live in, or both. Although the Southwest is the general locale for his first three novels, McMurtry is not merely a chronicler of a region. His themes are ones which do not know geographic boundaries, but he uses his knowledge of the Southwest to achieve memorable evocations of place and to indicate the qualities of initiatory experiences which occur there.

NOTES

1. This essay first appeared in *The Journal of Aesthetics and Art Criticism* 14 (1960): 221–228. It has been revised and reprinted in *Critical Approaches to Fiction*, ed. Shiv K. Kumar and Keith McKean (New York: McGraw-Hill, 1968): 201–213. My references are to this revised edition.

2. Ihab Hassan, *Radical Innocence: Studies in the Contemporary American Novel* (Princeton: Princeton UP 1961): 41.

3. See Eudora Welty, "Place in Fiction," *The South Atlantic Quarterly* 55 (1956): 57–72 *et passim*.

Damn the Saddle on the Wall: Anti-Myth in Larry McMurtry's *Horseman, Pass By*

MARK BUSBY

In the "Prologue" to Larry McMurtry's *Horseman, Pass By* (1961) Lonnie looks out on the early oats and leafing mesquites of the April plains and hears the zooming cars headed north to Amarillo or south to Dallas, the growling diesels moving purposefully across the prairie, and especially the whistling Zephyr whose "noise cut across the dark prairie like the whistling train itself" (Penguin Books, p. 6). The train makes Lonnie's grandfather Homer Bannon "tireder" and urges him to bed early, but it excites Lonnie and sends his imagination whirling down the track toward the "airplane beacons flashing from the airport in Wichita Falls." In many ways this scene is paradigmatic of the novel's movement: the old frontier order symbolized by Homer is dying and the new one represented by Lonnie and the trains and planes to which he is attracted is arriving. Does this passing indicate a new, more powerful beginning or a degeneration, an end to something suggestively beautiful?

Critics often conclude that *Horseman, Pass By* dramatizes the psychic indirection caused by the loss of nature and the healing values taught by a beneficent nature. In the Winter 1975 issue of *Western Humanities Review* E. Pauline Degenfelder notes that the title suggests an "elegy for the desecration of the land, the temporality of an older order, and the death of the patriarchal figure who is its embodiment" (p. 81). And in the Spring 1976 issue of *Western American Literature* Janis P. Stout finds that in *Horseman, Pass By* and several other novels McMurtry uses journeying as a "metaphor for modern life itself, which is seen as being impoverished by the demise of the old traditions and the lack of new structures of meaning and allegiance" (p. 38). According to this view, the "Prologue" demonstrates that the Edenic frontier of the old cowboy has been (to paraphrase Leo Marx) fatally corrupted by the machine's entry into the garden.

But another view of the novel, especially in light of some of McMurtry's comments in his non-fiction work *In a Narrow Grave* (1968), reveals that in many ways *Horseman, Pass By* demonstrates the enervation of the romanticized myth of the frontier. Rather than a saddened nostalgia for a past way of life, much of *Horseman, Pass By* indicates a goodbye–good riddance attitude which appears more directly in McMurtry's essays. Although McMurtry admits in one essay that he has a "contradiction of attractions," an ambivalence "as deep as the bone" (Encino Press, p. 141) toward Texas and the past, he strikes out at the frontier emphasis on the goodness of nature and open country. He also attacks the anti-intellectual, anti-woman, anti-minority, pro-violence attitudes which were part of the old value system. In both the novel and the essays McMurtry is anti-myth, countering much of what Larry Goodwyn defines as the Southwestern legend in his essay "The Frontier Myth and Southwestern Literature" in the February 1971 issue of *Library Journal:*

> The legend is pastoral: the courageous men conquered nature, but
> at the same time were "at one" with nature. The legend is
> inherently masculine: women are not so much without "courage" as
> missing altogether; cowgirls did not ride up the Chisholm Trail.
> The legend is primitively racialistic: it provides no mystique of
> triumph for Mexicans, Negroes, or Indians. (p. 161)

Old Homer Bannon, as representative of the frontier values, believes in the myth of a beneficent nature. Lonnie recalls that "he told me that nature would always work her own cures, if people would be patient enough, and give her time" (p. 5). The land, to Homer, is sacred; he will not think of allowing oil wells on his ranch: "'I guess I'm a queer, contrary old bastard, but there'll be no holes punched in this land while I'm here'" (pp. 87–88). Similar primitivist attitudes were held by the Big Three of Texas letters—J. Frank Dobie, Roy Bedichek, and Walter Prescott Webb, McMurtry points out in his essay entitled "Southwestern Literature?" For them, McMurtry notes, "Nature was the Real. Knowledge of it made a full man, and accord with it was the first essential of the Good Life" (p. 36). For his generation, however, McMurtry says that he doubts if "we could scrape up enough nature-lore between us to organize a decent picnic." He then makes his charge against the frontier emphasis on nature more explicit:

> I spent more than twenty years in the country and I came away
> from it far from convinced that the country is a good place to form
> character, acquire fullness, or lead the Good Life. I have had fine
> moments of rapport with nature, but I have seen the time, also,
> when I would have traded a lot of sunsets for a few good books.
> Sentimentalists are still fond of saying that nature is the best
> teacher—I have known many Texans who felt that way, and most
> of them live and die in woeful ignorance. When I lived in the
> country I noticed no abundance of full men. (Encino Press, p. 36)

This overwhelming emphasis on nature as a teacher resulted in what McMurtry believes is one of the major weaknesses of the frontier myth: a militant anti-intellectualism. If the only valuable learning comes from a life of action in the natural world, then any other education lacks worth. McMurtry notes that even Dobie and Bedichek "displayed a marked ambivalence toward the intellect" (p. 43), and he laments that he grew up in a "bookless town—in a bookless part of the state" (p. 33).

In *Horseman, Pass By* Homer's primitivism causes him to deny any emphasis on education. Disparaging "college fellers," he would not approve of Hud's desire to go to college. Hud tells Homer,

> "You thought I oughta drive that goddamn feed wagon for you,
> instead of goin' to college. Yeah. You held on tight then, but you
> sure let me go in a hurry when the draft board started lookin' for
> somebody to go do the fightin'. But hell, you were Wild Horse
> Homer Bannon in them days, an' anything you did was right. I even
> thought you was right myself, the most of the time. Why I used to
> think you was a regular god. I don't no more." (p. 66)

Homer, therefore, is largely responsible for creating the embittered Hud who mockingly says to him: "'You're the boss, you must be the one who knows if anybody does. I just work from the shoulders down, myself'" (p. 65).

As Hud's stepson status implies, he is a debased version of Homer. Homer's world has been sustained by the cowboy's mythos, but he cannot cope with a changing world, one with a frontier diminished by highways and railroad tracks. Nor can he help prepare the young to live full lives in a world dominated by cities and cars. By denying support for Hud's education, perhaps influenced by the anti-intellectualism of the frontier myth, Homer had closed to Hud one way of preparing for that changing world. By turning Hud against him, Homer contributes to his own downfall, just as he hastens it by buying diseased Mexican cattle which contaminate his herd.

Hud reveals in other ways that he is a product of Homer Bannon's world, especially its emphasis on violence. In the March 1975 issue of *Atlantic* McMurtry excoriated Texas, noting that one of the few vestiges of the old world which remains is the frontier emphasis on violence:

> If frontier life has left any cultural residue at all, it is a residue of a
> most unfortunate sort—i.e., that tendency to romanticize violence
> which is evident on the front page of almost every Texas newspaper
> almost every day. (p. 31)

McMurtry comments on the way that Hud is influenced by the violence of the fading myth in *In a Narrow Grave:*

> Hud, a twentieth century Westerner, is a gunfighter who lacks
> both guns and opponents. The land itself is the same—just as
> powerful and just as imprisoning—but the social context has
> changed so radically that Hud's impulse to violence is turned inward,
> on himself and his family. He is wild in a well-established tradition
> of western wildness that involves drinking, fighting, fast and
> reckless riding and/or driving, and, of course, seducing. (p. 24–25)

Not only does Hud's violent wildness manifest itself in seduction,
but with Halmea, the black cook, seduction becomes rape. He can rape
Halmea with impunity because she is a *black* woman. The innocent
Lonnie tells her that the "'law can take care of Hud,'" but she replies:
"'No law gonna hear about dis', you see dey don't. Tell de law, dey have
it my fault befor' you turn aroun'. I seen dat kinda law before'" (p. 96).
McMurtry notes that this violence toward minorities was often part of
the cowboy's world in "Take My Saddle From the Wall: A Valediction":

> The cowboy's working life is spent in one sort of violent activity or
> another; an ability to absorb violence and hardship is part of the
> proving of any cowboy, and it is only to be expected that the
> violence will extend itself occasionally from animals to humans,
> and particularly to those humans that class would have one regard
> as animals. (p. 168)

While Hud's treatment of Halmea seems to have been primarily the
product of racism, his attitude toward women may have been affected
by the fact that women were excluded from the cowboy mythos. In
"Take My Saddle from the Wall" McMurtry says that cowboys had a
"commitment to a heroic concept of life that simply takes little account of women" (p. 148). Hud certainly has learned no full way of
treating women from Homer. Women to Homer are just to be humored
as he does Hud's mother, sending her to Temple to get a few fake
stitches to quiet her hypochondria (p. 56). The scene which best exemplifies their separation has them listening to separate programs on
separate radios, "The two programs blaring . . . against each other"
(p. 71). These anti-women attitudes along with other anti-minority,
anti-intellectual, pro-violence ones of the frontier myth have helped
shape Hud.

If Hud is one product of the frontier myth, Jesse, the former rodeo
rider, is another. Jesse has followed the rodeo circuit in search of an
Edenic ideal: "'I went all over this cow country, looking for the exact

right place an' the exact right people, so once I got stopped I wouldn't have to be movin' agin, like my old man always done'" (p. 121). But Jesse has never found the "exact right place"; rather he has been worn out and crippled by the pursuit. In one essay McMurtry evaluated the rodeo as an alternative to the past:

> The cowboy's temperament has not changed much since the nineteenth century; it is his world that has changed, and the change has been a steady shrinkage. There are no more trail herds, no more wide open cattle towns, no longer that vast stretch of unfenced land between Laredo and Calgary. If the modern cowboy is footloose, there is only the rodeo circuit, for most a very unsatisfactory life. (p. 26)

What kind of world, then, is open for Lonnie—the new generation—to enter? Lonnie is vaguely aware that something is wrong with the world into which he is being initiated; from Marlet, the in-town kid who longs for the cowboy life, Lonnie learns how to embody that hazy feeling in an image: strangling. After talking to Marlet one night, Lonnie goes out into the dark and tries to realize himself through violence. He takes the .22, walks past a cottonmouth (the snake in the garden?), and begins shooting turtles and frogs in the tank. But, then, he feels that he too is strangling: "Suddenly the high weeds and the darkness made me feel like Marlet, like I was strangling. 'Oh, me,' I said, 'I wasted all those frogs'" (p. 72).

After Lonnie recognizes that mindless violence contributes to his feeling of strangulation, he then tries to become part of the world of wild and reckless riding. He saddles Granddad's significantly named horse Stranger and goes for a ride along Idiot Ridge. But just when he senses that he and Stranger may have reached an ecstatic peak as they race across the range, a fence, image of the diminished frontier, appears suddenly in front of them; and Lonnie takes an extremely hard fall.

While wild and violent activity is unavailable to Lonnie in this dry, dusty, diminished frontier, he does find new pastures: the world of the imagination which his reading of *From Here to Eternity* has opened. McMurtry too had found the world of literature as an alternative to the old wide-open spaces:

> In their youth . . . my uncles sat on the barn and watched the last trail herds moving north—I sat on the self-same barn and saw only a few oil-field pickups and a couple of Dairy trucks go by. That life died, and I am lucky to have found so satisfying a replacement as *Don Quixote* offered. And yet, that first life has not quite died in me—not quite. I missed it only by the width of a generation and, as

I was growing up, heard the whistle of its departure. Not long after
I entered the pastures of the empty page I realized that the place
where all my stories start is the heart faced suddenly with the loss
of its country, its customary and legendary range. (pp. 139–40)

So when Lonnie climbs into that cattle truck for a ride to Wichita
Falls as the novel ends, he will not light out for the circuit that Jesse
followed. Instead, he will head for the cities which have now filled the
wide-open spaces of the old frontier. There he can pursue the books
now open to him. There he will become the writer of his own story.
There he will escape the stifling, strangling world of the diminished
frontier. In this light, McMurtry's title is not a lament; it is a command.

Anatomy and *The Last Picture Show:*
A Matter of Definition

DONALD E. FRITZ

If one has both seen the film and read the book, it is difficult to
consider either version of Larry McMurtry's *The Last Picture Show* in
total isolation. Images and insights experienced in one version make
synaptic leaps to influence thoughts about the other version and,
generally, with useful gains in the illumination of whichever version is
being studied at the moment. Naturally, the overlap between the two
versions is considerable, yet, more interestingly, the differences between them are sufficiently significant to support the argument that
wholly different concerns are involved in the two works, despite their
surface similarity. To some extent, one can explain away the differences between the versions on the basis of the demands of the two
media: lacking the abundant experiential time available to the book,
the film necessarily had to restrict its focus, to reduce the diversity
and simplify the developmental lineaments of the book. The telling
point, however, seems to be that the two versions could have had the
same central concern, but do not.

It seems inescapable, for example, that the film is identifiable as a
distinctly recognizable literary type, namely an *Erziehungsroman,*
with Sonny as the clearly dominant interest. He may be off-screen
occasionally, but the film revolves around his education, and it is his
progression into adulthood that most engrosses us. Admittedly, the
same progression is present in the book; proportionately, however, it is
much less important. Other characters compete much more strongly

for our attention in the book than in the film. Characters who seem subordinate to Sonny in the film are essentially coequal in the book, because we are with them in the book more intimately than we are in the film, since the use of the omniscient point of view takes us *inside* their minds and forces us to share their lives as fully as we share Sonny's life. In the film, we watch; in the book, we share. The difference is considerable, and the conclusion seems inescapable that the book is not meant to engage us as exclusively with Sonny as was the film. In short, then, it seems that McMurtry's original intention in *The Last Picture Show* was not to give us a West Texas Wilhelm Meister, as he does in the film, but to give us something else instead.

A clue to McMurtry's original intention may be found in his essay, "Eros in Archer County," where he restricts his focus for that essay by remarking, "At the moment, however, I am not interested in describing or evaluating the sexual attitudes that prevail in present-day Texas. That pleasant task can be better taken up in the novel."[1] "Eros in Archer County" is concerned with the sexual attitudes and activities of Texas prior to the present day and with the difficulty of capturing in fiction the sexual dimension of the Texas experience. The essay reveals McMurtry's interest in recording that area of human activity, and I believe that a similar intention of recording a period's sexual history—"that pleasant task"—was one of the primary forces at work in the creation of *The Last Picture Show,* if not indeed the controlling concern of the book.

By this point, the astute reader of this essay may well have noticed an almost labored avoidance of the term *novel* when referring to the printed version of *The Last Picture Show.* The reason for this avoidance has been to establish in this essay the difference between the use of the term *novel* in the common sense and the more restricted use of that term by Northrop Frye in his *Anatomy of Criticism,* because, quite simply, *The Last Picture Show,* using Frye's classification of types of fiction, is not an unalloyed novel straightforwardly concerned with characters acting within a society, but more accurately a novel strongly pulled in the direction of an anatomy, that is, toward an encyclopedic investigation of one specific human concern, specifically, the sexual attitudes and activities of Texas in the 1950's.

The evidence supporting the argument for this clarification of nomenclature is the extraordinary emphasis on sex in the work, an emphasis manifested by its central position in the events recorded for almost every character in the book, major or minor. We do not see characters in the way they react to life, and the varied activities involved in living life, so much as we see them as they react to sex, and the various activities and attitudes connected with sex. The constancy of the focus on sex is striking; characters become noticeable largely to the degree that they are involved in some way with sex. Consequently, in the book, Jacy and Ruth are at least as memorable, if not more so, than Sonny, and relatively minor characters linger firmly in the mind as case studies of various sexual problems or experiences: Herman Popper as the latent homosexual, for example, or Joe Bob Blanton as a victim of repressed sexuality and masturbation phobias.

This case-study approach is further evidence of the degree to which *The Last Picture Show* moves away from the concerns of the novel and toward the concerns of an anatomy. Not merely does *The Last Picture Show* focus almost constantly on sexual matters, it also manages to present an impressively comprehensive collection of the attitudes and activities of the Texans of that period. It is, in short, the encyclopedic investigation of the subject that Frye argues is characteristic of an anatomy. The list of matters covered is impressively lengthy and includes, in addition to the examples of Popper and Blanton already given, such items as the various sexual initiations of the youthful characters, the sexual awakening of Ruth, the sexual frustration of Lois, the sexual adventures in Mexico and Fort Worth, the sexual exhibitionism of Jacy, and so on. Even the fringes of human sexual activities are examined, in the two episodes involving bestiality. Sex is not only central in *The Last Picture Show*, it is comprehensively examined, as is appropriate in an anatomy.

There are two advantages in recognizing the degree to which *The Last Picture Show* moves away from the concerns of the novel and toward those of an anatomy. The first advantage is that, as Frye argues, a work should be judged on the basis of the conventions the author chooses to follow, not on the basis of conventions not central to the work. A good romance may be judged harshly if considered as a novel, and so may an anatomy. In the case of *The Last Picture Show*, certain weaknesses it seems to have as a novel are less troublesome if it is recognized as an anatomy. Clearly, if *The Last Picture Show* is judged as a novel, W. T. Jack is justified in complaining that, "The whole, however, is not as satisfying as the parts. The characters lack depth . . . The novel loses focus when Jacy takes over."[2] If judged as an anatomy, however, the same complaints are less valid for *The Last Picture Show*, just as they would be for any other anatomy, such as *Brave New World*, to name one of Frye's examples of the type. The parts in an anatomy may be as important as the whole, and some characters are *meant* to be types, not fully developed individuals.

Even the exceptional emphasis on sex, which might be considered a weakness in a serious novel, becomes wholly justifiable in an anatomy investigating that topic; indeed, it becomes obligatory.

The second advantage in recognizing *The Last Picture Show* as an anatomy of the sexual condition of the society it examines is that such a recognition points our attention to statements the book is making that we might otherwise miss. The general view of McMurtry's gesture in *The Last Picture Show* (and one drawn partly, I suspect, from a famil-iarity with the film version and, perhaps, with *Horseman, Pass By*) is that he wishes to call attention to the movement from the relatively positive nature of Texas-past to the relatively negative nature of Texas-present. And I would not dispute this conclusion, in general. On the other hand, the emphasis on the sexual history of Texas-past in *The Last Picture Show* suggests that not all we have left behind was posi-tive. As McMurtry argues in "Eros in Archer County" and, more to the point here, presents in *The Last Picture Show,* the sexual situation in Texas-past was pretty awful, and its passing is not to be lamented.

The sexual situation McMurtry reveals in *The Last Picture Show* is undeniably negative. Virtually all the characters we see may be con-sumed by their absorption with sex, but not one of them derives any-thing resembling substantive pleasure from it. The pleasures won are won for the moment and are usually edged in some darkness that keeps them from being fully and richly rewarding. Sex for the Thalians was not a comfortable garden in which one could relax and enjoy; it was a dark forest from which one could win prizes but only by taking unnerv-ing risks. As McMurtry comments in "Eros in Archer County," "We never thought of Mother Nature as a fruitful female who was generous with Herself; what one got from Her one earned. From nature one got no sense of sex as gift, much less a sense that sex was something in which both partners could delight."[3]

It is precisely this failure of sex to be an act in which *both* partners delight that is most noticeable in *The Last Picture Show.* Of the nu-merous sexual relationships in the book, not one is a mutually reward-ing experience; sex is a matter of giving and taking, never sharing. There may be a degree of satisfaction for the giver and the taker, but satisfaction is experienced in isolation. No unification of individual passions is achieved, no lasting bonds are forged. In one extreme ex-ample of the imbalanced nature of the Thalian sex act, McMurtry illus-trates the utmost degree of one-sided sexual satisfaction-in-isolation by following a group of the young men as they copulate with a blind heifer, an incident, as he points out in "Eros in Archer County," that is not hyperbolic, and, he might have added, neither is it meta-phoric, though it is symbolic.

Less striking than the bestiality, but more central and more mean-ingful, are the numerous human couplings. Many of these are devoid of pleasure for either party, and in all of them the isolation is never over-come. The sex act may be presented as selfishness, as in the case of Jacy's use of Duane to prepare herself for Bobby Sheen, or as compas-sion, as when Lois gives herself to Sonny to reduce the pain of his loss of Jacy, but it is never shown as a means of bringing together two people and making them truly one. The individuals of Thalia remain trapped in isolation. Sex offers a way out, but never provides it.

By far the most interesting character actively engaged in the futile attempt to find fulfillment through sex is Ruth Popper, the coach's wife and Sonny's lover. McMurtry shows through her experiences the adamantine durability of the barrier between the sexes. In her role as a wife, Ruth has been forced into being a giver, never a taker, and a giver, primarily, of services other than sexual. Her duties as a wife have been performed mainly in the kitchen; those performed in the bedroom have been perfunctory, infrequent, and brief. Until her affair with Sonny, she has never achieved an orgasm. In the beginning of the affair with Sonny, she is initially cast again in the role of giver; her pleasure comes from making him happy. Soon, however, she begins to experience orgasms, taking pleasure as well as giving.

McMurtry gives considerable attention to Ruth's discovery of the orgasm, the "beautiful thing" she had read about but had never experi-enced until her affair with Sonny. Prior to Sonny, she had been condi-tioned not to enjoy sex. Herman (and one might note the ironic implications of her husband's name in passing) is revolted at any indication that Ruth might be enjoying sex with him. If she moved in an attempt to increase her pleasure, he would command her to be still and ask "What kind of a woman do you think you are, anyway?"[4] Consequently, in the initial sessions with Sonny, Ruth is reluctant to free herself and capture fully her own sexual pleasure, especially when her violent, and largely involuntary, reactions as she comes closer to achieving orgasm apparently drive Sonny from her for a few days. Fearful of losing him, she retreats into passive giving.

Eventually, despite herself, Ruth does achieve an orgasm, and Sonny's reaction to it is worth noting: "He had no doubt that Ruth had broken through, but her success was as strange and almost as fright-ening as her failures."[5] The period of their love making that follows Ruth's break through is the most positive picture of sex present in the book, but McMurtry presents it with a significant superficiality that is justified by the later events in the narrative. Both Sonny and Ruth conquer their fear of the female orgasm and become comfortable with it, but they are not able to go beyond comfort because each remains sexually isolated regardless of the mutuality of their orgasms.

A bit later, in a marvelous comic-tragic scene, McMurtry establishes the fact that Ruth, despite her achievement of orgasm, has continued to consider herself in the traditional womanly role of giver. In this scene, she surprises both herself and Herman when she achieves an orgasm during intercourse with him. Her first thoughts after they finish reveal her essentially unchanged self-realization: "Ruth was away, in a misty, drowsy country, but even there she felt a little worried and a little sad. She had not meant it and could not understand how she had done it, *given* Herman something she thought was only for Sonny."[6]

The italics in the quotation above are mine, but McMurtry underlines the essential problem Ruth is experiencing in the way he develops Ruth and Sonny's relationship. As Ruth continues as a giver, Sonny continues as a taker, first leaving Ruth for the chance to take from Jacy (a prize that he doesn't fully attain), then taking briefly from Lois, and ultimately again returning to take from Ruth, but not to take in the role of lover as before, instead ironically reduced to taking in the role his name has suggested all along he is destined for, the role of a child, the primary taker. The book closes with Ruth comforting Sonny as a mother comforts her child.

No one in *The Last Picture Show* pulls fully free from the constraints imposed by the sexual attitudes ruling the period and place depicted in the work. The concept of sex as something that can be fully shared by men and women has not yet arrived upon the scene. Sexual frustration remains dominant, and lasting, shared sexual satisfaction an elusive will o' the wisp. Of all the characters in the book, Ruth comes closest to a realization of the possibility of reciprocally enjoyable sex, ironically as an aftermath of the orgastic experience with Popper just cited. After her initial chagrin at having cheated Sonny by experiencing fully with Herman, she goes to sleep musing that perhaps it is "all the better that she could finally enjoy it," as long as "Herman was going to insist on his connubial rights."[7] She is, however, not allowed to attain full liberation; Herman's nature and Sonny's youth leave her trapped, like all the other residents of Thalia of the fifties. Liberation was for later times and other Thalians.

The shift in definition, then, from novel to anatomy reveals a shift in the statement made by *The Last Picture Show*. If positive qualities were left behind as Texas moved forward in time, so were negative qualities. McMurtry can thus be recognized as a perceptive critic of the continuing human comedy, not merely as a nostalgic malcontent lamenting the glories of past times. Indeed, his study in *The Last Picture Show* of the struggle for sexual liberation—both for males and females—suggests that he was well ahead of the majority of his peers. Currently popular studies of the sexual situations of women and men, such as *The Hite Report* and *Beyond the Male Myth,* are prefigured in the anatomy of sex McMurtry produced in the mid-sixties.

NOTES

1. Larry McMurtry, *In a Narrow Grave: Essays on Texas* (Austin: Encino Press, 1968), p. 55.

2. W. T. Jack, "Sex Wasn't Everything," *New York Times Book Review* (13 Nov. 1966), p. 69.

3. *In a Narrow Grave,* pp. 67–68.

4. Larry McMurtry, *The Last Picture Show* (New York: Dell Publishing Co., 1967), p. 99.

5. *The Last Picture Show,* p. 105.

6. *The Last Picture Show,* p. 120.

7. *The Last Picture Show,* p. 120.

M O V I N G

O N

The Houston Trilogy

ERNESTINE P. SEWELL

Hard on the heels of the success of the "Thalia Trilogy," Larry McMurtry shocked the Texas literary establishment with his "less than reverent" criticism of the "Holy Oldtimers"—Roy Bedichek, J. Frank Dobie, and Walter Prescott Webb ("Bridegroom" 1). In his opinion, they had fettered the talents and imagination of ambitious writers because of their focus on the frontier ethos as a writer's most viable stock in trade. McMurtry explained: "[T]he frontier ethos . . . apparently inhibited . . . the more introspective modes of expression. One may write on the frontier, but one must write about the world that is or was, not about the person one is or the world one might imagine" (*ING* 52). His radically divergent revisionist views begot clouds that darkened when he pointed out the obvious: Texas was no longer a rural state but, like most others of the fifty, was definitely urban. Writers, he advised, would do well to look to the city for those images that would enable them to write reflectively, introspectively, and realistically about Texas. And he continued, "[I]t would not be hard to find in today's experience, or tomorrow's, moments that are just as eloquent, just as suggestive of gallantry or strength or disappointment [as those that came out of Old Texas with its frontier values]" (173).

McMurtry's critique of Bedichek, Dobie, and Webb created a furor that has not been laid to rest. Any account of Texas letters necessarily has at the opposite poles of its axis the Oldtimers and McMurtry, and his opinions have become the catalyst for ruminations on literary traditions in Texas.

The exceptions McMurtry took to the traditional modes of writing about Texas were not just for other writers. A decade before "Ever a Bridegroom" was published, McMurtry hung up his saddle, dusted his boots, and set out for that most urban of Texas cities, Houston. But the strengths demonstrated so masterfully in his earlier fiction proved of little advantage to him as he undertook what would become the "Houston Trilogy": *Moving On, All My Friends Are Going to Be Strangers,* and *Terms of Endearment,* all three of which are concerned with places other than the cow country either in setting, characters, or coincidence. Despite his sensitivity to detail and the precision with which he made those details work for him, the Houston novels lack the sense of place which had brought him critical approval. The reason could be, as John Graves says, that the city shields its people from a very ancient kind of human awareness, the sense of place. He explains further:

> Sense of place is bound up with the way people are in that place
> and with the history of the people, and it's bound up even more
> with physical and natural detail, with trees and grass and soil,
> creatures, weather, water, sky, wild sounds, the way some weed
> smells when you walk on it. Those are the details of place, and an
> awareness of them is what I call a sense of place. (11)

McMurtry supports Graves's definition of "thereness." In "Ever a Bridegroom" he gives high praise not only to Graves but also to William Goyen, William Humphrey, and John Howard Griffin for their artistry in communicating the sense of rural Texas to their readers (13). But in the "Houston Trilogy" he himself is deprived of "thereness" by virtue of the limitations of the townspeople he characterizes—who are alienated from natural things—and the transition to New Texas—where there are no yesterdays. Given that the sense of place is bound up with nature, then the fact that he chose Houston for setting is of little note, as life in one city is very much like life in another. Achievement of a marked sense of place is unlikely whether the city be in Texas, California, or elsewhere.

City as setting effected other changes. The vigorous and colorful diction of his Westerners is replaced for the most part with a variety of cosmopolitan jargons having no distinct ties to geography. Another change from the earlier modes is structural. The confusion that typifies the lives of rootless, restless, directionless city folk lends itself to loose construction rather than to a "well made" narrative. And the unexplored dramas McMurtry anticipated in the emotional experiences of the urbanities—i.e., in their sexual encounters—fall short of meaningful.

McMurtry was convinced that the tensions created when rural folk from Old Texas confronted the sophisticates of the urbiculture, and vice versa, made for good fiction ("Southwest" 31). He found himself faced, then, with necessary stylistic and structural changes that would separate this work from his earlier work, the "Thalia Trilogy." The critics were harsh, even brutal, in their disdain for the new fiction, many of them measuring it by the earlier novels. However, because of the place McMurtry has been assigned in the literary history of Texas, and because this urban fiction can be viewed now in relation to his latter-day achievements, the time has come to review the criticism and to rethink the changes inherent in McMurtry's shift to the urban scene.

The failure of the marriage of Patsy and Jim Carpenter is the focus of *Moving On,* a 797-page chronicle, published in 1970. One can say "chronicle" for McMurtry seems to have taken a sociological rather than a narrational stance toward his characters. Patsy is central to a cross-view of the action and interaction of a generation of young people struggling with the social changes of the turbulent sixties, its uprootedness and its restlessness.

William Decker thinks the Carpenters belong to an "in-between generation." They came too late to share the traditions and values of frontier folk, and they came too early to be a part of the beat and hippie generations. Occasionally they suffer a twinge of conscience as if there were some dormant remainder of old-fashioned morality still available to them; often they rebel against the materialism of their wealthy Texas fathers and go on a poverty kick; just as often they use Daddy's money foolishly. They live chaotic lives because they are confused.

Details of the most trivial kind belabor the text. "The principal trouble with McMurtry's novel is that it is about 500 pages too long," L. J. Davis finds. "His characters are too amiable and ordinary, his action is too slight, his psychology is too shallow, and his incidents are just too damn normal to justify the incredibly extended treatment he has given them." Elroy Bode agrees: "The reader feels weighted down by details, and the book does not have enough drive or beauty or dramatic urgency to lure him on. . . . Thus the book is largely a misdirection of effort—as though Hemingway had decided to write a Sears Roebuck catalogue . . ." (428).

No doubt pictures of Patsy combing her hair, of Patsy taking a shower, of Patsy climbing into bed with Jim, of Patsy climbing out of Hank's bed are the kind of details, oft repeated, that cause readers like Bode to feel weighted down. Such minutiae suggest, however, similarities of *Moving On* to the traditional novel of manners, as do sociological signifiers (like woman's role in the home, child care, marital and extramarital relations, drink, drugs, and race); the shallow characterization of Patsy; the stereotyping of other characters; and the satiric thrusts at the intellectual types. On the other hand, there is an ambivalence that removes the novel from that genre, for McMurtry fails to maintain distance from his characters. Patsy is treated not so much with affection as gentleness, Emma with genuine warmth, his Westerners with pathos (often comic), and the university crowd with contempt. Among all of them, alienation is a constant, thus turning the novel toward existentialist themes.

One would expect Patsy to "come of age," or, rather, to come to an awareness of her selfhood that would allay her confusion. Reviewer Webster Schott finds a resolution for her in her "entry into love through the tangible presence of her child." Patsy, too, had thought little Davey would bring her to a "station where she would be content—not frightened and at a loss" (374). She was wrong. With the turning of the last pages, the reader sees Patsy "manless" and feeling "over the hill" (768). She is aware of the value of being attuned to natural things on the ranch, but she prefers the comfort of familiar things in the city. What cognizance the author grants her comes about through her consciousness that what she has missed in her life is attachment to the land and the principles to be derived from that attachment. She will continue on (there is no moving on for Patsy in this novel), existing in the malaise of alienated being. And though she relinquishes her own claim to the land, she believes that her sister Miri and Miri's young lover Eric, who represent the best of the hippie generation, will fulfill Uncle Roger's charge to come to the ranch, to bring their life's blood "back home, back to the place it [can nourish], the country it [can feed]" (797).

To sum up, *Moving On* is a big, sprawling novel. It is many other things as well: a novel of manners with random satire, a sociological study of urban life and marriage, and an existential tome complete with absurdities, all of which tracks are fraught with the poignancy of some characters looking on as their frontier culture dies, and other characters living confusedly in the city. Sadly, they will all suffer alienation unless they heed Uncle Roger's urgent plea: "The land needs you" (501). Reviewers, however, disregard such inferences and look to the marriage of Patsy and Jim for the pith of the matter. The criticism of Webster Schott may be taken for the consensus:

> McMurtry is a writer very serious about his work. He wants to tell us something important. He wears himself out trying to do it, finally giving up on Patsy, Jim, and their messy lives. . . . Rather than psychological investigation, his resolution of the conflict between his two principal characters is to introduce more events, more people, more of what he can do.

True, McMurtry loads this work with "more of what he can do," i.e., little stories: the romance between the King of the Rodeo and the Queen of the Ranch; the rescue of Patsy's sister from the San Francisco drug scene; the infatuation of a very young barrel racer for an aging rodeo clown; the search of a blasé Hollywood scriptwriter for a woman to suit him; life on Uncle Roger's ranch. Schott's judgment is that the little stories don't work, and he adds:

> The crisis in the lives of Patsy and Jim Carpenter is not other people and other places. The crisis is caused by unresolved conflicts within their own personalities which the author cannot identify. . . . If one senses what McMurtry has missed, all the words and lovelessness may come home. There's a message here, but not the one he wanted to send.

Reviewers had another opportunity to determine whether or not McMurtry was sending the message he wanted when *All My Friends Are Going to Be Strangers* appeared in 1972. Although second in the urban series, it is first in chronology. In *Moving On*, Emma tells Patsy that Danny "had written one book, had one child, broken up with his wife, and disappeared. His car had been found in Del Rio, Texas, near a bridge that crossed the Rio Grande" (789–90). In *All My Friends Are Going to Be Strangers,* the reader is taken back in time to 1961, when Danny, a student at Rice University, has a first novel accepted and there is interest in Hollywood in filming it. Danny is a naïf. McMurtry puts him on the road, moves the action away from Houston to West Coast cities and back again, and colors the whole with surrealistic happenings that have the effect of weakening the tensions of country-to-city transition.

Critics gave the book mixed reviews. Peter Dollard notes that once again McMurtry "demonstrates his affinity for a very popular sort of corn" (699). Martha Duffy praises him for his "indelible people" and "brilliant set-piece scenes" but compares his structure to "tumbleweed." An unnamed critic observes that the nostalgia of the earlier plains novels, used as a kind of sociology in this book, effectively aids characterization. Danny Deck creates "real affection in the reader as he yearns for the past and in journeying toward it, the random events, howsoever odd, contrast with humor and sense of place" ("Past Master").

Tom Pilkington considers Danny an anachronism. Strangely out of place because he cannot rid himself of the past, he is pitifully naïve in all his dealing with people in tune with the realities of present-day life. But McMurtry fails, Pilkington continues, when he attempts to communicate the conflict between past and present. Also, he finds the novel too loose and rambling: altogether simply not "a consistent work of art" (55).

"All about Sex in Tex" is Reed Whittemore's suggestion for an inscription on McMurtry's tombstone. He finds the lesson of *All My Friends Are Going to Be Strangers* to be "If you can't have sex in Tex, go jump in the Rio Grande." There are, Whittemore says, "good characters, witty comments on the current writing scene, good narrative, good dialog [sic], in short, the making of a good scenario for the movies, but the small talk, small scenes, small souls reveal the rut that Texas seems to have dug for its people" (28).

The problem with reviews is, of course, that they are written in haste, the critic hoping to be the first, or among the first, to make an evaluation. The intellectual exercise we anticipate to result from reflective thinking comes later, as in Alan Crooks's assessment of *All My Friends Are Going to Be Strangers*. His thesis is that Danny Deck is the alter ego of McMurtry, for the story is one of the self-destruction inherent in the relationship between a writer and his work (155). In this respect, *All My Friends Are Going to Be Strangers* is somewhat autobiographical, to which statement McMurtry lends credence:

> It is true that the better you write the worse you live. The more of yourself you take out of real relationships and project into fantasy relationships, the more the real relationships suffer. The popular theory is that writing grows out of a neurosis, but it doesn't cure it; if anything, it drives it deeper and makes it nearer to being a psychosis. I do not think that real writing is a purgative, though there must be some people who let off tensions by writing. I do not think that writing, or any art, pursued seriously is necessarily a health-producing activity. Writing involves a kind of gambling with the subconscious and the destruction of self-defenses. I don't encourage young people to write, for several reasons. For one thing, it's a very difficult profession. Not very many of them could conceivably make a living at it; not very many of them could conceivably have a very

satisfactory life—unless they are geniuses, and then they don't need advice from anybody. I'm just not sure that it is a health-producing or joy-producing activity. (Peavy 43)

In an interview following publication of the "Houston Trilogy" McMurtry addresses the same point:

> Being a writer sooner or later causes you to reflect on what you are doing and creates a kind of ambivalence. You get to wondering what it [writing] is doing to you, sitting in a corner with a machine, projecting your emotions [through characters on paper]. (Dunn)

Danny's troubles begin when he recognizes the hostility of former friends at the university after it is announced his book will be published. The estrangement which has set in is worsened by the beautiful bitch Sally whom he impetuously marries. They go to California, where Sally leaves him, and he holes up in a sordid hotel to write and wait for Sally to come back. Meantime he tries to recapture his "place" back in Texas on paper—Idiot Ridge, three hundred miles north of Austin, "where Granny Deck had lived and died," he reminisces. "It was just a little bluff, with lots of mesquite trees and rattlesnakes, but in a way it was the place most truly mine. The ridge was the northern boundary of a valley called the Sorrows" (212). But his "place" deserts him. The urban setting drives out the vitality of the rural scene.

Danny tries to move out of his isolation. He can find no circle of friendly writers. The women he meets want only casual sex, no relationships. An acquaintanceship with a Hollywood producer comes to an abrupt end when the man shows Danny his pet: the world's second largest rat. He goes to a hippie celebration but feels as apart as with the students at the university. He drives back to Texas to find the Old Texas where he can "connect." But when he stops at the Hacienda of the Bitter Waters to visit his ninety-two-year-old Uncle L, he finds the Old West he liked to believe in has disappeared. "[I]t was the bitter end of something," he said (199).

He comes to understand that writing has played havoc with his life. He had thought that, at least, his words were his friends, but they were really the agent of the estrangement he feels. So he walks into the Rio Grande with his new novel, *The Man Who Never Learned:*

> I looked at my pages under the flashlight. They looked odd. Pages. Words. Black marks on paper. They didn't have eyes, or bodies. They weren't people. I didn't know why I put marks on paper. . . . The marks didn't have faces, and I had forgotten the

faces that had been in my mind when I wrote them. . . . I had
never felt such black, unforgiving hatred of anything as I felt for the
pages in my hands. (278, 284)

Danny drowns his book.

Raymond L. Neinstein, in *The Ghost Country,* explains Danny's
estrangement from the "black marks" he had put on paper:

> [Danny's] search for a locus of value has taken him from simple
> nostalgic evocations of a more stable and heroic past, through an
> examination of the waning of that past . . . to the actual
> disappearance of that place. . . . This is the journey from
> regionalism to "neo-regionalism," from the environment as a
> powerful, shaping force to the imagination as locale and text as [the
> only] inhabitable place for those willing to live in it. (46)

A writer who is willing to live in the imagination as locus must pay the
price: alienation.

All My Friends Are Going to Be Strangers is an important book for a
study of the relationship between an author and his or her text. It is,
therefore, even more significant in any consideration of the development of McMurtry's art.

When *Terms of Endearment* was published in 1975, there was some
wonderment that McMurtry had planned the three books to stand as
a trilogy. The question persists. What holds these novels together?
Emma is the only character to figure in all three, but she is always cast
in a supporting role. The setting, Houston, is lacking for reasons already considered. One must settle on the urban-rural conflict and the
ensuant alienation for a constant to lend substance and a degree of
unity to the whole. The theme, however, is not easily discerned at
times. The excessive reportage in *Moving On* of Patsy's sex life and
failed marriage causes diffusion of the theme. The grotesqueries of *All
My Friends Are Going to Be Strangers* have the effect of lessening the
impact of city-country tensions. Likewise, the delightfully comedic
portrayal of Aurora Greenway in *Terms of Endearment* overshadows
whatever weighty ideas follow in her wake.

Even so, alienation is the thread that runs so true throughout the
trilogy. The sense of decorum Aurora insists upon as her proper
Bostonian heritage contrasts (rather than conflicts) with her "sense of
place" in Houston. Her experience differs from Patsy's, for her
"standards" structure her existence. At the same time, they separate
her from the fundamental virtues which are the heritage of those who
have known attachment to the land. Aurora is more fortunate than
Patsy, however, in that the author endows her with a sensitivity to

"place": she likes to feel the grass beneath her bare feet; she loves the flowers Alberto brings her and the trees in her yard; she listens for birdsongs and watches with pleasure as waves of clouds undulate across Houston skies. It is not only the gratification she derives from the things of nature but also her name that suggests she may be capable of finding a resolution.

Immediate reader interest in Aurora is fixed on her antics with her bevy of suitors, who, taken separately, fail in one way or another to be attractive enough to be invited up the stairs to her bedroom to see her Renoir. Taken all together, they make up the ideal man, Michael Mewshaw says: General Scott has a commanding masculinity; Alberto, an Italian tenor, though no longer able to sing, has all the ardor of his people; Trevor Waugh, a wealthy yachtsman, is an adventurer, not the kind to enjoy Aurora's "place" with her; and, finally, Vernon, the untutored, unmannered oil-rich Texan, has the wherewithal and the practical experience to take care of any and all eventualities.

Aurora keeps isolation at bay by manipulating her suitors, imposing on them as well as on herself the controls afforded her by her proper Bostonian standards. (Her daughter, Emma, thinks her mother's decorousness makes her ridiculous in hot, muggy, relaxed, boom-town Houston.) All the ingredients for humor are here, but not all critics are amused—or charmed. Robert Towers considers Aurora "who is supposed to be so charming . . . as little more than a termagant." He prefers the story of the "low-life, country-and-western counterpart" starring Rosie the maid and her husband Royce, who drives his delivery truck into a dance hall and demolishes it before he is stopped with a machete planted in his breastbone. Clay Reynolds places her among well-worn stereotypes, qualifying his opinions thus: "On the plus side, the book reads well. There is humor for those who have not become inundated with McMurtry's lampooning of Texas and Texans" (105). Others, like Roberta Sorensen, find Aurora "the saving element in the novel, although it takes some time to find her so," the book being altogether lightweight, "lacking insight or social satire" (358). Mewshaw thinks her arrangements "strange as they at first seem . . . eminently sane and reasonable . . . an interesting and provocative model" for older women who "are striving to redefine their roles" (44).

The last almost-fifty pages of the book are Emma's story, an authorial mistake, the critics complain. Sorensen's comment is typical:

Book II [Emma's section] neither adds structural or thematic unity to this novel nor provides a link with the previous two. Moreover, its tone is inconsistent with Book I. It is an oppressive conclusion,

> similar in effect to dropping a pile of Emma's dirty laundry on
> Aurora's dinner table. (358)

Towers says that "the ending—a real tear-jerker—dangles from the
rest of the novel like a broken tail."

After following Aurora's whimsies, the reader is treated to narration of the dullest sort about the boredom of keeping house and bearing children. It may be that McMurtry simply wanted to tell the rest of
Emma's story. When asked if Patsy was his favorite female character,
he answered, "Fickle novelist that I am, I think that I've gone on to
have other favorite characters. I think Emma is my favorite character.
Emma, who runs through three novels. For the moment, at least"
("Southwest" 39). It may be, too, that McMurtry had found a satisfactory resolution for the Trilogy. Emma's story, lugubrious though it be,
brings together the sophisticated Aurora of Bostonian "standards"
and the uncouth, comically pathetic oil-rich Vernon from the West.
They accommodate themselves to each other, each giving what he or
she has to fulfill the needs of the other. Intense suffering would be the
existentialist way of moving the characters to resolution.

It is tempting to see Aurora as the embodiment of Houston, a city
vested with the trappings of wealth, whatever is shiny and new and
extravagant. Overall it is a verdant and lush place—all surface, some
say—its people exuberant with the joy of following their dreams and
sadly unmindful of human suffering until brought face to face with it.
Aurora/Houston, so desirable, opens her arms, if not her heart, to all
who come to her, and she accepts their worship as her due. To complete the fantasy, one sees Vernon Dalhart as the rural folk who succumb to the charm and attractions she offers. They will adapt or they
will perish. She will not care. Though she is not unkind, she will never
ask them up the stairs to see her Renoir. But neither does she take
away hope.

The "Houston Trilogy" ends. The novels were not well received,
either singularly or as a whole, the connection between them tenuous
at best. Yet, their unfavorable remarks notwithstanding, some reviewers imply that the last word remains to be said. Towers, for example,
would have critics add another page—or pages—to their appraisals:

> A reader—or reviewer—should tread carefully whenever a writer
> decides to leave the turf on which he has established his success. It
> is too easy to chide him for not doing what he is good at. Admirers
> of Larry McMurtry will want to extend their close and sympathetic
> attention to [the urban novels].

Closer attention to the "Houston Trilogy" in the light of McMurtry's later novels up to and including *Lonesome Dove* must show that he was "taking large risks, that he [was] deliberately rupturing his tone and collapsing his structure in order to achieve a richer complexity or something like that," Towers adds. The urban novels would then stand as the transition from the stylistics of the earlier Old Texas novels to devices he would continue to develop. Structures are episodic, an on-the-road motif lending itself to this kind of movement and, at the same time, allowing metaphorical dimensions. There may be several themes, or levels of meaning, running concurrently. The episodic structure also allows a galaxy of characters. The grotesque and the absurd become more shocking. Sex, more than a trademark, continues to be the favorite source for exploring emotion. And characters continue to be drawn with precise and memorable detail.

Craig Edward Clifford offers this concluding remark:

> What I would like to see is not another *Horseman, Pass By* or *Leaving Cheyenne* . . . but an older, wiser, better-educated, more worldly, more skillful Larry McMurtry graduated from these first-rate accounts of the remnants of the frontier spirit to a great novel on the same themes. He's as capable as anyone of doing for the Texas frontier tradition what Faulkner did for the South. (21)

The evidence is strong that the "Houston Trilogy" moved McMurtry, if not to Faulknerian density, at least to his own "literary coming of age"—a phrase he uses in "Ever a Bridegroom" (9). It is also in that essay that one can elicit the goal he must have attempted to reach while composing the three novels. He appears to be seeking the "richer possibilities" of "intricate social networks" where a reader can sense "a mind actively in contact with other minds" (10, 11). To accept this as McMurtry's ambition for his own writing leads one to consider the impact on his work of the Russians—Dostoevski, Tolstoi, and Turgenev—inasmuch as he is known to have said they have been primary influences.

All of which encourages serious readers to rethink the hastily conceived impressions of the critics of the "Houston Trilogy" and to move on with McMurtry.

WORKS CITED

Bode, Elroy. "Moving On . . . and On . . . and On." *Southwest Review* 55 (1970): 427–31.

Clifford, Craig Edward. *In the Deep Heart's Core.* College Station: Texas A&M UP, 1981.

Crooks, Alan. "Larry McMurtry—A Writer in Transition: An Essay-Review." *Western American Literature* 7 (1972): 151–55.

Davis, L. J. Rev. of *Moving On. Book World* 21 June 1970: 6.

Decker, William. Rev. of *Moving On. Saturday Review of Literature* 17 Oct. 1970: 36.

Dollard, Peter. Rev. of *All My Friends Are Going to Be Strangers. Library Journal* 15 Feb. 1972: 699–700.

Duffy, Martha. "Moving On." *Time* 3 Apr. 1972: 64.

Dunn, Si. "Ex-native Son McMurtry." *Texas Observer.* 16 Jan. 1976: 13.

Graves, John. "The Southwest as the Cradle of the Writer." *The American Southwest: Cradle of Literary Art.* Ed. Robert W. Walts. San Marcos, TX: Southwest Texas State U, 1981. 5–20.

McMurtry, Larry. *All My Friends Are Going to Be Strangers.* New York: Simon and Schuster, 1972.

———. "Ever a Bridegroom: Reflections on the Failure of Texas Literature." *Texas Observer.* 23 Oct. 1981. 1+.

———. *In a Narrow Grave.* Austin, TX: Encino, 1968.

———. *Moving On.* New York: Simon and Schuster, 1970.

———. "The Southwest as the Cradle of the Novelist." *The American Southwest: Cradle of Literary Art.* Ed. Robert W. Walts. San Marcos, TX: Southwest Texas State U, 1981.

———. *Terms of Endearment.* New York: Simon and Schuster, 1975.

Mewshaw, Michael. "Moving On." *Texas Monthly* Nov. 1975: 44+.

Neinstein, Raymond L. *The Ghost Country: A Study of the Novels of Larry McMurtry.* Modern Authors Monograph Series 1. Berkeley: Creative Arts, 1976.

"Past Master." *Times Literary Supplement* 23 Mar. 1973: 313.

Peavy, Charles D. *Larry McMurtry.* Twayne's United States Author Series 291. Boston: Twayne, 1977.

Pilkington, William T[om]. Rev. of *All My Friends Are Going to Be Strangers. Southwestern American Literature* 2 (1972): 54–55.

Reynolds, R. C[lay]. "Trilogy-Adventures Rounded Out." *Southwest Review* 61 (1976): 102–05.

Schott, Webster. "Words, Words, Sex, Sex." *New York Times Book Review* 26 July 1970: 16.

Sorensen, Roberta. Rev. of *Terms of Endearment. Western American Literature* 11 (1977): 356–58.

Towers, Robert. "An Oddly Misshapen Novel by a Highly Accomplished Novelist." *New York Times Book Review* 19 Oct. 1975: 4.

Whittemore, Reed. "Texas Sex." *New Republic* 1 Apr. 1972: 28–29.

The reception of *Moving On* (1970), *All My Friends Are Going to Be Strangers* (1972), and *Terms of Endearment* (1975) was negative by and large, occasioning some attacks approaching the vituperative. Friendly reviewers often founded their praise on reminiscences of the McMurtry of the plains. However, now that McMurtry has won the Pulitzer Prize, it appears that serious readers may come back to the "Houston Trilogy" to see the usefulness of the three new novels to him, i.e., where they stand in the development of his art.

The following critiques fall short of calling for a reconsideration, but they do suggest it.

Kerry Ahearn's "More D'Urban . . ." rounds up about all the reviewers had to say, along with his commentary on what was good in the first novels and what was bad in the later ones (excluding the 1975 publication). His conclusion is open-ended: "The strange case of Larry McMurtry is still to be resolved."

Elroy Bode in "Moving On . . ." and Alan F. Crooks in "Larry McMurtry . . ." both see the writer in transition. Bode regrets that McMurtry gave the "best of himself first," only to find himself "caught in a kind of trap . . . created by East Coast critics." *Moving On* marks a critical point in McMurtry's career, Bode concludes and wonders what he will do to bring his readers back to cheers. Crooks questions whether the artist has "grown" enough at this stage to write novels about other than the West and proposes the transition to be a move away from novels to screen writing.

Michael Mewshaw and Robert Towers focus on Aurora Greenway and her entourage in *Terms of Endearment,* Mewshaw reveling in and wishing for more about the idiosyncratic figures, and Towers wondering what McMurtry was up to.

Finally, there is added Barbara Granzow's "The Western Writer . . . ," not for reassessment of the trilogy, but to note the literary relationship between Wallace Stegner and McMurtry. Granzow's Procrustean bed for comparing Danny Deck with Stegner's American Western writer has more to say about Western writers than about McMurtry's art.

.   .

More D'Urban:
The Texas Novels of Larry McMurtry
KERRY AHEARN

Recently, I met a young woman who adores the work of Larry Mc-
Murtry and who confided that she was first drawn to him when she
heard he often wears a sweatshirt inscribed, "I am a regional writer." I
don't know if the sweatshirt ever existed, but I am certain that at least
figuratively, McMurtry has taken it off. The irony of the "regional
writer" pose is no longer tolerable to him, and he has written off Texas.
A recent *Atlantic Monthly* essay explains why his fiction subsequent to
Terms of Endearment (1975) will feature an "international" cast:

> [Novelists] exploit a given region, suck what thematic riches they
> can from it, and then, if they are able, move on to whatever regions
> promise yet more riches. I was halfway through my sixth Texas
> novel when I suddenly began to notice that where place was
> concerned, I was sucking air.

Just a few years ago, his book of essays, *In a Narrow Grave,* defended
Texas as rich ground for the novelist:

> The state is at that stage of metamorphosis when it is most fertile
> with conflict, when rural and soil traditions are competing most
> desperately with urban traditions—competing for the allegiance
> of the young. The city will win, of course, but its victory won't be
> cheap—the country traditions were very strong. As the cowboys
> leave the range and learn to accommodate themselves to the
> suburbs, defeats that are tragic in quality must occur and may
> be recorded.

What went wrong? McMurtry's five Texas novels, from *Horseman,
Pass By* (1961) through *All My Friends Are Going to Be Strangers*
(1973), showed a writer eager to tell a good story and willing to experiment. He tried short novels and long (*Moving On* [1970] fell just short
of eight hundred pages); he has employed different points of view, rural
and urban locales, male and female protagonists. Such a course implies
a writer serious about his craft, and yet the differences may hint at
McMurtry's uncertainty with how to use Texas experience. The two
quotations above signal one difficulty: they imply different approaches
to fiction—the first presenting an obviously superficial conception of
setting, and the second an obviously deep sympathy for the intricacies
of human character and situation. The pair of statements charts a

change in McMurtry rather than in the Texas material; he has come more and more to subscribe to that peculiar Eastern parochialism which views the Great Plains only as a place, denying it the complexity of reality. We may take McMurtry at his word: he has become an "exploiter" rather than an explorer of Texas experience. His work shows an increasing absence of psychological depth and artistic refinement (from individual word choice to total vision). *Horseman, Pass By* is superior to the *Hud* Paramount made of it, more alive and more controlled; the film version of *The Last Picture Show* (1966) is a finer piece than the novel because it imposes restraint the book badly needs. That comparison hints at what might be called McMurtry's "decline to success."

The sudden disenchantment with place is not surprising. The writer of serious fiction in the West has always battled the cultural version of the Myth of the Great American Desert. McMurtry's *Atlantic* essay shows him especially vulnerable, since it pictures the novelist as a kind of carpetbagger who uses his repertoire of tricks before a regional backdrop and then moves on when the place will provide no more variety. At the time of his greatest successes, in fact, McMurtry wrote that being a Texas writer was leaving him in a progressively darker humor: "We [Texans] aren't thought of as quaintly vulgar any more. Some may find us *dangerously* vulgar, but the majority just find us boring."

McMurtry's first two novels, *Horseman, Pass By* and *Leaving Cheyenne* (1962), fight this majority view, exploring as they do the people, the rhythms of their lives, and the meaning they derive from life on the Texas plains, which tend to reflect their beholder's mood and emphasize it. Lonnie's first words in the prologue to *Horseman* convey something of this purpose:

> I remember how green the early oat fields were, that year, and how the plains looked in April, after the mesquite leafed out. . . .
> When I rode out with him on Saturdays, Granddad would sometimes get down from his horse, to show me how the grass was shooting its runners over the droughty ground; and he told me that nature would always work her own cures, if people would be patient, and give her time.

To Hud, the land is something to poke wellholes through, and from that contrast in views comes the tension that moves the novel to its sad end. It also moved McMurtry to subsequent novels. His center is Thalia, a North Central Texas cattle town similar to his childhood home, and though his focus has moved from adolescents to young adults and the scene has shifted to Houston, the plains remain vastly important as memory, escape, even value. His people are either from the plains or they go to them. The landscape moves people, and a consideration of how he explores and exploits its possibilities reveals a good deal about his difficulties and successes, and also about the problems of the contemporary Western writer, for McMurtry, like the best Western writers we have, Wallace Stegner and Wright Morris, attempts to escape the stereotypes of the Wild West myth and to free himself from our persistent frontier fantasies.

That stance is evident even in *Horseman, Pass By*, more than a eulogy to a vanishing, ennobling way of life, and more than a sentimental response to the Texas plains. The prologue hints too at the discouraging emptiness of the scene and the temptations in the distance. While his grandfather Homer sleeps, Lonnie climbs the windmill:

> Sitting there with only the wind and the darkness around me, I
> thought of all the important things I had to think about: my honors,
> my worries, my ambitions. . . . When it was clear enough I could
> see the airplane beacons flashing from the airport in Wichita Falls.

The plains setting, McMurtry implies, is important to Western fiction, but should not be presented as a formula influence because in sum it is everything everyone has described it to be, and at any given moment it could reflect a variety of those attributes. Considered in the abstract, McMurtry's attitude is deceptively simple, but because it avoids stereotypes, it allows the physical landscape to become the complex and subtle influence one would expect from the fiction of any region.

Remarkably, the few serious critics to deal with the novel have overlooked or misinterpreted this aspect of McMurtry's independence from traditional approaches. One of the most perceptive essays yet to appear on *Horseman, Pass By*, James K. Folsom's *"Shane* and *Hud:* Two Stories in Search of a Medium,"* argues that the book reflects a "belief, inherent in primitivism, that man reflects in moral terms the physical nature of his environment," in this case, "an attitude that has been present in Americans' treatment of their epic since the West was first assumed to be the most significant factor in the American experience." The "physical nature" in McMurtry's story he characterizes as "ugliness," implying that Hud's evil personality should be taken as a reflection of the place where he grew up. Such a position ignores the presence of old Homer as a moral touchstone, and Hud's absolute indifference to the land his stepfather loves. Their clearest confrontation on that issue concerns oil leases, which Hud favors: Homer says, "What good's oil to me? I can't ride out every day an' prowl amongst 'em, like I can my cattle. I can't breed 'em or tend 'em or rope 'em or chase 'em or nothin.' I can't feel a smidgen a pride in 'em, cause they ain't none a my doin'." Late in the novel, when Hud kills him, the act symbolizes the supplanting of Homer's traditional yeomanry by the get-rich-quick ethic that disconnects itself from nature's rhythms and depends purely upon exploitation. Homer had pointed with relief at grass roots spreading out to knit the land together; he knew the oilmen would work the opposite effect ("They ain't gonna come in and grade no roads, so the wind can blow me away").

Folsom correctly identifies ugliness as a basic quality in McMurtry's picture of Texas life, but it comes not as he would have us believe, from the "physical nature of the environment," which is actually neutral, but rather from human habitation. Thalia is ugly, but McMurtry portrays the town with the same restraint he exhibits in presenting the natural world. His most reliable technique is Lonnie's tone: ranch life might be monotonous, but at least it presses people together, directs their energies, and keeps them busy—when Lonnie speaks of Thalia, or other, larger towns, an unappeasable longing changes his voice. Yet Thalia offers nothing beyond the inevitable pool hall and all-night cafe, and two of the novel's finest "town" sequences detail, first, an adolescent night-out where nothing happens (adventure comes from their fantasies; they can't even get a fight started), and second, the final night of the annual rodeo—the biggest day on the social calendar—a mad whirl of drunken fights, banal honky-tonk tunes, and Lonnie's quiet anguish. As he gets closer to town, he leaves farther behind the close and (relatively speaking) satisfying human relationships of the ranch, which only increases his frustration. He looks to the city, to the distant places Homer's cowboy Jesse has been, and when the people he loves on the ranch disappear from his life— Halmea, the proud and understanding Negro cook who leaves after Hud rapes her; Jesse, released when the diseased Bannon herd is destroyed; Homer himself—his first impulse is to cross the great spaces that surround him and search for new people and good times. The reader recognizes, and Folsom has pointed out, that Lonnie views the adult, especially the urban, world with a romantic bias; Hud shakes that attitude just enough to leave Lonnie adrift—although in the final scene he is "tempted to do like Jesse once said: to lean back and let the truck take me as far as it was going," he suspects that such an escape won't bring him the satisfaction he once expected. Yet he knows that what lies behind offers him little. The spacious landscape which in stereotype acts as an oppressive influence, and which in Lonnie's occasional view separates him from life's real enjoyments, is also, ironically, an insulator. Lonnie's acceptance of that possibility leaves him in a true dilemma. The puzzled young man who at the book's end withdraws his savings and heads north, ultimate destination unknown, actually continues an initiation barely begun, and will learn some predictably hard lessons that may dwarf his Thalia-bred discontent. In Hud he has encountered real evil, but he still does not comprehend it fully; he ends his tale in a quiet daze, puzzled that "Hud seemed calm and fairly friendly, and he didn't act depressed at all." The truly pitiable fact is that when we leave him, Lonnie is a seventeen-year-old without a dream. And if the empty landscape becomes an analogue for his condition, it is because we make it so. Others, we know, lived well there.

McMurtry's distinguishing so completely between those living in harmony with the plains' natural rhythms, and the sordid, frantic world of violence, lust, and amorality Hud represents, may constitute overstatement. Homer, in his eighties, has passed the time of such excesses, though he admits to having seen another day: "I used to think [money] was all I was after, but I changed my mind." Lonnie is too young, too restless in the incipience of some of the drives from which the older Hud has made his life style. Yet even if the trio seems to represent the "ages of man" too systematically, they never become predominantly types. Homer, for example, maintains his individuality as a "contrary old bastard" (his own description). McMurtry's sentiment for the days of small ranches is more than balanced by his realism and the alternate focus upon town life.

The relative emphasis between ranch and town, so crucial in his fiction, goes far in explaining radical changes in the tactics of his next two novels, *Leaving Cheyenne* and *The Last Picture Show*. They sit on opposite ends of the Texas spectrum he introduced in *Horseman, Pass By,* the former a ranch novel, the latter a study of Thalia. Both are disappointing, for *Leaving Cheyenne* embodies too much of the sentiment, and *The Last Picture Show* too much of the distaste which, when mixed together in McMurtry's first novel, forced him to greater narrative caution and refinement than either of the following novels can match.

Leaving Cheyenne was born of what McMurtry called his special "interest in situations in which a person loves or is loved by more than one person. . . . I think, humanly, it's a very interesting question, how many people one can love." Depending upon what limitations one puts on that crucial term "love," the question might well be interesting, but the dangers of such exploitation in fiction are manifold. In this case, McMurtry's tendency to make characters represent vectors plagues the narrative. He emphasizes sexual love, and has his patently unselfish heroine Molly Taylor relating with three men; recognizing that his study must explore the psychological implications, he has each of the men represent a distinct "type"—for Eddie Taylor, the man Molly inexplicably marries, sex is a weapon; for Gideon Fry and Johnny McCloud (best friends from boyhood), it expresses affection, but whereas Johnny's free spirit allows him to enjoy it completely, Gid, whom Molly loves most, is bothered throughout his life by guilt. He can never, as she says, go "whole hog in love," so she refuses to marry him. Still, she bears Gid and Johnny each a son while Eddie stays conveniently away and finally dies in an oil-field accident. As though to prove that she is not simply a nymphomaniac or a mental case, McMurtry has her care for a mean and drunken father, and agonize in purest maternal fashion over her sons, both finally killed in World War II.

Even Hollywood's *Lovin' Molly* could not make the situation come alive. Because the ranch setting isolates the group, McMurtry can do little with them except have them go about their chores between couplings, forty years' worth. And because McMurtry shows such uncertainty in his psychological probings, it is impossible to take the novel seriously, though a Texas critic or two has tried. *Leaving Cheyenne* illustrates limitations both in a "just folks" approach to the rural West, and also in McMurtry's skills at writing problematical fiction.

The novel's three sections, first-person narratives by Gid, Molly, and Johnny, have a fatal sameness about them, an empty garrulousness signaling McMurtry's inability to establish the three minds as distinct, interesting, and worthy of our attention. Gid's opening lines capture the essential banality of the rest (one is never quite sure whether one is expected to laugh at the teller or the tale):

> When I woke up, Dad was standing by the bed shaking my foot. I opened my eyes, but he never stopped shaking it. He shook it like it was a fence post and he was testing it to see if it was in the ground solid enough. All my life that's the way he'd wake me up—I hated it like poison. Once I offered to set a glass of water by the bed, so he could pour that over me in the mornings and wake me up, but Dad wouldn't do it. I set the water out for him six or seven times, and he just let it sit and shook my foot anyway. Sometimes, though, if he was thirsty, he'd drink the water first.

Sometimes, too, one of them rises to such a line as "Sometimes you can't get around being lonesome for a while." So severely has

McMurtry limited himself in these narrators, who, as far as we know, never read even a newspaper, that any note other than banality rings false, as when the cowboy Johnny, thinking of his dead friend, says, "Gid was off in the Great Perhaps." The absence of "thoughts," the narrow uniformity of experience, vocabulary, and expression (people "tremble like leaves," are "pretty as a picture," etc.) are not implausible, but still boring. Had McMurtry chosen to limit the span of time and narrate the same events from three points of view, the differences in the three individuals' attitudes toward love might have been emphasized into significance. As it is, Molly begins her section when Gid is forty-seven, and Johnny's final section covers events of later decades. I can find nothing about the respective periods that demands to be told by any one of the narrators. Gid and Johnny go through life loving the same woman, remaining best of friends, and never, even by implication, revealing why they should be able to escape the savage, possessive impulses of that love. Explanations of a sort have obviously been planted in the story: Gid gets religion suddenly, and Johnny has little interest in marriage. What effect any of that has in real life upon the imperatives of male hormones is a question McMurtry must avoid.

The superficiality of the portraits, and the rather ineffective choice of the extended quotations initiating each new section, imply that *Leaving Cheyenne* was conceived and largely written before *Horseman, Pass By.* Its syrupy beginning, seeking to establish the close relationship between Gid and Johnny, reads like the archetypal First Novel. The rest moves clumsily and fitfully; at times, McMurtry's trio seem like antinarrators. Gid, for example, gives a single paragraph to relate his father's suicide and how he retrieved the body from a nearby pasture; Johnny tells how they raced over to a neighboring farm, grabbed a drowned boy from his mother's arms and brought breath back rolling him over a rain barrel, all in twelve lines. Ironically, words seem cheap to these people, and dramatic emphasis beyond them. Their low-key, long-suffering personalities make reader response equally weak. Where, one keeps asking, is the exploitation of human desire and its behavior? In the end, Molly has loved everyone, good and bad, as though conscious of the reader watching and determined that she can pull off the prodigious feat; now that all but she and Johnny are dead, none of it seems to have mattered much. Everyone has lost, and no one has learned much about love or anything else. The force within Molly and Gid that compels them to think of love in terms of singular possession, summarized in various lectures she gives him over the years, seems to answer the novel's central "question": we prefer to love one above all. Gid's inability to "go whole hog" forces

Molly to marry another man simply because "[she] thought Eddie needed a wife the worst." Gid marries an equally unlikely person for an equally implausible reason. Occasionally, one catches sight of the puppet-showman's strings. If, however, the novel is meant as an ironic commentary on the mind-reducing cultural poverty of the North Central Texas plains, it becomes a classic case of human stagnation and boredom conveyed through boring and stagnant fiction. Lonnie Bannon's narrative, infinitely more refined, avoids so many of the misleads and limitations McMurtry forces upon himself here that it is difficult to believe *Leaving Cheyenne* came after it.

In any case, McMurtry clearly saw the slim possibilities remaining to be exploited in his vision of rural Texas, and came for a time to distrust the first-person mode because it reveals more sentiment than he is comfortable with (he has formally repudiated *Horseman, Pass By* as "a slight, confused, and sentimental first novel"). Self-criticism is usually a symptom of health for an artist; a Western novelist must be especially careful of sentimentality, and McMurtry, who relies heavily upon his own life and family for some of the substance and much of the emotion in his first novels, is understandably wary. His next two novels, *The Last Picture Show* and *Moving On*, accordingly depart from the subject and manner of the earlier works, but they illustrate two very important problems for McMurtry: 1) when he leaves the first-person mode, he has great difficulty maintaining coherence, and 2) the distance between sentimentality and cynicism (like love and hate) is not vast.

His ability as a storyteller is brilliantly testified to by *The Last Picture Show*, which focuses upon another parentless boy of seventeen and traces the same themes of sexual awakening, initiation to evil and absurdity, and loss of human companionship that McMurtry dealt with in Lonnie's story. Hollywood made an excellent film by faithfully reproducing the feeling in his opening line: "Sometimes Sonny felt like he was the only human creature in the town," a desolation similar to Lonnie's at the end of his novel. By retaining the full variety of vivid and energetic characters (which it failed to do in *Hud*), Hollywood kept the texture of McMurtry's tale and emphasized serious themes without eliminating their dark comedy.

McMurtry's decision to focus upon the town signals a change in his use of landscape; his desire in *The Last Picture Show* to become a social critic of small-town life leaves physical setting without an important function in his work. Furthermore, his manner of criticism excludes most of Thalia itself from the scene. His preoccupation is sex; we should assume, I take it, that what he presents to us comments

metaphorically upon the quality of life in the general community. That
physical setting and the town at large enter McMurtry's picture only
to offer predictable effects—the land is desolate, isolating, depressing;
the town illustrates bigotry and/or stupidity on a large scale—implies
a shift in his interest to the purely popular, the exploitation of complex
human problems for less-than-complex portraits. My reservations
about this change come not from a bias against "popular culture," but
from the obvious fact that McMurtry's quality has suffered. What he
has written in the past seven or eight years has been too easy; his
concern for pleasing the audience has engendered a disappointing
carelessness in his work, so much so that I wonder what community of
writers he works in, and whether there is anyone to read and seriously
criticize him as he writes.

Nothing in McMurtry's sardonic view of Thalia demands the simplistic treatment he gives the town; he made the same point in *Horseman, Pass By,* without the excesses that characterize this novel. His
tactic here is to combine the purely popular concern with the sex lives
of Thalia's most adventuresome with his serious "invisible man"
theme, presented through Sonny Crawford, the victim-hero. In theory,
the two might mix, but in *The Last Picture Show* they don't, largely
because McMurtry never convinces the reader that he values the
"serious" above the "popular"—the latter is just too much fun. Although he displays sporadic sympathy for Sonny and Ruth Popper,
the football coach's wife with whom Sonny has a long affair, and to
some extent Sam the Lion and his retarded ward Billy, McMurtry
confuses the realism of their story with the grotesque buffoonery and
sideshow atmosphere of the rest of visible Thalia. The same adolescent qualities that make Sonny an object of his concern—especially
the boy's sexual problems—are employed with greatest enthusiasm to
make the rest of his friends maniacal masturbators, voyeurs, and
sodomites.

The most pervasive and disturbing evidence that McMurtry has
little interest in pursuing serious social criticism or psychological
complexity is the norm and texture of the narrative itself. Perhaps the
"invisible man" theme could have profited from the juxtaposition of
sensitive, recognizably human characters and a townscape of freneti-
cally sexed caricatures—the surreal metaphor might have worked.
McMurtry expends considerable effort presenting Thalia in terms of
stereotypes, but the narrative suggests that he considers the portrait
something other than surreal. Through most of the novel, the norm of
his language moves about so wildly that the teller often sounds like

one of the caricatures (though not in a systematic way; the narrator does not "imitate" the voice of the person being described). Had these modulations been used to emphasize a variety of voices in the town, and to reinforce the themes McMurtry attaches to Sonny's story, the combination would have strengthened the novel.

Before the story has really begun, McMurtry's uncertainties with the omniscient point of view become apparent; the narrator seems to have no sense of direction, as though unsure of what to do with the characters once they have been drawn together. Within a single paragraph, for example, the focus might jump to three or four different consciousnesses. A sentence seemingly dedicated to one character will shift to another for no better reason than mere proximity. Scenes habitually have their development interrupted three or four times by extended "asides" (bits of history, anecdotes to illustrate a personality trait just mentioned, etc.); these diversions, uniformly pursuing the eccentric, have an annoying monotony. The result is a fragmented, jerky narrative; we are, it seems, at the mercy of association, though this lack of shape and flow does not finally justify itself by creating out of its wandering course either a sense of the variety of experience or a Shandian personality. McMurtry may have had such a posture in mind; his use of incidental names such as Mr. Wean (the timid home economics teacher at rival Paducah High), Bobby Sheen (a smooth seducer), Charlene Duggs (who lets Sonny fondle her breasts, but nothing else), Frank Fartley (owner of the bottled-gas works), and Lois and Jacy Farrow (almost all the men in the novel plough one or both) sounds very faintly like Sterne, but also hints at the imaginative level of the general narrative. Whenever McMurtry can exploit that sort of humor, he does so, whether or not he violates impressions previously established. It would seem, for example, that Thalia has some good athletes (so confident is the town that the football team will win the championship that they present Coach Popper with a new shotgun two weeks before the season ends; the next year, Thalia wins every game), but when basketball season arrives, McMurtry shifts the boys into his formula for caricature and includes a long account of Thalia's 121-14 loss at Paducah (a not unusual score)—with all the predictable effects: players knocked out against the walls or hit in the groin by malicious passes; biased officiating which allows the home team to block, tackle, and gouge.

The narrator emerges not as a voice with consistent position or attitude, but as three separate voices. There is the high-toned, to convey humor and condescension:

The prospect of copulation with a blind heifer excited the younger boys almost to frenzy, but Duane and Sonny, being seniors, gave only tacit approval. . . . Sensible youths, growing up in Thalia, soon learned to make do with what there was, and in the course of their adolescence both boys had frequently had recourse to bovine outlets. At that, they were considered overfastidious by the farm youth of the area. . . .

And the low-toned, to capture the racy rhythms of street talk:

She was nostalgic for the days when boys necked with her and wanted her desperately and didn't get her. That was better than actually screwing, somehow. When she got to college she could start screwing again, and there it would probably be altogether great. Fraternity boys were gentlemen and would fall right in love with her when she let them screw her.

Most common is a more subdued, ungracious, matter-of-fact style, though it, like the second example above, does not maintain a completely consistent norm. A single scene might employ all three voices describing the same characters: the "copulation" is also referred to as "screwing heifers," and one of the participants is seen "beating his member against a cold aluminum gate." Sonny gets up one night with an erection "embarrassed by his own tumescence"; a little later he is described as "jacking off." McMurtry undercuts the seriousness of the Sonny-Ruth affair whenever a cute pun can be made: ". . . when Sonny was really beginning to get in touch with Ruth . . ." or "The thought of Ruth popped into his mind. . . ." In the middle of a serious analysis of Ruth's suffering after Sonny stops seeing her, the narrator notes: "From time to time she tried playing with herself. . . ." The variety of usage may add "color" to the account, but so unsystematically that the final effect is confusion. McMurtry's "social criticism" sounds in the end like cheap cynicism. The "invisible man" theme is something he comes back to periodically, but it never gets the serious treatment it demands. The crucial turn of the book's final scene, where Sonny returns in existential anguish to Ruth, concludes a movement from loneliness to involvement to lonely involvement that McMurtry has been uncertain with throughout. In a novel with the ironic inscription, "Lovingly dedicated to my home town," his creative energies have been directed toward presenting Thalia as a pitiable place where sex is the only available means of personal expression. The wasteland surroundings are somehow responsible, but he cannot capture their essence or explain their influence. Satisfied with merely showing the results, he never challenges himself to make the book out of the material he would like serious readers to think most important to him. The few "normal" people seem lifeless compared to the caricatures they move among; in the end, McMurtry doesn't demonstrate that they interest him as much as do the freaks.

With his first three novels, McMurtry answers the question of what he wishes to do with the Texas plains as raw material for fiction. All three contain the themes of male initiation, loss of loved ones, despair, and, to an increasing degree, sex. To make fiction out of a rural culture requires specific talents of an author, notably a touch for sensitive psychological portraits, for subtleties of growth, and for complexities of human relationships. These talents are, of course, essential to any serious writer, but their absence in rural stories is more obvious because less complex routines and a slower pace rule such scenes. McMurtry has not yet shown those talents. He tends to give more surface detail rather than probing deeper; since his Texas world offers, literally and figuratively, a severely limited amount of surface variation, he has understandably turned to sexual behavior as a major resource—it is the most obvious manifestation of psychology, and readers never tire of it.

McMurtry has also become increasingly influenced by his urban reading audience. His first two novels portray the life of ranch and small town with a clear effort to balance distaste for its limitations with recognition of the value of community, but *The Last Picture Show* seems to me a sudden turning to purest exploitation: he will tell the city people that all their myths about depraved country life are true. In doing so, he has become a popular writer, but I wonder what "truth" he seeks as an artist.

In *Moving On*, he brings his vision to the city and finds a new kind of anguish; it becomes apparent with this, the fourth novel, that though the settings may change, his view of life emphasizes a belief in the illusory nature of personal fulfillment—people do not progress, they move on. Although reviewer Martha Duffy complained that the novel has no "discernible direction," that "his books are constructed like tumbleweed" (presumably she meant that they move as the weed tumbles), McMurtry would surely defend those very qualities in *Moving On*. Consciously picaresque, it stops, not ends. Whether the novel can afford to be merely expansive and episodic is a question we will consider.

The picaresque structure does provide McMurtry with excellent opportunities to combine pictures of the rural and urban West into a single narrative. He makes the movement plausible because the prime mover, *pícaro* Jim Carpenter, is a rich dilettante afflicted with the ailment McMurtry finds endemic to young America: restlessness. First as a Kodak chronicler of the rodeo, then as a graduate student of literature in Houston, Carpenter runs himself and his wife Patsy through a gantlet of striking characters, rich and poor, Wild West and high society. McMurtry has many little stories to tell.

Moving On, an interesting novel because of its variety, finally suffers from an excess of that quality; it (and almost every important character except Patsy) seeks only diversity, and has only that to justify its movement. Patsy creates most of the tension by dragging her feet. At eight hundred pages, the book is about twice the length it should be; its very excesses tell something about McMurtry's problems in unifying his material into coherence, and his tendency to give more little stories instead of probing deeper into essential relationships. *Moving On* disguises that propensity better than *The Last Picture Show* or *Leaving Cheyenne,* because its narrative breaks in half (a term of emphasis, and to some extent sequence), one dealing with the rodeo world, the other with Houston. It reads like two separate but interfused novels. The problem is that they make the same effect, have the same organization, and feature the same cast of character types. Both halves are dominated by predatory males: Sonny Shanks, World Champion Cowboy, and William Duffin, English professor; both predators have a woman "accomplice" to attract Jim and reveal the instability of the Carpenter marriage (Eleanor Guthrie, Shanks's wealthy mistress, and Duffin's wife Lee); the rodeo and Houston sections each feature a sweet but eccentric married couple, the Tatums and the Hortons, respectively, and a true regional clown, Peewee Rankin and Dixie McCormack.

This diversity allows McMurtry to tell some good stories, especially in the early rodeo chapters, when Sonny Shanks dwarfs Jim and becomes a constant sexual threat to Patsy, a source of tension whether or not he is present. A fight scene in a low-life Houston Bar, Peewee's favorite off-season hangout, is one of the funniest sequences I've ever read. In fact, those portions of the novel dealing with the rodeo group contain so much more force than the long English Department section, I wish McMurtry had been satisfied with three or four hundred pages and eliminated the Houston academic scene altogether. The graduate-school experience might be material to arouse some imaginations, but McMurtry's failure to give it life (and his instinctive touch with the rodeo people) confirms what *The Last Picture Show* and *Leaving Cheyenne* implied about his creative temperament: he is not a novelist of manners; he finds his topics not in a positive, "realistic" vision, but rather from a strong reaction to themes which themselves have vast energy and mythic potential. Thus in Sonny Shanks's hyperglandularity he both exploits and spoofs the stereotype of cowboy virility, and also mocks the earliest literary tradition of the sexless six-gun hero; Peewee Rankin is Shanks's negative image. The rodeo scene, capturing the violence and transience of mythical Wild West cowboy life, is the kind of overstatement McMurtry handles best. When he applies his techniques to academe, the resulting eccentricities reveal nothing of the world they are meant to portray. Perhaps in America there are famous scholars like Duffin who move with their dissatisfied wives from one campus to another, seduction teams who separate students from the group the way Shanks would rope calves from a herd, and perhaps such scholars have developed come-ons like, "You're awfully pretty. Let's go out in the back yard and neck," and perhaps such methods work, but in all, it is not very interesting. When McMurtry published the first twenty-page section of the novel in *The Redneck Review* (1968), he claimed that it was the opening of a thousand-page novel; he came close to achieving his goal more by repetition than through the imperatives of his tale.

The two worlds of *Moving On* are valuable, however, in illustrating why McMurtry should seek "open" situations for his fiction, situations which provide much of their own movement. Rodeo life, for example, sweeps people along with such velocity that characteristic social encounters are short-lived, and he finds a richness there that allows him to leave the rodeo arena outside his narrative (except for the eerie scene where Shanks leaves Patsy calf-roped at midnight). Sport, hard enough to handle in fiction without the complications of cowboy myths, would be superfluous here. Unfortunately, the Houston college scene offers no such movement, and because McMurtry feels more confident with its routines, he spends a good deal of time describing them, though to little effect. Many times, he loses the reader's interest, and on occasion, the reader's confidence as well. Beyond mentioning the names of books and authors, and reporting in detached fashion the subjects of seminars and paper assignments, he seems at a loss. The few instances where he hazards comments upon literature in attempting to illustrate knowledge of it in his characters, he reveals both carelessness and his own limitations. For instance, he wishes to show that Jim and his few graduate-student friends have questionable aptitude for their chosen discipline, and so enlists Patsy as a foil. A voracious reader, she brings common-sense perceptiveness to literature and makes a mockery of the postures and formulaic thinking of the "professional students." Lightly handled, the contrast is effective, but he returns to it too often, and when he gets specific, it suffers. Early in the novel, for example, when he sets out to character-ize her as a very bright young lady, she goes to the film version of *Lolita,* a book she has read three times and loves; she enjoys the movie less, and thinks afterward:

> One reason she was annoyed by it was because she had been no nymphet herself, no Lolita, when she was that age. She had been thin . . . and had had no bosom at all. . . . The movie left her all the more convinced that as a teenager she had been a complete stick-in-the-mud.

So monumentally ignorant is she of the physical characteristics of nymphetry, its sexual attitudes and age limits, and so completely does this contradict the image McMurtry builds for her, that I suspect the mistake is her creator's. The scene is symptomatic of the absence of psychological clarity that plagues McMurtry's omniscient narratives, especially among the supposedly intelligent characters. He seems more comfortable demeaning his people and exhibiting their faults, and when he must present them seriously, he proceeds with less confi-dence and success. That more than anything else explains the slug-gishness of the Houston sections; McMurtry's intelligent characters can always be identified by their use of language, but he does not seem to have sorted out for himself what qualities make the relationships of highly intelligent people truly distinct.

Thus he seeks to demonstrate that the settled academics and the rodeo followers represent the same banality, and to do so finds the lowest common denominator: sexual behavior, which also illustrates the deterioration of the Carpenter marriage and keeps the book mov-ing. McMurtry might well have taken the advice of the psychiatrist who counsels the Carpenters, "Sex is not that important." All rela-tionships in the novel are defined sexually; every character either has or most obviously does not have a sexual problem. His point is clearly that the people in Houston, like their country counterparts, make physical coupling a refuge, acting out their frustrations, illustrating the emptiness of their lives. Yet the artist cannot become obsessed with what obsesses his characters, and long before the end of this novel he has narrated sex so many times in the same discreet tone that none of the episodes has special impact. For example, at least twenty times McMurtry records that the woman gets up and puts on her bra and panties; the garments appear so often as to imply a fetish. Sex plainly becomes his refuge—he seems unable to reveal his characters' problems any other way (another reason why they lack complex inner lives). The pairing of characters between Houston and rodeo groups was clearly intended to underline the theme of community likeness; it strikes me as the same kind of formulaic approach he has Patsy demolish among the graduate students.

The Carpenters give the novel its unity, and the dissolution of their marriage gives it a feeling of progression, if that term can be applied to the scores of sex-initiated spats they have. As several reviewers have pointed out, McMurtry doesn't know himself why Patsy and Jim fall apart. In the end, when he focuses upon Patsy's trip to save her sister Miri from a mindless black dopehead, he consciously diverts our attention from the marriage issue, the implication being that continuity in life is an illusion, and conclusions artificial. Maybe so. But when McMurtry's eye begins falling predictably upon the wildest Haight-Ashbury grotesquerie (Hell's Angels girls hand-pumping their guys' penises in the park, etc.), the reader who has made his way through nearly eight hundred pages in hope of something more than formula vision suspects he has been had.

Moving On represents an artist out of control, without a vision worthy of the name. Perhaps by some abstruse metaphysical architectonics or regional loyalties one could demonstrate that a book so long should result in a question mark (small at that), yet to hold that it is more than an often attractive but superficially conceived and carelessly written novel is to ignore evidence on every page. For an author who can write so well to commit so many blunders means, I think, that we should question whether he wishes to be regarded as a serious Western novelist or a "pop" writer. In this example of omniscient narrative voice, there is no distinction made between "horse manure" and "horse shit," "genitals" and "balls," "empty his bladder" and "piss," nor between "just became a man" and "became just a man." His people can, at various times, be "thrilled to the core," or "strangely incongruous," go "unawakably to sleep," eat "an enormous unstomachable meal" or a warm "unhandleable" candy bar, and feel "slightly inimical" toward their fellows. Worse still, McMurtry's penchant for repetition infects his style at the most basic level:

a lecture by a famous lecturer,
Jim had to teach a class for a friend who taught a class,
wash the pan of oatmeal before the oatmeal stiffened,
to wipe up spit-ups,
sipped sly sips,
a huge pile of papers and magazines piled . . .

> neither came or even came close to coming,
> he began to drive in his memory all the drives he had driven with
>   Patsy.

His prose, especially in this novel, is full of Whooery, Whichery, and
Thatery, padded in a host of careless ways, and repeatedly betrays or
confuses meaning in ill-considered descriptions such as "She felt as
cool and unpassionate as if she had become a virgin again," or "He had
never touched Clara, though he had looked up her dress a time or two
at boring points in the Chaucer seminar. . . ." This breakdown in
language is a further hint that McMurtry, having begun a story heavily dependent upon the complexity of its psychological portraits, finds
himself in uncongenial surroundings. A sentence like "Patsy pointed
out in the wittiest possible terms" characterizes his difficulty—he is
forced to name a wide range of attributes he cannot dramatize. Personalities like Sonny Shanks and the host of other eccentrics live
because they derive force from their very mysteriousness; the novel
does not depend upon them for anything but immediate effects. Patsy
and Jim sometimes come alive as well, but in general they, like Peewee
Rankin or Eleanor Guthrie or Lee Duffin, repeat themselves over and
over, for a single effect. The novel's last lines seem an abdication.

By the appearance of his fifth novel, *All My Friends Are Going to Be
Strangers,* the limits of McMurtry's vision have been established. His
eye watches for the eccentric details, especially in material related to
social, sexual, or Western myths (the *Library Journal* called it "a very
popular sort of corn"), and his pen puts them down in episodic narratives. In *All My Friends,* he returns to the lode: we find his young
novelist, Danny Deck, down and out (spiritually rather than finan-
cially) in Houston, San Francisco, Hollywood, and what is left of the
Wild West. Once again, McMurtry relies upon personal experience, as
in *Horseman, Pass By* and *Leaving Cheyenne,* to provide milieu, movement, and emotional tone. He seems intent upon exploiting this contemporary "Western experience" with the vision but not the stylistic
grace Philip Roth has used with middle-class Jewish life; Danny Deck
sells his first novel to Hollywood, and leaves for California to write a
second—McMurtry knows that, taken together, Texas and California
provide a greater variety of craziness than any artist could use.

His biggest problem is lack of a consistent comic touch; he tends to
overstate his characterizations, thus denying himself overstatement
as tactic of surprise (Danny's beating at the hands of two Texas
Rangers being a good example). Because he relies so heavily upon the

eccentric to make his fiction move, the extra effort of a really comic scene leaves visible marks of strain, the terminal symptom of comedians. Such is the case in Danny's brief confrontation with a rural gas-station attendant:

> "You oughtn't to sass around and use your goddam profanity with me," he said. Suddenly he hunched over, made a fierce face, and gave the air a hard karate chop.
> "See that?" he said. "I just finished a karate class, up in Midland. These hands is lethal weapons. I'd about as soon give a curly-headed fart like you a chop or two, for practice. Hai! Karate!"
> . . . . He looked forty, and foolish. I shook my hair at him and smote the air once or twice, for effect.
> "Hai!" I said. "Tire tool!"
> "Let me get them windshields for you," the man said.

Having met a host of fools before this one, the reader is unlikely to be doubled over by the "goddam profanity" gambit.

McMurtry apparently believes that large effects can be got from merely overstating the sexual, that the technique carries its own insurance, its sensationalism attracting readers and also serving as an ironic and devastating attack upon our preoccupation with sex. Two of the novel's most important women introduce themselves with the lines, "He wanted me to give him a blow job," and "Hi. . . . Does your wife like cunnilingus?" Danny, of course, has serious sex problems with both his wife and the girl he wants to live with. To make this procession seem inevitable, McMurtry creates in Danny Deck an energetic naïf who meets experience with wide-eyed wonder and narrates it straight. His peculiar combination of initiative and innocence explains the kinds of people he draws to him, but his narrative neither directly nor by implication supplies the coherence of an intelligent mind coming to terms with a theme worth considering. "Moving on" has become a necessity.

Evidence in this novel suggests that McMurtry has not from the beginning changed his ideas about the physical Texas landscape, but only rejected it as a valuable resource as he has drifted away from the realism of his early fiction. Occasionally, his feeling for the land appears, as in the *Moving On* sequences at old Roger Wagonner's ranch, quiet interludes away from Houston and the rodeo. He shows, too, that he can employ such scenes for thematic effect: when Patsy invites her lover Hank Morgan to stay with her at the ranch, its association with Roger's simple and honest life style nicely emphasizes her feelings of dishonesty and self-betrayal. Anyone familiar with McMurtry's earlier fiction will recognize that Danny Deck speaks not only for himself when, returning home after a year's writing by San Francisco Bay (as McMurtry did himself), he says,

> It was the sky that was Texas, the sky that welcomed me back. The land I didn't care for all that much—it was bleak and monotonous and full of ugly little towns. The sky was what I had been missing. . . . It had such depth and such spaciousness and such incredible compass, it took so much in and circled with such a tremendous generous space, that it was impossible not to feel more intensely with it above you.

Unfortunately, fiction comes from the ground and the ugly little (and big) towns, and McMurtry's distaste for them and much of their population emerges larger than ever in subsequent scenes, especially Danny's visit to the ranch of his Uncle L, the Hacienda of the Bitter Waters.

Nowhere else in McMurtry's fiction is there wilder grotesquerie or vituperation. Uncle L at ninety-two stands straight and mean as the mockery of all the qualities that made Homer Bannon a hero to his grandson. He punches holes in his land "because he hated the earth and wanted to get in as many licks at it as he could, before he died." There is no mystique about his herds, either ("he kept an assortment of animals he planned to eat"). He raises goats, pigs, buffalo, guinea hens, antelope, and camels, but always wanted an ostrich ranch and a few giraffes. He is a stubborn, crazy anachronism, living in this century but largely oblivious to it, squatting in a camp beside the twenty-eight-room ranch house, driving his car across country as though it were a horse, his attention always directed to the past. Every night he and his friend Lorenzo light a signal fire and sit by it, waiting for Zapata to return ("Uncle L actually kept a sack of gold in the jeep, in case Zapata needed money"). The manifold stupidities finally sicken even Danny Deck, and he notes: "The Hacienda of the Bitter Waters wasn't the Old West I liked to believe in—it was the bitter end of something." He had come with such enthusiasm and fond memories; to McMurtry it clearly represents the contrast between the essences and the myths we perpetuate about the West—his narrator admits that Uncle L has achieved self-reliance and a kind of timelessness, but also concludes that he is a "sonofabitch."

The Hacienda section shows considerable imagination in its attempt to dramatize McMurtry's antimythical attitudes, yet I wonder at his insistence on overstatement. What purpose, except distraction, does it serve to have a crazed Mexican ranch hand applying his erections to a posthole, Uncle L's camels, the truck's "gas hole" ("The other vaqueros were outraged at seeing a pickup fucked. To them it was unpardonable license")—anything, it would seem, for a joke?

McMurtry begins with the archetypal odyssey theme, the venture-and-return structure, and in doing so has many of his largest strategies set for him; his concern, then, is in the sequence of events and the development of character. Yet the result has no "intellectual resonance," little psychological complexity (for example, no one ever has the slightest idea what motivates Danny's wife Sally, who quietly disappears into a maternity ward); as Ruth Prigozy noted in *Commonweal*, "Although McMurtry catches just about the whole contemporary scene, he doesn't seem to know what to do with his [material]." In the end, he implies that experience smashes the romantic eagerness Danny Deck brings to it. The last scene, a bit of low-grade John Barth, where Danny acts out his suicidal urge in the Rio Grande, attempts what is by now almost a cliché in our fiction of despair; somehow, its choppy sentences and talkative tone seem out of place:

> . . . the river flowed down to me. I was so glad. I waded deeper. Such a wonderful thing to flow. I wanted to so badly. It was all I had ever wanted to learn. . . . Jill was gone.

Presumably, Danny does not, at least this time, kill himself; we are, after all, reading his narrative. His symbolic drowning of his second novel and the appearance of this personal tale make the final scene one of release, not from life, but into a new awareness of self-limitations. Even personal defeat is worth telling. The Rio Grande experience may be the "death" of a novelist, and its narrative the final statement of a sobered, beaten man. We know from Emma Horton in *Moving On* that his car was found, but that he remains missing; unlike Sonny Crawford, Danny cannot even maintain a superficial affair to keep himself from invisibility. I wish only that McMurtry had found a different world to move him through; his concentration upon the "shocking" and perverse seems to me akin to the sentimentality he criticized in *Horseman, Pass By;* both are sins of excess.

McMurtry must decide whether he wishes to be a serious writer or an exploiter of methods others have used better, notably absurdism and black humor. His last three novels have only pretended at meaning; their organization shows his tendency to dodge the responsibility of developing the serious themes they introduce. Danny Deck, in the agony of composing his second novel, laments that he has weaker capacities for analysis of life's raw data than he would like. Reading *In A*

Narrow Grave, McMurtry's collected essays on Texas, confirms what his fiction implies: social criticism and analysis of large public trends are not his forte, either. Many of the pieces, especially "Eros in Archer County," "A Handful of Roses," and "A Look at the Lost Frontier," reveal embarrassingly superficial thought along with an overabundance of detail and an absence of synthesis. Thomas Landess, his most perceptive critic, called the collection "disappointing"; his justification relates to McMurtry's uncertain course as a novelist: "The heart is McMurtry's true country, and when he strays far from it he usually winds up in trouble." His fiction has contained very few people he cares deeply about, and even they have received something less than his full creative attention as he continues to pursue his reactions against various myths, delusions, and strange life styles, victimized by the very qualities he speaks against because they distract him from the matter of the heart which he handled so well in his first novel. One thinks of Faulkner's or Reynolds Price's ability to create without idealization or condescension rural characters of sensitivity and enduring dimensions. The common folk in McMurtry's later fiction come alive only to exemplify viciousness or simplemindedness. Since the show must go on, he parades the freaks before us.

One irate Dallas reader wrote to the *Atlantic Monthly* editors, placing the Texas of McMurtry's mind "about five coon-ass miles southwest of reality," a judgment that would be merely humorous had McMurtry shown he possesses the delicate satirical touch his recent fictional strategies require. McMurtry writes that he is "tired of dealing creatively with the kind of mental and emotive inarticulateness that [he] found in Texas," where "drivers are complete solipsists," where the major university cannot "claim a single first-rate artistic talent, in any art," where "informed conversation is simply too hard to get." In general, his essays illustrate a simplistic, puritanical disillusionment he partially hides beneath the attractive flippancy of his fiction. As though he cannot rid himself of the puritanical ghost of Homer Bannon.

Faulkner reportedly said that in order to create, a writer must hate his region as he does his wife. McMurtry certainly possesses the detachment, but when he pulled off that regional-writer sweatshirt, his rejection was something like divorce. After all, the self-deprecating-regional-writer is a pose whose irony means self-protection, too. McMurtry has in a sense "made it" in Washington, D.C.; he no longer can use the irony, and out of his apparent security have come the overzealous attempts to bury the regional image by, of all things, attacking the region. Perhaps the move East, which McMurtry regards as the essential journey for artists of the plains, will provide him with a new vision. Perhaps it will merely supply a new cast of eccentrics. At any rate, the strange case of Larry McMurtry is still to be resolved.

WORKS QUOTED, CITED, OR CONSULTED

Primary

McMurtry, Larry. *Horseman, Pass By.* New York: 1961.
———. *Leaving Cheyenne.* New York: 1963.
———. *The Last Picture Show.* New York: 1966.
———. *In a Narrow Grave: Essays on Texas.* Austin: 1968.
———. *Moving On.* New York: 1970.
———. *All My Friends Are Going to be Strangers.* New York: 1972.
———. "The Texas Moon, and Elsewhere." *Atlantic Monthly* 235 (March 1975): 29–36.

Secondary

Dunn, Si. Letter to the editors, *Atlantic Monthly* 235 (May 1975): 26.
Folsom, James K. "*Shane* and *Hud:* Two Stories in Search of a Medium." *Western Humanities Review* 24 (1970): 359–72.
Landess, Thomas. *Larry McMurtry.* Austin: 1969.
Peavy, Charles D. "Coming of Age in Texas: The Novels of Larry McMurtry." *Western American Literature* 4 (Fall 1969): 171–88.

Reviews

New York Times Book Review (July 26, 1970): 16. (*Moving On*)
Library Journal 97 (February 15, 1972): 699. (*All My Friends*)
Time (April 3, 1972): 64. (*All My Friends*)
Commonweal (October 20, 1972): 71. (*All My Friends*)

Moving On . . . And On . . . And On
ELROY BODE

Just about everything that Larry McMurtry does in *Moving On* he has done better in his first two books, *Horseman, Pass By* and *Leaving Cheyenne*—which were beautiful and memorable.

His latest novel is an exasperating reading experience—exasperating because even though the book demonstrates McMurtry's immense capabilities it is nevertheless too tedious and too wrongly conceived.

As a McMurtry fan I lifted the huge book respectfully, assuming that nearly eight hundred pages of such an admirable writer was going to be a better reward, perhaps, than Katherine Ann Porter's *Ship of*

Fools. I thumbed through it, reading paragraphs at random, and the McMurtry touch seemed much in evidence: precise observations of countryside, natural-sounding dialogue among rodeo hands, frank sexual encounters and intimacies. So I settled down, ready to be impressed by the Big Book of the best novelist in Texas.

But reading it turned out to be less of a pleasure and more of a chore, for *Moving On* is flat-surfaced, lacking in bite, and at least five hundred pages too long.

The plot centers around a young Texas married couple, Patsy and Jim Carpenter. Jim, who has money enough to follow whatever hobby strikes his fancy, photographs rodeo life for a while before deciding to settle down as a graduate student at Rice Institute. Patsy, the main character, has a lot of time on her hands, both along the highways to rodeos and in Houston, and she spends much of it bitching at Jim— who remains vaguely preoccupied with his own work and who more or less takes Patsy for granted. Since Jim and Patsy are never quite interesting enough to make the reader care about them for 794 pages, McMurtry's narrative skills are misspent in chronicling their daily quarrelsomeness and general inability to get along. An ironic consequence is that they become almost faceless through McMurtry's massive overwriting about their lives.

This is the basic flaw in *Moving On*—that the reader becomes desensitized to events from the barrage of minutiae. He feels weighted down by details, and the book does not have enough drive or beauty or dramatic urgency to lure him on. McMurtry tells us everything we would need to know if we were deeply interested in what he is telling us, but we are not. Thus the book is largely a misdirection of effort— as though Hemingway had decided to write a Sears Roebuck catalogue and thereby obligated his readers to follow page after page of carefully chosen words about linoleum and sundresses and wicker baskets.

It's as if McMurtry knew *too* much about his subject. He gives the reader enormous amounts of information rather than groping toward a personal truth. By resolving to Tell All about Patsy Carpenter— the kind of soft drink she buys in a laundromat, the kind of gum she wants in a filling station—McMurtry fails to hint at, suggest, save back. Indeed, he forgets to be artful. He appears so hypnotized by his need to draw a full-length portrait of a girl who cries a lot and is constantly aggrieved that he does not seem to consider the possibility that someone else might find her a trifle dull. (You read along, and it is like being asked to look attentively at a very thick photograph album full of people you don't care about. . . . See, there's Patsy eating a package of cheese crisps in Big Spring . . . and that's Patsy and Jim arguing in Ogden, Utah, at a motel . . . here's one of Patsy fretting in bed after only having had a minor orgasm . . . and this is Patsy in Tucson, finishing Volume II of Gibbon. Dutifully, the reader continues to examine the snapshots—hoping, somewhere, to become enthusiastic about them. Yet as the pages keep folding back he remains hard-eyed, unaffected, uninvolved.)

The reader gets twinges of concern quite early in the book: Is McMurtry, the novelist whose characters in *Horseman, Pass By* and *Leaving Cheyenne* talked with such natural, bred-in-the-soil poetry— is he going to be as formal and distant as he was in *The Last Picture Show*? . . . And before you can say *avid* or *keen*—a couple of the words McMurtry was beginning to overwork—there it is in front of you: a sentence about Jim which tells us that "it took him much aback to be spoken to at a critical juncture in his waking."

Honky-tonks tumbling down! Larry McMurtry, sounding bookish: yes!

And all because of his heroine Patsy Carpenter, Girl Gripe. Patsy, who pouts and is continuously annoyed and who keeps responding to situations with her arch, A-in-high-school-English talkativeness. . . . All because of her McMurtry decided to surrender his own good voice— the voice of a native-son, spit-on-the-palms, natural-born storyteller of rural Texas life.

He is still a good storyteller in *Moving On* whenever he leaves Patsy to her moodiness and frustrations and gets to weaving his other characters into the plot. He is lean, straight-telling, unerring. He has always had a special knack in presenting characters with Hud Bannon–Cassius Clay arrogance and self-confidence; thus Hud-like Sonny Shanks, the rodeo star, is flawlessly done and throughout the book provides a strong, life-filled undertow that pulls hard against the small monotonous waves of the Patsy-Jim sections.

There are others who, like Sonny, are well conceived and who become a great deal more interesting than the two main characters: Pete Tatum, the rodeo clown; Eleanor Guthrie, the West Texas millionairess; Joe Percy, the Hollywood screenwriter; Peewee Raskin, the knockabout, wandering rodeo contestant. (There is one brief but glorious chapter—equal to the wild basketball game in *The Last Picture Show*—in which Peewee goes into the Gulf-Air Lounge in South Houston to have a couple of beers. As he sits among the Moon- and pool-playing regulars a mean-eyed husband comes barreling in to knock his two-timing barmaid wife about; then a neat little man in baggy green pants—who had stopped by to ask for directions—finds only two beans in his bowl of chili and proceeds to shoot up the joint.

It is a beautifully executed scene, putting into play McMurtry's fine sense of humor, and stands out from the rest of the book like the lights of a warm café on a long prairie road.) Actually, what McMurtry has in *Moving On* is a dozen very good short stories—not an epic about a Madame Bovary in curlers and jeans. Had he cut his material to the bone and presented his cast in separate, possibly even interconnecting stories, he would have made his people and his writing available to the public in a wholly successful way. As it is, I am afraid that the best sections of his novel will remain out of sight, buried in an intimidating swamp of words.

At one point in the novel Patsy is listening to Jim's old rancher uncle, Roger Wagonner, tell about his dead wife, Rosemary:

> Listening hurt Patsy more than the telling hurt Roger. A woman whose name was Rosemary had been alive and was dead—had sat where she sat and was gone. The old man sitting behind her had lived with the woman for almost forty years, had courted her, eaten her food, sat on that same porch with her thousands of nights, had fought with her, taken her places, made love to her. . . . And then one day without knowing it they did that act and each common act for the last time, rose from bed a last time, went to the morning's toilet, ate, spoke, rode the roads they had known, left their friends without being aware that they were leaving them, argued for the last time, touched for the last time, and, for the last time, were thrilled or hurt.

This is McMurtry writing with a passion that affects the reader— the kind of passion that characterized both *Leaving Cheyenne* and *Horseman, Pass By* and that is absent too much of the time from *Moving On.*

. . . Those first two excellent books: it is difficult to read any later work of McMurtry's without comparing it to their vigor and power. There was *authority* in *Leaving Cheyenne.* The sentences were as commanding as a boot heel struck against a metal bedstead; you did not read them as much as you were transfixed by their rightness and cool power. McMurtry's words were like ax strokes cutting strong, beautifully grained oak chips in the sharp light of a country daybreak. (In *Moving On* the words are too often the honings of a scalpel, making intricate balsa figures for a room of private exhibits.) The dialogue floated, effortlessly, and you felt stunned at language being handled so easily and well. Like Faulkner's Jason narrator in *The Sound and the Fury,* the narrator of *Leaving Cheyenne* suggested dimensions and realms of emotion lying beyond the page, in the reader's own imagination.

Thus *Leaving Cheyenne* and *Horseman, Pass By* were not *written*, the reader felt; they simply were. The novelist's art and his passion had been so subtly fused that both books lived effortlessly on their own, independent of their author. They were genuine creations, true and believable—living as natural phenomena in the world and apparently unattached to any creator.

This is the crucial difference, I think, between McMurtry's first and latest two novels: In *The Last Picture Show* and *Moving On* we too often feel the author's hand at work; we are constantly aware of his expertise, his word choice, his plotting. We marvel at his industry and admire his obvious gifts, but we know that we are merely reading books rather than having personal experiences.

With this novel McMurtry poses his readers a problem: What is a talented young novelist going to do if he keeps on writing—out of either habit or inner necessity—and fails to match his early excellence? There is no question, of course, of McMurtry's being now, as before, a tremendously good writer; there is a question, however, of why his more recent works fail to affect the reader deeply.

I think it is mainly a matter of voice. He has apparently given up the technique of having a narrator who uses the speech patterns and vernacular of McMurtry's Panhandle home territory, and has decided to write from the point of view of a rather detached novelist of manners. I believe that this change has been unfortunate, for it was a voice full of country poetry that spoke to us so well in his first books. . . . Also, I believe McMurtry is caught in a kind of trap—not the trap of success, as we generally think of success, but something closely associated with it: the need to shake loose from whatever image he has of himself as a Minor Regional Writer—the false role created by the prejudices of East Coast critics who failed to take seriously his first successes merely because of their Texas ranch-cowboy setting—and be considered now as a Major American Novelist. It could be that in order to be recognized as such a novelist, he is forcing himself away from the roots that have nourished his talent.

I frankly miss the Old McMurtry, and wonder what he can do to make us salute his work once again with cheers and gladness. So far he has given the best of himself first—as John O'Hara did with *Appointment in Samarra*—and that is certainly all right for posterity even though it makes things difficult for McMurtry who, like any writer, is undoubtedly driven to make today's creation a better one than yesterday's. . . . We can only wish him well at this critical point in his career and hope that he somehow manages to steer himself back into the deepest and truest channel of his art.

Larry McMurtry—A Writer in Transition:
An Essay-Review
ALAN F. CROOKS

The one moment of interest for me during the otherwise dull Academy Award presentations came when Tennessee Williams haltingly read the list of nominees for the best screenplays of 1971, for among those names was that of Larry McMurtry who, together with Peter Bogdanovich, wrote the script for *The Last Picture Show*. And despite the fact that McMurtry did not win the Oscar for his efforts, the film's great success is very likely to signal a transition in the career of the young Texas writer.

Less than two years before his Academy Award nomination McMurtry was drawing intense critical fire for his over-sized novel, *Moving On*. While some reviewers were content with drawing attention to the book's excessive length (794 pages), others were more vociferant in their criticism. Elroy Bode, for example, deemed the novel "tedious," "wrongly conceived," and "flat-surfaced."[1] L. J. Davis concisely wrote it off as an "obese catastrophe."[2] In short, few critics had anything positive to say about the extensive narrative of Patsy Carpenter.

However, with the recent appearance of McMurtry's latest novel, *All My Friends Are Going to Be Strangers,* it is possible to offer a more satisfactory appraisal of both *Moving On* and the new novel, for together they make up two volumes of a planned trilogy. *All My Friends Are Going to Be Strangers,* although the most recently completed, in design constitutes the trilogy's initial volume, taking place some eight years before the events in *Moving On,* the third volume. Due to the absence of the second volume the relationship between the completed parts is understandably somewhat difficult to perceive. Patsy Carpenter, the focal character of *Moving On,* is mentioned only briefly in *All My Friends Are Going to Be Strangers* by way of a letter from Emma Horton, Patsy's best friend, to the principal character, Danny Deck. Likewise, Danny is mentioned only once in *Moving On*. The character common to both novels is Emma, around whom the yet unwritten second volume will center—if it is ever completed.

Yet in spite of the frail connections between the two novels, *All My Friends Are Going to Be Strangers* throws enough new light on *Moving On* to warrant a reconstruction of its claimed superficiality. While it is true that Patsy fails to achieve any significant degree of self-awareness, her failure to do so may be considered less a structural flaw than a convincing commentary on the absence of substantial values in the contemporary West. Granted that the irony of Patsy's situation may not be easily discernible, it is ironic indeed that as a native of that geographical area which has become traditionally associated with courage, endurance, and self-reliance, Patsy neither possesses nor gains from experience these or other so-called "Western" values. She remains an innocent in the Garden, though the Garden is in reality a concrete-and-steel mechanized wilderness.

Supporting this ironic interpretation of the contemporary West are the situations of *Moving On*'s other characters. Patsy's husband, Jim, is another victim of the affluent society; blessed with sufficient means to pursue any career he chooses, he lacks the motivation to seriously pursue any. Other figures—such as Pete Tatum, the middle-aged rodeo clown; Peewee Raskin, the young, simplistic rodeoer; Joe Percy, the sensitive, and therefore miscast, Hollywood producer; Bill Duffin, the cynical, weary intellectual—further reflect modern man's inability to perceive his own problems. The most significant casualties, however, are presented in McMurtry's vivid portrayals of Sonny Shanks, the Hud-like World's Champion Cowboy, and his millionairess friend, Eleanor Guthrie, for whom fame and wealth are accompanied by boredom, frustration, and emotional paralysis.

Standing in opposition to these victims of the twentieth century is a lone figure from the nineteenth, Patsy's uncle Roger Wagonner. Through his West Texas ranching experience as well as an implied affinity with the land, he has gained the necessary insight to accept the world and himself as they really are. That the land itself played a role in the process of Uncle Roger's self-realization is suggested by Patsy's sense of its power during her final visit to his ranch:

> It was the silence of the house and land that made her slightly
> conscious of how isolated she was, and the sense was heightened
> when she stepped out on the cold front porch for a minute. It was
> not terribly cold, but cold enough, and the stillness, the moonlight
> and the stars over the plains gave the night air a cleanness and
> clarity that were tangible; everything in sight was very distinct. . . .
> It was the opposite of Houston, whose warm, foggy, mushy nights
> melted everything together, made neons pastel and figures blur. The

night was so beautifully clear that it was disturbing, and too dry
even for smells.³

But Patsy's realization of the landscape's influence is too fleeting to
have any lasting effect. The isolation she senses merely disturbs her
because she is unable to translate her perception of external differences into any personal awareness of the significance of those differences and their effects upon her.

This motif of existential alienation is carried over into the pages of
All My Friends Are Going to Be Strangers, the story of Danny Deck, a
young Texas writer who, says Patsy in *Moving On,* "had written one
book, had one child, broken up with his wife, and disappeared."⁴ Indeed, as the novel's title suggests, Danny's natural condition is that
which characterizes the existential dilemma; he is lonely, filled with
self-doubt, unable to communicate—except on the most superficial
level—and, therefore, unable to establish meaningful relationships.
His attempts to set his directionless life into some kind of order are
continually unsuccessful: he impulsively marries a promiscuous girl
because he likes the way she smells in the morning; moves from Texas
to San Francisco to try to save his marriage; fails in the attempt and
leaves his wife; finds Jill, a Hollywood illustrator, whose hang-ups
prevent her from participating in a sexualized relationship, and who
finally leaves him; moves back to Texas only to discover that he is
even more isolated than before. In despair, he drives to the Mexican
border, and after several futile attempts to establish communication
with other human beings, drowns himself and the manuscript of his
second novel in the Rio Grande.

Like its predecessor, *All My Friends Are Going to Be Strangers* is
episodic and, at times, rather dull. It is saved from absolute failure
only by McMurtry's knack of presenting colorful characters. And in
this novel, not only are Danny's friends "going to be strangers," most
of them are simply *strange.* Unlike Danny, whose problems are authentic and thematically significant, his friends are merely memorable
neurotics. Among them are such figures as Mr. Fitzherbert, Danny's
landlord, who drunkenly batters on the apartment's walls because he
is unable to bear the idea of his tenants indulging in sexual activity;
Godwin Lloyd-Jons, the English heterosexual sociologist; Jenny
Salomea, the sex-starved wife of a homosexual decorator; Leon
O'Reilly, a Harvard-trained Hollywood producer who keeps as a pet a
twenty-two-pound rat. Yet as memorable and as vivid as these figures
are, they give the distinct impression of being artificial supports to
help sustain an otherwise sagging narrative.

McMurtry's talent for grotesqueness is utilized for a thematic purpose only in the representation of Danny's ninety-two-year-old uncle Laredo, to whom Danny refers as his most colorful relative. And colorful he is. Though his ranch, the "Hacienda of the Bitter Waters" is dominated by a four-storied, twenty-eight-room parody of a Victorian mansion, Uncle Laredo prefers to sleep in a bedroll behind the house. Instead of cattle, he keeps a menagerie of camels, goats, buffalo, and antelope. Out of sheer revenge on the land he digs postholes he doesn't intend to fill. His wife lives thirty miles away on another ranch where she raises goats which, in turn, Laredo steals whenever he has the opportunity. His "cowboys" are a few half-starved, half-crazed Mexicans, one of whom attempts sexual relations with anything from a newly-dug posthole to a camel. And, together with his old Mexican cook, Lorenzo, Uncle Laredo keeps nightly vigils in anticipation of the return of Zapata.

What emerges from this portrait of the "Hacienda of the Bitter Waters" is an absurd parody of the "old man of the West" which effectively shatters the romantic myth surrounding the figure of the nineteenth century Westerner. McMurtry's portrayal of Uncle Laredo is essentially the demonic reflection of *Moving On*'s Roger Wagonner. Moreover, it may be the last of the type, for as McMurtry has recently commented,

> It seems to me I've taken these Western figures as far as I can take them, and that in Roger Wagonner . . . is the best I have to say about the old Westerner. . . . The treatment of the old man of the West in [*All My Friends Are Going to Be Strangers*], which I think is the last time I am going to do such a figure, is an ironic and rather savage treatment which takes all the glamor and all the romance out of him and he is presented really as a mean old son-of-a-bitch.[5]

Despite the exotic characterization and the ironic treatment, *All My Friends Are Going to Be Strangers* fails to move the reader deeply. Contributing to this failure may be the absence of a "sense of place" one has come to expect in a McMurtry novel. However, a part of this feeling for locale seems to be a conscious omission on the novelist's part, for on his return to Texas Danny concludes,

> It was the sky that was Texas, the sky that welcomed me back. The land I didn't care for all that much—it was bleak and monotonous and full of ugly little towns. The sky was what I had been missing, and seeing it again in its morning brightness made me realize suddenly why I hadn't been myself for many months. It had such

depth and such incredible compass, it took so much in and circled one with such a tremendous generous space that it was impossible not to feel more intensely with it above you.[6]

If, in fact, a portion of the novel's flatness is purposely depicted as such because it is reflective of the narrator's state of mind, it works *too* well. Hopefully, McMurtry will take his hero's conclusions to heart, for when he moves too far from Texas sky his writing suffers considerably from its absence.

Nevertheless, it is away from the Texas sky and the Western landscape that McMurtry openly wishes to move. As he says, "I would hope that I'm simply growing away from the West. One doesn't want to write the same book all one's life, and I have written three novels and a book of essays which are primarily . . . concerned with the West, and that's all I want to say about it, I hope. I hope I've grown in experience enough that I can write about other places and other things and not just have to go on writing about the West forever and ever."[7] Yet, whether he has in fact grown enough to completely abandon the West is questionable. Indeed, it is questionable whether any writer with genuine talent should—or could—give up his native region, even if his regionalism makes him "a square." Frankly, I miss the "old" McMurtry and, along with Elroy Bode and Wallace Stegner, hope that he will revaluate his position on future usage of Western material.

More importantly, I hope that he will not abandon the writing of novels completely. While it is not likely that his success with screenplay writing will "trap" him, Bode's question as to what a young, talented novelist will do if he keeps on writing and fails to match his early excellence is a critical one. Certainly a writer of McMurtry's sensitivity will react to the lukewarm reception of his latest novelistic efforts, especially if another field of writing is more personally rewarding. And for McMurtry the attraction of screen writing is very strong. Before the publication of his latest novel he revealed:

> I do want to go into screen writing. I've found that I enjoy it, that it is less lonely and much less isolating than writing novels, and that it may turn out to be just as satisfying creatively. . . . I don't have any very firm convictions about it yet, except that I am very fatigued with writing novels, and I would like to investigate screen writing either as a possible new line of work completely or, at the very least, as a balance to writing novels. . . . I don't believe it could possibly be good to go on pouring out book after book of fiction. . . . I think if you've been writing for fifteen years you very much need a change—maybe not quit writing completely, but

go into a kind of writing that uses your linguistic abilities in a different way.[8]

From these personal remarks and the unqualified success of his screenplay for *The Last Picture Show*, it seem only logical to conclude that McMurtry will be "movin' on." Certainly, whatever personal reservations he held before the film's release have been removed, and the possibility of his going into screen writing as a "completely new line of work" is very likely, indeed. Furthermore, it may be a very wise decision, for his fatigue and loneliness are easily discernible throughout the story of his alter-ego, Danny Deck. One can only hope, however, that he will not remove his exceptional talent to where all of his friends actually will become strangers.

NOTES

1. Elroy Bode, "Moving On . . . and On . . . and On," *Southwest Review,* 55 (1970), p. 427.

2. L. J. Davis, rev. of *Moving On,* by Larry McMurtry, *Book World,* (21 June 1970), p. 6.

3. Larry McMurtry, *Moving On* (New York: Simon and Schuster, 1970), p. 710.

4. *Ibid.,* p. 787.

5. Interview with Larry McMurtry, Salt Lake City, Utah, 10 June 1971.

6. Larry McMurtry, *All My Friends Are Going to Be Strangers* (New York: Simon and Schuster, 1972), p. 176.

7. Interview with McMurtry, 10 June 1971.

8. Interview . . . , 10 June 1971.

Moving On

MICHAEL MEWSHAW

Larry McMurtry's sixth novel is a significant event, perhaps a turning point, in the author's career. First, it completes the trilogy which started with *Moving On* and *All My Friends Are Going to Be Strangers* — although it's not clear in which order these books should have been published. Second, it is concerned almost exclusively with women. Third, it is not really about Texas, and many of the principal characters are out-of-state transplants, struggling to find roots in an area where even the bizarre indigenous foliage has difficulty flourishing.

Essentially *Terms of Endearment* is a comedy of manners populated by a cast of amusing and idiosyncratic characters who share similar, and sometimes interrelated, problems. Primary among the problems appears to be the impossibility of maintaining traditional male-female relationships, especially marriage.

Interestingly, Aurora Greenway, a wealthy, well-born, middle-aged Boston widow, the one character aware of conventions and tradition, learns the value of innovation and discovers a solution. Pursued by a number of suitors, she refuses to choose among them and instead decides to manage her own life and theirs so that they will all be able to ward off the twin enemies—emotional suffocation and loneliness. With a hugeness of spirit which harbors an infinity of contradictions—she is alternately sensible and nonsensical, decisive and capricious, charming and bitchy, engaging and insulting, yet invariably interesting—Aurora realizes that although she won't be satisfied with any one man, all of her suitors together add up to the perfect mate. General Scott provides the commanding masculinity, Alberto the Latin ardor and romance, Trevor the breeding and class, and Vernon a dash of Texas pragmatism and efficiency. So she encourages each of them, partly taking advantage of what they have to offer, but also presenting an appreciative and perceptive audience for what they do best.

In contrast, Aurora's daughter Emma (ironic shades of Jane Austen) wastes herself on a dreary, desultory husband. The conventional couple's trouble could be attributed almost entirely to their passive, hapless personalities. Unlike Aurora they never take command of their lives. But it is also clear that McMurtry believes the day-to-day events of domesticity produce tragedy as surely as character flaws do. A few random moves, a new job in a desolate town, a feckless affair or two, and suddenly the couple is adrift, not simply fading away from each other, but slipping beyond the borders they believed had defined them individually.

Aurora's maid, Rosie, is mired in a similar predicament, although her husband Royce is cretinous, while Emma's is merely phlegmatic. "Seven kids ought to mean somethin'," Royce insisted. . . . "Yeah, seven accidents," Rosie said. "Means you can't hold your liquor, or nothin' else either. We've had seven car wrecks too—maybe more. An' for the same reason." One of these car wrecks is dramatized in thunderously comic detail when Royce, drunk to the point of delirium, drives his delivery truck into a dance hall to run down Rosie in revenge for an imagined infidelity. He himself is later stabbed for a substantiated infidelity.

Compared to these catastrophes, Aurora's arrangements, strange as they at first seem, begin to appear eminently sane and reasonable.

Likewise her behavior, which at first strikes the reader as annoying and overbearing, even if funny, gradually assumes a sort of logic. Aurora is a stickler for precision, for fine distinctions and details, because she recognizes that a myriad of such dot-like details comprises the entire picture of our lives, and that imprecision in one area is bound to slop over into others. She insists on her own prerogatives to the point where she seems self-centered, but she does so only because she realizes that to underestimate one's "self," or to lose it altogether, is to forfeit everything. At a time when so many women, especially older ones, are striving to redefine their roles, the character of Aurora Greenway offers an interesting and provocative model.

One objection which might be raised is that *Terms of Endearment* is too long, too rambling and episodic. A few of the characters seem redundant, some of the scenes superfluous. But it would be very difficult to say what could be cut since so much of the book's pleasure depends upon marginal people and peripheral observations. There's Vernon, for example—an oil millionaire living in his Lincoln, which he parks each night on the twenty-fourth floor of a parking garage he owns. Then he climbs into the backseat and while gazing out over Houston, makes dozens of long-distance telephone calls to his holding companies throughout the world.

In the morning he eats breakfast at a cafe called the Silver Slipper. "It was run by a husband-and-wife team named Babe and Bobby, who made it their life. They had a tiny house trailer hitched to the back wall like a Shetland pony, and whichever one of them was tiredest slept in it while the other cooked. It was really an antique one-man trailer dating from the 1930s, and they had taken it in payment for two hundred dollars' worth of cheeseburgers owed them by a one-time friend named Reno, who had lived for a while in the smelly little trailer camp a few yards up the street. Reno had eventually found life in the trailer camp too stable and had moved downtown to the Trailways bus station, where he became a wino."

Some of this may indeed be irrelevant to the central story, but who would want to delete it?

Which raises another, more important question: Is Larry McMurtry, having completed his trilogy, finished with Texas? One hopes not. After all, what will become of Vernon, Babe and Bobby, and even old Reno and others like him who deserve to have their stories told in their entirety? For years McMurtry has mined a rich vein of material which runs the length and breadth of this state, but there is still much more waiting underground for a man of his energy, wit, and skill.

An Oddly Misshapen Novel by a Highly Accomplished Novelist

ROBERT TOWERS

A reader—or reviewer—should tread carefully whenever a writer decides to leave the turf on which he has established his success. It is too easy to chide him for not doing what he is good at. Admirers of Larry McMurtry will want to extend their close and sympathetic attention to *Terms of Endearment,* which moves even further than his last novel, *All My Friends Are Going to Be Strangers,* from the wide expanses and desolate small towns of western Texas, from the ranchers and waitresses and yearning adolescents who inhabit *Leaving Cheyenne, Horseman, Pass By (Hud)* and *The Last Picture Show.* They will discover McMurtry trying his hand at what seems, for most of the book's length, to be a kind of comedy of manners centered upon a well-to-do widow of forty-nine who lives in Houston with a Renoir, a Klee and a circle of aging admirers. And for as long as possible they will resist, I imagine, their swelling disappointment.

A displaced New Englander, with Bostonian antecedents, Aurora Greenway is imperious, self-indulgent, impulsive, good-looking, beautifully dressed, reckless in the driving of her old Cadillac, and a whiz at cooking up spectacular meals. Having dominated her deceased husband (an inert gentleman from Charlestown), she now bosses around her daughter Emma, who is overweight and drably married to a depressive student of literature named Flap Horton. The novel opens with Aurora's outrage at the news of Emma's pregnancy. The idea of becoming a grandmother is frightening. "Now I'll lose all my suitors!" she yells. But of course she doesn't, and for the next 350 pages we are invited to watch the way she handles her men.

These include a painfully submissive banker, whom Aurora ditches early in the book after overturning a plateful of pompano in an expensive restaurant to annoy an officious headwaiter; a sentimental Italian opera-singer, now retired, with a bad heart; a bristling retired general, who at one point actually says that old soldiers never die; a rich, tweedy, often-married yachtsman named Trevor, who sails in from Aurora's past with a final offer of marriage; and a humble, woman-shy oil-millionaire named Vernon, who lives and conducts his business within the confines of his luxuriously-appointed white Lincoln.

Except for Trevor, Aurora treats them brutally, ridiculing their manners and conversation, demanding services, rejecting their advances, correcting their English—leading them a merry chase in short. Despite, or because of, this abuse, they all adore her and keep coming back for more. The general finally wins access to her bed-room—a pyrrhic victory at most, for Aurora's behavior toward him remains as scornful as ever.

With all their eccentric variety, the suitors unfortunately remain thinly-rendered cartoons, and Aurora herself, who is supposed to be so charming, comes across as little more than a termagant.

To supplement his central comic action, McMurtry provides two subplots—one realistic and pathetic, the other farcical, with moments of pathos thrown in. The marriage between Emma and Flap slowly disintegrates as her pregnancy advances; it is a dispirited business from the start, seldom engaging the reader's interest or concern. Much livelier is the story of Aurora's long-suffering maid Rosie and her faithless husband Royce. It is treated broadly and bawdily, like a Chaucerian fabliau—a low-life, country-and-western counterpart to the goings-on of the lady and her suitors. Royce demolishes a dance hall with his delivery truck in an effort to run down Rosie and her date. Subsequently he has a machete planted (non-fatally) in his breastbone when a rival discovers him in bed with his girlfriend. Some of this material is funny; most of it strains to be funny. But at least McMurtry is able, in these sections, to display his much admired gift for rural Texan dialect.

In the last fifty pages of the novel McMurtry surprisingly abandons all that he has set up. He leaves Aurora and her suitors in Houston, relinquishes comedy, both high and low, sets the time forward nine years, and picks up the lugubrious story of Emma and Flap, who now live in Nebraska with their three children. The narration becomes perfunctory, underdramatized. Flap turns out to be a failed English professor who has affairs with students. Emma has two affairs of her own—both sad—but she and Flap keep the marriage going, partly from inertia, partly for the sake of the children. Emma visits an old friend in Hollywood, where she sees Ali McGraw, Ryan O'Neill, Peter Bogdanovich and Cybill Shepherd at a party. Then, back home, she discovers she is riddled with cancer. A softened Aurora arrives from Houston, bringing with her the general, Rosie, and the Renoir, which is installed in Emma's hospital room. The final scenes between the dying Emma and her stricken boys are the most affecting in the book, but the ending—a real tear-jerker—dangles from the rest of the novel like a broken tail.

It is hard to guess what McMurtry is up to. Is his main theme the unfairness of life, the unequal fates of the selfish, vital, surviving

mother and the decent, unattractive and helplessly trapped daughter?
If so, it remains undeveloped, lost among many distractions. Respect-
ing McMurtry's earlier achievements, one would like to think that the
author is taking large risks, that he is deliberately rupturing his tone
and collapsing his structure in order to achieve a richer complexity or
something like that. But the evidence does not support such a wish.
Terms of Endearment remains an odd, misshapen, surprisingly ama-
teurish novel composed of disparate parts that never cohere.

The Western Writer: A Study of Larry McMurtry's *All My Friends Are Going to Be Strangers*

BARBARA GRANZOW

In 1964, Wallace Stegner wrote "Born a Square: The Westerner's
Dilemma,"[1] an essay which isolates, characterizes, and therefore defines the unique species known as the American Western writer. That
is, Stegner gives a detailed account of the qualities and attitudes
which are typical of writers whose roots are in the West. In 1972,
Larry McMurtry wrote *All My Friends Are Going to Be Strangers,*[2] a
novel whose hero brings Stegner's generalizations to life and exhibits
the characteristics and attitudes which Stegner pinpointed eight years
earlier. Danny Deck fits Stegner's definition so well, in fact, that one
might think McMurtry created him primarily to give specificity to
Stegner's generalization.[3] McMurtry's novel and Stegner's essay both
point up the Western writer's "dilemma," his naïveté when confronted
with worldliness, his meliorism when surrounded with apparent nihilism, and his struggle for a new personal identity when faced with
literary success. Further, both works agree that once the Western
writer leaves his native land, he is both inhibited and sustained by his
heroic values—fortitude, resolution, and magnanimity.[4] That is, his
values prevent his full acceptance of corrupt standards necessary to
his fitting into the Eastern writer's world. At the same time, his attempts to fit into that world make his own standards seem inadequate. They are, however, the only viable ones for the Western writer,
and they are strong enough to keep him from getting utterly lost.

Stegner traces the Westerner's value confrontation and subsequent
struggle to regain his identity through, loosely, three stages.[5] The first
stage deals with the period just prior to and just after the writer's
having received his "invitation from the great world" (S 47), usually in

the form of a letter or telegram from a literary agent asking whether the writer has a novel. Up to this time, the writer lives in an essentially frontier atmosphere, is conditioned by the land, the weather, and the frontier experience; he is one of a group of local intellectuals, and for whatever reason, has written a novel, almost certainly about his region and the kind of people who live there. He is isolated from, and by extension, innocent of the forces beyond his geographically vast but intellectually small world. Once he receives his invitation to bigger things, however, that world becomes too confining, and the young writer moves to a literary center where opportunities are purportedly richer. Thus begins what Stegner calls the writer's "growth . . . away from the people and society [he knows] best" (S 46).

Alienation from the homeland continues in the second stage, when the Westerner tries to assimilate new values, those of the Eastern publishing and critical establishment. The younger writer meets "a literary generation that appears to specialize in despair, hostility, hypersexuality and disgust" (S 46). He does not feel comfortable with these people, but the Western writer draws upon his stiff-upper-lip Western tradition to make the most of a trying situation. He refuses to "demur at this literary model (S 47) by trying to accept standards alien to his own. His dilemma becomes more apparent: his frontier virtue will not allow him to go down this path: his frontier values will not tolerate "quitters."

Where, then, can he go in the third stage? Stegner's essay offers several possibilities, one of them positive. He suggests, for one thing, that the Western writer knows he can never become part of the Eastern establishment. Nevertheless, Stegner says, the Western writer may be tempted to borrow the themes and characters of Eastern writers. But this is not a suitable alternative, for the world of Eastern writers can never be home. And, according to Stegner, the Western writer "needs a present to come home to, even if his present is only his identity as an orphan with an inadequate tradition" (S 49).[6] While Stegner provides us with the understanding that the Western writer does not grow "through or beyond" (S 46) his heritage, but away from it, he yet insists that the Western writer must learn to accept his values and capitalize on them. John R. Milton terms the return process "another, larger, beginning."[7] The Western writer goes away, has his eyes opened, and returns to begin again—to see an old land from a new perspective.

McMurtry, at least insofar as *All My Friends* is concerned, seems to agree with Stegner's basic assumptions. In Danny Deck, McMurtry gives us a man of the land. Although Deck tells us little about himself and his background, we learn that he has grown up with the land and been nurtured by it. While Danny Deck is an English major at Rice University in Houston when we meet him, we learn that he comes from Idiot Ridge, somewhere near Van Horn, Texas. This decidedly frontier place, the homeland of Granny Deck and Old Man Goodnight, is, as Deck says, the place most truly his own. In friendly competition with the land, he has learned to hunt game, and he has learned to deal effectively with heat, wind, and flash flooding, the quirks of nature.[8] Throughout *All My Friends,* in fact, we hear Deck wish for the wide open spaces, the wind, the big blue skies of Texas where the most fragile of loves can grow. The land is magical—Deck thinks it might even cure his wife of her persistent infidelity, it might make Jill Peel love him.[9] John R. Milton would say that Danny Deck is the product of an "open-ended" world where environment and landscape influence the man, where "people still cling to the earth, exploiting it or loving it or questing across it."[10]

Danny Deck quests across the land equipped only with the Western system of values, the naïve inheritance which both inhibits and yet sustains him. We find the positive side of that system exhibited in Danny's daily life prior to the telegram accepting his novel for publication. He is, as Stegner's writer is, one of a group of local artists, in this case, Danny and his best friends Flap and Emma Horton. The three of them write stories for *New World Writing,* the ultimate publication as far as they are concerned, and Danny has had two stories published in *Texas Quarterly.* Danny writes seriously, but he cannot think of himself as a real writer, whatever that may mean, and his friends accept his view. Despite the fact that Professor Lloyd-Jons has heard that Danny is "'the best young writer in the state'" (3), Danny's friends, too, see him as just another student like themselves, and so long as his writing is but a minor part of his life, he poses no threat to them. But that will change once the novel Danny has written is accepted for publication. This "simple novel about a good old man whose one son had gone bad" (113) is the kind of novel Stegner would smile upon and understand; it is the kind Stegner says the budding Western writer produces.

The parochial attitudes Danny holds, in this first stage, toward monogamous sex, homosexuality, individual responsibility, and kindness toward others are also what Stegner would expect of him. Like Stegner's model writer, for example, Danny Deck accepts monogamy as a norm. Thus, we are not surprised that Danny resists the aggressive advances of his voluptuous neighbor, Jenny Salomea. Newly married, Danny believes he ought to "give monogamy a chance" (16). In addition, Danny admits that he has some "oddly decorous habits of speech" (38), particularly in the sexual realm. He has never heard the term "fuckist" and cannot recall ever having heard *cunnilingus* pronounced. Certainly he cannot refer to intercourse in four letters as Lloyd-Jons, Jenny, or his wife Sally can. Sex is good, but it is not to be taken lightly.[11]

Danny's innocence carries over into the areas of individual responsibility[12] and his attitudes toward other people. When, for instance, Mr. Fitzherbert, his landlady's son, delivers a tirade against students and sex, Sally believes in goading him on. Danny, on the other hand, believes it his duty to help the drunken Fitzherbert and closes the car door for him. Danny is magnanimous, too. When Godwin Lloyd-Jons makes sexual advances toward him, Danny gives him the benefit of the doubt, dismissing it as a "drunken friendliness" (1). When Jenny makes advances, Danny feels sorry that he cannot oblige her; she is, after all, a lady who has asked a favor of him. When guests at a cocktail party insult his intelligence and talk about the way he eats and smells, Danny can answer with "sir" and "ma'am" because he has not yet learned deliberate cruelty. In light of his obvious naïveté, his argument with Sally concerning whether he is clean-cut or not is genuinely amusing. Although Danny cannot be like them, he can fit in with and tolerate people who are essentially Eastern.

The situation becomes less amusing to us as the first stage progresses. Stegner does not tell us how long the separation process takes. It seems to be reasonably quick, and the hero seems to look forward to leaving home to learn another way of life. For Danny Deck the process is quick, but it is also terribly painful. He leaves Texas only when he no longer feels at home with his long-time and would-be friends. When Random House accepts Danny's novel for publication, for example, he is abruptly changed in the eyes of his old world. Without his wanting it to happen, Danny Deck is dislodged, rooted out of his place among friends. Because he has received the official stamp of success, others begin to impose upon him their concept of real writers: Rick Leonard, the reigning campus genius, is dismayed, for he knows Danny's success will outshine his own. Petey Ximenes, Danny's library-waxing friend, can think only "'you gonna be famous'" (19), a state resplendent with money and fancy women such as all writers (and no janitors) surely enjoy. Henry, the "executive-level" janitor who writes anachronistic Seventh Cavalry screenplays for Darryl F. Zanuck, answers "'Don't that beat all?'" (20), a bewildered reaction to the acceptance of a novel he considers deadly dull. Godwin Lloyd-Jons tells Danny that a writer must know tragedy, thievery, and lying if he is to succeed. Razzy Hutton, the essence of Houston's perverse culture, tells Danny, "'If you propose to walk among us as an equal you must begin to cultivate one or two of the more basic of the civilized graces'" (41). It is important to understand that Danny himself does not feel changed and consequently cannot imagine why others thrust perverse traits upon him. Except for having stolen Godwin's girl and made her his wife, Danny knows nothing of thievery, much less of lying or real tragedy. Certainly he does not understand that, through his contacts with Random House, he has asked to be admitted to a world of Razzy Huttons where perverted hostility, lust, homosexuality, and vulgarity are the alleged norm. Danny Deck, then, is not growing beyond or through the society he knows best; it is growing away from him and he away from it. Danny Deck cannot explain it; he has only an uneasy "sense . . . of bridges about to be burned" (44). The Texas world is closing in on him, forcing him to be something he cannot be.

As soon as Danny senses change among his old and new friends, he begins to feel uncertain of himself and his professional potential. Stegner says this uncertainty does not begin en force until the hero is actually among other writers. For Deck it begins sooner and it takes the form of vague uneasiness. When the telegram arrives, for example, Danny feels both excitement and fear, an anxiety which makes him think he may have found one dream but lost another, more important one. He begins to feel unsure about his novel, a comfortable part of his life for over a year. He fears that, after all, it will not measure up, that it may be too ordinary. In his fears we see, again, the Western writer's dilemma: two worlds impinging upon one another, each world just out of reach, neither really belonging to the writer. But Danny must meet the challenge of the publishing world, and that challenge exists beyond his small world. He has no choice but to leave Texas.

Emma Horton, Danny's friend, sees where Danny is heading. Better than anyone else, she understands what the challenge means. For her and for Danny it means that the fun of writing is over. The group is irrevocably broken apart because Danny is "'a real writer now'" (34). She knows that Danny cannot meet the challenge the new state will bring or live up to the standards it will demand of him. Her final words to Danny are the essence of the Western writer's dilemma. She says, "You can't take care of yourself. You just look like you can" (54). But Danny Deck, as "parochial [and] dewy-cheeked" (S 48) as Stegner's model, makes his break with Texas, appropriately enough, in the middle of the night, the proverbial darkest hour. With typical Western hope for a better day tomorrow, he heads, as Stegner predicts, toward

San Francisco. The alienation, physical this time, begins, and Danny Deck faces a world of people whose standards are even lower than Razzy Hutton's. From them, Stegner says, the Western writer will learn disgust, despair, and hostility, qualities Lloyd-Jons has already told Danny he must have in order to write.

The fact of Danny's exile and separation is accentuated, perhaps heavy-handedly, by the flash flood at Junction, Texas, an obvious juncture in Danny's life. His last chance to turn back, to ignore the request from the great world and hold on to what is left of his snug world, Junction is a place of prophecy. Danny proves to us that he can cope with natural disaster. He takes command on the hilltop, keeps his head above water, and gives vital instructions to Sally and Godwin. He proves that he can handle the physical state of Texas. But Godwin gives him more to think about. Godwin, a man whose value system makes him Eastern, advises Danny to get a divorce and give up writing *before* he leaves Texas or he will never have "'a chance for happiness'" (65). He fears that Danny cannot, because of what he is, ever learn to be a writer. When Godwin tells Danny that real writers cannot enjoy the earth, an idea incomprehensible to a Western innocent, he is warning Danny that he cannot have both worlds. Danny, of course, does not understand what Godwin means. He has a future now, and thinks it silly to think of giving it up, even if he could. Still, he has an uneasy sense that Godwin is telling him something vital, and he feels that somehow his fate is wrapped up in Texas. Danny comments that Texas is like "some genie, some god . . . whose vengeance might fall on me from behind" (67). Although he is unable to put the fear into practical terms, Texas's vengeance is his innocence, the training which forces him to keep a stiff upper lip and not turn back, even when things are most distasteful. Danny Deck in his naïveté seems determined to drift further away from the society and people he knows best and closer to a society "at bottom" (S 46) so unlike his own as to be virtually unacceptable.

Stegner gives us a fuller account of the writer's probable struggles during the second or exile stage. Eastern values clash more violently with Western ones, for example, and the writer is torn between embarrassingly inadequate standards (S 49) and decidedly worldly ones. Stegner's model makes us expect to find Danny Deck among people who are weary of life, people who are knowing and bitter, people who are empty and faithless. McMurtry does not fail us. He shows us the value struggle in Danny's social, private, and professional lives. He shows us that the Westerner's values inhibit him yet sustain him.

At first, for example, San Francisco seems, indeed, like Stegner's great world of "veritable Rome" (S 47), and Danny is infatuated with

the idea of meeting writers, feeling, at last, like he "*was* one, after all"
(68). The excitement fades quickly, however, and the anxiety takes
over. Danny Deck realizes that he is but one of "hundreds . . . maybe
thousands" (69) of writers who line the streets of San Francisco and
live in its basements. Not the best young writer in *this* state, Danny is
not even a member of a local group of intellectuals. On the contrary,
he finds he is not like any of these writers. He has no kinship with
them, and none of them become his friends. It might be easy for a
non-Westerner to fall into a nihilistic state of self-pity and anger, but
it is impossible for a Westerner. Certainly Danny is depressed with
the prospect that he is only a mediocre writer and that he has no
friends, but his Western inheritance forces him out of his unhappiness. To be unhappy without real cause, Danny tells us, is "unmanly,"
and a "healthy" man (76) has no room for anger. By implication, then,
Deck already feels that Eastern writers are cowardly quitters, suffering from self-caused moral sicknesses which debilitate them. Danny
Deck cannot be like them. On the other hand, he cannot run away
from them, either; to do so would make him as much a quitter as one of
them. Instead, Danny tries to think of Texas, but he cannot remember
it. In short, he cannot let Texas keep him from giving San Francisco a
fair try; he cannot imagine his going home yet.

Danny's values are further tested in his private life, and once again
his frontier values both inhibit and sustain him. When he learns that
Sally is unfaithful to him, he might, if he were Eastern, accept it as
normal behavior and allow himself the same privilege. Or he might feel
anger and self-pity. But Danny is not Eastern, as his Louisiana wife is,
and his first reactions to Sally's infidelity are hopeful, innocent, and
Western: he thinks perhaps it is not true; he thinks of taking Sally home
to Texas, as if that will make her magically monogamous; he still thinks
that "maybe monogamy is the way things should be" (85). It is important
to note that Danny says "maybe" as if he is not certain that monogamy
is, after all, the best way, and "should be" as if he understands that such
is not the way it *is*. Perhaps Danny could have dismissed Sally's adultery had she not made fun of Willis's having had only one woman, a
derisive attack against Danny's Western values. When she does that,
Danny is no longer uncertain: he shoves her to the floor, tells her to
clean up her language, disapproves of his loving her any more, and
leaves. But his break with Sally and her Eastern standard is not a clean,
uncompromising one as his break with the Eastern elements of Texas
had been. He takes a hotel room near Sally and decides to wait for her to
need him again. The hopeful implication, of course, is that she will need
him again and will somehow accept him as he is.

When faced with depressing actualities in his social and private lives, then, Danny Deck manages to be melioristic. But the second stage is not yet over. Stegner warns us that the Western writer is likely to meet people who speak "with appalling certainty and casualness of things [the Western writer] hardly even dares imagine" (S 47). The writer becomes ashamed of his inheritance and tries to hide it. Certainly it is true of Danny Deck. When Bruce, Danny's Random House editor, comes to visit, for instance, he looks askance at the Piltdown room, making Danny feel uneasy. He gushes about French cuisine, and Danny feels embarrassed that he prefers Fig Newtons, jalapeño peppers, Peanut Planks, and Dr. Peppers.[13] Bruce speaks of Hollywood knowingly and mentions $40,000, a fortune to Danny, nonchalantly. "Universally informed" (90), Bruce speaks comfortably of literary parties, events as abstract to Danny as triangles or cubes. Danny is impressed with Bruce's ability to know everything and everyone, but he is even more awed by the writers at the literary party. Philip Roth, James Baldwin, and Wallace Stegner are real writers whom Danny must emulate if he is himself to become a real writer. Uneasily, Danny remembers that he has written only "one slight book" (93) and wonders for a moment whether his Texas friends would be disappointed in him if he gave up writing. Once again, however, his Western tradition makes him fight the urge to quit, makes him refuse to cower before the Eastern standard. He does not, however, have to like it. In fact, Danny feels that these real writers who smile, know everyone, and talk so knowingly seem only to cheapen literature. He does not like these men who are to be his models. With Western hopefulness, then, Danny vows that he will continue to write "out of pride" (94) until he is good enough to quit. By implication, Danny believes he can be a better writer than any of these writers is, and he can be a better judge of good art than they are. When the time to quit comes, it will be judged by his Western standards and not their Eastern ones.

Still, however, Danny cannot forsake his effort to be a writer. He must accept their terms until he is better than they are. Danny, therefore, accepts the challenge to learn from them. Stegner points out that this is typical: "[Western writers] learn . . . in exile and often harbor [Eastern standards] in uneasy alliance with a great yearning nostalgia for the health they left behind them" (S 46). Thus, when Danny Deck forms an alliance with Renata Morris, a fellow novelist whose first book was *The Diary of a Jaundiced Woman*, we are not really surprised. Nor are we surprised that Renata is the archetype of the contemporary novel's heroine who, according to Stegner, conveys "the message that sex is the only thing that makes a rotten world bearable, the only possible means of human contact, and pretty grubby at that, closer to hostility than to affection" (S 47). Renata Morris is not Danny's kind of woman, but however much she goes against his standards, he will not back away from her. Danny takes her to bed, quite aware that she has a husband and he has a wife. He listens to her stories of what she calls "sexual adventures" with cats and then calls their own coupling a sexual adventure. All that her casual standards require is going through the motions, but Danny's Western standards keep him from enjoying the experience. He says, "Maybe saying dirty words worked for her, but hearing them didn't work for me" (96). Danny laments the fact that he feels nothing for Renata and suggests that being able to feel "would have made the morning different." As it is, he has only "a memory of disappointment" (97). Obviously, Danny does not yet feel comfortable in his new Eastern pose.

Danny's next chance to test his new role comes when he meets The New Americans, the family and friends of Teddy Blue, a writer who came to the great world from Forth Worth. Naked children, casual talk of sex and wife stealing, and mounds of young people high on mescaline and Mexican mushrooms disorient Danny. At first he is impressed with the peace they seem to have found and for awhile thinks that he has found some possible friends. But his values inhibit him when he cannot "feel comfortable naked" because they are yet "bourgeois shackles [he] still hadn't shaken off" (102). The following day, Danny finds that although he can still visualize The New Americans, he cannot "imagine what they might be doing" (105). That is, Danny allows them their life style but cannot himself enter it with more than his body. Danny's efforts to enter a new life seem thwarted at every turn.

And still he perseveres. Danny allows Bruce to fly him to Los Angeles, a shamefully new experience, to meet movie producer Leon O'Reilly. During this final half of the second stage Danny Deck meets Jill Peel, and his pose as an Eastern writer solidifies.

This further excursion into Hollywood's version of reality is, nonetheless, disquieting to Danny. As Danny sits in a room rented in Leon's name, looks at a bottle of scotch that magically appears, and wonders at secretaries and bellboys who perform as Leon's puppets, he has the uneasy feeling that he is in the presence of a stranger, that he is "living [his] first hours with someone [he] is about to become" (106). Not even Dr. Peppers, a small but symbolic spit in the eye of Leon's world, can give Danny comfort. The uneasy feelings, unlike earlier ones, are well-defined, dealing directly with Danny and his future. And the premonitions prove out: during a series of bizarre incidents with

Leon and his fat secretary, Danny finds himself becoming a "real" writer, despite his instinctive desire to avoid the world in which such writers move. He wants to be "thousands of miles away, in Texas" (112), where there are people with whom he has something in common. Danny does not "feel at all at home with Leon O'Reilly" (112), and home is where he most wants to be. Instead, Danny has temporarily lost the fight to retain frontier values. Danny is overwhelmed by Leon and his plans for the simple novel. Stegner tells us that the Western writer in contact with Eastern standards inevitably loses confidence in his own: "As he listens to the people around him it slowly dawns on him that his book and the stance from which he wrote it were both embarrassing mistakes" (S 47). So it is with Danny Deck.

Until Danny comes to Leon O'Reilly we do not know what his book is about or even its name. Danny tells us his book is *The Restless Grass,* in Stegner's terms a typical Western novel because it has "a hero, or at least a respect for the heroic virtues" (S 47), attributes which are not the staples of Eastern writing. Danny has written it from the life he knows best, and predictably, Stegner says, its content is the same as that of "nearly every Western novel" (S 48). Danny Deck sees no problem in turning his novel into a screenplay. Neither does Leon O'Reilly, but for reasons quite different from Danny's. Leon wants to fill it with the filth and sexy corruption he believes the public wants. In order to convert this simple story of Western life into "'a richer brew'" (113), he is willing to pervert every belief and every attitude Danny holds dear. To Leon, Danny's Western values and experiences are not only embarrassingly inadequate but, as Stegner would put it, "unusable" (S 47). Danny Deck acquiesces in O'Reilly's verdict. Because he does not object to Leon's changes, Danny tacitly accepts Eastern standards. And by accepting Leon's ideas as "better" than his own, Danny Deck becomes, in effect, just what "the great world" expects him to be.

At the beginning of the third stage, if Stegner's pattern is correct, we can expect Danny Deck to borrow the themes and characters of Eastern artists. Having given up his own themes and characters, Danny Deck chooses to capitalize upon an idea presented by Jill Peel, an Eastern girl he believes he loves. Danny cannot, of course, accept the suggestion out-of-hand; it occurs to him only after he and Jill develop a relationship. Because Danny and Jill have much in common, he comes to love her. They share easy things like holding hands, watching television, and just talking, things that are a familiar part of his Western experience. But whatever they share, Jill is not a Westerner. And when Danny's love causes him to accept her, by extension he partly accepts her Eastern standards. Jill, after all, loves someone else, is an irresponsible mother, has had an abortion, and cannot love Danny physically. Not the kind of relationship he had dreamed of back in Texas, it is temporarily acceptable, and Danny overlooks the fact that he is still married to Sally and is soon to be a father. Certain that he can win Jill sometime, Danny abandons some of his Western values.

This abandonment of some Western values, e.g., monogamy, is symptomatic and carries over into Danny's attitudes about writing. He discards his second Western novel, the one he began before he left Texas. Since those materials, the ones Danny knows best, have come to seem inadequate, he steals Jill's idea, becoming the thief that Godwin had said he would, as a real writer, become. He writes Jill's novel, a "baby-bed novel" (127), becoming, like Western writers before him, a writer who "must live in exile" and write of experiences not his own (S 49). Temporarily, Danny's heart lies with the characters of his new book, Jill's book, *The Man Who Never Learned*.[14] Not surprisingly, then, when his copy of *The Restless Grass* arrives, Danny is not moved by it, for it depicts an old, naive society from which he has grown away. He says of the characters in *Restless Grass*, "I was so dead to them that I didn't like seeing their names on the page" (141). Danny does not say that the characters are dead: he says that *he*, the boy who used to be, is dead to them. Danny has changed, has lusted after strange gods, but as Stegner knows, Danny, like other Western writers, has not changed "at bottom." He has not grown *beyond* the society he knew best; he has only grown *away* from it.

At the end of the third stage, according to Stegner's pattern, the Western writer will understand that he can never become a part of the Eastern establishment. Once Jill leaves him, once he learns that Sally has returned to Texas, and once *The Man Who Never Learned* is finished, then, there can be no Eastern life left for Danny. He goes home to Texas, looking, Stegner would say, for "a present to come home to." At Van Horn, Texas, Danny is almost back "to some part of [himself and] just on the rim of home" (149). The exile returns to the land of Granny Deck and Old Man Goodnight and Idiot Ridge, the place most truly his own. For the moment, Danny has forgotten that he is "dead" to the society at home.

In this third stage, Danny Deck searches for his "present." It seems to him that somehow his roots lie with Uncle Laredo and his Hacienda at Bitter Waters. As ludicrous and ugly as this representation of the Old West is, it is, nonetheless, the source of all the virtues that comprise Danny's character. The exile is cheerfully received and cared for, and Danny listens to the stories of old days, of Old Man Goodnight, the Zapatistas, and the horse El Caballo. They are things Danny likes to believe in, but they are things of the past, and they no longer exist except in myth. Instead, Danny can see that the Hacienda at Bitter Waters "was the bitter end of something" (170), a place he will never want to visit again. Rather than robust, manly cowboys who measure worth in terms of roping ability, Laredo's cowboys are scrawny specimens who can hardly rope at all. Instead of El Caballo, Laredo's transportation is a run-down Jeep with manhole covers for seats. Instead of an unpretentious ranch house, Bitter Waters sports a dilapidated castle built on work but filled by sand. Symbolically, two old men, far past the prime of life, wait patiently, not for a living legend, but for a dead hero to make them useful again. As Danny said of the literary party, he might also say of Bitter Waters now, "I didn't like the picture I had of things" (94). Bitter Waters makes Danny wonder whether he can "ever make life his" (170). Danny Deck cannot look back. This particular past holds no life.

Perhaps the only life for Danny is somewhere between East and West, somewhere "on the rim of home." At this time, nothing remains for him but "to rush on toward the battle" which awaits him in Austin and in Houston (171), one more past.

After his San Francisco experiences, Danny Deck can "see" better now. Godwin—Danny's first Eastern advisor and lesson giver—is a victim of his own casual standards and his perverted life who can no longer look Danny in the eye. Godwin understands that Danny can see him for what he is. A writer of real Eastern persuasion might well record Godwin's story, as Stegner puts it, in all its "misery, perversion, oversexed hostility, and hatred of life" (S 50). But Danny seems to realize, as Stegner says the Western writer should, that Godwin's story is not "a rule of the universe" (S 50); it is only one possible part of human experience. When Danny leaves, Godwin can smile and shake Danny's hand, confident that Danny is not Eastern enough to expose him in some upcoming novel.

Danny Deck's East-West character comes through again in his relationship with Jenny Salomea. Not the "kid" she had once known, Danny is no longer afraid of Jenny, and he tells her almost nonchalantly, "'I've given up on monogamy'" (183). But Jenny observes, "'You don't look healthy'" (1983)—as if somehow the two are cause and effect and it doesn't matter which is which. Despite the fact that Danny makes love to Jenny almost casually and seems undaunted when Sammy Salomea douses them with warm water, at bottom Danny has not really given up his Westernness. He feels embarrassed when they slip under the covers together and later refuses to move in with Jenny because it would be bad for her "reputation." Danny quickly comes to think of her as another responsibility. His Eastern casualness, then, exists only on the surface, and "at bottom" duty and honor are still essential parts of Danny Deck.

As if to prove that point, Danny confronts Sally by saying, "'I came home because you were having the baby'" (189). Sally's reaction to Danny is much like that of Razzy's lesbian guests. If Danny was just a "frontier genius" then, to Sally he is just a "real writer" now; he must have all the perversions the contemporary writer is supposed to have. Sally calls him a sex maniac and tells him he would not make a good father. She says Danny is a criminal and a disgrace to her family. Perhaps the only Eastern thing Danny is guilty of here is that he has learned at last "'to call a bitch a bitch'" (31) as Jenny long ago had advised him to do. Although Sally will not permit it, Danny wants very much to accept the responsibility for his child; he is still enough of a Westerner to believe in the idea of home and family.

Danny Deck's Westernness still shows through with Godwin, Jenny, and Sally, but it is less visible in his relationship to the people at his Random House autograph party. They hold to the dream, the fantasy of the great world, as Danny himself once held to it. And when he goes to Mr. Stay's book shop and meets Dorsey Ebbins's mother, he is to her something of a remote power, as Bruce or Leon O'Reilly had been to him. Danny plays the part of author, saying the nice things he is expected to say, sharing small talk about literature with Mr. Stay, extending invitations he never expects to be honored. The literary party on a small scale, Danny's autograph party becomes just as empty as the dream world has been. Jenny's buying his books and giving them to the first fifty people in the telephone book is an appropriate gesture, for Danny begins to hate the pile of books at the store, wishing he could dump them into a puddle. Ironically, Danny's personal story, the story of all Western writers, makes him an outsider. The people who once knew him and who now receive what is partly their own story from him are strangers. Were it possible for Danny to re-live that story and be snug again, he would gladly relinquish his talent to anyone "who would be made happy by it" (198). He cannot give it up now; other people, strangers, will let him be nothing but a writer.

When Danny tells Sally's parents that he is something more, they will hear none of it. As far as they are concerned, writers stay hog drunk much of the time, frequent bordellos, and delight in ruining the names of good girls. The Bynums recoil when Danny reminds them that he married Sally decently; writers, they feel, can do nothing decently. And once again, Danny plays the part of a writer, this time by defending himself with words, instead of fists as a Westerner should. His reaction to Razzy Hutton's insults had been "pure frontier." Now, in a degrading and disgusting scene, Danny displays all the sexual terms he knows, all those words he could never have used back when he had "some oddly decorous habits of speech." But Danny is still not comfortable with those words. Not having done the Western thing, this Westerner has not lived up to his own standards and must now "go limping home" after "a cheap victory" (203).

The home Danny limps to is Emma because he hopes that somehow there will be one person he is not "cut apart from" (204). But when he and Emma make love, "straining for something more than could be gotten from two bodies," they feel like "criminals" (205). In the end they resign themselves to the fact that it's going to be hard now for them even to be friends. Danny's fate seems to be borders, in-between places where his old friends have become strangers and any new "possible friends" are also strangers.

As if to symbolize his resignation to that fate, Danny Deck leaves Houston to travel to the Mexican border, "the rim of home," the edge of another country. A middle land where one does not have to be one thing or another to the exclusion of all else, the border is perhaps the only place where Danny can fit. Big enough to encompass extremes, the median holds E. Paul and Luther, the sadistic Texas Rangers, at the same time that it holds the gentle Juanita, a Mexican whore who—like Danny—prostitutes herself before a picture of home. Juanita, E. Paul and Luther are what they are not because of outside pressure, some force which controls them, but because they choose to be what they are. They are comfortable, perhaps even happy, with the roles they have chosen. And for some inexplicable reason, Danny seems to draw strength from them. As strange as they may be, even E. Paul and Luther are "normal" insofar as they know who they are. Neither the law nor the whore seem to want anything beyond that. Danny's money or the possibility of a home in the United States do not interest Juanita, for example. Unlike Jill, who is always on "brinks," or Jenny, who frightens people away, or Sally, who has no feelings, she is no more and no less than Juanita.

Stronger now, Danny decides to dispose of both the old life and the new life. Having given Wu his own copy of *Restless Grass* and having seen the others go to strangers, Danny has lost much of his early life already. To further break the tie, he gives away El Chevy, the car which has brought him full circle, and with it all the remainders of

both lives save one. As a final gesture, Danny carries the manuscript
of *The Man Who Never Learned* to a bluff overlooking Roma, a world
apart from "veritable Rome." Like the time of the flash flood, the
moment is another turning point for Danny, but this time the decision
is his. In this final scene, Danny Deck, the Western writer, completely
rejects the alternative to his "square" heritage, as Stegner says he
must. Inadequate as the West may be, however "culturally half-
baked," it remains the "last chance to be something better" (S 49).
Danny is finally brave enough, manly enough, to "drown" the San
Francisco novel. He hates the pages, those words that record a life not
his own, the life of an exile. Plunging into the Rio Grande, the border
river which periodically shifts the boundaries of Texas, Danny "beats"
the book, holding it under water until every page is squishy, until it is
dead.[15] Danny Deck swims well and he comes up victorious because
his superior strength prevails. Surprisingly, Danny's victory makes
him think of Jill Peel, "just an artist" and afraid to be anything else.
But Danny explains by saying, "Jill Peel would be proud of me, if she
could know. I had killed it in honorable battle and given it to the sea,
as she had wished" (246).

At the same time that he rejects the East, Danny reaffirms his
Western values. Because, unlike Eastern, contemporary writers, he
"'had no grounds for being mad at life,'" Danny can say, "I didn't feel
sorry for myself" (241).[16] Everything that has happened to him has
been simply what he deserved, the price for his rejection of Texas.
Part of that price is, as his friend Wu had told him, that Danny cannot
recapture the dream, cannot regain his innocence. But Danny thinks
the dream is still worthwhile. If, as Wu had warned, there are "too
many borders," and if "only heart can go home" (142), so be it.
Danny's heart goes home to Granny Deck and Old Man Goodnight.
Danny is good enough to quit writing now, but significantly, he saves
"the only good things in the box" (244), the only things not about his
California life. In one simple gesture, Danny sends the most Western
of his work to the most Western of his women: the old prologue about
Granny Deck and the old epilogue about Old Man Goodnight go to
Emma. Stegner claims that "in a time of repudiation, absurdity, guilt,
and despair, the Western writer still half believes in the American
dream" (S 48). Danny Deck knows that if he is a writer at all, he must
be a Western writer who accepts himself for what he is.

If it is true, as Stegner implies, that the Western writer must also be
"the symbolic orphan" (S 49), Danny's troubles are not over. He seems
destined, in fact, to seek out his new beginning in a "thin little strip

between the country of the normal and the country of the strange" (246). Probably this is as it should be. As Danny tells himself, "'Perhaps my true country was the borderland anyway'" (246). Even as an orphan doomed to borderlands, Danny Deck affirms that the Western writer "may be grateful to his Western upbringing for convincing him . . . that man, even Modern Man, has some dignity if he will assume it" (S 50). "The point," as Stegner puts it, "is to do the best one can in the circumstances, not the worst" (S 50).

NOTES

1. *Atlantic,* 213 (Jan. 1964), 46–50. Hereafter noted in text by (S + page).

2. (New York: Pocket Books, 1973). Hereafter noted by page numbers in the text.

3. Two likely explanations suggest themselves here and both may apply to the similarities between the essay and the novel. First, Stegner's ideas may have helped to "seed" *All My Friends.* Certainly McMurtry, who was once a student in Stegner's creative writing class at Stanford, would be familiar with Stegner's ideas, ideas stated in one form or another by many Westerners—Thomas Hornsby Ferril, for example—before him. On the other hand, it is probable that Stegner and McMurtry, as Western writers, simply share characteristics and views common to the species.

4. These are almost always included in lists of the Western virtues. See, for example, Delbert Wylder's discussion in "The Western Hero from a Strange Perspective," *Rendezvous,* 7, no. 2 (Winter 1972).

5. In the same *Rendezvous,* p. 19, John R. Milton's article, "The Western Novel: Whence and What?", considers the "death-descent into hell-resurrection motif" of archetypal novels. Western novels, of course, are special instances of the general hero pattern discussed definitively by Joseph Campbell in *Hero With a Thousand Faces* (New York: World Publishing, 1970); originally copyrighted 1949.

6. In "Conversation with Walter Van Tilburg Clark," *South Dakota Review,* 9, no. 1 (Spring 1971), p. 38, Clark notes that the Western writer must learn to deal with his past before he can develop a kind of continuity with his present. Clark's general discussion of the "orphan problem," pp. 34–35, seems basically to agree with Stegner.

7. Milton, p. 17, discusses the Western novel in terms of cycles. In five Western novels, including one by Stegner, Milton finds that the hero returns to the old ways to begin again. The typical quest does not end in a conclusion but in a *beginning.*

8. See Clark pp. 32–33 for a discussion of the typically Western attitude about animals, trees, land and pp. 35–36 for a Western writer's emotional response to landscapes. Easterners simply do not have the sense of the West necessary to understand how it can shape a man.

9. Max Westbrook in the "The Western Esthetic" chapter of *Walter Van Tilburg Clark* (New York: Twayne Publishers, 1969) notes that many artists feel the West "has the obligation to restore, or at least to husband, the American dream *after* it has already been corrupted in the East . . .", p. 39.

10. Milton, p. 21.

11. McMurtry explains the Westerner's attitude toward virtuous women and sex in "Take My Saddle from the Wall: A Valediction," reprinted in *The Literature of the American West,* ed. J. Golden Taylor (New York: Houghton Mifflin, 1971), pp. 554–555.

12. For a minority view, see Wylder, pp. 25–32. In his discussion of alpha-animals and their similarities to and differences from heroes, Wylder says basically that the hero is an egomaniac who shuns all responsibility and any close tie to others.

13. McMurtry, "Valediction," p. 560, tells us how "the son of someone's hired hand put all the young McMurtrys to shame by consuming twenty-six Dr. Peppers in the course of a single day." Dr. Pepper is undoubtedly a Texas drink; it was first concocted there.

14. In McMurtry's *Moving On* (New York: Avon, 1970), Emma Horton tells us that *The Man Who Never Learned* is "about a guy who had terrible troubles with women—I think he had himself in mind. It was structured around a baby bed—his little girl's baby bed—and the point of it was that everybody's apt to sleep with everybody they know, sooner or later," p. 784. *All My Friends* has Deck drown the novel. Patsy, Emma's friend in *Moving On,* says, "I wish he'd written it," p. 785, and Emma, too, seems to think Danny never wrote it.

15. *Moving On,* p. 784, Emma says Danny is dead.

16. See Stegner's "Specifications for a Hero" chapter in *Wolf Willow* (New York: Viking Press, 1963) for the genesis of Stegner's own adherence to Western standards.

L E A V I N G

T E X A S

The Trash Trilogy

MARK BUSBY

Although this section of McMurtry's work is sometimes called the "Trash Trilogy," the name is only partially appropriate. Unlike McMurtry's earlier work, *Somebody's Darling, Cadillac Jack,* and *The Desert Rose* have no interrelated quality; none of the characters, plots, or settings overlap. In fact, *Somebody's Darling* logically makes a quartet with his three previous novels, since two of its main characters appeared in them. (McMurtry, however, does not consider it part of the "Houston Trilogy.") Nor are these three books necessarily "trash," but of all of McMurtry's novels these three have been more generally abused by critics than his others. Therefore, it makes a convenient grouping to trash them, and certainly in the long look at McMurtry's fiction they rank low on the list of his significant work. But the "Trash Trilogy" designation also reflects the subject matter of the three novels: the glitzy but centerless worlds of Hollywood and Las Vegas and the trash and garbage through which Cadillac Jack McGriff sifts. While many critics excoriated these three books, all three novels contain praiseworthy elements, and each one received some positive reviews.

What makes these novels important is that they demonstrate some of McMurtry's continuing techniques and themes. Technically, the novels show McMurtry working with varying points of view, especially his fondness for using female narrators, and with different levels of realism. All three books are contemporaneous to the time of writing, and they are concerned with displaced characters searching for something to provide their lives with stability and purpose. They long for ways to combine love and work into a satisfying and enduring whole. Although their lives are ultimately fraught with difficulty, pain, and uncertainty, McMurtry demonstrates how these characters take pleasure in moments of creativity, love, or humor.

More significantly, the novels are important because of their transitional nature. Taken together, they reveal a writer's "dark night of the soul," for it was with *Somebody's Darling* that McMurtry lost his enthusiasm for writing, a condition that existed through *Cadillac Jack.* With *The Desert Rose* McMurtry recovered the lost excitement for writing. Thus, these novels exemplify that Larry McMurtry could continue to write when his life and world were in flux. They also document how McMurtry attempted what he had long called on Texas novelists to do: to write about the urban—and urbane—world beyond Idiot Ridge, Wichita Falls, Fort Worth, and Houston. In these three books we find Larry McMurtry leaving Texas for Hollywood, Washington, D.C., and Las Vegas.

A publisher's note on the dust jacket of *Somebody's Darling* recognizes that McMurtry's "background is the Frontier" and asserts that this novel about Hollywood has simply moved the frontier "farther west than Texas." And "Book One" hints that *Somebody's Darling* concerns the way Hollywood replaced the West in the American imagination as the place symbolic of youthful hope and promise. Book One is narrated by Joe Percy, a sixty-three-year-old hack screenwriter and former novelist, who was a minor character in *Moving On.* As the novel opens, Percy is about to accompany his old friend Jill Peel (a refugee from McMurtry's 1972 novel *All My Friends Are Going to Be Strangers*) to New York where she is about to achieve success as a director. She wants Joe to be there for the opening of the film which will establish her reputation.

Joe, a Hollywood veteran, knows how Hollywood had satisfied the needs of innocents who wanted to "make a life of the games of childhood" (71), but now he describes Los Angeles "with the reptilian coil of freeways rippling like golden boas" and understands that he has "lost the habit of hope" (126–27). With these observations, Joe Percy moves McMurtry's novel toward substance, and critics have been quite positive toward McMurtry's presentation of Joe Percy's character.

The first part ends when Jill Peel meets Owen Oarson at a party celebrating her film. Oarson becomes both her lover and the narrator

of Book Two. A former Texas Tech football player and farm equipment salesman, Oarson sees that Jill will give him an easy ride to
success as a producer. In the mold of the Texas cowboy, Oarson cannot
articulate his feelings; Oarson's narration is also inarticulate and,
most critics felt, boring. Perhaps McMurtry tried to dramatize Hollywood enervation by allowing the manipulators to demonstrate that
they are unimaginative and dislikable. The problem is that the book
begins to show the same characteristics.

Book Three is narrated by Jill as she continues her affair with
Owen knowing it is based purely on his selfish motives. They copro-
duce a Western movie set in West Texas, which Jill directs, but soon
Owen is advancing his career by sleeping with Sherry Solare, the star.
The circumstances deteriorate and conclude with the gratuitous death
of a child. Much of Book Three recounts the strange sexual and personal misadventures of the characters. Near the end of the novel, Jill
and Joe capture a brief moment of pleasure as Jill—in a purely unselfish act—helps Joe regain sexual vigor. But the novel ends with
Joe's death and with Jill's uncertainty about the ties that bound them
together.

The result of all this, as I asserted in a *Houston Chronicle* review, is
"that *Somebody's Darling* tears promisingly out of the chute, but soon
stumbles, falls, and wallows in the mire." McMurtry has called the
book an example of bad timing. He initially was drawn to Jill Peel's
character after he created her in *All My Friends Are Going to Be
Strangers,* but by the time he got around to writing about her, he could
not sustain his interest.

McMurtry told Patrick Bennett that writing *Somebody's Darling* was
"an unpleasant writing experience" because he did not feel "really engaged; it was forced" (30). He attributes the novel's difficulty to two
problems. First, he tried to force two impulses: one was to write a novel
about Hollywood; the second was to write again about Jill Peel. When
he finally merged the two and began writing, the "original energy had
gone" (29). The second problem arose from his unfamiliarity with California culture: "Because you happen to know how people talk, you feel
you know more about Californians than you really do" (29).

In the ten years following *Somebody's Darling*'s publication, only
one critical article, an updated entry in *Dictionary of Literary Biography,* focused specifically on the novel. Some critics have referred to it
briefly. Kerry Ahearn in his *Fifty Western Writers* article finds some
value in the novel, noting that the "focus on a non-Texas milieu seems
to ease McMurtry away from the stereotypes, punning, and facile
black humor of the previous four novels and toward a more subtle and

sensitive use of character." He points out that it "continues the theme of skepticism about marriage, and its preoccupation is with loss and the inevitable victimization of sensitive and kind human beings" (288). Jane Nelson writes that McMurtry has seemingly disowned the novel and finds that it lacks the power of McMurtry's best work because "none of these Hollywood characters faces the loss of a home that forms the emotional center of his previous novels" (617).

Standing on a street corner in Washington, D.C., Larry McMurtry found his next title before he had a novel to hang it on. A man in a Cadillac pulled to a stop, and a black man on the street sang out, "Ho, ho, Cadillac Jack." Soon, McMurtry had a character and then a plot that moved away from Texas. *Cadillac Jack* is set mainly in Washington, but it provides a sympathetic treatment of a Texan for the first time in a decade of novels and essays critical of almost all things Texan. Jack McGriff is by no means completely positive because he is a wanderer who cannot accept the permanence of love, but he is much more admirable than most of the other characters in the novel.

McGriff, a thirty-three-year-old former bulldogger from Solino, Texas, stands six feet five inches in his yellow armadillo boots. With his brown beaver Stetson and doeskin jacket, Jack is an antique and doodad scout always on the lookout for the unusual as he travels the country in a pearl-colored Cadillac with peach velour interior. In some ways Jack brings to mind McMurtry himself, for during this period McMurtry lived in Washington and ran his used book store, Booked Up, and roamed the area searching for rare books.

Previously, the gaudy, materialistic, womanizing Texan would have received the brunt of McMurtry's satire, but not in *Cadillac Jack*. In fact, McMurtry embraces much of Jack's Texas outlook, and the satire is directed outward—at the effete and the snobbish, the social climbers and bureaucrats of Washington.

But satire is not McMurtry's major purpose here. Mostly, *Cadillac Jack* is a rollickingly humorous trip through the detritus of contemporary America. It's a picaresque ramble with a man who is trained to find something of value in the trash heaps and flea markets of American life. It is also, McMurtry has written, a novel about the instability of human love, either for objects or for other human beings. In fact, the novel's use of objects emphasizes McMurtry's phenomenological theme in which he demonstrates the meaning people place on objects, whether a doghouse in *Texasville* or Billy the Kid's boots in *Cadillac Jack*.

As the novel begins, Jack has come to Washington to dump a load of cowboy regalia in the middle of the urban cowboy craze. His friend

Boog Miller, a wealthy oilman who owns Winkler County, Texas, introduces him to Cindy Sanders, a dabbler in antique dealing and full-time beauty and social climber. Because too many of the people in Washington are "shrimps," Jack provides Cindy with a tall diversion. Jack, object connoisseur, is inspired by Cindy's physical perfection.

Cindy soon introduces Jack to her Washington friends, a crew as odd as the bar gang from *Star Wars,* with names like Sir Cripps Crisp, Moorcock Malone, Khaki Descartes, Freddy Fu, Spud Breyfogle, Oblivia Brown, Prub Bosque, and Brisling Bowker. The names indicate how McMurtry moved away from the realism of *Somebody's Darling* and into the lightly satirical comedy of manners in *Cadillac Jack.*

Between bouts of lovemaking, Jack convinces Cindy that she should replace the bread sculpture exhibit in her shop with a boot display built around Billy the Kid's boots, owned by a 108-year-old friend of Jack's in Fort Sumner, New Mexico.

But Jack, forever the scout, soon finds something else to attract him at an estate sale: Jean Arber, another antique dealer. Jean is a soon-to-be-divorced young mother of two daughters whose down-to-earth family life offers a stability that Cindy's Dickensian society does not, and Jack's deflected interest reinforces McMurtry's point about the instability of human love.

While Jack's sexual forays make up a good part of the book (too much, in fact: better editing could have made this an even stronger book), much of the best that is here comes from Jack's straightforward, good-humored approach to the possibility of life for one who is on the lookout. He takes his motto from Zack Jenks, a Coke bottle scout, who once told him: "Anything can be anywhere" (23).

On this expedition to Washington, though, Jack also casts a critical eye. His response to the people of Washington demonstrates the contrast between his Western openness and their tiny timidity. The bureaucrats, the GS-12s, come under his scrutiny, and, in an effective metaphor, he finds their dull similarity limiting:

> I was getting the sense that Washington was a very cellular place.
> The motif of the cell recurred. All the men in trench coats and
> woolen hats probably spent their days in cell-like offices in vast
> gray buildings. Then when the government let them out they
> squirmed like larvae into small cell-like cars and rushed across the
> river or around the Beltway to vast gray apartment buildings,
> where they inhabited cell-like apartments. (123)

A man who hears the song of the open road, Jack finds the cellular life disgusting. But all is not sweetness and treasure for Jack in this book, for his faith in himself is shaken when Jean refuses to marry him, telling him that he lacks the ability to love. As the novel ends, Jack hits the road, continues to find unusual objects in odd places, and refuses to realize that he has substituted objects for emotion.

Although Jane Nelson concludes that *Cadillac Jack*'s "political and social intrigues . . . are . . . no more convincing than the Hollywood scenes of *Somebody's Darling,*" she finds that "[i]n learning to accept himself as a perpetual wanderer, Jack becomes the most satisfying male character McMurtry had yet created, almost a match for his strong female characters." Nelson also notes the interesting contrast between *Cadillac Jack* and McMurtry's first two novels:

> Idiot Ridge and any corresponding nostalgia for the western landscape have disappeared from his novels in *Cadillac Jack.* Now the western past is represented by a cattle rancher who is a drug addict; the modern West is run by a network of female real estate agents who are directed by a powerful and dynamic woman living in the East. In his first two novels, lonely women are encircled and engulfed by men who both love and abuse them. *Cadillac Jack* is peopled largely by women, many of whom use and then discard the lonely men in their lives. Because of Jack's quiet acceptance of his fate, *Cadillac Jack* becomes the first McMurtry novel in which man and woman seem almost equal. (618)

If McMurtry's treatment of the sexes changed, his use of what Raymond Neinstein has called his central theme, displacement, continues to be important in *Cadillac Jack.* In *The Ghost Country,* Neinstein concludes: "Displacement is the central concern of the first five novels of Larry McMurtry. In four of the novels, the protagonist is either breaking away from a place, or has already done so, only to find himself rootless and lost" (i). McMurtry told Patrick Bennett that Jack Kerouac's *On the Road* was a significant influence (17), and and *Cadillac Jack* provides ample evidence of Kerouac's legacy, for Jack is a rootless, searching figure who finds life on the road. Like some of McMurtry's earlier characters, Jack spends his life searching for a center, a home that will again allow lost virtues to be regained.

McMurtry was working on *Lonesome Dove* and had gotten bogged down in the details of his trail drive novel when a call came from a Hollywood producer who wanted him to write a film script about a Las Vegas showgirl. Loaded with the names of people to contact and needing a break, he headed to Las Vegas where he met a real former showgirl who raised peacocks. Soon, he noted in the preface to the paperback edition, he sensed a connection that interested him:

> I have always been attracted to dying crafts—cowboying is one such. It became clear that the showgirls were the cowboys of Las Vegas; there were fewer and fewer jobs and they faced bleak futures, some with grace, and some without it. (7)

The story's outline came next: "Dying breeds aren't the only thing I'm attracted to. I also like mother-daughter stories. Why not a mother-daughter story in which the daughter replaces the mother on her own stage in the show in which she's been a star for some years?" What resulted was the character of Harmony, the mother, and Pepper, the daughter, and a variation on the "old-matador-going-down-vs-the-young-matador-coming-up motif, except with a family twist" (7). McMurtry wrote the novel in three weeks.

Many reviewers were disappointed in *The Desert Rose*. For example, I wrote:

> *The Desert Rose* reads like a novel that leaped from Larry McMurtry's imagination and into print without the intervening process of evaluation—or editing. While the conception may be there, the execution is as arid as McMurtry's subject: the life of an aging Las Vegas showgirl.

My initial response to *The Desert Rose* was similar to my earlier reaction to *Somebody's Darling,* where McMurtry had used Owen's tedious narration to demonstrate the character's distastefulness. To replicate the paltriness of Harmony's imagination, McMurtry chose to tell the story first from her point of view and then later from that of her sixteen-year-old daughter. Committed to a realistic approach, McMurtry decided to use the language and thought of people like them. The result is vapid vocabulary and anemic thought.

For example, in the following passage, Harmony considers her wardrobe:

> After all, wearing those costumes every night, being a feathered beauty as Bonventre used to call her, sort of changed your attitude toward clothes. After the costumes it was sort of hard to know you were there if you didn't wear clothes with a little color in them. Pepper just didn't realize that, she was so beautiful she didn't even need makeup yet. (14)

Remove the "sort ofs" and "kind ofs" from this book, I asserted in my review, "and the result would be a short story."

Other reviewers responded similarly. D. Keith Mano in *National Review* found the novel "brain-sphinctering," noting that by choosing dumb characters for point of view, McMurtry's vocabulary is reduced. Charles L. Adams in *Western American Literature* pointed to the same weakness:

> The fundamental technical problem with the novel is this
> presentation through the eyes and voices of two women of limited
> intelligence. The use of an outside narrator might perhaps have
> made it an amusing fantasy, and indeed, McMurtry's almost
> patronizing tone does come through, but all in all, the lives of these
> women as told by them are anything but amusing.

Ever since his first editor insisted on changing the ending of *Horseman, Pass By*, Larry McMurtry has resented editorial interference. After he became a reasonably famous writer, he no longer had to listen to editorial suggestions, but *The Desert Rose* demonstrates that even a good writer could benefit from editing.

The novel's strength derives from its poignant human story: Harmony, a thirty-eight-year-old showgirl who has long been called the most beautiful woman in Las Vegas, is aging; Bonventre, the hard-hearted dance manager, has decided to hire Pepper, Harmony's daughter, as the lead dancer and to fire Harmony.

To his credit, McMurtry gets many readers to care for these figures and some of the other weird ones in this menagerie—Myrtle, an alcoholic neighbor who sits in the yard drinking, waiting for customers to come to her rummage sale and watching her goat Maude eat either Cheerios or the bottoms out of the chairs; Myrtle's boyfriend, Wendell, who cleans the MGM Grand pool and works at the AMOCO station; Gary, the gay wardrobe manager who is confidant for all the girls; Mel, the mysterious former fashion photographer who is so taken by his films of Pepper in old lingerie that he decides to marry her and watch her grow up. Given the language and level of mind McMurtry chose to portray, it is an accomplishment that we begin to feel anything about these characters. McMurtry is, in fact, taken with them, noting that they taught him that "optimism is a form of courage" and stating that he may some day return to Pepper in a later work.

There are other elements with potential here. For example, Harmony is often concerned about the pet peacocks that she keeps around her house. Harmony's caring for these beautiful natural creatures suggests that she is worthy of our interest. McMurtry juxtaposes these beautiful birds to Harmony, who often wears a dance costume that makes her a "feathered beauty," but he allows the irony of the two images to remain undeveloped. In the hands of a writer like Flannery O'Connor, the universe in the pattern of a peacock's feathers became symbolic of the wonders of the invisible world; but McMurtry's world here, unlike O'Connor's, lacks a transcendent power that gives life meaning.

In the long view of McMurtry's work, *The Desert Rose* is interesting because it includes a number of McMurtry themes, images, and techniques: nostalgia for a dying craft, the complex intertwining of affection and anger in mother-daughter relationships (explored earlier in both *The Last Picture Show* and *Terms of Endearment*), the process by which emotions become reified as objects of barter, varying of points of view, and the metaphor of journeying. As the novel ends, Harmony takes the bus to Reno, where she faces her limited future with grace and dignity.

Ultimately, what is most important about *The Desert Rose* is that it marks a turning point in Larry McMurtry's career. With this book McMurtry regained the enthusiasm for writing that he had lost writing *Somebody's Darling*. With his renewed energy, he returned to the trail drive novel—and to Texas as both a part-time home and the subject for his fiction. He soon finished the novel he had been tinkering with for years, *Lonesome Dove;* the Pulitzer Prize and other accolades followed. No longer was Larry McMurtry the "Minor Regional Novelist" as proclaimed on a T-shirt he once liked to wear.

WORKS CITED

Adams, Charles L. Rev. of *The Desert Rose*. *Western American Literature* 20 (1985): 167–68.

Ahearn, Kerry. "Larry McMurtry." *Fifty Western Writers: A Bio-Bibliographical Sourcebook*. Eds. Fred Erisman and Richard W. Etulain. Westport, CN: Greenwood, 1982. 280–90.

Bennett, Patrick. "Larry McMurtry: Thalia, Houston, and Hollywood." *Talking with Texas Writers: Twelve Interviews*. College Station: Texas A&M UP, 1980. 15–36.

Busby, Mark. "McMurtry, Out of the Chute, Stumbling." Rev. of *Somebody's Darling*. *Zest [Houston Chronicle]* 14 Jan. 1979: 35.

———. "McMurtry's Cardboard Characters." Rev. of *The Desert Rose*. *Book Week [Bryan-College Station Eagle]* 8 Oct. 1983: 1BB.

———. "The Junk Man." Rev. of *Cadillac Jack*. *Texas Books in Review* 5 (1983): 31–32.

Mano, D. Keith. "Vegas Deserta." Rev. of *The Desert Rose*. *National Review* 25 Nov. 1983: 1495–96.

McMurtry, Larry. "Preface." *Cadillac Jack.* Touchstone ed. New York: Simon and
Schuster, 1986.

_____. "Preface." *The Desert Rose.* Touchstone ed. New York: Simon and Schuster,
1986.

_____. "Preface." *Somebody's Darling.* Touchstone ed. New York: Simon and
Schuster, 1987.

Neinstein, Raymond L. *The Ghost Country: A Study of the Novels of Larry McMurtry.*
Modern Authors Monograph Series 1. Berkeley: Creative Arts, 1976.

Nelson, Jane. "Larry McMurtry." *A Literary History of the American West.* Ed. J.
Golden Taylor, et al. Fort Worth: Texas Christian UP, 1987: 612–21.

Larry McMurtry's works covered in this section—*Somebody's Darling* (1978), *Cadillac Jack* (1982), and *The Desert Rose* (1983)—have received less academic scrutiny than many of his other works. The extended studies of McMurtry by Charles Peavy, Thomas Landess, and Raymond Neinstein had already appeared when these novels were published, and none of these works achieved the critical response that leads to intensive scholarly analysis. In fact, after the books' initial reviews, only two critical articles had been published by 1988, one on *Somebody's Darling* and one on *Cadillac Jack*. Both of those articles follow.

Also included in these selections are initial reviews that demonstrate the basis for the reviewer's judgments and go beyond simple responses. Although many of the initial reviews were unfavorable, this section includes both positive and negative reactions to the novels.

Brooks Landon's analysis of *Somebody's Darling* was written for the *Dictionary of Literary Biography Yearbook: 1980* and has the benefit of hindsight. Since it is not a review, the tone is usually objective, but Landon is generally positive about the novel. Gene Lyons's review in *Texas Monthly*, which always treats a McMurtry publication as an important event, criticizes the novel, primarily for McMurtry's choice of characters.

Dominique Browning's review of *Cadillac Jack* demonstrates that *Texas Monthly* has no party line on McMurtry's work, for Browning praises the novel on the grounds that its main character is a true American eccentric in a comic novel that mines significant American themes. Clay Reynolds, on the other hand, finds Jack's directionless wandering symptomatic of his creator's loss of roots.

The last novel treated in this section, *The Desert Rose,* has likewise drawn both positive and negative responses. Emily Benedek finds an effective "contrapuntal pattern" in the careful organization of the novel. Rod Davis, on the other hand, sounds a critical refrain heard about the other novels in this section as he takes McMurtry to task for creating shallow characters.

No comprehensive articles that synthesize these three novels and demonstrate their relationship to McMurtry's other work have yet appeared. It is, of course, one of the purposes of this casebook to stimulate just that kind of analysis.

Larry McMurtry
BROOKS LANDON

In a biting 1975 essay in the *Atlantic,* "The Texas Moon, And Elsewhere," Larry McMurtry bade a not-so-fond farewell to the region his novels had so richly mined. "I was halfway through my sixth Texas novel," he explained, "when I suddenly began to notice that where place was concerned, I was sucking air. The book is set in Houston, but none of the characters are Texans." Pinning his fatigue on "the kind of mental and emotive inarticulateness" he found in Texas, McMurtry concluded: "The move off the land is now virtually completed, and that was the great subject that Texas offered writers of my generation. The one basic subject it offers us now is loneliness, and one can only ring the changes on that so many times." In 1978 McMurtry put away his "Minor Regional Novelist" T-shirt (actually, he reports he lost it in a laundromat) and published his seventh novel, *Somebody's Darling*— leaping from the frying pan of Texas literature into the well-stoked fire of novels about Hollywood.

Somebody's Darling, a comedy of manners and of vulgarity, is about movie people and movie-making and has all the earmarks of the Hollywood novel: hopeless dreamers, bitchy stars, cynical writers, artless directors, colorful has-beens, and sad hangers-on. McMurtry's Hollywood is all about "frippery, pretense, indulgence, overconspicuous overconsumption." It is a place where gofers hold elevators for their bosses and a dalmatian can, unnoticed, eat $800 worth of caviar at a director's party. It is a place where *whatever* is the word to end all conversations and equivocation is the order of the day.

It should come as no surprise to his readers that McMurtry would set a novel in Hollywood. As early as 1968 he was indicating in his essays that California and Texas had much in common, going so far as to predict that "the new Texas is probably going to be a sort of kid brother to California, with a kid brother's tendency to imitation." And McMurtry was quick to acknowledge the challenge this "big brother" posed: "California, whether as a subject or a place to live, is almost too taxing. There the confusion is greater, the rivalries of manners more intense: the question is whether anyone can live in California and comprehend it clearly now. Nathanael West would have a harder time with the state today than he had in 1939."

Certainly, McMurtry's knowledge of Hollywood is extensive. Charles Peavy, author of the most systematic study of McMurtry's work, notes that "few contemporary American novelists have been as intimately associated with motion pictures" as has McMurtry. Three of his novels have been made into movies (*Horseman, Pass By* as *Hud*, 1963; *The Last Picture Show*, 1971; and *Leaving Cheyenne* as *Lovin' Molly*, 1973); two others sent Texas characters to Hollywood, and McMurtry—an avowed aficionado of "bad movies"—has been a contributing editor of *American Film* magazine. One critic has claimed that his involvement with Hollywood makes him "a pivotal figure who demonstrates how an exchange between film and fiction can each enrich the other."

Against such a background, the surprising thing about *Somebody's Darling* is that it never really tries to be much of a Hollywood novel: Hollywood provides its context, but not its subject. While Jonathan Yardley contended in the *New York Times Book Review* that the novel's "principal concern is the ambiguous relationship between craft and art as it manifests itself in Hollywood," *Somebody's Darling* seems much more concerned with familiar McMurtry themes, ringing one more change on the subject of loneliness. Indeed, everything about the book is familiar: its three-narrator structure is very similar to that of *Leaving Cheyenne* (1963); two of the three narrators—Joe Percy and Jill Peel— and a couple of minor characters reappear from *Moving On* (1970) and from *All My Friends Are Going to Be Strangers* (1972); and the third narrator—Owen Oarson—is a Texan, a slightly more urbane and complicated version of Paul Newman's Hud. Two of the most memorable characters in *Somebody's Darling*, Elmo Buckle and Winfield Gohagen, are good ol' boy screenwriters from Austin, Texas, and that native Texas delicacy, chicken-fried steak, even makes a guest appearance. In one humorously self-conscious moment, one of McMurtry's narrators laments: "There's no getting away from cowboys, no place I've ever been." In another such moment, one of the two puckish Texan screenwriters counsels that "Texas is the ultimate last resort. . . . It's always a good idea to go to Texas, if you can't think of anything else to do."

Somebody's Darling, a frequently hilarious, finally sad, always engaging book, does indeed "go to Texas" twice, but not because McMurtry runs out of ideas. (Some of the novel's most effective scenes are set in New York and much of its important action occurs in Rome.) McMurtry has acknowledged the danger of self-imitation ("that monster that lurks eternally outside the writer's window") and in this wide-ranging story he studies the love that is friendship in a way not seen before in his novels.

Somebody's Darling tells the story of thirty-seven-year-old Jill Peel, Hollywood's first female director, a woman somewhat randomly catapulted by her directorial debut into success and out of her long-standing and deep friendship with Joe Percy, a sixty-three-year-old contract screenwriter. Joe, the first of the novel's three narrators and easily its most endearing character, has been reduced to writing plots for a television series based on the song "Witchita Lineman." He is a dapper widower, a self-styled "pseudo-sage," who manages to be both avuncular and sybaritic. One of Hollywood's last gentlemen, Joe is a man whose consideration and simple kindness prove irresistible to a string of young Hollywood wives. Joe feels himself to be the last of an old breed, but unlike so many of McMurtry's earlier patriarchal dinosaurs, he can accept change: he misses the old days of Hollywood, but does not delude himself that they were idyllic. Joe lives his life knowing that at any moment, in any relationship, "the bottom could always drop out." And, when Jill begins an affair with Owen Oarson, an opportunistic ex-football star now determined to become a Hollywood producer by bedding the right women, the bottom does drop out of their long friendship. "Friendship, too, is ruinable," Joe sadly notes, "and can be destroyed as quickly and as absolutely as love."

Owen detests Jill's respect for old-timers such as Joe and, in fact, detests most of her characteristics. She is as principled as he is not, as sentimental as he is callous. However, Jill has an intellectual toughness that Owen grudgingly admires, a kind of integrity he cannot understand since "a woman like her destroys all the simple appetites." For all his unpleasantness and cruelty, Owen remains the book's most pathetic figure: his hustling never slows, but his own recalcitrant complexity keeps betraying him. "I've always aspired to pure opportunism," he complains, "but I never make it."

Jill Peel is the momentary darling of the movie industry, the recipient of "more general love than anybody." But specific love has always been her special problem, a chronic victim of her complicated principles and pride. She recognizes all of Owen's flaws, but his crude attraction to her counters her debilitating need for overintellectualizing relationships. Jill is one of McMurtry's most complex characters, paradoxically strong and weak at the same time. Recently, McMurtry told interviewer Patrick Bennett that his women characters give him the problem of "finding men worth having in the same book with my women." McMurtry elaborates: "Women are always the most admirable characters in my novels. . . . I feel I write about them well, but that's not necessarily to say that I understand them. My writing frequently convinces women that I understand them, but I don't know whether that means I really do, or whether it means they are easily persuaded, or that my writing is especially persuasive when it comes to descriptions of women."

Although she is torn by her conflicting feelings for Owen, Jill's greatest concern is for her old friend Joe Percy. Even more than she had disapproved of Joe's affairs with young wives, Joe had disapproved of her involvement with Owen, and Joe and Jill had quietly grown apart. Jill worries: "We're such old friends we've forgotten how to be friends. Maybe we really aren't friends any more and just don't want to admit it." The nearly symbiotic Texan screenwriters, Elmo Buckle and Winfield Gohagen, remind Jill that friends should complement each other. ("When one was down, the other could be counted on to be up. They were sometimes both up, but never both down.") However, the problem facing Jill and Joe is that *both* of them are down: a stroke has robbed him of his potency and spirit; her relationship with Owen and various studio intrigues have robbed her of precision and purpose.

The most compelling scenes in *Somebody's Darling* deal with Jill's and Joe's fumbling attempts to make sense once more of "the little roads that lead people up to and then away from one another." The great poignancy of their final scene together probably stems, at least in part, from the pivotal role his endings play in McMurtry's writing. He explained to Patrick Bennett: "I consider it a process of discovery, writing a novel. But I always start with an ending. My novels begin with a scene that forms itself in my consciousness, which I recognize as a culminating scene. . . . It's been to the point where I see the people, and I hear the conversation, and I know what the last words are going to be, and I know that something's ended. I don't know exactly what's ended, and the writing of the novel is a process in which I discover how these people got themselves to this scene."

While reviewers variously grumbled that *Somebody's Darling* failed to answer "important questions," or that it set its sights too low, the novel's critical reception was by and large genial, as critics acknowledged the appeal of both McMurtry's characters and his prose. McMurtry uses the device of multiple narrations to refract his characteristic concerns with kinds of initiation, with loneliness, and with the passing of old orders through the prism of Jill's relationships with Joe and Owen. In Joe Percy and Jill Peel, McMurtry has created two of his most mature and most fully realized characters. In Elmo and Winfield ("neither of them quite trusted a woman until she'd slept with them both"), McMurtry has created two screamingly funny characters—crazy but endearing Texans.

Yet, McMurtry was not satisfied with *Somebody's Darling,* seeing it as "an enjoyable read," but as no more than an interesting failure. Calling it the only unpleasant writing experience that he had ever had, McMurtry specified in the Bennett interview: "I've often wished that I had done only the first section and used it as a short novel or something. The first section has life. I struggled with several technical problems in that novel that I don't think I overcame. Perhaps my approach was a bit conservative. That first section should have been the last section somehow, and it should have been the only section in the first person. . . . I always felt there was something misfitting about the conception of that book. Oh, well, water under the bridge. I'm not one to brood."

Currently, McMurtry divides his time among his writing, his prolific reviewing and incidental journalism, and his Washington, D.C., rare-book shop, Booked Up. His exploits as a book scout have been detailed in a 1976 *New Yorker* article by Calvin Trillin. Indeed, talking about his book collecting, McMurtry wryly notes, "the strange thing is that in the book trade my reputation as a dealer is a good deal better than my reputation as a novelist." McMurtry has indicated his interest in writing a serious novel about Washington and has recently worked on a screenplay about coal development in Montana, but he says only that his current projects are "vague."

Periodical Publications

"The Texas Moon, And Elsewhere," *Atlantic Monthly* (March 1975): 29–36.

Interviews

Patrick Bennett, "Larry McMurtry: Thalia, Houston, & Hollywood," *Talking With Texas Writers: Twelve Interviews* (College Station: Texas A&M University Press, 1980), pp. 15–36;
David W. McCullough, "Larry McMurtry," *People Books & Book People* (New York: Harmony Books, 1981), pp. 117–118.

References

E. Pauline Degenfelder, "McMurtry and the Movies: *Hud* and *The Last Picture Show,*" *Western Humanities Review,* 29 (Winter 1975): 81–91;
Charles D. Peavy, *Larry McMurtry* (Boston: Twayne, 1977);
Dorey Schmidt, ed. *Larry McMurtry: Unredeemed Dreams* (Living Author Series, 1), (Edinburg, Texas: School of Humanities, Pan American University, 1978);
Calvin Trillin, "US Journal: Washington, D.C.—Scouting Sleepers," *New Yorker* (14 June 1978): 86–92.

Day of the Hocus
GENE LYONS

Larry McMurtry's seventh novel, *Somebody's Darling,* is a classic example of a genre that has led many another talented author into an artistic morass: the Hollywood Novel. Since Nathanael West's *Day of the Locust,* published in 1939, nobody who has tried seems to have got much beyond what one might call the vulgar-vulgar paradox, that is, portraying the loan-shark ethics, the gargantuan egos, the crudity and the almost unimaginable pettiness of the movie-making world without writing a book that itself partakes of those same sleazy values. Another way of putting it, in McMurtry's case, is that he has attempted a manners novel about a group of people who have none and in so doing comes on all too often like a cross between Harold Robbins and the gossip writers at *Women's Wear Daily.* But with Robbins you get a tightly constructed plot, however absurd, and with *WWD* you get real gossip; you don't have to guess who they are talking about. Not so with McMurtry.

Somebody's Darling begins quite promisingly. Lunching with his dear friend Jill Peel, who has just completed directing a "women's" movie that will make her famous, washed-up screenwriter Joe Percy is bemused and touched by the way she chides him for his womanizing: "I was always a sucker for dogmatic women. The absolute and unassailable confidence with which they deliver their judgments on human behavior charms me to my toes—the more so because I've noticed that it usually exists side by side with an almost total uncertainty as to how to proceed with their own lives." It is not so much a question of agreeing or disagreeing with such a sentiment as it is a matter of texture and prose style; if McMurtry hasn't the exactness of Anthony Powell or even of Philip Roth—both "sucker" and "charms me to my toes" weaken the passage—he begins, nevertheless, with two interesting and intelligent characters who are at critical points in their lives. At 63, Percy considers himself a hack and is facing old age "writing Westerns, jungle movies, serials, shorts, and propaganda pictures. I wasn't destroying my sensitive, artistic soul, either, because I didn't have one." His penchant for young women—always other men's wives—seems a way of avoiding emotional commitment since the death of his own wife, to whom he had been devotedly faithful. "Life wasn't really life anymore—it was just a straight imitation of bad art. Nine-tenths of the time I found myself playing the roles I was typecast for: the jovial drunk, the versatile hack."

Friend Jill, on the other hand, faces the terrors of success. Her film, *Womanly Ways,* is about mistreated housewives, exactly the sort of thing, since Jill is uninterested in feminism or politics, to bring her misplaced notoriety and attention in terms that embarrass her. Indeed her press conference at the New York Film Festival quite early in the novel, with its strident idealogues and pompous academic reviewers on parade, may well be the best thing in the book. Seeking comfortable companionship, perhaps even love, Jill convinces Joe to accompany her and share a suite in New York. But Joe blows his big chance—perhaps out of fear, that part never becomes clear—and spends most of the time holed up in another hotel room with his young mistress. Jill takes up with a former football player and farm equipment salesman from Lubbock named Owen Oarson, who is eager to become a producer.

From the moment Oarson enters the book, the narrative descends to his crude level and stays there: "You can stand on Hollywood Boulevard any day of the week, and if you just watch the asses and the legs, you'll think you're in ass heaven. The mistake is ever looking at the faces." Of probably a hundred such passages, that is one of the few Oarson narrates that can be printed in a magazine that eschews the Anglo-Saxon verb meaning "to copulate," as well as the more common one-syllable nouns referring to the anatomical parts with which the deed is performed. As a person who grew up in a climate where such language is used constantly in discussions of everything from politics to baseball and the weather report, I am hardly squeamish about it. Coarseness and crudity, as novelists from D. H. Lawrence to Philip Roth have proved, are not necessarily the same thing. Using Jill to advance his own career, and making his way finally into the bed of Sherry Solare, *the* Bitch Queen of Hollywood and its reigning sex symbol, while Jill is directing her on a Western being shot outside Amarillo, Oarson is finally too boring even to make an interesting villain. If Jill Peel is such a wonderful woman, what is she doing with such a crumb?

The reader hoping to find an answer in Book III, the section Jill narrates, will not so much be disappointed as simply annoyed and confused. "Owen was virtually a textbook case," she says, "a man who violated all the rules, who had shown zero consideration for me and my feelings; and yet I guess I still would have slept with him if my body hadn't been suddenly like a rock." But why? Only a few pages earlier she was saying, "I had genuinely tender feelings for his body, only his dumb personality kept getting in the way." The problem seems to be that, while Jill is dedicated to her craft, she really does not seem to differ sufficiently from the alley cat ethics of the people who surround her to act upon her convictions. Perhaps, like other

McMurtry heroines, she is victimized by men's seeming inability to know or even to care what women need in an intimate relationship. But if that is so, McMurtry has failed, in my opinion, to articulate a feminine point of view that differs convincingly from that of Owen Oarson. *Somebody's Darling* turns to pulp at the end, the climax of all the bed hopping coming in the accidental shooting death of a child—a killing for which we are quite unprepared and which seems to have been cooked up out of the *Novelist's Book of Cheap Tricks* as a way of punishing the characters for their sins. It is an ending terrible without being understandable, inexplicable without being mysterious.

After that Jill jumps into a car with two Texas screenwriters and old Joe Percy and heads for Austin. "Texas is the ultimate last resort," says one of the screenwriters, a cruder type even than Oarson, but with a touch of humor meant to redeem him. "It's always a good idea to go to Texas, if you can't think of anything else to do." Ostensibly they are stealing the only print of Jill's movie in order to prevent a jealous and bitter Sherry Solare from having it reedited according to her whims. But they ship it back on a bus with no real explanation given. McMurtry characters are always driving through Texas; and instead of a resolution this trip reads as if the novelist himself had run out of ideas and fell back upon self-imitation. In the end Joe has a stroke and Jill assists him manually to his last erection. It's supposed to be affecting. It's not.

Joe dies some time later while reading a girlie magazine. His own words about his life are a fitting summary of the novel as well. "Life ought to be like a good script. The incidents ought to add up, and the characters ought to complement each other, and the story line ought to be clear, and after you've had the climax it ought to leave you with the feeling that it has all been worth it. . . . [But] there never was a clear story line, and most of the incidents were just incidents." Of course many lives are like that; it is one of the things we have art for. But what McMurtry has fallen for used to be called, when the New Criticism was riding high, "the fallacy of imitative form." He has written a vulgar, muddled book about vulgar, muddled people.

The Knickknack Cadillac

DOMINIQUE BROWNING

Sometimes a man's just got to take a long drive and think things over, and that's what Jack McGriff does, many times, in *Cadillac Jack* (Simon and Schuster), Larry McMurtry's eighth novel, and one of his best. Cadillac Jack is a scout. He makes a living combing through junk stores, antique shops, and flea markets, discovering and then reselling objects of exceptional value. He roams America in a pearl-colored 1960 Cadillac with peach velour interior. Jack lives by a law fundamental to scouts, articulated by his friend Zack Jenks, the world's greatest Coke bottle scout: "Anything can be anywhere." All Jack loves as much as truly beautiful things is women, and he finds women to love everywhere, too. "My kind of buying is like my kind of falling in love," he says, "a matter of immediate eye appeal." Scouting has taught Jack a lot about life.

Cadillac Jack, which chronicles its hero-narrator's comic misadventures as he travels across the country, fits squarely in the tradition of the picaresque novel. It begins in Washington, D.C., where Jack goes to unload a carful of cowboyana and to visit his old friend and customer, Boog Miller. Boog, who has a penchant for slime-green suits and cheap women, is one of the wealthiest (he owns Winkler County— with its many oil wells—back home in Texas) and most powerful political consultants in town. He sends Jack to a trendy antique store in Georgetown, where Jack promptly falls in love with the owner, a stunning California beauty named Cindy Sanders. Dating Jack means downward mobility for Cindy, an energetic social climber, but she has an affair with him anyway, because "this town is full of shrimps." In fact, Washington doesn't often see the likes of Jack, a six-foot-five, 33-year-old retired bulldogging champion from Solino, Texas, who cuts a dashing (if studied) figure in a white doeskin jacket, brown beaver Stetson, and yellow armadillo boots.

Since Cindy has to be seen in all the right places, she and Jack spend their evenings at the parties of the very rich along with pompous senators, insufferable columnists, and curvaceous, airheaded talk show hostesses. They cover ground that's de rigueur in any Washington novel, but that's where the resemblance of *Cadillac Jack* to other books in that genre ends. McMurtry's D.C. is a depraved, hilarious place, caving in under the weight of too much food, money, sex, self-importance, and boredom. McMurtry is the Rabelais of Washington; under his eye the most banal of social affairs, an embassy dinner, turns into an orgy of rich people's appetites:

> All the food was roped off behind thick velvet ropes. They were the kind of ropes used in the foyers of movie theaters, to restrain eager crowds.
>
> This crowd was eager, too. Most of the people in the receiving line had looked half dead, but the sight of a feast had brought them back to life. They were massed three deep behind the velvet ropes.

. . . The sight of so much food must have released internal floods of gastric juices, causing sweat to pop out on many faces. The people were oblivious to one another. Lamb, caviar, and big pulpy shrimp were what they wanted. . . . It was hard to imagine that such a well-dressed crowd could look so hungry. I've been to some wild barbecues down in Texas, where whole beeves were consumed, and yet I'd never seen a Texas crowd crammed up together, beaded with sweat.

During the day, Jack gets back to his own element, moving out of the "civilized" circles of Washington to the suburbs of Virginia and Maryland, where the real people live. His world is an eccentric one, full of collectors like Benny the Ghost, from Baltimore, in danger of being smothered by a secret hoard that fills every inch of a five-story house, and Bryan Ponder, a retired spook who traded a secret for a wife with a voice unlike any he'd ever heard and happily spent 34 years filling his songbird's house with 10,000 bird's nests. Each of these characters is sparely but precisely drawn. With them, McMurtry captures the essence of what it means to traffic in objects: the furtiveness of the hunt, the blood-rush on spotting a treasure, the fierce attachment to a loved thing that separates the collector from the dealer or trader, the empathy of certain people for certain things ("Basket scouts were among the nicest people I know. They tend to be simple, spare, graceful, unaggressive. They had a kind of dry quiet humor that I liked").

Life gets complicated for Jack when at a downtown auction he bids for a rare quadripartite icon against lovely Jean Tooley, soon-to-be divorced mother of two charming daughters. Jean, "a trunk person: delicate, wistful, a little withdrawn," is a kindred soul, a woman who will spend her last dollar on a beautiful object. She runs an antique store in a lousy cinder-block shopping center in Wheaton, Maryland. Jack is immediately smitten with her and her two girls. (Some of the funniest dialogues in the book are between Jack and three-year-old Belinda; McMurtry's ear is well tuned to the cadence of conversations with children.) Around Jean and her family, Jack is his tenderest, most loving self, and around Cindy—and lots of others—he's a generous, saucy, slightly self-deprecating stud. Cindy, his high-society girl, turns his head; Jean, his frontier (such as it is these days) woman, turns his heart. He is passionate about both but can't really have either, and somehow all this frustrated wanting throws him into a confusion that brings on a crisis of professional confidence:

Something had suddenly gone wrong in my relationship to objects, and my relationship with objects was more or less the basis for my life. Women came and went from me, or I came and went from women, but there were always objects, in their endless, infinite variety.

Poor Jack. While all around him marriages are collapsing, people keep telling him to settle down, get married, and have children. He's a happy enough fellow until he starts listening. He doesn't really want a conventional life; he wants everything—he can't help himself. Desire is the motor of his soul. Jack's open to anything, anywhere; that what makes him a great scout, and a great character. He's at his best when he's devouring mile after mile of America (what the Mississippi River was to Huck Finn, I-40 is to Cadillac Jack), turning up treasure after treasure, falling in love with woman upon woman. He isn't indiscriminate; he's got such a strong lust for life that he *does* manage to find the truly exceptional where most people see only the commonplace. He's not a cad, either. He's more committed to his friends, in his odd way, than most people are. He's a loner, and countless like him have wandered across America.

And wandered through American fiction. Some great novels—*Moby Dick* and *The Great Gatsby* and *All the King's Men*—deal straightforwardly with major themes like power and love. But there's another tradition of American fiction, one in which a novel can be straightforwardly humorous and deal with major themes obliquely. Such novels are about an idiosyncratic human condition—they portray the world view of a particular, often eccentric character writ large as another way of thinking about what it all means. *Cadillac Jack* is in this second tradition. Jack isn't going to preach about what constitutes the good life or what it means to do right by others, but it's easy to see what his values are by watching him yearn his way across America. "I guess I buy and sell in hope of style—or maybe as a style of hope, and . . . there are always others as restless as myself, who constantly buy and sell, too, for their own reasons."

Come Home Larry, All Is Forgiven:
A Native Son's Search for Identity

CLAY REYNOLDS

Texas novelist Larry McMurtry struck gold with his first book, *Horseman, Pass By,* which was filmed as the Oscar-winning *Hud,* and he followed that with another blockbuster, *The Last Picture Show,* a novel and a film that quickly found their ways into classrooms and livingrooms across America. *Leaving Cheyenne,* filmed as *Lovin' Molly,* also enjoyed modest success as both book and movie, and McMurtry left Texas for California in spirit if not in person for a brief and reportedly mutually dissatisfying flirtation with Hollywood. He mapped out his westward movement in a quartet of loosely related novels—*Moving On, All My Friends Are Going to Be Strangers, Terms of Endearment* (also a successful film), and *Somebody's Darling*—that revolve around a set of characters and situations ranging from Houston to Los Angeles to the anonymous midwest, including a frustrated Texas writer, Danny Deck.

After California, however, and during the process of writing these four books, McMurtry found himself living in Washington, D.C., from where he has recently issued two more volumes, *Cadillac Jack* and *The Desert Rose.* On the surface, at least, these new books seem to indicate his contentment with characters, themes, and situations that are only incidentally connected to his home state.

Among those who read McMurtry's early works and hailed him as a perceptive voice to speak to and about Texas and Texans, who enjoyed his special, humorous understanding of this special, humorous place, and who appreciated his ability to articulate the romance of the Southwest without miring down in nostalgia or nonsense, a feeling has grown that insofar as he is a representative of the Southwest, McMurtry is dead. Even such an unlikely critic as Gary Cartwright, feature writer for the state's slick, public relations magazine, *Texas Monthly,* has seen fit to attack McMurtry's relationship to his home state as bogus.[1] Even the most ardent fans of the novels must admit that the work produced since leaving Texas exhibits a certain flatness, a loss of the inspiration that gave his early books their freshness and appeal.

But in one of these recent books, *Cadillac Jack,* McMurtry seems to be signalling, perhaps unconsciously, his awareness of this authorial identity crisis, and the careful reader can perceive a recognition on McMurtry's part of the need to return to his roots and make peace with his homeland. *Cadillac Jack* tells the disorganized and ungainly tale of one Jack McGriff, displaced Texan, who finds himself in the middle of Washington's highest society. He is a "scout," a trader in second-hand merchandise acquired from flea markets, garage sales, and junk stores from coast to coast and transported in Jack's pearl-colored Cadillac to other dealers who he knows will pay fat profits for his finds. Although little is said about Jack's education, where he learned to estimate the value of a quadripartite icon in the midst of lots of snow tires and used garden implements, he is at thirty-three a

highly skilled judge of antiques and rare merchandise and supposedly
has a vast knowledge of everything from Coke bottles to Mogul leaves.
Further, he claims to be a shrewd haggler and to know everybody who
is anybody in the second-hand world of collectables.

Jack is also knowledgeable of second-hand women: Cindy Sanders,
herself displaced from Southern California and now introduced to a
wealthy Washingtonian, alternately seduces and drives Jack to distraction with her siren-like beauty and capricious selfishness; Jean
Arber, an attractive, homey, motherly divorcée who deals in *objets
d'art*, charms him with visions of ready-made home and family; and
Coffee, his own ex-wife, who never actually appears in the novel except as a nagging call on his car phone, tempts him to come back to
Austin, where he left her.

Between bouncing beds, Jack finds himself at stuffy Washington
parties populated with the absurdly wealthy and successful of the
capital's society. He saunters through the crowds of the prominent and
powerful in his armadillo boots and Stetson hat, saying little that
fails to offend and, incredibly, revealing his ignorance of the antique
trade at every turn. Whenever he has a chance to demonstrate his
expertise, he is surprised to learn of the "biggest," "most famous," or
"most notorious" deal or dealer in the country for the first time, casually accepting the challenge to his self-proclaimed knowledge without
rebuttal.

The book is, to borrow a word from the jacket blurb, "slouchy,"[2] as
unanchored and disorganized as McMurtry's hero. Although there are
several promises of plot development—the clandestine sale of the
Smithsonian's contents, for example—none of them ever get anywhere.
In fact, the book is full of dead ends, sloppy summations, and helplessly
dangling loose threads that continue to tantalize as Jack finds himself
at the novel's end alone in a Colorado motel room reading the classified
ads and wondering what in the world he might do next.

Even the several romantic interests remain unresolved at the
novel's close. Jack has been abandoned by Cindy, turned down by
Jean, and continues to resist the idea of going home to Coffee. Thus,
nothing in the way of Jack's lovelife is concluded, and nothing in his
professional life has come to resolution either. He has failed to break
into Washington society, failed to find a new home, and failed to
return to his roots. His options in all these areas seem to remain open,
and he finds himself spent, weary, with no place to go and no particular motivation to go there if he had one.

One reason for the novel's progress, of course, is McMurtry's attempt at humor in his broadly drawn caricatures of the people of the

nation's capital. In fact, as one trips along behind Jack as he bumbles his way through fancy parties, engages in shady real estate deals, and holds secret meetings with ex-spies to trade antiques, one gets a very clear offering of McMurtry's version of east coast society that roughly parallels television's view of Texas in such a series as *Dallas*. Like the Ewings on that program, McMurtry's Washingtonians are broad, one-dimensional characters whose very names—Brisling Bowker, Cunny Cotswinkle, Pencil Penrose, Bessie Lump—suggest through alliteration and onomatopoeia that one is not supposed to take them seriously; they have as much resemblance to real people as J. R. or Miss Ellie do to real Texans—millionaires or otherwise.

Even Cadillac Jack, the narrator's trade name, reminds the reader of the scout's chief mode of transport, his pride and joy, his home and castle—his car. And his women, Coffee, who has an awakening impact on the footloose trader, Cindy Sanders, who affects his eyes and ears and gives him a frustrating itch, and Jean Arber, who represents stability and roots in the city that houses the branches of government, all have names that illustrate their roles in the novel and their relationships with Jack.

But if McMurtry's aim in this novel is merely to spoof those who would stereotype his home and folks by stereotyping his adopted home and its people, he does not quite succeed. In spite of some outrageous scenes where food and drink are extravagantly mixed with million dollar deals and political intrigue, the novel fails to spark the flame of satire and sputters out as weak slapstick, an array of hopelessly confusing scenes that lead nowhere but occasionally and too infrequently back to each other.

Ironically, the best of McMurtry's satire seems to be revealed when he gently portrays his fellow Texans. Boog Miller, for example, who spends his time in hot tubs romping with prostitutes when he is not negotiating exorbitant antique deals, is drawn just as broadly as any of the Washingtonians, but McMurtry's portrait of the Winkler County oil baron is both tender and compassionate. Likewise, his depiction of Uncle Ike Spettle, the possessor of Billy the Kid's boots, and a couple of other small town Southwestern types recalls a richness of characterization that was evident in his earlier books.

The major problem with the humor of *Cadillac Jack*, however, is that McMurtry's satiric norm, Jack McGriff, is himself neither normal nor believable. He is not even original, but comes to the novel second-hand, though altered. Drawn rather loosely from a minor character in an earlier novel, Vernon Dalhart, Jack is at least as improbable as the Washingtonians who find him curious. Like Vernon, Jack lives in his car and has most of the comforts of home there, and like Vernon he enjoys associations with beautiful and wealthy women. But Vernon was McMurtry's vehicle for humor; Jack seems to represent the reasonable world; unfortunately, he is neither reasonable nor particularly realistic.

Apparently traveling without luggage, he wears the same clothes all the time, bathes only after sex, and totes around every conceivable kind of gee gaw and gimcrack a dealer or potential lover might want. He drives his Cadillac at excessively high speeds from Washington to New Mexico, Baltimore to Seattle, and back again without a thought to such trivialities as oil changes or tune ups. He regularly deals in enormous sums of money, always seems to have thousands of dollars on his person, but he never visits a bank, makes a deposit, or cashes a check on his apparently unbalanced account. He is handsome, apparently irresistible to women, but he has no common sense, is indecisive, and, alas, underdeveloped.

Furthermore, Jack lacks any apparent, honest connection with Texas at all. His attempts at folksy witticisms fall flat, as his description of one character indicates: He calls a party goer a "mean little rat terrier . . . As long as you're looking at them they let you alone, but the minute you turn your back they bite you in the leg" (p. 131). And he describes Boog at one point as wearing a "raspberry tuxedo that would have nicely outfitted the maitre d' of a dinner theatre in Killeen, Texas, or somewhere" (p. 112).

In all, Jack seems to be more of a caricature of Texas than the Washingtonians are caricatures of Eastern society and wealth. His first-person narration is sprinkled with words such as "bethought," "bespeak," and "beringed," as well as other atypically Texas samples of vocabulary such as "lubricity" and "sere," and there is no self-consciousness in such inflated usage. He cites Spinoza with ease, and he seems to be as cozy with the absurd characters McMurtry draws from Washington society as he is with Uncle Ike and his domino partners in New Mexico. In this sense, Jack's lack of dimension is summed up in a single introduction that is offered at a Washington party: "Spud Breyfogle," Boog's wife blithely says without noticing anything odder about their names than if they were Smith and Jones, "meet Cadillac Jack" (p. 115). Still, Jack is offered as McMurtry's version of an erudite cowboy "gone East," and perhaps it is here, in this Texas-scout-turned-darling-of-the-jet-set that the point of *Cadillac Jack* rests.

If seen on a symbolic level, the women in Jack's life take on a poignant and significant meaning. Cindy Sanders, for example, flirts with the trader, takes him in for a while to see if he will "work out," but ultimately dumps him. Originally introduced to Jack by the trader's Texas connection, Boog, Cindy is initially drawn to Jack's Texas background and cowboy mannerisms; to her he is exotic as well as erotically appealing. Although he recognizes that their relationship is temporary, and although her illogical demands frustrate and anger him, he commits himself to her, happily risking his own integrity.

On their Southwestern trip to find Billy the Kid's boots, Jack is dismayed to find that Cindy is unable to see anything beautiful or impressive about Texas. Complaining about the food, the weather, the lack of a New York *Times,* she finally declares: "This is an awful place. I think it's the worst place I've ever been" (p. 242). Ultimately she cuts the trip short, abandons Jack, and flies to Florida to meet Spud Breyfogle, a "proven success" who is sexier than Jack, and who, presumably, will place fewer demands on her.

For solace, Jack turns to Jean Arber. Her symbolic representation of security and acceptability tempt him to quell his wanderlust and settle down with Jean and her two daughters under the bower of family life and permanent address. Although his dashing good looks almost win her over, she sees through him too well and tells him: "I think you're just getting lonely. You're leading a more interesting life than you think. You just don't realize it's interesting . . . I think you're romanticizing all this middle class domesticity we've got around here" (p. 325). Jean understands that Jack does not belong in a family, in a home, or in Washington. He belongs on the road, playing the role of the modern drifter, the contemporary cowboy, searching for dreams and success at the trail's-ends of the world symbolically represented by junk yards and garage sales: "You really find wonderful things," she tells him. "It's a kind of art. You shouldn't give that up just because you've met a woman with a couple of cute kids" (p. 326). Although her refusal of marriage does not preclude future romantic involvement, Jack is again dismayed.

Finally, there is Coffee, the symbolic representation of Texas and, not covertly, of home. Although Jack is frequently angered by her always inconvenient phone calls, he never tries to discourage her from making them. Although they are divorced, although he left her back in Austin, and although he admits that "she had never heard of places no farther away than Waco" (p. 93), he carries a burden of guilt for their marriage's demise. He acknowledges that he left her to go galavanting all over the country searching for something she probably could give him, that she is abandoned to the mercies of a mad Italian dope dealer who beats her and misuses her, that he possibly wants to go home to her more than he wants Cindy and Washington's glamor or Jean and a home and family; but he cannot admit, even to himself, that returning

to her and to Texas is what he ought to do. Even in her simpering
naïveté, however, she manages to put a hard finger on Jack's tenderest
nerve:

> "If you keep dreaming about me you must want something," she
> said. "Anyway, I don't want to talk anymore. Now everytime I talk
> to you I want to cry."
> "I don't see why," I said.
> "You don't want me enough, that's why." (p. 298)

Coffee's accusation forces him to admit: "I was very fond of her, but I
probably didn't want her enough—particularly since I was not the one
who got to measure enoughness . . . Enoughness admits of no sub-
traction: either one's desire is enough, or it's a failure" (p. 298). In this
admission, Jack may reveal something about the author who created
him and that author's definition of success and relationship to a home
he abandoned.

But it is Cindy who brings the meaning of the female symbols home
in one angry summation of Jack's relationship to Coffee—and possibly,
by extension, McMurtry's relationship to Texas—"The fact you've divorced somebody doesn't mean you stop knowing them," she tells him
(p. 236). And here Jack's whole problem in the novel, and perhaps
McMurtry's whole problem as a contemporary Texas writer, is pinpointed. The trader continuously tries to stop "knowing" his ex-wife
just as the writer tries to stop "knowing" Texas. Coffee's constant
phone calls, coming as they always do when the scout is trying to
straighten out a problem with one or another of his women, remind
Jack of home in a painful way and make mockery of his attempts to
"play Texan" in yellow boots and a doe-skin jacket, of his putting on a
show to prove that he is what he claims to be—a genuine Texan—even
though he desperately wishes he was not.

Hence the anomaly in his character is revealed. He is a successful
man, but he is also a failure because he cannot evade the responsibility
of deciding whether or not he wants what he can have enough to
possess it. Instead, he wanders around with no direction at all and
hunts for a life, a symbol, to call his own.

He almost finds such a symbol in Boss Miller, Boog's wife. Ironically, she is the one woman he can never possess, even temporarily.
She represents exactly what Jack cannot attain, either sexually or
socially—a sense of identity. Her vast real estate holdings make her
wealthy and successful, but she maintains her ties to her roots
through such activities as making her own biscuits for breakfast. She
is both confident and acceptable, although outrageously ethnic at

times, and she is as well connected in Washington society as any other socialite. But she is neither pure Texan nor pure Washingtonian. She collects lovers the way some of the dealers in the novel amass antiques, but she maintains her distance from her possessions, never allowing them to take over and own her.

She understands Jack's dilemma, assesses what he needs to do, and neatly sums up his problems for him: "I'll tell you what's wrong with you . . . You're too romantic on the one hand. On the other hand, you don't know the first thing about romance." All he has done is hurt himself, she goes on: "There's just two romantic relationships," she tells him. "Sexy friendships and adultery" (p. 147). When Jack learns that the Miller marriage is falling apart, he is forced to re-evaluate his definitions of success and failure: "Their long defiance of convention had been so successful that you tended to forget that no success is necessarily permanent," he admits to himself (p. 291). Finally understanding that none of these lives, these symbols, will satisfy him, the scout abandons Washington to roam the country in pursuit of new trail's-ends, new second-hand dreams.

Cadillac Jack, therefore, offers something more than a lampoon of Washington society, or even of the mania for possession of semi-worthless and second-hand things. It reveals that the object of McMurtry's satire is the narrator—or perhaps the author—himself, who finds himself rejected by California after a brief period of wild fantasy and promises of endless success, uncomfortable in Washington which insists on seeing him as an oddity who may know something about Texas but very little about anything or anywhere else, and unable to return to his home and face the triumphs and mistakes of the past. The desire to go back to "Cheyenne" may be overwhelming the guilt he feels for having left in the first place, hence leaving both the scout and his story inconclusive as the novel closes.

But Jack is still young at thirty-three, and the direction of his future is yet to be determined. He is not yet completely lost; nor is he as hopeless as many of McMurtry's former heroes have found themselves: Lonnie, Sonny, or even Danny Deck, who drowns himself in the Rio Grande in an attempt to kill the novel that is destroying his life. Jack might still go home to Coffee and save her, or he might continue to wander the second-hand stores of the country looking for salvation and fulfillment in a haven he has yet only to dream of.

As a young writer with many stories yet to tell, McMurtry has decisions to make about his future as well. He must reflect on the feeling he attributes to Jack, a feeling that Texas is calling him home to reacquaint himself with the Homer Bannons, the Mollys, the Sam the Lions, and certainly the Danny Decks he left behind. He must learn to recognize such fickleness as Hollywood's which places capricious and compromising demands on its lovers, to acknowledge that wherever he hangs his hat, home will always be Texas, and to understand the importance of saving that home from malevolent foreigners who would invade it and try to tell its story as their own.

As Cadillac Jack scans the want ads of the future, one tends to hope that he is looking for something more than auction announcements and estate sales. One tends to imagine that he also glances over the "personals," seeking, perhaps, to find a cryptic line of invitation printed under the name of this lost Texas scout: "Come Home Larry, All Is Forgiven!"

NOTES

1. Gary Cartwright, "I Am the Greatest Cook in the World," *Texas Monthly* (February 1983), p. 149.
2. Larry McMurtry, *Cadillac Jack* (New York: Simon and Schuster, 1982), jacket. All citations are from this edition and will be noted by page number in parenthesis in the text.

An Author Recaptures His Voice
EMILY BENEDEK

For years, Larry McMurtry has steered clear of the world of his early and most successful books—the Texas that was. He has, in fact, harshly criticized himself and other writers from his home state for what he sees as a desire to cling to the "country-and-western" genre while ignoring the realities of the contemporary urban Southwest. Yet until now his attempts to break away have been flawed by a ponderous determination to write "literature" and by a rambling search for focus. Happily, in his ninth novel, McMurtry has once again found a form and setting that allow his story to tell itself. And when it comes to just plain unfolding a tale, he has few rivals.

In McMurtry's first three novels—*Horseman, Pass By, Leaving Cheyenne,* and *The Last Picture Show*—the texture of life is deeply rooted in a sense of place; the characters face broad moral choices that stem from an effort to reconcile their larger yearnings with their ties to the soil. Because films were made out of *Horseman* (retitled *Hud*) and *The Last Picture Show,* they are the author's most famous works.

His best, though, is *Leaving Cheyenne,* an American masterpiece about the love of a woman and two men. The three—particularly the heroine, Molly—are bound to one another above all by the few square miles of ranch land where they spend their lifetimes.

In *The Last Picture Show* McMurtry opens the vista a bit, introducing the possibility of escape by motor vehicle. The major players are the restless youth of Thalia, a poor West Texas cattle town. Their short excursions—to Mexico to look for whores, to sports events on the school bus, Saturday nights in the pickup—provide a backdrop for their most intense emotions and for decisions that seemed impossible within walking distance of home.

McMurtry takes another step in what currently constitutes the middle third of his *oeuvre, Moving On, All My Friends Are Going to Be Strangers* and *Terms of Endearment.* Here most of the action involves leavetaking. The characters pass in and out of urban Texas, graduate school, money, and relationships. But the direction of their wanderings, beyond a vague compulsion to wrestle with the Lone Star State's mythical past, is unclear. Many of the writer's trademarks are present: humor, a laconic ingenuousness, resilient, good-natured characters. His once impeccable sense of pacing, though, has deserted him.

With *Somebody's Darling, Cadillac Jack* and now *The Desert Rose,* McMurtry abandons Texas altogether for the more ephemeral locales of Hollywood, Washington, D.C. and Las Vegas, respectively. The last seems to be exactly what he has been looking for, a city dominated by transients. The only history to contend with is the accumulation of days in a life. The present is measured by beauty, the most valuable commodity in Vegas after money. The future is determined by luck.

The Desert Rose charts the last weeks in the career of a 39-year-old showgirl named Harmony. Despite her 20 years of hard work in the famous Stardust Hotel floor show, and the once-prevailing opinion that she had "the best legs in Las Vegas and maybe the best bust too," she has been told by manager Jackie Bonventre that she must leave on her 40th birthday. Later, Harmony discovers that Bonventre has kicked her out because he intends to hire her 16-year-old daughter, Pepper, and thinks little of topless mother-daughter acts.

The novel is carefully constructed, its six parts focusing alternately on Harmony and Pepper. Their stories run in opposite directions, with Harmony's luck falling as her daughter's rises. Their fates are inevitably the same. McMurtry uses the contrapuntal pattern effectively to emphasize the curious routes of human sympathy and the quality of bonds in the lives of the dislocated.

Harmony and Pepper share a duplex with Myrtle, "a tiny redhead in her early sixties who had no intention of letting age or anything else get in the way of pleasure." She raises goats, thinking she may train them for an act, but between garage sales, vodka and frolics with her favorite beast, Maude, she hasn't much time to be an educator. She eats only Cheerios, unless someone takes her out to Wendy's for a burger binge.

Ross, Harmony's husband, left her soon after Pepper's birth. The couple had gotten along, Harmony explains, yet Ross "liked to change lives once in a while and he was such a good light man he could always get work." Her most recent boyfriend, Denny, ran out on her after precipitating the cancellation of her Visa card, destroying her car, and stealing a $1,300 insurance check from the mailbox. Pepper, who has just become engaged, is aloof and rebellious; Harmony hears about the betrothal from friends. Still, the over-the-hill dancer remains cheerful: "For herself she didn't worry too much, she still loved being in the show, plus there was a lot to like about life if you could make a little effort and look on the bright side. Even a nice morning was a form of happiness, plus having a sweet guy around for a while was another form, a major form actually, major even if usually sort of brief in her experience."

Harmony is reminiscent of McMurtry's early female characters, winning us by giving without hesitation: ". . . she was like a beautiful car, a Mercedes or something, that had everything it needed except brakes. . . . Generally when a guy left her love would be going at full speed." McMurtry is skillful enough to demonstrate her generosity and compassion without making her a caricature, a fool, or even a victim. Rather, she has the mixed blessing of living in good faith in a world that hardly reciprocates. However distressing the situation, she finds a way to make a big breakfast (one of McMurtry's favorite signs of affection), run an errand, flash a smile, squeeze a hand. She is weak enough to love and strong enough not to wound her loved ones.

Harmony still has pretty much her pick of the men in town. But the choice is between one second-rate card shark and another. McMurtry's men tend to pale beside his women, and in this book, instead of deriving strength from their partners, they drift away. The one man who is different—rich, self-sufficient, intelligent—is Mel, Pepper's fiancé. Like Godwin Lloyd-Jons, the British sociologist and professed Flaubertian who pops up in two of McMurtry's earlier books, Mel appears on the provincial landscape to challenge the inhabitants' limited worldview.

The power of the land is recognized in *The Desert Rose,* too, for McMurtry makes it clear that those who ignore it are condemned to atrophy in the neon city. Moreover, to the few denizens of Las Vegas who are moved to explore beyond their immediate surroundings the desert expanses offer a chance for transcendence: "When she turned off the pavement onto the bumpy dirt road Harmony looked back at the Strip, eight miles away. It looked so miniature, like a wonderful toy place, with all the lights still on, whereas on her other side there was a bright band of sun behind the mountains, from horizon to horizon." As a substitute for owning land, many residents of McMurtry's glitter palace keep animals that reflect their personalities. Harmony has peacocks; Myrtle her goats; and Jessie, another veteran showgirl nearing mandatory retirement, a toy poodle.

Texas, old and new, remains a fertile literary landscape, as the work of such writers as Larry L. King, Beth Henley and Thomas McGuane attests. It is easy to understand why McMurtry felt the need to search for material elsewhere. Since he finally seems capable of writing about the modern West without being derailed by ghosts or stylistic artifice, though, one hopes he will soon take us back to his native habitat.

A Surfeit of Bimbos

ROD DAVIS

The Desert Rose, Larry McMurtry's ninth novel (Simon and Schuster) stars a voluptuous and leggy dancer named Harmony, who is approaching her thirty-ninth birthday having gained nary a pound in 22 years as the most beautiful showgirl in Las Vegas. For the last 12 years she has been dancing at the Stardust casino. She's a trouper, always looking for the bright side no matter what, even as the bags of sleeplessness begin to puff under her eyes, even as her sixteen-year-old daughter, Pepper, berates her for her garish taste in clothing, men, and makeup. Unlike her inexplicably sunny mother, Pepper is a pouty-mouthed, dark-haired Kinski cat, who mesmerizes Mama the way she does men.

Harmony and her husband, Ross, have been separated for thirteen years, ever since Ross ran away to "change lives" and wound up in Reno. After her marriage failed, Harmony developed a habit of falling for men who don't last, losers like Denny, who exits after wrecking Harmony's car, stealing her insurance check, and asking Pepper to perform a sexual act illegal in some parts of the United States. Or Dave, an ex-Marine who invites Harmony to his apartment for a breakfast of K rations and beer. Dave is altogether a scary guy, but Harmony decides to treat him to her torso anyway because "after all he had needed her a lot and she did like the gray streak. . . . She couldn't help feeling a little love."

It is tempting to ridicule Harmony for her sexual servility, flakiness, and insufferable sunniness, but it's not really her fault. For reasons best known to McMurtry, she was created without a functioning brain and is incapable of resolving her simplest problems. McMurtry reduces Harmony to a caricature of the honky-tonk angel and then punishes her for her sins—beauty, womanhood, an offbeat job—by having her ceaselessly minister to all comers. She is neither angel nor rose but eternal bimbo: "The sadness of men, once it got into their eyes, affected her a lot, she sort of couldn't bear it and would usually try and make it go away if the circumstances permitted her to, often they didn't but sometimes they did, it was mainly a desire to kiss their sadness away that had caused her to bring so many of them home."

Pepper, a calculating bitch of Freudian dimension who wants to take the world by the throat, chooses the same route to fame that Harmony did. As a seventeen-year-old knockout, Harmony was kept by a wealthy and influential older man who died not long after helping her break into the Stardust limelight. Pepper, in turn, is discovered by a wealthy and influential middle-aged voyeur named Mel, who meets her when she goes to his house for a modeling session. Mel is love-struck by Pepper's nubility and indifference, and she is intrigued by his desert house, his expensive gadgetry, and his willingness to give her thousands of dollars for scampering around before his lens in old underwear. He asks Pepper to marry him, and she obliges. Mel then uses his contacts to arrange an audition for her at the Stardust, where she wows the casino manager and is offered a job as lead dancer. The manager promptly fires Harmony— just before her birthday—because he doesn't want a mother and a daughter onstage at the same time.

This final perfidy might have inspired a veteran of one of the most cynical cities in America to do some serious stock-taking. But not Harmony. She accepts her firing as inevitable, hops in the sack with another man, and then gets a bus to Reno to meet Ross. His pregnant girlfriend has just left, and he is amenable to trying again with Harmony. He's even pretty sure he can get her another job.

You don't have to have much more prescience than Harmony does to detect something rotten in *The Desert Rose*, for although this is a bad novel, it is not just that. It is, from an author touted on the dust jacket as having an "ability to write about women," a wholesale indictment of the female gender.

Harmony and Pepper allow themselves to be used by men and then discarded when firmer flesh comes along, even—perhaps especially—

if the firmer flesh is in the form of a daughter. Harmony remains, start to finish, a shallow character, a pliant and easily duped womanoid whose fate at every turn depends upon men. She does not rebel, does not wake up, does not escape. Never is her character elaborated enough to explain this wholesale dependency, which coats the book like a suffocating film.

The problems in *The Desert Rose* are exacerbated by McMurtry's use of what might be called pseudo new journalism. New journalism, a mode of reportage created in the sixties and seventies by authors like Tom Wolfe and Hunter Thompson, uses the dramatic devices of fiction to lend pacing and tension to nonfiction. Some writers of contemporary fiction try to reverse that process, applying the data—"detail" is too generous a term—of real life to novels. McMurtry, for example, attempts to convince us that he knows the social milieu he writes about by sprinkling his text with the mundane. Brand names (Taco Bell, Cheerios, Visa) and famous places (Caesar's Palace) are a kind of secret wink to the reader: hey, this guy's been there. Even the choice of Las Vegas is derivative of Hunter Thompson, a link duly noted by Thompson's vacuous blurb on the dust jacket. But McMurtry comes up short as a social reporter—too glib, too cute, too lacking in authority. The fake realism of pseudo new journalism is only name-dropping compared to the social observation that is characteristic of great novels.

The middle-class alienation implicit in the selective use of ultrabanal facts works when it is combined with a larger, more critical vision and a firm grasp of crackling minimalist rhetoric. But McMurtry has no vision worth sharing, and his loose, affected style prickles about as much as a bubble bath. His attempts to write in the conversational syntax of his characters come out sounding phony: "Pepper would just about never have even a how-do-you-do for any of Harmony's boyfriends, no matter how sweet they were or how nice they tried to be to her, except with Denny it was not just ignoring it was kind of more like hate, Denny wasn't a guy you could just ignore, he was something but probably sweet wasn't a good word choice for what Denny was." Stretched page after page, McMurtry's herculean effort to capture the nuances of Harmony's airhead stream of consciousness and Pepper's teenage hip talk becomes not authenticating but embarrassing, like watching Dick Clark get *down.*

McMurtry purports to make Harmony's life believable and, worse, typical by setting it amid matter-of-fact contemporary banality, the wackier the better. He pretends to convey "real life," but he does so from a point of retreat and disengagement, and his data barely mask his contempt.

COMING

HOME

Fear and Loathing in Texasville

ROBERT FLYNN

My first visits to Archer City were on the school bus carrying the Chillicothe football team, and those visits consisted of trotting to and from the gymnasium where we changed into and out of uniforms, and sitting on the bench and watching the game. That was as close as I got to being one of Texas's Friday Night Heroes. I was a secret weapon saved for those occasions when the issue was no longer in doubt, and I could be inserted into the game without posing a threat to either side.

I did not notice Larry McMurtry, although he probably was present at the games. If I had noticed him, I doubt I would have spoken to him. We had nothing in common. He was the enemy, and we hated Archer City more than anything non-Texan, except Crowell. Chillicothe and Archer City were as far removed from one another as Vernon and Quanah, or Fort Worth and Dallas, or Texas and Oklahoma.

I don't know about the rest of the team, but I was always a little intimidated by Archer City. They had a courthouse. In the Texas tradition it was an imposing block structure with the requisite square. In Archer City you knew you were there when you saw the courthouse. Chillicothe had no courthouse, no square, and like Oakland, there was no "there" there. Infrequent visitors looked in vain for "town."

Besides, Archer City was only twenty-five miles from Jacksboro, a real town with history and an old fort that was mentioned in the

Texas History books we studied. The only "real" town we had, as opposed to towns whose names appeared only on maps and that were named after someone's sister, was Quanah. Quanah was real because it was named after an Indian whose name appeared in our Texas History books.

Archer City was also twenty-five miles from Wichita Falls, which wasn't a real town either, but Wichita Falls had a courthouse, more than one drugstore, more than one picture show, and a Woolworth's so big you could spend all day just looking around. We were seventy-five miles from Wichita Falls, and in order to get home in time to pen the chickens, gather the eggs, and milk the cows, we were able to enjoy only one movie, one malted milk, and one aisle of Woolworth's. Which was scarcely better than going to Quanah.

But the real advantage Archer City had was its proximity to Fort Worth. Fort Worth not only appeared in the Texas History books, it was Mecca to every kid in every dusty town in West Texas. If you lived in Archer City, you could drive to Fort Worth, scarcely a hundred miles away, and return the same day, although it's doubtful that many ever tried. In Chillicothe, we visited Fort Worth once a year on the school bus that took the Future Farmers of America to see the splendor of the Fort Worth Fat Stock Show. But we found more than splendor. We found a Texas more multifarious and exciting (read "wicked") than we had ever imagined.

If Chillicothe had a male rite of passage it was probably the F.F.A. trip to the Fat Stock Show where boys smoked their first cigarette, saw their first pictures of seminudity outside *National Geographic,* rode something scarier than a horse and noisier than a combine, and for the first time got lost within sight of houses.

Fort Worth gave us something else. While gagging over unfamiliar cigarettes, I pondered the fact that you could be a Texan without being from Chillicothe or Archer City, without wearing boots or an F.F.A. jacket, without playing football or cowboy, without driving a combine or a Cadillac, without saying "shoot," "shucks," or "I swan." You could, in fact, be a Texan while looking like a Yankee and talking like a fairy. When I conquered the heaves and lighted another cigarette, I searched down the red brick streets of Fort Worth for a definition of what it meant to be a Texan. Or, more specifically, what it meant to be a human in a geographical setting called Texas. That search was to take me through several cigarettes, more heaves, and a few epiphanies.

I once asked some Kickapoos how they learned what it meant to be a Kickapoo. How they learned what it meant to be a man or a woman who was identifiable as Kickapoo. They said they learned from the stories the grandmothers and grandfathers told them. Of course they wouldn't tell me the stories because then I would know how to be a Kickapoo. That was an epiphany.

How did I learn to be American? To be Texan? Growing up in a Chillicothe cotton patch, my notions of how to be an American came from near-equal portions of Yankee Doodle, Davy Crockett (the autobiography, not the television series), Ichabod Crane, Simon Legree, Horatio Alger, and Clark Kent.

I learned what it means to be Texan from the Fort Worth Fat Stock Show, the classroom study of Texas History, and yes, Roy Rogers.

The classroom was probably the most influential in helping with my self-interpretation as a, specifically, Texas-brand human. It was also the most corruptive, with its portraits of invincible, incorruptible, ruthless, and contentious super-Texans who could whip ten Meskins and a passel of Injuns, own slaves and feel self-righteous about it, threaten to invade Mexico with thirty Rangers, or sever relations with France over a pig.

My father, who had a sixth-grade education, scoffed at the classroom view of Texas and was enraged by Roy Rogers. He saw all movies as corruptive, not in the narrow moral sense—in movie Westerns, the good guys always won and eschewed tobacco, alcohol, strong language, and strong women—but degrading to what he considered appropriate. Cowboys who carried guitars on their silver-trimmed saddles and wore fringe on their trousers were as offensive to him as a man wearing an evening dress on the main street of Chillicothe. And as shameful. A real cowboy, at least Hardeman-Wilbarger County style, had as soon milk a cow as milk the public.

My father was born in 1887, fifty-one years after the fall of the Alamo, forty-two years after the end of the Republic. When he was eight years old, his father was shot to death. That left my father, his two brothers, and their mother at the mercy of a Texas that was almost as harsh to widows and orphans then as it is today. It gave him a fine sense of what was appropriate.

My father, who detested movies as much as he did coyotes and for somewhat the same reasons, would have changed his mind had he lived long enough to see the films of Horton Foote. He would have believed the characters, their language, their manners, morals, and dress. He also probably would not have spoken to them. Too fancy for his taste, their collars too stiff, their shoes too tight.

Texas writers like Horton Foote, George Sessions Perry, Katherine Anne Porter, and William Humphrey have waged a "Victory or Death" effort to delineate the character and nature of Texas and have fared no better than William Butler Travis at the Alamo. Despite Sam

Houston, Stephen F. Austin, John Wesley Hardin, Babe Didrikson, Sammy Baugh, J. Frank Dobie, T. Boone Pickens, and Phyllis George, among others, Texans have not shaped the Texas image.

Texas artists, of whatever stature or medium, have had almost no effect upon our understanding of what it means to be a human of the Texan persuasion. The image of a Texan was formed by the Penny Dreadful Western books and the movies that succeeded them. The work of the movie image makers has been pervasive. You can write anything about a New Yorker. He can be dumb or urbane, poor or wealthy, conservative or liberal. The same is not true for writing about Texans.

The image of a Texan has been formed, and a writer contradicts that image at the risk of disbelief because his characters do not talk or behave the way Texans are supposed to talk and behave. No one outside Texas, and few inside, will accept a view of Texas that does not include television's "Dallas," Paul Newman, or Trigger, or at least one of them. We remain cartoon figures and movie characters. One can argue or deny the image, but it is as real as Santa Claus and as insidious.

How do you learn to talk Texan? Why, you go to Hollywood. It doesn't matter that you're a native Texan; the way you learned to talk in Texas is not appropriate for movies about Texas. So Texans, and other actors, learn to speak "Hollywood Texas," and from the screen teach Texas teen-agers to talk Texan. And dress Texan. And act Texan. And that's why Horton Foote's movies aren't hits at the box office. Not even Texans recognize the images and sounds from the screen as Texas. Not close enough to television's "Dallas." As they say in the White House, "Only Hollywood is spoken here."

Maybe that's all right for foreign consumption. But is it all right for us? For our children? How do we represent ourselves to ourselves?

That's why Larry McMurtry has been so important to us, not just to those who write about Texas, but to those who try to understand Texas and Texans. Because McMurtry transcended Texas, found a nationwide readership, was baptized in Hollywood, and was raised to Pulitzer Heights. And this man returned to Texans and "Texas subjects" and gained a national audience for them.

"Texas subjects" are cows, Cadillacs, and country. Small towns in the valley don't count. Small towns that look like and toward Mississippi don't count. No town with a high school named after Beauregard counts. Big towns like Houston and Dallas don't count. San Antonio is acceptable because God and Davy Crockett put the Alamo there, but only its past is acceptable, let's say before 1890. Fort Worth remains defiantly "Cowtown." Neither television nor movies, fiction writers nor Baptists have been able to corrupt it, or do anything else with it.

But neither *Lonesome Dove* nor *Texasville* is treated in the Texas manner. No one, so far, looks like Paul Newman, Trigger, or J.R. Unscathed from, or by, Hollywood, McMurtry gives us two stories by which to measure ourselves. The two books are bookends—who we were and who we are.

In *Lonesome Dove* men, overgrown and overage boys, are brutish and playful, but they have a code. It is a code that countenances righteous arrogance and racial bigotry. Nevertheless, it is a code that gives substance, or at least interest, to otherwise overblown characters like Judge Roy Bean, John Wesley Hardin, Shanghai Pierce. Without a code, they are empty, vacuous, and dull. Not just dull-spirited, they are uninteresting people. In *Lonesome Dove,* men are strong but silent, their strength beyond words. Young men are high-spirited, rambunctious, ignorantly destructive in their pranks. Old men philosophize, or more accurately, speculate, in a generally humorous way.

In *Texasville* men are still overgrown boys, still brutish and playful, but without a code. More nearly incoherent than silent, young men are equally destructive but without the spirit, without a moral or personal code. Old men, even middle-aged ones, ruminate in despair, and their advice is generally a discouraging word.

If the men are boys, at least good ol' boys, their women are ambidextrous, disappointing, and disappointed. In *Lonesome Dove* women are "mothers or others," largely others, and even the mothers sometimes long for the freedom and gaiety of the soiled and spoiled doves. Mothers are as utilitarian as washboards and as handsome and ill-used, but they gain something close to wisdom.

In *Texasville* women are both mothers and others, spoiled and soiled doves without the freedom or gaiety of a whore, and they wear their wisdom stenciled on T-shirts.

McMurtry has given us models of endurance. In *Lonesome Dove* men and women patiently endure loneliness and physical hardship. Without much patience, the residents of *Texasville* endure ennui, conspicuous consumption, and themselves. It's hard to tell which is more courageous: cowboys who hang a friend for violating an unwritten code of honor, or Thalians who forbear putting themselves out of their misery.

One wonders how cowboys rather than slaves became models of endurance—slaves lasted longer than cowboys, endured at least as much hardship, and died as heroically. Or why literature deals with the guilt of the descendants of slave owners, or the mental and spiritual anguish of slave owners with nothing to wear to the ball, rather than the spiritual resources and inner strengths of those in bondage. But that is a reflection less on our literature than on our values as a nation.

It isn't fair to expect McMurtry to give us a comprehensive past and present view of what it means to be human, Texan, or even West Texan. Nevertheless, something is missing in the portrait. Something of the spirit. There is an absence of religion, or at least the religious fervor that seems to have been a characteristic of the state from the beginning. George Slaughter, one of the messengers sent from the Alamo, survived to become both cattleman and preacher. Colonel D. H. Snyder rested his trail herds on Sunday. And Colonel Travis, in his message to all the Americans in the world, in a postscript after "Victory or Death" added, "God is on our side."

Travis's spiritual and historical descendants have enjoyed the same certitude. As patriotism has been our usual excuse for owning guns, religion has been our excuse for using them. And use guns we did. And do. After Indians and Mexicans became off-limits, and when there were no Germans or Orientals to shoot at, Texans turned to mailboxes, streetlights and doghouses for targets.

Is no one ever the wiser? Does ignorance extend forever without challenge? Is there no one with vision beyond the immediate, beyond nostalgia for what is gone? Any futuristic, or even visionary people? Any planners, even schemers? Does anyone try, or even think of measuring up to Old Sam's standards, or Tom Jefferson's? Sam Houston was no boy. Nor was Stephen F. Austin.

McMurtry has taken the romance out of Texas, out of the West. What has he given us in its place?

I think he has given us a near-perfect picture of Ronald Reagan's America. The real walking-tall-and-looking-proud, dressing-up-in-cowboy-suits-and-aping-movie-stars-aping-cowboys thing. The whole country has imitated the West, not the real by-God mange-and-manure range, but the painted backdrop that we so deeply love with singing cowboys, dancing horses, and posses of white hats ready to string up the bad guys who invariably look like Communists, no matter what their color.

It is an America of law-and-order men who steal, kill, and maim without guilt or penalty, who regard an international border as a King's X and foreign territory as opportunity for private gain. It is an America that celebrates its past deeds of derring-do by trivializing its genuine heroes and accomplishments with gaudy movies, gaudy centennials, and gaudy reenactments for private profit and political gain. Where a minor movie star attempts to recapture a motion-picturesque Garden of Eden. Where people have never had anything in their lives more valuable than money and have now lost that.

It is an America deeply in debt but living high on the hog, where boys never grow up and girls never grow old, where adults destroy each other while preaching traditional values, where immoral parents want the government to require kids to quote prayers by rote while their children race pell-mell toward a disaster everyone can see but prefers to ignore, instead celebrating greatness with a leader who doesn't know where he is and sits in a destroyed picture show watching nonexistent movies about a nonexistent past. Would I make this up?

Americans can't stand much reality. Maybe no one can. Or maybe our country is so new and so raw and so barren of images—are we Yankee Doodle or Rambo, Horatio Alger or J.R.?—that we have to borrow the old myths whole cloth, although the ill-fit tends to show how misshapen we are.

We've never been happy with George Washington or Thomas Jefferson or Abraham Lincoln because they were too smart, too noble, too big. They make us feel inferior. Our real heroes are Jesse James, Elvis Presley, and John Wayne, heroes for whom we have to invent virtue.

That was not King Arthur at the Bay of Pigs. Or at Cam Ranh either. And it was neither Niobe nor Guinevere who married Aristotle Onassis. East of the Pecos, there ain't no God either.

Lyndon Johnson had the virtue of revealing politics for what it is, the reality rather than the romance. Johnson saw the world in frontier "coonskin on the wall" terms. But Johnson, who was closer to Theodore than Franklin, wasn't the kind of cowboy we wanted. The kind of cowboy we wanted was the kind who could pin Libya's ears back and force Gorbachev to smile when he called you a son of a bitch. The kind of cowboy who could walk into the Near East bar and shoot Libya because he's the least dangerous one present—Syria and Iran can shoot back—and not look like a bully. Or kick Grenada's ass to show Cuba and Nicaragua how tough he is, and still wear a white hat. "Yes ma'am, I hit him just as hard as I could." As every movie fan knows, you must save the really bad guys for a shoot-out at the end of the movie.

In *Texasville,* Duane says that whatever they do in the future they will do less well than what they did in the past. It is a decidedly pessimistic view. On the other hand, maybe we have been looking in the wrong places. What if our salvation was not in movie theaters and television evangelists? Or even in oil and high tech. Could it be that our redemption lies in our artists who continue to tell the stories and paint the pictures and sing the songs that tell us who we were, what we have become, and the way to human being?

In *Lonesome Dove* and *Texasville,* we see a writer who has reached his stride and whose career has fulfilled its early promise in the first book and then turned back upon himself and itself in the second. In this section, *Lonesome Dove* has received more attention because it is the larger book, has been in print longer, and has received more serious treatment by critics.

Robert M. Adams's "The Bard of Wichita Falls" represents the sweep and panorama of *Lonesome Dove* and the loneliness and desolation of Thalia. The writer isn't familiar with Western humor, but makes important connections between the two books, particularly the balance of tenderness and toughness.

In *"Lonesome Dove:* Butch and Sundance Go On A Cattledrive," Don Graham does little to explore the themes of the book, but does an excellent job detailing the events and characters of the novel and outlining sources in movies, history, and other novels.

Ernestine P. Sewell describes how *Lonesome Dove* is the natural consequence of McMurtry's earlier opinions and ideas as expressed in *In a Narrow Grave.* In addition, McMurtry has singled out "McMurtry's Cowboy-God in *Lonesome Dove*" as one of his favorite pieces of criticism of his work, justification enough for including it here.

Nicolas Lemann describes the scope of *Lonesome Dove* as McMurtry portrays the American West and outlines Western frontier types. In addition, "Tall in the Saddle" compares the novel to themes from previous books.

Clay Reynolds reminds us of minor problems of credibility and structural dead ends in *Lonesome Dove,* but also outlines the size and scope of the book and how it combines themes and characters that have been McMurtry's mainstay. Perhaps more than anyone else, Reynolds points the way to new directions and even greater success.

Jan Reid is a novelist and critic, a native of Wichita Falls, and one who understands rough Western humor. That would seem to make him the ideal reader for *Texasville.* But Reid is not enamored of *The Last Picture Show,* and "The Next Picture Show" casts a cold and jaundiced eye on *Texasville.* Nevertheless, Reid makes the clearest and strongest statement regarding McMurtry's developing study of the war between the sexes.

Louise Erdrich's "Why Is That Man Tired?" captures the metaphorical strength and breadth of a *Texasville* where waste is celebrated, political leaders have VCRs in their brains, and being rich drives people to insanity.

. .

The Bard of Wichita Falls

ROBERT M. ADAMS

Wichita Falls lies in north central Texas, with the Oklahoma line just a few miles to the north and the Texas Panhandle sticking up just a few more miles to the west. It is not now and never was one of the scenic beauty spots of North America. Under the heading of "What To See," the AAA Tour Book lists nothing whatever. More sedate books of reference speak unenthusiastically of Wichita Falls as the center of an agricultural district, the home of Sheppard Air Force Base, and as surrounded by oil and gas fields. Set in a vast expanse of level plateau country, Wichita Falls lies on the Wichita River, indeed, but the "Falls" are hypothetical. Something must have been there when the town was named and a set of artificial falls are being built now—but for most of the town's history, there weren't any that you could notice.

Heading west from Wichita Falls on Route 287, one reaches after some sixty miles Vernon; and then, cutting a little southwest, another twenty miles brings one to the hamlet of Thalia. There one is in the heart of Larry McMurtry country. Larry McMurtry is the author of twelve novels, published over the last twenty years, two of which have been made into successful movies (*The Last Picture Show* and *Terms of Endearment*), and another of which won the Pulitzer Prize for fiction. McMurtry was born and to some extent bred in Wichita Falls. As a "serious" novelist he hasn't received much consideration, probably because his western settings have led eastern critics to confuse him with writers of cowboy melodramas. He can do cowboy melodrama, and do it very well, but even as he does it, there are overtones and nuances of feeling that transcend the formulas. Comparison with classic American writers is probably premature (if one ventured on such comparisons, they might be with Bret Harte, not Mark Twain; Sherwood Anderson, not William Faulkner; Frank Norris, not Stephen Crane), but it is safe to say that Wichita Falls has produced an artist. An account of one early and two late novels can give some impression of the shape and quality of his career. Though one of these books is panoramic in its scope and historical in period, the other two are firmly set in Thalia, Texas, which is not just a backdrop but a powerful presence.

Whatever it may be in real life, Thalia in McMurtry's fiction is one of the most dreary, ugly, depressing small towns imaginable. Set in a flat, semi-arid plain, it is swept when the wind blows with storms of gritty sand and thickets of tumbleweed. The town has minimal commercial life, most of it moribund, practically no opportunities for amusement, zero culture. People in Thalia do not read books under any circumstances; the only music they listen to is Willie Nelson; they take no interest in politics above the local level, watch TV torpidly, and drink as much as they can afford to. Conversations when they occur are apt to be blunt, sarcastic, and brief; the prevailing mood of the town is sullen. For brief periods, some Thalians may be very rich and spend their money, out of boredom, on things they don't really want or need; but there's really no elite group to show off before. The lively social event is the high school football season; but the activities of the town are largely channeled into fornication. It is continuous, barely concealed, and cuts across all boundaries; it takes place day and night (once notably at the town's only traffic light where the two main streets cross). In this respect, and this alone, Thalia is a lively town.

The Last Picture Show is an early (1966) novel about Thalia; it introduces us to Duane Moore and Sonny Crawford, two boys in their last year at Thalia High School. Both are curiously detached from their families; they live in a boarding house and support themselves doing a variety of handyman and roughneck jobs. Both are avid in their pursuit of sexual initiation. Jacy Farrow is the sex queen of the high school, and reserved for Duane the football captain; but she is an elusive prey, and though both boys successively attain her—sort of— it can't be said that either really enjoys her. Nor indeed does she enjoy them, or anybody else; the various *grandes affaires* end invariably in fiasco or ludicrous comedy. Meanwhile the book's background is enlivened with many more bizarre couplings. Sonny in particular bounces around like a sexual billiard ball, from dull Charlene to Ruth Popper, wife of the football coach, to Jacy herself to Jacy's mother— who, having prevented the consummation of his marriage to her daughter, calmly takes the young groom off to spend the wedding night with her.

Around the margins of the Duane and Sonny stories a good deal of yokel sex-play goes on—callow experimentation and barnyard buggery, plus a trip by Duane and Sonny to a Mexican whorehouse. None of these episodes bestows anything in the way of enlightenment or pleasure on the participants; indeed, the book's happenings, especially when they are deliberately intended, have very few consequences of any sort. On the other hand, when Duane and Sonny (despite their long friendship) get into a barroom scuffle over Jacy, things turn unexpectedly ugly. Though the fight is perfunctory, one of Sonny's eyes is so badly damaged that he loses the sight of it. An obvious irony is that the girl over whom they are fighting cares for neither of them, and probably at the moment for nobody except herself.

Sonny's affair with Ruth Popper, who is at least twenty years older, is the most carefully developed and movingly described element of the book.

> "I see you feel you've missed a chance," Ruth said, when they were at the door. She looked at him frankly. "You see, I'm very confused, even if I look like I'm not. That's why you must go. I've got on a great many brakes right now—what I was thinking about a while ago is nothing I've ever done except with Herman, and for a long time I haven't even believed a man could want me that way. I don't know if I believe it now, even though I see you do. But then I think it isn't really *me* you want, it's only *that* . . . sex. Not that there's anything wrong with you wanting that, it's perfectly natural. . . ." She was talking faster and faster, but suddenly she stopped.
>
> "You must really think I'm crazy," she said. "I am crazy I guess."
>
> "Why's that?" Sonny asked.
>
> "What?" Ruth said, caught by surprise.
>
> "I mean why do you feel crazy? I guess I shouldn't be askin'."
>
> "Of course you should," she said. "I was just surprised you had the nerve. The reason I'm so crazy is because nobody cares anything about me. I don't guess there's anybody I care much about, either. It's my own fault, though—I haven't had the guts to try and do anything about it. . . ."
>
> She shut the screen door and they stood for a moment looking through the screen at one another.

Ruth, though atrociously misused by her loathsome husband and then almost as cruelly by her callow lover, shows signs of being a survivor; but Sonny has been overwhelmed in his manhood. He will never, it seems, be anything but the whimpering, shamed puppy that he is at the end. Sonny isn't in any way a sensitive soul crushed under the iron wheels of life; there aren't more than two sensitive souls in Thalia. It's the dumb innocence of the young people in their thoughtless cruelty, as in their blind despair, that gives the book its very moving balance. The boys don't know they're pathetic, but older people achingly do— Genevieve, night waitress at the local café, and Sam, who runs the pool hall; they realize the only thing to be in Thalia is young and foolish, and they realize the hopeless fragility of that temporary condition. The book touches the throbbing nerve of American loneliness; it is relatively gentle with its people, but hard as nails about their desolate condition.

Lonesome Dove is a bigger and very different novel. It is set sometime in the undefined past, between 1869, when the first cattle drive from Texas to Montana was made, and a decade later, when Custer's Last Stand (1876) was a much-talked-about event. Once again the balance of the novel is between toughness and tenderness, and once again the central figures are a pair of cooperating and contrasting males. Augustus McCrae and Woodrow Call are retired Texas Rangers who run a rather dubious cattle-and-horse ranch, the Hat Creek outfit, at Lonesome Dove, not far from the Rio Grande. The mythology of the Texas Rangers (who from the days of the Republic had been the principal and in many districts the only agents of law in Texas) is extensive and romantic. They are said to have been omnicompetent and invincible, Supermen before their time. Tales are told of a single Ranger being dispatched to capture a raiding party of two hundred Mexican soldiers, and of similar heroic deeds involving desperadoes, Comanche war parties, and assorted hard cases of the ragtag frontier.

McCrae and Call have given up "rangering," as they call it, and now are business partners, breaking and making the law as they see fit along a frontier where there is properly no law at all. Sometimes they raid Mexican ranches across the border, sometimes they are raided. As the novel opens, the business run by these two soldiers of fortune does not seem much better than hit-or-miss. They have very few hands, most of their stock is running loose on the open range, and since it is very poor range, the commercial side of their enterprise hardly seems likely to prosper. As for Lonesome Dove itself, it seems to be little more than a saloon/whorehouse surrounded by a few houses and perhaps a general store: not being described, they have to be imagined. But the grubbiness of the hot, sandy, savage environment is thoroughly rendered. The sandy land is crawling with red-legged centipedes, a couple of bites from which can lead to an amputation; food consists mainly of beans laced with chopped rattlesnake and goat fried in a substance like tar; and when someone has a chunk bitten out of him by a vicious horse, the treatment is axle grease and turpentine.

McMurtry clearly relishes these details. In the opening scene Augustus McCrae is sitting on his porch, sipping whiskey from a jug, and watching with mild interest as two blue pigs try to devour a single rattlesnake, starting from opposite ends. There are other scenes to turn the stomach, and a steady undercurrent of *macho* (or is it sadistic?) violence that sometimes seems excessive. For example, when Woodrow Call finds one of his men being assaulted in Ogallala, Nebraska, by a nasty, domineering soldier, it is natural for him to come to the rescue, natural for him to knock down the aggressor, even to kick out a handful of his teeth; but when he drags the prostrate victim to a nearby blacksmith shop and beats his head against the anvil till he has to be dragged away by a horse and lariat, a reader may feel it's been a bit much. Again, on a visit to Fort Worth, Augustus McCrae is offended by an uppity young barkeeper; so he smashes the man's face on the bar, breaking his nose, and then puts an end to the contretemps by knocking him cold with the butt of his revolver. They are tough hombres, these Texas Rangers, but not invariably *sympathique*.

It's a desperate situation in which Call and McCrae engage themselves; they are to drive a thousand head of cattle, more or less—most of them rustled from Mexican ranchers across the border—north over some two thousand miles of open plains, never far from hostile Indian tribes and gangs of frontier outlaws, to the unclaimed range lands of Montana. They have some assurance that good grass and plentiful water will be waiting for them there; on the other hand, they will have to build shelter for themselves and their stock before winter sets in. Call and McCrae know next to nothing about Montana, and haven't given so much as a thought to where they can sell their cattle, once established. But the long trek is the frame on which the book's many events hang; it is a spacious, romantic, and dangerous venture, and the author clearly luxuriates in it.

Men die en route of lightning strokes, of snakebites, of wounds from Indian lances; to punish thieves and killers, there are a good many impromptu hangings along the way. The band of cowboys fights off Indians and captures outlaws, struggles through sandstorms and clouds of grasshoppers, survives a dry stretch, and negotiates the sinful snares of Ogallala. Because their difficulties are so many and various, they don't need, and as a rule don't get, meticulous solutions; one simply succeeds another. The ex-Rangers don't have any compunction about hanging horse thieves on the spot—that, after all, is the code of the Old West. They don't pause to reflect that the horses they themselves are riding had been stolen. Perhaps the fact that they were stolen from Mexicans, not "white men," makes the difference.

Inward complications are provided, as usual, by women. In the distant past, taciturn Captain Call had, apparently, an affair whose sole product, a young cowboy named Newt, is riding with the gang. Call cannot bring himself to talk about the relationship or acknowledge his son; he is, to the distress of his friend Augustus, very up-tight about the whole matter. Though he trembles on the verge of saying something to Newt, the novel ends without his actually having done so. Captain McCrae, though the more loquacious of the two, also has inhibitions, caused by the memory of a lost love, Clara, who had been a bit too tough for him, and he a bit too elusive for her. With regrets on both sides, they had gone their separate ways, and their rediscovery of each other in darkest Nebraska is similarly inconclusive—it is a nostalgic but not enthusiastic meeting.

The most vividly present of the ladies in the book is Lorena, a "sporting woman" in the whorehouse at Lonesome Dove, who is picked up by Jake Spoon, an old associate of Call's, carried off on the Montana trek, abandoned by Jake, abducted by a bestial Indian, sold to a war party, gang-raped, rescued by Captain McCrae, and finally left to the care of Clara. But neither she nor any of the other women has a strong part in the novel. One can say that *Lonesome Dove* is "a man's book": emphasizing traditional male codes and values and including the less attractive ones. A grandiose but moving climax is reached in the final pages. McCrae, having been mortally wounded in a single-handed stand against some Indians, asks his partner Call to bury him in a little peach orchard by the Guadalupe River in southern Texas, where he had once been idyllically happy with Clara. Call gives his word; and single-handedly, on a disintegrating wagon, carries his partner's mummified body two thousand miles cross-country to bury it in the right spot. It is a barbaric, stately, Homeric cortege; it is also Quixotic and absurd as well as a dazzling piece of imaginative writing:

> Before he reached Kansas, word had filtered ahead of him that a man was carrying a body home to Texas. The plain was filled with herds, for it was full summer. Cowboys spread the word, soldiers spread it. Several times he met trappers, coming east from the Rockies, or buffalo hunters who were finding no buffalo. The Indians heard—Pawnee and Arapahoe and Ogallala Sioux. Sometimes he would ride past parties of braves, their horses fat on spring grass, come to watch his journey. Some were curious enough

to approach him, even to question him. Why did he not bury the *compañero*? Was he a holy man whose spirit must have a special place?

No, Call answered. Not a holy man. Beyond that he couldn't explain. He had come to feel that Augustus had probably been out of his mind at the end, though he hadn't looked it, and that *he* had been out of his mind to make the promise he had.

Lonesome Dove won McMurtry the Pulitzer Prize for fiction, and probably more popular success than any of his other novels; it moved, after all, largely in the soft tradition of the cowboy romance–adventure story, along trails well worn by Zane Grey and Clarence E. Mulford; it would have been relatively easy to reprise with modifications. But McMurtry's latest fiction, *Texasville,* undertakes to break new ground, paradoxically by returning to Thalia some thirty years after the events of *The Last Picture Show.* Many of the adolescents of the earlier novel reappear, somewhat timeworn, and Thalia is as unappealing as ever. But in the interval the Texas oil business has been through an unparalleled cycle of violent boom and bust. Duane Moore, back from the Korean War, caught on to the boom and made out of it more millions than we can do anything but guess about. But the bust caught him with four new oil rigs, bought on credit at three million dollars apiece. Now they are sitting on a vacant lot and quietly rusting, piling up interest he cannot pay, while the price of oil sinks somewhere near fifteen dollars a barrel.

Throughout *Texasville* the remains of his former prosperity surround Duane like an assembly of mocking mourners. He has a twelve-thousand-square-foot house with an uncountable number of water beds, a hot tub, a satellite-dish antenna, a two-story log doghouse, a BMW plus pickups, and a $60,000 condo that his wife has just bought for their older son and his new (but obviously impermanent) wife. But the house is too big and the kitchen appliances don't work, the hot tub is ridiculous in a climate where the temperature rises to ninety-five or one hundred degrees most days, the VCR is used only occasionally to look at a porn movie, the BMW is shaking itself to pieces on dirt roads, and the dog won't sleep in the doghouse. As the novel opens, Duane is sitting in his hot tub, idly shooting the doghouse to pieces with a .44 Magnum. He has $850 in the bank and debts of twelve million. He has recently accepted chairmanship of a committee to help Thalia celebrate its hundredth birthday. In its early days, the town was called Texasville, hence the title of the novel; but neither the past, the present, nor the future of the town offers much in the way of consolation for disconsolate Duane.

His family life is just as much in disarray as his finances. Karla, his strident, still-beautiful wife, who has read in *Cosmopolitan* about open marriages, has opened hers up to any likely male she can attract; daughter Nellie is out to set a world record for short-term marriages, and son Dickie not only sleeps his way through the town but peddles marijuana for kicks and cracks up automobiles at the rate of four a year. There is also a pair of twins about twelve years old, on whom Duane says the best word: "They got personalities like wild dogs."

Various other characters from *The Last Picture Show* survive in *Texasville,* but they are scarcely a source of animation. Sonny Crawford, convinced he is a total failure, slips into more and more frequent fits of mental vacancy; his wife has left him, and he divides his time between living in Duane's big house and jail, where he's convinced he belongs. Lester Marlow, who had once aspired after Jacy, is now the town banker, under indictment on seventy-three counts of bank fraud. In this wasteland Karla is loudly dissatisfied with her sex life, Duane's mistress Janine is bored with him, and his new girlfriend Suzie talks too persistently about the sexual prowess of Duane's son Dickie. Not surprisingly, Duane is tired most of the time, given to frequent headaches.

What are the hopes for growth, if not redemption, in this stony, sterile heap of apathetic lives? The oldest and tritest logic of fiction is that things have to move; if they're at the bottom, there's no way to go but up. And indeed, phantoms of recovery do now and then drift across Duane's horizon. One of his rigs hits a big pool of oil; but by then the price of oil is so low that the stuff is not worth taking out of the ground. In return for a share of his future production, he tries to get a crusty and immensely rich oil man in Odessa (Texas) to buy his rigs; but the answer is no. And Jacy Farrow, the girl with whom he was in love thirty years before, comes back to town after years in Europe, including two failed marriages and a small-time career in the movies.

Given the conventions of fiction, Jacy's return—she lives in a big house full of unread books—ought to provide some sort of climax, but it doesn't. When she takes part in the halfhearted, ludicrous centennial pageant, playing Eve to Duane's embarrassed Adam, there is no scene of passionate congress; there is no avowal (nothing much to avow), no hot-eyed restraint (nothing much to restrain).

The ground bass of the book is silent despair, and efforts to rise above it end, almost invariably, in fiasco. The centennial celebration falls apart under the impact of two explosive, irrelevant events: an over-size windstorm fills the town with impenetrable thickets of tumbleweed, and the kids of the town, finding an unguarded truck laden with sixty thousand eggs, stage an egg fight that leaves the town dripping with slime. During the celebration, there is a battle between Prohibitionists and beer drinkers; but nothing comes of it, and next morning the whole thing is forgotten. The novel ends in a tableau of sorrow and frustration, with Jacy weeping on Duane's shoulder for her lost son, Karla cradling the increasingly imbecilic Sonny, and the kids careening around them in their joyous, idiotic games.

On the face of things, what could sound more repellent—a long novel about dumb, mostly disagreeable people, without manners or intelligence, caught in a dreary village, to whom nothing significant ever happens? This is a fair description of *Texasville,* yet in retrospect it is larger than the materials of which it is made. The characters have endurance and they have vitality; the very landscape partakes of their cruel, sour humor, blowing up ugly, violent jokes out of its everyday monotony. In a late chapter Duane takes a moment to sit alone on the courthouse steps and see his life as a threadbare sheet being ripped up for rags; there's nothing in the scene of self-pity, but a sense of inevitability as deep as anything in Thomas Hardy. *Texasville* is far from conventional storytelling; perhaps for that reason, the impression it makes is strong, maybe indelible.

Long ago I saw a picture painted by a wretchedly unhappy young woman. I have never forgotten it, and for me it summarizes the world of *Texasville.* It showed a desolate landscape, all rocks, sand, and brush, painted in Daliesque detail. Across the desert from foreground to horizon were scattered stone structures of different sizes but all the same shape. A flight of stairs went up one side to the top; the other side was a sheer drop. Years ago they didn't look to me like oil rigs, but now, in a kind of retrospective rearrangement, they do.

Lonesome Dove:
Butch and Sundance Go on a Cattledrive

DON GRAHAM

Lonesome Dove, Larry McMurtry's eleventh novel, has achieved a measure of success far above that of any of the rest of his previous efforts. To date it has racked up three awards: the Spur Award of the Western Writers of America, the Texas Institute of Letters Prize for fiction, and the Pulitzer Prize for fiction. It also made the Best Seller List of the New York *Times*. Heretofore McMurtry had had to depend on the movies to convert the dross of fiction into precious metals. No less than four of his novels have been turned into films, and three of them, excepting only the execrable *Lovin' Molly,* were very fine films indeed. But it was something new for a McMurtry novel to create such a sensation in the literary marketplace.

Who would have thought that a traildriving novel would turn the trick? The book appeared in June, 1985, poised strategically to catch the summer-poolside reading audience, the up-scale crowd that takes its literary cues from National Public Radio. But there was something else either calculated or lucky about its publication; it beat James Michener to the gate by two full months. Did McMurtry have his eye on the Sesquicentennial Sweepstakes of 1986? One can't imagine that he did not. Career-wise as they say on the coast, *Lonesome Dove* accomplished several things for McMurtry. His lecture fee jumped straightaway from $1500 to a cool $4000, his picture appeared in *People* magazine in a story about his close personal friend, Cybill Shepherd, and he got invited to the White House reception for Princess Di. The advance copy of the novel that I received for review bore portents of his new eminence. The agent who handled this book was none other than Irving "Swifty" Lazar, who numbers among his clients Richard Milhouse Nixon.

Down Texas way, the most surprising thing about *Lonesome Dove* was the fact that it was written at all. Just three years before, McMurtry had cast a cold eye on Texas letters, in a long article in the *Texas Observer.* Taking the measure of his fellow writers and of himself, McMurtry couldn't find much to be happy about. Texas writers were lazy and unproductive, they were ill-read in the 19th century masters of the craft, and they spent far too much of their time gazing backwards nostalgically at the vanished and superior past, the days of the cattlemen and the land-centered values of small farmers, small towns, and small Dairy Queens. Ever helpful, McMurtry had a prescription for curing Texas letters. Texas writers should turn to the state's urban centers and explore the "less simplistic experience of city life."

In the meantime, it appears, McMurtry was holed up somewhere churning out 843 pages of nostalgia, 19th century realism, and Hollywood-like heroes. The novel had its roots in a screenplay that McMurtry wrote "not long after *The Last Picture Show.*" He called it *The Streets of Laredo,* and in an interview in 1980 he described the project in these terms: "It was an end-of-West western. Three old men stumble into a last adventure, and they're old, and the West is over. Everybody loved it except the three actors, so we didn't make it. I've

sometimes thought I might see what would happen if I did it as a novel."
The three actors were John Wayne, Jimmy Stewart, and Henry Fonda.

Now, over a decade later, McMurtry resurrected the traildrive scenario and fleshed it out. The herd doesn't actually hit the trail until page 220, by which time we are fully informed of what life is like in a fly-blown dusty little nowhere border town where a mixed crew of likely lads, veterans of the Indian wars, and other assorted types try to figure out what it is they should do. Once on the trail, things pick up considerably, though, and McMurtry, good popular writer that he is, uses every cattledrive obstacle that has ever been invented to kick his story along. There are dry drives, wet drives, dusty drives, river crossings with snakes, river crossings without snakes, hail storms, wind storms, lightning storms, stampedes, Indian attacks, Comanchero attacks, boredom attacks. As if all these weren't enough, McMurtry packs along a young prostitute to provide a certain whiny amusement for various love-stricken cowboys. Lorena is not one of McMurtry's triumphs in the characterization of women, a point worth mentioning because of several of his quite vividly drawn women characters in some of his earlier novels. The only interesting woman character in this novel doesn't appear until around page 500 or so.

Clearly, it seems to me, this novel derives from two broad sources: the movies and history. The first does not serve McMurtry as well as the second, as I hope to demonstrate. By and large, when McMurtry taps into history in this novel, the results are satisfying, but when he follows the traditions of popular culture, the novel crosses over from history into something else, caricature or comedy, and, for me at least, ceases to be interesting. With one exception: Blue Duck. The meanest character in the book, Blue Duck, a Comanchero, may in fact be based upon an historical figure, but if so, I am unaware of who that might be. In this case I don't care, because Blue Duck has the kind of energy and presence that jumps off the page. Blue Duck has the capacity for truly malevolent actions, and his method of eviscerating captives when he is bored with them conveys a memorable sense of absolute evil. At the end when Blue Duck is himself held captive and is about to be hanged, I was quite convinced that he was actually going to fly from the upper story of the courthouse, simply leap into space and soar beyond the grasp of his enemies.

The movies first. The figure of Lorena, the whining prostitute, derives from a long tradition in traildriving movies, from the first, *North of 36* (1924), to the greatest, *Red River* (1948). Now we know that there were women who went up the long trail. Amanda Bourke was one, and Emerson Hough's novel from which the 1924 film was

made was based in part upon her story. In his novel and the film, the
woman is young, beautiful, plucky, but essentially helpless to accomplish the great task. She can get the cowboys to start the drive, but in
order to finish it, she needs the help of a stalwart cowboy hero. Nearly
all subsequent traildriving films saw the need of having a woman
along. She could be genteel or tainted, but what she offered was romance. Lorena, who is tainted, springs from *Red River,* not from history. Remember how Joanne Dru damn near wrecks that film when
she enters it about three-quarters of the way through. The dynamics
of empire-building, fatherhood, and patrimony require the presence of
a good "breeder," which is the way Dru's character is presented in the
film. Wayne looks her over like a prize heifer, and Montgomery Clift
falls in love with her. The film recovers, only just barely, and surely its
worst moment is the high-pitched oratory delivered by Dru who has to
tell the Duke and Clift that by god, you big lugs really love each other,
don't you know that. Imagine how the film would have been if Joanne
Dru had been along from the beginning. They'd never have gotten the
herd out of Texas.

Another movie-inspired, or rather, TV-inspired character in the
novel is the bumbling deputy of the bumbling sheriff. July Johnson is
the sheriff's name, and his deputy by all rights should have been
named Chester. Imagine a *Gunsmoke* episode in which Chester gets
laid, and you have the whole conception of this character in a nut-
shell. Fortunately in this bloody book the deputy gets wiped out fairly
early, and we don't have to heed the further adventures of this hapless
creature adrift on the great plains.

The three main characters, of course, all derive from the movies, as
might be expected from a book that began as a movie script. There is
Call, taciturn, tight-lipped, flinty-eyed, capable, and hard, the strong
silent type from a thousand Westerns. John Wayne. And there is his
opposite, the loquacious, philosophical-minded, and supposedly charming Augustus, who chatters from the early pages until his death near
the end. Jimmy Stewart. Recast with actors today: Robert Redford and
Paul Newman. The third member of this predictable trio is the dandy,
and in Howard Hawk's *Rio Bravo* Dean Martin played him to a *T*. The
dandy is a great bore in the novel, and fortunately, he too is killed fairly
early in the proceedings. If there is one movie source lying behind the
novel, it might be King Vidor's *The Texas Rangers* (1939), a quite bad
Western, or its equally bad remake, *Streets of Laredo* (1949). Both trace
the story of three Texas Rangers, all former outlaws, two of whom are
converted to truth and justice by the Ranger way, and the third of whom
has to be eventually tracked down by his old pals. It's not the plot but

the conception of the triad of two good/one bad that seems to be reprised in McMurtry's hands.

So much for the movie sources, and there are doubtless echoes of other Westerns that may strike you as you read the novel. From history McMurtry has taken both details, incidents, and a feeling for authentic recreation of the traildrive experience. McMurtry has long been conversant with the major historical texts of the cattledrive era, and I would suggest that certainly one of his sources was E. C. "Teddy Blue" Abbott's marvelous *We Pointed Them North*. This as-told-to narrative has a jaunty tone to it that makes the book far more attractive than the recognized classic in the field, Andy Adams' *The Log of a Cowboy*. I will quote one passage to give its flavor. Abbott is describing how he and his fellow cowpunchers left Miles City after having spent time and money with the girls they married for a week: "I still had Cowboy Annie's ruffled drawers that she gave me that night, and I put them on a forked stick and carried them that way to the mouth of the Musselshell, like a flag. And before we left, my girl took one of her stockings off and tied it around my arm, you know, like the knights of old, and I wore *that* to the mouth of the Musselshell." At its best *Lonesome Dove* does a fair job of capturing that carefree banter and rollicksome ways recorded by Abbott.

As for the numerous incidents of travail, danger, and work practices that inform the narrative and give it an air of dusty authenticity, McMurtry may have drawn upon numerous authentic accounts of the era, in fact undoubtedly did. The best single source of such information is *The Trail Drivers of Texas*, a two-volume collection of oral history and written accounts produced in the 1920s and reprinted on several occasions, including a recent edition by the University of Texas Press. Many of these first-person accounts are flavored with colorful incidents, but many are written in a stiff, rather genteel manner as well. Any novelist wanting to find accounts of incidents that took place on the trail could find plenty in the 1044 pages that make up the two volumes. Need a good hail storm? Here is an account by Jerry M. Nance, who went to Cheyenne, Wyoming with 2,100 cattle in 1877: "There was no timber on our side of the river, and when the hail began pelting the boys and myself made a break for the wagon for shelter. We were all naked, and the hail came down so furiously that within a short time it was about two inches deep on the ground." There are many similar details about stampedes, lightning storms, encounters with Indians, even one incident where a tom-boy girl dressed up like a boy in order to go along on a drive. There are also moments of tedium and dry-as-dust accounts of drives that offer little to the novelist looking for action and color. Consider a drive that Jack Potter made in 1882: "There was no excitement whatever on this drive. It was to me very much like a summer's outing in the Rocky Mountains." The only thing that relieved the pleasant tedium was medical in nature: "The itch . . . had broken out on the trail and in those days people did not know how to treat it successfully. Our manager sent us a wagon load of kerosene and sulphur with which to fight the disease." The itch might have comic possibilities, but it is hard to see how a novelist would be captivated by this incident.

The most moving sequence in the novel is surely the return of Augustus's body by his old friend Call. At the point of death Augustus asks to be packed in ice and hauled back to his beloved Texas to be buried. The request seems both absurd and touching. In Texas history the most likely analogue for this action is Charles Goodnight's carrying out of his friend and partner Oliver Loving's last request. Goodnight and Loving together blazed one of the first cattle trails out of Texas, to New Mexico. In 1867 Loving got caught by the Comanches in a skirmish on the Pecos River and was severely wounded. The best account of this episode appears in J. Evetts Haley's biography, *Charles Goodnight: Cowman and Plainsman* (1936). Haley describes Loving as a man "blessed with a constitution of iron." His wounding and eventual death prove that assertion. At one point after he had eluded the Comanches, he tried to eat his buckskin gloves. Later, after he was found and taken to Fort Sumner, New Mexico, where, because of gangrene, amputation of his arm became necessary, Loving knew he might die. He summoned his friend Goodnight to his bedside and almost the last thing he said to him was, "I regret to have to be laid away in a foreign country." Goodnight made a solemn promise that his remains would be returned to his home cemetery in Weatherford, Texas. On September 25, Loving died and was buried at Fort Sumner. Five months later, in February, 1868, the body was exhumed. Haley's account of the incident is worth quoting in its entirety:

> From about the fort the cowboys gathering scattered oil cans, beat them out, soldered them together, and made an immense tin casket. They placed the rough wooden one inside, packed several inches of powered charcoal around it, sealed the tin lid, and crated the whole in lumber. They lifted a wagon bed from its bolsters and carefully loaded the casket in its place. Upon February 8, 1868, with six big mules strung out in the harness, and with rough-hewn but tenderly sympathetic cowmen from Texas riding ahead and behind, the strangest and most touching funeral cavalcade in the history of the cow country took the Goodnight and Loving Trail that led to Loving's home.

In the novel Call's return of Augustus's body is a one-man version of the Goodnight-Loving episode, or if not, it is certainly reminiscent of that homage paid to one old friend by another.

In suggesting these combined sources of film and history, I have by no means exhausted the literary and imaginative materials that McMurtry drew upon for his novel. Anybody conversant with the field could suggest other possible influences including Andy Adams' *Log of a Cowboy* and J. Frank Dobie's *The Longhorns* and *A Vaquero of the Brush Country*. McMurtry, a rare-book dealer of considerable stature, may well have drawn upon less familiar works as well. In part, though, he drew also upon that common fund of cattledrive lore gleaned from having watched, growing up, hundreds of Western movies. As a writer with a keen eye for the marketplace, McMurtry must have been concerned with the problem of keeping his largely urban readers turning the pages and believing they were getting the straight stuff and not Louis L'Amour. The reviews suggest that he was very successful indeed. But few of the reviewers seemed aware that there have been other traildrive novels, and the professor in me makes me want to mention two of these for anyone who wishes to see how other Texas novelists have handled similar material. One is Benjamin Capps's *The Trail to Ogallala*, a straightforward novel with no women characters along for the ride. Capps's theme is the nature of leadership, of what is required to trail a herd of some 3,000 cattle from south Texas to Ogallala, Nebraska. The second is Robert Flynn's *North to Yesterday*, a novel with serious comic overtones. It traces a cattledrive undertaken twenty years after the cattledrive era had closed due to barbed wire, increased settlement, and the extension of railheads into Texas. Placed in the context of such novels, *Lonesome Dove* begins to seem like a novel too crowded with incidents, with everything that could possibly happen on one drive but never did. Still, it's not a bad read, and that apparently was McMurtry's main goal from the beginning.

McMurtry's Cowboy-God in *Lonesome Dove*

ERNESTINE P. SEWELL

A panoply of big sky, the surging of mighty waters, vast expanses of grassland, a cattle drive studded by adventure and misadventure: these—with or without a camp cook for comic relief, a soiled dove for romance, a thundering herd of horses, and some Indians—will fulfill the expectations of those readers who judge western fiction by the use of conventions set to a formula. For that audience, Larry McMurtry's novel *Lonesome Dove* proves eminently satisfying.

The story line is simple: McMurtry places Captains Woodrow Call and Augustus McCrae, aging Texas Rangers, at Lonesome Dove, where they had set up the Hat Creek Cattle Company, a ranch close to the Rio Grande, within easy raiding distance of Mexico. For ten years they have dealt in cattle and horses, a dull way of life after resplendent careers marked by triumphant battles against frontier hellraisers, Indians, Comancheros, and border Mexicans.

Jake Spoon, who also held a captaincy with the Rangers and had ridden with Call and Gus in their glory days, comes to the ranch unexpectedly—on the run. He entertains his friends with tales of his wanderings, stirring up Call's yearning for the old life when he suggests a cattle drive to Montana, a Garden of Eden where a man can have all the land he wants just for the taking.

Call springs into action to make ready for the drive. He and his men rustle up cattle and horses on both sides of the river, and he gathers together several local cowboys, one top hand, two Irishmen, and some inexperienced youths for drovers. McMurtry loses no time putting them into motion and then assails them with an omnium-gatherum of the accidents of weather, wild creatures, and man. Sandstorms, hailstorms, lightning, floods, drought, heat, and snow. Grasshoppers, mosquitoes, snakes, and bears. Horsethieves, Indians, bandits, and eccentrics. Nevertheless, they reach Montana just as winter storms set in—not without losing horses and cattle and men.

Even a naive reader, however, is aware soon that this Western offers more than action. There is clearly a focus on the Texas Rangers, not without reason it would seem. McMurtry had accused Walter Prescott Webb of failing to be true to his commitment to write as a historian in *The Texas Rangers* (*In A Narrow Grave* 43). Though Webb had published his tome in 1935, no one had faulted his glorification of the Rangers. The public gullibly accepted the "glaring whitewash" until McMurtry's critique in *In A Narrow Grave* in 1965 (40). Nor did that publication really set the record straight. Instead, McMurtry was labeled the enfant terrible of Texas letters for attacking Webb and his fellows of the literary triumvirate—J. Frank Dobie and Roy Bedichek. The fact is that only now are academicians interested in an unbiased picture of the Rangers. True, they served Texas in her hour of need, but they were violent, ruthless men who thought all non-whites to be subhuman. Should one look on Call and Gus and Jake as a composite of the Texas Ranger, he emerges as a man capable on the one hand of rustling, murder, hanging, atrocity, and injustice; and on the other of sentiment, gentleness, and heroism. In other words, the Rangers were men with feet of clay, not deities to be sanctified by a historian practicing "symbolic frontiersmanship" (*Narrow Grave* 43).

History, however, is not McMurtry's territory: storytelling is. About his technique, he has written: "My first concern has commonly been with textures, not structures" (*Narrow Grave* 142). As the trail drive, which gives the novel structure, moves along, so the texturing process, which gives the novel depth, develops. McMurtry's texturing may be thought of as interlarding, enriching the whole.

The search motif is major. Each of the characters is a seeker after something. As they pursue their separate dreams, their stories are interlarded into the texture of the whole.

Call's dream is for a life of adventure and excitement where he can be again a captain of men, where he can ride the Hell Bitch, his horse, into the face of danger and prove to himself and his men that his strength lies in upholding frontier ideals of masculinity. Gus throws in with Call though he attempts to dissuade him from making the drive. They had done their duty, made Texas "safe for bankers and Sunday-school teachers" (*Lonesome Dove* 83). Why should they subject themselves to the hazards of the trail? Texas is their place. Why not stay at Lonesome Dove and enjoy life? However, Gus is willing to go, for the trail will take him to Ogallala, where he will see Clara, whom he has dreamed about and loved from afar for fifteen years. Jake's aim in life is aimlessness. He is a gambler, a womanizer, and a bluff. Not a mean sort, just childlike, he wants only to satisfy his appetites: the challenge of a game of cards and the pleasure of a woman.

Lorena, the soiled dove, wants a cool place to escape the wretched heat of Texas and a man she can trust. San Francisco sounds cool and Jake appears willing to assume responsibility for her (*Lonesome Dove* 146). Newt, the sixteen-year-old waif, may be said to be searching for love. He holds fast a secret and hallowed love for Lorena and anticipates the time when he will speak to her. Also, he seeks a father.

To sum up texture thus far, a reader may begin to see parallels with Don Quixote. McMurtry writes that when he was twelve, he discovered the old knight on his adventures, imperiling the lives of others as well as himself for a ridiculous dream. Further parallels with Don Quixote would be counterproductive, though with little imagination one could construct a Procrustean apparatus, with particular reference to the Absurd: two herds of rustled horses collide head-on in the night; Call leaves in April with cattle enough for five ranches, knowing they will not reach Montana until winter; the cook gives the boys foods a survivalist would turn down; a swarm of snakes kills one of the boys; the Kiowas and Comancheros, led by the most villainous Blue Duck, commit inexpressible atrocities; a corpse is hauled from Montana to Texas. Are these instances for real? Or is McMurtry creating effect? Or is the absurdity an example of the ambivalence common to his works? Perhaps this statement from *In A Narrow Grave* will clarify McMurtry's use of borderland incredibilities: "nowhere else, except possibly California, can one find a richer mixture of absurdities" than in Texas (54).

More significant to this study is McMurtry's further comment about Don Quixote: "Not long after I entered the pastures of the empty page, I realized that the place where all my stories start is the heart faced suddenly with the loss of its country, its customary and legendary range" (*Narrow Grave* 140). This is the dilemma of the three Rangers. Call is restless for the old life and "tried hard to keep sharp" in the event some threat arose (*Lonesome Dove* 27). Gus, humorously philosophical about the sociological changes coming about in the land he had helped to tame, intends to enjoy life, keeping his whiskey jug handy and frequenting the Dry Bean, where the alluring Lorena keeps an upstairs room. Jake, uncaring, feels "rather impermanent" about life and makes no laments (*Lonesome Dove* 145).

With this insight into the characters, one may continue to penetrate the density of the novel. McMurtry has written: ". . . our emotional experience remains largely unexplored, and therein lie the dramas, poems, and novels. An ideal place to start, it seems to me, is with the relations of the sexes" (*Narrow Grave* 54).

The self-destructiveness of love negated is found in Call's story. Except for the close like-marriage feeling he has for his horse, the Hell Bitch, he rejects relationships for they may lead to emotional involvement. Yet Call is not infallible. He had made a mistake once, a mistake that "seemed to undermine all that he was, or that people thought he was. It made all his trying, his work and discipline, seem fraudulent, and caused him to wonder if his life made sense at all" (*Lonesome Dove* 360). The saloon girl Maggie, whose love for him had shone from frightened, despairing eyes, had borne his child, but Call had rejected her and her child, for he could not bring himself to admit that he had betrayed his tenets. Call is an empty shell, committed only to the image of himself as a Texas Ranger.

Jake's lack of emotional depth brings him to a tragic end. Incapable of love and the loyalty love asks, he drifts ever downward to an ignominious end.

The loss of humanity when sex is abused is dealt with by McMurtry in some minor sequences about the men into whose hands Lorena fell when she was but seventeen, men who sold her body for their own profit. And the depravity man is capable of is sickeningly revealed when Lorena is stolen from the cowcamp and turned over to Kiowa renegades and Comancheros.

But the depths of emotional experience that make *Lonesome Dove* literature in the most respected sense are found in the relationship Gus has with Lorena and the love he entertains for Clara. Lorena, at twenty-four, is distractingly beautiful. Her abundant soft blonde hair falls over her shoulders, and her hollow cheeks, the small scar above her upper lip, her long silences all add to her charm and her mystery. There is something about her that makes Gus think of Clara (*Lonesome Dove* 46). For her part, Lorena "knew he would probably even help her if she ever really needed help. It seemed to her he had got rid of something other men hadn't got rid of—some meanness or some need" (*Lonesome Dove* 40–41). It is Gus who watches over Lorena on the drive, after Jake's default. It is Gus who goes alone into the camp of the fearsome Kiowas and Comancheros to rescue her. It is Gus who tenderly cares for her until she overcomes the muteness with which her terror has left her, until she is able to control her tears, until some of the scars fade. She becomes entirely dependent upon him, knowing life cannot go on for her without him but knowing also that his love for Clara is the stronger.

Clara had been a vivacious, intelligent young woman he had known in Austin, "a girl with some sand" (*Lonesome Dove* 175). Left without parents, she had kept store in Austin, and her experience had shaped her to make use of all her inner forces and outward strengths. Knowing well that in a marriage with Gus the two of them would be forever competing for the lead, she married a man with whom she plays out the maternal role expected of a woman and at the same time exercises the masculine traits she has assimilated in her adopted role of ranch-woman—cowgirl may be a better term. Clara, denying the sexual self its gratification and growing in independence as she matures, is the counterparted alter-ego of Lorena, for whom sex is a natural activity and in whom the inner force lies dormant.

Lonesome Dove is, then, a work of art that makes use of a cattle drive for structure and receives texture mainly through the search motif and the love theme, with the Absurd lending ambivalence to the credible and the incredible.

There are other symbolic interlardings. The wild Texas bull is zoomorphically the three Ranger/Cowboys themselves. Uncontrollable,

he bellows and paws the ground, frightens the boys, falls behind to
lollygag with the cows, or lopes ahead to lead the herd. He dashes fear-
lessly into battle with an enormous grizzly, and, one-eyed and one-
horned, wearing the scars of that unequal battle, he brings the herd to
Montana.

Gus has two pigs that go along on the drive. They symbolize the
change of Texas from a land of ranching empires to a state cut up into
small farms for Tennesseans and others who bring domesticity to the
frontier.

Newt's initiation into manhood is confirmed by Call's gift of the
Hell Bitch, for the measure of a cowboy is how well he rides and Newt
had proved himself on the trail. Also, Call gives him his Henry, his
buffalo gun, an act which marks the surrender of his phallic self to
which he, Call, has been untrue. A last gift is his father's watch, the
traditional gift of father to son.

Further, there is the symbolic subplot of July Johnson and Elmira,
which serves as a foil to the Gus-Clara story. July, the Fort Smith
sheriff, searches for Jake to bring him to the gallows for shooting the
major. But he gives up that search to follow his soiled dove, Elmira,
who has run away on a whiskey boat to follow her gunman-lover Dee
somewhere north. Elmira, murdered by Indians, disappears from the
story line and July is drawn into Clara's community, the fate awaiting
Gus had Clara allowed him to remain with her.

Obviously the trail drive satisfies the aficionados of western fiction, appealing to the frontier spirit that Americans share and to the
American dream that there is an Eden awaiting the stalwart. The
search motif and the love relationships give the book universal appeal.
But the power of the book rests in the awesomeness of the myth of the
cowboy. The myth, heretofore foisted upon gullible audiences by Hollywood, can now be drawn from the fiction of one who knows the
myth, Larry McMurtry, who admits to being haunted by it and recognizes that he will never be free of it (*Narrow Grave* xvii).

In the myth the Cowboy is the God. And "the god has abandoned
Texas. Only the guards hear the music of his leaving. . . ." (*Narrow
Grave* xvii). The God may have been Old Man Goodnight, or Teddy
Blue, or McMurtry's own Uncle Johnny—any horseman whose
"mythos celebrates those masculine ideals appropriate to the frontier" (*Narrow Grave* xvii). McMurtry, heir to the legacy of ranchers,
heard the music of the god's leaving, and he believes that, though the
last cowboy has made the last drive, the Cowboy has become a mythic
"figure of romance as remote and appealing as King Arthur" (*Narrow
Grave* 28).

In *Lonesome Dove* the Cowboy-God is a Freudian composite of the three old Rangers: Call is Super-ego; Gus, Ego; and Jake, Id. Taken as one, the three embody the idea of Cowboy, the man on horseback, full of the joy of life, accepting the tragedy of life, brave, daring, hard-working, loyal, reliable, proud, stoic, often ascetic, straightforward, restless, independent, and not without a sense of humor. Each of the Rangers is consistent within the Freudian concept. When Jake the Id dies, nothing seems to go right anymore. When Gus's tempering Ego is gone, Call becomes a confused old man. He had adhered rigidly to the higher conscience and had achieved his goals. He had performed his duties, but he had failed to become ennobled by his acts, for he lacked the chastening of the Ego which would allow him to compromise his ideals and descend to Gus's level of humanity where all men make mistakes and redeem themselves someway. To view the three as one is to realize the Cowboy-God.

That the three-in-one figure is by authorial intent is strengthened by the motto Gus painted on the sign of the Hat Creek Cattle Company: *Uva uvam vivendo varia fit* (*Lonesome Dove* 89), which may be translated "The cluster of grapes—many-sided, parti-colored, diverse—through living, begets one grape." The three, like a cluster of grapes, so various, are finally, after much ripening by the vagaries of life, one, the Cowboy-God.

The boy Newt cannot bear his father's name. He may be of Call's seed, but he is actually the product of the Cowboy-God. Perhaps he hears the music of the God's leaving—ironically, the bellowing of the Texas bull? The impact becomes even more dramatic when the reader sees that Newt and the other boys will eventually be drawn into the feminine urban world, for there are no more frontiers, only a world tamed for townbuilders.

During the latter decades of the 1800s the West became less and less a man's world. The Feminine Principle, symbolized by Clara, inexorably swallowed up the cowboys, pulled them into her domain, be it her growing ranch community in Nebraska or, to move to the contemporary scene, one of the metropolitan centers spreading out over what was once rural (*Narrow Grave* 128). The Feminine Principle will diminish the cowboy, for his confidence will be destroyed when he leaves his man's world (*Narrow Grave* 73). July Johnson will become Clara's husband, bereft of his manly stature; Dish, top hand on the trail, will stay on at her ranch, "the extreme romantic, sentimental to the core" (*Narrow Grave* 149), idealizing Lorena and responding to Clara's will.

Lorena is the Cowboy-God's Love-Goddess. Despite all the abuse she has suffered and the horror she has faced, Lorena remains beautiful and worship-worthy. Jake had admitted: there was "a distance in her such as he had never met in a woman. Certain mountains were that way, like the Bighorns. The air around them was so clear you could ride toward them for days without seeming to get any closer. And yet, if you kept riding, you would get to the mountains. He was not so sure he would ever get to Lorie" (*Lonesome Dove* 195). Within the household of the ranchwoman, the Love-Goddess may or may not live on: she is forever unreachable. Her spirit has gone with the Cowboy-God.

One reviewer of *Lonesome Dove* has said: McMurtry "writes with a new power and harnesses his awesome skills to the fullest" and "has distilled the westering experience to the essence" (Leonard Sanders, *Fort Worth News-Tribune,* Aug. 16, 1985). Let it be added that McMurtry, who has himself heard the music of the departing God, has elevated the Cowboy in the Call-Gus-Jake figure to that mythically heroic stature where he remains forever superior to other men and to his environment, his legends, however exaggerated or absurd they may seem, firmly rooted in the true western frontier experience.

WORKS CITED

McMurtry, Larry. *In A Narrow Grave.* Austin: Encino Press, 1968.
McMurtry, Larry. *Lonesome Dove.* New York: Simon and Schuster, 1985.

Tall in the Saddle

NICHOLAS LEMANN

The practice of trail-driving herds of beef cattle over long distances from ranch to railhead flourished for just a moment after the Civil War and before the widespread use of barbed wire. It was the tiniest fraction of our national experience and did not directly involve more than a few thousand people. But maybe more than anything else— more than wars, more than slavery, more than urbanization or immigration—it has animated a part of our imagination out of which flows a vital branch of popular culture. Cowboyana in the form of dime fiction and stage shows flourished even before the short era of the trail drives ended. It nourished movies and television when they were young. Even today, it seems to be everywhere: in clothing, in advertising, in political rhetoric.

Unlike other themes that have obsessed us, though, the trail drive has not made the transition from low art to high art very well. The

South has "Gone With the Wind" but also Faulkner; the cowboy has "Red River" and J. Frank Dobie. It seems mysterious that so rich a subject has not produced a great novel—perhaps it has become so stylized that there is no juice left in it.

Readers who held out hope have been getting sustenance for years from the rumors that Larry McMurtry was writing a big trail-driving novel. As much as anyone, he knows the subject: he comes from a large west Texas family that he has described as "cowboys first and last," and his essays show that he has done considerable digging around in obscure first-hand accounts of trail drives. Also, if the myth-making machine has expropriated the subject, well, Mr. McMurtry knows about that too. It is hard to think of an American novelist who has been so lucky in Hollywood for so long ("Hud," "The Last Picture Show," "Terms of Endearment") without becoming a part of it. By now a cowboy novel probably would have to show some underlying awareness of the movies. Mr. McMurtry seems ideally equipped for that.

At its beginning, "Lonesome Dove" seems to be an antiwestern, the literary equivalent of movies like "Cat Ballou" and "McCabe and Mrs. Miller." The novel's title comes from the name of a Godforsaken one-saloon town on the dusty south Texas plain near the Rio Grande. Two former captains in the Texas Rangers have retired from the long wars against Indians and Mexicans to run the Hat Creek Cattle Company—when a customer wants horses or cattle, the former lawmen drop into Mexico at night and steal them. One of the captains, Augustus McCrae, is a lazy, hard-drinking, falsely erudite old coot; the other, W. F. Call, is strong and silent in circumstances that don't call for strength or silence. Surrounded by a motley crew of cowboys, Mexicans, old Rangers and flea-bitten animals, they have been living this funky life for nearly 15 years.

Then an old Ranger comrade of theirs rides into town, on the lam because he accidentally killed a man in Arkansas. He suggests they drive a herd of cattle to the unsettled country in Montana, where he has been on his wanderings. In no hurry to stop the picaresque fun, Mr. McMurtry lets the idea of a cattle drive gradually take hold among his characters. Call steals some horses and a herd of cattle and lines up some cowhands; grumbling and wisecracking and pulling on his jug, McCrae ambles along; the old friend brings the town prostitute as his guest.

As they get under way, the novel's scope begins to become clear. Mr. McMurtry weaves a dense web of subplots involving secondary characters and out-of-the-way places, with the idea of using the form of a long, old-fashioned realistic novel to create an accurate picture of life on the American frontier, from Mexico to Canada, during the late 1870s. He gives us conversationless cowboys whose greatest fear is that they will have to speak to a woman, beastly buffalo hunters, murderous Indians, destitute Indians, prairie pioneers, river boat men, gamblers, scouts, cavalry officers, prostitutes, backwoodsmen; open plains and cow towns, the Nueces River and the Platte and the Yellowstone. Everything about the book feels true; being antimythic is a great aid to accuracy about the lonely, ignorant, violent West.

Mr. McMurtry plows right into the big themes. The lack of a good reason for Call and McCrae's epic trail drive—"Here you've brought these cattle all this way, with all this inconvenience to me and everybody else, and you don't have no reason in this world to be doing it," McCrae says to Call at one point—makes the drive seem oddly profound. It becomes a way of exploring whether what gives our lives meaning is the way we live (as Call and McCrae believe, though in different ways), or what we accomplish, or nothing at all. The trail drive and the turns of plot provide many loves and deaths by which to measure the degree of meaning in the frontier's codes and imperatives. Even Call and McCrae's ages—just at the far edge of middle age—are conducive to mellow, sad tallyings-up.

The characters in "Lonesome Dove" seem always to be putting their horses into easy lopes that could be sustained all day, and this is the way Mr. McMurtry writes. His writing is almost always offhand and laconic, with barely any sustained passages intended to be beautiful or fervent. He always has time for another funny minor character to pirouette on stage, or for McCrae to produce a new bon mot. And he leisurely pursues familiar themes—two friends in love with the same woman ("Leaving Cheyenne"), a 17-year-old coming of age ("The Last Picture Show"), a formidable middle-aged woman surrounded by terrified men who love her ("Terms of Endearment"). During the last decade or so, the idea that eccentricity is the best way to deal with life has permeated Mr. McMurtry's work, and he makes an awfully good case for it again here. The question is whether it is possible to be eccentric and "major" in the same novel.

The scenes that best put the matter to rest are the most traditionally Western ones—the gunfights, stampedes, hangings and horse-stealings. Every one of these is thrilling and almost perfectly realized in describing violence. Mr. McMurtry does not need to raise the stakes with labored prose—they are already high. When a young boy rides into a nest of poisonous snakes in a river and dies of the bites, or when McCrae single-handedly fights off a band of Indians on an open plain with only a dead horse for shelter, it is unforgettable.

Such moments give "Lonesome Dove" its power. They demonstrate what underlies all the banter, and they transform Call and McCrae from burnt-out cases into—there is no other word—heroes. They are absolutely courageous, tough, strong, cool, loyal, fabulously good fighters. They and their men live through incredible travails, and, once they get to Montana, it is a paradise, worth everything. When McCrae explains the journey to the woman he loves by saying "I'd like to see one more place that ain't settled before I get decrepit and have to take up the rocking chair," it is moving, not silly. Whether this response is justified by the grandeur of their mission to tame the frontier, or conditioned by popular culture, it is there and cannot be denied.

All of Mr. McMurtry's antimythic groundwork—his refusal to glorify the West—works to reinforce the strength of the traditionally mythic parts of "Lonesome Dove," by making it far more credible than the old familiar horse operas. These are real people, and they are still larger than life. The aspects of cowboying that we have found stirring for so long are, inevitably, the aspects that are stirring when given full-dress treatment by a first-rate novelist. Toward the end, through a complicated series of plot twists, Mr. McMurtry tries to show how pathetically inadequate the frontier ethos is when confronted with any facet of life but the frontier; but by that time the reader's emotional response is it does not matter—these men drove cattle to Montana!

The potential of the open range as material for fiction seems unavoidably tied to presenting it as fundamentally heroic and mythic, even though not to any real purpose. If there is a novel to be written about trail-driving that will be lasting and deep without being about brave men—and about an endless, harsh, lovely country where life is short but rich—it is still to be written. For now, for the Great Cowboy Novel, "Lonesome Dove" will do.

Back Trailing to Glory: *Lonesome Dove* and the Novels of Larry McMurtry
CLAY REYNOLDS

It would be positively unpatriotic both as a Texan and as an American to begin reading this Pulitzer Prize–winning *magnum opus* by Larry McMurtry without the anticipation of starting a truly great novel. Just knowing the general theme and topic from reading newspaper reviews is sufficient to excite most readers' imaginations, even those imaginations who don't particularly like Westerns and who overdosed on *Rawhide* years ago. I, however, was skeptical even as I began turning the opening pages and found the immediate immersion into nineteenth century Texas culture and history as warm and inviting as a hot bath on a cold night; and by the time I reached "Trail's End"—somewhere north of the Yellowstone deep in Montana territory—with McMurtry's main characters, I had long since come to the conclusion that while this was an excellent novel in many ways, while it was intense and terribly well written in many places, it lacked the dimension and quality of work of which Larry McMurtry is capable. It's a good story, no doubt, and it captures an important part of the "American experience" and utilizes a vital part of the Western American mythos, but I have serious reservations about seeing it proclaimed as the novel for which this fine writer and native son of the Lone Star State will be remembered, and I wonder if the Pulitzer Committee didn't jump the gun a bit. I would hope that *Lonesome Dove* will be only one more notch on McMurtry's publication list, and that his big novel, his truly great novel, is yet to come.

The mere size and scope of a novel like *Lonesome Dove* is intimidating and demands attention. Few "serious" novelists these days devote such time and energy to a particular chapter in Western American history without sensationalizing it or centering it on some well-known happening such as a war or political controversy or significant and well-known historical event. To chronicle the movements of a cattle herd northward from the Rio Grande to the Yellowstone in the mid-1870s, movements that in no way take in a major battle of the Indian wars or demonstrate some political viewpoint, is ambitious at the least. But through McMurtry's capable storytelling, such important actual historical developments form a background for his fiction, a background that readers ignorant of the history of the American West will find oblique and confusing in places. This is, however, to McMurtry's credit. He is not presenting historical romance here, nor is he writing a "Western." Instead, he is offering an examination of a greater myth or combination of myths, most of which McMurtry has dealt with before; and by doing so he illustrates both the triumph and the sadness of the end of a brief era in American history which continues to dominate this nation's sense of honor and codes of behavior as much as it tends to dominate the novels of Larry McMurtry.

Lonesome Dove tells the story of two retired Texas Ranger captains, Augustus McCrae and Woodrow F. Call, who have thrown in together in the evening of their lives to run a cattle company near the town of Lonesome Dove on the Rio Grande. Call is a workhorse, losing himself and his old memories and sense of adventure in the day-to-day chores of ranch work. Gus, by contrast, works no more than he absolutely has to and is content to sit on his porch and drink from a jug and recall the days of glory he and Call enjoyed when they were fighting Indians and Mexican bandits along the Texas frontier. Their ranch is peopled with misfits and boys the two old rangers have collected from their bygone days as rakes and Indian fighters, and their lives have settled into a kind of ennui that depends upon routine to cloud their advancing ages and lack of new challenges.

Into this complacent and boring atmosphere rides an old *compañero*, Jake Spoon, who is fleeing murder charges in Arkansas. He tells his friends of the wonderful grasslands of Montana and recommends that they gather a herd and drive north to claim a ranch and a new life for themselves in the valleys of the high Rockies. This they do, after several midnight raids against their old adversary, a bandit across the river in Mexico, to put together 3,000 head of longhorn cattle and a remuda, and the drive begins.

Matters complicate in a hurry. Jake, whose idea the drive was in the first place, refuses to work the herd as it heads north, but in a move to continue to enjoy protection from his old ranger comrades, he follows along at a distance in company with Lorena, a "soiled dove" from the town's saloon, whom he has promised to take eventually to San Francisco but for whom he has no real affection at all. Gus also goes along, although he does little actual work on the drive, and Call is left to contend with about a dozen teenagers, inexperienced immigrants, and ignorant and superstitious cowboys—only one or two of whom have any knowledge of cattle at all—as he moves the massive herd farther and farther north, past Dodge City, past Ogallala, past the Powder, and into the valleys of the high Rockies.

Along the way, the herd experiences just about every adversity save tornadoes and Indian raids any reader familiar with the considerable body of works on Texas cattle drives might expect. There are swollen rivers, quicksand bogs, thunderstorms, sandstorms, hailstorms, grasshopper storms, stampedes, horse rustlers, snakes, bears, drought, and the overwhelming insecurity of taking a herd of semi-wild cattle where no man—at least no white man—has gone before. It's quite a mission, and it satisfies Call's need for adventure and Gus's need to see a long-lost love, Clara, who he knows resides in Nebraska and, he hopes, awaits his coming. Call and Gus make wonderfully contrasting personalities in the book, although by mid-way, the loquacious and affable Gus comes to dominate the main plot, even though he has less and less to do with the cattle drive and more and more to do with ironic expressions of philosophical comments on the uselessness of Call's determination to live out what has already become a myth, the search for a true frontier that offers day-to-day challenges and the constant threat of violent death. Gus also becomes a connection to the subplots, thereby taking the reader away from the herd and into ancillary adventure along the trail north.

Gus is a talker and a frontier philosopher. A smattering of education somewhere in his background gives him vast reservoirs of knowledge, most of which he deliberately misuses as he liberally shares it with whoever is in earshot. Call, by contrast, is a taciturn, quiet man who treasures his solitude and goes about life with a serious determination that borders on a maniacal dedication to hard work and suffering. Both men epitomize the mythic bravery of the Texas Ranger, however; their commitment to the lawless codes which govern the unsettled West is as unwavering as is their personal loyalty to each other. They easily risk their lives to save a principle as much as they do to rescue a friend. Their capabilities and heroic actions are taken as much for granted by those who know and respect them as they are found to be marvelous by the uninitiated who meet them and are awestruck by such displays of hard-bitten dedication to law and order that would lead Gus to ride guns blazing into a gang of desperadoes all alone, or that would lead Call to hang his best friend for violating codes of honesty and decency.

Overall, then, the novel is packed with adventure and excitement and is heavily spiced with McMurtry's wonderful capability to describe people and scenery with a homey detail that is almost tactile in its completeness. Certainly McMurtry's sense of suspense and ability to spin a yarn take the reader by surprise as he demonstrates the quick death and intense violence that inhabit the empty plains of the American West. But even so, the book is not without problems.

Although McMurtry carefully avoids pinning the book down to a specific year, his characters mention the battle of Adobe Walls, which took place in June 1874, as having happened two years before. Later in the drive, however, Custer's destruction at the hands of the Sioux on the Little Bighorn, which took place in the summer of 1876, is also mentioned in the context of the past to the extent that one cowboy has named a mature horse for the ill-starred commander of the Seventh Cavalry. There also seems to be a problem in contrasting the vast emptiness in the Kansas plains the cowboys experience on their way north with the heavy traffic Call meets only a year later. Toward the end of the novel, Call encounters so many herds moving north through the plains of Kansas and Nebraska that he detours to Denver to avoid meeting people; yet major cattle drives *that* far north did not commence in great numbers until the eighties—well after the Indians had been pacified—and he was more likely to meet herds in the mid-to-late seventies in Colorado and northern New Mexico than on the Kansas plains north of Dodge City. Such vagueness in dates might be deliberate, but it is nonetheless confusing; and such confusion is complicated by a series of incredible coincidences where characters who know one another continually meet each other by accident in the utterly void expanses of the Great Plains with the casual familiarity of old acquaintances running into themselves on the crowded streets of San Antonio.

Another structural difficulty in the book involves the relationship of the main plot to the three or four subplots McMurtry introduces. The principal subplot involves Arkansas characters July Johnson, the sheriff who sets out to track Jake Spoon, his stepson, Joe, and July's deputy, Roscoe. McMurtry goes to great length to develop these characters, particularly Roscoe, and yet leads them to a quick and decisive dead-end, effectively writing out everyone but July in a page and a half. Similar structural dead-ends are applied to Elmira, July's estranged and runaway wife, and one or two other minor characters who find themselves at the center of the main plot or a subplot's action only to be quickly disposed of as the herd moves on. The major difficulty here is that these subplots as well as one or two others that tend to "spin off" from the main plot of the cattle drive often become more intense and more interesting than the major plot line. At times, it seems, coming back to the herd is accompanied with an authorial sigh that leaves the reader anxious to get through whatever natural trial is about to threaten the herd and then back to the more interesting characters elsewhere on the plains. One wonders if McMurtry did not sense that his lesser plot lines threatened to take over the novel and simply kills off characters and snuffs out the secondary plots to keep the reader's attention focused on the herd, to which very little of an intense nature happens.

In a similar vein, McMurtry's characters in the main plot, the drovers and attendant cooks and hands, are completely introduced during the first one hundred fifty pages of the book; yet after the subplots begin to develop, these characters tend to fade so much into the background that he feels obliged to reintroduce them and to remind the reader of their major traits in nagging repetitions that slow down the reading and add little to the development of these itinerant cowboys and hangers-on. In some cases, these minor figures of the major plot re-emerge to take on significant roles later in the story. Pea Eye and Dish, for example, take on important parts toward the end of the book; however, by the time they do, their static characterizations for hundreds of pages have robbed them of reader interest and sympathy, and repetitious reminders of their major character traits become intrusive and boring.

An additional but related problem comes with McMurtry's narrative voice, which tends to "bleed over" into his characters' vernacular from time to time. Inconsistency also plagues his dialogue. Gus, for example, says "et" for "ate" but only about half the time; the narrator from time to time says "drownded" for "drowned"; and no one in the book—neither character nor narrator—seems to know the difference between a hanged and a hung man, although dragged and drug are used more or less correctly throughout. Finally, there are minor problems in credibility: horses that seem capable of riding almost a hundred miles without water or food; men exposed to the roughest natural elements imaginable who never become ill; watches, firearms, and other equipment that seem impervious to dust, mud, and water immersion; and some men and animals who seem to have wonderful night vision while comrades or fellow beasts are completely blinded by darkness.

But such flaws, if that's what they are, fade into nit-picking caveats in the brilliance of the sweeping scope of *Lonesome Dove*. In his main characters, Gus, Call, Lorena, and possibly Clara, McMurtry presents well-rounded archetypes who represent an enormous cross section of the Western American myth. Even the chief "bad guy," Blue Duck, the buffalo hunters, prostitutes and whiskey-soaked sawbones of the infrequent towns join the cowboys, drifters, gentleman ranchers, and cut-throat ne'er-do-wells of the empty plains to round out the myth, although they sometimes slip from their archetypal levels into stereotypical examples of the American Western and B movie of a few decades ago.

Perhaps the most amazing, and laudable, characteristic of *Lonesome Dove* is its subject—a cattle drive through the American West—and its relationship to McMurtry's canon to date. The drive is fraught with peril and evocative of images and symbols, all of which may be associated with the well-established mythos of the American frontier. In a 1981 essay in the *Texas Observer,* Larry McMurtry condemned such "back to the country" excursions as being backward and hardly worth considering as literature. Instead he calls for Texas letters to look to the city, to the future, and he denigrates his early efforts, *Horseman, Pass By, The Last Picture Show,* and *Leaving Cheyenne,* as immature attempts at nostalgia, obviously seeing his newer work, *Terms of Endearment* and *Cadillac Jack,* as more representative of what Texas literature should be doing.

But *Terms of Endearment* is part of a loose quartet of novels that actually begins with *Moving On* and proceeds through *All My Friends Are Going to Be Strangers* and concludes obliquely with *Somebody's Darling*. Taken as a whole, these books do represent the moving from rural to urban life, commencing as *Moving On* does in Wilbarger County at the Santa Rosa Rodeo and taking the reader to Houston, California, and ultimately the anonymous Midwest. Looking backward through his novels, in fact, one can trace the development of a number of McMurtry's characters that tend to parallel characters in *Lonesome Dove*. Certainly readers familiar with McMurtry's novels will recognize vestiges of Jacy from *The Last Picture Show* and Patsy from *Moving On* in Lorena, of Jacy's mother, and Molly from *Leaving Cheyenne*, and Emma from *Moving On* and *Terms of Endearment* in Clara. The friendship between Gus and Call is reminiscent of the rivalry and bonding between Gid and Johnny in *Leaving Cheyenne*, and Call's character recalls Roger Wagonner from *Moving On* as much as it does the old horseman, Homer Bannon, from McMurtry's first novel; and Gus's personality evokes memories of Sam the Lion from *The Last Picture Show*. Similarly, Jake Spoon reminds McMurtry's readers of the rakish rodeo rider who seduces Patsy in *Moving On*, of Flap in *Moving On* and *Terms of Endearment*, and also of Cadillac Jack, characters who are not bad so much as simply lost and seeking a kind of happiness and a kind of identity that doesn't really exist. In some if not many of the minor characters, readers will find familiar "McMurtryisms," personalized character types which have become the novelist's stock-in-trade and seem to recur in different guises at different times, always to delight the reader and to complete a cast which is somehow unique and at the same time eminently recognizable.

In this sense, then, *Lonesome Dove* represents a culmination of Larry McMurtry's career as a novelist, and by way of risking contradiction of my opening statement, it is perhaps well that it did receive the nation's highest book award, for the book tends to combine themes and characters which have been so vital to this important Texas and American novelist. However, culminations and combinations are the sorts of things one usually talks about at the end of a novelist's career, not at a point somewhere in the middle. And while it is encouraging that McMurtry has finally received the literary recognition he has long laid unofficial claim to, it is also dangerous to speculate on the career-mark that a novel like *Lonesome Dove* might represent.

In his earlier works, Larry McMurtry treated the myths of the American West much more specifically than he does in the enormous boundaries of *Lonesome Dove*. Certainly one of his more prominent themes, the end of the Western Frontier, is explored here in much more subtle ways even than in Lonnie's observation of the old horseman and his world passing by. As Call and Gus set out on their drive, they learn that their old adversary across the river has died, apparently of natural causes; their discussion frequently leads them to speculate on how long it will take for civilization to come and occupy the vast emptiness of the Great Plains; and even the ultimate end of one of the West's worst villains is anticlimactic and mundane in light of the violent and sensational life he led. One can hardly read these segments of *Lonesome Dove* and not think of the slaughter of Homer's herd in *Horseman, Pass By,* or the death of Sam the Lion in *The Last Picture Show,* or the attempt of Danny Deck to drown himself and his life's work in the Rio Grande in *All My Friends Are Going to Be Strangers.* And other themes are recognizable as well. Symbols such as the Texas bull, Call's horse, the Hell Bitch, Gus's sign for the Hat Creek Cattle Company, the ever-present violence and suddenness of death, and even the eventual fate of the saloon in Lonesome Dove all point to McMurtry's more mature handling of his principal theme of the close of the frontier.

In all, then, *Lonesome Dove* represents a major milestone for Larry McMurtry's novels. It is not the first or perhaps even the best novel about a trail drive and the end of the frontier—certainly Benjamin Capps and Robert Flynn, among others, have some claim on that distinction. *Lonesome Dove,* though, demonstrates McMurtry's recognition of the importance of the Western myth and its attendant codes and characters as a part of present reality, and it brings together many it not most of his previous themes and characterizations into a single epic-length tale of the American West. It is, arguably, the most mature and most artistic book he has written in two decades, and it indicates forcefully the power and intensity of this comparatively young writer. We can all, therefore, hope that in spite of the hype and recognition that go with the Pulitzer Prize, *Lonesome Dove* will herald a new direction and a new beginning for this talented Texas novelist and that his next work will be even better.

The Next Picture Show

JAN REID

Larry McMurtry's third novel, *The Last Picture Show,* was the least of his early North Texas books, a trilogy that also included *Horseman, Pass By* (1961) and *Leaving Cheyenne* (1963). McMurtry grew up on a cattle ranch in Archer County, and in the first two novels his laconic voice caught the tang and rhythms of uncles and cowhands whose way of life had fallen prey to the twentieth century. In a scene of brute terror and slow madness from *Horseman, Pass By,* an old man's entire herd—everything he had to live for—was driven into a pit and shot on the orders of a bureaucrat. In *Leaving Cheyenne,* McMurtry wrote about lovers who sprinkled water on their sheets to make the hot nights bearable. But for *The Last Picture Show,* published in 1966, he shifted to a third-person voice, and while the adjustment sharpened his narrative skill, it cost him style. The prose fell slack, and the tone went flat.

McMurtry had scant sympathy for area settlements and less still for the oil industry that supplanted the ranch economy. *"The Last Picture Show,"* he wrote, "is lovingly dedicated to my home town." Thalia, his fictionalized Archer City, was a moribund place where green slime dripped from cattle trucks parked along the courthouse square. Teenage boys sodomized heifers. As one read on, the space between the lines of that dedication seemed to fill with the rancor of a parting shot.

But because of Peter Bogdanovich's well-cast black and white film, McMurtry's vision of small-town life holds up two decades later. The scenes in the 1971 movie glowed and flickered like a kerosene lantern. They gave the story presence and flair that McMurtry, who cowrote the screenplay, just missed in the original fiction. The images from his book and the movie are further blended now that McMurtry has followed *Lonesome Dove*—the cowboy epic that won him the Pulitzer— with *Texasville,* a sequel to *The Last Picture Show.* The success of the film obscured the novel, perhaps even for the author. With scarcely a face described in *Texasville,* McMurtry assumes that the readers—or viewers—already know his characters well. In large type the new dedication page reads, "For Cybill Shepherd," the actress who played the high school bitch Jacy in Bogdanovich's movie.

Teenagers in the first book, the primary characters now talk about their upcoming thirtieth high school reunion. The sequel shifts the focus from doleful Sonny (the Timothy Bottoms character) to his one-time best friend, Duane (Jeff Bridges). Sonny, the mayor of Thalia, has all sorts of problems: he is blind in one eye from the beer bottle that Duane bashed over his head in a fight about Jacy; he's stiff in one arm from a bullet fired by the cuckolded Coach Popper, since deceased. And now Sonny is losing his mind. He sits in the roofless shell of the old theater and thinks he's watching Tab Hunter. The bank president, Lester, who used to take Jacy skinny-dipping, now

checks into the hospital's "quiet room" because he faces certain im-
prisonment for fraud. In her seventies, Ruth Popper (the role that won
Cloris Leachman an Oscar) jogs daily and works for Duane, who got
rich in the oil boom but now has a bank balance of $850 and debts of
$12 million. Despite his own woes, Duane somehow has to put a cheery
face on plans for the downtrodden county's centennial anniversary
celebration. And the hard-shell Baptists even want to deny the town-
folk drink.

For several years McMurtry has made a frequent home of the ranch
where he grew up, and nobody knows those plains better. Age has
mellowed him: he even lightens up on Wichita Falls, which he glee-
fully tormented in the early fiction and essays. Odessa, not Wichita
Falls, now takes his prize as the ugliest town on earth. McMurtry has
a grand time describing a plague of tumbleweeds that blows through
Thalia, and the story of nearby Texasville, once the county seat but
now a ghost town, is quite funny. When a town father hoped that oil
would rescue the settlement, he drilled too close to a rocky bluff and
opened up what was believed to be the world's largest rattlesnake den.
But mostly the ghost town digression serves as the pretext that
McMurtry needs to call a novel *Texasville:* the humdrum title takes an
oblique swipe at James Michener's knighted sesquicentennial novel of
similar name. Thalia cannot escape the irony that its grand celebration coincides with the hardest times in Texas since the Great Depression. Shortly after the bank fails, Duane reads in the *Wall Street
Journal* that the price of crude has sunk to $8.89 a barrel.

> He had seen the pumps working all his life, like patient, domesti-
> cated insects, bringing up their three or four barrels every day: not
> enough to make anyone rich, but enough to give the old folks a little
> edge on their social security, or to keep the kids in school. As
> long as they kept pumping, pumpers would be hired to pump them,
> well-service crews to clean out the wells, truckers to haul the oil
> and equipment, welders to fix what broke down. Now much of that
> life would stop. The pumps would cease to peck at the stained
> plains. Little businesses would fold, and little lives.

Hoping for a lease extension on his own life, Duane sits in his hot tub
and shoots at a doghouse with his .44 Magnum. Duane's wife, a new
character, is a tart, beautiful, and alienated woman named Karla. Their
older son sells drugs, the older daughter marries every nitwit she takes
to bed, and the foulmouthed twins disgrace themselves at church camp.
Thalia is so incestuous that Duane finds himself sleeping with an old
friend's wife who may be pregnant by Duane's dope-dealing son. Seeking

privacy, Duane sneaks off with his dog, a memorable pooch named Shorty, and spends the night in a fishing boat on Lake Kickapoo. In a fine and sparing scene his old girlfriend Jacy swims up through the golden sunrise, taking her morning laps. Grieving over her dead child, she has returned to Thalia in the wake of failed marriages and a career as an Italian movie star.

The life Jacy breathes into the prose is too little too late. Narrative force often enables McMurtry to overcome his slow starts and pipe-wrenched syntax, but this time he shows up without much story. Comedic scenes resort to slapstick, the first conversation at the Dairy Queen drags on for six chapters, and the novel ultimately stumbles over worn-out soil. Even with poetic license, it doesn't seem likely that so many pillars of the community would sleep around so openly—or, given the looks of the crowd in most Dairy Queens, that they'd even want to. And the results are not erotic poetry. McMurtry sails past a tender and critical moment by the handy means of a paragraph break. "'Gosh, that was an intense orgasm, thanks, Duane,' Karla said, later."

Whatever the time and setting, McMurtry always comes back to his war of the sexes. The taciturn male, though a decent sort, runs afoul of enigmatic women who think faster, talk smarter, and know life better. Thalia's bank president passes on rumors that Karla and Jacy, immediate friends, may be lovers as well. "We're not half as advanced as they are," he says. "It's only logical that they'd come to prefer their own company, sooner or later." In *Leaving Cheyenne, Terms of Endearment, Lonesome Dove,* and even the aimless *Moving On,* McMurtry's premise about females holds because the characters are well drawn. Here the reliable position has turned into a pose. McMurtry indicates that the dead child is the key to knowing Jacy, but he doesn't reveal much more about her than that. From what we see and hear, these women harbor contempt for everything. Do yourself a favor, Duane. Take the dog and go.

McMurtry drops a hint of another reprise in the offing. We learn that Danny Deck, the young novelist featured in McMurtry's Houston novels, is still alive. Deck writes screenplays and looks after Jacy's kids in Europe. When he described his dreams and approach to the craft in *All My Friends Are Going to Be Strangers,* he seemed to speak for the prolific McMurtry: "With great luck I might, by accident mostly, write something fine, sometime in my life, particularly if I kept myself in shape by writing books that were decently good for twenty years or so." With half a dozen fine books to his credit, McMurtry deserved his Pulitzer, but in this novel the haste of the workout shows. It could have used another draft, and it badly needs a coat of polish.

Why Is That Man Tired?

LOUISE ERDRICH

In the 1950's Texas of Larry McMurtry's novel "The Last Picture Show," the movies cost 30 cents if you missed the cartoon, Ronald Reagan adorned a poster in the lobby, teen-agers numbed their lips with hours of steady kissing, and the intricate class differences in the small town of Thalia were rigidly based on scarce cash. In the contemporary Thalia of "Texasville," the picture show that closed in the earlier novel has burned down, but most people have satellite dishes and cable-television hookups. One woman buys thousands of dollars' worth of video movies in an afternoon of boredom. Ronald Reagan's picture, presumably, now hangs framed in the courthouse lobby. Adultery and sexual treachery of all kinds are openly practiced, tolerated and discussed, and the economy has exploded—first the oil boom, then the glut and bankruptcies.

"Texasville" is intended as a companion to "The Last Picture Show," but the two works do not mesh easily, though the setting and leading characters' names have remained constant. The leisurely, lyrical character development, description and complexity that distinguished the first book are absent from the sequel. Many of Mr. McMurtry's novels ("Horseman, Pass By," "The Last Picture Show," "Terms of Endearment") have been translated into film, and "Texasville" often reads like a movie script, all dialogue and situation. The individual scenes are sharp, spare, full of longhorn humor and color, but motivation is sketchy, rarely described, clued by action rather than reflection.

When depressed, Duane Moore, the former high school football captain turned oil baron, shoots at his two-story log doghouse. His wife, Karla, relieves her frustration by driving her BMW back and forth over 85 Willie Nelson cassette tapes. Irritated at her daughter's boyfriend, she snags his little Datsun pickup and drags it with her Supernova—like a sheriff capturing a cattle rustler. These grandiose gestures, piled so close and fast on one another, are cinematic, entertaining, although at times they render the characters mere props for slapstick set pieces.

"Texasville" aims to be farcical and uproarious. It is filled with local idiom, tall stories and unabashed one-liners, many of which fall flat or offend, but some of which are dead-on funny. One rejected but persistent suitor warns, "I'm a hard dog to get out from under the porch." A daughter mourns her father "I get on him for missing his tobacco can when he spits. He can't hit the can in the dark in a moving car. I got on him and he opened the door and tried to spit. The next thing I knew he was gone."

This anecdote seems a metaphor for the fates of Mr. McMurtry's characters. They are missing, but from themselves. They have stopped having thoughts. They simply act out their emotions by destroying things, shooting things, throwing expensive collections of guns into ravines. Waste is celebrated. Sixty thousand eggs are smashed in a town egg fight. But although broken and depressed, Mr. McMurtry's people are talkative. The laundromat owner, file clerks, desperate oil men, suicidal bankers and marginally employed oil drillers meet at the local Dairy Queen to discuss a question—Who likes sex more, men or women?—that seems dated and adolescent for all of the novel's libidinal disorder. The other burning topic of conversation, Hardtop County's centennial, serves as a device that moves along a plot less concerned with telling a story than with recording a town's collective, often grimly funny, nervous breakdown.

Well into the last quarter of this long novel, a banker, Lester Marlow, gloomily asserts that if the price of oil plunges to $5 a barrel, "People will start foaming at the mouth or having sex in the middle of the street. Every marriage in the town will break up." He's a bit late with his prediction since most marital unions in Thalia have already collapsed at least once.

The characters who seemed, at the conclusion of "The Last Picture Show," destined to carry on the kindliest of small-town virtues have turned cartoonish and begun to crack. Sonny Crawford, the owner of the town's Kwik-Sack convenience store, laundromat, hotel and various other small enterprises, forgets to mind the till. He sits in the balcony of the burned-out movie house and seems to see "The Burning Hills" (starring Natalie Wood and Tab Hunter) projected on the "blue morning sky." "It's like I have a VCR in my brain," he says. Ruth Popper, Sonny's former lover and almost twice his age, has become a sensible and ludicrously spry jogger. Jacy Farrow, the teen-age goddess, has gone on to star in a few B movies and has now returned with a shattered heart to live in a secluded adobe mansion.

In "The Last Picture Show," Jacy's interior monologues were elegant pieces of wit that revealed a budding monster of self-absorption. In "Texasville," one expects an enlargement of the portrait. But Jacy is curiously vacant. Although she exerts a pull on those around her, the reader is not sure why. She is beautiful, but pales beside Karla, the novel's most outrageous, vulnerable, exasperating and vibrant character. She is the one who wears her heart on her sleeve, she has her opinions, culled mainly from country-western songs, printed on T-shirts: "INSANITY IS THE BEST REVENGE." "I'M NOT DEAF I'M JUST IGNORING YOU." "LEAD ME NOT INTO TEMPTATION. I'LL FIND IT FOR MYSELF."

She is also the best at being depressed, and the most concise and snappy when she talks about herself, "I haven't got a thought left in my head that I'd care to be alone with for five minutes." She makes no bones about her inspiration, either: she reads USA Today in her hot tub and discovers in Cosmo "the source of many of her concepts."

The word "concepts" is, of course, used ironically. Nobody in Thalia has ideas, or even warmed-through opinions. Worry over money has sucked away the populations' mental energy. Nobody wonders about anything any more. In "The Last Picture Show," people puzzled and brooded and tried to make sense of their lot. Once they did, their outlook was often cruelly pessimistic. That novel's most affecting character, Jacy's mother, Lois, says, "Life's too damn hard here. The land's got too much power over you. Being rich here is a good way to go insane. Everything's flat and empty and there's nothing to do but spend money." Karla complains of the same thing in "Texasville," but without Lois's intelligence: "Sex and dope and making money. . . . That's all people around here ever have on their minds."

Being rich *is* a good way to go insane. We see the town's collapse through Duane's eyes, through conversations he overhears or rumors that are brought to him. He is bewildered at his fellow Thalians' stubborn inability to change their view of him as the town's most successful man, "although his personal life was bizarre, his children uncontrollable and his business on the verge of ruin." Duane is $12 million in debt, has $800 in the bank and spends lots of time resting, because "getting rich had been tiring, but nothing like as tiring as going broke." Outspoken women dominate his life, and his inability to satisfy any one of them sends him stumbling from one bed (or pickup seat) to another.

In "The Last Picture Show," the quest was not only for sex, but sex linked to tenderness and mystery, to love. In "Texasville," sex is just sex. It happens everywhere and often. It is sometimes graphic but is no more exciting than the raunchy and repetitious language Duane's women use in their attempts to galvanize or awaken him.

"Texasville" is a novel about going broke, not about getting along without money. Nobody suffers material deprivation. People don't go hungry or wear out their clothes. As their bank balances decline, people seem to eat more steak, to keep on buying houses and cars and video tapes and throwing away guns. It is a book about what sudden affluence does to a community, and about the anxiety of losing it.

For all the novel's unrestrained humor, Mr. McMurtry suggests that human nature is at least partly a function of human circumstances and, at its worst, a function of money. He doesn't ask us to feel sorry for his characters, but to laugh at their crude one-liners and to be appalled at, and yet admiring of, their raw material decadence. Like the eponymous Texasville, the bygone county seat of Hardtop County, Thalia is no more than a ghost town of bones and rattlers, a tall tale, a few boards kicked up out of dirt.

FILMING

McMURTRY

The Regionalist Imperative

DON GRAHAM

Until *Lonesome Dove,* none of Larry McMurtry's novels were best sellers. But throughout his career he has benefitted from something almost as good—the three hit movies that have been adapted from his novels. *Hud* in 1963, *The Last Picture Show* in 1971, and *Terms of Endearment* in 1981 each racked up Academy Awards and built up McMurtry's readership. (There was also one clunker, *Lovin' Molly,* in 1974.) In a sense, then, the movies helped make Larry McMurtry, a point he has himself conceded more than once.

In the beginning, with *Hud,* he was very lucky. The country's taste for Westerns hadn't yet been killed by television. McMurtry has argued that if the novel had been set in Iowa, it wouldn't have attracted filmmakers so readily. What he meant, correctly, is that *Horseman, Pass By* fit nicely into a familiar and beloved genre, the Western. But both the novel and film were a Western with a vengeance, each projecting a gunfighter manqué, a Zane Grey hero without a nineteenth-century frontier as backdrop.

Art-house serious and shot like European cinema in black and white, *Hud* dealt with the end of the Technicolor West. It was in good company, preceded in 1961 by John Huston's *The Misfits,* a threnody for the end of the wild free days of the open range; in 1962 by John Ford's *The Man Who Shot Liberty Valance,* a meditation in black and white about the legendary West versus the real West; and again in 1962, by David Miller's *Lonely Are the Brave,* another black-and-whiter that lamented the displacement of the free-spirited cowboy by bureaucracy and technology. Of these films, *Hud* was easily the most commercially successful.

In specifically Texas terms, *Hud* offered a mordant version of the state's favorite movie about itself, George Stevens's epic *Giant* (1956). If *Giant* presented the Texas myth at its fullest, most glorious moment, *Hud* turned it upside down. Dark, bleak, ironic, this drastically scaled-down version of *Giant* reduces the shimmering vistas of the color epic to a flat, closed-in wasteland. The cattle grazing on the open plain are now diseased, and in the film's most powerful visual moment they are driven into scooped-out pits where they are executed, covered with quicklime, and buried by bulldozers. The cattle drive and ranching era closes grimly. *Hud* feels like World War II footage (Graham, "Myths" 42).

It is precisely here, in the film's rendering of the landscape, that the connections with both *Giant* and McMurtry's novel are severed most completely. In an early chapter of the novel the narrator, Lonnie, a sensitive and precocious seventeen-year-old—a kind of Holden Caulfield of the plains—imagines, in a dream, a moment of sympathetic merger with his grandfather, the old-time rancher and cowboy whose memory goes all the way back to the glory days of the trail-drives in the nineteenth century. In the dream Lonnie and his grandfather pause to contemplate the fair countryside:

> We stopped our horses on the edge of a hill, a high, steep hill, maybe
> it was the cap rock, and rested, our legs across the horses' necks.
> There below us was Texas, green and brown and graying in the sun,
> spread wide under the clear spread of sky like the opening scene in a
> big Western movie. There were rolling hills in the north, and cattle
> grazing here and there, and strings of horses under the shade trees.
> . . . Finally he [Grandfather] swung his feet into the stirrups and
> we rode down together into the valley toward some ranch I couldn't
> see, the Llano Estacado or the old Matador. . . . (HPB 60)

In this pastoral scene, typical of many in the novel, the observer, a modern swain, a shepherd in training as it were, understudy to the patriarchal figure of Homer Bannon, gazes upon the source of all bucolic beatitudes: the land. But the lens of observation is modern, and Lonnie *sees* the landscape, has been taught to see it thus, as an open-ended frame in a "big Western movie." He sees it, that is, in terms of something like *Red River,* a movie of sufficient scope and the greatest of the cattle-drive epics—a point of course not lost upon Peter Bogdanovich, who uses a clip from *Red River* in *The Last Picture Show*. McMurtry also underlines the dreamlike dimensions of his little pastoral by alluding to storied ranches of a bygone era, ones that Lonnie can't see because they belong to the myths of the past—the Llano Estacado, the Matador.

In the film, no scene like this occurs. Mostly, the camera gives us a flat terrain that seems to lead nowhere except to metaphorical deadness. The landscape of the film is as empty as the nothingness surrounding the train depot in *High Noon*. Only in the roundup scenes do we have any sense of rolling range or perspectives of low-lying ridges, swales, or, stretching the term, valleys. Never once is there any sense of the grandeur of landscape evident in the novel's more traditional evocation of Western space. Rather the movement in *Hud* is the other way, and the wide-open scenes of cattle being rounded up narrow to one of the bulldozed burial pit into which the cattle are jam-packed and shot. At the end, the ranch has become a place where nothing lives. Alma (the white cook based on Halmea, the black cook) has left, with nobody remaining to attempt to grow flowers where Hud carelessly used to park his Cadillac; old man Homer Bannon is dead; Lonnie is leaving; only Hud remains. The landscape mirrors the wasteland perfectly: there are no lowing herds, only the wind to rattle the gates on the pens.

One has only to visit the location site where filming took place, in Claude, Texas, near Amarillo, to see how deliberately the possibilities of scope, grandeur, and beauty have been severely—one might say systematically—eliminated from the film's *mise-en-scène*. The "Hud house" as the locals call it (in the eighties now prettified and yuppified beyond recognition) is situated on the brow of a slight elevation, from which one can see a great distance across gently rolling prairie. The view is quite striking and, coupled with the overarching sky, affords a sense of majestic space radically different from the existential bleakness of the viewless space recorded in the film.

Like *Giant, Hud* sets up a stark contrast between the good (ranching) and the bad (selfish oil interests). Homer Bannon, the elderly rancher, is supposed to carry the moral message of the novel and film. His character does so better in print than in film. Even J. Frank Dobie, Texas's most renowned chronicler of cattle culture and a reader who was unsympathetic to McMurtry's brand of four-letter realism, liked the portrait of the old rancher and said so in his private copy of the galley proofs of the novel (Graham, "Dobie" 7–9). Looking back on his novel, though, McMurtry condemns the old rancher as a "sentimentalized version of the 19th century cowman. He's far more pious and far more sententious and nobler than many of those cowmen actually were" (qtd. in Walts 33). In the film the character's basic sentimentality is exposed and he comes across as a moralizing old-timer whose defeat, while pathetic, is also inevitable. Certainly contemporary film audiences could not stomach the old man's preachiness. Director Martin Ritt found himself bushwhacked by an unexpected audience reaction: "It shocked me the first time I got a letter and it said that the old man is a pain in the ass; Hud is right!" (Graham, *Cowboys* 63).

Standing against the old man is his hard-driving, unprincipled son, Hud. Taking the Jett Rink role in *Giant* one step farther, Paul Newman completely steals the movie. When the old man says he's not going to let any oil companies ruin his land by drilling holes in the ground, Hud is furious. He'd drill and he'd sell the diseased cattle to unsuspecting buyers. In 1963 Hud's argument had a very contemporary ring to it when he said, hell, the rest of the country is crooked, from rigged game shows on TV to souped-up expense accounts to cheating on income taxes. Everybody does it. The Hud of the novel, a pure bastard, has been transformed into a figure of honest if unscrupulous vitality. Opening in early summer, months before the tragic events of November 22, *Hud* and its grim—at times didactic—prefiguring of America in conflict with itself foreshadowed the generational antagonisms to come.

Where the novel was strong, the film was weakest. Lonnie, whose narrative voice sounded one of the freshest notes in Texas writing, is in the novel a lonely, appealing, sympathetic figure who, contrary to most alienated narrators in American literature, is not angry with his provincial culture. At the end of the book he says he misses everybody, even Hud. In the film, however, Lonnie is a wimp, a proto–English major, sensitive and morally priggish. He's at his best when he's listening to country-and-western music on a pocket transistor radio, a nice reflection of with-it American pop culture, or spinning the rack of paperbacks at the local drugstore, where he pauses to read a page of *From Here to Eternity,* his favorite novel. In one of the film's best scenes, one not in the novel, he and Hud go to a bar where Lonnie attempts a heart-to-heart talk with Hud, flirts with a grown-up woman, gets in a brawl. At the end, though, he reverts to rampant priggishness and shuns Hud and all his ways. Hud, revealed in his essential aloneness too, asks Lonnie to stay on the ranch; but after all that has happened, the assault on Alma and the circumstances surrounding Homer Bannon's death, Lonnie must repudiate Hud and his rapacity.

The music of *Hud* helps set the generic boundaries that tell us we're seeing a traditional form, a Western. In doing so, the music also departs from the novel and oversimplifies the cultural situation caught so accurately by McMurtry. Everywhere in the film, directorial decisions seem to have been predicated upon making it into a recognizable form, a shit-kicking Western. The musical score, directed by Elmer Bernstein, opens with a melody played on a mandolin. The tone is melancholy and sounds faintly Mexican, though not flamenco. The effect is to convey a sense of the Southwest, perhaps also to evoke Mexico, the place where Homer Bannon bought the twenty steers that are thought to have infected his herd. The surprising thing is that the film does not begin with a country-and-western motif, because all the rest of the music in the film, with one exception, is authentic country music. In the opening scenes Lonnie walks down the streets of Thalia with a transistor radio in his pocket. He's listening to a country-and-western deejay named Bobby Don Brewer (a name lifted from the truckdriver in the novel's epilogue). The song is an immediately recognizable hillbilly classic, "Wabash Cannonball," known to everybody in the fifties from Dizzy Dean's renditions on radio broadcasts of baseball games. The next song is also pure hillbilly, the mournful "Driftwood on the River," a great song whose title is mentioned in the novel. ("Fraulein," another classic, is quoted in the novel but does not appear in the film.) We hear "Driftwood on the River" one other time in the film, along with snatches of unidentified country-and-western instrumentals. We also hear two nineteenth-century classics: "My Darling Clementine," in a follow-the-bouncing-ball rendition at the local movie house, virtually the only time in the film that Homer relaxes his bumper-sticker tendency to moralize and actually enjoys himself; and an overheard scrap of "Rock of Ages" sung at the old man's funeral. The novel's "Shall We Gather at the River" would have been a superior choice, evoking both the pastoral setting and John Ford's signature music in his best Westerns.

In the film, there is only one hint of a different musical style, and that's a bit of twist music played during a dance contest for teenagers in Thalia. The twist, however, belongs to the early sixties, not to the midfifties when the film appears to take place. In the novel we know, musically speaking, exactly what era we are in. It's 1954, back before Elvis (though he was already beginning to make records at Sun Studio in Memphis). Halmea, the black maid, hears some sounds of a new era on her radio. They insinuate their way into ranch culture. She hears Fats Domino, and she hears a really great song called "Honey Love." It went something like this: "I want it, I need it, I want yuh honey love," and it was as sexy, as deliciously dirty, as shocking as anything coming out of England in the next decade. The novel doesn't say where these songs were being played, but Dallas's KLIF must have been the station McMurtry had in mind. In the midfifties KLIF blasted out the likes of Chuck Berry, Fats Domino, and scores of hot-sounding bluesy black singers with a new idiom and sound, new to white folks anyway, and with a new name that was going to catch on: rock 'n' roll.

Nineteen fifty-four, then, was a transitional year, both musically and racially: the year of the *Brown vs. Board of Education* decision would change the legal conditions of Halmea's life just as black music would change the way white people regarded black culture. McMurtry, by rich implication, has all of this material in his novel; but the film, made in 1963 when the Civil Rights Movement was in full swing, ducked the whole question of race and music too, transforming Halmea into an earthy, flirtatious white maid and avoiding the explosive issue of a white man's unpunished rape of a black woman, and confining the music almost exclusively to country-and-western tunes, keeping it simple so we'd know we were seeing a Western and not a more culturally complex form. The best sign of the film's conservatively transforming impulse is that a song containing the words "honey love" actually appears in the film; only it's a traditional hillbilly tune and not a powerful black song at all. Did the filmmakers include the hick "Honey Love" because they mistook McMurtry's reference in the novel, or did they intentionally substitute the hick song for the black one? One more point about the music. If Lonnie weren't such a retrograde sentimentalist, he'd tune in to the new music and take off his boots and put on some sandals and get down at some coffeehouse in San Francisco with Kerouac and the other beatniks (Kerouac being arguably the most important early influence on McMurtry's writing).[1]

Still, *Hud* was more faithful to its source than many films have been. McMurtry has even claimed that the film is better than his novel. And in one of his later novels, *All My Friends Are Going to Be Strangers,* as if to exorcise the first novel once and for all, he turned the filming of it into self-reflexive comedy. His feckless hero, Danny Deck, has written a first novel called *The Restless Grass* that his agent has sold to the movies. Danny finds what Hollywood intends to do with it very amusing because he has already disowned the novel himself, feeling completely alienated from it by the time it appeared in print, the creative excitement belonging to the past and having nothing to do with the actual product. Danny regards *The Restless Grass* as "a simple novel about a good old man whose one son had gone bad" and thinks it would be easy to turn it into a movie. But the Hollywood producer Leon O'Reilly has other ideas. He wants the old man to have two sons, one good, one bad, for the purposes of conflict. Cooperative and malleable as ever, Danny agrees to such changes as this one: "We decided to have the bad son get killed while illegally roping antelope from the hood of a speeding Cadillac" (136).

McMurtry had a direct hand in the second and best film to be made of one of his novels. With Peter Bogdanovich he coauthored the script of *The Last Picture Show,* a film about Texas and about the fifties that still stands as a work of quite superior merit.

In the novel broad satire often dominates over sympathy for the characters. In the film the comedy remains but is subordinated to respect for the people trapped in the backwaters of America, circa 1952. Actually *circa* is not correct: the time is precisely marked, 1951–1952, with references to the Korean War and the nomination of Adlai Stevenson in 1952. Again the music provides a nice cue to time and place. In *The Last Picture Show* the dominant mode is country music, and there is popular music of the Hit Parade variety—such as "Shrimp Boats Are A'Comin'" and "Glow, Little Glow Worm"—what later came to be known as "easy listening." There is no hint of a musical revolution to come. Of the country-and-western songs, most are sung by the great Hank Williams. We hear at various times snatches of "Cold, Cold Heart," "Why Don't You Love Me Like You Used to Do?," "Hey, Good Lookin'," "The Wild Side of Life," "Kaw-liga" (Sonny's choice at the jukebox), and "Lovesick Blues." The films at the Royal, the last picture show of the title, frame a similar pastness too: *Father of the Bride* and *Red River.* References to television indicate the transformative powers of that new medium, but everytime we see a TV set the context is one of terminal boredom, and it is from TV sets that we hear bits from the Hit Parade.

Anarene, Texas, 1952, is a dead town in a cultural wasteland where all the resources for growth and enlargement of perspective are denied. The high school English teacher struggling to present the meaning of Keats's "Ode to a Nightingale" has to debate the question of immortality with a preacher's son named Joe Bob who knows the answer already: Christ is the answer. The forbidden paperback novel in this film indicates a loss of richness, too: it is not James Jones's *From Here to Eternity* but Mickey Spillane's *I, The Jury* which one kid passes furtively to another during class. Jesus, Keats, and Mickey Spillane compete for the attention of bored teenagers.

The film opens with the wind banging the doors of boarded-up buildings, and near the end, in the next-to-last scene, the wind, still blowing, contributes to the death of the retarded boy Billy who is futilely sweeping the streets when a truck hits him and kills him. When Sonny, in a rage of loss and grief, drives out of town to escape, there's no place to go. The land stretches level and empty as far as the eye can see. The film's most touching moment with regard to landscape nearly always brings a wry laugh from audiences. Sam the Lion, played beautifully by Ben Johnson, has taken Sonny and Billy fishing at a tank (pond) outside of town. He comes out here, he says, to "get a little scenery," and the camera pans to the far bank. The scenery looks like a Beckett set: water, sparse "shore" line, a few scraggly mesquite trees. Sam knows he is sentimental about this place and about the past, but given the cultural desiccation of the present, his feelings are perfectly validated.

When Sam dies, the last cultural institution that connects with the mythic past, the movie house, is doomed as well. The last picture that the boys see is *Red River,* about which there has been considerable critical commentary. In a detailed analysis Robert Wilson has argued that the original film mentioned in the novel—Audie Murphy's *The Kid from Texas*—would have been a better choice. As Wilson sees it, quoting from the novel, "it would have taken *Winchester'73* or *Red River* or some big movie like that to have crowded out the memories the boys kept having." By selecting *Red River,* the greatest of the cattle-drive epics and one of the all-time best Western films, Bogdanovich wanted the movie house to close with a bang, with an evocation of the heroic past—John Wayne paralleling Sam the Lion. Wilson prefers the Audie Murphy reference, but for the wrong reasons. He says, "Audie Murphy and Gale Storm, who was herself to become a TV star, strike me as inspired choices to suggest the reduction of legends to seven-inch dimensions" (168). But his argument depends upon thinking of *The Kid from Texas* as a "made-for-TV variety," an anachronistic statement that ignores the high production values of this glossy Universal Technicolor feature release. He also ignores the specifically Texas association carried by World War II's best-known soldier. Murphy, the most decorated soldier of World War II, was a major celebrity in postwar Texas, and his films were extremely popular throughout the Southwest. Thus Duane's comment that "this here's a dog" is really McMurtry's judgment. A boy like Duane would have admired Audie's skill with guns, his menacing baby face, and his war record, and considering that Duane himself enlists in the army, the *Kid from Texas* motif works splendidly. On the other hand, there is a somewhat puzzling note on this very point in McMurtry's recent novel, *Texasville.* Late in the novel Duane observes a painting done by his friend Sonny. Entitled "Hometown," it contains essential elements of the earlier novel: an empty street, a high school letter jacket, a poolroom, the football field. It also contains the picture show with the marquee reading "The Kid from Texas," a "movie Duane had never heard of" (465).

The end of possibilities signaled by the closing of the picture show is mirrored in the lives of the characters in the film. Jacy, the bitch goddess of the dying frontier, lures two boys to near despair and nearly destroys their friendship in her quest for local celebrityhood. At the end she is absent, away in Dallas attending school at SMU where there will be plenty of opportunity to work her charms on rich boys. Duane is headed for Korea from where, if he doesn't get shot, he expects to return to live in Anarene. Sonny is making his peace with the aging coach's wife, Ruth Popper. At eighteen most of the youths in this film seem like defeated people. (Of course, we know, after *Texasville,* that they survive into the eighties. In a sense the film version has already been made; it was called *Middle Aged Crazy.*)

To viewers outside of Texas, *The Last Picture Show* seemed less regional than national in focus: it seemed to be a film about everybody who had attended a small high school in a small town in the 1950s. Iowa, South Carolina, Minnesota, Utah—the Texasness didn't matter unless you happened to be from Texas. But in retrospect, the film achieves its power, in part, because it is so rooted in a particular place. Like Woody Allen's films set in Manhattan, *The Last Picture Show* is regional in the best sense of the word. When the kids graduate from high school, it's "Texas, Our Texas" that they sing.

The only false moment in the film occurs, however, because of this very regionalism. That is the redneck-bashing scene that takes place at Billy's death. The old men of the town, who throughout have appeared as hard-talking, crude, yet humorous, here take on the worst aspects of the Southern redneck as lampooned in such counter-culture films as *Easy Rider* and such mainstream films as the Burt Reynolds *Smoky and the Bandit*–type comedies. The men stand around commenting callously on the death of the boy, calling him a simpleminded retarded kid and expressing not one ounce of human sympathy. They just let the body lie there, bleeding on the pavement; nobody thinks to call an ambulance. Except for the striking detail that the truck is a cattle truck (carrying cattle to slaughter, one supposes, the end result of the cattle business that ends in *Hud*), the rest of the scene seems contrived to present Sonny with a chance to call them "sons of bitches" and to cradle the body of his beloved friend, whom he too had earlier in the film allowed to be brutalized by the harsh rituals of this society, participating as an onlooker in the crude defloration of the unwitting boy by the grotesque Jimmy Sue.

McMurtry's black and white Westerns represent the best transla-
tions of his fiction into film, though some might argue that *Terms of
Endearment,* a smash popular hit, is superior to one or both of the
earlier films. Nobody would argue for the merits of *Lovin' Molly*
(1974). The two color films, however, should be bracketed together,
just as the two modern Westerns are, and one way of seeing the contrast turns upon the question of relation to region. A truism of criticism of McMurtry's writing is that his regional fiction is stronger
than those novels set outside the boundaries of the Lone Star State,
and one can stir up arguments only as to which is the weakest of the
so-called expatriate fiction: *Somebody's Darling, Cadillac Jack,* or *The
Desert Rose.* My argument is that the two color films, insofar as they
depart from a realized Texas context, fail to be as effective as the
more regionally grounded earlier films.

With *Lovin' Molly* the case is almost ludicrously easy to make.
McMurtry himself has written a very funny essay about the miscar-
riages of justice committed by director Sidney Lumet and his array of
miscast actors headed by Tony Perkins and Beau Bridges. All one has
to do is look at a still of this film to see what's wrong with it. Tony
Perkins, looking as if he wishes he were back in the Bates Motel where
he belongs, wears overalls, an L. L. Bean–style lumberjack shirt (lots
of broad plaid squares), flat shoes, and so on. The wardrobe looks like
it came from *Deliverance.* The landscape, lush with streams and leafy
green trees and soft, undulating hills, is another cue to what's wrong,
intrinsically, with this film. The decision to shoot at Bastrop, east of
Austin, was one from which this film could never hope to recover.
McMurtry's Western novels require the integrity of authentic location
shooting. Near Bastrop there is a stand of pine trees.

From the Third Coast to the East Coast, reviewers had fun attacking the absurdities of this film. Katherine Lowry in *Texas Monthly*
indicted both the director and scriptwriter (Steve Friedman) as
"born-and-bred New Yorkers who capture the flavor and essence of
Texas about as accurately as I could draw a map of the Manhattan
subway system" (34). *New Yorker* reviewer Penelope Gilliatt put her
finger on another failure of this film: the portrayal of the central
character Molly, whose earth-motherhood provides the cohesive bond
that ties everything together. Attacking the film from a feminist perspective, Gilliatt's review parodies with devastating results the language and assumptions of Molly's down-home stand-by-your-men
attitude. The review mocks Molly's voice: "They tell me that all my
lovin' and breedin' through the years since then has made me prettier

than ever, like the times when my father would hit me and one of my men comforting me for my black eye would admire me for my beauty. Guess that was because a black eye's natural now and then in Texas." Gilliatt never lets up: "But I guess those magazines [women's liberation magazines] would say my great fondness for lovin' and breedin' ain't liberated. Well, you should see my men burying their faces in my hair when I've just rinsed it in vinegar and they enjoy it like eating vinegar cobbler" (136).

To Texans, the film was a pastiche; to outsiders, it purveyed the worst of stereotypes. Its deracination from McMurtry's place—the ranch country around his hometown, Archer City—was the cause of it all, though McMurtry himself, in characteristic fashion, has dismissed the novel on which it was based, *Leaving Cheyenne*, as "another sentimentalized treatment of conditions and life in Texas in the 20's and 30's." He thinks the book is a favorite among his readers because it "incorporates a popular fantasy," namely that two friends can share the same woman without murdering one another (qtd. in Walts 35).

The most recent of McMurtry's books to be filmed is *Terms of Endearment,* which McMurtry has called his favorite among his novels. The Academy Award–winning film is a movie beloved by many people, especially, I think, by women viewers who respond to the complexities of the mother-daughter portrayals rendered by Shirley MacLaine and Debra Winger. (On the other hand several women reviewers have taken the film to task for its compromises and slick emotionalism.[2]) From the regional perspective, *Terms of Endearment* has less of a specific-place feeling than any of his other films, including even the wretched *Lovin' Molly*. Not so the novel. Houston is a slippery city to capture, but McMurtry here and in the longish but affecting *Moving On,* as well as the early scenes of *All My Friends Are Going to Be Strangers* (the three works making up the "Houston Trilogy") does a good job of capturing the feeling of a city so close to frontier chaos that it barely deserves the name *city.* McMurtry, who has always been unabashedly in love with the nineteenth-century novel, tried in *Terms of Endearment* to cross Jane Austen with Balzac: a mix of manners and money of the cruder sort commingling with low comedy and soap-opera melodrama. The film takes out the low comedy, the specific density of Texas as revealed in Houston, and builds up the melodrama—Emma's pathetic death from cancer. Houston might be any city, and the Texas characters in the novel, including the redoubtable eccentric millionaire Vernon Dalhart (named after a pioneer country-and-western singer), disappear into the background.

In the Iowa scenes there is one brief attempt to talk about Texas. Debra Winger's lover (John Lithgow) asks her what is special about Texas, and she thinks for a minute and decides that there's a "wildness" there that's absent from tamer places like Iowa. But there is nothing in the film, objectively speaking, to confirm this judgment. Again deracination moves the film away from a Texas setting towards a generalized, unlocalized "national" setting. This sense of the film's unrootedness was confirmed in a minor way by producer Martin Jurow's remarks upon accepting the Oscar for Best Film. Jurow, who could not get the film made in Hollywood, took the occasion to say that it was after all a "Hollywood film." By that he meant box-office big. And Texas, fittingly, was not even mentioned, though much of the film had been shot on location in or near Houston.

McMurtry remains an author to watch as well as read. The pleasures his films provide are often directly proportional to their fidelity to the region in which the novels are rooted. The complete failure of a film like Lovin' Molly began with the decision to shoot it in farming and piney-woods country. Casting such actors as Beau Bridges and Tony Perkins simply completed the process of deracination. And Terms of Endearment, for all its popularity, fails to convey any specific sense of Houston or of Texas—admittedly a difficult task in the first instance.

One test, then, by which one measured the merits of the television miniseries Lonesome Dove, which aired in February 1989, was whether the cattle ran to Montana as they do in all bad cattle-drive films, or walked as they do in the good ones, and whether they ran or walked through a landscape unadorned with snow-clad mountains in the middle distance. Surprisingly, I can report that they walked and that Texas never looked better. Australian director Simon Wincer gave us a Texas of scrawny mesquite trees, rocky escarpments and bluffs and dunes and high ground that was never too high, and never, not once, were the Rockies visible. Bringing McMurtry's vast open-aired epic to the little screen turned out to be a resounding success, as Lonesome Dove finished fourteenth among all-time top-grossing miniseries productions in the U.S. and first among miniseries of the past five years. Once again McMurtry's cinematic novelistic imagination has hit pay dirt. Now there's talk of video production, a "prequel," even a TV series based on Lonesome Dove. All in all, the gloomy predictions for American culture forecast in the closing of the last picture show seem to have turned into something sunny and bright for McMurtry and the Western.

NOTES

1. See Patrick Bennett, "Larry McMurtry: Thalia, Houston, and Hollywood," *Talking with Texas Writers* (College Station: Texas A&M UP, 1980) 15–36. On the matter of Kerouac's importance, McMurtry is emphatic: "One sort of historical influence on me was Kerouac. I think it was because, at the time *On the Road* was published, American writing had been stodgy for quite a while. . . . Kerouac came along and opened it up. It was a breath of air. A lot of writers of my generation were stimulated by Kerouac" (qtd. in Bennett 17). The Kerouac presence in McMurtry's fiction is most apparent in *All My Friends Are Going to Be Strangers.*

2. See, for example, Marcia Pally, "World of Our Mothers," *Film Comment* Mar.–Apr. 1984: 11–12; and Pauline Kael, "Retro Retro," *New Yorker* 12 Dec. 1983: 149–52.

WORKS CITED

Biskind, Peter. Rev. of *Terms of Endearment. Nation* 14 Jan. 1984: 28–29.

Folsom, James K. "*Shane* and *Hud:* Two Stories in Search of a Medium." *Western Humanities Review* 24 (1970): 359–72.

Gilliatt, Penelope. "The Current Cinema." *New Yorker* 22 Apr. 1974: 136+.

Graham, Don. *Cowboys and Cadillacs: How Hollywood Looks at Texas.* Austin: Texas Monthly, 1983.

———. "When Myths Collide." *Texas Monthly* Jan. 1986: 42+. See for extended comparison of *Giant* and *Hud.*

———. "J. Frank Dobie: A Reassessment." *Southwestern Historical Quarterly* XCII.1 (July 1988): 1–15.

Kael, Pauline. "*Hud,* Deep in the Divided Heart of Hollywood." *I Lost It at the Movies.* Boston: Little, 1965. 78–94.

King, Larry L. "Leavin' McMurtry." *Texas Monthly* Mar. 1974: 70–76.

Lowry, Katherine. "From Badlands to Worselands." *Texas Monthly* June 1974: 31–35.

McMurtry, Larry. *All My Friends Are Going to Be Strangers.* New York: Simon and Schuster, 1972.

———. *Horseman, Pass By.* 1961. New York: Penguin, 1979.

———. *Texasville.* New York: Simon and Schuster, 1987.

Silver, Isidore. "*The Last Picture Show:* A Concurring Opinion." *Commonweal* 14 Jan. 1972: 348–50.

Speidel, Constance. "Whose *Terms of Endearment?*" *Literature/Film Quarterly* 12.4 (1984): 271–73.

Walts, Robert W., ed. *The American Southwest: Cradle of Literary Art.* San Marcos: Southwest Texas State, 1981.

Wilson, Robert. "Which is the Real 'Last Picture Show'?" *Literature/Film Quarterly,* 1.2 (April 1973): 167–69.

Published criticism of films based on Larry McMurtry's novels is fairly extensive, chiefly in the form of reviews appearing in newspapers, magazines, and journals. There are also a few longer journalistic pieces and a few academic pieces that appeared in scholarly journals. The selections in this volume are intended to provide a sample of responses drawn from a cross section of such material.

Pauline Kael's "*Hud*, Deep in the Divided Heart of Hollywood" represents this famous critic at her best. Kael wittily shows how *Hud*, a movie that viscerally undercuts the pieties of its liberal social-message faith, represents the "schizoid" nature of serious film-making in Hollywood. Taking a different approach to the same question, James K. Folsom's essay "*Shane* and *Hud:* Two Stories in Search of a Medium," part of which is excerpted here, is the best of a thin substratum of academic criticism on McMurtry's films. Utilizing the novel-into-film approach, Folsom discusses, though not always with enough thoroughness, the choices that the scriptwriters and director made in translating the novel into film.

By contrast, Isidore Silver's wide-ranging review, "*The Last Picture Show:* A Concurring Opinion," relates the film to its roots in the Western tradition of Ford, Hawks, and Peckinpah. Her commentary also reflects the low standing of Texas in the national consciousness at the beginning of the 1970s. Coming closer to home, fellow Texan Larry L. King's account of the making of *Lovin' Molly,* called "Leavin' McMurtry," besides being very funny, offers several real insights into the perils of how regional culture can get completely scrambled in the hands of outsiders who don't know the difference between a chicken-fried steak and a cow-patty.

Finally, the audience-pleasing Shirley MacLaine–Debra Winger vehicle, *Terms of Endearment,* comes in for dissenting critical examinations in Peter Biskind's review for the *Nation* and Constance Speidel's short article in *Literature/Film Quarterly.* Biskind finds an unsettling rightist view of male-female relations in this film, arguing that its ideology derives from pro-life arguments based on a deep distrust of men. Speidel uses the lens of the novel to explain a number of disappointments and shortcomings in the film.

All in all, the films made from McMurtry's fiction have stimulated some lively personal responses, but as yet not many full-fledged analyses—a statement that is also true of responses to his fiction.

. .

Hud, Deep in the Divided Heart of Hollywood
PAULINE KAEL

As a schoolgirl, my suspiciousness about those who attack American "materialism" was first aroused by the refugees from Hitler who so often contrasted their "culture" with our "vulgar materialism" when I discovered that their "culture" consisted of their having had servants in Europe, and a swooning acquaintance with the poems of Rilke, the novels of Stefan Zweig and Lion Feuchtwanger, the music of Mahler and Bruckner. And as the cultural treasures they brought over with them were likely to be Meissen porcelain, Biedermeier furniture, oriental carpets, wax fruit, and bookcases with glass doors, it wasn't too difficult to reconstruct their "culture" and discover that it was a stuffier, more middle-class materialism and sentimentality than they could afford in the new world.

These suspicions were intensified by later experience: the most grasping Europeans were, almost inevitably, the ones who leveled the charge of American materialism. Just recently, at a film festival, a behind-the-iron-curtain movie director, who interrupted my interview with him to fawn over every Hollywood dignitary (or supposed dignitary) who came in sight, concluded the interview with, "You Americans won't understand this, but I don't make movies just for money."

Americans are so vulnerable, so confused and defensive about prosperity—and nowhere more so than in Hollywood, where they seem to feel they can cleanse it, justify their right to it, by gilding it with "culture," as if to say, see, we're not materialistic, we appreciate the finer things. ("The hunting scene on the wall of the cabana isn't wallpaper: it's handpainted.") Those who live by making movies showing a luxurious way of life worry over the American "image" abroad. But, the economics of moviemaking being what they are, usually all the producers do about it is worry—which is probably just as well because films made out of social conscience have generally given an even more distorted view of America than those made out of business sense, and are much less amusing.

The most conspicuous recent exception is *Hud*—one of the few entertaining American movies released in 1963 and just possibly the most completely schizoid movie produced anywhere anytime. *Hud* is a commercial Hollywood movie that is ostensibly an indictment of materialism, and it has been accepted as that by most of the critics. But those who made it protected their material interest in the film so well that they turned it into the opposite: a celebration and glorification of materialism—of the man who looks out for himself—which probably appeals to movie audiences just because it confirms their own feelings. This response to *Hud* may be the only time the general audience has understood film makers better than they understood themselves. Audiences ignored the cant of the makers' liberal, serious intentions, and enjoyed the film for its vital element: the nihilistic "heel" who wants the good things of life and doesn't give a damn for the general welfare. The writers' and director's "anti-materialism" turns out to be a lot like the refugees' anti-materialism: they had their Stefan Zweig side— young, tender Lon (Brandon de Wilde) and Melvyn Douglas's Homer, a representative of the "good" as prating and tedious as Polonius; and they had their protection, their solid salable property of Meissen and Biedermeier, in Paul Newman.

Somehow it all reminds one of the old apochryphal story conference—"It's a modern western, see, with this hell-raising, pleasure-loving man who doesn't respect any of the virtues, and, at the end, we'll fool them, he doesn't get the girl and he doesn't change!"

"But who'll want to see *that?*"

"Oh, that's all fixed—we've got Paul Newman for the part."

They could cast him as a mean man and know that the audience would never believe in his meanness. For there are certain actors who have such extraordinary audience rapport that the audience does not believe in their villainy except to relish it, as with Brando; and there are others, like Newman, who in addition to this rapport, project such a traditional heroic frankness and sweetness that the audience dotes on them, seeks to protect them from harm or pain. Casting Newman as a mean materialist is like writing a manifesto against the banking system while juggling your investments so you can break the bank. Hud's shouted last remark, his poor credo, "The world's so full of crap a man's going to get into it sooner or later, whether he's careful or not," has, at least, the ring of *his* truth. The generalized pious principles of the good old codger belong to nobody.

The day *Hud* opened in San Francisco the theater was packed with an audience that laughed and reacted with pleasure to the verve and speed and economy, and (although I can't be sure of this) enjoyed the surprise of the slightly perverse ending as much as I did. It was like the split movies of the war years—with those cynical heel-heroes whom we liked because they expressed contempt for the sanctimonious goody guys and overstuffed family values, and whom we still liked (because they were played by actors who *seemed* contemptuous) even when they reformed.

It's not likely that those earlier commercial writers and directors were self-deceived about what they were doing: they were trying to put something over, and knew they could only go so far. They made the hero a "heel" so that we would identify with his rejection of official values, and then slyly squared everything by having him turn into a conventional hero. And it seems to me that we (my college friends) and perhaps the audience at large didn't take all this very seriously, that we enjoyed it for its obvious hokum and glamour and excitement and romance, and for the wisecracking American idiom, and the tempo and rhythm of slick style. We enjoyed the *pretense* that the world was like this—fast and funny; this pretense which was necessary for its enjoyment separated the good American commercial movie—the good "hack" job like *Casablanca* or *To Have and Have Not*—from film art and other art. This was the best kind of Hollywood *product:* the result of the teamwork of talented, highly paid professional hacks who were making a living; and we enjoyed it as a product, and assumed that those involved in it enjoyed the money they made.

What gave the Hollywood movie its vitality and its distinctive flavor was that despite the melodramatic situations, the absurd triumphs of virtue and the inordinate punishments for trivial vice—perhaps even because of the stale conventions and the necessity to infuse some life that would make the picture seem new within them—the "feel" of the time and place (Hollywood, whatever the locale of the story) came through, and often the attitudes, the problems, the tensions. Sometimes more of American life came through in routine thrillers and prison-break films and even in the yachting-set comedies than in important, "serious" films like *The Best Years of Our Lives* or *A Place in the Sun,* paralyzed, self-conscious imitations of European art, or films like *Gentleman's Agreement,* with the indigenous paralysis of the Hollywood "problem" picture, which is morally solved in advance. And when the commercial film makers had some freedom and leeway, as well as talent, an extraordinary amount came through—the rhythm of American life that gives films like *She Done Him Wrong, I'm No Angel,* the Rogers-Astaire musicals, *Bringing Up Baby, The Thin Man, The Lady Eve, Double Indemnity, Strangers on a Train, Pat and Mike, The Crimson Pirate, Singin' in the Rain, The Big Sleep,* or the more recent *The Manchurian Candidate* and *Charade* a freshness and spirit that makes them unlike the films of any other country. Our movies are the best proof that Americans are liveliest and freest when we don't take ourselves too seriously.

Taking *Hud* as a commercial movie, I was interested to see that the audience reacted to Hud as a Stanley Kowalski on the range, laughing

with his coarseness and sexual assertiveness, and sharing his contempt for social values. Years before, when I saw the movie version of
A Streetcar Named Desire, I was shocked and outraged at those in the
audience who expressed their delight when Brando as Stanley jeered
at Blanche. At the time, I didn't understand it when they laughed their
agreement as Stanley exploded in rage and smashed things. It was
only later, away from the spell of Vivien Leigh's performance, that I
could reflect that Stanley was clinging to his brute's bit of truth, his
sense that her gentility and coquetry were intolerably fake. And it
seemed to me that this was one of the reasons why *Streetcar* was a
great play—that Blanche and Stanley upset us, and complicated our
responses. This was no Lillian Hellman melodrama with good and evil
clay pigeons. The conflict was genuine and dramatic. But Hud didn't
have a dramatic adversary; his adversaries *were* out of Lillian Hell-
manland.

The setting, however, wasn't melodramatic, it was comic—not the
legendary West of myth-making movies like the sluggish *Shane* but
the modern West I grew up in, the ludicrous real West. The comedy
was in the realism: the incongruities of Cadillacs and cattle, crickets
and transistor radios, jukeboxes, Dr. Pepper signs, paperback books—
all emphasizing the standardization of culture in the loneliness of vast
spaces. My West wasn't Texas; it was northern California, but our
Sonoma County ranch was very much like this one—with the frame
house, and "the couple's" cabin like the housekeeper's cabin, and the
hired hands' bunkhouse, and my father and older brothers charging
over dirt roads, not in Cadillacs but in Studebakers, and the Saturday
nights in the dead little town with its movie house and ice cream
parlor. This was the small-town West I and so many of my friends
came out of—escaping from the swaggering small-town hotshots like
Hud. But I didn't remember any boys like Brandon de Wilde's Lon: he
wasn't born in the West or in anybody's imagination; that seventeen-
year-old blank sheet of paper has been handed down from generations
of lazy hack writers. His only "reality" is from de Wilde's having
played the part before: from *Shane* to *Hud*, he has been our observer,
our boy in the West, testing heroes. But in *Hud*, he can't fill even this
cardboard role of representing the spectator because Newman's Hud
has himself come to represent the audience. And I didn't remember
any clean old man like Melvyn Douglas's Homer: his principles and
rectitude weren't created either, they were handed down from the
authors' mouthpieces of the socially conscious plays and movies of the
thirties and forties. Occupied towns in the war movies frequently
spawned these righteous, prophetic elder citizens.

Somewhere in the back of my mind, Hud began to stand for the people who would vote for Goldwater, while Homer was clearly an upstanding Stevensonian. And it seemed rather typical of the weakness of the whole message picture idea that the good liberals who made the film made their own spokesman a fuddy-duddy, worse, made him inhuman— except for the brief sequence when he isn't a spokesman for anything, when he follows the bouncing ball and sings "Clementine" at the movies. Hud, the "villain" of the piece, is less phony than Homer.

In the next few days I recommended *Hud* to friends (and now "friends" no longer mean college students but academic and professional people) and was bewildered when they came back indignant that I'd wasted their time. I was even more bewildered when the reviews started coming out; what were the critics talking about? Unlike the laughing audience, they were taking *Hud* at serious message value as a work of integrity, and, even in some cases, as a tragedy. In the New York *Herald Tribune,* Judith Crist found that "Both the portraits and the people are completely without compromise—and therein is not only the foundation but also the rare achievement of this film." In the *Saturday Review,* Arthur Knight said that "it is the kind of creative collaboration too long absent from our screen . . . by the end of the film, there can be no two thoughts about Hud: he's purely and simply a bastard. And by the end of the film, for all his charm, he has succeeded in alienating everyone, including the audience." According to Bosley Crowther in the New York *Times:*

> Hud is a rancher who is fully and foully diseased with all the germs
> of materialism that are infecting and sickening modern man . . .
> And the place where he lives is not just Texas. It is the whole
> country today. It is the soil in which grows a gimcrack culture that
> nurtures indulgence and greed. Here is the essence of this picture.
> While it looks like a modern Western, and is an outdoor drama,
> indeed, *Hud* is as wide and profound a contemplation of the human
> condition as one of the New England plays of Eugene O'Neill. . . .
> The striking, important thing about it is the clarity with which it
> unreels. The sureness and integrity of it are as crystal-clear as the
> plot is spare . . . the great key scene of the film, a scene in which
> [the] entire herd of cattle is deliberately and dutifully destroyed . . .
> helps fill the screen with an emotion that I've seldom felt from any
> film. It brings the theme of infection and destruction into focus
> with dazzling clarity.

As usual, with that reverse acumen that makes him invaluable, Crowther has put his finger on a sore spot. The director carefully builds up the emotion that Crowther and probably audiences in general feel when the cattle, confused and trying to escape, are forced into the mass grave that has been dug by a bulldozer, and are there systematically shot down, covered with lime, and buried. This is the movie's big scene, and it can be no accident that the scene derives some of its emotional power from the Nazis' final solution of the Jewish problem; it's inconceivable that these overtones would not have occurred to the group—predominantly Jewish—who made the film. Within the terms of the story, this emotion that is worked up is wrong, because it is not Hud the bad man who wants to destroy the herd; it is Homer the good man who accedes to what is necessary to stop the spread of infection. And is all this emotion appropriate to the slaughter of animals who were, after all, raised to be slaughtered and would, in the normal course of events, be even more *brutally* slaughtered in a few weeks? What's involved is simply the difference in money between what the government pays for the killing of the animals and their market value. It would not have been difficult for the writers and director to arrange the action so that the audience would feel quick relief at the destruction of the herd. But I would guess that they couldn't resist the opportunity for a big emotional scene, a scene with *impact,* even though the emotions don't support the meaning of the story. They got their big scene: it didn't matter what it meant.

So it's pretty hard to figure out the critical congratulations for clarity and integrity, or such statements as Penelope Gilliatt's in the *Observer,* "Hud is the most sober and powerful film from America for a long time. The line of it is very skillfully controlled: the scene when Melvyn Douglas's diseased cattle have to be shot arrives like the descent of a Greek plague." Whose error are the gods punishing? Was Homer, in buying Mexican cattle, merely taking a risk, or committing hubris? One of the things you learn on a ranch, or any other place, is that nobody is responsible for natural catastrophes; one of the things you learn in movies and other dramatic forms is the symbolic use of catastrophe. The locusts descended on Paul Muni in *The Good Earth* because he had gotten rich and *bad:* a farmer in the movies who neglects his humble wife and goes in for high living is sure to lose his crops. *Hud* plays it both ways: the texture of the film is wisecracking naturalism, but when a powerful sequence is needed to jack up the action values, a disaster is used for all the symbolic overtones that can be hit—and without any significant story meaning. I don't think the line of *Hud* is so much "controlled" as adjusted, set by conflicting aims at seriousness and success.

It hardly seems possible but perhaps Crowther thought the *cattle* were symbolically "fully and foully diseased with all the germs of materialism that are infecting and sickening modern man." Those sick cattle must have *something* to do with the language he uses in describing the film. "It is a drama of moral corruption—of the debilitating disease of avaricious self-seeking—that is creeping across the land and infecting the minds of young people in this complex, materialistic age. It is forged in the smoldering confrontation of an aging cattleman and his corrupted son." Scriptwriters have only to toss in a few bitter asides about our expense-account civilization and strew a few platitudes like, "Little by little the country changes because of the men people admire," and the movie becomes "a drama of moral corruption."

The English critics got even more out of it: Derek Prouse experienced a "catharsis" in *The Sunday Times*, as did Peter John Dyer in *Sight and Sound*. Dyer seems to react to cues from his experience at *other* movies; his review, suggesting as it does a super-fan's identification with the film makers' highest aspirations, is worth a little examination. "From the ominous discovery of the first dead heifer, to the massacre of the diseased herd, to Homer's own end and Hud's empty inheritance of a land he passively stood by and watched die, the story methodically unwinds like a python lying sated in the sun." People will be going to *Hud*, as Charles Addams was reported to have gone to *Cleopatra*, "to see the snake." Dyer squeezes out more meaning and lots more symbolism than the film makers could squeeze in. (A) Homer just suddenly up and died, of a broken heart, one supposes. It wasn't prepared for, it was merely convenient. (B) Hud's inheritance isn't empty: he has a large ranch, and the land has oil. Dyer projects the notion of Hud's emptiness as a human being onto his inheritance. (C) Hud didn't passively stand by and watch the land die. The *land* hasn't changed. Nor was Hud passive: he worked the ranch, and he certainly couldn't be held responsible for the cattle becoming infected—unless Dyer wants to go so far as to view that infection as a symbol of or a punishment for Hud's sickness. Even Homer, who blamed Hud for just about everything else, didn't accuse him of infecting the cattle. Dyer would perhaps go that far, because somehow "the aridity of the cattle-less landscape mirrors his own barren future." Why couldn't it equally mirror Homer's barren past? In this scheme of symbolic interpretation, if there was a dog on the ranch, and it had worms, Hud the worm would be the reason. Writing of the "terse and elemental polarity of the film," Dyer says, "The earth is livelihood, freedom and death to Homer; an implacably hostile prison to Hud"—though it would be just as easy, and perhaps more true to the audience's experience of the film, to interpret Hud's opportunism as love of life and Homer's righteousness as rigid and life-destroying—and *unfair*. The scriptwriters give Homer principles (which are hardly likely to move the audience); but they're careful to show that Hud is misunderstood and rejected when he makes affectionate overtures to his father.

Dyer loads meaning onto Hud's actions and behavior: for example, "Instead of bronco-busting he goes in for a (doubtless) metaphorical bout of pig-wrestling." Why "instead of"—as if there were bronco-busting to do and he dodged it—when there is nothing of the kind in the film? And what would the pig-wrestling be a metaphor for? Does Dyer take pigs to represent women, or does he mean that the pig-wrestling shows Hud's swinishness? Having watched my older brothers trying to catch greased pigs in this traditional western small-town sport, I took the sequence as an indication of how boring and empty small-town life is, and how coarse the games in which the boys work off a little steam. I had seen the same boys who wrestled greased pigs and who had fairly crude ideas of sex and sport enter a blazing building to save the lives of panic-stricken horses, and emerge charred but at peace with the world and themselves.

Are the reviewers trying to justify having enjoyed the movie, or just looking for an angle, when they interpret the illustrative details *morally?* Any number of them got their tip on Hud's character by his taking advantage of a husband's absence to go to bed with the wife. But he couldn't very well make love to her when her husband was home—although that would be par for the course of "art" movies these days. The summer nights are very long on a western ranch. As a child, I could stretch out on a hammock on the porch and read an Oz book from cover to cover while my grandparents and uncles and aunts and parents didn't stir from their card game. The young men get tired of playing cards. They either think about sex or try to do something about it. There isn't much else to do—the life doesn't exactly stimulate the imagination, though it does stimulate the senses. Dyer takes as proof of Hud's bad character that "his appetites are reserved for married women." What alternatives are there for a young man in a small town? Would it be proof of a *good* character to seduce young girls and wreck their reputations? There are always a few widows, of course, and, sometimes, a divorcee like Alma, the housekeeper. (Perhaps the first female equivalent of the "white Negro" in our films: Patricia Neal plays Alma as the original author Larry McMurtry described the Negro housekeeper, the "chuckling" Halmea with "her rich teasing laugh.") But they can hardly supply the demand from the married men, who are in a better position to give them favors, jobs, presents, houses, and even farms. I remember my father taking me along when he visited our local widow: I played in the new barn which was being constructed by workmen who seemed to take their orders from my father. At six or seven, I was very proud of my father for being the protector of widows.

I assumed the audience enjoyed and responded to Hud's chasing women because this represented a break with western movie conventions and myths, and as the film was flouting these conventions and teasing the audience to enjoy the change, it didn't occur to me that in *this* movie his activity would be construed as "bad." But Crowther finds that the way Hud "indulges himself with his neighbor's wife" is "one of the sure, unmistakable tokens of a dangerous social predator." Is this knowledge derived from the film (where I didn't discover it) or from Crowther's knowledge of life? If the latter, I can only supply evidence against him from my own life. My father who was adulterous, and a Republican who, like Hud, was opposed to any government interference, was in no sense and in no one's eyes a social predator. He was generous and kind, and democratic in the western way that Easterners still don't understand: it was not out of guilty condescension that mealtimes were communal affairs with the Mexican and Indian ranchhands joining the family, it was the way Westerners lived.

If Homer, like my father, had frequented married women or widows, would Dyer interpret that as a symbol of Homer's evil? Or, as Homer voiced sentiments dear to the scriptwriters and critics, would his "transgressions" be interpreted as a touching indication of human frailty? What Dyer and others took for symbols were the clichés of melodrama—where character traits are sorted out and separated, one set of attitudes and behavior for the good characters, another for the bad characters. In melodrama, human desires and drives make a person weak or corrupt: the heroic must be the unblemished good like Homer, whose goodness is not tainted with understanding. Reading the cues this way, these critics missed what audiences were reacting to, just as Richard Whitehall in *Films and Filming* describes Newman's Hud as "the-hair-on-the-chest-male"—although the most exposed movie chest since Valentino's is just as hairless.

I suppose we're all supposed to react on cue to movie rape (or as is usually the case, attempted rape); rape, like a cattle massacre, is a box-office value. No doubt in *Hud* we're really supposed to believe that Alma is, as Stanley Kauffmann says, "driven off by his [Hud's] vicious physical assault." But in terms of the modernity of the settings and the characters, as well as the age of the protagonists (they're at least in their middle thirties), it was more probable that Alma left the ranch because a frustrated rape is just too sordid and embarrassing for all concerned—for the drunken Hud who forced himself upon her, for her for defending herself so titanically, for young Lon the innocent who "saved" her. Alma obviously wants to go to bed with Hud, but she has been rejecting his propositions because she doesn't want to be just another casual dame to him; she wants to be treated differently from the others. If Lon hadn't rushed to protect his idealized view of her, chances are that the next morning Hud would have felt guilty and repentant, and Alma would have been grateful to him for having used the violence necessary to break down her resistance, thus proving that she *was* different. They might have been celebrating ritual rapes annually on their anniversaries.

Rape is a strong word when a man knows that a woman wants him but won't accept him unless he commits himself emotionally. Alma's mixture of provocative camaraderie plus reservations invites "rape." (Just as, in a different way, Blanche DuBois did—though Williams erred in having her go mad: it was enough, it was really *more,* that she was broken, finished.) The scriptwriters for *Hud,* who, I daresay, are as familiar as critics with theories of melodrama, know that heroes and villains both want the same things and that it is their way of trying to get them that separates one from the other. They impart this knowledge to Alma, who tells Hud that she wanted him and he could have had her if he'd gone about it differently. But this kind of know-ingness, employed to make the script more clever, more frank, more modern, puts a strain on the credibility of the melodramatic actions it explicates—and embellishes. Similarly, the writers invite a laugh by having Alma, seeing the nudes Lon has on his wall, say, "I'm a girl, they don't do a thing for me." Before the Kinsey report on women, a woman might say, "They don't do a thing for me," but she wouldn't have prefaced it with "I'm a girl" because she wouldn't have known that erotic reactions to pictures are not characteristic of women.

The Ravetches have been highly praised for the screenplay: Penelope Gilliatt considers it "American writing at its abrasive best"; Brendan Gill says it is "honestly written"; *Time* calls it "a no-compromise script." Dyer expresses a fairly general view when he says it's "on a level of sophistication totally unexpected from their scripts for two of Ritt's least successful, Faulkner-inspired films." This has some special irony because not only is their technique in *Hud* a continuation of the episodic method they used in combining disparate Faulkner stories into *The Long Hot Summer,* but the dialogue quoted most appreciatively by the reviewers to illustrate their new skill (Alma's rebuff of Hud, "No thanks, I've had one cold-hearted bastard in my life, I don't want another") is lifted almost verbatim from that earlier script (when it was Joanne Woodward telling off Paul Newman). They didn't get acclaim for their integrity and honesty that time because, although the movie was entertaining and a box-office hit, the material was resolved as a jolly comedy, the actors and actresses were paired off, and Newman as Ben Quick the barn burner turned out not really to be a barn burner after all. They hadn't yet found the "courage" that keeps Hud what *Time* called him, "an unregenerate heel" and "a cad to the end." It may have taken them several years to learn that with enough close-ups of his blue, blue eyes and his hurt, sensitive mouth, Newman's Ben Quick could have burned barns all right, and audiences would have loved him more for it.

In neither film do the episodes and characters hold together, but Ritt, in the interim having made Hemingway's *Adventures of a Young Man* and failed to find a style appropriate to it, has now, with the aid of James Wong Howe's black and white cinematography, found something like a reasonably clean visual equivalent for Hemingway's prose. Visually *Hud* is so apparently simple and precise and unadorned, so skeletonic, that we may admire the bones without being quite sure of the name of the beast. This Westerner is part gangster, part *Champion*, part rebel-without-a-cause, part the traditional cynic-hero who pretends not to care because he cares so much. (And it is also part *Edge of the City*, at least the part about Hud's having accidentally killed his brother and Homer's blaming him for it. Ritt has plagiarized his first film in true hack style: the episode was integral in *Edge of the City* and the friendship of Cassavetes and Poitier—probably the most beautiful scenes Ritt has directed—drew meaning from it; in *Hud* it's a fancy "traumatic" substitute for explaining why Hud and Homer don't get along.)

When *Time* says *Hud* is "the most brazenly honest picture to be made in the U.S. this season" the key word is brazenly. The film brazens it out. In the *New Yorker* Brendan Gill writes, "It's an attractive irony of the situation that, despite the integrity of its makers, *Hud* is bound to prove a box-office smash. I find this coincidence gratifying. Virtue is said to be its own reward, but money is nice, too, and I'm always pleased to see it flowing toward people who have had other things on their minds." Believing in this coincidence is like believing in Santa Claus. Gill's last sentence lacks another final "too." In Hollywood, a "picture with integrity" is a moneymaking message picture. And that's what Crowther means when he says, "*Hud* is a film that does its makers, the medium and Hollywood proud." He means something similar when he calls his own praise of the film a "daring endorsement"—as if it placed him in some kind of jeopardy to be so forthright.

If most of the critics who acclaimed the film appeared as innocent as Lon and as moralistic as Homer, Dwight Macdonald, who perceived that "it is poor Hud who is forced by the script to openly practice the actual as against the mythical American Way of Life," regarded this perception as proof of the stupidity of the film.

But the movie wouldn't necessarily be a good movie if its moral message was dramatically sustained in the story and action, and perhaps it isn't necessarily a bad movie if its moral message is not sustained in the story and action. By all formal theories, a work that is split cannot be a work of art, but leaving the validity of these principles aside, do they hold for lesser works—not works of art but works of commerce and craftsmanship, sometimes fused by artistry? Is a commercial piece of entertainment (which may or may not aspire to be, or pretend to be, a work of art) necessarily a poor one if its material is confused or duplicit, or reveals elements at variance with its stated theme, or shows the divided intentions of the craftsmen who made it? My answer is no, that in some films the more ambivalence that comes through, the more the film may mean to us or the more fun it may be. The process by which an idea for a movie is turned into the product that reaches us is so involved, and so many compromises, cuts, and changes may have taken place, so much hope and disgust and spoilage and waste may be embodied in it or mummified in it, that the tension in the product, or some sense of urgency still left in it, may be our only contact with the life in which the product was processed. Commercial products in which we do not sense or experience divided hopes and aims and ideas may be the dullest—ones in which everything alive was processed out, or perhaps ones that were never alive even at the beginning. *Hud* is so astutely made and yet such a mess that it tells us much more than its message. It is redeemed by its fundamental dishonesty. It is perhaps an archetypal Hollywood movie: split in so many revealing ways that, like *On the Waterfront* or *From Here to Eternity,* it is the movie of its year (even though it's shallow and not nearly so good a film as either of them).

My friends were angry that I'd sent them to *Hud* because, like Macdonald, they "saw through it," they saw that Hud was not the villain, and they knew that though he expressed vulgar notions that offended *them,* these notions might not be unpopular. The film itself flirts with this realization: when Homer is berating Hud, Lon asks, "Why pick on Hud, Grandpa? Nearly everybody around town is like him."

My friends, more or less socialist, detest a crude Hud who doesn't believe in government interference because they believe in more, and more drastic, government action to integrate the schools and end discrimination in housing and employment. However, they are so anti-CIA that at Thanksgiving dinner a respected professor could drunkenly insist that he had positive proof that the CIA had engineered the murder of Kennedy with no voice but mine raised in doubt. They want centralized power when it works for their civil-libertarian aims, but they dread and fear its international policies. They hate cops but call them at the first hint of a prowler: they are split, and it shows in a million ways. I imagine they're very like the people who made *Hud,* and like them they do rather well for themselves. They're so careful to play the game at their jobs that if they hadn't told you that they're *really* screwing the system, you'd never guess it.

From

Shane and *Hud:*
Two Stories in Search of a Medium

JAMES K. FOLSOM

The different treatments of the same story in the novel *Horseman, Pass By* and the film *Hud* . . . show clearly the difficulty of translating the "mood" of a work of fiction into film and the necessity imposed by a visual medium of having characters act as visible foils to each other. . . . *Horseman, Pass By* . . . is remembered in retrospect through the eyes of Lonnie, its now older boyhood observer, who reflects upon the significance of a series of events that had happened on the ranch of his grandfather, Homer Bannon. Homer, a man past eighty years old, his wife, and Hud, her son by a former marriage, live on a ranch in Texas together with Lonnie and Halmea, the black cook and housekeeper. At the beginning of the novel a dead heifer has been discovered that turns out to be a victim of hoof-and-mouth disease. Homer's cattle must all be destroyed in order to halt the spread of the disease, and the reactions of the characters in the novel to the worst disaster which can strike a cattleman form both the conflict in the novel's plot and the catalyst for Lonnie's transition to adulthood.

In a sense the differences between the two treatments of the story are indicated by the change in title from *Horseman, Pass By* to *Hud*. Specifically, of course, the novel's title is a direct reference to the self-epitaph with which Yeats concludes his poem "Under Ben Bulben"—an epitaph also fitting to Homer Bannon. The title is generally relevant too, especially to the fifth section of "Under Ben Bulben," in which Yeats exhorts the Irish poets to celebrate native Irish themes rather than conventionally genteel ones, and more specifically, "well made" themes of "other days," of "heroic centuries" now past. Something like this feeling is basic to the thematic structure of *Horseman, Pass By,* which is, as a recent critic perceptively points out, a historic study of "the evolution of the Southwest . . . embodied in . . . three central characters," all of whom turn out to be different aspects of the "single image of the cowboy"[1]—a figure which itself exists in an uncomfortable and inconsistent world composed partly of myth and partly of reality. The point is nicely emphasized through the name of the town near which the Bannon ranch is located and where much of the novel's action takes place. For the town is named "Thalia" after the Greek muse of history and epic poetry.

This ambiguity inherent in the nature of "the West"—that part of the American experience that we like, conventionally at least, to think of as having epic potentialities—has been seen by many of the critics of the West as one important reason for the failure of Western themes to produce a literature of epic proportions. The West, it is alleged, is simply too close to us in historic terms to be viewed from what is conventionally considered to be an epic perspective; the prosaic reality of the cowboy's life intrudes involuntarily upon the mythic grandeur of the epic story. Whether this objection is ultimately true is beside the point here, but it does point up one factor in the "epic of the West" of which McMurtry is cognizant and of which in *Horseman, Pass By* he makes considerable esthetic use. For, to oversimplify, the adult world toward which Lonnie yearns at the beginning of the story he conceives in essentially heroic terms, a perspective that his experience ultimately teaches him is a false and childish one. Neither Hud nor Homer, however each may appear to the childhood observer, is wholly a walking embodiment of mythical characteristics. Both are characters of flesh and blood, with problems conceived of in human rather than epic terms.

The film's difference from the novel, to return, is nicely exemplified by the change in title. For the motion picture concerns itself with Hud in a way the novel does not, Hud becoming if not the film's moral hero very definitely its focal character. Again the film has had to make specific the various generalized aspects of the novel's "single image" of the cowboy and to present them in terms of direct foils. Hence the values that in the novel are scattered among a number of characters, in the film are polarized between Hud and Homer Bannon, both of whom come to represent two distinct and mutually exclusive models for adult life. Rather than having a general view of the adult world as presented retrospectively through a number of characters, the film Lonnie must make a specific choice between two models who are conceived of as being directly opposed to one another. Though at the beginning Hud seems to Lonnie more attractive, by the end of the film Homer has replaced him as the desirable model.

This overly schematic analysis of *Hud* may give the quite erroneous impression that it is less subtle than *Horseman, Pass By.* Such is most emphatically not the case. The difference is rather that in the film subtlety is expressed through the nuances of conflict between the two major characters, Hud and Homer, while in the novel subtlety is expressed through proliferation of characters and . . . through the retrospective musings of Lonnie himself upon the meaning of his own experience.

Horseman, Pass By is quite consciously conceived of as a mood piece, and McMurtry does a brilliantly effective job of presenting, through Lonnie's thoughts, the inchoate but very real yearnings of adolescence for something, it knows not what. In *Horseman, Pass By,* then, Lonnie's adolescent perspective may effectively be presented in terms of his yearnings for some kind of escape from the world in which he finds himself.

Although it is immediately clear what Lonnie wishes to escape *from,* it is not at all evident exactly what he wishes to escape *to;* nor in fact does he himself know. He expresses his yearnings in terms of sex and travel, two generalized metaphors which he sees embodied respectively in the figures of the cook Halmea and Jesse, one of the ranch hands. Quite the opposite is true of the symbolic pattern of *Hud,* in which, if only because we must see both Homer and Hud, we understand very clearly what Lonnie is drawn *toward,* and not so clearly what exactly he is reacting *against.* The respective endings of novel and film emphasize the point: for while the metaphor of the novel is of escape, that of the film becomes exile.

Again, the very real difference between the two versions of the story may best be seen by analysing some of the changes from the novel made in the film. First of all is the fact that Halmea is changed in *Hud* from a black to a white woman, and Hud's rape of her, successful in *Horseman, Pass By,* is abortive in the film. Though this change

originally may well have been prompted by non-esthetic consider-
ations, it is nevertheless an effective one. The rape of Halmea in the
novel is accomplished by Hud while Lonnie, who loves her, stands
passively by. Though thematically this may make good sense, it is
impossible to visualize except upon the screen of retrospective memory. In the novel Lonnie can tell us that this is what happened, without
further explanation, and we accept his statement, though not without
some mental reservations. But when the scene is actually presented to
us we withhold our assent. When we must actually see the scene
rather than having it reported to us, the basic improbability of the
action becomes evident.

A more important change in the film is in the development of Hud's
character. In the novel Hud's attractiveness to Lonnie as an image of
successful sexuality is not really insisted upon until the rape of
Halmea, while in the film this aspect of Hud's character is emphasized from the beginning. Early in *Hud* Lonnie is seen searching for
Hud, whom he finds in the house of a married woman whose husband
is away. The adolescent devil-may-care attractiveness of Hud to Lonnie is clear in this scene, which stands in clear symbolic contrast to
the unattractive aspect of the same side of Hud as presented through
the attempted rape of Halmea. In *Horseman, Pass By* the contrast can
be, and is, more abstracted.

The necessity in the film to place Hud and Homer Bannon in
direct contrast issues in one other really major change, the almost
total omission of Jesse, the ranch hand. In *Hud* Jesse's role is reduced
to that of a walk-on part, while in *Horseman, Pass By* he is a major
character.

The reason behind the change is again visual. In the novel both Hud
and Jesse act as direct comparisons to Homer. Hud's morality is
placed in specific contrast to Homer's, in both novel and film, in terms
of the two men's different reactions to the discovery of hoof-and-
mouth disease in their cattle. After the initial shock has worn off,
Homer realizes that the only moral choice open to him is to have his
cattle slaughtered, and he accepts the necessity for the destruction of
his entire herd. Hud, in contrast, proposes to Homer that they sell the
cattle before the disease is diagnosed and the herd quarantined. If
someone is "stupid enough to buy" the cattle, Hud sees no objection to
selling them. In short, *caveat emptor*. "That ain't no way to get out of a
tight," Homer says, and refuses.[2]

Jesse, in contrast, acts as a foil to Homer in terms of the theme of
escape. For he has been everywhere, Lonnie thinks, and Lonnie's own
yearnings for distant places are gratified by listening to Jesse talk of

his experiences "on the rodeo circuit." "Just hearing the names," Lonnie says, "was enough to make me restless."

Hud eliminates the theme of Lonnie's yearning for escape that is central to *Horseman, Pass By,* and therefore of necessity decreases Jesse's significance and eliminates the minor subplot of the Thalia rodeo and Jesse's failure to perform creditably at it. The need inherent in a visual medium to establish an explicit polarity between Hud and Homer is again the explanation. While in the novel both Hud and Jesse may act as contrasts to different aspects of Homer, in the film the distinction between Hud and Jesse must inevitably be blurred because of the fact that since Homer must be visualized as a person they must be seen in contrast to all of him rather than to specifically differentiated qualities of his character. Therefore Hud and Jesse, had they remained of equal importance in the film, would inevitably have become redundant rather than complements to each other. The difference between them, in short, which is of basic importance to the novel, would have appeared less striking on the screen than their overpowering similarity in terms of their not being Homer.

This point is perhaps best illustrated by a scene from the novel that was carried into the film almost intact. In both *Hud* and *Horseman, Pass By,* Homer keeps on his ranch three longhorn cattle in addition to his beef herd as a reminder of the old days. "Cattle like them make me feel like I'm in the cattle business," he says. These three longhorns must be destroyed with the rest of the herd, since they too are presumably infected with hoof-and-mouth disease.

In the novel, when the longhorns are being rounded up Jesse suggests to Homer that he let them go. "If the government wants 'em, let the government go find 'em," he says. Homer brushes off the suggestion by saying, "I don't know what to think yet"; but when the diagnosis of hoof-and-mouth disease is confirmed he has these cattle killed along with the others. In the film, significantly, the suggestion to Homer is made not by Jesse but by Lonnie, and his remark to his grandfather that the longhorns ought to be let go is very clearly reminiscent of Hud, who has made almost exactly the same suggestion about how best to get rid of the infected herd. Again, the film has concentrated its effect rather than spreading it out over a number of characters, since visually the most important thing is not which particular character makes the suggestion but that the suggestion itself is one totally antithetical to Homer's own values. In the film Lonnie has received a direct lesson in terms of two diametrically opposed characters; in the novel, by contrast, the same opposition can be expressed without redundance by more than one character, if only because each character, if not seen, is visualized by the reader as representative of a more or less isolated point of view rather than as a person of flesh and blood, someone who stands in opposition to relatively specific qualities in Homer Bannon rather than to his entire character.

This necessity to condense all the foils to Homer in the character of Hud inevitably implies the one major change between novel and film—a total reversal of the ending. Lonnie learns, through the action of *Horseman, Pass By,* the futility of his own generalized longings for escape. The world, he discovers, when viewed with, in Yeats's phrase, "a cold eye," is not the romantic place he had thought it was at the beginning of the novel. Captive at the beginning of the story of the common adolescent belief that somewhere there must be more "life" than there is in one's own environment, Lonnie learns the truth symbolized by the name of the town—Thalia—where the story's action has taken place: that the stuff of life and history and epic poetry may be discovered in one's own surroundings if one has the intelligence to know where to look for it.

In the novel, then, Lonnie's education culminates in his acceptance of the world for what it is and his rejection of the unreal attitudes toward it he had held at the beginning of the story. In the novel's final scene, after Homer's death, Lonnie hitches a ride on a truck to visit a friend injured in the Thalia rodeo and taken to the hospital at Wichita Falls. For a while, Lonnie says, "I was tempted to do like Jesse once said: to lean back and let the truck take me as far as it was going." But his newly achieved maturity enables him to reject this temptation, and he decides to stop at Wichita Falls, see his friend, and then return to Thalia.

In *Hud* the ending is quite different. Here, Lonnie's newly won maturity has taught him not to accept the world as it is, but rather to see the validity of Homer's attitude toward life and to reject the tempting but ultimately immoral standpoint represented by Hud. Lonnie has, therefore, no choice but to leave the world dominated by Hud that the Bannon ranch has become after Homer's death; and so at the end of the film he sets out to make his own way in the great world he has rejected in the novel. While the ending of *Horseman, Pass By* showed Lonnie's new maturity by emphasizing his realization of the flimsiness of his adolescent longings for escape, the ending of *Hud* shows it in terms of his symbolic acceptance of Homer's attitude toward the world and his rejection of Hud's.

The major differences between the stories of Shane and Hud as they are presented on film or on the printed page are largely implicit in the very different points of view required by the two media. The primacy of vision in the film, though perhaps an obvious point, cannot be too strongly insisted upon. It results first of all in the necessity for an almost complete denial of both the retrospective mood and the nostalgic point of view upon which the fictional versions of both stories heavily rely. The internalization of the fictional point of view implied by the reminiscences of an older hero reflecting upon his past is simply impossible to achieve with either success or consistency upon film for two reasons: first of all, the narrator of the novel must inevitably become one among many characters in the film; and secondly, the action of the story when seen must be seen as occurring in the present.[3]

An equally important, and less obvious, difference between novel and film also follows from the primacy of vision implied by the latter. For although the phrase "cast of thousands" has become a cliché for describing the so-called "epic" film, in fact the necessity for externalization implicit in the film results in an overwhelming tendency to simplify by reducing the number of characters. Most of the cast of thousands are background characters whose function is analogous to the consciously generalized mood-painting used by the novelist as a way of establishing his setting.

For all their specific differences, however, both media have in common one basic attitude toward their material—an attitude that has been present in Americans' treatment of their epic since the West was first assumed to be the most significant factor in the American experience and the unique part of that experience which set it off from other lands and other peoples. This attitude comes ultimately from an environmentalist belief, inherent in primitivism, that man reflects in moral terms the physical nature of his environment. This belief, which is in fact nothing more than an assumption, is treated as though it were axiomatic for interpreting the materials of the great American epic. Whether, as with Natty Bumppo, the American hero directly reflects the glory of his environment or, as with Emerson's strictures upon New Hampshire, the comment that "The God who made New Hampshire/ Taunted the lofty land/With little men" is ironic,[4] the importance of the analogy is never doubted. And the Western film has absorbed this analogical comparison between man and his environment. In the film, Shane has picked up, along with his other attributes, the quality of a mountain spirit, representative of the brooding grandeur of the Grand Tetons against which he is filmed, an analogy specifically evoked by the mountain man's buckskin shirt he wears and by the theme song of the film, "The Call of the Faraway Hills." In *Hud* the analogue is more ironic, but the bleak Texas landscape, the stark ranchhouse on the

Bannon ranch, and the ugly town of Thalia make much the same symbolic point: for Hud expresses them exactly as Shane reflects the mountains.

The great problem, then, shared by both the Western film and Western fiction is the problem of presenting man against the landscape. What is the landscape, first of all: the beauty of the Grand Tetons or the ugliness of the Bannon ranch? And how does man stand against it: does he stand *for* it, symbolizing in detail what it expresses in general? or does he stand *in contrast to* it, repudiating everything it represents? There are of course no simple answers to these questions, all expressions of a basic ambiguity in the American identity; no answers, that is, except for the statement of the metaphorical problem and of its ritual solution.

NOTES

1. Thomas Landess, *Larry McMurtry* (Austin, Texas: Steck-Vaughn Company, 1969), pp. 10, 14. Landess's study of McMurtry is generally excellent, though his interpretation of certain aspects of *Horseman, Pass By*—notably the ending—differs from my own.

2. *Horseman, Pass By* (New York: Harper & Brothers, 1961). All further references are to this edition.

3. This is true, I think, even of films—unlike these two—that use technical variations of the flashback as ways of insisting upon a film's action having happened in the past. Such action, even when we are assured by such violations of point of view that it did actually happen in the past, nonetheless seems to me to be happening in the present.

4. "Ode Inscribed to W. H. Channing," II. 24–26.

The Last Picture Show: A Concurring Opinion

ISIDORE SILVER

Undoubtedly—and perhaps rather quickly—a bevy of "revisionist" critics will arise to honor or assail Peter Bogdanovich. No motion picture receiving the initial, unanimous and enthusiastic acclaim of *The Last Picture Show* can long be immunized from skeptical second assessments. The nature of both Art and its choleric commentators make such reappraisal inevitable. Before the battlelines crystallize, however, a modest disclaimer entered in the form of a concurring opinion, as we lawyers say, might be in order. Such an opinion would acknowledge that the movie is, indeed, an impressive work of art; it would also recognize that, at its core, it perpetuates the hoary American myth that the "Old" West was a golden age, an Eden from which we have expelled ourselves and to which we must return to cure our wounded collective psyche. One staking out the middle ground might also be tempted to conclude that the myth, though generally held under tight control, ultimately flaws the Art.

In general, the Art is remarkable. The petrifaction of Anarene, Texas is brilliantly caught by the camera eye of a Martian who fortuitously landed there twenty years ago (or twenty years from now, or two hundred years—does it make any difference?). The ossification of the people, in their relationships, in their faces, is mercilessly caught and held by the innumerable close-ups which depict each character's loneliness and isolation. Bogdanovich does achieve the remarkable feat of managing to sequester each individual within a closed space by distancing him from every other person, even in group scenes. Even the physical violence seems distant and remote, mere slight intrusions into each cell of isolation, from the characters as well as the audience. Indeed, the violence in the film, when it does occur, is strangely muted, almost laconic. After Sonny is slashed in the eye by a beer bottle, we are surprised to find that only a slight scar remains after the patch is removed. The wounds are clearly inner ones, although the scene itself leads one to believe that there will be nothing less than total disfigurement or even removal of the eye.

Because of the constant background of space which operates to create a vacuum between characters, even conversations float off into a void and are never so much completed as lost. Bogdanovich fills the space not with the noises of life but with the mechanical roars and gasps of broken-down trucks and other inhuman junk. One has the eerie feeling that when all of us have expired the only thing left will be a cacophony of grunts, the wheezes of machines which are taking longer to die and which will die with more protest.

The space of the film is also filled by the vitality (artificial though it be) *within* the movies intermittently flashed on the screen of the decaying Anarene theater. Spencer Tracy embracing Elizabeth Taylor in *Father of the Bride* is an aching and poignant reminder (to us) of what family life could be—and a devastating counterpoint to the boredom and aimlessness of the Anarene audience over which it flickers. Watching Tracy, the Sam the Lion of our fantasy lives, we almost shout out—"Come on Peter, it's too easy." Since Bogdanovich is addressing the over-thirties generation, his choice of Tracy and the young Taylor (today she is a different person) is like shooting emotional ducks in a barrel. The counterpoint—between not only Anarene and the vitality of the old movie, but also between us and the art form—is heightened by those few seconds of *Red River* at the end. Bogdanovich here does more than pay tribute to Howard Hawks and John Wayne (about which more later): he captures the exuberance— the possibilities—of Man himself. Those quick cuts in *Red River*—in such contrast to the almost stately framing of *The Last Picture Show* itself—of men screaming "yip" on the cattle run are immediately played off against the stillness of the audience itself, the stillness of death (or its equivalent, life suspended). And if we are inclined to laugh at the ludicrousness of Wayne's cry, "Let's go to Montana," we are quickly caught short by our knowledge that this dreadful cliché is better than the blank silence of the Anarene movie house. Interestingly, the novel of *The Last Picture Show* is less symbolic: the last movie is an old Audie Murphy Western clinker and McMurtry laconically notes that it wasn't *Red River*.

Inevitably, the bits and pieces of old movies (a distinctly subordinate theme of the McMurtry novel) raise the question of sentimentality. The sentimentality lies in Bogdanovich's belief that the Old West was the repository of a unique American character. He honestly thinks that Howard Hawks and John Wayne are right. Since *The Last Picture Show* is not a political tract, and since Bogdanovich gives no indication of any facile assumption that we can recreate that character, I shall not dwell on what some may see as a neo-fascist, or at least callous conservative, tinge. As an artist, Bogdanovich is evidently not concerned with the contemporary implications of rugged individualism. The picture is not as fundamentally undemocratic as is, for instance, *High Noon*—with its lone, brave hero contrasted to an effete and cowardly citizenry—and cannot be judged as if it were a Stanley Kramer or Carl Foreman epic. Indeed, Bogdanovich has no room for Political Man on his barren landscape.

The thematic analysis must commence with Sam the Lion, the appropriately named last survivor of the Old West. As played by Ben Johnson (another Hawks tribute) Sam is the moral cement that, increasingly failingly, holds the community together. Sam is the tie to the past—the past of human decency, hope, and vitality—and when he dies, everything becomes unglued. All sense of community vanishes, the violence so latent in many of the relationships escalates precipitately (though, as we have seen, without great harm), and the only hope for Sonny becomes a retreat into the self. In a world where giants have trodden, Bogdanovich tells us, the only possibility is personal growth (along with the limited and obviously temporary hopes of one to one intimacy).

Ben Johnson has become a sort of apolitical John Wayne and his casting here resembles—and recapitulates—his use by Sam Peckinpah in *The Wild Bunch*. Bogdanovich adds the extra tribute of a brief shot of a poster advertising *The Wagon Master,* a picture, the cultist will note, featuring none other than Ben Johnson. The Johnson character symbolizes both the toughness and the tenderness, the wisdom and the compassion of that timeless relic of the American screen, the cowboy. Yet, surely, the myth of the Old West, while durable aesthetically, has been proven to be somewhat less than grandiose, historically, and, in contemporary times, has given us Lyndon Johnson and John Connally.

If *The Last Picture Show* had merely made the point that an era of rugged individualism had died, to be replaced by a bloodless, frustrated anomic suburban America (the true theme of the movie is not just the death of a small town but its increasing suburbanization), then it could only be faulted for redundancy. The theme would be more provocative here than it was in such movies as *The Wild Bunch, The Ballad of Cable Hogue, Hud* (also a McMurtry creation) and, perhaps the best of all, *Lonely Are the Brave*. But, Bogdanovich is striving for something more. The key line in the picture is given to the old woman who has taken over the management of the movie house from Sam the Lion after his death, when she explains her decision to close down the theater. After attributing that decision to changing times, including the advent of television, she muses, "If Sam had lived, I believe we could have kept it going. But me and Jimmy just didn't have the know-how" (the line, incidentally, is taken directly from the novel). Is a return to Eden possible? Is our civilization and its technology not necessarily inevitable? Can we rouse ourselves from our torpor and make one more effort of will? Although the picture quickly retreats from this exposed position, there is a lingering wistfulness which neither the movie nor audience can completely shake.

Bogdanovich's belief in the myth is enhanced by the contrasts between the middle-aged and the young on the one hand and the elderly, on the other. Sam the Lion is not the only "honest" character in the film. There are those anonymous town elders who jeer Sonny and Duane for their inability to tackle during the high school football games. Although the sure directorial hand of the film falters in these sequences—there were at least four forced, allegedly "humorous" references to "tackling" in about two minutes—that is not the main problem. Obviously, the elders have seen and know "real" football, the bone-crushing kind, while the youngsters are unable to make the kind of commitment, both emotional and physical, to the violence required by the sport. They are afraid to use their bodies, to test their bodies, to risk their bodies. Although some of the elders are later depicted as being cruelly oblivious to the death of the dumb boy, Billy, that is readily attributable to the increasing callousness of life in general, and in no way detracts from their characterization as being more aware of life.

The mythical treatment of the death of small-town America creates one more aesthetic problem. Except for the prevalence of the myth itself and the accents of the characters, there is nothing specifically "Texan" about the decline. The depicted frustrations and unfulfillment become characteristic of *all* of middle-America. Perhaps Anarene, Texas is as dreary as Winesburg, Ohio, but surely there must be some differences. Small-town America did die, but not all at once at a particular time. Surely, the circumstances of the demise must have varied by region, if not by town. The nationalization of American culture, abetted as it was first by radio and then (at an accelerated pace) by television, could not have had the same, simultaneous results everywhere. The failure to particularize, or rather the reliance on the myth to create particularity, makes the movie less than a completely satisfying aesthetic experience.

Of course, this discussion has omitted certain cultural questions such as whether small-town life was *always* boring, or at best, boring and violent. Perhaps the migration of American youth to the cities (let us forget the suburbs for a moment) was, on the whole, a more satisfying life experience for the migrants than remaining behind was for the others like Sonny. Would it be too heretical to suggest that even those who left *before* the advent of television led happier lives than did their settled brethren? Perhaps the advantages of "civilization" on balance outweigh the banalities and cruelties of small-town life (after all, *Winesburg* was written long before television and the Korean war)? That other master of the "dying West" genre—Peckinpah—is more ambiguous about these questions. On the whole, I have tried to judge *The Last Picture Show* on its own terms and to put aside these troublesome questions (although, doubtlessly, the latter influenced the former).

On its own terms, then, the movie is flawed, but still remains an impressive artistic achievement. When the inevitable "revision" occurs, when (perhaps) *Targets*, Bogdanovich's first full-length movie, is compared to his second—and (perhaps) found to be more valuable—it would be wise to keep in mind that both extremes may be wrong. If we who "wish to keep our heads while all about us are losing theirs" savor the virtues of a fine, though not seminal work of Art, for its own considerable merits, that will be an accomplishment indeed, especially when the winds of debate start to churn.

Leavin' McMurtry

LARRY L. KING

A little over a year ago the movie folk came to Texas—to Bastrop—to film Larry McMurtry's *Leaving Cheyenne*, which remains my favorite among that good writing man's novels of the old home state. *Life* magazine offered me money to write what I saw of Tinseltown's efforts to capture McMurtry's Texas on film. Perhaps foolishly, I took it.

About a month later, while I was accomplishing some real serious mid-afternoon research over beer at Scholz's in Austin, a New York lawyer tracked me down to report a death in the family: *Life,* as of two hours earlier, had expired. But to assuage my grief, I could keep the money.

I also kept my notes and memories against the day when *Molly, Gid, and Johnny*—the shooting title—might be loosed upon an unsuspecting world. Well, neighbors, it soon will be, under the title *Lovin' Molly* (which won out, at the final gun, over *The Wild and The Sweet*) and unless you are careful you soon may find yourself trapped with it in some Texas theater. Should you find more than a modicum of true Texas in the film—excluding John Henry Faulk's bit role—why, then, I'll buy you a two-dollar play purty. *Lovin' Molly* has no sense of Time or Place: a curious development, indeed, when you consider that Larry McMurtry's writing strength derives from evoking Time-and-Place about as well as you will find it done this side of Faulkner.

McMurtry writes of a real and human Texas. It is that part I know best—"my blood's country and my heart's pastureland," he puts it—where the land is flat, the people narrow, and their small, pinched lives beyond even Hollywood redemptions. Tales of "legendary" Texas, blessedly, are not McMurtry's cup of Pearl: not for him blazing six-guns, noble Pioneers taming the land by killing Indians, granite-jawed sons of the Alamo, the excesses of the Big Oil New Rich—all those characters and situations which long ago passed across the great divide of willing suspension of disbelief to take firm root in Cliché Land.

What I like about McMurtry is that he sees those hypocrisies, attritions, perversions, and absurdities common to the universal human condition and then isn't afraid to admit, in print, that they exist even in Texas Our Texas. Not all "Texas writers" are entirely bold in telling truths on the home-folks, a condition reflecting our Boosterism Heritage, traditional Yahoo-ism, and dogged, unnatural institutional and family pressures to conform: to put a good face on all things Texas and Texan and to unite against critics from within or without.

Introspection has never been highly prized in the land of my birth, or hard looks at why we operate as we do or feel as we feel. For too many years writing was considered "woman's work" by most Texans and still is by some.

Our writing antecedents, including the revered J. Frank Dobie, too often hurrahed or gung-hoed and looked away from painful truths. Younger "Texas writers" are more honest than their elders. McMurtry, now a doddering 38, got in the truth-telling business early: *Leaving Cheyenne* was written at a precocious 23. He knows more truths now than he knew then, and has recently said of the book that it often seems to him the gropings of a somewhat dreamy very young man. Still: it's a fine job; it rings true in the basics.

Not that I never quarrel with McMurtry. He sometimes harbors a touch too much romanticism, especially in his early work. His women strike me as a bit much, too heroic and long-suffering and strong. Too *good*. He sees 'em tough, but seldom does he see 'em mean. And Texas probably has as many mean, bitchy, neurotic women as any place on earth, with the possible exception of Manhattan; there, of course, they've gathered from all points of the compass, while our own crop is largely homegrown. McMurtry recognizes their ability to fight back, to survive in tough country, and knows that Texas women may often be stronger than their men. But I think he misses the extent to which large numbers purely enjoy wrecking and plundering and flashing their stingers.

And in *The Last Picture Show*, it's my feeling that McMurtry too gently judges what a small town would tolerate should word get around that a high school kid was regularly diddling the coach's wife—especially in the 1950s. There are just too many busy bodies and bored avengers to permit anything short of catastrophe in retribution. I believe one—or several—bad things would have happened: the coach would have been fired, his wife would have been chased out of town, and the cuckolded would have killed (1) the student and/or (2) the wife.

But no matter. McMurtry writes of Texas and Texans as well, or better, than anyone and with a rare honest bite. If I green with envy at the thought of a fellow-author's Texas book, it's McMurtry's *In a Narrow Grave: Essays on Texas*. That high standard will last awhile. So he is a favorite with me, and I am saddened and angry when—as in *Lovin' Molly*—I find him foully used. Let us fade, now, into the recent past—back to Austin and Bastrop, in November and December, 1972—to discover how professional film folks could have so botched and perverted McMurtry's Texas.

THE REGIONALIST IMPERATIVE

Arriving at Austin's Chariot Inn, I found the film company from technicians to Biggies—Director Sid Lumet, "Stars" Tony Perkins, Beau Bridges, Blythe Danner, Edward Binnes—understandably torpid in their enthusiasms toward the local culinary arts. Like starving Prisoners of War, they sat over their burned steaks or soggy tacos dreaming of the ideal: bagels and lox, frog's legs provencale paysanne, duckling a l'orange with wild rice, vichyssoise. When one of their number, fresh off the airplane from New York, recounted his recent dinner—artichokes Juan-les-Pins, soup aux Choux paysanne, caviar and cucumber aspic and, maybe, candied Yak's rump or salt-pickled hummingbird tongue—much of his audience cheered; others wept into their neglected barbecue.

The scene offered my first clue to the immediate future. "Billie Lee"—I said to writer William Brammer—"do you reckon people who don't appreciate chicken-fried steak with cream gravy can do justice to McMurtry on film?"

"Naw," he said. "No way. I bet they don't even drink Dr. Pepper."

I kept that in mind when Producer Steve Friedman offered the opportunity to invest a few thousand in his upcoming production.

Leaving Cheyenne is a triangular love story spanning 40 years, set in Wichita Falls country with side excursions to Fort Worth's old North Side bars and smelly cattle pens and to the Panhandle's taller points. It is a story of small ranchers and their evolutions forward from the 1920s. You get this bleak sense of landscape, of drought and semi-arid soil, of prayers sent to high, dry skies pleading for enough rain that the cattle won't finish skinny at market time. True, the family patriarch disturbs his only son, Gid Fry (Tony Perkins), by diversifying with a little wheat. What McMurtry is telling us is that even in 1925 *some* Texans knew that cattle wouldn't make it forever, that the last Big Herd had passed, that one day irrigated farming and perhaps even oil wells would come. But he obviously intended a yarn of cattle country and of the last stubborn independent men in it; he well-clued the reader that his people wore coiled hats, boots, jeans, and retained a certain fierce saddleback pride.

So director Sid Lumet trots everybody out in clod-hoppers and bib-overalls; they plant and reap as if in the best bottomlands of the rich Mississippi Delta.

First day on location I said to Producer-Screen Writer Friedman: "Jesus, Steve, what's all this sowing-and-reaping shit about?" He didn't understand the question. I said, "Look, you've got scenes bustin' wild broncs, shippin' cattle, birthin' calves. And folks just didn't *do* those

things, back then, while rigged out in Li'l Abner overalls. Texans—
especially North and West—surrendered most reluctantly to the
plow. Up there in cowboy country, people simply wouldn't have gone
around 50 years ago dressed like Arkies on the way to pick prunes in
California."

"So?"

"So, goddamn it, there was a beginning *shame* to farming up there.
It wasn't considered quite . . . manly. It broke with tradition. And if
anything would make them uneasy, it would be cracking tradition.
They would have—and did—cling to their cattleman's garb."

"Yeah?"

"Yeah! See Steve, the difference between ranching and farming
is . . . well, hell . . . between riding, I guess, and walking. Between
being served by animals, or *serving* them. Understand?"

The producer-writer stared into the distance. "I see what you
mean," he said, in a way perfectly indicating that he did not.

They had a fence-mending scene. Tony Perkins held a post atop the
good earth while his buddy and hired man Johnny (Beau Bridges)
whomped on it with a sledgehammer.

"Jesus, Steve," I said, "the goddamn ground's near to *rock* just
below top soil. You couldn't hammer fence posts in the ground!"

"How would you do it, then?"

"You'd use post-hole diggers! You'd have to dig deep, and you'd feel
the shock all through your body. And when you'd finished your back
would ache like you'd been kidney punched. But you'd know the fence
would *hold*. It would turn back a stud horse trying to reach a mare in
heat. Christ, even if you *could* hammer a fence post in the ground, the
damn thing would collapse the minute you strung wire and pulled it
tight."

"So who's gonna know?" Friedman asked. "How many movie-goers
ever saw a fence made?"

Gid and Johnny—buddies, and rivals for Molly's bed and love—
had a fight on a cattle car while transporting their lowing charges
to Fort Worth market. Each accused the other of having first slept
with Molly and then of failing to make an honest woman of her via
matrimony.

It was the sissiest, most awkward fight I've seen outside
Elaine's—which is where New York's high-rent literati gather to
juice, back-bite, screech and scratch out their professional frustrations or petty jealousies.

I sought out Director Lumet: "Jesus, Sid, that fight scene's a real pussy-cat. It just won't do."

Lumet chuckled: "That's my point. We're getting away from the obligatory standard Texas *machismo.*"

"You're wrong," I said. "See, back then, two guys fighting over the honor of their mutual girl friend would be as mean and unreasoning as rattlesnakes. They'd literally beat shit and blood out of each other."

"But these guys are *good friends,*" Lumet said.

"Beg your pardon, Sid, but that's why it'd be so fierce. The only way it'd be worse is if they were brothers. In which case somebody might be seriously maimed."

"We're trying to reject the old myths," Lumet said.

I said, "Look, I appreciate that. I'm sick of tough, tall Texans myself. And I feel about half-foolish insisting on blood. But given the emotional circumstances, I think blood would flow."

The director smiled and touched my arm, forgiving my standard Texas parochialism. He moved away before I could say that the most damage I had ever inflicted, or *had* inflicted, came in fistfights with a good friend or two. Except the time when I was 15, and had a bloody knock-down with my father.

Over drinks that night I tried to persuade Friedman. "It's funnier Sid's way," he said.

"Maybe so, baby. But it ain't real."

One finally grew weary of approaching the film folk with unsolicited advice. Also, it got more difficult to slip up on their blind sides. When they spotted that certain outraged gleam or heard the beginning echos of "Jesus, Steve" or "Jesus, Sid," they moved with all deliberate speed to safer quarters. Lumet reached the point of fleeing the Chariot Inn bar should he discover me in it.

At great expense to my soul I said nothing when a 1945 scene presented a Rural Route mail carrier *not* in khakis or tattered blue jeans but in a sparkling, tailored U.S. Mail costume which even Houston's city letter-carriers would not adopt until years later.

I held my tongue when Gid and Johnny abandoned the Fry place to briefly cowboy in "the Panhandle"—maybe five minutes worth on film—where they were constantly in the company of lush Delta growths, lakes, and rivers.

I stood silently when Molly, accepting a telegram telling of her son's death in World War II, expressed her grief in front of a pastel-hued building which no Texas town had that early. Nor did I complain that she supported herself by clutching a huge, modern red-and-white stop sign even though stop signs in them days, pardner, were teensie-tiny and announced themselves in blacks and yellows.

I said not a word when Mr. Fry, son Gid, and buddy Johnny sat on horses near a cattle-loading chute—*outside* the corral—to chat of their market worth while, apparently, the cattle accommodatingly loaded themselves.

Watching the filming and the daily rushes, one knew the final product would offer no sense of place: that geography, somehow, was being judged unworthy of attention. Throughout *Lovin' Molly* people canter by horse, wagon, buggy, or pickup-truck to this ranch or that farm or another town, without any sense of direction. You don't know if a given trip implies a journey of a hundred yards or an equal number of miles: all you know is that wherever people go—whether to Fort Worth or to the Panhandle or to an adjoining spread—the landscape is as unvarying as the moon's. Though it all looks as if it might yield 40 bales to the acre.

I grin and am warmed by recollecting an Early-Dewline warning flashed by Amarillo's Buck Ramsey. Ole Buck for years was the quintessential Texas cowboy; he rode for wages, fought in bars, and his neck was red. Some years ago Buck Ramsey's horse tricked him off, stomped him, and dragged him far enough that Buck has since been assigned a wheelchair. This cut down on Buck's riding and fighting, though not on his drinking or sense of humor. As a side effect, Buck was caused to read and mull Camus, Dickens, Twain, McMurtry and better. So when I called Buck Ramsey one night to inform that *Leaving Cheyenne* would soon be filmed near Austin, Buck gave the perfect literary criticism: "Shit, when will them folks learn not to film cowboy stories down yonder in that damn swamp country?"

Stars, producer, and director jangled in anticipation of Larry McMurtry's heralded visit to the shooting location. He disappointed them by arriving in Austin after the day's wrap. Though McMurtry had—and has—no responsibility for the flick, other than having sold its screen rights, Lumet and Friedman sought him out for dinner and to court his good will. McMurtry, who does not flower in the presence of excessive praise, squirmed and wouldn't look anybody in the face while being told of what a grand, perfect "vehicle" he had provided.

"You know what your book's about?" Lumet curiously asked.

Startled, McMurtry said something sounding like er-ah-whonk-oh.

Lumet leaned in, grasping McMurtry's arm, frowning to show Deep Artistic Insight: "Larry, it's about . . . well, it's about . . . *the glory of no reward!*"

"Hmmmmmmmmmm," McMurtry perfectly responded, failing to look up from his cucumber salad.

Later, McMurtry witnessed the latest daily rushes flown down from New York processings: rough cuts and retakes of scenes put on celluloid three, four days earlier. Often he snorted or muttered to himself.

By now they were filming some scenes from the 1960s portion of the book, when the principals have aged 40 years over the film's beginning. Tony Perkins, who in the opening reel appeared much too used and scabby for the 23-year-old he portrayed, now appeared to be about two years older than Christianity: possibly the worst make-up job since Nixon's in that first debate against Kennedy; he spoke in a voice cracking near to a yodel, and exaggerated the shakings of terminal palsy. In the darkness of the Chariot Inn's make-shift screening room, generally a meeting place of Lions and Rotarians, McMurtry took one look and grunted like somebody had poked his ribs with a pitchfork.

He suffered the sissy mock fistfight, Blythe Danner's pitiful attempts at a West Texas accent (it sounded as if it had been shipped in from Philadelphia by way of Pascagoula), and a 1925 scene where Gid and Molly, semi-sensually roistering in an open field, groped in passion near a fresh cow-plop obviously and recently tracked by a 1972 giant-type tri-wheeler. When a scene depicting "the Panhandle" revealed green foliage, and many running brooks, McMurtry breathed: "Is that Vietnam, or Missouri?"

McMurtry talked near to dawn in a motel room with old Texas friends, instructing how, for all their millions, movie folk seemed to possess natural talents for being unable to distinguish asses from elbows. He philosophized that, well, hell, you wrote something and then you moved on to write something else and the devil take the hindmost.

As a perfect counterpoint to the Technicolor turkey then in the making, he reported on his old cattleman daddy who—aged, ill, long past any hopes of Big Herds—had freshly battled a mad cow to at least a moral victory though suffering a bootful of blood and a major fracture. It was a symbolic story, almost as poignant as the old yarn of the dying Indian tribe buying a Longhorn steer and then killing it the way they—and their ancestors—had once killed countless buffalo. And I thought it an affirmation of that which McMurtry writes about life's natural attritions, and inevitable change, and the stubborn surrenderings they force. You knew damn well that tough old Jeff McMurtry hadn't worn bib-overalls—or given a thought one way or

another to Texas *machismo*—in playing out one of the final natural
dramas of a hard-scrabble ranch life.

One night on location outside Bastrop, as a few dozen of us shivered
in a chill wind and klieg lights, I cornered a big, cheerful, robust
native-Texan rancher who supplied cattle and horses for *Lovin' Molly*
and also was being paid as a technical advisor. True, he had taught the
principal actors how to mount horses without appearing totally foolish or getting hurt, how to toss a rope or to saddle-up and other
"techniques" that were to him second nature, but how—I asked—
could he permit the make-believe cowboys to miss or misinterpret so
much, to commit so many dozens of small boo-boos he certainly must
have recognized?

He was a good ole boy, not without a certain country ambition, and
we'd poured enough booze together that I knew he owned more smarts
than he'd publicly revealed. He lowered his voice and carefully checked
for outsiders: "Listen," he said, "them people payin' me $3600 for six
weeks a-work. And I got three buttons to educate. This is the best and
quickest money I ever seen. Maybe, you know, them people may come
back down here from New York to make another picture one day. You
want me to screw up easy money by quarrelin' with 'em *now?* Whatever
pleases *them* people, cousin, just tickles me plumb to death. . . ."

All prevailing deceptions were not hatched by Texans. Governor
Preston Smith and several state legislators "starred" in a cattle auction
scene ending with the auctioneer crying out, "Sold for forty dollars to
Preston Smith." I remarked to Producer Friedman that the scene didn't
appear all that vital to moving his story line. He grinned: "Well, it never
hurts to politick with the politicians. Meanwhile, when we need cooperation from the authorities—well, this scene hasn't hurt us."

I said, "And there's always the cutting room floor. You can always
decide during the final editing that maybe Governor Smith's scene is
expendable."

Friedman laughed: "You're pretty damn smart for a Texan. You sure
there's not a little New York hustler somewhere in your bloodline?"

P.S.: If Preston Smith made the movie as released, I neither saw
him nor heard his name.

Beau Bridges, cast as the happy-go-lucky Johnny, noted that many
real-life cowboys chewed tobacco. Concluding that perhaps Johnny
would take a chaw, too, he wrote that bit into his part. "A guy passed me
some of this stuff that looked like a pressed rag," he said, "and I chewed

it and nearly passed out." By now Director Lumet loved the tobacco-chawin' idea, and Bridges was stuck with it. He tried substitutes: licorice, black bubble gum; nothing seemed to work but the real thing. Beau spent a lot of off-camera time rinsing out his mouth, and gagging.

The cast and crew grumbled of a spartan social life. One night a party was arranged in the home of a congenial Austin man who supplied booze, music, deposits of minor dope, and friendly girls attracted to the possibility of meeting Tony Perkins. It was the flop of Austin's social season: only the technicians among the film folk appeared, and after nervous introductory drinks and chatter they segregated themselves to talk of Joe Namath, cream cheese, the New York Giants, and how wonderful it would be to see the spires of Manhattan.

Since Producer Friedman had made much—in press conferences and local speeches—of how at home New Yorkers were being made to feel in Texas, I asked one of the crewmen—by then drunk—what he really thought of the cowboy life and the region. "I get enough of these salt-of-the-earth types in a hurry," he said. "Hell, they don't even know what *stick*-ball is!"

Finally, it was over. At the cast party—attended, again, only by technicians and, this time, Beau Bridges from among the "stars"—there were mutters that anti-Semitism had been felt in Bastrop. How so? "Well," said an assistant producer, "when we needed to lease farms or ranchers or equipment for certain scenes, people tried to hold us up. And one old rancher said to me, 'Listen, you New York Jews come in here and git rich makin' fun of us and try to git out for six-bits.' I can't say I won't be happy to get home."

I saw McMurtry last summer, shortly after he'd witnessed the first rough-cut screening of *Lovin' Molly;* he was in a state of mild shock.

"It's simply dreadful," he said. "Tony Perkins plays a swishy boy until the final reel, and then suddenly he's older than rocks or water. The old-age make-up on everybody is simply grotesque. There's no sense of direction: Lumet apparently shot the thing in track shoes—zip, zip, zip. People at the screening kept laughing in all the wrong places, and some walked out. Near the interminable end, I realized a woman behind me had been crying for 20 minutes. I wondered what kind of woman would cry at such a film. When I risked a look behind me, it was my agent."

With some 20 minutes clipped from the original cut—mercifully, most of it in the mismanaged "old age" sequence—Columbia Pictures held a recent New York screening.

I was surprised to find Larry McMurtry sitting alone near the front row. "Glad to see you," he said. "I'll probably need your moral support."

What in hell was he doing there?

"Well, I've been asked to write a review for *The New York Times.*"

We laughed for the only time that day.

The longer the film ran, the lower McMurtry sank in his seat: "It's not so bad if you see only the top half of the screen." We suffered it all again: sowings and reapings, technical boo-boos, lush growths and rivers allegedly indigenous to Panhandle country; Blythe Danner clasping a bloody, wet, newborn calf to her generous bosoms and then—yes!—*kissing* it. McMurtry covered his face with his hands; his shoulders shook. I don't know if he was giggling or crying. We felt no sense of how hard-scrabble ranch life might be on the high Texas plains; received no notions of sandstorms, summer parchings, winter freezes, wild lonesome winds, or incessant jangling country tunes.

We escaped to a bar, drinking silently and shaking our heads.

I asked McMurtry what he intended to call his review for *The New York Times.* He perked up and smiled for the first time in two hours. "I'm gonna call it," he said, "'Leavin' Lumet.'"

Review of
Terms of Endearment
PETER BISKIND

It's hard to hate *Terms of Endearment.* James Brooks's new film is so appealing, so unassuming and good-hearted, so funny, intelligent and well crafted, that to break its spell seems churlish, like knocking Christmas. There's no way it won't sweep the Oscars, enabling Shirley MacLaine or (less likely) Debra Winger to edge out Meryl Streep (*Silkwood*) and Barbra Streisand (*Yentl*) for best actress. Then there's Jack Nicholson, a shoo-in as best supporting actor for his marvelously antic performance as the lecherous neighbor who ogles MacLaine across the hedge. But let's face it, *Terms of Endearment* is an obnoxious movie. It's a right-to-life soap opera; it does for the family what *An Officer and a Gentleman* did for the military.

Based on Larry McMurtry's first-rate novel of the same name, *Terms* focuses on the fortunes of Aurora Greenway and her daughter, Emma. Played by MacLaine with enormous charm, Aurora is a caustic Texas widow who alternately tempts and terrorizes a bevy of fatuous admirers. Emma, played by Winger, is considerably more conventional than her eccentric mother. She marries a feckless graduate student named Flap (Jeff Daniels) and follows him to a teaching post in Iowa. *Terms* crosscuts between the parallel lives of mother and daughter, who keep in constant contact by phone. While Aurora is tutored in the joys of sex by the amorous astronaut next door (Nicholson), Emma, despite a romantic interlude with a banker (John Lithgow), sticks close to the kitchen and breeds like a rabbit. When Aurora suggests that Emma stanch the flow of babies with an abortion, Emma recoils in shock. But Flap turns out to be a bad investment, spending all his time reading books in the library while Emma's changing diapers in the nursery. When he is offered a position as head of the English department at a cow college in Nebraska, Emma doesn't want to go. She follows him anyway, only to discover that he's followed one of his female grad students with whom he's been having an affair.

So far, unlike any film since *The Turning Point, Terms* has distinguished itself by its close, sympathetic attention to the bonds between mother and daughter; it presents relationships with men exclusively from a feminine point of view and raises interesting questions about those relationships. Should men change diapers too? Should wives subordinate themselves to their husbands' careers, following them to the ends of the earth, for better or for worse, till death do them part? Should Emma leave Flap, or stick it out? We never find out the answer to that last question, because Emma gets cancer.

At this point, midway in the film, *Terms* ceases to make any serious claim on our intelligence, despite the excellent performances. The questions of sexual politics raised explicitly in the film's first half are resolved in the second half by shameless emotional manipulation. The momentum is so great that most people in the audience won't care, but while he's tugging at our heartstrings, director Brooks is getting away with murder. Before we can blink our tears away, Emma is on a last fling in Manhattan, beset by career women, divorcées and victims of genital herpes. Even hospitalization is preferable to this, and Emma cuts short her trip to rush back to Nebraska General. In the New York sequence, Brooks finally lays his ideological cards on the table, and the film deteriorates into clumsy caricature. All the career women in this film are jerks, including Flap's grad student.

Not that the men are much better. They're either infantile and foolish or sex-crazed and irresponsible. Aurora always said Flap was bad news, and at the end, we see it's true. Emma's cancer is discovered right after she stumbles on his girlfriend. Are we meant to think that his affair has killed her, that male infidelity is the cancer that is destroying the family? (Emma's affair is excused because her lover isn't being satisfied by his wife—no Total Woman.) Moreover, Flap gives up his kids to Aurora to raise, turning *Kramer vs. Kramer* upside down. But if *Kramer vs. Kramer* attacked feminism from the vantage point of the liberal human potential movement, *Terms of Endearment* attacks it from the vantage point of the pro-life movement. Its contempt for men comes from the right, not the left. It's an expression of the deep-seated distrust of men that permeates pro-life literature, the fear that sexual equality threatens to erode the conventional constraints on male behavior by which errant breadwinners have traditionally been bound to the family. Even Nicholson's swinger is right out of George Gilder. He takes to the hills at the first whiff of commitment.

Debra Winger has made a specialty of post-feminist performances, which is to say she displays the surface characteristics of liberation—she's scrappy, direct, unglamorous—without its substance. From *Urban Cowboy* to *An Officer and a Gentleman,* the characters she plays have fought tooth and nail for equality until they're swept off their feet in the very last frame, as if to reassure anxious viewers that despite the sound and the fury, nothing much has changed after all.

Here the terms of endearment are slightly different. Emma can't be swept off her feet because Flap is too weak. But she can't divorce him either, as Aurora suggests, because that is the province of the New York herpes-infected harpies whom she detests. Under these circumstances, cancer becomes the moral equivalent of divorce. It allows her to escape from (and punish) Flap, without the stigma the right connects with dissolving the sacred bonds of matrimony.

When Emma finally dies and Flap retreats in disgrace, Aurora saves the day. The same Aurora who once had recommended abortion now embraces adoption. Since the astronaut makes a better role model than a wimpy college professor, she succeeds in transforming him into a surrogate father to Emma's oldest boy. As the dissidents fall into step, the new family takes shape before our very eyes. Will they make it legal? Hang in for the sequel.

Whose *Terms of Endearment?*

CONSTANCE SPEIDEL

Larry McMurtry's novel, *Terms of Endearment,* is not likely to be considered an enduring or endearing classic. It does, however, deserve better treatment than it receives from James L. Brooks. The novel, third in a trilogy (*Moving On,* 1970, and *All My Friends Are Going to Be*

Strangers, 1972) chronicling the lives of four Texas friends (Patsy Carpenter, Emma Greenway Horton, Flap Horton and Danny Deck) is divided into two unequal parts. The first, and longer, portion of the book deals with the escapades of Emma's mother, Aurora Greenway, a transplanted New England widow. Its basic theme is sexual frustration as Aurora's suitors attempt to make their way into her bed. The suitors are a most improbable collection of swains: an ossified, retired armored-tank commander, General Hector Scott; an Italian tenor, Alberto, who now owns a music store; Aurora's first love, Trevor, a yachtsman and big-game hunter; and the consummate McMurtry character, Vernon Dalhart, a fifty-year-old virgin Texas millionaire oilman, who lives atop his twenty-four-story parking garage in his white Lincoln. Aurora, an updated Auntie Mame, manipulates her suitors and eventually welds them into a cohesive group who commiserate with each other as they attempt to keep Aurora happy.

A major subplot of the novel concerns Aurora's maid of twenty-three years, Rosie, and Rosie's husband, Royce. One of the funniest chapters in the book is a previously published short story (*Playboy,* July 1975), in which a drunken and enraged Royce drives his delivery van into the J-Bar Korral dance hall in pursuit of his estranged Rosie and her Cajun dancing partner, the chauffeur of Aurora's General. Rosie and Royce's problems weave in and out of Aurora's machinations, adding an element of drama to the otherwise frothy story. Through it all Aurora moves blithely on, selecting the correct dress, jewels, and menu for every occasion, totally unaware that the world may come tumbling down around her at any moment, happy to blame everyone around her for any inconvenience she experiences.

In the second, shorter portion of the novel, the focus moves from Aurora's life to Emma's, from Houston to the Midwest. Emma's marriage to Flap, a minor disaster in the first part of the book, falls apart in this second section. Flap fulfills his expectations of failure, but blames Emma. Eventually their only form of communication becomes arguments about money, and they both take a series of lovers. The trilogy concludes with the tragic death of Emma at 37, leaving behind her two insecure sons and a daughter who promises to grow up in the image of the two people Emma loves and envies most, her mother and Patsy Carpenter.

This is not a great novel. The characters are not always fully developed; some of them tend toward stereotypes. Aurora's suitors appear briefly, do their comic turns and disappear for a chapter or two; chronology is sometimes confusing, and Emma's grim fate at the conclusion of the novel seems out of keeping with the earlier froth. And yet the novel is entertaining. There is humor in it; Aurora is as fascinating as she is infuriating, as engaging as she is egotistical. The lampooning of Texas and Texans is funny; Texas has more than its share of rednecks like Royce and millionaire innocents like Vernon. As distasteful as Emma's death is, the realistic portrayal of cancer and the egotistical responses of those around her enlighten, though they don't entertain.

The March 15, 1976 issue of *The New Leader* featured a review of the novel written by playwright Charles Deemer. He contends that the book is a natural for a television series. "It would be inefficient to make a film from all this when a TV series would get so much more mileage" (p. 20). The Aurora Greenway role would be sought after by every middle-aged actress in Hollywood, and most character actors would jump at the opportunity to play Aurora's suitors. "I'm convinced" he concludes, "we shall be seeing them all soon" (p. 20).

Inefficient or not, the film became an Academy Award–winning blockbuster. At the risk of swimming upstream against the current of public opinion, I cannot like this film. I cannot understand the multitude of encomiums heaped upon it, nor can I understand James L. Brooks's Academy Award for Best Adaptation; for the two works are similar only in skeletal structure and identity crisis. Each begins as a comedy and ends as a melodrama; each seems unsure if it is an in depth study of the female psyche, an often hilarious exploration of human relationships, or a screwball comedy. I find it difficult to resolve the two separate stories, and the epilog, or Emma's story in both novel and film, covers too much territory in too short a time, and leaves me feeling manipulated as McMurtry and Brooks strive for pathos. It is, however, the epilog that is the more faithful adaptation of the two parts of the novel. In the interests of film economy Brooks has eliminated all but one lover for each of the Hortons. Emma has an affair with her ursine banker, charmingly played by John Lithgow, and Flap has an affair with his graduate assistant. Emma's ordeal in the hospital is realistically handled, but her friendship with a Nebraska farmer's wife is sacrificed in favor of a pointless trip to New York with her friend Patsy Carpenter in the film. Emma's good-byes to her sons and their response to her are painfully detailed. The essential truth of the story, it is vital for us to remember what the terms of endearment between us are, is in the film, although the idea is somewhat weakened.

It is with the Aurora portion of the film that I have the most trouble. Shirley MacLaine's Aurora is a self-centered, uptight, bitchy, unsympathetic middle-aged woman, totally without the charm that is the saving grace of the novel's Aurora. Only once in the entire film is MacLaine's Aurora human. Emma is in the hospital, nearing the end of her life; her pain is intense; her medication is overdue. Aurora goes on a rampage around the nurses' desk screaming, demanding, crying, until Emma is given her injection. Shirley MacLaine has been applauded for looking like a fifty-year-old woman in this film, and I suppose it took courage in this youth conscious age, but my sixty-year-old mother has looked at least that for twenty years, and she still doesn't have an Oscar.

Rosie, the housekeeper, one of the most fully developed characters in the novel, is little more than a walk-on in the film, and Vernon Dalhart, the short, sandy-haired white knight of the book, suffers the same fate. Danny DeVito who plays Vernon in the film could have brought Vernon to life. Instead he is limited to hanging around the edges of Aurora's retinue, making cow-eyes at her. None of Aurora's other suitors survive Brooks's adaptation; it might be a fate DeVito could wish on Vernon.

In the interest of economy one can understand compressing all of Aurora's suitors into one person, but it is fascinating to speculate about how a seventy-year-old General, a former opera star, a yachtsman and an oilman could all be turned into an alcoholic ex-astronaut.

Garrett Breedlove, an interestingly named character portrayed by Jack Nicholson, is eccentric in the mold of Vernon Dalhart, though he lives on his past glory rather than in a white Lincoln. This beer-bellied satyr has been given the dubious honor of arousing Aurora's long dormant sexual desires, a chore which takes almost as long as the building of the Great Pyramids. When they finally get to bed, and one is never quite sure who is the pursuer and who is pursued (and who really cares?), the post-coital scene is winsome enough for an "R" rated Brady Bunch. Aurora immediately calls Emma in Iowa to tell her Momma is in bed with the astronaut. Nicholson is cute as Garrett Breedlove with his pot-belly, his bald spot, and his "I'm a bad little boy" grin, but it would be good to see him take on a role in which he has to stretch rather than relying on his bag of tricks from *One Flew Over the Cuckoo's Nest*.

There are some good things in the film. The opening scene, with MacLaine as a young mother trying to climb into Emma's crib to check on her, is funny. Emma's younger son, played by Huckleberry Fox, is superb. Jeff Daniels as the hapless Flap Horton is appealing, and John Lithgow is loveable. The main reason for seeing *Terms of Endearment*, however, is Debra Winger. Her loose-jointed walk, her raucous laugh, her mobile face, these are the reasons, I think, so many people adore this movie. They get caught up in her spell; they care about her. Who can care about a self-centered mother, an unfaithful husband, an alcoholic ex-astronaut?

James L. Brooks has proved once again that a successful film does not need to be a faithful adaptation, but *Terms of Endearment* raises the question, why bother to adapt? Why not write an original screenplay? With the exception of the epilog, that is what this is. Nothing is more essential to the book than Aurora's fey, capricious personality; nothing in the film is less observable. Without the distinguishing characteristics of McMurtry's novel, one does not have *Terms of Endearment*; one has television soap opera. When I called the Washington-based novelist Larry McMurtry and asked him what he thought of the film, this laconic, politic Texan would only say, "Waaall, I liked it." And after all, who can argue with success? Instead of thanking Larry McMurtry for "a wonderful book" as Brooks did at the Oscar ceremonies in April, he should have apologized.

S U M M I N G

U P

Thalia and the Real Texans

HAMLIN HILL

Begin with an individual," Scott Fitzgerald said in "The Rich Boy," "and before you know it you find that you have created a type; begin with a type and you will find that you have created—nothing." The stereotype of The Texan is so familiar to us all that it hardly needs comment—something between Lyndon Johnson and John Wayne; beneath that stereotype lies an equally unique personality, from which the distortion itself evolved. Larry McMurtry recognizes that the source of both the true Texan and his parody began on the frontier: "The tendency to practice symbolic frontiersmanship might almost be said to characterize the twentieth century Texan, whether he be an intellectual, a cowboy, a businessman, or a politician" (*ING* 43).

I

It would be fair to argue that the original Texan, or at least his forebear, was born in icy, barren New England in the middle of the seventeenth century, when a scraggy band of Puritans tried to persuade themselves that God had chosen them for an errand in the wilderness, to found a city on a hill and become the American Adam, while other Puritans claimed a Holy War on the other side of the Atlantic, with beheadings of Stuart kings and Anglican divines, was in fact the occupation upon which God smiled his fondest smile.

The Colonists did their best: they covered their feelings of inferiority with promotion tracts, extolling the flora, fauna, climate, agricultural richness, and healthfulness of a region that was decimating their ranks a lot faster than the victims die in *The Texas Chainsaw Massacre*. In the process, they invented the tall tale.

Reminded constantly of their inferiority to Mother England, the Americans just had to fight. In addition, they adopted a curious defense mechanism to deal with their second-class status: they became violently anti-intellectual; they exaggerated those very qualities for which they were criticized. They appropriated from the British and their Tory sympathizers the loutish bumpkin "Yankee Doodle" and made him their own. They measured, after the Great Awakening, salvation by the decibel. They so studied bad manners in front of English travelers that their vulgarity was mistaken as always unintentional. The pantheon of American types consisted of the Yankee peddler, the Negro minstrel, and the frontier backwoodsman, each of whom Constance Rourke has delineated in *American Humor: A Study of the National Character*. None of the three made any claims to book-learning. They were, indeed, suspicious first of English and then of New England gray matter.

Once the frontier and the frontiersman moved south and inland to Tennessee, Kentucky, and later, Mississippi, Alabama, Louisiana, it distilled its qualities into a single person, Davy Crockett. Crockett became the apotheosis of crudity and vulgarity. His address to Congress, printed in one of the *Crockett Almanacks,* was a model of modesty, self-effacement, and propriety:

> In one word I'm a screamer, and have got the roughest racking
> horse, the prettiest sister, the surest rifle and the ugliest dog in the
> district. I'm a leetle the savagest crittur you ever *did* see. My father
> can whip any man in Kentucky, and I can lick my father. I can
> outspeak any man on this floor, and give him two hours start. I can
> run faster, dive deeper, stay longer under, and come out drier, than
> any *chap* this side the big *Swamp.* I can outlook a panther and
> outstare a flash of lightning: tote a steamboat on my back and play
> at rough and tumble with a lion, and an occasional kick from a
> *Zebra.* To sum up all in the one word *I'm a horse.* . . . I can walk
> like an ox; run like a fox, swim like an eel, yell like an Indian, fight
> like a devil, and spout like an earthquake. (Meine 106–07)

Americans (except for a few supercilious New England Whigs) loved him for it.

The Old Southwest, as the region is called, added a number of other qualities to the emerging form that was to become The Texan. In the

Old Southwest, life was cheap and Nature, hostile. Men lived by their wits or physical prowess; both the con man and the Ring-tailed Roarer flourished in the canebreaks. Morality became relative ("It is good to be shifty in a new country," Simon Suggs proclaims in backwoods Tennessee). Isolation or a retreat from advancing civilization became a way of life. In the small settlements, a frenetic energy erupted constantly, lest time for introspection allowed the frontiersman to brood on his fragile hold on his universe:

> In one day, they recently had two street fights, hung a man, rode three men out of town on a rail, got up a quarter race, a turkey shooting, a gander pulling, a match dog fight, had preaching by a circus rider, who afterwards ran a footrace for apple jack all round, and, as if this was not enough, the judge of the court, after losing his year's salary at single-handed poker, and licking a person who said he didn't understand the game, went out and helped to lynch his grandfather for hog stealing. (Blair 69)

Physical violence, often sadistic, was common; sublimated violence (turkey pulls, shooting contests, procreation—the football game was yet to come) was equally common.

But the time to brood was available. Sut Lovingood, George Washington Harris's and one of American literature's finest fictional creations, knew long before Henry Adams that beneath the fighting and fornicating, chaos was the law of Nature and order was the dream of man.

> "Men wer made a-purpus jis' tu eat, drink, an' fur stayin awake in the early part ove the nites: an' wimen wer made tu cook the vittils, mix the sperits, an' help the men do the stayin awake. That's all, an' nuthin more, onless hits fur the wimen to raise the devil atwix meals, an' knit socks atwix drams, an' the men to play short cards, swap hosses wif fools, an' fite fur exersise, at odd spells. . . . " (Harris 88)

> "Whar thar ain't enuf feed, big childer roots littil childer outen the troff, an' gobbils up thar part. Jis' so the earth over: bishops eats elders, elders eats common peopil; they eats sich cattil es me, I eats possums, possums eats chickins, chickins swallers wums, an' wums am content to eat dust, an' the dust am the end ove it all." (Harris 228).

A variant of the Ur-Texan became a fixture of the Deep South. (As McMurtry astutely knows, Texans in the Piney Woods are in fact Southerners: "they had more in common regionally with the people who might gather on the courthouse lawns of Georgia and Alabama than with the Texans who lived in Lubbock, San Antonio, or El Paso. East Texans are moulded by the South, West Texans by the West, and the two cultures are no longer correspondent" [*ING* 101]). The Southerner, in short, stopped and took root. He built his plantations, developed his obsession with genealogy and heritage, and protected himself as best he could from the world with what Mark Twain called the "Walter Scott disease," a mixture of aristocratic and medieval qualities which could render violence socially acceptable in the guise of duels, feuds, lynchings, and tarring-and-featherings. It was a thin veneer, however; and if the Southerner looked too deep into his heritage, he became Quentin Compson and committed suicide from the burden of his guilt. If his gentility failed him, he could turn into one of Flannery O'Connor's many Misfits. It is in those characters, in many of Faulkner's, and some of Eudora Welty's that the original prototype from the Old Southwest crops up like a recurrent nightmare.

Indeed, motion is so integral to the frontiersman archetype that stopping is always fatal. Stay in Winesburg, and you become a Grotesque; light out for the Territory ahead of the rest or you will get "sivilized"; stay long enough in Lake Wobegone and you become the subject of a bittersweet pathos.

The frontiersman did of course move to Texas, and he brought with him those virtues and vices which had been forming for just about two hundred years. Crockett and Bowie insured their permanence far beyond the fact of dying at the Alamo. Unlike the Deep Southerner, the Texan remained restless; his sense of place always included a nervous insecurity and a strong awareness of the mutability of things.

Lonesome Dove illustrates, epically, these characteristics of the frontier Texan. Although Augustus and Call had "to go along establishing law and order and making it safe for bankers and Sunday-school teachers," (*LD* 83) they have nevertheless remained basically restless and rootless. Gus muses early in the novel that "it was that they had roved too long. . . . They were people of the horse, not of the town. . . . They had been in Lonesome Dove nearly ten years, and yet what little property they had acquired was so worthless that neither of them would have felt bad about just saddling up and riding off from it" (81). Once on the trail, Gus muses philosophically about the constant encroachment of civilization, before which he and Call instinctively retreat:

> "We'll be the Indians, if we last another twenty years," Augustus
> said. "The way this place is settling up it'll be nothing but churches
> and dry-goods stores before you know it. Next thing you know they'll

have to round up us old rowdies and stick us on a reservation to keep us from scaring the ladies."

"I'd say that's unlikely," Call said.

"It's dern likely," Augustus said. "If I can find a squaw I like, I'm apt to marry her. The thing is, if I'm going to be treated like an Indian, I might as well act like one. I think we spent our best years fighting on the wrong side." (326–27)

"If I'd have wanted civilization," Augustus observed earlier, "I'd have stayed in Tennessee and wrote poetry for a living" (319–20).

And so Call's relentless drive goes on, not toward Montana or the Yellowstone or Milk Rivers, but toward some ineffable goal which constantly remains just out of reach, like a mirage on an asphalt highway. Compelled, like Old Dog, the lead steer, to move onward at the head of the herd, Call—even near the Canadian border—obeys an instinctive compulsion. "He kept on going north because it had become a habit. . . . Some days he felt so little interest in the herd and the men that he could simply have ridden off and left them to make the best of things" (796).

Gus's deathbed request, to be buried in Clara's orchard in Texas, is phrased enigmatically: "'The favor I want from you will be my favor to you,' Augustus said" (783). And Call must then return to Lonesome Dove, to Texas. Even though "he had never felt that he had any home on the earth anyway" (841), Call alone of the Hat Creek gang returns home at the end of the novel.

Meanwhile, the carnage and death that splatter *Lonesome Dove* are a violent testimony to the meaninglessness of life on the frontier. Death is a constant companion on the trail; some characters seem to enter *Lonesome Dove* for a few pages only to serve as victims of violence and as emblems for the unpredictability of survival. Individuals perish, but the instincts which motivate them in *Lonesome Dove* survive to the present.

McMurtry acknowledges that the frontiersman has remained in several senses immune to destruction: "On the rims of the West—and perhaps, in America, only there—one can still know for a moment the frontier emotion, the loneliness and the excitement and the sense of an openness so vast that it still challenges—in Gatsbian phrase—our capacity for wonder" (*ING* 108). He evolved, to be sure. Financial prowess replaced physical in many arenas: the cattleman, the oil entrepreneur, and the Houston dowager socialite may use other weapons than the Bowie knife; but theirs are just as lethal and just as envied.

McMurtry believes (erroneously, I think) that Texas

is at that stage of metamorphosis when it is most fertile with conflict, when rural and soil traditions are competing most desperately with urban traditions. . . . The city will win, of course, but
its victory won't be cheap—the country traditions were very
strong. (*ING* xv)

In fact, the scale may be grander, the stakes higher, the consumption
more conspicuous, but the values remain the same and the character
of The Texan who embodies them has them embedded too deeply for
mere geography to eradicate them. There are as many Kodiak bears in
the living rooms of River Oaks mansions as there are in Thalia. And I
suspect that as many deceased women lie in state in their pink plastic
curlers in Dallas as in Lubbock. McMurtry is correct (and Donald
Barthelme wrong) that Texas writers must "render the particularities
of their own place" (*ING* 54), but, except for the slight sense of history
which Thalia communicates from one generation to another, the large
city is just as Texan as the sprinkling of small towns whose very
existence mystifies the rational mind.

II

That sense of place (but not, like Southern literature, of heritage or
genealogy) hovers over the Thalia tetralogy. Duane leaves, for the
army, in *The Last Picture Show,* but returns, drawn inexorably to
spend his middle age there in *Texasville.* Jacy does the same. When
Gid and Johnny leave, in *Leaving Cheyenne,* Gid points out that after
only a week,

I just minded feeling that I wasn't where I belonged. Home was
where I belonged. . . . It wan't that I liked being in Archer County
so much—sometimes I hated it. But I was just tied up with it;
whatever happened there was happening to me, even if I wasn't
there to see it. The country might not be very nice and the people
might be onery; but it was my country and my people, and no other
country was; no other people, either. You do better staying with
what's your own, even if it's hard. . . . If you don't stick with a
place, you don't have it very long. (93–94)

Lonnie Bannon leaves Thalia at the end of *Horseman, Pass By,* but
with that sense of loss and depression that preoccupies him throughout the novel. Mitch Mott (in *Texasville*) "had lived in Thalia for a
mere ten years," and therefore he "was not deeply versed in its lore,
which only a lifetime's residence could make intelligible—and sometimes not then" (47). Curiously, though, when Sonny suggests that
Sam the Lion and Billy be included in the centennial pageant, Duane

thinks that the collective memory of Thalia would not recognize them: "People had heard of Adam and Eve, and had some vague idea of who Ben Franklin was, but local figures, dead so long, were almost as lost to memory as Texasville itself. Duane couldn't remember Sam and Billy very well himself" (137). In spite of her elaborate plots in *The Last Picture Show* about losing her virginity, Jacy cannot remember in *Texasville* that it was Duane to whom she lost it. In the latest novel, Duane notices at the class reunion that "in most cases he was unable to remember whether it had been a wife or a husband who was his classmate" (399).

The "lore" is not objective history or factual information; it is more a mood or a conviction which, however absurd it might be, holds its power over Duane, who

> had never supposed that people really lived as they ought to live, but he had gone through much of his life at least believing that there was a way they ought to live. And Thalia of all places—a modest small town—ought to be a place where people lived as they ought to live, allowing for a normal margin of human error. Surely, in Thalia, far removed from big-city temptations, people ought to be living on the old model—putting their families and neighbors first, leading more or less orderly, more or less responsible lives. (314)

But, of course, the evidence of all the Thalia novels masses to show that abstract values, "the old model," constantly eludes the characters as reality smashes their hopes and aspirations.

The most obvious aspiration of the prototypical Texas is to achieve the superlative: the richest, the poorest; the ugliest, the prettiest; the meanest, the kindest; even the vulgarest. ("Lyndon, honey, cover up your gut. You're the President of the United States, and shouldn't be showing your scar to the world!" "You think *that* was crude; just watch me swing these beagles by their ears.") It is Davy Crockett's heritage, of course, the blustering search for perfection that misses its target and camouflages a deep insecurity. It produces violent desperation: shooting frogs out of water tanks or blasting two-story doghouses to release the depression, depriving your best friend of the sight in one eye with a beer bottle, racing your Cadillac or Porsche as fast as its engine will permit. In *Leaving Cheyenne*, Johnny muses to Gid,

> "I can't figure you out," I said. "As much money as you got, and you're still fighting a goddamn windmill. Why do you do it, Gid?"
> "Sometimes I wonder myself," he said. (243)

In Gid's case, the irresistible challenge proves fatal.

In other cases, it becomes tragic or pathetic. Much earlier in *Leaving Cheyenne,* Gid's values, then idealistic, conflict head on with his father's pragmatic realism:

> "I still wish I'd gone to the Panhandle. I ain't training to be no oat planter. I intend to enjoy my life."
> "If that ain't a fine ambition," he said. "Why, any damn fool can enjoy himself. What makes you think life's supposed to be enjoyed anyhow?"
> "Well," I said, "if you ain't supposed to enjoy it, what are you supposed to do with it?"
> "Fight it. Fight the hell out of it." (27)

In a sense, the Thalia tetralogy's basic theme is that of an older, disillusioned generation attempting to provide its children with exactly that message.

But, almost always, the inhabitants of Thalia miss the dream. Lonnie says at the dance in *Horseman, Pass By* that people "wanted more and seemed to end up with less; they wanted excitement and ended up stomped by a bull or smashed against a highway; or they wanted a girl to court; and anyway, whatever it was they wanted, that was what they ended up doing without" (117–18). Molly ponders the missed possibilities when Gid suggests that they should have married: "I never did like to think about how much better things might have turned out if we hadn't acted like we did. We *did* act like we did, and some bad things happened, but others would have happened if we had acted some other way" (177). In *Texasville,* the motif becomes a persistent refrain: Duane contemplates the fact that at seventy-two, Ruth Popper "seemed girlish—a living example of how seldom life turned out to be as advertised" (64). In the hospital quiet room, Lester announces, "I'd rather be anything than what I am" (125). In his first encounter with Suzie Nolan, Duane "had a sense that life was about to jump the fence of credibility and become completely unbelievable. He wanted to stop it, to keep it from racing into hopeless emotional chaos, but, unfortunately for his ethical sense, desire was growing faster than dismay" (129). Jacy analogizes life with a television game show: "You win things that look great at the time but turn out to be junk, and you lose things you might want to keep forever, just because you're unlucky" (217). Genevieve Morgan declines Duane's offer to teach her to run his boat so that she can fish in the middle of the lake; she refuses, explaining that she would rather keep her dream . . . "that there's a big fish out there in the lake somewhere that I could catch" (316–17). Small a dream as it is, it is the only one intact in Thalia.

If the consequences of following the dream are disillusionment and depression, losing the dream too soon or not having one at all produces even greater despair. Both Lonnie Bannon and Sonny Crawford, while still teenagers, forfeit the vision. We do not know what happens to Lonnie or to Hud, but Sonny's personality in *Texasville* is by far the bleakest in the Thalia chronicle. The residents of Thalia echo the themes of *The Great Gatsby,* transferred to the West Texas plains: Sonny and Gatsby embody their illusions in Jacy and Daisy. Foreshadowing more mature adults in *Texasville,* Sonny learns too young in *The Last Picture Show* that "he was never going to get to sleep with Jacy. . . . Somehow his whole life had worked out to keep that one thing from happening, and it was the one thing he wanted most of all" (195). Although Gatsby dies, Sonny in *Texasville* is literally borne back ceaselessly into the past, as his mind blurs and he returns to the nonexistent past. Ruth attempts to reassure and console Sonny at the conclusion of *The Last Picture Show,* but cannot verbalize the elusive insight which she tries to convey:

> She was on the verge of speaking to him, of saying something fine. It seemed to her that on the tip of her tongue was something it had taken her forty years to learn, something wise or brave or beautiful that she could finally say. It would be just what Sonny needed to know about life, and she would have said it if her own relief had not been so strong. She gasped with it, squeezed his hand, and somehow lost the words. . . . (219–20)

The paragraph echoes Nick Carraway's failed insights into Gatsby's romantic illusions about Daisy:

> Through all he said, even through his appalling sentimentality, I was reminded of something—an elusive rhythm, a fragment of lost words, that I had heard somewhere a long time ago. For a moment a phrase tried to take shape in my mouth and my lips parted like a dumb man's, as though there was more struggling upon them than a wisp of startled air. But they made no sound, and what I had almost remembered was uncommunicable forever. (Fitzgerald 249)

Many of the inhabitants of Thalia, at least before the oil bust, echo the Buchanans: "they smashed up things and creatures and then retreated back into their money or their vast carelessness, or whatever it was that kept them together" (Fitzgerald 300). In Thalia, "tomorrow we will run faster, stretch out our arms farther," in a pursuit of a lost dream that "was already behind [us], somewhere back in that vast obscurity beyond the city, where the dark fields of the republic rolled on under the night" (Fitzgerald 301). Finally, except for Genevieve, Ruth, and Molly, all of Thalia's women have voices, like Daisy's, which have the sound of money.

McMurtry has claimed that "the tough-minded Texan is a rarity" (*ING* 38), but he is clearly exempting Jacy and her mother Lois and Karla Moore and most of the bed-hopping women of Thalia. They are domineering women, whose amorality makes jelly of the weak-minded males of the Thalia novels. Controlled by their libidos and their materialistic self-aggrandizement, they are all daughters of Daisy Buchanan. They survive because they have never been deluded by tenderheartedness or illusory idealism. Jacy plots her future at SMU based on merchandizing her sexuality. Hedonism, mixed with a bitter sardonic world view, immunizes them from both the idealism and the sense of loss that the male inhabitants of Thalia feel.

The morose nature of the men of Thalia mixes, as it did for Sut Lovingood, with raucous humor. McMurtry and the quintessential Texan as well leaven the despair and alleviate the gloom of the basic premise. The tumbleweed invasion and the great hens-of-hell egg fight are masterful Old Southwestern humor. The homespun poetry and comic similes come straight from the frontier vocabulary. Duane's first unsuccessful attempt to rid Jacy of her exasperating virginity belongs to barnyard humor. The Reverend G.G., who mixes piety with prurience, has a lineage that traces back to Parson John Bullin and other frontier circuit riders. Aphoristic one-liners utilizing the commonplace pepper the Thalia novels, as do prime examples of Texas vernacular. The energy and vitality of the comic relief suggests that another inheritor of the frontier tradition in humor, Mark Twain, was correct when he said that "against the assault of laughter nothing can stand." The mythic Texan can feign seriousness and yearn for superiority, but he can never take himself completely seriously. He can laugh at himself, even in his most preposterous poses, and then laugh at censorious outsiders who do not understand his rituals, his personae, his whistling in the dark of an improbable universe, and his nervousness at being such a microscopic speck in the vastness called Texas. Larry McMurtry has succeeded in delineating him more skillfully than any other writer, and, even more impressively, in suggesting the ways that beneath his uniqueness, the essential Texas is blood kin to modern man.

WORKS CITED

Blair, Walter. *Native American Humor.* New York: Harper, 1960.

Fitzgerald, F. Scott. *The Great Gatsby.* 1925. New York: Scribner's, 1951.

Harris, George Washington. *Sut Lovingood's Yarns.* New York, 1860.

Meine, Franklin J., ed. *The Crockett Almanacks.* Chicago: Caxton Club, 1955.

McMurtry, Larry. *Horseman, Pass By.* 1961. New York: Penguin, 1979.

———. *In a Narrow Grave.* Austin: Encino, 1968. New York: Simon and Schuster, 1968.

———. *The Last Picture Show.* 1966. New York: Penguin, 1979.

———. *Leaving Cheyenne.* 1963. New York: Penguin, 1979.

———. *Lonesome Dove.* New York: Simon and Schuster, 1985.

———. *Texasville.* New York: Simon and Schuster, 1987.

Rourke, Constance. *American Humor: A Study of the National Character.* 1931. New York: Harcourt, 1959.

BIBLIOGRAPHY

CHARLES WILLIAMS

This is a comprehensive secondary bibliography listing all the major books and articles about Larry McMurtry published before the end of 1988 as well as many minor publications and a few items published in 1989. It lists over five hundred writings in a broad range of publication types, including specialized reference works; monographs, dissertations, and theses; books that discuss McMurtry in the context of some larger focus; and a variety of periodical literature, including professional journals, popular magazines, and newspapers.

The bibliography organizes writings about McMurtry under six major headings, as follows:

1. *Bibliography*

   Includes only stand-alone bibliographies; does not include the numerous lists of works cited and bibliographies accompanying many critical studies listed elsewhere on this bibliography.

2. *Biography*

   Includes entries in biographical reference works; interviews; and news items concerning McMurtry's public appearances, bookselling interests, awards, etc.

3. *General Criticism*

   Includes studies of theme and style when based upon more than one

McMurtry title, comparative criticism, and studies of region and
genre that discuss McMurtry.

4. *Criticism of Individual McMurtry Titles*
   Includes reviews and other articles focused primarily on one work,
   with articles gathered under individual McMurtry titles introduced
   according to publication date.
   • Novels
   • Essays

5. *Film Criticism*
   Includes studies of films adapted from McMurtry novels.
   • Comparative Studies
   • Criticism of Individual Film Titles
     Gathers articles and reviews under individual film titles intro-
     duced according to original release date.

6. *Masters' Theses*

Though masters' theses are listed separately at the end, doctoral dissertations are listed under appropriate subject headings. Throughout
the bibliography, entries are alphabetized by author's name, with unsigned items listed separately at the end of each section.

Users of the bibliography who are interested in particular McMurtry
titles should study not only section four, Criticism of Individual
McMurtry Titles, but also sections two and three, Biography and General Criticism, where annotations, together with article titles and dates,
help identify the McMurtry titles discussed in the publications cited
there.

To be listed, a publication needed to directly consider McMurtry's
life or work, if only briefly. However, reviews of the film versions of
McMurtry novels are cited even when they do not mention McMurtry,
who was directly involved in the filming of only *The Last Picture
Show,* which he co-scripted with director Peter Bogdanovich. Reviews
of other "McMurtry" films—*Hud* (adapted from *Horseman, Pass By*),
Lovin' Molly (*Leaving Cheyenne*), *Terms of Endearment,* and *Lonesome Dove*—are included for anyone interested in the relationship
between McMurtry's books and the films they inspire. (Incidentally,
that relationship has already been explored in several articles, some of
the most interesting by McMurtry himself, whose essays about the
films *Hud, The Last Picture Show,* and *Lovin' Molly* are the only
primary items listed on this bibliography.) One review of *The Ballad of
Mary Phagan,* with television screenplay co-written by McMurtry, is
also included.

Many articles are from Texas-based periodicals, including *Balcones,*

Texas Books in Review, Texas Humanist, Texas Monthly, Texas Observer, Texas Quarterly, Texas Review, and about a dozen Texas newspapers. Of course most of these periodicals are not covered by the usual indexes. This bibliography tries to answer that inconvenience for scholars and students by listing as much as possible of Texas writing about McMurtry.

Probably, this bibliography just begins to account for the newspaper attention McMurtry's home state has given him, with only two Texas newspapers represented systematically: the *Houston Post,* whose published index identified many articles, beginning with 1976, and the *Dallas Morning News,* which I searched through its Sunday book sections to find reviews for all of McMurtry's novels. Correspondence gave me articles from other Texas newspapers, both large and small. Encouraged by Don Graham's view that "[s]ome small-town Texas newspapers do much better by Texas literature than the big dailies" (*Texas: A Literary Portrait* 233), I included them all the same.

The style of the entries follows *The MLA Style Manual* (1985), with a few exceptions. Most notably, for items published in a regularly featured column, such as the *Texas Observer's* "Books and the Culture," the column name appears after the title of the article, if it is titled, and without quotation marks or italics. For many unsigned, untitled articles, the column name begins the entry. Asterisks mark entries for articles reprinted or excerpted in *Taking Stock.*

Annotations appear mostly in the Biography and General Criticism sections. At minimum, they identify the McMurtry books considered in the cited article, but some more detailed annotations summarize arguments or point to major concerns. No judgment on the value of the cited article is ever intended.

For an accounting of primary works, see Charles D. Peavy's selected bibliography at the end of his *Larry McMurtry* (Boston: Twayne, 1977). Peavy lists McMurtry's books up to the publication of *Terms of Endearment* (1975) as well as the poetry, essays, film criticism, and numerous book reviews McMurtry published before 1976. He also describes McMurtry's manuscripts and letters in the Special Collection Room at the University of Houston Library.

Scholars seeking primary materials will also be interested in the McMurtry holdings at the University of North Texas, where the Rare Book and Texana Collections include originals of McMurtry's submissions to some student publications; undergraduate and graduate papers, including McMurtry's master's thesis; typescripts of *Horseman, Pass By* and *Leaving Cheyenne;* early correspondence with publishers; and screenplays.

Dwight Huber's selected bibliography in *Larry McMurtry: Unredeemed Dreams,* edited by Dorey Schmidt (Edinburg: Pan American U, 1978), provided the basis for this compilation, which attempts to correct some errors (of spelling and of page and volume numbers) as it extends the coverage.

Of more immediate help to this bibliography was the expert attention given it by several people, whose contributions I am pleased now to acknowledge. Three graduate students were exceptionally kind, granting me the benefit of the McMurtry bibliographies they compiled for their thesis or dissertation work. They are Jane Jackson Lewis, at Hardin-Simmons University; Thora Thurn, at Tarleton State University; and Roger W. Jones, at Texas A&M University. Each checked my work against his or her own and offered corrections and additions. Further such help came from P. Martin Sarvis, librarian at the University of North Texas, who also reviewed the bibliography and recommended improvements. Together these people saved me from numerous errors, especially omissions. They have my sincere thanks. At Lamar University I owe thanks to Linda Dietert, librarian in charge of interlibrary loans, who efficiently answered my requests for scores of articles, and Marion Ingham, lecturer in the Department of English, who generously took time from her own research in the library at the University of Texas to verify many entries on the bibliography.

• •

The following indexes were among those consulted in compiling this bibliography: *Access, Book Review Index, Essay and General Literature Index, Humanities Index, An Index to Book Reviews in the Humanities, Magazine Index* (a computer database), *MLA Bibliography,* and *Reader's Guide.* Indexes for the following periodicals were also consulted: *Houston Post* (from 1976), *National Observer* (1969–77), *New York Times, Texas Observer, Wall Street Journal,* and *Washington Post.*

Abbreviations

McMurtry titles:
AFB	*Anything for Billy*
AMF	*All My Friends Are Going to Be Strangers*
"Bridegroom"	"Ever a Bridegroom: Reflections on the Failure of Texas Literature." *Texas Observer* 23 Oct. 1981: 1+.

CJ   *Cadillac Jack*
DR   *The Desert Rose*
FF   *Film Flam: Essays on Hollywood*
HPB   *Horseman, Pass By*
ING   *In a Narrow Grave: Essays on Texas*
LC   *Leaving Cheyenne*
LD   *Lonesome Dove*
LPS   *The Last Picture Show*
MO   *Moving On*
SD   *Somebody's Darling*
T   *Texasville*
TE   *Terms of Endearment*
"Texas Moon"   "The Texas Moon, and Elsewhere." *Atlantic Monthly* Mar. 1975: 29–36.

Other titles:

CLC   *Contemporary Literary Criticism.* 51 vols. to date. Detroit: Gale, 1973– . An ongoing series that prints excerpts of reviews and articles concerned with contemporary writing. This bibliography cites *CLC* reprints parenthetically after the entry for the original publication. Citations are to volume and page numbers, in the form "*CLC* 7: 214–15."

Magill Magill, Frank N., ed. *Magill's Literary Annual* [formerly *Masterplots*]. 32 vols. to date. New York: Salem, 1957–70; Englewood Cliffs: Salem, 1971– . An ongoing series that collects new essay-reviews in annual volumes devoted to "outstanding books published in the United States." To cite items from this series, this bibliography cross-references to Magill and gives the year (printed on each annual's spine and title page) and page numbers, in the form "Magill 1976: 317–20."

Schmidt Schmidt, Dorey, ed. *Larry McMurtry: Unredeemed Dreams.* Living Author Series 1. Edinburg: Pan American U, 1978. A symposium of critical essays, an interview, and a bibliography, written mostly by faculty members of Pan American University after McMurtry appeared there in 1978. The nine pieces of the collection are here listed individually, cross-referenced to Schmidt with page numbers, in the form "Schmidt 52–61."

1. Bibliography

Huber, Dwight. "Larry McMurtry: A Selected Bibliography." Schmidt 52–61.

Landess, Thomas. "Larry McMurtry." *Southwestern American Literature: A Bibliography.* Ed. John Q. Anderson, Edwin W. Gaston, Jr., and James W[ard] Lee. Chicago: Swallow, 1980. 352.

Peavy, Charles D. "A Larry McMurtry Bibliography." *Western American Literature* 3 (1968): 235–48.

2. Biography

Ahearn, Kerry [David]. "Larry McMurtry." *Fifty Western Writers: A Bio-Bibliographical Sourcebook.* Ed. Fred Erisman and Richard W. Etulain. Westport: Greenwood, 1982. 280–90. Includes biography, criticism, and bibliography.

Amory, Cleveland. Trade Winds. *Saturday Review* 13 June 1970: 12+. Recounts details of an interview in Washington, D.C. Provides some background biographical information and briefly quotes McMurtry in conversation about his father and his writing.

Anders, John. "McMurtry's New Store One for the Books." Notes. *Dallas Morning News* 18 May 1984: 1C. Reports McMurtry's plan to open a bookstore in Dallas. Briefly mentions controversy over his "Bridegroom" essay.

Bennett, Elizabeth. "Larry McMurtry: Best Seller." *Houston Post* 29 Mar. 1988: 1C+. Reports McMurtry's purchase of a Houston bookstore and quotes him on his interest in rare-book collecting and selling.

Bennett, Patrick. "Larry McMurtry: Thalia, Houston, and Hollywood." *Talking With Texas Writers: Twelve Interviews.* College Station: Texas A&M UP, 1980. 15–36.

Berger, Joseph. "Herding Words." *New York Times Book Review* 9 June 1985: 7. Based on a telephone interview; quotes McMurtry on LD's source in his uncles' stories about cattle drives.

Brown, Norman D. "Larry McMurtry." *Southern Writers: A Biographical Dictionary.* Ed. Robert Bain, Joseph M. Flora, and Louis D. Rubin, Jr. Baton Rouge: Louisiana State UP, 1979. 293– 94.

Curtis, Gregory. "The Power of Polite Discouragement." Behind the Lines. *Texas Monthly* Dec. 1986: 5–6. On McMurtry's manner of teaching writing at Rice, as recalled by one of his former students.

Davis, Peyton. "Checking in with Larry McMurtry." *Westward* [*Dallas Times Herald*] 12 Oct. 1980: 77+. Based on an interview given by

McMurtry at his Washington bookstore. McMurtry discusses a screenplay he wrote for Francis Ford Coppola, about ranchers and Indians in Eastern Montana who form an alliance to preserve the environment from strip mining, and works then in progress—CJ, LD, and a book-length essay on Archer County.

Dunn, Si. "Ex-native Son McMurtry." *Texas Observer* 16 Jan. 1976: 13. Reports McMurtry's appearance at a Southern Methodist University literary festival, with quotations taken both from McMurtry's speech and from an interview.

———. "Larry McMurtry Moves On." *Scene: The Dallas Morning News' Sunday Magazine* 18 Jan. 1976: 18–20. Includes much the same material as Dunn's *Texas Observer* article cited above.

Flood, Mary. "McMurtry Winner of Pulitzer." *Houston Post* 18 Apr. 1986, final ed.: 1A+. Reports a telephone interview with McMurtry.

Greene, A. C. "Larry Remembered as Dedicated Bookman." *Texas Books in Review* Sept. 1987: 14. Describes McMurtry's long-time interest in book collecting and selling.

Grumbach, Doris. "Talking with McMurtry." *Washingtonian* June 1976: 119+. An interview ranging over such topics as literary influences, contemporary fiction and nonfiction, film writing, Hollywood novels, Washington novels, and the reading public.

Lee, Richard. "Cadillac Larry." *Washington Post Magazine* 5 Dec. 1982: 12+. A profile based on an interview.

McCullough, David W. "Larry McMurtry." *People, Books and Book People.* New York: Harmony, 1981. 117–18. Based on a 1976 interview for the *Book-of-the-Month Club News.*

O'Keefe, Ruth Jones. "The W. J. McMurtrys." *Archer County Pioneers: A History of Archer County, Texas.* Hereford, TX: Pioneer, 1969. 64. A brief history of McMurtry's antecedents in Archer County. Jeff (W. J., Jr.) is the novelist's father. Cf. Lich's account of McMurtry's ancestry in *Larry McMurtry's Texas* (6–7), listed below with General Criticism.

Papincheck, Robert Allen. "Getting Personal with Larry McMurtry: Texas Put His Fiction on the Map." *Family Weekly* 18 Nov. 1984: 20.

Parks, Louis B. "'Lonesome' Larry: McMurtry Has Little to Say When Push Comes to 'Dove.'" *Houston Chronicle* 9 Feb. 1989: 1D+. Based on a telephone interview occasioned by the success of the miniseries.

Rigler, Judyth. "Bookfair Focuses on Film." *Express-News* [San Antonio] 9 Oct. 1988: 1-H. Briefly discusses films of McMurtry's novels and reports his participation in events of the Inter-American Bookfair.

———. "Conference: Literary Texas Alive, Well." Books. *Express-*

News [San Antonio] 5 Oct. 1986: 6H. Includes a brief account of McMurtry's speech at the Texas Sesquicentennial Conference on the Literary Arts, at North Texas State University.

———, Judy[th]. "Larry McMurtry: Pressing at the Barriers." Books. *Monitor* [McAllen, TX] 1 Nov. 1981: 9C. A full-page account of McMurtry's participation as an instructor at the University of El Paso's Summer Writer's Conference in August 1981.

———. "McMurtry: A Hit Today and Tomorrow." The Texas Shelf. *Fort Worth Star-Telegram* 24 Jan. 1988, sec. 6: 7. In describing McMurtry's success, reports numbers of copies in print for editions of T and LD.

———. "McMurtry: It Seemed More Like a Pulitzer Price." *Express-News* [San Antonio] 29 Mar. 1987: 4-H. Reports McMurtry's speech to the Texas Institute of Letters, "Adventures with *Lonesome Dove,*" about the numerous prizes the book won and their effect on the author's relationship with his readers.

———. "McMurtry to Speak at Texas Literary Meet." Books. *Express-News* [San Antonio] 1 Mar. 1987: 6-H. Reports plans for the annual meeting of the Texas Institute of Letters.

———. "NTSU Took Tough Task and Made It into Reality." *Denton Record-Chronicle* 12 Oct. 1986: 10D. Reports events of the Texas Sesquicentennial Conference on the Literary Arts, briefly mentioning McMurtry's participation.

Rosenfeld, Arnold. "Larry." Books. *Spotlight [Houston Post]* 30 Oct. 1966: 26. A profile based on an interview. McMurtry discusses sex in LPS; the differences in country, small-town, and city life; his regional-novelist status; and female characters in LPS.

Rothstein, Mervyn. "A Texan Who Likes to Deflate the Legends of the Golden West." *New York Times* 1 Nov. 1988: C17+. Reports a phone interview in which McMurtry criticizes the myth of cowboys who are "simple, strong and free, and not twisted, fascistic and dumb."

Schmidt, Dorey, and Dwight Huber. "Larry McMurtry: Unredeemed Dreams." Schmidt 1–4. Transcription of a telephone interview.

Shales, Tom. "The Author: He'd Rather Sell Books." *Washington Post* 12 Dec. 1971: E1+. Based on an interview occasioned by the Washington opening of the movie LPS.

Sweeney, Louise. "A Bookstore Owner Who Writes His Own Best-sellers." *Christian Science Monitor* 6 Feb. 1976: 16. Based on an interview.

Trillin, Calvin. "U.S. Journal: Washington, D.C.: Scouting Sleepers." *New Yorker* 14 June 1978: 86–92. Describes the author's experience of rare-book hunting for McMurtry.

Weems, John Edward. "Ruminations on Texas Writing: UT Literary Symposium." *Texas Observer* 22 Apr. 1983: 18–20. Reports a conference in Austin at the University of Texas: "The Texas Literary Tradition: Fiction, Folklore, History." McMurtry was a participant.

Weisser, Patti. "So the 'Real' Larry McMurtry Stood Up." Schmidt 62–63. A student-written profile occasioned by McMurtry's appearance at Pan American University.

West, Richard. "Book Bound: The Rare Passion of Larry McMurtry and Friends." Working. *D Magazine* June 1985: 46+. Partially based on an interview with McMurtry, who was in Dallas to purchase a private library of fine books. McMurtry describes his beginnings as a book scout in the early sixties.

Wyckoff, Peter C. "Why Do You Do What You Do?" *Houston Post* 16 Feb. 1986, final ed.: 11F. Gives McMurtry's response to the article's title question, put to him when he spoke at a gathering of the Houston Advertising Federation.

——. "Larry McMurtry's Hardtop County." *Houston Post* 19 Apr. 1987, final ed.: 3F. Profiles McMurtry's hometown, Archer City, Texas.

UNSIGNED

"Larry McMurtry." *Current Biography Yearbook: 1984.* Ed. Charles Moritz. New York: Wilson, 1984. 276–79.

"McMurtry, Larry (Jeff)." *Contemporary Authors: A Bio-Bibliographical Guide to Current Authors and Their Works.* Ed. Barbara Harte and Carolyn Riley. 1st revision. Vols. 5–8. Detroit: Gale, 1969. 100 vols. 767.

"Notes and Comment." The Talk of the Town. *New Yorker* 19 May 1986: 27+. Briefly quotes from and comments on McMurtry's contribution to "Texas in Transition: A Sesquicentennial Forum," in Austin, Texas.

"A Writer's Trail." *Time* 24 Oct. 1988: 92. A profile, accompanying R. Z. Sheppard's review of AFB.

3. General Criticism

*Adams, Robert M. "The Bard of Wichita Falls." *New York Review of Books* 13 Aug. 1987: 39–41. Considers T, LD, and LPS.

Ahearn, Kerry David. "Aspects of the Contemporary American Western Novel." *DAI* 35 (1974): 2975A. Ohio U. Includes discussion of

*Indicates that an item is reprinted or excerpted in *Taking Stock.*

McMurtry as one of several writers who "seek detachment from
Western myth."

*_____, Kerry [David]. "More D'Urban: The Texas Novels of Larry
McMurtry." *Texas Quarterly* 19.3 (1976): 109–29. (Rpt. in *Critical
Essays on the Western American Novel.* Ed. William T[om] Pilkington. Boston: Hall, 1980. 223–42.) Charts "McMurtry's 'decline to
success'" in the first five novels (HPB, LC, LPS, MO, AMF), which
show "an increasing absence of psychological depth and artistic
refinement."

*Baker, Christopher. "The Death of the Frontier in the Novels of
Larry McMurtry." *McNeese Review* 28 (1981–82): 44–54. Represents principal characters of LPS and AMF as throwbacks to their
nineteenth-century, frontier-settling ancestors. Thus, in LPS Sam
"embodies the silent aloofness of the frontier rancher," while Sonny
suffers from the *"anomie"* characteristic of mountain men and
trappers. To establish the relevant frontier personality types, cites
historians Frederick Jackson Turner and Ray Allen Billington and
sociologists Georg Simmel and Robert E. Park.

Bold, Christine. "Anti-Western Westerns." *Selling the Wild West: Popular Western Fiction, 1860–1960.* Bloomington: Indiana UP, 1987.
155–65. Briefly cites HPB as an example of the "New Western
[that] overturns the conventional attributes of the Western hero to
chart and even celebrate the new, unheroic West."

Busby, Mark. "McMurtry, Larry (Jeff)." *Twentieth-Century Western
Writers.* Ed. James Vinson. Detroit: Gale, 1982. 534–36.

Byrd, James W., Scott Downing, and Art Hendrix. "McMurtry Circles
His Wagons: An East Texas Roundup." *Southwestern American
Literature* 14.2 (1989): 4–19.

Clark, L. D. "Texas Historical Writing: A Sample of the Myth at Age
150." *American West* Jan.–Feb. 1986: 80–81. Considers LD.

Clifford, Craig Edward. *In the Deep Heart's Core: Reflections on Life,
Letters, and Texas.* Tarleton State University Southwestern Studies in the Humanities 1. College Station: Texas A&M UP, 1985. No
index; see references to McMurtry on pages 3–6, 8, 9, 13, 14, 19, 21,
34–35, 38, 42, 45, 46, 47, 51n, 66–67, 86–87, 92n, 112, 115, 117, 121,
and 123.

_____. "Myth in Texas Letters: Horseman, Hang On." Books and the
Culture. *Texas Observer* 12 Feb. 1982: 20–24. (Rpt. with revisions as
"Horseman, Hang On: The Reality of Myth in Texas Letters" in
In the Deep Heart's Core, listed above. 11–22.) Discusses three
McMurtry essays: "Bridegroom," "Southwestern Literature?" (in
ING), and "Texas Moon."

Cochran, Mike. "'Texasville' Tale Raises Eyebrows in Archer City." *Houston Post* 10 May 1987, final ed.: 5B. Recalls Archer City's hostile reaction to the filming of LPS there and cites the varied critical response in Texas periodicals to T, sequel to LPS. Quotes McMurtry's sister and other Archer City residents.

*Crooks, Alan F. "Larry McMurtry—A Writer in Transition: An Essay-Review." *Western American Literature* 7 (1972): 151–55. Identifies existential alienation and vivid characters as notable elements of the "episodic and, at times, rather dull" novels MO and AMF. Briefly quotes from an interview with McMurtry, who describes his loss of interest in writing novels about the West and his increasing attraction to screen writing.

*Davis, Kenneth W. "The Themes of Initiation in the Works of Larry McMurtry and Tom Mayer." *Arlington Quarterly* 2.3 (1970): 29–43. (Revised for *Taking Stock* and reprinted here as "Initiation Themes in McMurtry's Cowboy Trilogy.") Discusses HPB, LC, and LPS.

Dean, Patricia E. "Names in Larry McMurtry's 'Thalia Trilogy.'" *The Dangerous, Secret Name of God; Fartley's Compressed Gas Company; The Barf'n'choke; And Other Matters Onomastic.* Papers of North Central Names Institute 2. Ed. Laurence E. Seits. Sugar Grove, IL: Waubonsee Community College, 1981. 71–76. Examines connotations of characters' names in HPB, LC, and LPS.

D[ugger], R[onnie]. "Fallow Fields." *Texas Observer* 5 Nov. 1971: 21–24. In a survey of contemporary Texas writers, assesses McMurtry as a "serious talent," though one whose "best work [is] ahead of him."

English, Sarah. "Larry McMurtry." *Dictionary of Literary Biography Yearbook: 1987.* Ed. J. M. Brook. Detroit: Gale, 1988. 265–74. Discusses CJ, DR, LD, T, and FF and reviews the critical reception of the four novels. Concludes by pointing to signs of a new, serious critical regard for McMurtry.

Gerlach, John. "Larry McMurtry." *American Novelists Since World War II.* Ed. Jeffrey Helterman and Richard Layman. Detroit: Gale, 1978. 328–31. Vol. 2 of *Dictionary of Literary Biography.* 61 vols. to date. 1978–   . Discusses HPB, LC, LPS, MO, AMF, and TE.

Giesen, Tom. "Novels by Larry McMurtry." *Northwest Review* 9.1 (1967): 120–21. Examines themes of loneliness and loss in HPB, LC, and LPS.

Giles, James R. "Larry McMurtry's *Leaving Cheyenne* and the Novels of John Rechy: Four Trips Along 'the Mythical Pecos.'" *Forum* [U of Houston] 10.2 (1972): 34–40. Takes two ideas from McMurtry's ING as the basis for a comparison of McMurtry and Rechy: (1) the

writer's rebellion against restrictions on language and subject matter and (2) the writer's replacement of the lost physical frontier with
a new literary frontier, the "mythical Pecos" that is often "lonely and
bitter."

Goodwyn, Larry. "The Frontier Myth and Southwestern Literature."
American Libraries Feb. 1971: 161–67; Apr. 1971: 359–66. (Rpt. in
Regional Perspectives: An Examination of America's Literary Heritage.
Ed. John Gordon Burke. Chicago: ALA, 1973. 175–206. Excerpted in
CLC 27: 328–29.) Criticizes the frontier myth for its pastoralism,
sexism, and racism, "a debilitating literary frame of reference," and
analyzes variously inadequate responses to this myth in many works
of Southwestern literature. Singles out McMurtry for questioning
the received myth in HPB and LC, where "[a] kind of drawing back
from the frontier mystique on McMurtry's part" represents a
new, serious literary approach to the frontier. Notes abandonment
of frontier materials in LPS and MO but detects ambivalence in
McMurtry's "personal declaration of independence from the frontier
mystique" in ING.

Graham, Don. "Is Dallas Burning? Notes on Recent Texas Fiction."
Southwestern American Literature 4 (1974): 68–73. Points to
McMurtry's consciousness of a vanishing frontier in HPB, LC,
LPS, MO, and AMF. Contrasts his effective depiction of "Old
Texas" with his unconvincing presentation of "New Texas."

———. "Regionalism on the Ramparts: The Texas Literary Tradition." *USA Today* July 1986: 74–76. This survey of Texas fiction
considers "what the proper province of the Texas writer should be"
and concludes with a defense of regionalism. Briefly describes J.
Frank Dobie's dismissal of HPB and LC, and discusses LD as a
"seeming repudiation" of McMurtry's "Bridegroom."

———. *Texas: A Literary Portrait.* San Antonio: Corona, 1985. No
index; see references to McMurtry on pages 11, 101, 165–66, 172–
73, 185, and 230–31.

Graham, Don, James W[ard] Lee, and William T[om] Pilkington, eds.
The Texas Literary Tradition: Fiction, Folklore, History. Austin: Col-
lege of the University of Texas and the Texas State Historical
Association, 1983.

Greene, A. C. *The Fifty Best Books on Texas.* Dallas: Pressworks, 1981.
Includes estimates of HPB and LC as among the fifty.

———. "The Texas Literati: Whose Home Is This Range Anyhow?"
New York Times Book Review 15 Sept. 1985: 3+. A survey of the
contemporary Texas literary scene. Discusses McMurtry's "Bridegroom," LD, and ING.

Hulbert, Ann. "Rural Chic: Fiction and Films Are Living Off the Fad of the Land." *New Republic* 2 Sept. 1985: 25–30. Discusses LD.

Kehl, D. G. "Thalia's 'Sock' and the Cowhide Boot: Humor of the New Southwest in the Fiction of Larry McMurtry." *Southwestern American Literature* 14.2 (1989): 20–33.

*Landess, Thomas. *Larry McMurtry.* Southwest Writers Series 23. Austin: Steck-Vaughn, 1969.

Lee, James Ward. *Classics of Texas Fiction.* Dallas: E-Heart, 1987. Discusses HPB, LC, and LD on pages 102–04.

———, James W[ard]. "The Deep South Experience in Texas Fiction." *Texas Humanist* Apr. 1980: 1+. Briefly mentions McMurtry's work as the best fiction about "the new Texas of industry, oil, banking, and politics."

Lemann, Nicholas. "Today's Best Journalism: Better Than Fiction." *Washington Monthly* Mar. 1983: 24+. CJ is one of four Washington novels discussed.

Lich, Lera Patrick Tyler. *Larry McMurtry's Texas: Evolution of the Myth.* Austin: Eakin, 1987. Biographical criticism; includes photographs of McMurtry's hometown, Archer City, TX.

Limón, José E. "A 'Southern Renaissance' for Texas Letters: A Literary Flowering in South Texas." Books and the Culture. *Texas Observer* 28 Oct. 1983: 20–23. (Rpt. with revisions as "A 'Southern Renaissance' for Texas Letters" in *Range Wars: Heated Debates, Sober Reflections, and Other Assessments of Texas Writing.* Ed. Craig [Edward] Clifford and [William] Tom Pilkington. Dallas: Southern Methodist UP, 1989. 59–68.) Includes discussion of "Bridegroom."

Lindsey, Daniel Lee. "Staying on the Road: The Ironic Journey of the Youthful Protagonist in Contemporary American Fiction." *DAI* 37 (1976): 4354A. Northwestern U. Discusses Danny Deck's plight in AMF.

Lindstrom, Naomi. "The Novel in Texas: How Big a Patrimony?" *Texas Quarterly* 21.2 (1978): 73–83. The first paragraph mentions McMurtry's "Minor Regional Novelist" T-shirt.

Major, Mabel, and T. M. Pearce. *Southwest Heritage: A Literary History with Bibliographies.* 3rd rev. ed. Albuquerque: U of New Mexico P, 1972.

Melichar, Don. "Recommended: Larry McMurtry." *English Journal* Dec. 1986: 49–50. An "appreciation" occasioned by McMurtry's Pulitzer.

M[iller], L[antz]. "Is There Life in Texas after McMurtry?" *Balcones* 1.2 (1987): 88+. Argues that McMurtry's novels represent his own failure to live up to the challenge of his "Bridegroom" essay, which calls for an urban Texas literature.

Mogen, David. "Sex and True West in McMurtry's Fiction: From Teddy Blue to *Lonesome Dove* to *Texasville.*" *Southwestern American Literature* 14.2 (1989): 34–45.

Morrow, Patrick D. "Larry McMurtry: The First Phase." *Seasoned Authors for a New Season: The Search for Standards in Popular Writing.* Ed. Louis Filler. Question of Quality 2. Bowling Green: Bowling Green U Popular P, 1980. 70–82. Reads HPB as "a direct attack on *Shane,*" discovering in various parallels "a punishingly extensive antiphony-response relationship" that "can hardly be accidental." Focuses on characterization in LPS.

———. "Mental Retardation in *The Sound and the Fury* and *The Last Picture Show.*" *Re: Artes Liberales* 6.1 (1979): 1–9.

*Neinstein, Raymond L. *The Ghost Country: A Study of the Novels of Larry McMurtry.* Modern Authors Monograph Series 1. Berkeley: Creative Arts, 1976. Traces McMurtry's journey "from an old-fashioned regionalism to a kind of 'neo-regionalism,' his characters, and the novels themselves, turning from the land as the locus of their values to an imaginary, fictive 'place.'" Discusses HPB, LC, LPS, ING, MO, and AMF.

———. "Neo-Regionalism in America." *DAI* 38 (1977): 5482A–83A. State U of New York-Buffalo. Discusses McMurtry's development from an "early mode of nostalgic re-creations of the past to a 'neo-regional' sense that place has disappeared or become unavailable."

Nelson, Jane. "Larry McMurtry." *A Literary History of the American West.* Ed. J. Golden Taylor, et al. Fort Worth: Texas Christian UP, 1987. 612–21. A chronological, critical account of McMurtry's major publications through LD.

O'Conner, Patricia T. New and Noteworthy. *New York Times Book Review* 3 May 1987: 40. Notes paperback reissues of SD, MO, DR, and CJ.

Peavy, Charles D. "Coming of Age in Texas: The Novels of Larry McMurtry." *Western American Literature* 4 (1969): 171–88. (*CLC* 27: 324–26.) Studies themes of loneliness, adolescent sexuality, and the achievement of manhood ("the most important theme") in HPB, LC, and LPS.

———. *Larry McMurtry.* Twayne's United States Authors Series 291. Boston: Twayne, 1977. Includes biography, criticism, and bibliography.

Phelan, Richard. "Waiting for a Texas Writer." Books and the Culture. *Texas Observer* 3 Sept. 1982: 12–14. Discusses "Bridegroom."

*Phillips, Billie. "McMurtry's Women: 'Eros [Libido, Caritas and Philia] in [and out of] Archer County.'" *Southwestern American Literature* 4 (1974): 29–36. Categorizes McMurtry's women as "travellers," "settlers," or "searchers" as it analyzes their experience of love. Discusses characters from HPB, LC, LPS, MO, and AMF.

*Phillips, Raymond C. "The Ranch as Place and Symbol in the Novels of Larry McMurtry." *South Dakota Review* 13.2 (1975): 27–47.

Pilkington, [William] Tom. "Contemporary Texas Writers and the Concept of Regionalism." *Texas Humanist* Apr. 1980: 1+. Discusses Texas's transition from the country to the city in ING, HPB, LC, LPS, and MO and the abandonment of Texas themes in TE and SD.

*———, William T[om]. "The Dirt-Farmer and the Cowboy: Notes on Two Texas Essayists." *Re: Arts and Letters* 3.1 (1969): 42–54. (Rpt. in *My Blood's Country: Studies in Southwestern Literature.* Texas Christian University Monographs in History and Culture 10. Fort Worth: Texas Christian UP, 1973. 163–82.) Compares Larry King's essays and McMurtry's ING.

———, William T[om]. "The Recent Southwestern Novel." *Southwestern American Literature* 1 (1971): 12–15. In a survey of Southwestern fiction of the 1960s, singles out McMurtry as the region's most promising novelist. Discusses Texas's transition from the country to the city in HPB, LC, LPS, and MO.

Reid, Jan. "McMurtry-Kesey Reunion: Two Old Friends Find They Don't Have Much in Common." *Houston City Magazine* Mar. 1980: 72+. Reports the panel discussion of McMurtry and Ken Kesey, who appeared together at North Lake Community College, Irving, Texas. Includes discussion of movies *Hud* and LPS.

*Reynolds, R. C[lay]. "Showdown in the New Old West: The Cowboy vs. the Oilman." *Lamar Journal of the Humanities* 6.1 (1980): 19–31. Identifies antithetical values of adult characters in HPB and LPS, where "romantic visions of the past" compete with "pragmatic demands of the present," confusing the novels' adolescent protagonists.

Risser, Katherine Lynn. "The Mexican Setting in the Contemporary American Novel." Diss. U of Arkansas, 1985.

Scheel, Charles. "Narrative and Character in Larry McMurtry's Novels of the 1970's." Diss. Université Des Sciences Humaines De Strasburg, 1985. Discusses AMF, MO, TE, and SD. Available at the U of Houston.

Shockley, Martin. "Larry McMurtry." *Southwest Writers Anthology.* Austin: Steck-Vaughn, 1967. 230–33. Reprints a selection from HPB, "The Slaughter of the Herd," with a brief biographical and critical headnote.

Smith, Roland Hinojosa. "McMurtry Work Inspired Early Critic to Cry Foul." *Austin American-Statesman* 22 Mar. 1987: D7.

Sonnichsen, C. L. *From Hopalong to Hud: Thoughts on Western Fiction.* College Station: Texas A&M UP, 1978.

_____. "The New Style Western." *South Dakota Review* 4 (1966): 22–28. Represents McMurtry as one of a group of "High-Road Western writers" who seek to revive the Western novel. Discusses HPB and LC.

_____. "Sex on the Lone Prairee." *Western American Literature* 13 (1978): 15–33. (Rpt., with minor revisions, in *From Hopalong to Hud,* listed above. 157–75.) Posits a "Larry McMurtry school of realism" in Western fiction, a "Tribe of Larry" that evokes "obscure corners of human sexuality." Discusses zoophily in LPS and AMF.

Stegner, Wallace. "History, Myth, and the Western Writer." *American West* 4.2 (1967): 61–62+. Briefly mentions HPB and LPS.

*Stout, Janis P. "Journeying as a Metaphor for Cultural Loss in the Novels of Larry McMurtry." *Western American Literature* 11 (1976): 37–50. (*CLC* 27: 329–31.)

*Summerlin, Tim. "Larry McMurtry and the Persistent Frontier." *Southwestern American Literature* 4 (1974): 22–28.

_____, Charles T[im]. "Late McMurtry." *Lamar Journal of the Humanities* 2.1 (1975): 54–56. Discusses MO and AMF in relation to McMurtry's statement in "Texas Moon" about Texas settings that leave him "sucking air"; argues that the novels belie the statement.

Thurn, Thora. "McMurtry's Settlers: Molly and Emma." *CCTE Studies* 47 (1982): 51–56.

Underwood, June O. "Western Women and True Womanhood: Culture and Symbol in History and Literature." *Great Plains Quarterly* 5 (1985): 93–106. Cites LC's Molly as an example of a modern Western's depiction of "the 'good' woman who actually likes sex."

Ward, Carol Marie. "Movie as Metaphor in Contemporary Fiction: A Study of Walker Percy, Larry McMurtry, and John Fowles." *DAI* 42 (1982): 3996A. U of Tennessee. Considers LPS and SD.

Wood, Susan. "Lone Star Literary Society." *Book World* 2 May 1982: 15. In discussing changes in Texas literature, mentions "Bridegroom" as the culmination of a year's self-examination by several Texas writers.

Wyckoff, Peter C. "With McMurtry, the Contrasts Remain." *Houston Post* 21 July 1985, final ed.: 1F+. Discusses McMurtry's relationship to Texas and his regional-novelist status.

_____. "They Have Finally Picked a Winner." *Houston Post* 27 Apr. 1986, final ed.: 11F. Discusses the appropriateness of McMurtry's Pulitzer for LD.

Wylder, Delbert E. "Recent Western Fiction." *Journal of the West* Jan. 1980: 62–70. Describes Western fiction since 1975, briefly discussing TE and SD.

Yardley, Jonathan. "All in the Family." *Commonweal* 11 May 1979: 265–66. Briefly mentions TE as one of many examples of contemporary American fiction dealing in family situations.

Zafran, Robert L. "An Analysis of the Novels of Larry McMurtry for Oral Interpretation of Script Adaptation." Diss. Southern Illinois U, 1982.

UNSIGNED

"Larry McMurtry (Jeff)." *Encyclopedia of Frontier and Western Fiction.* Ed. Vicki Piekarski and Jon Tuska. New York: McGraw, 1983. 230–31. A peculiarly unsympathetic entry for a reference volume. Opens by identifying McMurtry as a "[m]agazine writer and book reviewer whose early novels were set in contemporary Texas"—as if McMurtry were primarily a journalist. In discussing McMurtry's fiction (HPB, LC, LPS, MO, AMF, TE, and SD), focuses almost exclusively on McMurtry's "obsession . . . with sexuality, including sexual intercourse with animals."

"McMurtry, Larry (Jeff)." *Contemporary Authors: A Bio-Bibliographical Guide to Current Writers in Fiction, General Nonfiction, Poetry, Journalism, Drama, Motion Pictures, Television, and Other Fields.* Ed. Linda Metzger. New revision. Vol. 19. Detroit: Gale, 1987. 25 vols. 329–34. Includes biographical data, overview of criticism spanning McMurtry's career (through LD), and bibliography.

"Notes and Comment." The Talk of the Town. *New Yorker* 26 Aug. 1985: 19–22. (*CLC* 44: 258–59.) Discusses LD and McMurtry's prefaces to paperback reissues of CJ and DR. Emphasis on McMurtry's "on-going capacity for fashioning fully living characters."

4. Criticism of Individual Titles

NOVELS

Horseman, Pass By (1961)

*Busby, Mark. "Damn the Saddle on the Wall: Anti-Myth in Larry McMurtry's *Horseman, Pass By.*" *New Mexico Humanities Review* 3.1 (1980): 5–10.

Gard, Wayne. "Grandfather Knew Best." *New York Times Book Review* 18 June 1961: 27.

Hartley, Margaret L. *Southwest Review* 46.3 (1961): viii+.

Kelley, David Otis. *Library Journal* 1 Sept. 1961: 2818.

Macdonald, Andrew. "The Passing Frontier in McMurtry's *Hud/ Horseman, Pass By.* Schmidt 5–11.

Minter, David L. "To Live and Die in Texas." *Texas Observer* 15 Sept. 1961: 6.

Pore, Charles. *New York Times Book Review* 10 June 1961: 21.

Serebnick, Judith. "Texas Is Home Country." *Library Journal* 1 Feb. 1961: 603.

Tinkle, Lon. "Raw and Rough Look at Ranching Texas." Reading and Writing. *Dallas Morning News* 28 May 1961, sec. 5: 9.

UNSIGNED
Now in Paperback. *Los Angeles Times Book Review* 15 Sept. 1985: 8.

Leaving Cheyenne (1963)

Bogie, Thomas M. *Library Journal* 1 Oct. 1963: 3644+.

Cole, William. "Easy Reading, Woody to Wodehouse." *Saturday Review* 26 June 1976: 41.

Clemons, Walter. "The Last Word: An Overlooked Novel." *New York Times Book Review* 15 Aug. 1971: 39.

D[ooley], S[ally]. *Review of Texas Books* 1.1 (1986): 1. Brief notice of the reissue by Texas A&M UP.

Markus, Kurt. *Western Horseman* July 1982: 73–74.

Phillips, Al. *Best Sellers* June 1986: 86.

Sprague, Marshall. "Texas Triptych." *New York Times Book Review* 6 Oct. 1963: 39.

Tinkle, Lon. "Of Fate and Doom in Ranch Country." Reading and Writing. *Dallas Morning News* 13 Oct. 1963, sec. 1: 24.

The Last Picture Show (1966)

Bode, Elroy. "The Last Picture Show." *Texas Observer* 20 Jan. 1967: 17–18.

Dubose, Thomas. "*The Last Picture Show:* Theme." *Re: Artes Liberales* 3 (1977): 43–45.

England, D. Gene. "Rites of Passage in Larry McMurtry's *The Last Picture Show.*" *Heritage of Kansas* 12.1 (1979): 37–48.

*Fritz, Donald E. "Anatomy and *The Last Picture Show:* A Matter of Definition." Schmidt 12–18.

*Hickey, Dave. "Elegy and Exorcism: Texas Talent and General Concerns." *Texas Observer* 20 Jan. 1967: 14–16.

Hobby, Diana. "The Boys and Girls of Thalia." *Spotlight* [*Houston Post*] 30 Oct. 1966: 26.

Jack, W. T. "Sex Wasn't Everything." *New York Times Book Review* 13 Nov. 1966: 68–69.

Lask, Thomas. *New York Times Book Review* 3 Dec. 1966: 37.

Macdonald, Andrew, and Gina Macdonald. "Values in Transition in *The Last Picture Show*, or How to Make a Citybilly." Schmidt 19–28.

Peavy, Charles D. "Larry McMurtry and Black Humor: A Note on *The Last Picture Show.*" *Western American Literature* 2 (1967): 223–27. Focuses on McMurtry's treatment of sex.

Petersen, Clarence. *Books Today* [*Chicago Tribune*] 30 July 1967: 8.

Stern, Daniel. "Paper Worlds." *Book Week* [*Washington Post*] 23 Oct. 1966: 16.

Tinkle, Lon. "Critical Spirit in Texas Fiction." Reading and Writing. *Dallas Morning News* 26 Feb. 1967: 2G.

UNSIGNED

Kirkus Reviews 1 Aug. 1966: 783.

"Pick of the Paperbacks." *Saturday Review* 22 Jan. 1972: 70.

Publishers Weekly 18 July 1966: 74–75.

Publishers Weekly 15 May 1967: 42.

Moving On (1970)

Barthelme, Steve. "McMurtry's *Moving On.*" *Texas Observer* 8 Jan. 1971: 13–16. See also McMurtry's point-by-point rebuttal, "Answer from McMurtry" (*Texas Observer* 26 Feb. 1971: 22–24).

————. "Barthelme's Response to McMurtry's Answer to Barthelme's Review of McMurtry's *Moving On.*" *Texas Observer* 12 Mar. 1971: 15. See annotation to the entry above.

*Bode, Elroy. "Moving On . . . and On . . . and On." *Southwest Review* 55 (1970): 427–31.

Comp, Linda. *Best Sellers* 1 July 1970: 129–30.

Davis, L. J. "Daily Life in Texas." *Book World* 21 June 1970: 6. (*CLC* 27: 326.)

Decker, William. *Saturday Review* 17 Oct. 1970: 36.

Greene, A. C. "McMurtry's Mammoth Novel." *Dallas Morning News* 31 May 1970: 7C.

Griffin, Lloyd W. *Library Journal* July 1970: 2517.

Landess, Thomas. *Southwestern American Literature* 1 (1971): 38–39.

Leonard, John. *New York Times Book Review* 10 June 1970: 49. (*CLC* 2: 271.)

Perkins, Bill. "The Details Pile Up in a Story of a Marriage That's Running Down." *National Observer* 13 July 1970: 19.

Schott, Webster. "Words, Words, Sex, Sex." *New York Times Book Review* 26 July 1970: 16. (*CLC* 2: 272.)

UNSIGNED
Kirkus Reviews 15 Mar. 1970: 346.
Publishers Weekly 6 Apr. 1970: 53.

All My Friends Are Going to Be Strangers (1972)

Baker, Roger. *Books and Bookmen* Nov. 1973: 101–02. (*CLC* 3: 333–34.)
C[lemons], W[alter]. "Drowning a Book." *Newsweek* 20 Mar. 1972: 110.
Dollard, Peter. *Library Journal* 15 Feb. 1972: 699–700.
Donald, Miles. "Lone Ranger." *New Statesman* 2 Mar. 1973: 314.
Duffy, Martha. "Moving On." *Time* 3 Apr. 1972: 64.
Gordon, Roxy. "McMurtry's *All My Friends.*" *Texas Observer* 25 Aug. 1972: 14–15.
*Granzow, Barbara. "The Western Writer: A Study of Larry McMurtry's *All My Friends Are Going to Be Strangers.*" *Southwestern American Literature* 4 (1974): 37–51.
Harrison, Jim. "Women Impossible Not to Love and Impossible to Love Right." *New York Times Book Review* 19 Mar. 1972: 5+. (*CLC* 2: 272.)
Hill, William B., SJ. *Best Sellers* 1 May 1972: 55–56.
Hollwedel, John. Magill 1973: 12–16.
Metz, Violette. "The Inner Child of Danny Deck: A Hypothetical Assessment." Schmidt 33–45.
Pilkington, William T[om]. *Southwestern American Literature* 2 (1972): 54–55.
Prigozy, Ruth. *Commonweal* 20 Oct. 1972: 70–71. (*CLC* 3: 333.)
Ricklefs, Roger. "A Trip through McMurtry Land." *Wall Street Journal* 6 June 1972, eastern ed.: 26.
Terry, Marshall. "Larry McMurtry Tightens Craft." *Dallas Morning News* 19 Mar. 1972: 10E.
Van Brunt, H. L. "McMurtry's Picaresque Tale in Grand Tradition." *Southwest Review* 57 (1972): 340–42.
Whittemore, Reed. "Texas Sex." *New Republic* 1 Apr. 1972: 28–29. (*CLC* 27: 329.)
Wood, Scott. *America* 15 Apr. 1972: 410–11.

UNSIGNED
Booklist 15 May 1972: 796.
Briefly Noted. *New Yorker* 1 Apr. 1972: 106.
Kirkus Reviews 1 Jan. 1972: 21.
New York Times Book Review 4 June 1972: 22.
New York Times Book Review 3 Dec. 1972: 72.
"Past Master." *Times Literary Supplement* 23 Mar. 1973: 313. (*CLC* 3: 333.)

"Potpourri." *Best Sellers* 1 Feb. 1973: 503.
Publishers Weekly 7 Feb. 1972: 91.
Publishers Weekly 18 Dec. 1972: 41.
"A Selection of the Year's Best Books." *Time* 1 Jan. 1973: 61.

Terms of Endearment (1975)

Adams, Phoebe-Lou. *Atlantic Monthly* Nov. 1975: 126.
Chamberlain, Ethel L. *Best Sellers* Jan. 1976: 302.
Deemer, Charles. "A Pro Strikes Out." *New Leader* 15 Mar. 1976: 19–20.
Eyth, Mary Jo. *Library Journal* 15 Dec. 1975: 2343.
Getlein, Frank. "Very Good McMurtry." *Washingtonian* Nov. 1975: 255–56.
Hardison, O. B., Jr. *New Republic* 29 Nov. 1975: 37+. (*CLC* 7: 215.)
Lehmann-Haupt, Christopher. "A Messy Vehicle That Runs." *New York Times* 22 Oct. 1975: 43.
*Mewshaw, Michael. "Moving On." *Texas Monthly* Nov. 1975: 44+.
Mittleman, Leslie B. Magill 1976: 317–20.
Rabinowitz, Dorothy. *Saturday Review* 10 Jan. 1976: 57. (*CLC* 11: 371.)
Reynolds, R. C[lay]. "Trilogy-Adventures Rounded Out." *Southwest Review* 61 (1976): 102–05. (*CLC* 7: 215.)
Schmidt, Dorey. "What to Make of Aurora Greenway." Schmidt 46–51.
Sorensen, Roberta. *Western American Literature* 11 (1977): 356–58.
Terry, Marshall. "A Texas Talent Growing Still." *Dallas Morning News* 2 Nov. 1975: 11F.
*Towers, Robert. "An Oddly Misshapen Novel by a Highly Accomplished Novelist." *New York Times Book Review* 19 Oct. 1975: 4. (*CLC* 7: 214–15.)

UNSIGNED
Booklist 1 Oct. 1975: 220.
Briefly Noted. *New Yorker* 27 Oct. 1975: 166.
"Forging into Fall." *Book World* 31 Aug. 1975: 1.
Kirkus Reviews 15 Aug. 1975: 935–36.
Publishers Weekly 8 Sept. 1975: 50.
Publishers Weekly 16 Aug. 1976: 122.
Time 20 Oct. 1975: c. 86.

Somebody's Darling (1978)

Bartholomew, David. *Library Journal* 15 Oct. 1978: 2134. (*CLC* 11: 371.)

Browne, Joseph. *America* 5 May 1979: 379.

Busby, Mark. "McMurtry, Out of the Chute Stumbling." *Zest* [*Houston Chronicle*] 14 Jan. 1979: 35.

Caplan, Brina. "Existential Struggling." *Nation* 3 Feb. 1979: 121–23. (*CLC* 27: 331–32.)

Coers, Donald. *Texas Review* 4.1 (1979): 79.

Dunn, Si. "McMurtry Followers Get a Disappointment." *Dallas Morning News* 5 Nov. 1978: 7G.

Esposito, Joseph J. "Faltering Realism." *Prairie Schooner* 53.2 (1979): 181. (*CLC* 27: 332.)

Gault, John. "Ah, Ah, Ah, Ah, Stayin' Alive." *Maclean's* 25 Dec. 1978: 45–46.

G[old], P[at]. *West Coast Review of Books* Jan. 1979: 26.

Hall, Joan Joffe. "McMurtry Is Writing Splendidly, As Usual." *Houston Post* 12 Nov. 1978: 21AA.

*Landon, Brooks. "Larry McMurtry." *Dictionary of Literary Biography Yearbook: 1980*. Ed. Karen L. Rood, Jean W. Ross, and Richard Ziegfield. Detroit: Gale, 1981. 71–74.

Leffland, Ella. *New York* 25 Dec. 1978: 99.

Lehmann-Haupt, Christopher. Books of the Times. *New York Times* 20 Dec. 1978, late city ed.: C25.

*Lyons, Gene. "Day of the Hocus." *Texas Monthly* Dec. 1978: 220+.

Robinson, Jill. "Hollywood in the Age of Longing." *Book World* 12 Nov. 1978: E5+. (*CLC* 11: 371.)

Van Laan, James R. Magill 1979: 689–92.

Yardley, Jonathan. *New York Times Book Review* 19 Nov. 1978: 15+.

UNSIGNED

Booklist 15 Oct. 1978: 354–55.

Kirkus Reviews 1 Sept. 1978: 966–67. (*CLC* 11: 371.)

New and Noteworthy. *New York Times Book Review* 16 Dec. 1979: 31.

Picks and Pans. *People Weekly* 6 Nov. 1978: 14.

Publishers Weekly 18 Sept. 1978: 162.

Publishers Weekly 29 Oct. 1979: 81.

Time 13 Nov. 1978: c. 121.

Cadillac Jack (1982)

B[rosnahan], J[ohn]. *Booklist* 1 Sept. 1982: 2. (*CLC* 27: 333.)

Browne, Joseph. *America* 5 Mar. 1983: 179–80. (*CLC* 27: 334.)

*Browning, Dominique. "The Knickknack Cadillac." *Texas Monthly* Oct. 1982: 177–78+.

Busby, Mark. "The Junk Man." *Texas Books in Review* 5 (1983): 31–32.
————. *Saturday Magazine* [*Bryan-College Station Eagle*] 11 Dec. 1982: 10.

Crooks, Alan F. *Western American Literature* 19 (1984): 146–47.

Gerber, Eric. "Mr. McGriff Goes to Washington." *Houston Post* 10 Oct. 1982: 21AA.

Greene, A. C. "McMurtry's *Cadillac Jack* Is a Just Good Ol' Time." *Dallas Morning News* 17 Oct. 1982: 4G.

Hendricks, David. "McMurtry Hitches Fun Ride with 'Cadillac Jack.'" *Express-News* [San Antonio] 21 Nov. 1982: 7H.

Jones, Roger W. "A Review of Larry McMurtry's *Cadillac Jack.*" *Lamar Journal of the Humanities* 9.2 (1983): 53–55.

Judell, Brandon. *Village Voice Literary Supplement* Oct. 1982: 5.

Koger, Grove. *Library Journal* 1 Oct. 1982: 1896.

Latham, Aaron. "McMurtry Rides High with His Comic Tale of an Urban Cowboy." *Chicago Tribune Book World* 17 Oct. 1982: 3.

Lipson, Eden Ross. *New York Times Book Review* 21 Nov. 1982: 13+. (*CLC* 27: 333–34.)

M[acPike], L[oralee]. *West Coast Review of Books* Jan. 1983: 27.

Mallon, Thomas. "Laying Rubber." *National Review* 26 Nov. 1982: 1492–93.

Parsell, David B. Magill 1983: 90–95.

Prince, Peter. "A Good Ol' Antique Dealer." *Nation* 20 Nov. 1982: 536+. (*CLC* 27: 333.)

*Reynolds, R. C[lay]. "Come Home Larry, All Is Forgiven: A Native Son's Search for Identity." *Cross Timbers Review* 2.1 (1985): 65–72.

Rigler, Judyth. "Another Winner for McMurtry." Lone Star Library. *Texas Weekly Magazine* [*Brazosport Facts*] 12 Dec. 1982: 11.

Rips, Geoffrey. "A Bumpy Ride with Cadillac Jack." Books and the Culture. *Texas Observer* 10 Dec. 1982: 26–27.

Roman, David R. *Best Sellers* Jan. 1983: 370.

See, Carolyn. *Los Angeles Times Book Review* 14 Nov. 1982: 1.

Spitz, Bob. *Penthouse* Dec. 1982: 74–75.

Yardley, Jonathan. "McMurtry's Lemon: *Cadillac Jack* Is Nobody's Darling." *Washington Post* 13 Oct. 1982, final ed.: B1+.

UNSIGNED

Briefly Noted. *New Yorker* 13 Dec. 1982: 184.

Kirkus Reviews 1 Aug. 1982: 894. (*CLC* 27: 332–33.)

Picks and Pans. *People Weekly* 15 Nov. 1982: 18.

Publishers Weekly 30 July 1982: 63.

The Desert Rose (1983)

Adams, Charles L. *Western American Literature* 20 (1985): 167–68.

Anderson, Patrick. "Grit Amid the Glitter: Tale of Showgirl Mother and Daughter in Las Vegas Is Vintage McMurtry." *Dallas Morning News* 25 Sept. 1983: 4G.

*Benedek, Emily. "An Author Recaptures His Voice." *New Leader* 14 Nov. 1983: 18–19.

Busby, Mark. *Book Week* [*Bryan-College Station Eagle*] 8 Oct. 1983: 1BB.

Cole, William. "Beyond the Neon." Trade Winds. *Saturday Review* Sept.–Oct. 1983: 46.

*Davis, Rod. "A Surfeit of Bimbos." *Texas Monthly* Nov. 1983: 192+.

Gerber, Eric. "Harmony and Pepper in Las Vegas." *Houston Post* 4 Sept. 1983, final ed.: 13F.

Grant, Lyman. *Texas Humanist* Mar.–Apr. 1984: 51.

J[onas], L[arry]. *West Coast Review of Books* Nov.–Dec. 1983: 35.

Koger, Grove. *Library Journal* 1 Sept. 1983: 1721.

Mano, D. Keith. "Vegas Deserta." *National Review* 25 Nov. 1983: 1495–96.

McCaffery, Larry. "A Gallant Flower of the Sere Las Vegas Sands." *Los Angeles Times Book Review* 4 Sept. 1983: 7.

McFadden, Cyra. "McMurtry's Heroine an Unendearing Las Vegas Showgirl." *Chicago Tribune Book World* 25 Dec. 1983: 30.

Parsell, David B. Magill 1984: 225–29.

Pompea, Irene N. *Best Sellers* Oct. 1983: 239.

Tesich, Steve. "Lament in Las Vegas." *New York Times Book Review* 23 Oct. 1983: 12+.

Yardley, Jonathan. "Larry McMurtry: Harmony in Las Vegas." *Book World* 28 Aug. 1983: 3.

UNSIGNED

Booklist Aug. 1983: 1422.

Books. *Playboy* Nov. 1983: 32.

Brief Reviews. *Texas Books in Review* 6 (1984): 30.

Briefly Noted. *New Yorker* 24 Oct. 1983: 162.

Kirkus Reviews 1 July 1983: 723.

Picks and Pans. *People Weekly* 10 Oct. 1983: 14.

Publishers Weekly 24 June 1983: 53.

Lonesome Dove (1985)

Abernethy, Francis E. "Strange and Unnatural History in *Lonesome Dove*." *Texas Books in Review* 8.2 (1988): 1–2.

Balliett, Whitney. "Captain McCrae and Captain Call." *New Yorker* 11 Nov. 1985: 153–54. (*CLC* 44: 259.)

Biffle, Kent. "'Dove' Still Ruffling a Lot of Feathers." *Dallas Morning News* 19 Feb. 1989: 45A+. Identifies McMurtry's sources for the Latin motto on Gus's sign for the Hat Creek Cattle Company. Quotes from McMurtry's letters to Ernestine P. Sewell, whose reading of LD draws support from the significance she finds in the motto. See also Sewell's article, listed below.

B[rosnahan], J[ohn]. *Booklist* 15 May 1985: 1274.

Clemons, Walter. "Saga of a Cattle Drive." *Newsweek* 3 June 1985: 74. (*CLC* 44: 254.)

Clifford, Craig Edward. "The Last Roundup." Books and the Culture. *Texas Observer* 2 Aug. 1985: 15–16.

Englade, Ken. *Atlanta* Oct. 1985: 24.

Fiffer, Sharon Sloan. *Chicago* Oct. 1985: 128–29.

F[ord], G[ary] [D]. "Books about the South." *Southern Living* Nov. 1986: 132.

Fox, H. B. "Roasting *Lonesome Dove:* A Humorous Look at Western 'Authenticity' in Larry McMurtry's Pulitzer Prize Winning Novel." *Texas [Houston Chronicle]* 29 Jan. 1989: 4+.

Garrett, George. "McMurtry Pens Western Masterpiece." *Chicago Tribune Book World* 9 June 1985: 33+.

G[eeslin], C[ampbell]. Picks and Pans. *People Weekly* 8 July 1985: 12.

*Graham, Don. "*Lonesome Dove:* Butch and Sundance Go On A Cattledrive." *Southwestern American Literature* 12.1 (1986): 7–12. Points to a seeming conflict between McMurtry's anti-nostalgia prescription for Texas literature in his "Bridegroom" essay and his own performance in LD. Identifies cinematic and historical sources for the novel.

——. *Texas Humanist.* July–Aug. 1985: 39–40.

Groseclose, Everett. "Once upon a Time in the West." *Wall Street Journal* 15 Aug. 1985, eastern ed.: 25.

Hearon, Shelby. "The Strong, Silent Men of the West: Cowpunching Speaks Louder Than Words." *Houston Post* 23 June 1985, final ed.: 12F.

Hendricks, David. "McMurtry Writes His Best Book." Books. *Express-News* [San Antonio] 21 July 1985: 2-H.

Horn, John. *Los Angeles Times Book Review* 9 June 1985: 2. (*CLC* 44: 254–55.)

Lehmann-Haupt, Christopher. *New York Times* 3 June 1985, late city ed.: C20. (*CLC* 44: 253–54.)

*Lemann, Nicholas. "Tall in the Saddle." *New York Times Book Review* 9 June 1985: 7. (*CLC* 44: 256–57.)

Marvel, Bill. "A Book Larger Than Life Revived a Dying Genre." *Dallas Morning News* 5 Feb. 1989: 1C+.

Michaud, Charles. *Library Journal* July 1985: 94.

Milazzo, Lee. "*Lonesome Dove* Is the Great Texas Novel." *Dallas Morning News* 30 June 1985: 12C.

Morris, Jan. "Going Whole Hog." *Texas Monthly* June 1985: 160+.

Morsberger, Robert E. Magill 1986: 533–36.

———. *Western American Literature* 21 (1986): 165–66.

Mosiman, Billie Sue. "Defending *Lonesome Dove*." Letter. *Texas [Houston Chronicle]* 12 Mar. 1989: 7. Responds to H. B. Fox's article, listed above.

O'Conner, Patricia T. New and Noteworthy. *New York Times Book Review* 27 July 1986: 28.

———. "Notable Paperbacks." *New York Times Book Review* 7 Dec. 1986: 84.

Perrin, Noel. "Larry McMurtry's Western Epic." *Book World* 9 June 1985: 1+. (*CLC* 44: 255–56.)

Prokop, Mary K. *Best Sellers* Aug. 1985: 169.

*Reynolds, [R.] Clay. "Back Trailing to Glory: *Lonesome Dove* and the Novels of Larry McMurtry." *Texas Review* 8.3–4 (1987): 22–29.

*Sewell, Ernestine P. "McMurtry's Cowboy-God in *Lonesome Dove*." *Western American Literature* 21 (1986): 219–25. (*CLC* 44: 259–62.) Topics include the "search motif," the "love theme," "symbolic interlardings," and the mythic "Cowboy-God" realized in the "Freudian composite" of Call (Super-ego), Gus (Ego), and Jake (Id). See also Biffle's article, listed above.

Sheppard, R. Z. "It's a Long, Long Tale Awinding." *Time* 10 June 1985: 79. (*CLC* 44: 258.)

Stuewe, Paul. *Quill & Quire* Nov. 1985: 29.

UNSIGNED

Books. *Playboy* Aug. 1985: 30–31.

Kirkus Reviews 15 Apr. 1985: 341–42.

New in Paperback. *Book World* 3 Aug. 1986: 12.

Publishers Weekly 19 Apr. 1985: 71.

Publishers Weekly 4 July 1986: 65.

Texasville (1987)

Brooks, David. "Summertime Best Sellers: Irrationality Pays." *Wall Street Journal* 2 June 1987, eastern ed.: 28. T is the last of five "irrational" books reviewed.

Busby, Mark. *Saturday Magazine* [*Bryan-College Station Eagle*] 15 Aug. 1987: 14.

Clute, John. "Ghosts at the Feast." *Times Literary Supplement* 11 Sept. 1987: 978.

Diehl, Digby. *Modern Maturity* Apr.–May 1987: 113.

D[onavin], D[enise] P. *Booklist* 15 Feb. 1987: 857

Dubose, Louis. "One Hundred Years of Turpitude." *Texas Observer* 17 July 1987: 14–15.

*Erdrich, Louise. "Why Is That Man Tired?" *New York Times Book Review* 19 Apr. 1987: 7.

Frye, Bob J. "A Festival of Cynicism." *Fort Worth Star-Telegram* 26 Apr. 1987: 6D.

Greene, A. C. "A Place Called Texasville." *Dallas Morning News* 26 Apr. 1987: 8C.

Heaberlin, Dick. *Southwestern American Literature* 13.2 (1988): 37.

Hendricks, David. "McMurtry at His Funniest in Fast-paced 'Texasville.'" Books. *Express-News* [San Antonio] 12 Apr. 1987: 6–H.

Johnson, George. New and Noteworthy. *New York Times Book Review* 28 Feb. 1988: 34.

Jones, Nicolette. "A Feast of New Fiction." *Books* [London] Sept. 1987: 10–11.

Kakutani, Michiko. Books of the Times. *New York Times* 8 Apr. 1987, late ed.: C24.

King, Florence. *Los Angeles Times Book Review* 12 Apr. 1987: 1+.

Latham, Aaron. "McMurtry Country: What Once Was Tragic Is Now Too Funny for Tears." *Books* [*Chicago Tribune*] 5 Apr. 1987: 1+.

Lee, James W[ard]. "McMurtry's Sequel Pure Zaniness." *Denton Record-Chronicle* 26 Apr. 1987: 5C.

Michaud, Charles. *Library Journal* 1 Apr. 1987: 163–64.

Pilkington, [William] Tom. "*The Last Picture Show* — Part II." *Dallas Times Herald.* 12 Apr. 1987: D-8+.

———. "*Texasville:* A Review of Reviews." *Texas Books in Review* 7.1 (1987): 15–16. Surveys the critical response to T in a discussion of twelve newspaper and magazine reviews.

Rafferty, Terrence. "The Last Fiction Show." *New Yorker* 15 June 1987: 91–94. Includes review of *The Thanatos Syndrome,* by Walker Percy, with whom McMurtry is briefly contrasted.

*Reid, Jan. "The Next Picture Show." *Texas Monthly* Apr. 1987: 152+.

Reynolds, [R.] Clay. *Southern Humanities Review* 23.1 (1989): 92–94.

Rigler, Judyth. "McMurtry Returns to Thalia." Texas Books. *Abilene Reporter-News* 3 May 1987: 7E. (Also published under various

headlines in *Kingsville Record* 31 May 1987: 4C; and, with the last
two paragraphs cut, *Valley Morning Star* [Harlingen, TX] 3 May
1987: C3.)

Ronald, Ann. *Western American Literature* 22 (1988): 373–74.

Skow, John. "After the Last Picture Show." *Time* 20 Apr. 1987: 71.

Wyckoff, Peter C. "30 Years Later, A Return to McMurtryville."
Houston Post 19 Apr. 1987, final ed.: 12F.

Yardley, Jonathan. "Deep in the Heart of Larry McMurtry." *Book
World* 12 Apr. 1987: 3.

UNSIGNED

Books [London] Dec. 1987: 27.

Kirkus Reviews 15 Jan. 1987: 87.

Publishers Weekly 6 Feb. 1987: 87.

Anything for Billy (1988)

Butler, Jack. "The Irresistible Gunfighter." *New York Times Book
Review* 16 Oct. 1988: 3.

Clemons, Walter. *Newsweek* 26 Sept. 1988: 76.

Diehl, Digby. *Playboy* Dec. 1988: 37.

Gish, Robert. *Southwestern American Literature* 14.2 (1989): 46–48.

Graham, Don. "Blood on the Saddle." *World & I* Jan. 1989: 326–32.

Hansen, Ron. "The New Adventures of Billy the Kid." *Book World* 9
Oct. 1988: 1+.

Hendricks, David. "He's Still Mything Around: McMurtry Takes on
the Kid." Books. *Express-News* [San Antonio] 9 Oct. 1988: 6-H.

Koenig, Rhoda. *New York* 3 Oct. 1988: 70.

Mathews, Laura. *Glamour* Nov. 1988: 188.

Michaud, Charles. *Library Journal* 15 Oct. 1988: 104.

Milazzo, Lee. "'Billy' Misfires: McMurtry's Uneven Dime Novel Falls
Short." *Dallas Morning News* 16 Oct. 1988: 10C.

Pilkington, [William] Tom. "McMurtry's 'Kid' Doesn't Square with
History." *Dallas Times Herald* 11 Sept. 1988: K-6.

————. "Revising the Myth." *World & I* Jan. 1989: 343–47.

Reynolds, [R.] Clay. "It's Billy the Kid, Even Better Than His Own
Legend." *Fort Worth Star-Telegram* 16 Oct. 1988, sec. 6: 7.

————. *Western American Literature* 24.1 (1989): 65–66.

R[eynolds], [R.] C[lay]. *Review of Texas Books* 3.2 (1988): 2.

Rigler, Judyth. "*Billy* a Myth of West." *Denton Record-Chronicle* 4
Dec. 1988: 8C. (Also published under various headlines in *Abilene
Reporter-News* 25 Dec. 1988: 6B; *Monitor* [McAllen, TX] 11 Dec.
1988: 7C; *Valley Morning Star* [Harlingen, TX] 4 Dec. 1988: D4.)

Sheppard, R. Z. "The Terms of Fatal Endearment." *Time* 24 Oct. 1988: 92–93.

Tatum, Stephen. "Hopelessly Devoted to You." *World & I* Jan. 1989: 333–42.

Topping, Gary. "McMurtry's *Billy* Better Than *Lonesome Dove.*" *Texas Books in Review* Spring (1989): 1.

Winckler, Suzanne. "The Old West, The New South." *Texas Monthly* Oct. 1988: 146+.

UNSIGNED
Briefly Noted. *New Yorker* 23 Jan. 1989: 118.
Kirkus Reviews 1 Aug. 1988: 1088
Publishers Weekly 19 Aug. 1988: 59.

ESSAYS

In a Narrow Grave: Essays on Texas (1968)

*Hickey, Dave. "McMurtry's Elegant Essays." *Texas Observer* 7 Feb. 1969: 14–16.

Skinner, Izora. "Description: The Lyrics of Strange Music." Schmidt 29–32.

Tinkle, Lon. "Native Son Scans State's Culture." Reading and Writing. *Dallas Morning News* 8 Dec. 1968: 6C.

UNSIGNED
Book World 18 Dec. 1983: 12.
"On Larry McMurtry's Essays." *Texas Observer* 29 Nov. 1968: 10.
Western Books in Brief. *American West* Mar.–Apr. 1984: 66.

"The Texas Moon, and Elsewhere" (1975)

Dunn, Si. Letter. *Atlantic Monthly* May 1975: 26. Scoffs at McMurtry's depiction of Texas in "Texas Moon."

"Ever a Bridegroom: Reflections on the Failure of Texas Literature" (1981)

*Barthelme, Donald. "Terms of Estrangement." *Texas Monthly* Jan. 1986: 172+. Responds to McMurtry's "Bridegroom" essay with a defense of Texas's literary distinction and an argument for "a more liberal definition of what is Texian" than McMurtry allows.

Givner, Joan. "The Lady from Indian Creek." *Texas Observer* 7 May 1982: 29–30. Challenges McMurtry's assessment of Katharine Anne Porter.

H[olley], J[oe], ed. "For McMurtry: Terms of Endearment and Otherwise." Letters. *Texas Observer* 18 Dec. 1981: 18–24. Twelve readers respond to "Bridegroom."

Pickens, Donald K. "Webb Defended." Books and the Culture. *Texas Observer* 9 Apr. 1982: 23–24. Challenges McMurtry's assessment of Walter Prescott Webb.

Slung, Michele. "The Great Texas Divide." *Book World* 18 Oct. 1981: 15. Reports the controversy over "Bridegroom."

Film Flam: Essays on Hollywood (1987)

Bartholomew, David. *Library Journal* 15 June 1987: 82.

*Bawer, Bruce. "Tinsel Talk." *New Criterion* June 1987: 77–81.

Champlin, Charles. *Los Angeles Times Book Review* 16 Aug. 1987: 12.

H[ooper], B[rad]. *Booklist* 1 June 1987: 1486.

Kakutani, Michiko. "A Kind of Ego Zoo." Books of the Times. *New York Times* 27 June 1987, late ed.: 7.

Lenihan, John H. "Entertaining Views of Hollywood's 'Ego Zoo.'" *Texas Books in Review* 8.2 (1988): 2.

Murray, William. "Waste the Money and Run." *New York Times Book Review* 31 May 1987: 35.

R[eynolds], [R.] C[lay]. *Review of Texas Books* 2.1 (1988): 3.

Ward, Robert. "Reeling and Writing in L. A." *Book World* 26 July 1987: 7.

UNSIGNED
Films in Review Feb. 1988: 111.
Kirkus Reviews 15 April 1987: 620.
Publishers Weekly 17 Apr. 1987: 58–59.

5. Film Criticism

COMPARATIVE STUDIES

Degenfelder, E. Pauline. "McMurtry and the Movies: *Hud* and *The Last Picture Show.*" *Western Humanities Review* 29 (1975): 81–91. (*CLC* 7: 213–14.) Follows McMurtry's lead (in ING's second chapter) in using Northrop Frye's terms in seeking to identify elements of the "high mimetic," "low mimetic," and "ironic" modes in the two films. In discussions of character portrayal, animal metaphor, and cinematographic technique, *Hud*'s imperfect projection of the modes is contrasted with LPS's consistent employment of them.

*Folsom, James K. "*Shane* and *Hud*: Two Stories in Search of a

Medium." *Western Humanities Review* 24 (1970): 359–72. (*CLC* 27: 326–28.) Includes analysis of the movie adaptation of HPB.

Gerlach, John. "*The Last Picture Show* and One More Adaptation." *Literature/Film Quarterly* 1.2 (1973): 161–66. Analyzes alterations the film makes to the novel.

Graham, Don. "When Myths Collide." *Texas Monthly* Jan. 1986: 42+. Compares the conflict between the cattleman and the oilman in the movies *Giant* and *Hud.*

Haseloff, Cynthia. "Formative Elements of Film: A Structural Comparison of Three Novels and Their Adaptations by Irving Ravetch and Harriet Frank, Jr." *DAI* 33 (1972) 438A. U of Missouri-Columbia. Includes treatment of HPB's adaptation as *Hud.*

Robertson, Richard. "New Directions in Westerns of the 1960s and 70s." *Journal of the West* Oct. 1983: 43–52. Briefly considers *Hud.*

*Speidel, Constance. "Whose *Terms of Endearment?*" *Literature/Film Quarterly* 12.4 (1984): 271–73. Compares the McMurtry novel and the Brooks film.

Willson, Robert. "Which Is the Real 'Last Picture Show'?" *Literature/ Film Quarterly* 1.2 (1973): 167–69. Finds significance in the novel's having *The Kid from Texas,* a B movie starring Audie Murphy, as Thalia's last picture show and objects to the loss of this significance in the Bogdanovich film, which substitutes *Red River.* Cf. Degenfelder's endorsement of the substitution on page 84 of her article "McMurtry and the Movies," listed above.

Wright, Lawrence. "Coming Soon to a Theater Near You: Dwarf." *Texas Monthly* Oct. 1987: 122+. Considers the significance of Texas settings in movies that are "either playing into the myth or playing against it." Includes discussion of the films *Hud,* LPS, and TE, as well as many other Texas movies.

CRITICISM OF INDIVIDUAL FILM TITLES

Hud (1963)

Coleman, John. "Going West." *New Statesman* 7 June 1963: 873.

Crowther, Bosley. "Hurrahs for 'Hud': A Present-day Western Drama Has an Apt, Compelling Theme." *New York Times* 9 June 1963, sec. 2: 1.

_____. "'Hud' Chronicles a Selfish, Snarling Heel." Screen. *New York Times* 29 May 1963: 36.

Dent, Alan. "A Week of Aitches." *Illustrated London News* 8 June 1963: 902.

Gill, Brendan. "Two Good Ones." *New Yorker* 8 June 1963: 166.

Hartung, Philip T. "Siblings Hissing." The Screen. *Commonweal* 14 June 1963: 328.

*Kael, Pauline. *"Hud,* Deep in the Divided Heart of Hollywood." *Film Quarterly* 17.4 (1964): 15–23. (Rpt. in *I Lost It at the Movies.* Boston: Little, 1965. 78–94.) "[P]rovides all that is needed in the way of criticism of *Hud,"* McMurtry says (ING 16).

Kauffmann, Stanley. "A Near Hit: More Art than Matter." *New Republic* 25 May 1963: 27–28.

Knight, Arthur. "Deep in the Heart of Texas." *Saturday Review* 25 May 1963: 40.

MacDonald, Dwight. "A Masterpiece—And Some Others." *Esquire* Sept. 1963: 50+.

McMurtry, Larry. "Here's *Hud* in Your Eye" and "Cowboys, Movies, Myths, and Cadillacs: An Excursus on Ritual Forms in the Western Movie." *In a Narrow Grave: Essays on Texas.* 1968. Albuquerque: U of New Mexico P, 1987. 3–29.

Walsh, Moira. *America* 15 June 1963: 871–72.

UNSIGNED

"Heel vs. Homer." *Newsweek* 3 June 1963: 84.

"Panhandle Punk." *Time* 7 June 1963: 100.

The Last Picture Show (1971)

Alpert, Hollis. "The Last Shall Be First." *Saturday Review* 16 Oct. 1971: 63.

Austin, Charles M. "The '50s Revisited." *Christian Century* 1 Mar. 1972: 259–60.

C[allenbach], E[rnest]. Short Notices. *Film Quarterly* 25.3 (1971–72): 59.

Clurman, Harold. Theatre and Films. *Nation* 25 Oct. 1971: 410–12.

Denby, David. "Visions of the End." *Atlantic Monthly* Dec. 1971: 130–33.

Farber, Stephen. "The Last—and Most Overrated—'Picture Show'?" *New York Times* 23 Jan. 1972, sec. 2: 11+.

Kael, Pauline. "Movies in Movies." *New Yorker* 9 Oct. 1971: 145–47+.

Kanfer, Stefan. "Festival Prize." *Time* 11 Oct. 1971: 80.

Kauffmann, Stanley. *New Republic* 16 Oct. 1971: 18+.

Kirvan, John J. *"The Last Picture Show* and *Sunday, Bloody Sunday." New Catholic World* Mar.–Apr. 1972: 63–64.

Larson, Magali, and Sherri Caven. "Hollywood Dream Factory." *Society* Sept. 1972: 68–70.

McMurtry, Larry. *"The Last Picture Show:* A Last Word." *Colonial Times* [Washington, D.C.] 21 Dec. 1971–12 Jan. 1972: 1+.

Pechter, William S. "Youth; Manhood; Middle Age." *Commentary* Jan. 1972: 78–80.

Schickel, Richard. "Some Lessons in Growing Up." *Life* 15 Oct. 1971: 14.

*Silver, Isidore. *"The Last Picture Show:* A Concurring Opinion." *Commonweal* 14 Jan. 1972: 348–50.

Sittel, Edward. *Vogue* 1 Nov. 1971: 170.

Smith, Julian. "They Don't Make Picture Shows Like That Any More." *New York Times* 23 July 1972, late city ed., sec. 2: 7.

Westerbeck, Colin L., Jr. "Remembrance of Things Past." The Screen. *Commonweal* 5 Nov. 1971: 132–33.

Zimmerman, Paul D. "The Streets of Anarene." *Newsweek* 11 Oct. 1971: 57.

Lovin' Molly (1974)

Canby, Vincent. "Texas Farm Woman Not True to Type." *New York Times* 15 Apr. 1974: 41.

Gilliatt, Penelope. *New Yorker* 22 Apr. 1974: 136+.

*King, Larry. "Leavin' McMurtry." *Texas Monthly* Mar. 1974: 70–76.

Lowry, Katharine. "From Badlands to Worselands." *Texas Monthly* June 1974: 31–35.

McMurtry, Larry. "Approaching Cheyenne . . . Leaving Lumet: Oh, Pshaw!" *New York* 29 Apr. 1974: 64–66.

Schickel, Richard. "Baby Makes Three." *Time* 22 Apr. 1974: 68+.

Whitehorn, Ethel. *PTA Magazine* Apr. 1974: 6.

Zimmerman, Paul D. "All for One." *Newsweek* 15 Apr. 1974: 101+.

Terms of Endearment (1983)

Ansen, David. "Extraordinary People." *Newsweek* 21 Nov. 1983: 91–92.

*Biskind, Peter. Films. *Nation* 14 Jan. 1984: 28–29.

Benson, Sheila. *CoEvolution Quarterly* Winter 1983: 19.

Blake, Richard A. "Hatchets and Heartburn." *America* 7–14 Jan. 1984: 13.

Bosworth, Patricia. "Some Extraordinary People and Places." *Working Woman* Feb. 1984: 132.

Canby, Vincent. "Talented Actors Enrich a Fine Script." *New York Times* 4 Dec. 1983, sec. 2: 21.

Cheney, Harry. "Best Picture of the Year?" *Christianity Today* 17 Feb. 1984: 54.

Clarke, Gerald. "The Night of the Great Prom: James Brooks' *Terms of Endearment* Wins Five Oscars." *Time* 23 Apr. 1984: 74.

Denby, David. *New York* 5 Dec. 1983: 143–44+.

Dowell, Pat. *Washingtonian* Feb. 1984: 48.

Dworkin, Susan. "There's No Divorce for Mothers and Daughters: Behind the Scenes with the Producer/Writer/Director of *Terms of Endearment.*" *Ms* Mar. 1984: 26+.

Harmetz, Aljean. "Coming to Terms with Success." *New York Times Magazine* 8 Apr. 1984: 47+. A profile of director James Brooks.

Haskell, Molly. "Ten Hankies, 2¾ Stars." *Vogue* Jan. 1984: 55.

Hey, Kenneth R. *USA Today* Mar. 1984: 93–94.

Kael, Pauline. "Retro Retro." *New Yorker* 12 Dec. 1983: 149–52.

Kauffmann, Stanley. "The Way Some People Live." *New Republic* 26 Dec. 1983: 24–25.

Lithgow, John. "Coming to 'Terms': Diary of an Itinerant Actor." *Film Comment* Nov.–Dec. 1983: 28–32.

Orth, Maureen. "Larry McMurtry: A Woman's Best Friend." *Vogue* Mar. 1984: 456+.

O'Toole, Lawrence. "The Silent Contract of Love." *Maclean's* 5 Dec. 1983: 69.

Pally, Marcia. "World of Our Mothers." *Film Comment* Mar.–Apr. 1984: 11–12.

Schickel, Richard. "Sisters under the Skin." *Time* 28 Nov. 1983: 84+.

Shipman, David. "Cinema: A Quarterly Review." *Contemporary Review* June 1984: 325–26.

Simon, John. "Little Big Screen." *National Review* 9 Mar. 1984: 54–55.

Turan, Kenneth. "On His Own 'Terms': James L. Brooks Interviewed by Kenneth Turan." *Film Comment* Mar.–Apr. 1984: 18–23.

——. *California Magazine* Dec. 1983: 112+.

Ventura, Michael. "Endearment, Pass By." Books and the Culture. *Texas Observer* 27 Jan. 1984: 15–17.

Wolcott, James. "Terminal Endearment." *Texas Monthly* Dec. 1983: 194+.

UNSIGNED
People Weekly 5 Dec. 1983: 14.

The Ballad of Mary Phagan (1988)

Klein, Andy. *Los Angeles* Jan. 1988: 169.

Lonesome Dove (1989)

Bark, Ed. "The Miniseries Writes a New Page in TV Excellence." *Dallas Morning News* 5 Feb. 1989: 1C+.

Calhoun, John. "Lonesome Dove." *Theatre Crafts* Feb. 1989: 40+.

Describes efforts at authenticity in the production design, including sets and costumes.

Carman, Tim. "'Dove' Flies above Traditional Western." *Houston Post* 3 Feb. 1989, state ed.: D-7.

Carter, Bill. "'Dove's' Bountiful Trail Isn't Over Yet: Western Saga Storms Foreign Shores, Stirs Talk of 'Prequel.'" *Zest* [*Houston Chronicle*] 12 Mar. 1989: 10+.

Chapman, Art. "'Dove' Comes to End of Viewers' TV Trail." Television. *Fort Worth Star-Telegram* 9 Feb. 1989, sec. 4: 6.

———. "*Lonesome Dove:* The Revered Novel Comes to TV Tonight and a Previewing Shows That It Surpasses All Expectations." *Fort Worth Star-Telegram* 5 Feb. 1989, sec. 6: 1+.

Gerber, Eric. "CBS Is Betting the Ranch on 'Lonesome Dove.'" *Houston Post* 3 Feb. 1989, state ed.: A-1+.

———. "'Lonesome Dove': This Texas Epic Stays True to Its Roots." *Houston Post* 3 Feb. 1989, state ed.: D-1+.

———. "Take the Long, Dusty Trail of 'Lonesome Dove.'" *Houston Post* 3 Feb. 1989, state ed.: D-6.

Harrigan, Stephen. "The Making of *Lonesome Dove.*" *Texas Monthly* June 1988: 82+.

Loeffler, Mark. "The Big Round-up." *Theatre Crafts* Feb. 1989: 47+. Describes production difficulties with the use of animals.

Madigan, Tim. "The Range of Opinion." *Fort Worth Star-Telegram* 9 Feb. 1989, sec. 4: 1+. Gives several Texas cowboys' estimates of the miniseries, which they judge for its authenticity; also includes an American Indian leader's charge that LD is racist.

Parks, Louis B. "Home on the Range with 'Lonesome Dove.'" *Houston Chronicle* 7 Feb. 1989: 1D+.

———. "On the Set of 'Lonesome Dove.'" *Houston Chronicle* 17 Apr. 1988: 24+.

Shales, Tom. "The Splendors of 'Lonesome Dove': CBS Brings Larry McMurtry's Western Epic to Television in a Breathtaking Miniseries." *Washington Post* 5 Feb. 1989: G1+.

Swindell, Larry. "Book to Teleplay, Story True to Form." *Fort Worth Star-Telegram* 5 Feb. 1989, sec. 6: 1+.

———. "'Dove' Sales Flying on a Surge." *Fort Worth Star-Telegram* 9 Feb. 1989, sec. 4: 4. Reports effect of the miniseries on local sales of LD.

Waters, Harry F. "How the West Was Once." *Newsweek* 6 Feb. 1989: 54–55.

Westbrook, Bruce. "'Dove' on Tape: The Question Remains When." *Zest* [*Houston Chronicle*] 12 Mar. 1989: 10+.

Wright, Jim. "'Dove' Gave Us the Simple Life." *Dallas Morning News*
    21 Feb. 1989: 13A.
Zoglin, Richard. "Poetry on the Prairie." *Time* 6 Feb. 1989: 78.
Zurawik, David. "'Dove' to Soar as Mini-series." *Dallas Times Herald*
    29 Dec. 1988: E-1+.

UNSIGNED
"'Dove' in Texas: McMurtry Novel Slated for CBS Miniseries." *Houston Post* 21 Mar. 1988, final ed.: 5C.

6. Masters' Theses

Allen, Elizabeth Browning. "*Leaving Cheyenne:* The Evolution of the
    Cowboy in Larry McMurtry's Fiction." Southwest Texas State U,
    1975.
Buford, Susan L. "The Transition from Adolescence to Adulthood: J.
    D. Salinger's *The Catcher in the Rye* and Larry McMurtry's *The
    Last Picture Show.*" West Texas State U, 1974.
Fort, Myrna Randolph. "Larry McMurtry's Texas: Myth and Real-
    ity." West Texas State U, 1974.
Frost, Martha Toles. "Small-town Teenagers in Modern American
    Fiction: *Red Sky at Morning, The Last Picture Show,* and *American
    Graffiti.*" West Texas State U, 1976.
Gilbert, Richard A. "McMurtry and Bellow: Individualism in Amer-
    ica." Trinity U, 1968.
Lewis, Jane Jackson. "Blest Be the Tie That Binds: The Ambivalence
    Toward Legacies in Selected Novels of Larry McMurtry." Hardin-
    Simmons U, 1987.
Ross, Janet Fowler. "From Hero to Misfit: The Mythic Cowboy in the
    Novels of Larry McMurtry." Texas Christian U, 1974.
Smith, Gordon Bennett, Jr. "Sectarian Religion in the Early Novels of
    Larry McMurtry." Texas Christian U, 1975.
Sniffen, Jimmie Clifton. "The Emergence of Woman in the Novels of
    Larry McMurtry." Stephen F. Austin State U, 1972.
Tovar, Inez Hernandez. "The Quest Theme in the Fiction of Larry
    McMurtry." U of Houston, 1972.

NOTES ON CONTRIBUTORS

Mark Busby is associate professor of English at Texas A&M University. He has published numerous articles on modern American literature and is the author of *Preston Jones* and *Lanford Wilson* in the Western Writers Series. He coedited *The Frontier Experience and the American Dream: Essays on American Literature* (with David Mogen and Paul Bryant). Busby's latest work, *Ralph Ellison* in the Twayne U.S. Authors series, is scheduled for publication in 1990.

Robert Flynn is novelist-in-residence at Trinity University in San Antonio. He is the author of four novels—*North to Yesterday, In the House of the Lord, The Sounds of Rescue, the Signs of Hope,* and *Wanderer Springs*; a collection of short stories, *Seasonal Rain*; and a memoir of his experiences as a war correspondent, *A Personal War in Vietnam.* He is also the author of *Journey to Jefferson,* a dramatic adaptation of William Faulkner's *As I Lay Dying,* and "A Cowboy Legacy," a two-part television documentary for ABC.

Don Graham is J. Frank Dobie Regents Professor of English and American Literature at the University of Texas at Austin. He has published numerous articles on American literature and film and is the author of

The Fiction of Frank Norris: The Aesthetic Context, Cowboys and Cadillacs: How Hollywood Looks at Texas, and *Audie Murphy: No Name on the Bullet.* He is the editor of *The Texas Literary Tradition, Texas: A Literary Portrait,* and *South by Southwest: 24 Stories from Modern Texas* and coeditor of *Western Movies* (with Tom Pilkington).

Hamlin Hill is Ralph R. Thomas Professor of Liberal Arts at Texas A&M University. A well-known scholar of Western American literature as well as a specialist on the works of Mark Twain, he is the author of *Mark Twain: God's Fool,* coauthor of *America's Humor from Poor Richard to Doonesbury* (with Walter Blair), and editor of *Mark Twain's Letters to His Publishers.*

James Ward Lee is chair of the English Department and director of the Center for Texas Studies at the University of North Texas in Denton. He is the author of *Classics of Texas Fiction* and was general editor of the Southwest Writers pamphlet series published by Steck-Vaughn in the late 1960s. He is a longtime active member and past president of the Texas Folklore Society.

Tom Pilkington is professor of English at Tarleton State University in Stephenville. He is one of the general editors of *A Literary History of the American West* and is coeditor with Suzanne Comer of Southern Methodist University Press's Southwest Life and Letters series. He has published numerous books and articles on Southwestern and Texas literature, including *My Blood's Country: Studies in Southwestern Literature* and *Imagining Texas: The Literature of the Lone Star State.* He is the coeditor of *Range Wars: Heated Debates, Sober Reflections, and Other Assessments of Texas Writing* (with Craig Clifford).

Clay Reynolds is associate professor of English and novelist-in-residence at the University of North Texas. He is the author of two novels, *The Vigil* and *Agatite;* a scholarly study, *Stage Left: The Development of the American Social Drama in the Thirties;* and numerous articles, essays, and reviews, many of which are concerned with Southwestern and Texas authors. His third novel, *Franklin's Crossing,* is forthcoming from E. P. Dutton in 1990.

Ernestine P. Sewell is former professor of English at the University of Texas at Arlington and past president of the Texas Folklore Society. At present she is a book reviewer, lecturer, and author of articles related to the Southwest and, with her husband, Charles Linck, operates Cow Hill Press. She is the coauthor of *Eats: Texas Foods and Foodways* (with Joyce Gibson Roach).

Charles Williams is a graduate of Bard College. He taught high school math and English in Port Arthur, Texas, before taking up graduate study at Lamar University in Beaumont, where he is a teaching fellow completing work toward an M.A. in English.

Grateful acknowledgment is made for permission to reprint the following:

"Larry McMurtry and the Persistent Frontier" by Tim Summerlin is reprinted from *Southwestern American Literature* 4 (1974) by permission of the publisher.

"Journeying as a Metaphor for Cultural Loss in the Novels of Larry McMurtry" by Janis P. Stout is reprinted from *Western American Literature* 11 (1976) by permission of the publisher.

"The Ranch as Place and Symbol in the Novels of Larry McMurtry" by Raymond C. Phillips, Jr., is reprinted from *South Dakota Review* 13.2 (1975) by permission of the publisher.

"McMurtry's Women: 'Eros [Libido, Caritas, and Philia] in [and out of] Archer County'" by Billie Phillips is reprinted from *Southwestern American Literature* 4 (1974) by permission of the publisher.

Excerpt from "The Dirt-Farmer and the Cowboy: Notes on Two Texas Essayists" by William T[om] Pilkington is reprinted from *Re: Arts and Letters* 3.1 (1969) by permission of the publisher.

"McMurtry's Elegant Essays" by Dave Hickey is reprinted from *The Texas Observer* 7 Feb. 1969 by permission of the author.

"Terms of Estrangement" by Donald Barthelme is reprinted with permission from the January 1986 issue of *Texas Monthly.* Copyright 1986 by *Texas Monthly.*

"Tinsel Talk" by Bruce Bawer is reprinted from *The New Criterion* June 1987 by permission of the author.

Excerpt from "Elegy and Exorcism: Texas Talent and General Concerns" by Dave Hickey is reprinted from *The Texas Observer* 20 Jan. 1967 by permission of the author.

Excerpt from *The Ghost Country: A Study of the Novels of Larry McMurtry* by Raymond L. Neinstein, Modern Authors Monograph Series 1 (Berkeley: Creative Arts, 1976) is reprinted by permission of the publisher.

Excerpt from *Larry McMurtry* by Thomas Landess, Southwest Writers Series 23 (Austin: Steck-Vaughn, 1969) is reprinted by permission of the author.

"Showdown in the New Old West: The Cowboy vs. the Oilman" by R. C[lay] Reynolds is reprinted from *Lamar Journal of the Humanities* 6.1 (1980) by permission of the publisher.

"The Death of the Frontier in the Novels of Larry McMurtry" by Christopher Baker is reprinted from *McNeese Review* 28 (1981–1982) by permission of the author.

"Initiation Themes in McMurtry's Cowboy Trilogy" is a revised version of "The Themes of Initiation in the Works of Larry McMurtry and Tom Mayer" by Kenneth W. Davis published in *Arlington Quarterly* 2.3 (1970); revised by the author and used by permission.

"Damn the Saddle on the Wall: Anti-Myth in Larry McMurtry's *Horseman, Pass By*" by Mark Busby is reprinted from *New Mexico Humanities Review* 3.1 (1980) by permission of the publisher.

"Anatomy and *The Last Picture Show*: A Matter of Definition" by Donald E. Fritz is reprinted from *Larry McMurtry: Unredeemed Dreams,* edited by Dorey Schmidt, Living Author Series 1 (Edinburg, TX: Pan American U, 1978), by permission of the publisher.

"More D'Urban: The Texas Novels of Larry McMurtry" by Kerry Ahearn is reprinted from *The Texas Quarterly* 19.3 (1976) by permission of the author.

"Moving On . . . and On . . . and On" by Elroy Bode first appeared in *Southwest Review* 55 (1970). Copyright © 1970 by Elroy Bode. Reprinted by permission of the author.